ROBERT HART
AND CHINA'S EARLY MODERNIZATION

His Journals, 1863–1866

HARVARD EAST ASIAN MONOGRAPHS, 155

*The preparation of this volume
was made possible in part by a grant from the
National Endowment for the Humanities,
an independent agency.*

Robert Hart and China's Early Modernization

HIS JOURNALS, 1863–1866

edited and with narratives by

RICHARD J. SMITH
JOHN K. FAIRBANK
KATHERINE F. BRUNER

Published by the Council on East Asian Studies, Harvard University
and distributed by the Harvard University Press
Cambridge (Massachusetts) and London   1991

Index by Katherine F. Bruner

The Council on East Asian Studies at Harvard University publishes a monograph series and, through the Fairbank Center for East Asian Research and the Reischauer Institute of Japanese Studies, administers research projects designed to further scholarly understanding of China, Japan, Korea, Vietnam, Inner Asia, and adjacent areas.

Library of Congress Cataloging-in-Publication Data

Hart, Robert, Sir, 1835-1911.
    Robert Hart and China's early modernization : his journals,
1863-1866 / edited and with narratives by Richard J. Smith, John K.
Fairbank, Katherine F. Bruner.
        p.   cm. — (Harvard East Asian monographs ; 155)
    Includes bibliographical references and index.
    ISBN 0-674-77530-9
    1. Hart, Robert, Sir, 1835-1911—Diaries.   2. Customs
administration—China—Officials and employees—Diaries.   3. Customs
administration—China—History—Sources.   4. China. Hai kuan tsung
shui wu ssu shu—History.   I. Smith, Richard J. (Richard Joseph),
1944-   .   II. Fairbank, John King, 1907-   .   III. Bruner,
Katherine Frost, 1907-   IV. Title.   V. Series.
HJ7071.A3H373   1991
354.510072'46'092—dc20
[B]   91-10378
                                                            CIP

*This volume
is dedicated to*
WEN-HSIANG
文祥
1818–1876

The Manchu high official Wen-hsiang was a major figure in the Ch'ing leadership that made peace with the Anglo-French invaders of Peking in 1860 and brought the Ch'ing Restoration into power in 1861. As the principal official under Prince Kung in the Grand Council and its foreign affairs subcommittee, the Tsungli Yamen, Wen-hsiang was the most influential Manchu that Robert Hart dealt with while building up the Maritime Customs Service. He sought Hart's advice, valued his reporting, and influenced Hart in turn.

Together, the two worked to maintain the Anglo-Ch'ing entente that in the 1860s included foreign support of the Manchu dynasty against rebels and its acquiescence in the growth of foreign contact and trade.

In his day Wen-hsiang was a modernizer, in ways that historians may debate. His background seems to have been rather conventional. He was both a classical scholar and a military commander. One of his outstanding qualifications to be an insider at Peking was his intense loyalty to the Ch'ing cause.

Wen-hsiang was born in Liaoyang, Southern Manchuria, into a family of the Manchu Plain Red Banner. He passed the provincial examination at Peking in 1840 and became a metropolitan graduate (*chin-shih*) in 1845. Serving in various posts at the capital, he attained the third rank in 1855 and became a Grand Councillor in 1858 at age 40. He was an incorrupt and conscientious official of unusual objectivity and intelligence. We esteem him especially for his skill in dealing with Robert Hart. The balance between them is still to be determined.

Contents

Illustrations

Acknowledgments

GERALD E. BUNKER's original reading of Hart's journals onto tape made him almost a fourth member of our editorial team. Gordon Wheeler of the Queen's University Library in Belfast has been unfailingly helpful. Professor Kwang-Ching Liu of the University of California at Davis has helped us especially with the probable meaning of some of Hart's renditions of Chinese phrases in his own pre-Wade romanization. We thank Vice Chancellor Wang Gungwu and Elizabeth Sinn of the University of Hong Kong for the letters in Appendix C. We are indebted to Mei Ching of the Harvard Graduate School of Arts and Sciences and to Timothy E. Connor of the Chinese-Japanese Library for bibliographical assistance, to Joan Hill for unremitting editorial assistance, to Nancy Deptula for fiscal help beyond the call of duty, and to Florence Trefethen for superb editorial management of production at Harvard. For financial help in various forms we thank the Harvard Council on East Asian Studies, the National Endowment for the Humanities and the American Council of Learned Societies, the American Philosophical Society, and the Harvard University Press.

RJS
JKF
KFB

Editorial Note

W<small>E HAVE TRIED</small> to present the journals exactly as Hart wrote them, without omissions or corrections, and retaining his parentheses and underlines, the latter often used to indicate not italics but special emphasis. One or two minor exceptions have been mandated by the need to avoid confusion for the reader and, in certain cases, by the difficulty, even impossibility, of deciphering Hart's handwriting.

We have inserted before each entry the date, month, and year, e.g., 1 January 1964, whereas Hart frequently wrote only "Friday 27th" or "9th Oct." When Hart's entry includes the day of the week, we also include it.

If Hart provides only a transliterated term in the text, we have included our "best guess" at a translation in brackets — unless, of course, the meaning is clear from the context, or Hart has provided his own rendering or explanation of the term or phrase. A direct translation (if we are relatively sure of what has been transliterated) appears in quotation marks; a paraphrase without them. In any case, the Wade-Giles equivalent is then included in the notes. Thus, if Hart writes keuen in the text, we have rendered it in the corrected version as follows: . . . keuen ["authority"]. . . . Then, in the endnote for that line or paragraph of the text, we have supplied: keuen: *ch'üan,* followed by further explanation if necessary. If we cannot figure out all or part of Hart's transliteration, we have put a question mark in brackets in the text, and have tried to say as much as possible about the transliteration in the note.

If a personal name and title (either honorific, such as ta-jin [*ta-jen*] or substantive, such as footae [*fu-t'ai*] appear together (e.g. Teen Tetuh or Pwan tajin), the explanation in the notes reads: Teen Tetuh: T'ien *t'i-tu:* Provincial Commander-in-Chief T'ien Hsing-shu (if we know the person's full name) or Pwan tajin: "his excellency" P'an (if we don't know his full name). A number of honorific terms such as ta-jin [*ta-jen*] are repeated so often that it seems unnecessary to translate them in the notes every time they appear in the text.

If only a title appears in the text (e.g. Leang Kwang Tsung-tuh), it is translated in brackets (e.g. Leang Kwang Tsung-tuh [Governor General of Liang-Kuang]) with the Wade-Giles equivalent relegated to the endnote (i.e. Leang Kwang Tsung-tuh: Liang-Kuang *tsung-tu*).

For characters written in the text, we indicate in brackets: [characters for *ch'eng-k'ou;* lit. "city port"]. except for dates, which are simply translated, since there is no ambiguity with them. Thus: [characters for the 1st day of the 5th month of the 4th year of the T'ung-chih reign].

In the notes, we italicize transliterated titles and honorific terms (e.g. *fu-t'ai, tsung-tu, ta-jen,* etc.), but not the names of offices, places, persons, etc.

Preface

THE CAREER OF Sir Robert Hart in nineteenth-century China becomes more significant with the passing years, both as a personal story of outstanding success in far-off places, and as a record documenting the development of Chinese foreign relations. We began the story in *Entering China's Service: Robert Hart's Journals 1854–1863*, published in 1986; we continue it now, with the journals from 1863 to 1866. It is carried still further by earlier work by John K. Fairbank, Katherine F. Bruner, and Elizabeth M. Matheson, *The I.G. in Peking: Letters of Robert Hart, Chinese Maritime Customs, 1868–1907*, published in 1975. The focus on one man, far from narrowing the prospect, brings insight into an ever-widening scope of his contacts, his working savoir faire, his goals, his successes and failures.

In the preface to *Entering China's Service* we explained in some detail how the journals of Robert Hart came to our attention. To recapitulate briefly, the journals—numbering 77 volumes and covering the entire span of Hart's years in China—were left to The Queen's University in Belfast by the last Sir Robert Hart, his great-grandson, who died without heirs in 1970. During the summer of 1971, several researchers connected with the Harvard East Asian Research Center journeyed to Belfast to have a look at the journals, but determined that for various reasons—not least, the huge volume of material and Hart's increasingly enigmatic handwriting—they could not be incorporated into *The I.G. in Peking*, which reproduces and annotates in two volumes Hart's extensive correspondence with his London agent, James Duncan Campbell.

The Hart journals thus languished at The Queen's University Library until the mid-1970's when Dr. Gerald Bunker, who had published his history PhD dissertation at Harvard in the field of Chinese studies, moved with his family to Belfast to attend medical school. In his spare time, Dr. Bunker began to investigate the journals with an eye toward eventually writing a biography of Hart. As a preliminary step, he started reading Hart's journal entries from 1854 to 1866 into a battery-powered recorder and sending the tapes back to Katherine

Bruner to be transcribed. Unfortunately, the recorder produced a very uneven product, and the transcriptions, although tantalizing, ultimately proved to be unusable: too many questionable readings, unclear words, and all but undecipherable Chinese phrases.

By 1978, Dr. Bunker's medical career had taken him away from Hart's journals, and Professor Richard Smith of Rice University was invited to join the editing team. He had just published a book entitled *Mercenaries and Mandarins: The Ever-Victorious Army in Nineteenth Century China*, which centered on the specific circumstances of Sino-foreign relations in Shanghai during the 1860s as well as the general issue of China's employment of foreign talent in the pursuit of military "self-strengthening" (*tzu-ch'iang*). Smith's ongoing interest in the values, institutions, and rituals of the Ch'ing era, which found expression in his book of 1983, *China's Cultural Heritage: The Ch'ing Dynasty, 1644–1912,* provided additional incentive for him to investigate Hart's early career as a Chinese bureaucrat.

With financial help from both the American Philosophical Society and Harvard University, Professor Smith made three visits to The Queen's University Library. There, he compared the Bruner typescript with the original journals, made extensive corrections, added Chinese characters when Hart used them, and investigated other research materials in the Hart collection, including letters to and from Hart, photographs, scrolls sent as presents from Ch'ing officials, books, Pin-ch'un's diary, and various other Chinese documents. Where seemingly illegible words remained in the journals, he made a tracing for communal scrutiny—in a few cases still to no avail. Thus in 1986 the extant parts of the first ten years of Robert Hart's journals 1854–1863 were published. We add now the eventful three succeeding years 1864–1866, beginning in late 1863.

How far is the present volume a continuation of the first? How does it break fresh ground? In *Entering China's Service* we followed a bright young man learning the ropes. Circumstances favored the process; they gave him time to observe, to watch the management styles of others—especially of the Chinese—and above all, to mature. At the end of that volume we saw him at 28 come into a position of grave responsibility and potential power for the development of much that the nineteenth century looked upon as "progress"—what we now routinely call "modernization." In the 1860s neither of these concepts had an equivalent in the Chinese language. Chinese "modernizers" knew only that China needed to change in order to contend with its internal and external challenges, and that the West offered certain technological and perhaps even institutional advantages. Modernizing change, unlike reform, assumed an external standard of judgment.

We have stressed the theme of modernization in this book because Hart's journal entries of 1863–1866 reveal that he played a significant part in the early stages of this tortuous process in China. His role during the period went well beyond his earlier support for modernizing projects such as the ill-fated Lay-Osborn Flotilla, discussed at some length in *Entering China's Service*. After receiving his appointment as Inspector General (I.G.) of the Chinese Imperial Maritime Customs Administration in late 1863, Hart became what his predecessor as I.G., Horatio Nelson Lay, could never have been—a close and trusted adviser to the Ch'ing central government. As a result, throughout the remainder of his long career, Hart was the most influential Westerner in all of China. The Ch'ing writer Ch'en Chih observed in the 1890s, for example, that Hart wielded enormous political power, that his counsels prevailed at Court, and that "high officials at both the capital and in the provinces honor and trust him."[1]

Hart's experience in the period from 1863 to 1866 proved to be critical to his later success. As I.G., he walked the corridors of Chinese officialdom—tentatively at first—and learned from the inside what could and could not be attempted. And, as he carefully negotiated his way between the Ch'ing bureaucracy on the one hand, and foreign diplomats and merchants on the other, he began to acquire ever greater confidence, ever broader vision. During the mid-1860s, in addition to championing "progress" in the form of Western science and technology, he inaugurated institutional changes within the Customs Inspectorate, and even advocated reforms in other spheres of Chinese administration. In so doing, Hart became an active partner with the Chinese in their quest for "wealth and power" (*fu-ch'iang*)—the same essential motivation that underlies China's present effort to achieve the "Four Modernizations."

Hart's journals do more, however, than simply shed light on his accomplishments as a modernizer. They also reveal much about the inner workings of the Ch'ing bureaucracy, and about the men who staffed it at various levels—particularly those at the top. Written from a unique vantage point, the journals tell us more about the private thoughts and personal characters of high-ranking officials in the early 1860s than most contemporary writings, Chinese or Western. Certainly they are far more detailed than the private writings of any of the principal metropolitan officials with whom the I.G. came into regular contact. In Hart's candid and often confidential conversations with ministers of the Tsungli Yamen (three of whom were also Grand Councillors) he heard a great deal of political gossip, which he dutifully recorded in the pages of his journal. His informal conversations with Yamen secretaries also proved to be illuminating, as did his periodic chats with leading provincial officials and their underlings on his tours of the treaty ports.

Little escaped Hart's notice, and his prodigious memory assured that his observations would find their way onto the pages of his journal. With remarkable objectivity and considerable cultural sensitivity — at least for a mid-Victorian — Hart shows us the human side of the Ch'ing bureaucracy: the weaknesses and strengths of its officials; their quirks of personality and idiosyncratic beliefs; their fears and their insecurities; their factional struggles. But, if Hart holds a close lens to his Manchu and Chinese colleagues, he is no less scrupulous in examining himself and his Western acquaintances. His journals overflow with revelations of self-discovery and self-analysis, as well as insights into his management style and social life. He also provides us with numerous evaluations of foreign diplomats at all levels and other Western sojourners in the Middle Kingdom.

Hart's journals provide a particularly valuable record of the intricate and fragile fabric of Sino-foreign relations in the 1860s. As head of the multi-national Customs Administration — which by 1864 boasted employees from Great Britain, the United States, France, and Prussia, as well as Chinese superintendents and other lower-ranking Chinese functionaries — the I.G. established an unshakable reputation for honesty, integrity, reliability, and efficiency among the foreign diplomats at Peking as well as the Ch'ing government. Western and Chinese officials alike took Hart into their closest confidence. He thus became involved in every major Sino-foreign diplomatic problem that arose, as well as a number of more minor disputes. Hart's significance as a bridge between Chinese and Western points of view was magnified by the wide range of activities undertaken by the Inspectorate, and facilitated by his sympathy both for China's interests and for what he took to be the positive contributions of Western "civilization."

In order to appreciate Hart's outlook and accomplishments, we should naturally begin with an examination of his nineteenth-century milieu.

CHAPTER ONE

Robert Hart in China's History

WHO THINKS NOW of travel by stagecoach, illumination by candlelight, or cobblestone paving? The givens of one era that do not survive into the next may soon be forgotten. For a full century from 1842 to 1943 foreigners lived and worked in China under the special protection of their own laws administered by their own national consuls. Known as extraterritoriality, this protection was a given feature of the foreigner's semi-colonial life in China. He could ogle the severed heads of bandits impaled on spikes along the street without fearing for his own neck. It was an era of foreign dominance in the Middle Kingdom. Today in this later era of China's national equality (and occasional superiority) in Sino-foreign relations, the nineteenth century can be recalled only by an effort of imagination. How did it happen that Western intruders had such a special position in late imperial China and the early Republic?

The explosive growth of modern science and technology, which has us all in its grip now more than ever, hardly needs recounting here. Its political and social impact is what concerns us. To see China in a world context, let us begin by noting the worldwide expansion of industrial Europe that set in during the latter half of the nineteenth century. The rise of nationalism in Europe, marked, for example, by the unification of Italy and Germany in 1870–1871, was accompanied by the spread of European colonialism abroad. The imperial powers divided up Africa and Southeast Asia. After the rebellion of 1858 ended the reign of the British East India Company, India was ruled by Imperial Britain, and the Indian Civil Service was built up as an arm of its local administration. Meanwhile, Japan's unification (1868) and subsequent modernization led to her defeat of China in 1895 and the inauguration of Japanese colonialism in Taiwan (1895–1945). In a parallel way, the United States's coming of age as a nation after the Civil War of the early 1860s encouraged the unacknowledged American colonialism in the Philippines after 1898. Nationalism at home and colonialism abroad characterized this era of expansion by industrial-commercial peoples over the less technologically advanced

1

parts of the globe. Christian missionaries from the Atlantic community made bold to explain to the colonial peoples that this often violent expansion was God's inscrutable way. For those of little faith but greater rationality there was the concept of Social Darwinism, that nations naturally struggled for the survival of the fittest. You could see it unfolding.

In this context, Robert Hart entered upon his Customs career as an early modernizer of China. The country was not yet a nation, but the training of the scholar elite made it culturally homogenous, and it was too politically unified under Peking to be made a European colony. The result in China was a semi-colonialism with its own distinctive features. Descendants of the Manchu invaders of 1644 would continue to rule at Peking until 1912. Western-style armaments would help their loyal Chinese generals to subdue the several mid-century rebellions by 1873 and thereafter to forestall further big-scale peasant risings until 1900. The domestic peace necessary for foreign trade was simultaneously encouraged by the presence and patrols of treaty-power gunboats, especially those of the British navy. Since the treaty system allowed foreign trade not only at coastal ports but also at inland river ports, particularly along the Yangtze, the foreign military power on the waterways of South China was a pervasive strategic influence. The Ch'ing dynasty survived partly by its acceptance of a British condominium, not only in keeping the peace but also in selected aspects of administration.

In this sense China became part of Britain's informal commercial empire of the late nineteenth century. (Britain's position as *primus inter pares* among the imperialist powers came to be marked by her maintenance of naval power double that of any other nation.) In colonies like Burma or Malaya the need of the imperialist power to promote trade by modern, impartial taxation of it, could be met by direct fiscal administration. In a semi-colony like China, however, this task could be performed effectively only by entrusting it to a capable foreign employee of the still sovereign (or semi-sovereign) native government.

In historical perspective, Robert Hart's career illustrates several themes in the international relations of the nineteenth century. First of all, he was one of those Westerners ("white men") who rose to power in a non-Western land. The annals of the Victorian era teem with such people. India was only the main focus, and British administration expanded into Burma and the rest of Southeast Asia as an offshoot from British India. In Borneo in 1841 (Sir) James Brooke was made rajah and governor of Sarawak, where his family successors would rule for more than a century. After (Sir) Stamford Raffles founded Singapore as a British port in 1819, Sir Frank Swettenham would become the first Resident General of the Federated Malay States in 1896. Meanwhile in Africa Sir Evelyn Baring (Lord Cromer after 1892) as Resident and British Consul General dominated the government of Egypt from 1883 to 1907. Hart's service as a Chinese official from 1859 to 1910 was a variation on a common theme in Britain's commercial empire.

Second, the feat of British administrators fostering law and order was primarily in the service of trade and economic growth. Combined with the expansion of Christian missions, both Catholic and Protestant, the European-American penetration of the continents beyond Europe and North America took the form of colonialism when feasible but of imperialism in any case. As the exchange of British manufactures (and Indian opium) gave way to the growth of Chinese industrialization (and Chinese opium), British commerce with China began to be accompanied by foreign and Chinese investment in port cities, steamship lines, banks, industries, mines, and railways. After Japan's defeat of China in 1895 the loans of British, German, French, and Russian banks to pay the indemnity would usher in the era of financial imperialism that Hobson, Lenin, and others decried as the highest stage of capitalism. (How little they really saw!) Saddled with the huge Boxer indemnity in 1901, the ailing Ch'ing dynasty found both its maritime and native customs revenue, and even its salt gabelle, hypothecated to pay its foreign creditors instead of, perhaps, financing domestic reform.

Imperialism had thus become an oppressive fact *pari passu* with the belated growth of Chinese nationalism. In patriotic Chinese eyes, Hart and the Customs became in the end the central actors in the triumph of foreign aggression. Needless to say, the modern patriotic Chinese view of the foreign commercial, cultural, and technological invasion, seen in retrospect, was bound to be quite different from the rather self-congratulatory view of foreigners at the time. This means that we are dealing in this volume with a controversial subject, and much can be asserted and illustrated on either side. Our own view is that imperialism can best be understood as an aspect of modernization, which is an even larger and more complex subject.

The inadequacy of imperialism as a concept to explain China's modern history lies in its one-sidedness. It puts the ball in the foreigner's court, as though China were a passive recipient of foreign aggression and that was all. This is illogical, implausible, and flies in the face of much evidence of vital growth and change within China.[1] Quite the contrary, imperialism began as a two-way street along which a traffic of goods and ideas, strategies and policies, flowed in both directions. China had been invaded before and China's response to the foreign aggression of Hart's day was well rooted in China's long history.

Just as Hart had his counterparts elsewhere in Queen Victoria's empire, so he had his predecessors in earlier periods of China's foreign relations. The famous exemplars are, of course, Yeh-lü Ch'u-ts'ai (1190–1244), the Sinicized Khitan Mongol who advised Genghis (Chinggis) Khan and later helped administer North China; Marco Polo, the Venetian who served the Chinese Emperor Kublai (Qubilai) Khan from 1275 to 1292; and the Jesuit fathers Adam Schall (1591–1666) and Ferdinand Verbiest (1623–1688) who served as Chinese officials in the Board of Astronomy at Peking under the late Ming and early Ch'ing dynasties. There are a host of other non-Chinese who served as officials in China under various dynasties. Their number is already legion, but it will increase as the dynastic histories are more intensively studied. The lore concerning them is immense, a major study in itself. So Robert Hart, the British insider at the Court of Peking, was only the latest in an ancient lineage — whether he knew it or not.[2]

In a similar fashion the opprobrious "unequal treaty system" that the British in particular felt they had invented had its Near Eastern predecessors, and in the Far East was only the latest in a long series of arrangements set up to mediate contact between China and the outside world. The predecessor of the unequal treaties as a means of managing Sino-foreign relations had been the Ming-Ch'ing tribute system that underlay the Canton trade until 1842 and in fact continued to coexist with the treaties — though with increasing pallor — down to 1894 (or 1908 if we count a tribute mission to Peking from Nepal that year).

The above suggests that China's "modernization" (a catch-all term even less precise than "imperialism") was a process influenced from within China even more than from without. This is, of course, what we should expect. The activities of China's modernization, after all, had to occur mainly within China and to be carried on mainly by Chinese persons. When we call Hart a "modernizer" we are classifying him essentially as a reformer who was trying to play a role that many Chinese and others were also attempting.

Behind this reforming role lay countless examples of Confucian reformism at work in China's long history. Christian righteousness was no more compelling than the moral dictates of Confucianism. Filial piety, which obliged even the highest official to leave office for

4

almost three years to mourn the death of a parent, was still an active force. No one has made a count, but the ancestral temples in China of Chinese lineages that reverenced their ancestors probably outnumbered the Christian churches in Western countries. Hart's Christian faith that found expression so often in his journal had its counterpart among his Chinese employers, though their faith did not impel them to assume anything like the Western "white man's burden."

What did Hart's "modernizing" activities consist of? Did he contribute principally by building a revenue arm of the failing dynasty? Or by advising it on its problems of foreign relations? Did he put the capstone on the treaty system that ushered China into the modern world? Or did he prolong the life of a moribund regime that held China back? Such questions can best be raised here and answered at least tentatively in subsequent chapters.

HART MEETS THE PROPER TIME

There is a type of Chinese poem entitled "Meeting the proper time." Specifically this refers to the scholar who has the good fortune to be needed and employed by the emperor as an official, thus having his talent recognized and recorded in history. The term is found most often in the poems of disappointed scholars, who lament that they did not meet the proper time to figure in great events.[3] The obvious and quite valid assumption is that greatness usually comes to those people of talent, like F. D. R. and Churchill, whose availability happens to coincide with an urgent historical need for leadership.

Plainly, young Robert Hart met the proper time. How he succeeded H. N. Lay as Inspector General of the Chinese Imperial Maritime Customs Service in November 1863 has been told in our first volume, *Entering China's Service*. It has presented the portions of Hart's journals that survived from his first decade in China after his arrival in 1854. In that earlier volume our narrative chapters followed Hart's personal growth during his twenties as he moved into the new bicultural environment of the treaty ports, and studied the Chinese language and social customs. In particular he learned the ways of the Ch'ing dynasty's Chinese and Manchu officials with whom the British consuls and interpreters had to deal. It was during this decade that Hart acquired the proficiency in Chinese that enabled him to become an interpreter—that special officer who mediated between the two sides, speaking to the hapless Ch'ing officials with the authoritative voice of his British superiors and yet representing the Chinese

side by explaining to his uncouth countrymen the facts and considerations that confronted the emperor's servants. This was the focal
point at which the Chinese and Western cultures and polities met and
clashed. Interpreting gave the two parties the verbal data that helped
to shape their decisions. It could be a positive, creative act, depending on the interpreter's intellectual grasp of the issues and interests on
each side.

By 1858 Robert Hart was interpreter for the Allied (Anglo-French)
Commissioners who governed the ancient entrepôt of Sino-Western
trade at Canton. There he had to deal with the proud and humiliated
puppet officials through whom the foreign invaders governed the city.
Governing involved fighting against the local terrorism of the popular
resistance movement that was backed by the Canton gentry with
imperial encouragement. The tangled fighting and negotiating in
which the young interpreter had to function put him truly in the eye
of the storm.

When Interpreter Hart resigned from the British service and from
1 July 1859 became Deputy Commissioner of Chinese Maritime Customs at Canton, he remained a British citizen but became a Chinese
civil servant. In the next four years, until his appointment as Inspector General on 15 November 1863, we see his career carried forward
by two trends of events. One was the institutionalization, after the
Anglo-French invasion of 1858–1860, of the Western imperialist
treaty system. The other was the coming to power of new leaders in
the Chinese government in an era of dynastic "Restoration."

The Unequal Treaties and the Customs Service

In brief, the Ch'ing dynasty that had ruled China for two centuries
was unable in 1856–1860 to stem the onslaught of the Western powers'
new steam gunboats and cannon. To avoid being toppled by the violent
popular rebellions of the Taiping and other movements in South and
Central China, the Manchu rulers at Peking, in November 1860,
finally accepted the Anglo-French demands and confirmed the institutional structure known as the unequal treaty system. Hart was on the
spot and became a chief agent in the elaboration of this system for the
management of Sino-Western intercourse. (With gradual modifications, the system would last until the 1940s.)

How can we appreciate the complexities that Hart and his generation confronted in China? We must begin by noting several historical
trends and institutional features that shaped his situation. The most
unusual feature of China's international contact in Hart's day, which
distinguished it from that of other countries, was the fact that the for-

eigners' trade did not remain foreign but also became domestic. Western merchants and their vessels traded from one open port to another along the coast and up the Yangtze River, carrying Chinese produce and Chinese-owned goods as part of their business. Some China traders ("old China hands") stayed in China for years on end, not going home until they retired.

This semi-colonial situation had several causes. First of all, it harked back to the expansion of the India-China opium trade in the 1820s and after from outside the single open port of Canton to the whole coast of South China. Under the 1842–1844 treaties until 1858, the China trade was part legal (at the treaty ports) and part illegal (at the opium-receiving stations offshore outside the treaty ports). In fact, the opium trade for the first 16 years of the treaty system was delimited by an unrecorded smuggler-gentlemen's agreement. On the one hand, the British opium duopolists (Jardine and Dent) did not sell outside the established receiving stations on the southeast coast nor did they go north of the Yangtze. On the other hand, the Chinese authorities, after Peking had been unable to suppress by force the opium trade in foreign and Chinese hands, tolerated and profited from it *faute de mieux*. The opium trade was legalized by treaty in 1858.

Meanwhile, enterprising Westerners had begun another invasion of China from Hong Kong in small craft operating under sailing letters given out by the British superintendent of trade. Originally for small craft plying the waters of the Canton-Macao-Hong Kong triangle, these sailing letters soon were not only giving the protection of the British flag to British masters but were also providing Chinese junks with convoy protection against pirates, all the way up to Shanghai.

The final impetus to Western invasion of China's domestic trade routes was the arrival of the steamship. It offered faster and more reliable carriage of cargo, which could also be insured. The British and American steam navigation companies found Chinese shippers to be good customers and in plentiful supply. Soon the foreign steamers were taking the carrying trade in Chinese waters away from the guilds of junkmen, and the junk owners were in trouble.

The result was that foreign shippers and foreign goods in China's domestic trade gave Hart many headaches. Western traders were persistent and ingenious, especially when assisted by Cantonese or, later, Ningpo compradors. By breaking the law consistently and then claiming it was an "old custom," they piled up one extra-treaty privilege after another. Hart and his commissioners, being committed to facilitating trade, went along with this expansion of foreign "rights." Imperialism kept encroaching on the Middle Kingdom.[4]

This encroachment was symbolized in the use of four kinds of documents or "certificates" that we find Hart referring to in his journal. They related to transit duties, exemption certificates, drawbacks, and coast-trade duties, respectively. The first, *transit-duty* passes or certificates, derived from the Anglo-American traders' ardent belief in free trade. Made arrogant by victory, they applauded the treaties as curbing the ancient predilection of Chinese officials for impeding trade by taxation. The free flow of commerce into China (and of profit to themselves) was constantly obstructed, they believed, by inland exactions. To limit this evil the treaties provided that transit dues were to be paid on all foreign-owned goods transported through the interior either as imports or for export. These transit dues were to be one-half the amount of the treaty-tariff import or export duties. They would be collected by the Maritime Customs, whose transit-duty certificates would free foreign imports from all domestic (or "native") tariff charges on goods in transit along the routes of domestic trade. Chinese goods purchased in the interior by a foreign merchant for export would similarly need to pay only a transit duty of one-half the export duty and then be free from taxation at the native customs collection barriers en route to the port (where they would pay export duty on export).

One result was to limit the rate of taxation on foreign-owned goods moving through the Chinese interior, just as the treaty tariff limited the rate of taxation at the ports. Another result was to allow enterprising compradors of foreign firms to extend the reach of foreign enterprise and treaty privilege far into the Chinese hinterland. And for Hart the most immediate result was that the new Maritime Customs Service asserted its supremacy over the old native customs collectorates as the agency for taxing all foreign-owned goods moving anywhere into or within China.

From one activity, however, the Foreign Inspectorate held rather sedulously aloof: Under the 1858 treaty tariff, opium imports were legalized and taxed 30 taels (Tls.) per picul (approximately 133 pounds; about the weight of an opium chest) by the Maritime Customs at the port of entry.[5] From there on, taxation of this high-value, erstwhile contraband drug was to be entirely a Chinese affair. The import tax of Tls. 30 on each of, say, 70,000 chests (the India-to-China trade in the 1880s would reach a height of 87,000 chests) gave Peking a very considerable revenue. Meanwhile, Chinese local authorities, who had always profited from opium the most, could deal with it as they wished. As it left Shanghai, for example, they might slap on a tax of Tls. 50, quite within their treaty rights. Hart's proposal for a transit duty on opium was rejected by the Ch'ing government because opium had always caused dirty work and violence among its handlers. The further revenue from its taxation was left to the provinces. Opium continued to make its way into China on its own merits (so to speak) until the production within China took over the market in the twentieth century. Evidently, by the 1860s, the deeply entrenched opium interest that paid its way by corrupting officials in the provinces was too well established for Peking to tangle with.[6]

Aside from opium, the sphere of Hart's revenue collecting kept expanding. As foreign vessels began to participate in domestic interport trade, both foreign and Chinese goods increasingly were carried in foreign bottoms accompanied by the second kind of document noted above, *exemption certificates*. The use of exemption certificates had resulted from the Western merchants' desire to treat China as a single market where foreign imports, if unsalable at one port, could be sold at another port free of duty. Caleb Cushing in the American treaty of 1844, Article XX, had specified that imported goods on which duty had been paid, if re-exported to another treaty port, would be exempted from a second duty payment. Originally this was done by the Chinese superintendent of customs, who would make a "memorandum in the port clearance" for the vessel concerned. But British consuls arranged in the late 1840s to have it done by the Customs issuance of an exemption certificate. Similarly, they arranged that, if imported goods proved unsalable in China and were shipped out to a foreign country, the owner could secure a duty credit or *drawback certificate* equal to the amount paid as import duty, which could be used thereafter to pay customs duties. These conveniences, like the interport trade itself, represented the growth of treaty-port privileges. They damaged both the old-style collectorates and the Chinese shipping interest.

Informal negotiations between the foreign ministers and the newly created Tsungli Yamen led to a compromise arrangement notified to the trading community on 30 October 1861. Exemption certificates would be only for duty-paid *foreign* goods moving from one port to another. All native goods arriving in foreign bottoms from another port (if the treaty export duty had been paid there) would now pay a *coast-trade duty* of one-half the treaty import duty. If taken to a third port, they could enter free under a duty-paid certificate. Thus, the new half-tariff coast-trade duty would be parallel on the coast to the half-tariff transit duty on inland trade.

The new coast-trade duty, like exemption and drawback certifi-

Russell & Co. Buildings, Shanghai, 1866
Ground floor: Chinese comprador's offices; Main floor: General business office;
Top floor: American clerks' quarters; On the right: Partners' residences;
On the left (not shown): Godown, tea taster's, and silk inspector's offices.

cates, began as a Chinese extra-treaty concession to the aggressive foreigners — another privilege granted them willingly or otherwise. But not for long. Imperialism in China progressed by using the most-favored-nation clause ("anything others get hereafter, I get too"). New treaties with Denmark (1863), Spain (1864), Belgium (1865), Italy (1866), and so on included as treaty law the right to ship Chinese-owned goods coastwise in foreign bottoms.[7] This foreign participation in China's domestic carrying trade was an extraordinary privilege not normally granted by the nation-states of the West.

The preceding account is, of course, an extraordinarily simplified picture of a situation comparable to the United States Internal Revenue Service income-tax system today. A smart firm in the China trade always had some staff member keeping close track of treaty provisions, consular notifications, and customs regulations, much like a present day tax lawyer.

Overall, we must see the China of the 1860s as a vast and intricate hive of commercial activity on the fringes of which foreign firms and their compradors were nibbling away to increase their share of China's trade. Meanwhile, as the Ch'ing government struggled to reestablish its superficial control over areas ravaged by the Taiping (1850–1864) and Nien (1853–1868) Rebellions, it received much-needed and increasing revenues from its new Maritime Customs Service. But this was only one part of China's financial structure.

The fact is that the Ch'ing government at Peking administered China in tandem with the provincial governments. It was a highly decentralized fiscal system, which foreigners could not imagine and tended to discount. True, the emperor exercised central power over officialdom, appointing, transferring, promoting, rewarding, and disciplining the bureaucracy all over China. His political prerogatives remained unchallenged. But his centralized power coexisted with a fiscal administration that was, in the words of a late Ch'ing encyclopedia, as confused as "tangled silk." Provinces credited to Peking their assigned quotas of taxes but kept the above-quota tax receipts for local use, primarily to maintain the official establishment at various levels. These receipts, together with gifts, also helped line the pockets of bureaucrats. "To become an official and get rich" (tso-kuan fa-ts'ai) was still the major motive that inspired the hard study of many thousands of degree candidates competing in the civil-service-examination system.

Peking ran the empire by assigning a multitude of revenue quotas to meet a myriad of established needs — whether to feed Manchu garrisons, maintain granaries, dikes and waterways, or reward virtuous widows for not remarrying. To meet emergencies of flood, drought, rebellion, or invasion, Peking called for special expenditures from the provincial administrations, whose officials had the primary responsibility for all events within their jurisdictions. The frequent result was financial chaos, a situation ripe for abuse. The British solution for China's ills was "more power to the emperor"—but a large gap existed between modern Western state theory and ancient Chinese practice.

To enlarge this gap in the 1860s came a new development, the growth of the provincial tax known as likin (*li-chin*, lit., "a levy of one thousandth [of a tael]"). Inaugurated after 1853 by provincial officials fighting the Taiping rebels, likin began as a very small tax, say 1 percent, on the value of goods in transit past a collecting point, or where produced or marketed. But there soon turned out to be many collecting points on China's internal trade routes. Provincial likin receipts rose quickly in the 1860s. Though Peking demanded provincial accounts and payments of likin revenues, the capital could never catch up with the provinces. All collectors had sticky fingers.

The reason for the rise of likin as a ready form of new revenue gives us one final clue to the Chinese puzzle that Hart confronted as Inspector General. Parallel to the growth of steamships, foreign trade, and Maritime Customs revenues so visible to foreign eyes, there was a vigorous growth of China's internal trade which the foreigners were less able to see. A long secular rise in China's domestic commerce had set in during the eighteenth century along with the doubling or more of China's population. The growing domestic market stimulated inter-provincial and countrywide staple trade in raw cotton, silk, textiles, tea, timber, salt, iron, ceramic wares, and the like, as well as opium. The growth of trade guilds and native-place associations evidenced the rise of a merchant class that officialdom could no longer dominate. A public sector of economic enterprise and community action grew up distinct from the official and private sectors of the past, and, although merchants never threatened the established Chinese social order the way their counterparts did in late Tokugawa Japan, they did become part of a new gentry-landlord-merchant elite that played an increasingly significant role in China's modernization. Provincial likin taxes, which foreign goods might avoid by paying transit duties, were harbingers of accelerating changes in China's domestic environment—changes that had begun before the foreign intrusion that brought Hart and the Maritime Customs to the scene.[8]

Once aware of these trends of the 1860s, we can more easily define Hart's role, or roles, in the complex events of his time. Like other foreign observers he was inclined to see the struggle as one between Western "progress" and Chinese "backwardness." In building the Customs Service, he felt that the forces of history were on his side. Hart's modesty about his personal attainments testified not only to his own objectivity but also to the apparent inevitability of the "progress" that seemed so evident in the world throughout the Victorian age. Hart's problem was not *whether* to help the forces of progress (now known with equal ambiguity as modernization). His problem was simply how to do it.

In this enterprise he was aided, as we have already suggested, by the long tradition of non-Chinese rulers of China employing other foreigners to help them govern. One secret of the efficiency of China's imperial government had been its longstanding custom of co-opting alien chieftains on the frontiers to become servants of the emperor. In the great tradition of "using barbarians to control barbarians" (*i-i chih-i*), the Manchu rulers of the Ch'ing dynasty knew that Hart could help them in the distasteful task of managing foreign merchants if only he himself could be controlled. They (and he) succeeded admirably. As a loyal Chinese official who appraised for Peking the customs duties due it from foreign traders, Hart gave employment to and closely supervised several thousand Europeans (mainly British) as well as Americans who worked under his Maritime Customs service.

He did not, however, create the system. Let us pause here to examine briefly how it developed, how British administrators trapped themselves. Experience under the Canton system of trade before 1842 had led the British to want two incompatible things — the extraterritorial jurisdiction of British consuls over the person (and property) of British nationals in China, and at the same time a "fair and regular" taxation of British trade according to a published treaty tariff. In other words, no more Chinese-style justice, no more Chinese-style taxes on trade. The dilemma arose when the new British consuls at the first five open ports were given responsibility both for applying British (and treaty) law to British persons and for applying the treaty tariff to British goods. They soon found that in facilitating Britain's China trade they could usefully do the former but not the latter. After all, they had to deal with the living institutions and practices of China, not Utopia.

Specifically, in creating the treaty system to take the place of the Canton system, the Treaty of Nanking in 1842 decreed that British consuls should take the place of the Security Merchants (the firms of the licensed guild or Cohong at Canton), one of whom took responsibility for the proper conduct of each foreign ship. Applying this idea, the Rules of Trade appended to the Anglo-Chinese Supplementary Treaty of 1843 provided that the consuls should see to it that British merchants paid their proper customs duties. Unfortunately, the American and French treaties had no such provision. This imbalance soon led to British "consular interference for the prevention of smuggling," as it was called by aggrieved British merchants, who found themselves unable to compete with merchants of other nations who colluded with the Chinese customs houses to pay lower duties to their mutual, and corrupt, profit. After all, the Emperor was far away, and who was to mind if Chinese collectors and foreign merchants connived to defraud the imperial revenue and split their ill-gotten gains? Even today, merchants in many parts of the world find it suicidal to pay full duties when their corrupt competitors are making deals with local collectors. Moreover, in China after the Opium War aggressive foreign merchants were not above browbeating timid Chinese collectors who lacked the power to coerce or punish them. In this way consular jurisdiction (extraterritoriality), when added to unscrupulous foreign competition, made the treaty tariff unenforceable. By 1851 Britain had to give up consular protection of China's revenue. The treaty system thus faced collapse. China could quite possibly tax the foreign trade inland, outside the treaty ports, and so disregard the treaty tariff entirely.

The solution to this institutional crisis evolved at Shanghai in the 1850s, as recounted in our earlier volume. The "foreign-inspectorate" principle—that the Chinese customs house should employ foreign officers to appraise the duties properly due from foreign merchants—was, as we have already indicated, quite compatible with Chinese tradition. As the system developed, opposition to the foreign-inspectorate principle turned out to be greater from the foreign than from the Chinese side. British consuls, in particular, found that foreign customs commissioners often cramped their style, stole some of their prerogatives, and had local power and prestige that rivaled their own.

The foreign-inspectorate idea was put across by a series of vigorous administrators: On the foreign side were the British Consul Rutherford Alcock, who invented the system in 1854 at Shanghai with the help of the American Commissioner to China, R. M. McLane; T. F. Wade and H. N. Lay, who served in succession as the principal Inspector at Shanghai in the 1850s; Sir John Bowring, the British Minister to China and a Benthamite reformer who pushed for the extension of the Shanghai system to all the ports in 1858; and Sir Frederick Bruce, first British Minister in Peking (1861–1864).

The counterparts of these men among Ch'ing officials included the

Shanghai Taotai (Circuit Intendant), Wu Chien-chang, a scalawag capable of creative opportunism; his successors, especially Lan Wei-wen, Wu Hsu, and Hsueh Huan; their superiors as Nanking Governor General, the Manchu I-liang and then the Chinese Ho Kuei-ch'ing; the Hoppo Heng-ch'i and Governor General Lao Ch'ung-kuang, both at Canton; and at Peking, Wen-hsiang, the astute Manchu who led the Tsungli Yamen along with the head of the Grand Council, Prince Kung. These men who figure in *Entering China's Service* are listed here for a purpose — to indicate the momentum that had accumulated behind the institution of the Inspectorate before Hart became I.G. in 1863. The way was cleared for him. An edifice had been started, not least by himself as acting I.G. in place of Lay in 1862.

Before looking more closely at the Chinese institutional framework within which Hart operated, we should note the degree to which, by 1863, the Maritime Customs had taken over several of the duties originally expected of the Chinese authorities or assigned under the treaty system to the British (and in varying degree to the other foreign) consuls. Shanghai, the chief port, had set the style. There the foreign Inspector of Customs had taken on the management of the harbor. The British consul no longer had to find and appoint a harbormaster who could direct traffic or settle the fees to be paid the local pilots who guided ships in and out of port. The marking of port limits and the installation of aids to navigation, such as buoys, beacons, and eventually a lighthouse service, were now handled by the foreign inspectorate. So also were the complaints of merchants, who could often get satisfaction without appealing to their consuls. The tidewaiters who met the ships and superintended discharge and loading of cargo soon formed the nucleus of a Customs Out-Door Staff.

A preventive service of Customs small craft armed to control smugglers began to take shape. This idea was behind Hart's scheme to get for China a fleet of foreign-officered steam gunboats to police waterways. The failure of the Lay-Osborn Flotilla program, already recounted in *Entering China's Service*, did not long delay the necessary growth of a small-scale Customs preventive fleet at each port.

Meanwhile the Customs In-Door Staff, headed at each port by a foreign commissioner and peopled by foreign assistants and Chinese clerks, shroffs (money-changers), and other underlings, devoted itself to one absorbing but limited goal — to ascertain the duties due by the tariff and certify that they had been paid into the Customs bank designated by the Ch'ing government's superintendent of customs (usually the top local official, a taotai). The foreign inspectorate itself received no payments. It only told Peking what had been received at each port each quarter. Until after Hart's death in retirement in 1910, in fact until the end of the dynasty in 1911, this practice continued to be the basis of the Customs' success. On this foundation of a well-trained civil-service staff that functioned day by day, year after year, Hart would maintain his position at Peking in control of the whole service. When we find Hart in his journal absorbed in problems of high-level personnel management, active in diplomacy, resolving problems of jurisdiction or *amour propre*, proposing reform, or creating new institutions in the arena of China's foreign relations, we will do well to remember that such activity was only the tip of Hart's iceberg. His main day-to-day job was comprehensive administrative supervision. The post of Inspector General was properly named.

In the period of 1859–1863, both Lay and Hart had scrambled in order to acquire buildings and staff and find competent administrators for their 13 offices. The buildup of this bureaucracy as an appendage grafted onto the Ch'ing official system would owe much to the procedures of both the Ch'ing and the British Empires. In titles of lower staff and forms of correspondence the Customs followed the example of the British Consular Service from which both Lay and Hart had transferred. But the British Consulates answered to a single parent, the British minister to China, resident after 1860 in Peking. The Customs offices were of mixed breed, part Chinese, part foreign, and their central authority was a young British subject employed by the Ch'ing dynasty.

The confusion of authority was not lessened by two factors: the Ch'ing government's civil war to suppress the Taiping rebels, and H. N. Lay's disorderly and insecure personality. It was the civil war that led to Lay's deep commitment to acquiring for Peking a powerful fleet of warships, but his trait of personal insecurity and aggressiveness (if we may psychologize) prevented his surrendering control of it to its Chinese purchasers. Having started out as tsar of the Customs Service he vaingloriously thought he could parlay this into controlling a Ch'ing navy.

While the Hart-Lay-Osborn scheme for instantaneous Chinese naval power was getting started, Lay's absence in England and his division of the Inspector Generalship between Fitzroy, who stayed mainly in Shanghai, and Hart, who traveled about setting up Customs offices in the treaty ports as well as an office in Peking, left the Customs without a single head. Remnants of correspondence indicate its floundering.

Take the newly opened port of Swatow, where in early 1860 W. Wallace Ward was Commissioner but traveling with Lay. This left F. Wilzer in charge as Acting Commissioner. Lay's letters to him offer a classic case of how not to administer a widely dispersed bureaucracy.[9] In April 1861 Lay tells Wilzer from Hong Kong that he is now to be Deputy Commissioner in charge at Swatow at a salary of 300 Tls. a month, and his "immediate Superior will be the Canton Commissioner of Customs at Canton . . . through whom you will receive Hoppo's instructions. Mr. Fitzroy, and Mr. Hart are appointed to discharge the duties of Inspector General during my absence, and you will transmit to their address your monthly returns, Cash Account, and act upon any instructions you may receive from them." In other words, Deputy Commissioner Wilzer at Swatow was to accept instructions from a four-headed Sino-foreign monster—the Canton Commissioner, the Hoppo, Fitzroy, and Hart. Who was his boss?

Such fragments from the early days reveal a nascent Customs Service ill-organized and poorly led—still another reason for the new I.G. to become the central authority, and to work out comprehensive regulations and instructions for his service. History was waiting upon Hart.

The T'ung-chih Restoration

History was also waiting on Hart's Chinese employers. The death of the Hsien-feng Emperor in 1861 brought his 5-year-old son, Tsaich'un, to the throne as the T'ung-chih Emperor (reigned: 1862–1874), under the co-regency of his biological mother, the Empress Dowager, Tz'u-hsi. This coup d'état turned out to be a blessing in disguise, for it resulted in an immediate and overdue change in China's metropolitan leadership. Prince Kung, brother of the deceased Emperor, received the designation "Deliberative Prince," and he soon emerged as one of the most "able and enlightened" officials in the empire. Together with Wen-hsiang, Prince Kung endowed the newly formed Tsungli Yamen with heightened stature in the eyes of foreigners, and this stature, in turn, gave the Western powers greater faith in China.[10]

A year earlier, Shanghai's *North China Herald* defied its English-language readers to "find one bright spot in . . . [the Ch'ing dynasty's] government or morals, one single spot that is not black and utterly decayed." But, by the end of 1861, the newspaper could describe the new regency as "powerful and vigorous," and claim that a "revolution in the [Chinese] state, as sudden, sharp and decisive as that at Paris, which astounded Europe in 1848, has just happened at Peking."[11] Whether such judgments were warranted is not our primary concern here; the point is that they were made, and that they provided the justification for much of Western policy toward China in the 1860s.

Foreigners were not alone in their enthusiasm for China's new political order. The term *Restoration* (*chung-hsing*; lit. "a rising at mid-course") was used by both contemporary scholars and by later Chinese historians to describe the reign of the youthful T'ung-chih Emperor. It implied precisely the timely emergence of "talented individuals" who could occupy civil and military posts in the Ch'ing government and arrest dynastic decline. The ascendency of Prince Kung, Wen-hsiang, and others in Peking was paralleled by the emergence of men such as Tseng Kuo-fan, Tso Tsung-t'ang, and Li Hung-chang in the provinces. Without this kind of leadership, Hart might never have had his chance.[12]

What were the values that bound Restoration leaders together? Despite striking differences in age, life experience, and even ethnic origin, most Ch'ing bureaucrats were the products of a sophisticated educational system that focused on a mastery not only of the hallowed Confucian Classics, but also over 20 dynastic histories, and various orthodox commentaries. These works emphasized above all the moral wisdom of the ancients, and the value of studying the past for lessons relevant to the present. Most Chinese thinkers of the T'ung-chih period rejected the idea of progress in the sense of progressive improvement, but they continued to be moved by a powerful impulse to improve society by harkening back to earlier history.

The prevailing orthodoxy of the Ch'ing dynasty, defined by the official commentaries of the Ch'eng-Chu school of Neo-Confucianism, viewed ethics as the single most important factor in Chinese administration. The emperor and his officials ruled primarily by moral example, with guidance from both the Classics and the histories. Neither bureaucratic specialization nor abstract law could therefore ensure good government. In the words of Confucius: "If a ruler is upright, all will go well without orders; but if he is not upright, even though he gives orders, they will not be obeyed." And again, "If the people are led by laws and regulated by penalties, they will try to avoid the punishment but have no sense of shame. If they are led by virtue and given uniformity by means of ritual, they will have a sense of shame, and become good."[13]

Ch'ing officials of the Restoration era relentlessly stressed this idealistic view of government. Tseng Kuo-fan, for example, believed that China's greatest need was for "earnest and solid scholars who would act on their own ideas," and that men who were both "virtuous and wise" could transform the morale and behavior of an entire generation.[14] The primary means of self-cultivation for such individuals was a rigorous review of the Classics and the dynastic histories, coupled with a strict adherence to ritual and propriety. Conformity to ritual would, in the orthodox view, preserve the all-important distinctions of status and inspire proper behavior at all levels of Chinese government and society.

But Ch'ing government was not simply a matter of ethical idealism. Most officials of the T'ung-chih period, including Tseng, saw the need to apply time-honored principles of practical statecraft (*ching-shih*) to solving the concrete problems of their time. To be sure, these administrative solutions tended to seek classical sanction and historical precedent; but, by the 1860s, increasing numbers of Ch'ing officials had come to realize that China was in the midst of a fundamental change — some referred to it as an "unprecedented situation" (*ch'uang-chü*) — for which classical formulas and traditional expedients might not suffice. It was this pragmatic realization that gave impetus to China's "self-strengthening" movement in the 1860s — a concerted attempt to acquire Western scientific and technical knowledge, as well as weapons and machinery, in order to contend with both internal rebellion and external aggression.

Hart's employment was a vital part of the process. Though only one of many foreigners employed by Ch'ing officials in the 1860s to provide technical advice and assistance, he quickly emerged as the most influential. In the first place, he was the only Westerner occupying an official post in the metropolitan bureaucracy. He thus had daily access to China's highest officials in the Grand Council and the Tsungli Yamen. As a foreigner, but also a trusted servant of the Ch'ing, his views on progress and foreign relations had special weight. Secondly, the regular customs revenues that his administration guaranteed financed a large number of self-strengthening projects, from the foreign training of Chinese troops to the establishment of shipyards and arsenals.

Hart still had to work, however, within a bureaucratic system that had evolved over some two thousand years, and did not lend itself easily to Western-style modernization. The most characteristic feature of this system was its elaborate pattern of checks and balances, inherited from the Ming dynasty and refined for Manchu purposes. Ch'ing administration was designed above all to assure maximum political stability, even at the expense of administrative efficiency. This was a particularly important consideration to the Manchus, who as alien conquerors outnumbered at least 100 to 1, were obsessively anxious to maintain control over all spheres of civil and military government. True, a time-honored principle of Chinese government was to grant wide leeway to provincial officials and, in Hart's words, to "localise responsibility." But the corollary principle of Ch'ing government was to maintain a high degree of centralized supervision, undertaken both by specially designated censors and by regular officials with overlapping jurisdictions.[15]

In civil affairs, Ch'ing administration featured the balanced appointment of high-ranking Manchu and Chinese officials in all major metropolitan agencies, including the Grand Council. Mutual supervision was the obvious purpose, and mutual suspicion the occasional result. In provincial administration, Chinese officials generally outnumbered Manchus, particularly at the lower levels. But the responsibilities of Manchu and Chinese officials often overlapped — as when, for example, a Manchu governor general and a Chinese governor were required to act on and report matters jointly. The balance of power in this carefully crafted Manchu-Chinese dyarchy, like the hoary institution of censorial supervision, strengthened the hand of the Throne against potential rivals for power, both at the capital and in the provinces.

Another distinctive feature of Ch'ing administration was the so-called "rule of avoidance" (*hui-pi*), which mandated that an official could not serve in his home locale (e.g., a county magistrate could not hold office in his home county, and so forth). The practice, designed to prevent an official from relying too heavily on personal contacts and from patronizing local interests at home, arose from a longstanding recognition of the enormous strength in Chinese society of personal "connections" or *kuan-hsi*. These relationships might be based on any number of social common denominators: blood or marriage ties, the same home origins (village, town, city, and province, in roughly descending order of importance), shared occupation, common educational experience (including receipt of a civil-service-examination degree in the same year, known as *t'ung-nien kuan-hsi*) and so forth. These connections — which reflected the personalism and particularism of Confucian values — were constantly reaffirmed and strengthened by the pervasive practice of gift giving, itself a manifestation of highly specific Chinese notions of reciprocity.

In a society that lacked the Western ideal of equal and impartial law, *kuan-hsi* provided a sense of security as well as a way of getting things done in the face of a ponderous, impersonal, and often inefficient bureaucracy. "Connections" were thus likely to be more carefully cultivated and far stronger in China than in any analogous Western system of personal relationships, including the "old-boy" network of political patronage known to Hart. But the practice of gift giving that characterized Chinese society as a whole proved to be a special problem within the Ch'ing government — particularly since officials were paid such low official salaries and had such high administrative costs. The opportunities for giving gifts to superiors, which might foster personal relationships within the bureaucracy, were numerous and manifold, as were the occasions for abuse. Ch'ing law stipulated that all such gifts were normally prohibited, and that it was illegal to ask an official "to take into account one's personal connection to him by handling a particular piece of public business in a partial way"; but the line between a "present" and a "bribe," between personal protocol and personal corruption, was difficult to draw. How much did a colleague need for "travel money" (*ch'eng-i*) or as a "parting gift" (*chin-i*)? What was an appropriate congratulatory present (*ho-i*) on the occasion of, say, a festival, or the birthday of an official's mother? The diary of Li Tz'u-ming, a low-ranking bureaucrat at Peking in Hart's time, indicates that from 1863 to 1888 nearly half of his total income came from gifts. And yet Li had comparatively little influence to peddle! Hart's journal entries refer repeatedly to the corruptive potential of Chinese gift giving, and his official circulars demonstrate a concerted effort to control it within the Customs Service; but the practice was too pervasive and multifaceted to eradicate entirely.[16]

In order to keep officials from becoming too deeply enmeshed in patterns of personal indebtedness — not to mention too firmly entrenched in their posts — Peking transferred its officials at all levels regularly, usually every three years or so. Here was more evidence of the Confucian assumption that personal character rather than specialized administrative or technical competence was the key to good government. The uniform training of all scholar-officials in preparing for the Chinese civil-service examinations made this policy feasible, but not necessarily efficient. Indeed, short tenure encouraged corruption and discouraged innovation. What official wanted to run the risk of starting a new venture, only to see his successor reap the hard-earned benefits? A Ch'ing official with progressive ideas might think twice before trying to implement them.

In military affairs, the system of checks and balances included the same overlapping jurisdictions, the rule of avoidance, and frequent transfer. Two distinct armies existed under separate commands. The Banner Army, numbering about 250,000 soldiers during the mid-nineteenth century, was a multi-ethnic fighting force composed primarily of Manchus, but also of Mongols and Chinese. It remained the principal military arm of the Ch'ing dynasty, at least in theory, under the direct control of either the Imperial Household or the Manchu-controlled Banner Office in Peking. The other regular army, known as the Green Standard, was an exclusively Chinese force designed primarily to serve as a provincial constabulary. It was responsible directly to the Boards of War and Revenue. Although the Green Standard Army boasted some 500,000 soldiers, it was fragmented into a number of small garrisons so that no single Green Standard detachment had as much concentrated strength as a single Banner garrison in any area. In addition, the command structure of the Green Standard Army was especially diffused, with a great number of overlapping jurisdictions and responsibilities.

Although "temporary" mercenary armies known as *yung-ying* (lit. "brave battalions") supplanted the degenerate Banner and Green Standard Armies as the bulwark of the Ch'ing dynasty's defense during the Taiping Rebellion, these provincially based imperial forces, too, were subject to a number of constraints. The Throne, for example, made a conscious effort to play the sponsoring provincial officials off against one another, to manipulate the funding and deployment of *yung-ying* forces, and to mandate their reduction or demobilization as soon as militarily feasible. The "regionalism" of the T'ung-chih period never devolved into warlordism.[17]

This carefully designed Ch'ing system of civil and military control made rapid change difficult enough. But an added problem was the regency of the Empress Dowager. Although Prince Kung and Wen-hsiang played the leading roles in most areas of Ch'ing administration during the early T'ung-chih period, Tz'u-hsi soon emerged as a potent political power in her own right. Only she controlled the Emperor's official seal necessary to validate his orders. One measure of her growing strength was her ability to dismiss Prince Kung from all offices in April 1865, on the rather vague grounds of carelessness at Court and partiality to his relatives. Although she relented after ten days and restored the Prince to most of his previous official positions, she permanently deprived him of the title of "Deliberative Prince," and left the metropolitan bureaucracy with no doubt about who held the reins of power.[18]

In this political maneuver and others, Tz'u-hsi had the support of conservative officials at the capital. As an astute but politically vulnerable female ruler, who had executed a coup d'état to gain power, Tz'u-hsi proved to be extremely defensive and particularly inclined to use conservative support and Neo-Confucian orthodoxy to serve her own political ends. Although she was not always as capricious and uncompromising as many critics averred, her policies were often misguided — particularly when she remained so far removed from the scene of Sino-foreign problems in treaty ports like Shanghai.

Given the context sketched above, we can read Hart's journal as a record of conflicting tendencies — the foreigners' constantly expanding their position in China, the Chinese instinctively seeking some advantage from the foreign activity. Our first section of the journal opens with Hart in Shanghai. In what circumstances did he find himself?

SHANGHAI 1864: THE ANGLO-CH'ING PARTNERSHIP

Unlike the Peking of Hart's day, built four-square around the cosmic power center known as the Forbidden City, Shanghai focused on a narrow strip, the Bund along the Whangpu River. As at other treaty ports, the shorefront installations of trading firms, banks, hotels, and consulates were the landward extension of maritime trade. The Shanghai Bund in the 1860s was about 65 feet wide, enlarged from the old junk towing path, and it extended 3,500 feet from the Soochow Creek (Wusung River) where it entered the Whangpu River, south to the French Concession and the old Chinese walled city. A dozen or so sloping wooden jetties, rising and falling with the tide, gave access to the anchorage. Toward the south end of the Bund was the Shanghai Club, a building four stories high with dining rooms, bedrooms and other accommodations for transients, though its bar was not yet "the longest in the world." In 1862 the American settlement to the north and east of Soochow Creek had been incorporated in the British to make the International Settlement under the Shanghai Municipal Council. As of 1864, it maintained 126 constables, had built 1,000 yards of sewers, and had macadamized most of the streets on a budget of Tls. 289,000. By 1866 the police force would include 40 Chinese.

Shanghai's rise had followed inevitably from the geographic fact that it was halfway between Hong Kong and Yokohama at the midpoint on the China coast where the waterborne trade of the Yangtze basin, all of Central China, joined the coastal and international trade. Shanghai's phenomenal growth was indicated by the population figures. In 1858 there were 70 firms with 330 foreigners plus families, 8 consulates, and 36 Protestant missionaries. By March 1865 the foreign resident population was 2,700 with the addition of 5,500 British military. From 1860 to 1865 Shanghai had experienced five years of military occupation, which included the use of temples in the Chinese city as barracks. In 1861 Defense Creek had been constructed on the west of the racecourse, running south from Soochow Creek to the Yang-king-pang, a small stream marking the northern boundary of the French Concession, later Avenue Edward Seventh.

The Chinese population, which had swelled with the influx of Soo-

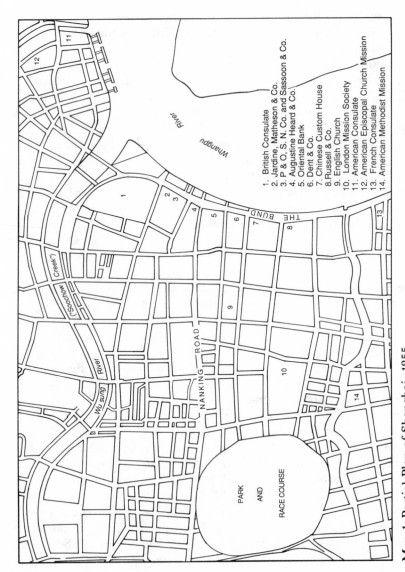

Map 1 Partial Plan of Shanghai, 1855

Adapted from Hosea Ballou Morse, *The International Relations of the Chinese Empire*, Vol. 1 (London, Longmans Green & Co., 1910).

chow gentry families fleeing the Taipings in 1853–1854, had fallen after the end of the rebellion to an estimated 146,000. The foreign settlement experienced a period of depression after an era of enthusiastic land speculation and profit at the expense of the large Chinese refugee population. The Chinese walled city to the south of the French Concession was estimated to have a population of 125,000 living in what foreigners routinely described as "extreme native filth and squalor."[19] Shanghai in the winter of 1863–1864 was still a raw product of invasion and rebellion.

For Hart as Inspector General of Chinese Customs, Shanghai was as important as all of the other ports put together. While Peking had been the center of diplomacy between the Tsungli Yamen and the foreign ministers to China, Shanghai harbored the British commercial interests (led by Jardine Matheson & Co. and Dent & Co.) that had helped precipitate and win the Opium War of 1839–1842. The second war of 1856–1860 and the final opening of China had heightened the merchants' sense of their role in the forefront of progress, which they saw in simplistic terms as Right backed by Might. Devotees of the Shanghai mind with its aggressive contempt for Chinese officialdom were quick to feel hostility for the Customs Inspectorate under Hart and for its expansion to form a branch of the Chinese government at every port.

Robert Hart, whose bronze statue would 60 years later be a tourist attraction on the Bund, kept a low profile in Shanghai during his first year as Inspector General. The title "I.G." as yet conveyed no aura of concentrated institutional power. Quite the contrary. In 1864, Hart was a nice, friendly young man, soft-spoken and unassuming in manner, although tenacious in his aims. He had to speak gently to the Shanghai-minded, especially after the assertive Harry Parkes returned to China to be British Consul at Shanghai. (Recall that Parkes's return from England in 1856 had soon been followed by his finding a *casus belli* for the warfare at Canton.)

An example of Hart's personal style can be found in his handling of the *Heron* case in late 1863. On 19 December 1863, Hart confides in his journal that he is perplexed because Dent & Co.'s *Heron* arranged to go on a pleasure trip without cargo, but outside the port found other boats loading cotton with local officials' permission and so did the same. The Shanghai Customs therefore seized their boat for smuggling. Since the trading outside the port limits was going on uncontrolled, Hart released the *Heron* but refused to let it move freely on the river again. Hart hinted that Dent & Co. had committed a breach of good faith. Dent objected, not wanting to be placed in a false position; and later H. N. Dent wrote a long letter "somewhat plausible, but yet [containing] fallacious arguments. I talked with him on the bund tonight: he admits I had cause for complaint — and that's enough. I must now let them down gently: and, Robert my boy!, no hurry in future!" (24 December 1863).

Hart's social life was largely institutional. He made it a practice every ten days or so to have a dinner party for five males guests, usually young staff members of the Customs. Sooner or later, all would be invited. Only once, on 20 April 1864, did he invite the high brass of British Shanghai — Consul Parkes, Colonel Hough, Major Jebb, Captain Murray plus Thomas Dick, his local Commissioner of Customs. Hart called it "a rather slow party," which was probably an understatement; he had little respect for Sir Harry's intellect, having been his interpreter in governing Canton in 1858–1859. Hart went out to dinner occasionally and paid many calls, both socially and for business, but he seems to have eschewed as a matter of policy the active social life of the Shanghai foreign business community at large.

On the side of Chinese officialdom, the young I.G. maintained steady relations with the Shanghai Taotai (in 1864 Ying Pao-shih), who was both the local Superintendent of Customs and the representative of the Governor of Kiangsu, Li Hung-chang. Hart and Ying, when both were in the city, kept in close touch, calling on or writing to each other on an almost day-to-day basis. Ying conveyed messages from Governor Li, wrote (2 March) to convey the Tsungli Yamen's approval of Hart's action in a case of confiscation, and sometimes simply reported news of events. Relations were so close, in fact, that Hart became aware "from word that Ying Taoutae let drop the other day" that Hart's Chinese amanuensis, Sun, evidently sent Ying copies "of all my correspondence — the old blackguard! Still what can I do? Any other Chinese that I could get hold of wd. require years of drilling before he could do what Sun does, and wd. then play false just in the same way." (18 March 1864)

Hart's Customs Administration by 1864 boasted employees from Great Britain, the United States, France, and Prussia, as well as Chinese superintendents of customs and lower-ranking Chinese functionaries. As the multi-lingual head of a multi-national body, he was a cultural middleman — British by birth, Chinese by choice. In this position, Hart constantly became involved in negotiations of many sorts: between Chinese and Western employees in his own organization; between Western merchants and Chinese officials; between Chinese and Western officials, and among the Western officials themselves.

By virtue of Great Britain's predominant commercial interests in

China, not to mention its superior naval power and colonial network (including Hong Kong after 1842), British officials took the lead in most policy matters relating to treaty-port affairs. This was particularly the case during the Taiping Rebellion. British policy in the early 1860s aimed to restrict direct Western intervention in the rebellion; instead, to assist the Ch'ing government in military reform ("self-strengthening"), and to bolster Peking's central authority, even against encroachments on that authority by British residents in China. In pursuing these goals, the Foreign Office limited the field of direct British military operations against the Taipings to a 30-mile radius around Shanghai; but at the same time it sanctioned the employment of British officers as advisers and instructors in the Chinese military service.

Hart's military counterpart in the Shanghai area was Major Charles "Chinese" Gordon, who headed the much publicized Ever-Victorious Army (EVA). Where Hart commanded his commissioners and their Chinese staffs to bring the Ch'ing government new sources of funds for military operations (including those of the EVA), Gordon commanded his foreign officers and Chinese troops to bring modern cannon fire to bear on Taiping strongholds. Gordon's ingenuity in using steamers and cannon in amphibious warfare in the Yangtze Delta waterways gave the Ch'ing forces a crucial strategic advantage; it also introduced special problems of responsibility and restraint. Although Hart and Gordon were both British subjects taken into the Chinese service, Gordon remained an officer of the Royal Engineers, more accountable to the British government than to the Chinese, while Hart operated solely as a Ch'ing employee. For this reason, among others, Gordon lasted less than 2 years as a Chinese officer; Hart, more than 40.

Shanghai's Chinese Establishment

Although Hart was a Ch'ing official, he neither lived nor worked in the Chinese walled city. He did, however, have regular and sometimes intimate contact with his bureaucratic colleagues there — notably the Shanghai Taotai. Moreover, he paid extremely close attention to the activities of the Chinese as well as the Western merchants at the treaty port. Although Shanghai in the 1860s had a split personality typical of colonialism, the International Settlement and French Concession were more than simply bastions of foreign privilege. They also served as havens for growing numbers of Chinese from other parts of the empire. The first wave of refugees arrived at Shanghai when Nanking fell to the Taipings in 1853. By early 1863, the Chinese population of the city as a whole was estimated at 1.5 million, about a third of whom lived in the foreign settlements. At that time, the Western residents totaled probably fewer than 2,000. Predictably, real-estate values skyrocketed, and profits from land rents tended to mute foreign grumbling about the influx of Chinese refugees. Wealthy gentry from the rich Yangtze Delta sought physical safety in Shanghai, while Chinese merchants found a secure environment for business.

Among the Chinese merchants at Shanghai in the 1850s and 1860s, two main groups vied for commercial supremacy. One consisted of natives from Kwangtung and Fukien — primarily from the port cities of Canton and Foochow. The other, sometimes known as the Chekiang financial clique, was led by merchants from the nearby city of Ningpo. Although Canton, Foochow, and Ningpo had all been opened along with Shanghai as treaty ports in the 1840s, a number of merchants from the three ports had foreseen their inevitable eclipse by Shanghai even prior to the Opium War. The fifth early treaty port, Amoy, had long been the base of an international trade conducted by Chinese merchants with Southeast Asia.[20]

In competing for Shanghai's profits, the Canton and Foochow merchants initially enjoyed the advantage of greater experience in foreign trade; but the Chekiang clique was firmly entrenched in the lower Yangtze Valley, where it dominated the native banks (ch'ien-chuang, lit. "copper-coin shops"). This gave the Ningpo guild a great advantage. In the absence of effective Ch'ing central government control over fiscal matters such as coinage, the distribution of currency, and the issuance of credit or bank notes, their native banks had considerable control over both currency exchange and interest rates — a situation that would not change appreciably until the first modern Chinese bank was established in 1897. Ch'ien-chuang handled traditional transactions between government and private interests, as well as between Chinese borrowers and lenders of different social classes; in addition, they played an increasingly significant role in business with foreigners. One analyst of Chinese native banking cliques noted how the Ningpo element at Shanghai relied on their common loyalty to their native place "to contain the profits of trade within the circle of a group of merchants" from that place, even when doing business elsewhere. In this way, Ningpo merchants "left their local system and abandoned their stake in its prosperity as a port of foreign trade, precisely in order to preserve that prosperity." In other words, they pinned their collective future as members of one local system (at Ningpo) on the success of another (at Shanghai), thereby building on the profits of two central places instead of one.[21]

At Shanghai, the Western firms and the Chekiang merchants developed a symbiotic relationship. On the one hand, the Chinese merchants grew increasingly dependent on foreigners for capital, for protection, and for political leverage with the Ch'ing government. On the other, foreigners needed the Chinese merchants and native banks in order to trade successfully in the interior. For this reason they were willing to lend the Chinese capital, entreat for them with the Ch'ing authorities, and allow them to operate in the International Settlement and French Concession. Western firms circulated investment capital to native banks through their Chinese compradors (*mai-pan*, managers), and the banks, in turn, lent this capital to other Chinese merchants, who controlled trade between Shanghai and the interior. Some native banks made loans for foreign trade staples such as opium, tea, and silk, while others concentrated on raw cotton and rice for the domestic market. Native banks increasingly owed their economic position to foreign capital, which would not have been so readily available if the foreigners themselves could have traded easily in the interior.

Compradors, in their dual capacity as Chinese merchants and employees of Western business firms, were uniquely situated to facilitate Sino-foreign trade. Their knowledge of both the foreign and domestic market, as well as their personal and professional connections, enabled them to serve several financial interests simultaneously. Acting as agents and brokers, they provided foreign firms with their Chinese personnel, and guaranteed the solvency of Chinese merchants who dealt with Westerners, all for a price. Furthermore, their skill at "barbarian management," and their ability to raise money for charitable and military purposes, made them of enormous value to Ch'ing officials.

The career of Yang Fang (also known as Takee) illustrates the several roles a well-connected comprador could play at Shanghai during the turbulent 1850s and 1860s. Yang became a comprador with Jardine, Matheson & Co. from 1849 to 1851, and proceeded in the next decade to amass a vast fortune, estimated at several million taels. As a native of Ningpo, enjoying excellent connections with other Chekiang merchants, he became a leading member of the influential "Ningpo guild" at Shanghai. Meanwhile, Yang's association with the prestigious Jardine firm — a product of his own extensive Chinese connections — assured him of many valuable foreign contacts, especially since he seems to have spoken English comparatively well.

While employed by Jardine's, Yang displayed a special talent for bringing opium from Shanghai to Soochow for sale and at the same time purchasing silk at Soochow for his Western clients. But he also dealt in a number of other commodities, including tea, and invested heavily in pawnbroking. He arranged for foreign merchants to lend steamships to the Chinese, bought his own steamers under foreign auspices, and served as treasurer for the Shanghai "Houseless Refugees Fund"—a somewhat questionable "charitable" undertaking sustained largely by Western contributions. With the vast wealth he had accumulated both legally and illicitly, Yang purchased official rank, and became a close associate of Wu Hsu, also a native of Chekiang, who served as Shanghai Taotai from 1859 to 1862 and concurrently as Provincial Financial Commissioner. According to the *North China Herald*, Wu had "the purse of Fortunatus" and "a small army of English friends."[22]

During the crisis of mid-1860, when the Taipings threatened Shanghai and the British and French were advancing on Peking, Yang and Wu negotiated with the foreign powers on behalf of the Ch'ing government, while making all kinds of feverish arrangements for the defense of the treaty port. The United Defense Bureau and the Ever-Victorius Army were two noteworthy products of their collaborative labors in the early 1860s—each organized with the assistance of compradors and sustained by private subscriptions as well as customs revenues that fell under Wu's direct control as Superintendent of Customs and Financial Commissioner. The first commander of the EVA, Frederick Townsend Ward, became a close friend of Yang and married the merchant-official's daughter in the spring of 1862. Together Yang and Ward not only headed the Sino-foreign mercenary force as imperially designated co-commanders, but also engaged in several defense-related business enterprises at Shanghai, not all of which were entirely above board.[23]

The military aspirations of individuals such as Yang Fang and Wu Hsu overlapped, but did not coincide, with those of gentry refugees from Soochow and other Taiping-held cities in southeastern Kiangsu. Shanghai officials and members of the Chekiang financial clique were concerned primarily with the protection of the treaty port and its immediate environs, while gentry members from the hinterland naturally sought the rapid pacification of their home districts and the restoration of their once-lucrative landlord economy. Among these latter individuals, P'an Tseng-wei serves as a typical example. A scion of the illustrious P'an family of Soochow, and a former senior secretary of the Board of Punishments, Tseng-wei boasted close connections with many influential literati in southeastern Kiangsu as well as a host of powerful relatives and friends in Peking. It was P'an who helped arrange for the joint defense of Shanghai by Western forces in early 1862, and who played a role in bringing Li Hung-chang's Anhwei Army to the treaty port in the spring.

The motive behind these actions was not, of course, simply the protection of Shanghai, but rather the recovery of Soochow and its surrounding areas. P'an and his elite associates, including the well-known scholars Wu Yun and Feng Kuei-fen, correctly perceived that, in order to achieve this object, local powerholders with entrenched financial interests at Shanghai—notably Wu Hsu, Yang Fang, and their numerous fellow provincials from Chekiang—had to be eliminated. Although the Governor of Kiangsu, Hsueh Huan, was the ranking official in Shanghai, he proved to be nothing more than Wu Hsu's "yes man," and therefore of no help against the pervasive power of the Chekiang clique. He had long been under fire by the Soochow gentry, and would soon be replaced by Li Hung-chang, who became Acting Governor upon his arrival at Shanghai in April of 1862.

Li wasted no time in mobilizing his gentry allies against Wu and Yang, while providing his erstwhile mentor, Tseng Kuo-fan, with a wealth of information on their various malpractices. On 6 June 1862, Yin Chao-yung, a Soochow native then serving as a metropolitan official, presented a secret memorial to the Throne impeaching Wu, Yang, and Lin Fu-hsiang—respectively in charge of Chinese customs at Shanghai, the Su-Sung-T'ai tribute grain collectorate, and the Shanghai likin bureaucracy—for financial misconduct. By the end of the year, all three had been replaced—Wu and Yang by men from Tseng Kuo-fan's home province of Hunan (Huang Fang and Kuo Sung-t'ao), and Lin by Feng Kuei-fen. In addition, Li Hung-chang placed a number of his own fellow provincials from Anhwei in positions of fiscal responsibility at Shanghai.

Meanwhile, highly sensitive to the interests of his local gentry supporters, the new Acting Governor made detailed plans for the recovery of Soochow, pressed successfully for tax reduction in the area (a plan championed by Feng Kuei-fen), and made arrangements with a relative of Wu Yun to support the establishment of a "rent bureau" that empowered local landlords to collect "donations" from their tenants in the name of defense and rehabilitation. By the terms of this arrangement, two-thirds of the receipts went to Li's war chest and to local philanthropies, while a third remained in the hands of the property owners. In the period from 1862 to 1864, the Yuan-ho Rent Bureau contributed over a million taels to Li's military operations.[24]

Li Hung-chang's rapidly expanding financial and political power allowed him to build the Anhwei Army to some 40,000 well-trained *yung-ying* soldiers by mid-1863. But he was still not strong enough militarily to dispense with the Ever-Victorious Army. Despite its relatively small size, high cost, and Li's persistent problems with its foreign commanders after Ward's death in late 1862, the EVA continued to be a valuable adjunct to Li's Anhwei Army and a crucial element in his strategy to recapture Soochow.

Unfortunately, Li's difficulties with the Sino-foreign contingent — which included his failure to pay the force regularly and on time — had implications that went well beyond domestic administrative and strategic considerations. On 14 January 1863, following the tumultuous dismissal of Ward's successor as commander of the force, Henry Burgevine, Li was compelled by the terms of the so-called Li-Staveley agreement to accept a British officer as commander of the EVA. Since this instantly increased Great Britain's stake in the EVA's affairs, British diplomatic and military officials at Shanghai began complaining bitterly over Li's management of the contingent. In particular, they chafed over problems of payment, resenting the fact that, although Gordon held a regular commission from Peking, Li treated him as no more than a local British mercenary (which, of course, he was). Once this situation came to the attention of the British authorities at Peking, it raised acutely the issue of provincial versus metropolitan responsibility in China's financial and military administration.

From the Ch'ing government's standpoint, no real problem existed. The dynasty's basic administrative strategy, as we have already indicated, was to grant comparatively wide leeway to its local officials, but to maintain unremitting supervision over them. In the 1850s and 1860s, as rebellion raged throughout most of China, the Throne was forced as a military necessity to surrender an unprecedented degree of control to provincial officials. But the establishment of so-called regional armies, as well as the privately arranged exploitation of regular tax revenues and the use of irregular sources of support such as the likin tax to support them, were possible only if provincial leaders enjoyed a large measure of confidence from Peking. Officials like Tseng Kuo-fan, Tso Tsung-t'ang, and Li Hung-chang could not operate independently of Peking's will without grave risk. Still, the lack of a means of supervising domestic tax collection analogous to that of the Imperial Maritime Customs for foreign trade taxes made it virtually impossible for the Throne to monitor precisely either the collection or the disposition of likin revenues.

Although the Ch'ing government was satisfied with this arrangement, the British assuredly were not. During the 1840s and 1850s,

Great Britain had built up an unwarranted assumption of imperial omnipotence, such that access to the emperor would be the key to securing treaty enforcement or any other local demand made at the ports. In the midst of empire-wide rebellion in the 1860s, British officials repeatedly encouraged the Ch'ing government to centralize its military forces and to unify its various provincial self-strengthening programs, not only in order to enhance the dynasty's power and national prestige, but also to protect foreign commercial and missionary interests.

Yet ongoing problems with both the Ever-Victorious Army and the Lay-Osborn fiasco demonstrated that British hopes did not conform to Ch'ing administrative realities. As Thomas Wade wrote to Gordon in mid-1863: "I find no willingness in the Central Govt. to commence organizing [the Chinese military], as from the centre, so long as it can get the giant *local* evils *topically* treated." The British Minister, Sir Frederick Bruce, made the same point: "So long as Governors can obtain on their own terms foreign officers and steamers officered by foreigners sufficient to repel the insurgents, it is idle to expect that the Government in Peking will undertake the organization of an Imperial force either on land or on sea, and thereby relieve local Governors from the responsibility of maintaining tranquility in their provinces, which is the established principle of Chinese administration."[25]

Thus, when Bruce bluntly informed the Tsungli Yamen in June of 1863 that he could not authorize the employment of British naval or military officers unless the forces in which they served were directly under central-government control and financed directly by centrally dispensed customs revenues, Prince Kung responded self-confidently: "The decision of the question whether (British) officers shall be authorized to serve China or not must undoubtedly lie with the British Minister, . . . but if they be authorised to lend their aid, it will be for the Prince alone to decide under whose command they are to be, and from what source they are to be paid."[26] Faced with the choice of withdrawing Gordon and his fellow officers from the Chinese service to make his point, or backing down, Bruce backed down. In his opinion, and that of most foreigners both at the capital and in Kiangsu province, the defense of Shanghai was too important to entrust to Li Hung-chang's forces alone. Hart himself held this view.

The Soochow Incident and Its Aftermath

When Hart arrived at Shanghai from Peking in early September 1863, and "took over charge" of his new responsibilities at the treaty port, he hoped that he would be able to confine himself solely to Customs business. But, as would so often be the case during his career, the new I.G. soon found himself involved in matters well beyond his official purview. Although by mid-1863 the tide in the Ch'ing-Taiping war had turned decisively against the insurgents, the threat to Shanghai lingered on. In August, the former commander of the Ever-Victorious Army, Henry Burgevine, joined the Taipings with over 200 foreign mercenaries, throwing both Ch'ing officials and the Western authorities at Shanghai into a panic. Hart, then still in Peking with Lay, recorded in his journal on 20 August that Bruce felt "the British would in all probability have to do what he had predicted some years ago, namely, turn out the officials from Shanghae, and hold it until affairs became quiet." In fact, however, Burgevine soon surrendered meekly to Gordon, and no such takeover occurred.

Meanwhile, imperial forces under Tseng Kuo-fan's younger brother, Kuo-ch'üan, had entrenched themselves outside the Taiping capital of Nanking, Tso Tsung-t'ang's troops were advancing on Chekiang's provincial capital of Hangchow, and the armies of Li Hung-chang and Gordon had driven to the walls of Soochow, capital of Kiangsu. For years the capture of Soochow had been a key element in Tseng Kuo-fan's grand strategy of hemming in and destroying the Taipings at Nanking, not to mention the fond hope of the city's influential gentry members in temporary residence at Shanghai. After months of battle and negotiation in the later half of 1863, the Taiping garrison at Soochow finally surrendered to Li Hung-chang's forces on 4 December, in a well-planned about-face that had been facilitated by Gordon. Hart's laconic journal entry of 6 December, recording the fall of the Taiping-held city, masks the delight such news must have given him — not least because the recapture of Soochow presaged the revival of Shanghai's commercial vitality.

But Hart's pleasure was short-lived. Two days after the capture of Soochow, Li Hung-chang had the major rebel leaders executed, contrary to the terms of surrender stipulated by Gordon. Gordon was outraged, and, although formally commissioned as a Chinese officer, he threatened to restore Soochow to the rebels, attack Li's troops with his foreign-led Ever-Victorious Army, and even join the Taipings. Although Gordon eventually decided against such a rash course, he retired to his headquarters at K'un-shan, "humiliated and heartbroken" over Li Hung-chang's breach of faith. Meanwhile, the British Commander-in-Chief, General W. G. Brown, took the Ever-Victorious Army under his own command and directed Gordon to "suspend all active aid to the Imperialist [i.e. Ch'ing] cause." The British Minister, Bruce, informed the Ch'ing government that Gordon could

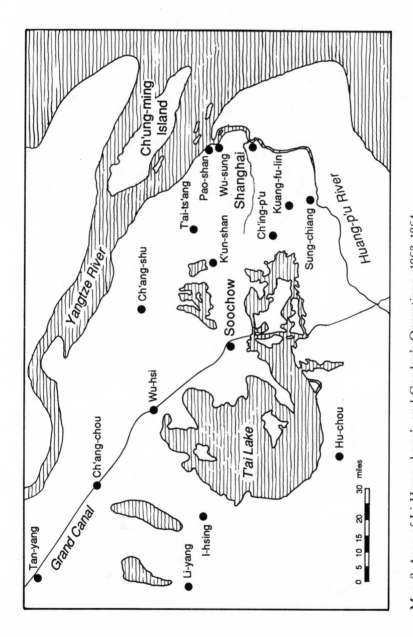

Map 2 Area of Li Hung-chang's and Gordon's Operations, 1863–1864

From Richard J. Smith, *Mercenaries and Mandarins: The Ever-Victorious Army of Nineteenth Century China* (KTO Press, 1978).

hold no communication with Li Hung-chang, "or in any way be under his orders."[27]

Li's traducing of Gordon's honor, as it turned out, was not so stark as it at first seemed. But for almost two months, until a reconciliation on 1 February 1864, the "Soochow Massacre" was a hot issue — ample ammunition for the Shanghai-minded critics of foreign cooperation with the Ch'ing. Looking back on the event, we should remember Victorian England's sense of superiority over other breeds in its moral code. One's personal honor was sacrosanct, a badge of worth acknowledged by fellow empire-builders around the world as well as by Kiplingesque local chieftains who joined the empire. In point of fact this moral code was not at all incompatible with the Confucian teaching that a superior man is known by his righteous conduct. Hart himself was determined to do right and in the process cement the Anglo-Ch'ing partnership that his career represented. The several extenuating circumstances that justified Governor Li's action are all laid out in Hart's journal as he tortures himself over the question of whether he followed morality or expediency in his treatment of the case.

Most foreigners in China suffered no such torment. For them, the execution of the eight rebel "kings" (*wang*) could never be justified. Little more than a week after the incident, consular officials in Shanghai, representing all the major powers in China and a number of minor ones, signed a unanimous resolution which, speaking for the entire foreign community, viewed with "unqualified disapprobation the late proceedings of the Futai [Governor, Li Hung-chang] at Soochow, as acts of extreme treachery abhorrent to human nature, calculated to withdraw from the Imperial cause the sympathies of Western nations, and the aid of gallant officers who have hitherto assisted them." The Chinese, for their part, felt that Li Hung-chang's response to the situation at Soochow had been perfectly reasonable in light of the threatening attitude of the rebel leaders, and that in any case the foreign powers had no right or reason to become involved in the matter.

Hart could not avoid embroilment in the controversy. Although his primary purpose at Shanghai was to settle the Lay-Osborn accounts and to take care of other Customs-related business at the treaty port, he became an essential intermediary between his Chinese employers and his British compatriots. Having no official authority in the affair, he could be relied upon for both his diplomatic skills and his language abilities. All parties in the matter sought his counsel, and all benefited from his advice.

From the outset, Hart believed that Gordon should take the field

Li Hung-chang, as Governor of Kiangsu, 1863–1864, age 40

From J. Thomson, *Illustrations of China and Its People* (London, Sampson Low, Marston, Low and Searle, 1874).

against the Taipings rather than remain in garrison at his K'un-shan headquarters. His reasons, enumerated in a revealing journal entry of 17 December 1863, reflect a mixture of motives. Above all, Hart sought the rapid suppression of the rebels — a development which, he reasoned, would benefit both the foreign powers and the Ch'ing government. Unquestionably, he saw the Ever-Victorious Army as a potent weapon in the Ch'ing-Taiping struggle, despite its recent problems with pay and discipline. Hart also sought to protect Gordon from "impeachment" (ts'an) by Li Hung-chang for insubordination — a possibility he foresaw based on the Lay-Osborn affair and his own experience with the Ch'ing bureaucracy. Finally, he believed that, since the Chinese supported the Ever-Victorious Army, they had a right to its services.

The foreign establishment did not share Hart's opinions. General Brown, for one, urged that the Ever-Victorius Army be disbanded immediately, "leaving the Chinese to fight their own battles." In typically intemperate language, the *North China Herald* editorialized on 19 December 1863: "We are glad that . . . Major Gordon will refrain from farther [*sic*] operations. It is by such means only that the Chinese can be acted on. It is hopeless to appeal to their sense of honour, for they have none; but they are keenly alive to their interests, and, rather than sacrifice these, may accommodate their actions to European principles. . . . [If Li Hung-chang finds] that the consequence of his conduct has been to deprive him of the all-important aid of the disciplined Chinese contingent [Gordon's Ever-Victorious Army], he will in future refrain from acts of treachery." The British Consular Interpreter, W. F. Mayers, as Hart's journal indicates, proved to be especially hostile to Li Hung-chang's actions and to the idea of Gordon's remaining in Li's service.

Hart had a running argument with Mayers about the affair, including, at one point, an earnest debate in the pages of the *North China Herald*. Mayers was a well-informed, capable man, but totally British in spite of his cosmopolitan experience. He had been educated in France, the son of a consular chaplain at Marseilles; had spent several years as a journalist in New York; and had gone to China in 1859 as a student interpreter, accompanying Lord Elgin to Peking. In 1872 he would become secretary at the legation there. He also became the author of a number of well-researched and respected books, including *The Treaty Ports of China and Japan* (co-edited), *The Chinese Government*, and *Treaties between the Empire of China and Foreign Powers*. For all his intimate knowledge of the workings of China, however, it never crossed his mind that the Chinese were anything other than a backward nation requiring guidance, and often perversely in the wrong.

But the logic of events as they unfolded favored Hart's pragmatic position. In the first place, Li was anxious to placate Gordon. His memorial announcing the capture of Soochow recommended, for example, that the British hero be given Tls. 10,000 as a reward for his services. Li also sent his able foreign assistant, Halliday Macartney, to see Gordon immediately after the execution of the Taiping leaders in an attempt to placate the enraged foreign commander. Gordon refused the monetary reward (which he later claimed he would have done in any case) and denounced Macartney for interceding on behalf of Li; but it is clear that he was in fact anxious to return to the field. Hart's journals suggest, and Gordon's correspondence confirms, that Li and Gordon maintained contact during "the late troubles," despite Gordon's initial anger and Bruce's early orders.

Gordon, for his part, wanted to return to action for a number of reasons. One was simply his love of battle. Another was his view that the Ever-Victorious Army would grow increasingly degenerate and difficult to manage if it remained in garrison at K'un-shan. Yet another seems to have been his recognition that Li Hung-chang's Anhwei Army was capable of achieving victory in the field without his assistance. Furthermore, according to General Brown, Gordon had received direct hints that Li Hung-chang would dismiss him if he refused to take the field against the Taipings. In a letter to Bruce dated 6 February 1864, Gordon claimed: "I know of a certainty that Burgevine meditates a return to the rebels; that there are upwards of 300 Europeans ready to join them, of no character, and that the Foo-tae will not accept another British officer if I leave the service, and therefore the Government may have some foreigner [sic] put in, or else the force put under men of Ward's and Burgevine's stamp, of whose action at times we should never feel certain."[28]

With his status as a Ch'ing official and his inside information and contacts, Hart soon stood forth as Li's champion against the Shanghai charges of perfidy. His journal entry of 18 December contains his own detailed interpretation of Governor Li's "somewhat inexplicable" beheading of the "wangs"—a view he later pressed successfully upon both Gordon and Bruce. In his opinion (and probably in fact), Li Hung-chang had not originally planned to execute the Taiping leaders. When, however, they began making extraordinary and threatening demands, Li felt compelled to eliminate them to forestall future difficulties. It was an interpretation that made sense to Prince Kung and his colleagues at the Tsungli Yamen, who requested Hart to act as mediator between Gordon and Li.

With such considerations in mind, and in the light of his recent experience with the Lay-Osborn episode, Hart decided to try to induce Gordon to rejoin Li Hung-chang's service. As early as 9 January we find him planning to "bring about some understanding between the two men," and on 18 January he tells us: "My intention is to endeavor to get Gordon to work again, and to find out all the circumstances connected with the Footae's [Governor Li's] action in beheading the Wangs at Soochow." Significantly, this entry reveals that Hart's primary goal was Gordon's return to the field, and that his principal justification was his fear that the Chinese would read Gordon's refusal to fight as evidence of the unmanageability of "an able and reliable" man. Apparently, as a Chinese employee himself, in a position in some respects similar to Gordon's, the Soochow incident hit Hart a little too close to home. The problem of reconciling his personal morality with the demands of expediency would continue to plague Hart in his ruminations on the affair throughout 1864.

On the afternoon of 19 January, Hart left Shanghai by boat with his secretary, Stuart Man, in search of Gordon. Traveling slowly in tiny boats through the byzantine maze of intersecting canals west of the treaty port, they passed by desolated villages and trampled fields, encountered wandering Ch'ing mercenaries (*yung*, or "braves"), and did some hunting. Weather conditions were miserable, but Hart was no stranger to uncomfortable travel. The two men persevered through icy winter rain to track down the restless and mercurial commander of the EVA. On the 23rd (a "lucky day" according to the Chinese almanac), they arrived at Soochow, a city newly liberated, still displaying defense gear on its walls and skeletons in the streets. There, Hart called on Li Hung-chang, who talked about the execution of the *wangs* and directed him to the peripatetic Gordon's supposed whereabouts.

On the morning of the 24th, Hart and Man left Soochow with "a high head wind," only to arrive at a bridge that rendered the canal impassable for their boats. (It must have been an unlucky day!) They detoured in the rain through a marsh, and eventually discovered that Gordon was not at the village that had been their original destination. They bought some fish and set off again across the marshes. So it went, day after day, for four more days. The wind blew a gale; the canal froze; the captain cursed, smoked opium, and to no one's surprise "was very disagreeable." They managed to get as far as Ta-wei-t'ing by 30 January, and the next day reached Gordon's headquarters at K'un-shan, having walked the last 6 miles ("a long day," as Hart put it). There, the two exhausted travelers encountered one final obstacle: They were stopped at the city gate until Gordon sent out to admit them. In conversation with the elusive and eccentric British commander, they learned that they had almost missed him again. He was, Gordon said, on the verge of setting off again, this time, to Hart's satisfaction, for Soochow to call on Li Hung-chang.

Although Gordon had already decided to make up with Li, Hart would still prove valuable, not only as an interpreter but also in persuading Li that paying the EVA more regularly would make the men feel less dangerously rebellious. On 1 February, Hart, Li, and Gordon at Soochow agreed that "Gordon should take the force into the field after the China New Year, and . . . the Footae [Li] is to issue a proclamation, taking responsibility of the execution upon himself, and showing that Gordon knew nothing about it." Thus a face-saving formula eased Gordon's return to the military action he loved so much. Once reconciliation had been achieved and Gordon's force had returned to action, Hart received credit for having resolved the problem. It was neither the first nor by any means the last crisis the I.G. would handle.

The records left by Li, Hart, and Gordon allow us to appreciate the critical importance of Hart's role as a conciliator. By the time Hart arrived at Soochow, Li and Gordon had already come to some sort of meeting of the minds, or were at least in communication; but Hart's presence provided both men with a convenient, face-saving device for publicly joining forces once again. According to a memorial written by Li Hung-chang on 25 February 1864, it was Li himself who initiated the formal reconciliation with Gordon, using Hart as his intermediary. Gordon, meanwhile, benefited greatly from Hart's vigorous defense of Li's actions, first expressed at length in a letter to Bruce (written, one might add, at Gordon's request) soon after Hart's meeting with Li on 23 January.

In this letter, dated 6 February 1864, Hart explained that the Taiping *wangs* had agreed to surrender "almost unconditionally," but that, when they visited Li Hung-chang, "their demeanour was rather that of men who had terms to dictate than of people who had just been allowed to participate in an act of clemency." Further, he remarked: "The tone they assumed, and the language they used, were alike unbecoming; but both tone and language might have passed without remark had it not been for the demands they then proffered. They not only refused to disband their followers, but they stated their intention of holding three of the city gates, strongly fortified positions, and demanded pay for their troops." By Hart's account, it was the failure of the Taiping leaders to submit to Li Hung-chang's authority that precipitated their execution, although he also indicated that Li had in mind all along the treachery of the Taipings at T'ai-ts'ang in April of 1863, when the rebels shaved their foreheads, feigned submission, and then attacked the Anhwei Army after it had entered the city.

Hart's long letter to Bruce masterfully addressed all of the criticisms leveled against Li and Gordon. He pointed out that the execution of the rebel leaders at Soochow had not prevented other Taiping leaders from surrendering to Ch'ing government forces; that it was not Gordon but the Anhwei Army commander, Ch'eng Hsueh-ch'i, who had actually engineered the surrender of the Taiping kings; and that, at the time of the execution, Gordon was supposed to have gone to K'un-shan already, so that, "even had the Footae deemed it proper to have communicated with him before acting, neither the urgency of the occasion nor the pressure of time would have allowed him with safety to have done so."

Hart concluded his letter to Bruce with a discussion of his meeting with Gordon and Li on 1 February—an account that corresponds closely to Hart's journal entry of that date but is much more detailed. Here, Hart argues that, even if the propriety of Li Hung-chang's actions at Soochow were to be put aside, it seemed to him that Gordon was "right in deciding on again taking the field." He goes on to state: "Disaffected people—rowdy foreigners and low-class Chinese—have been immensely delighted with the inaction of the last two months. Merchants fear to return to Soo-chow, not knowing but that Gordon in his wrath may with his men join the rebels, and their continuance at Shanghae is delightful to the owners of land and houses. The rebels themselves don't know what to make of the occurrence, and their expiring energies are again fanned into a flame. His appearance in the field will have immediate results; rowdies will commence to see that their game is hopeless and that they had better leave China; Chinese traders will again flock back to Soo-chow; and the rebels will again lose heart. Chang-chow-foo [Ch'ang-chou] will soon fall, and that will be followed very probably by the capitulation of Hang-chow, Woo-chow [Hu-chou], and Kea-hing [Chia-hsing], and the other two or three small cities still held by the Taepings in this province and Che-keang. Whether a stand will be made or not at Nanking Gordon thinks very problematical, but he is rather of [the] opinion that it will not fight. The destiny of China is at the present moment in the hands of Gordon more than of any other man."[29]

One condition for Gordon's return to action was a public proclamation by Li Hung-chang explaining that the Kiangsu Governor and not Gordon was responsible for the execution of the Taiping leaders.

Interpreter Mayers's translation of this proclamation, initially issued on 14 February 1864, appeared in the 27 February edition of the *North China Herald*. It reads in part: "At the time when the rebel Kao, falsely styled the Na Wang, and his associates, were summarily put to death, the overthrow of settled arrangements was imminent from one moment to another, and General Gordon, not being on the spot, could not be cognisant of the circumstances involved. . . . At first, in the negociations [*sic*] for the submission, for the murder of the so-styled Mo-Wang, for the surrender of the North-east gate, and the fixing of a time for the interview at the camp, every step was known to General Gordon; but on his arrival at the camp, the so-styled Na-Wang had not shaved his head, and his rebellious designs were patent to the view. . . . Whilst his speech was evasive and ambiguous, his expression of countenance was ferocious and bold to an extreme, and all this took place after the surrender had been completed. The Futai could, therefore, for his own safety, not do otherwise than guard against a departure from the arranged conditions; and these were all particulars with which Gordon was not acquainted."[30]

As Hart's journal entries for 5 March and 20 March indicate, he disagreed with Mayers's rendering of Li Hung-chang's proclamation. His anonymous critique, published in the 5 March issue of the *North China Herald*, faults Mayers for failing to "catch the sense of the Chinese version." His particular concern was the sentence beginning "At first. . .," in which, according to Hart, "the word 'for' is incorrectly repeated . . . in such a way as to make the Futai say that Gordon had been cognizant of, and a part to, negotiations *for the murder* of the Mo Wang." This is essentially the view expressed in Hart's journal entry of 20 March. Mayers's rebuttal, printed in the 20 March edition of the *Herald*, indicates that there were at least two different versions of the proclamation, which, the consular interpreter acknowledges, may account for different renderings. But Mayers stands by his use of the word "for" to precede each of the four clauses in question, and includes the Chinese text for illustration. Although Hart's journal admits, in turn, that the phrasing is ambiguous, he takes obvious satisfaction in learning eventually that both Li Hung-chang and his illustrious colleague in the Tsungli Yamen, Wen-hsiang, agreed with his own interpretation.

Two things about the proclamation catch our attention. The first is that Hart's obvious antipathy toward Mayers (see his journal entry of 22 February 1864) seems to have made him especially anxious to criticize the latter's work. The second is that Hart's desire to see Gordon return to the imperial service unquestionably affected his response to the entire Soochow incident, including his understanding of Li Hung-chang's proclamation. This is quite evident in Hart's long-winded journal ruminations that follow his discussion of Mayers's rebuttal in the *North China Herald*. At all events, Hart achieved his main object, to the relief of nearly everyone—Chinese and foreigners alike—with the obvious exception of Mayers. Even Bruce, who continually stressed the need for negotiating matters with the Ch'ing central government rather than the provincial authorities, was pleased with the local arrangements.

In late February, Gordon began mobilizing his forces, together with imperial troops under Kuo Sung-lin and others. On 1 March he forced the submission of I-hsing, and on 9 March, Li-yang. Later in the month, however, Gordon suffered severe repulses at Chin-t'an, where he was wounded (21 March), and at Hua-shu (30 March). In the meantime, imperial troops under Ch'eng Hsueh-ch'i had captured Chia-hsing on 25 March, and the forces of Tso Tsung-t'ang and Gordon's French counterpart, Paul d'Aiguebelle, had occupied Hang-chow on 31 March.

In mid-April, Gordon advanced on the city of Ch'ang-chou, which had been under siege for some time by Li Hung-chang's troops. By this time, Hart had become very actively involved in the Ever-Victorious Army's affairs. He corresponded regularly with Gordon and continued to serve as a mediator between Li Hung-chang and the British commander. He urged Li to pay the force more regularly, and gave material assistance to the Ever-Victorious Army—not least in supplying an interpreter from the Customs Service (Herbert E. Hobson) in order to help Gordon communicate more effectively with the Chinese authorities. His only stipulations were that Gordon should pay Hobson no more than the 100 pounds salary he received from the Customs administration and that Gordon should see to it that Hobson did not get shot![31]

In scattered action from 23 April to 27 April, Gordon's forces pressed upon Ch'ang-chou. The fall of this stronghold, the British commander believed, would carry in turn Tan-yang and Chin-t'an, thus isolating Nanking. Repeated efforts to storm the Taiping-held city failed, however, leaving 27 of Gordon's officers dead or wounded. Commenting on this failure, Li Hung-chang wrote: "Gordon could see for himself the ineffectiveness of the Ever-Victorious Army." It was after this repulse, according to Li, that Gordon asked for his troops to be placed behind the Anhwei Army in recognition of the superiority of Li's forces.[32]

Eventually, on 11 May, the Ever-Victorious Army played a significant role in the recovery of Ch'ang-chou, and Hart had a front-row seat for the spectacle. In an episode that brings home to us the relative intimacy of small-scale operations during the nineteenth century and the dramatic evolution of methods of warfare thereafter, Hart's niece later described the battle for Changchow as she had heard it from him. Gordon, it seemed, invited Hart and a few other acquaintances to be present at the taking of the city, fixed for 11 May; it would be a sight worth seeing, he promised — the culmination of his entire campaign. Hart left Shanghai on 28 April, and in due time moored his small flotilla on the Grand Canal outside Ch'ang-chou, next to Gordon's headquarters. The largest vessel of Gordon's fleet became the common dining room, which "owed its excellent ventilation to two holes opposite each other torn out close to the ceiling by a shell while Gordon had been lunching a few days before."[33]

On 10 May, Gordon took a small party including Hart and his bodyguard out to reconnoitre but was recognized and fired upon — as usual, without injury. The attack on the 11th was scheduled for noon, and all morning Gordon had his guns bombard the city. At noon, when he gave the order for a cease-fire, he explained that "the beggars inside" would conclude he had "finished work for the day." Snatching a hasty lunch, at 1 o'clock he gave the signal for attack, while Hart and Li Hung-chang stood together on a hillside to watch operations. Three rushes were made simultaneously — two feints and one led by Gordon himself. Typically, Gordon was first through the narrow breach, and the dramatic moment was over.

Ch'ang-chou had fallen, and Gordon was duly rewarded.[34] But, by this time, the EVA had clearly passed its prime, and both Li and Gordon hastily made plans for disbandment. Hart, on the other hand, felt that the force should not be disbanded too precipitously; and in fact he argued that at least part of the Ever-Victorious Army should be "kept up permanently." In a letter to Gordon, dated 17 May 1864, Hart addressed the various objections raised to retaining the Ever-Victorious Army, including Li's view that the force was too expensive, too ineffective, and too "local" in its loyalties, and Gordon's belief that the Anhwei Army was a superior and sufficient instrument for the protection of Kiangsu province. As to Li's objection that the Ever-Victorious Army could not be employed outside of Kiangsu because the Western commander might not get on well with the officials of other provinces, Hart rejoined (with more conviction than he probably possessed) that "an Imperial Decree could at any moment authorize the force to act elsewhere."[35]

In the end, a compromise was reached whereby a portion of the

Ever-Victorious Army would be retained as the nucleus of a foreign-training program in the vicinity of Shanghai, at Feng-huang shan (see chapters 5 and 7). Meanwhile, imperial forces under Li Hung-chang and others went on to capture the cities of Chin-t'an and Tan-yang, contributing to the eventual fall of Nanking to Tseng Kuo-ch'üan's forces in July of 1864—a denouement far from Hart's expectations eight months before.

CHAPTER TWO

Journal

6 DECEMBER 1863–15 MAY 1864

6 DECEMBER 1863: News came in today that SooChow was taken yesterday morning at 8 a.m. The Moo Wang was previously beheaded by a frightened faction in the city.[1] [Between this entry and the next is written, in a different ink, "Sacrament Sunday."]

Sacrament
Sunday

7 DECEMBER 1863: Rec'd Brown's letter of the 27th Nov. today: telling of the monies given to Lay, &c. Last night a letter from John Meadows advising me not to resign.[2]

Today recd four despatches from Ts. Le Yamun, of 10th m. [lunar month] of 12th d. [day] and one from <u>Le</u> Footae [Governor Li Hung-chang] of the 10th m. 25th d. about the Fleet a/c, &c. and payments to Lay.

9 DECEMBER 1863: Lay arrived from Peking. News in to the effect that <u>Le</u> Footae beheaded seven Wangs [Taiping "kings"], and that his troops went into SooChow, slaughtered right and left, burning, ravishing and pillaging. Sun tells me the Wangs refused to disband their men. Public opinion blames the Footae strongly, and Gordon, it is said, has retired with his men, for whom he vainly sought a two-months' gratuity, to Quinsan.[3]

10 DECEMBER 1863: The Genl. goes up to the front to make enquiries & arrangements. I beg him not to be in any way precipitant, to avoid greater complications.[4]

11 DECEMBER 1863: Lay has handed to me the a/c of the fleet; but I fear I shall find it no easy work to get through them.[5]

12 DECEMBER 1863: The last of the ships, the "Keangsoo", left with Osborne today for Bombay. Please God! I'll carry out my plans yet.

I wanted to effect the following ends with the fleet:

1°. to place a strong & easily moved force at the disposition of the govt. at Peking, & in a measure centralize as far as the system of Chinese govt. wd allow of it;

2°. to clear the Chinese coast of pirates;

3°. to remove one of the incitements to piracy, by giving boats such a protection as shd. enable the govt. to disarm all the heavily armed traders;

4°. to protect the revenue, & put down smuggling, &c.;

5°. to put down rowdyism on the Yangtsze;

6°. to defend all ports & places accessible by water, from the rebels;

7°. to prevent rebels from crossing the Yangtsze; &

8°. to take Nanking.

Lay's reticence has smashed everything—himself too, to wind up the series of disasters. His disappearance, however, will not grieve our service much; for his want of tact, and his arbitrary way of doing things, made every one feel unsafe and unsettled. Osborne,—thank him for his good will!—thinks that I shall find them all in revolt! We'll see. I shd. like to see one of them try it. I'll read him such a lesson that none will dare to follow his lead: by Jove! I will. I am, however, very sorry for Lay; for he has served the Chinese long, and has, I believe, acted very conscientiously throughout: working hard, and in all that he did believing he was acting for the best of all concerned. But conscientious action requires good sense and judgment in the pilot, and tact & [advising? word unclear] in the man at the helm! He was deficient in tact; he would not give them—the Chinese—time & he cut off the branch of future management by his own doings.

I have lived too much apart during the past; I must now mix more with others, and assert myself a little more. I fear I have too much of the <u>Seang-jang</u> <u>taou-le</u> [principle of yielding to others] in my composition: must try and remedy that.[6]

16 DECEMBER 1863: Have been busy with the a/c & commence to see land.

Prince Wittgenstein called today, & wishes me to write to Gordon; he says he saw horrid work,—women ill-treated & children thrown into the flames, &c.[7]

Mayers showed me a couple of letters this morning, one from Sir. F. [Frederick Bruce] and the other a reply from Gordon. Sir F's letter commences in a very diplomatic manner: says his previous one was not intended to ask G. to resign, but to support him if he wished to do so. On the whole, it is very complimentary, and asks him to hold on for the present, until the wish of the govt., on hearing of the flotilla break-up, is known as regards the Neutrality Act. Gordon's reply is good, and carries through feeling for the people.[8]

Mayers was deliberating about going to Tsäng Kuo fan: I said: "If you do good, Sir F. will be glad; if you gain nothing, he will be furious. Better have his action [word unclear]! Besides, T. K. F. can do nothing."[9]

17 DECEMBER 1863: [a red curlicue over this entire entry] Genl. Brown called today; he has ordered Gordon to remain in Quinsan, and to do nothing but act on the defensive—protect SooChow, & other places if threatened, but he fears the Footae may refuse to pay the troops, and he wants my advice. I say, as a Chinese official, I can do nothing; but I tell him the consuls, if they find the Footae likely to endanger the neighborhood by refusing to pay, & thereby leading to a mutiny at Quinsan, can write a letter to H. E. informing him they will call on foreign merchants to pay duties into a foreign bank, pay the force and hand him the surplus. [By this passage Hart has written the Chinese characters for "foreign bank," *wai-kuo yin-hao*, in the margin.]

I tell him that I think to keep Gordon idle at Quinsan is not good policy: for, 1°. the cause for which the British govt. was lending its aid & for which Gordon was working was not to support an admired [?] Footae in reducing his province to quiet; but,
2°. was in support of general interests & the Imperial cause;
3°. if that cause & these reasons were worth fighting for before, they are still;
4°. the Chinese pay the troops, & have a right to their services;
5°. one object in view of disciplining the men was to teach the Chinese, with a view to the better govt. of their own Country, the utility of having a proper military organization to fall back upon; and, inasmuch as the good will & support of the provincials is necessary to induce the people at Peking to act— the Lords & Commons—twould be well not to make the provincial now dislike this force; now, from the first Le has feared it, and now he will, finding it will not obey his orders, try to put it down;
6°. if Gordon will not take the Footae's orders, Le will "tsan" ["impeach"] him, and an insult to a most deserving officer will result; now such a step cd. not be stood;[10]
7°. I think the force ought to go on, put down as much rebellion as possible, then be disbanded or divided,—and trust to the future for regeneration [?].

I shall write to the above effect to Gordon, but more at length: not advising him, & not suggesting, but merely ventilating the matter from other points of view than he in his excitement is likely to stand on. The General goes to Hongkong tonight.

Woosieh was taken a few days ago without a fight: I think Taepingdom is on its last legs: I hope for the integrity of China things may quiet down here before the arrival of [Pa; Parkes].[11]

18 DECEMBER 1863: The Footae's conduct in beheading the seven Wangs is somewhat inexplicable. I have never before heard of cold-blooded or treacherous murder of men that had given in their submission.

It is said that the Wangs, when they visited the Footae refused to disband their men, and they attempted to force upon him sundry conditions,— conditions which it wd. have been dangerous for him to have objected to, so long as their men were together, & while his own had not mastered the position, the more especially as Gordon's force had returned to Quinsan. It seems to me that on the refusal of the Wangs to disband their men, the Footae:

1°. feared to consent to their proposal;

2°. thought it dangerous to refuse consent, and at the same time allow them to reenter SooChow;

3°. that he thought safety lay in putting them to death without delay;

4°. that he feared to keep them in custody, lest their nonappearance shd. cause suspicions and troubles in the city;

5°. that having decided on their death,<u>ª</u> either he thought it best to forestall the Taepings, by letting his men at them, or<u>ᵇ</u> they heard of what had occurred, and were commencing trouble; &

6°. the slaughter, if any & pillage, &c. were only what follow the capture of every city, and are doings of which even the civilized warfare of the West is not incognizant.

I think that the plan now wd. be for Gordon to go on vigorously, and end the rebellion with all speed. The force shd. then be disbanded, or sent to India, as a British force, & so rid China of a body of men which Chinese officials cannot control. Le Footae is a long headed man, & his objections to this force, recruited in such a way, have been sound from the first, & counts now prove him right: the people at Peking ought to have taken my advice and drilled only Tartars — Sir F. Bruce was right too, in writing them to drill officers.[12]

Yesterday took some 600 stand of arms in a cargo boat that was placing them on board an American Lorcha, the "Jupiter" [?] for Chefoo, below the anchorage.

Mail in by the "Yangtsze".

Getting on with the Fleet a/c.

19 DECEMBER 1863: The other night I read some of my Essays written in '53 at Belfast: good Heavens! I could not write such pieces now! I am sinking into utter mental stagnation: what shall I do?

I recd a note from Meritens today dated the 16th informing me that the authorities had communicated to him, at FooChow, Lay's "resignation" and my appointment; he thinks it will — & says it already has a bad effect at Foo-Chow & other places; advises me to organize the Service on a safe basis — "seniority & merit", enquires about my successor at Shanghai, & says he is coming up in the "Fohkien" to arrange matters, & say goodbye to Lay. I must be careful here; one thing's flat, I shan't stand any interference: he, & everyone else, will have to obey, or they shall go.[13]

Dent and Co.'s case of the "Heron" rather perplexed me today: they engaged she shd. not carry cargo, got a special permit to send her on a pleasure trip, brought up cotton — producing the local permit & proof of payment of tax, from Tsung Ming, a non-treaty-port, said in excuse, their shroff found other foreign boats loading cotton and that in consequence saw no reason why the "Heron" shd. not do likewise, the more especially as the local official made no objection. I said their explanation was unsatisfactory; but the fact of there being other boats there, & of the local official giving permits & accepting taxes, tied my hands. I released their boat, but refused to give them permission to move freely on the river, applied for on the 12th. I must look after Tsung Ming, & regularize the doings of foreign owned craft in the Chinese waters.[14]

Wrote to Rameau about Bovet Bros. who neglected to send their goods for examination to the jetty. Confound it! China is so weak, we can do nothing: and where one can't bite, a wise dog ought to avoid the superfluous trouble of barking.[15]

Saw Stewart of Linnies [?] today about sending Tae Pings to Col. Phayre [?]: the Footae wd., I'm sure, gladly get rid of the SooChow set: but Phayre only wants a thousand, & the Footae has 20000 to dispose of. Besides, the delay of communicating with him is a hindrance.[16]

Invitation to dine with the Lays on Monday. The mail seems to have got in: Heard two guns at eight o'clock.

Out of sorts this afternoon. [Chinese character *Mei*; Meritens] letter upset me.[17]

20 DECEMBER 1863: I was somewhat puzzled, when talking with Dick last night about Christianity.[18] His idea is that Christ was merely another Confucius or Mohammed, and he disbelieves the history of the miracles. I drew on the conversation myself, for I wish to state firmly that I am a Christian, and to talk usefully when I have an opportunity; but my tongue was tied, and I was not fit to go on with the argument which I myself originated. However, I pointed to four things as corroberation of the divine nature of the Savior, and the divine nature of the Christian revelation:

1°. the fulfilment of the prophetical sayings contained in books known to have existed before Jesus appeared;

2°. the peculiarity of his teachings, in giving such pictures of the life a disciple had to expect to lead as wd. be most likely to deter people from following Him;

3°. the high morality & purity of conduct required—so unlikely to attract followers;

4°. the conduct of his Apostles, who gave up all, & suffered everything, to preach his Gospel.

But I am not satisfied with myself atall, & must try to make myself more able to give "a reason for the faith".

Tonight heard a stranger preach: his text was from Corinthians, "Godly sorrow" & "worldly sorrow". He had previously read a chapter from "Samuel" relative to Nathan's rebuke of David when he took Uriah's wife and Herod's act in beheading John to placate the daughter of Herodius. The latter he took as illustration of worldly, the former of godly sorrow: the idea was good, but he did not work it out well, & his discourse was rather tame on the whole.

The mail in this morning. Lord Elgin dead! "Such is life!" Hale is dead too, and Mongan married to Hewlett's sister. Parkes to leave home on the 4th Jany next.[19]

21 DECEMBER 1863: Dined at W. Lay's: pleasant party.[20]

22 DECEMBER 1863: Curious correspondence with Dent & Co. relative to the "Heron". That lugger got permission to go to the light ship on a pleasure trip: then, however, took treasure to Tsung Ming and brought cotton back. I looked on the occurrence as a breach of good faith, & hinted as much; H. W. Dent now requires some explanations, thinking the tone of my letters "particularly peculiar", and "not wanting to be placed in a false position".

With Lay this morning, going through his private a/c; he is, as far as the a/c show, deficient by about 1200 Taels: Campbell, his secretary, did not leave things in proper order.[21]

Called on the Taoutae, whose language I have great difficulty in understanding: Lay refuses to meet him to settle the flotilla a/c, but the Taoutae says the Footae has ordered him to look into them.[22]

Mrs. L. had a miscarriage before leaving Peking: it seems to have done her no harm, as she was able to travel immediately after. Lay is now in no great hurry to get away.

Cd. not get the Taoutae to talk about SooChow: he pretends to know nothing of what goes on outside — the old humbug!

The "Hellespont" sank yesterday by the "Hydrafie" [?]

23 DECEMBER 1863: Lay again in with me today. While together, I thought I had got to the bottom of his private a/c; but now that he is gone, I cannot make things come straight. I don't know whether to call myself an ass for not being able to make them out, or a fool for attempting them from such materials.

A Letter from the Tsung Le Yamun today about the ground Kirby and Co. bought at Ningpo, & which Brown claimed.[23]

Also long and polite letter from Li Footae about SooChow, &c.: written in a somewhat deprecatory tone, and saying Gordon has listened erroneously to the [yen; character for talk] of other folk.

I saw a note today from Gordon to Mayers, which says there has been a French priest thrashed at SooChow. Does the Padre tell the truth, I wonder?

Corresponding today with Rameau about Savelle boat. Nothing more from Dent & Co.

Ground white with snow tonight!

24 DECEMBER 1863, CHRISTMAS EVE! a most lovely night: a dark blue sky without a cloud: a bright pale moon, nearly at the full, and a few tiny twinkling stars, whose little deathlike-steady gleams rather draw the eye into the far-off depths, than send light down to earth.

Great God! Christmas Eve! Nearly nineteen hundred years ago the shepherds watched their flocks by night: the angel of the Lord appeared, the message of goodwill was spoken, and the star moved towards Bethlehem! Ah me! When is there to be peace among men?

I feel sad and dispirited: and why? My life has been singularly successful: not yet twenty-nine, and at the head of a service which collects nearly three millions of revenue, in, — of all countries in the world! — the exclusive land of China, and in a position which can be easily abused for evil, but which too may be so taken advantage of as to cause great good. Sad, I say, and dispirited: and why? Simply because looking back on the past, notwithstanding my success, I plainly see time wasted, energies wrongly directed, opportunities for improvement neglected, evil indulged in, the reverse of a good example set, and after all little achieved and many failures! I must change;: "Lives of Great men all remind us, we may make our lives sublime!" And yet I seek not fame or praise: I like to be well thought of by my friends, and I love to make them happy. But what I long for is the approbation of myself: I see my shortcomings, I see what stains the doings for which others praise me, I see what might have been done and yet has not been done; I see how little fit I am for making the best of my present position! and yet, God knows I pray to act right, — pray for guidance, — and pray to be useful!

God help me! I am weak, and, perhaps, a bit of a humbug: and yet, I have got on without aid, without interest, and without asking for anything! My aim at school was to be first of my class: at college to be first too: and in China, since I entered on public life, my aim has always been to understand and fit myself for the head work of whatever department fate attached me to.

I started from home nearly ten years ago, to commence life with an appointment for which I had none to thank but myself — my determined, patient, plodding at school & at college — of some £170 a year, allowing for deductions: I now have £4000 a year, could get as much more, I believe, as I liked, am independent, and am the Chief of the Service. Not a bit proud I am! I am more conscious of defects — I am sensible of more deficiencies than is anyone that chooses to criticize me. Well: I must just go on doing my best; but I must now begin to take broader views of things than I have ever done before; and I must, too, assert myself somewhat more. Indeed, one of my great defects is my want to self-assertion: I don't fear responsibility, and I am cool and unflustered; but I keep to myself, and am content to be unknown, and I always yield. Now what objects have I to live for, to act for officially in China?[24]

1°. I must whip the Foreign Inspectorate into shape, getting good commissioners, good office men, and seeing that all do their work properly; the duties must be properly collected; office work must be thoroughly performed; the merchant not only must have no cause to grumble against the

Customs, but must be assisted; his business must be facilitated, & in that way increased, and increase of business will in the end swell the Imperial coffers.

2°. I must learn more about the Chinese; about the littoral provinces, about taxation, about official duties—all with an eye to being useful, and preserving myself from being "trapped".

3°. I must try to induce among such Chinese as I can influence a friendlier feeling towards foreigners: right conduct: and in that way keep things straight and ensure peace.

4°. I must do what I can to prevent any growth of or encouragement to antiforeign feeling on the part of the Imperialists, [i.e., the Ch'ing government] now that the rebellion is being put down.

5°. I must endeavour to ascertain what products of our Western civilization wd. most benefit China: and in what ways such changes could most affirmatively be introduced.

6°. I must set a good example, in conduct, to all my subs.

7°. I must assist those who are engaged in the noblest of all works, the preaching of the Gospel, & the teaching of Christianity,—this highest & purest morality, the most comforting religion, and the most civilizing of all influences in its purity & entirety.

Lots of other things too have to be done. God help me to work: and to work well! [Curlicue under the last sentence, separating it from what follows.]

H. N. Dent wrote this morning a long letter, in a very good spirit about the "Heron",—somewhat plausible, but yet fallacious arguments. I talked with him on the bund tonight: he admits I had cause for complaint—and that's enough. I must now let them down gently: and, Robert my boy! no hurry in future!

SUNDAY, 27 DECEMBER 1863: A good but rather lengthy sermon tonight from Mr. Muirhead on "God manifest in the flesh."[25] His sermons are weakened by his attempts at explaining the points inexplicable by the human mind, and by attempts at describing what God, in His wisdom, has left hidden. But he is an earnest preacher. His sermon tonight was too long: and what made it doubly tedious was the great cold. I was half [stoned?, unclear] before the first hymn was half sung through.

This morning, lying in bed half asleep, I almost heard the choristers in Hillsborough church singing "Oh joyful in the Lord," to the anthem-air they use there on Christmas mornings.[26] I could see Robert Rosborough, & could hear Jonny Watkins' tenor voice: and the fat burly good humoured face of the melodious shoemaker bellowing forth his tremendous bass [unclear] down from the organ loft. Oh dear! Oh dear! When shall I again attend service in that church? How I shall delight in going there. I'm sure I'll feel inclined to "blubber" the first time I'm there.

Read today two of Whately's sermons: "On Search after Infallibility" &

"On Christian Saints."[27] The first requires study: the second is a gem. In the latter, one part of the antiquity of the New Testament struck me: viz. that the believers are not spoken of in the books as <u>Christians</u>, but as Saints, Brethren, &c. Now after the Apostolic age, the word Christian was in common use: and if these books were written after that apostolic age, they wd. certainly have used the word repeatedly. As they were written at the time they are [unclear] to have been written, there is then the moral proof of their truth in the fact, that had their narrations been false, they wd. have been contradicted. The word Christians Whately conjectures to have been given by the Romans to characterize a sect comprised of both Jews & Gentiles, before the spread of the gospel, the Romans merely called its disciples Jews, while the unbelieving Jews called the believers, as to this day Nazareans.

A preacher's sermons shd. be timed, not by his own enthusiasm, but by his common sense. He ought to form a rational idea of how much his people can listen to with attention and profit: and when a man must not read his sermons, but preaches extempore, he ought to remember that going on a single text, he cannot, without touching on other subjects, & in short preaching the whole gospel, talk well & profitably for an hour and twenty minutes.

Awfully cold the last three days have been: I have felt nothing like it since I came to China, I think. Strange to say I have got a tremendous, & very painful boil, on my left arm: odd at this time of year.

Had Andrew Happer & some others to dinner last night.[28] [Red curlicue over this sentence.]

29 DECEMBER 1863: Campbell & Butler together in my office this morning. [Next sentence undecipherable.]

31 DECEMBER 1863: Dined with Morton at the Beloochee Mess, and saw the Old Year out with Dick.[29] To bed at 1/2 past one. Letters from Mamma, Cha, and Mary: "they count the days"— Farewell, eighteen 'sixty-three!

1 JANUARY 1864: Not up till ten today: and then feeling rather seedy—thanks to punch & cigars on New Year's Eve. A great many calls today, the loveliest New Year's Day, I ever knew.

2 JANUARY 1864: Lay wants me to sign the legal discharge: I object, for I say that if the wind-up is to be a legal document of such technicality, the preceding examination ought to have been correspondingly exact, legal and technical. It's not fair of him: but now that he's down, one does not like to be hard! Still if I don't take care, I may burn my own fingers most horribly.

3 JANUARY 1864: [No entry]

4 JANUARY 1864: This morning at eleven a.m., Lay came to me, Dick and Man being present, to make the final settlement of the various a/c. We signed:

1°. the a/c of the Peking Establishment:

2°. the " of the Steam Fleet from 1st Augt. 1862 @ 31 Oct. 1863;

3°. a document in which Lay certifies that he has paid me all money, & declares that he neither holds money of, nor is indebted to the Chinese govt.:

4°. a document signed by me in token of receipt of all the sums handed to me by Lay:

5°. a document signed by Lay in token receipt of various sums claimed by him, and agreed to by me:

5°. a discharge.

All documents signed in quadruplicate.

Lay wanted me to sign a legally worded discharge; I refused to do so alleging that that wd. leave it to be inferred that I had legally & technically audited all the a/c: which I have not done, &c. & cd. not at this stage do — I told Lay that I only signed the discharge, worded as it was, because I believed his statements: & that had I not known him, I would not at this stage have signed any discharge atall. [Red curlicues on this paragraph]

Antrobus called too about volunteers: I said if 50 men wd. join, I wd. authorize it — but not otherwise.[30]

9 JANUARY 1864: Exactly eight months ago, on the 9th May 1863, I returned to Shanghae from the Yangtsze ports, and about two o'clock met Lay, who had just returned from England. I then ceased to be Officiating Inspector General, & his duties as Inspector General were ventured upon by him. And very odd today at two o'clock, Lay went on board the "Ganges" en route for England.

Well: as I look back, I can see nothing to blame myself for in the slightest degree — I was true to him all through: I acted properly in the Steam Fleet affair, I am sure, and I'm likewise confident it would have been a success had my views been acted on. He, however, took his own way: smashed the fleet; smashed himself: and nearly smashed all of us too. However, all's well that ends well: he is gone, and now I must try if I cannot set things right after my own fashion.

Gordon still inactive at Quinsan. The Imperial Edict sent him Tls 10000, and a decoration of the first class: he received nothing, and, under present circumstances, I don't see how he could accept anything. I shall go up to see him and the Footae in a few days and endeavour to bring about some understanding.

The Footae has memorialized saying he was guilty of an imprudent act when he promised Gordon to spare the Wangs, & he now asks for Choo fun [punishment] He is too able a man though, to be thrown overboard: they'll probably wig him, but lew jin [retain him at his post].[31]

Chinkiang is said to be threatened just now; and the "Firefly" is somewhere in that neighborhood.[32] If she gets out on the Yangtsze, she may do damage: she could cover a party of rebels if they wished to land on the north bank.

Ping wang taken the other day by Ching and Major Bailey.[33] Considerable slaughter on both sides: Ching's actions are generally attended with a butcher's bill.

At Nanking 30 tls [?] a picul is offered for rice, and none is to be bought.[34]

I must put the "Elfin" down near Chinkiang.[35]

Brown, Moffitt, Kleinwachter, Bowra, and Wright to dinner tonight.[36]

Recd. a letter yesterday from the Tsung Le Yamun about confiscation cases and other matters.

Today placed Dick in charge, and took leave of the office people as Commissioner for Customs. [Red curlicue]

[Last page of this volume signed "Robert Hart."]

Volume 5 *Journal* of Robert Hart
9 January 1864–19 July 1864

18 JANUARY 1864: Lay, as I have noted in the preceding volume, left Shanghae on the 9th instant. Since then I have been chiefly engaged with drafting replies to four semi-official letters recd from Ching and the other Tsung Pan of the Yamun. I number them under the [*kung* "public" or "official"] character: theirs to me are under the character [*shui* "duties;" i.e. customs].[37] My first had reference chiefly to the steam-fleet as originally proposed: my second to the dispute at Ningpo about the ground — said by Brown to have been set apart for the Customs — purchased by Kirby & Co.: my third to 'mixed tribunal for investigation of infractions of revenue laws': and my fourth explained why I had been so long in answering their first three. I sent these letters through Le Footae on the 16th, and suppose they will reach Peking about the 10th February — somewhere near the Chinese New Year.

In the same cover I forwarded a long letter to Sir F. Bruce: do. to Brown, with a note for St. John: a cover containing chits for Brett, Hobson, and Sibbald: and a despatch ordering Mackey, with Sibbald, to NewChwang.[38]

Today I wrote to Chefoo ordering Baker to Tientsin.[39]

The Taoutae [circuit intendant] called today; I got little out of him, but that little corroborates the report that Kea-Hing has surrendered: Hoo-Chow too is said to have tendered its submission. Hsieh Wae-lung is the man connected with the capitulation of the former place. Genl. Ching is said to have been shot before ChangChow, where, as well as at Chinkiang and Keang-yen, the Imperialists appear to have been suffering of late.[40]

Now I start, taking Man with me, for Quinsan and SooChow, to see Gordon and Le Footae.[41] My intention is to endeavour to get Gordon to work again, and to find out all the circumstances connected with the Footae's action in beheading the Wangs at SooChow. This is a matter that must be gone into with perfect coolness and self-possession; and [on] its settlement hang very important <u>results</u>. [Underlined later in red pencil; and written in red pencil across the paragraph, "Successful in every respect!"]

Were Gordon to resign, the brigade wd. go over to the rebels: holding the command he refuses to fight: refusing to fight, he disobeys orders: disobeying orders, he shows the Chinese that even an able and reliable man, such as he is, is unmanageable: seeing him unmanageable, they find his men so too; and, such being the result, they are not likely to be very favorably impressed with the military system, which brings together a powerful body of men in no way, when a crisis arrives, under their control. Quixotry does not do at the present moment in China; an expediency that aims at the right — not an adherence to the right that allows wrong to continue uninterfered with — is what is now requisite. 'Tis a hard task indeed to decide between the onward party [the Taipings], whose course though tending towards liberalism is marked with so many atrocities, and must be unsuccessful for so many years to come, and the Imperialist [Ch'ing] party, not very liberal (and perhaps for good reasons) in its tendencies, but yet conservative of law and order.

There have been some murders in the vicinity lately: two of Gordon's officers coming down from Quinsan have been among the victims; I hope Man and myself may not get into any difficulty. I hope to be back in less than a fortnight; but, perhaps, if I get Gordon to move, I may stay up there, and see things out — or at least well started.

Gave yesterday Tls <u>1000</u> to the "Union Chapel". Wm Lay & Swinhoe applicants for Customs' Employ: the latter wd like the berth I vacated, the former anything! Saw Wadman a few days ago: he hardly knew me. Wonder where Meritens in the "Volunteer" has got to.[42]

11 FEBRUARY 1864: My dearly beloved journal, isn't it about time to commit to your keeping the record of my wanderings and doings during the last three weeks?

TUESDAY, 19 JANUARY 1864: Started, accompanied by Man, with a couple of boats, at 3 1/2 p.m. The boat men presented their compliments on the usual congratulatory red card; the joss-stick was brought; the gong beaten; and we got away. Day chilly, with rain: no pleasant prospect.

20 JANUARY 1864: By 9 in the morning got to <u>Wong</u> <u>Doo</u>, passing through the bridge of "a thousand autumns." Tsing poo to our left, & Keating to the right:[43] country very desolate and pheasants numerous; Man's gun went off at half cock, fortunately pointed heaven wards, otherwise I might have become the recipient of the charge. Many wandering Braves.

21 JANUARY 1864: Got to Kwän-shan at noon, and found that Gordon had started the night before on a surveying trip to the west of SooChow. Walked to the top of the hill; visited some of the barracks and the hospital, and dined with Moffitt.

22 JANUARY 1864: 12th m. [lunar month] 14th d. [day] arrived at SooChow at 3 1/2 p.m. Sent my card to Le Footae, who said he wd see me on the following day at 11. Walked about under the city wall, near the Low-mun; the wall spiked in triple rows, and beams hung up to let fall on the heads of whoever attempted to scale; many skeletons, and much ruin everywhere.

SATURDAY, 23 JANUARY 1864: Today being the 15th of the moon is a lucky day. Saw Le Footae at 11 in his new quarters, lately occupied by the Chung Wang—the Chung Wang foo: well built and clean, but awfully cold. He went into the details of the execution of the Wangs, and what he did seems to have been right and necessary, and not the result of premeditated treachery. He wishes me to endeavour to get Gordon to meet him. Spoke of compensation for wounds, and money to be given to Brennan dismissed by Gordon: advised him to pay everything without delay. Talked for an hour or two, and then came away. He said I shd. find Gordon at Muh-tuh or Tung-ting-shan. Met General!!! Rhodey.[44] Left SooChow at 3 1/2, and arrived at Muh-tuh, some twenty miles S.W. at dark; learned that Gordon had passed through the day before. The boatmen said we should have to retrace the steps as Tung-ting Shan is divided from Muh-tuh by a lake they daren't cross. The rebels had been thrice at Muh-tuh, and last left it on the 24th of the 11th moon. The people are gradually returning to their homes; this place was once famous for its gardens; population formerly over 10000.

SUNDAY, 24 JANUARY 1864: Left Muh-tuh with a high head wind at 9 a.m.: got as far as the village Mondi [?] Jiu-tsin-keaou, a fine 9-arched bridge.[45] Could not get through.

MONDAY, 25 JANUARY 1864: Got to a place through a marsh, called Too-chuh [Hart crossed out that name.] Rain. Very few people, and much ruin in the villages.

TUESDAY, 26 JANUARY 1864: Through a dreary marsh, with rain and wind. Crossed a stream leading to WooChowfoo, and some Hoonan gunboats, who said Gordon was not at Tung-ting shan: I passed some large stockades at a place called Too Chuh, and about noon got to Tung-ting-shan, a long—3 miles—village running along the base of some hills.[46] Gordon had not been there. Bought some fine fish, and started to return at 3 1/2. Rain. Again through the marshes.

27 JANUARY 1864: Last night blew a hurricane: this morning biting cold, with a high wind. Tried to move a little, but had to give it up. Stopped near "Dza-boo-dziaou". Find nearly every place takes its name from a bridge; all the people more or less easily understand Mandarin.[47] Many mulberry trees.

28 JANUARY 1864: Awoke and found the ice an inch thick in the canal. Make a little way at many attempts: our captain smoked opium, cursed, and was very disagreeable. Got to WanKin 50 le from SooChow.[48]

29 JANUARY 1864: I am bound again this morning. In the afternoon got to Jiu-tsin-keaou, many "divers"; Man's gun got us only two hare however. arrived at SooChow S.W. gate at 8 P.M.

30 JANUARY 1864: City moat frozen: however got away, and managed to get down as far as Ta Eding.[49]

SUNDAY, 31 JANUARY 1864: Left the boats and walked on to Quin-san, about six miles: long day. Were stopped at the gate, until Gordon, fortunately caught at last, sent out orders to admit us. Met Gordon for the first time: about thirty years of age; slightly made; with a restless and very blue—light blue—eye. Had a long talk with him: found the Footae had paid all claims; and said Gordon—"You nearly missed me again; for I was near going to Soo-Chow today to call on the Footae." He asked me to go with him, saying I wd. increase my influence with the Footae; but I told him the first thing I shd say to the Footae wd be that G. had of himself, before I met him, determined to visit H. E. He sd., "You surely wd not induce me to visit him:["] To this I made no reply: no use striking fire, when things were found to be in train. Gordon introduced me to his Comprador & Linguist, and to the Na Wang's son, a fine youth named Le native of the same prefecture in Ganwhuy from which Le Footae comes: he is only the adopted son of the Wang, whose name was Kaou.[50] Got my small boat alongside the "Hyson" and started in tow, at 11 P.M. for SooChow. Much ice; freezing Keen [?]. My boat people in an awful funk. After an hour's going, they began to yell the boat was sinking: and sure enough she was making water enough. Cast adrift; got the boat close to the bank, put Leang ashore with orders to go to Quinsan for another boat; put my blankets on board the "Hyson", lay down in my clothes on a trunk, & tried to sleep: couldn't do so. At 3 1/2 arrived at Wae-quau-dong.[51]

1 FEBRUARY 1864: Up at 7. breakfasted with Gordon in his boat at 8, he had got up before the steamer; he then showed me over the scene of the fight at the Low mun stockades, and then we went into the city: I visited the Footae alone first, & told him the execution of the Wangs, and the Emperor's presents, were not to be talked about. Then Gordon came in: he presented Davidson, Tapp, & Kirkham; and the Na-wang's adopted son, who was made a Show-fei [second captain], and told to be a good boy.[52] It was agreed that Gordon shd. take the force into the field after the China New Year, and cooperate even with Ching, unless told not to do so by Sir. F. Bruce; the Footae is to issue a proclamation, taking the responsibility of the execution on himself, and showing that Gordon knew nothing about it. Gordon then left: I had some further chat with the Footae, & got him to authorize the payment of the $7000 expended by Gordon from his own funds, when getting Burgevine out of SooChow. Called at Pwan Tajin's; but he was out. Ching is not dead; Kirkham saw him in the city. Left the Footae at 3 P.M. Saw Mandel & someone else, dealers in arms, in the court yard: they had gone in before 11, and had to cool their toes for four hours. Footae said that Macartney did all he wanted, and, so long as he did so, he would keep him: was very anxious about the Shot Manufactury left behind by Osborn for sale.[53]

Got back in Quinsan at 8.

2 FEBRUARY 1864: Gordon had out the men, 2400, to let me see them. Talked in the afternoon. He thinks Sir F. will consider him rather unstable; I'm to write explaining matters to the chief: Gordon says the force must be broken up. Bade him good bye at 10.

3 FEBRUARY 1864: Having worked [the boat] during the night, got well down towards Shanghae. My left knee very painful.

4 FEBRUARY 1864: Arrived back at Shanghai, about noon. Meritens arrived from FooChow on the 21st. Found many letters awaiting me.

Thus my trip, uncomfortable as it was, had been completely successful. Gordon hd seen both the Footae and Ching, & had determined on future operations! Never say die!

I need not recount here what I said to Gordon, what he sd to me, or what we talked about with the Footae; my letters of the 7th to Sir F. Bruce and of the 8th to Brown explain all these things.[54]

FRIDAY, 5 FEBRUARY 1864: Dined at Dent's, and met the Taoutaes Hwang, Woo: Ting, and the Defense people two of the name of Chin.[55]

SUNDAY, 7 FEBRUARY 1864: Tiffined with Mayers, who is opposed to any move on Gordon's part: sent a note to Gordon by Creamer [?].

MONDAY, 8 FEBRUARY 1864: Gordon's letter of 7th to hand: Mayer's [sic] in an awful frame.

TUESDAY, 9 FEBRUARY 1864: Wrote to Gordon.

WEDNESDAY, 10 FEBRUARY 1864: —again wrote to Gordon: my letters to Sir F. B. & Brown and the Yamun went to SooChow yesterday. Hobson ordered [forth] for special service.[56]

SATURDAY, 13 FEBRUARY 1864: Dined at Heard's, meeting Mr. Robinson and others.

MONDAY, 15 FEBRUARY 1864: Tea'd at Dr. Andersons.

TUESDAY, 16 FEBRUARY 1864: Another chit from Gordon, saying he is to move out today, leaving 250 men at Quinsan. People at Shanghai are savage that he moves; he says it will harm him personally (which I doubt), but that to put a stop to the misery of the people, he is willing to sacrifice himself. Markham wants to know whether I wrote, at Mayer's urgent desire, to ask G. not to go: in order that he may write the exact facts to the F. O.!!!! Very like a whale!

Busy the last few days preparing replies about all Lay's affairs for the Yamun.

On my trip, I asked a man if such a place had been important. "Important!" said he, "why, it had two pawn shops!"

THURSDAY, 18 FEBRUARY 1864: The mail in today from England. Letters from Cha & Brazier. Thackeray dead! What a loss!

Sir R. Alcock arrived <u>en route</u> for Japan.

This afternoon I recd. a letter from the Tsung Le Yamun dated 27th of the 12th m. 4th Feb. informing me that my letters from this on the 16th Jany arrived on the 1st Feb: 15 days from Shanghai to Peking! They defer discussion of all matters till I visit Peking, & tell me to set my mind at rest: that the fleet failure is not in any way attributed to me.

A despatch from Le Footae authorizing Gordon's $7000: and another with a valid copy of the Proclamation. Mayer [*sic*] wrote round to ask me for my English draft of the proclamation I had drawn up for the Footae! Good?[58]

FRIDAY, 19 FEBRUARY 1864: Had a letter today from Gordon, in which he blames Mayers for talking so much. G. is quite right; had M. held his tongue, there wd. have not been half the criticism on G's movements that now go about S'hae. He also sent me for perusal, and to be deposited with Mayers, a copy of Sir F. Bruce's desp. to the Genl. and a private letter to himself: Sir F. wrote on the 25th Jany, and though he said the main points for which we had been all along working, and must be kept steadily in view, he thinks G. has been duped by the Footae, and says "it is clear that he cannot take his orders"—which opinion he has conveyed to the Prince.[59] The Yamun promises an enquiry into the Footae's conduct. Gordon nevertheless goes on, and will answer all enquiries & stop all condemnation by crushing the rebellion.

Called on Sir Rutherford & Lady Alcock.

SATURDAY, 20 FEBRUARY 1864: My 29th Birthday! Goodbye to the Twenties, and all hail the advent of what may be called the second-half of the Three Score. "Surely goodness and mercy have followed me all the days of my life!"

Mayers very anxious to get Gordon's papers today: he says Sir F.'s letter to the Genl. is stronger than he expected, and that it "amply indicates the position he took up."

Col. Hough says his instincts are strong against M., and that he wishes some one else had the keeping of G's papers.[60]

Dick, Wright, Chase, Mercer, & St. Croix to dinner tonight: a very pleasant evening.

Jebb and Clements called in today.[61]

Snow falling for the last three days.

Ying came in today and told me that Ting-heang hein & Han-yin chow have submitted. Keahing foo daily expected to surrender; and then the Kwan-ping [official troops] can go on at WooChow.[62]

SUNDAY, 21 FEBRUARY 1864: Not up till near eleven o'c! Snow still on the ground, but the cold not very severe. My knee cap continues to show some symptoms of being still out of order.

MONDAY, 22 FEBRUARY 1864: Sent Sir F.'s private letter to Gordon round to Mayers, who writes back that he "thinks Gordon does not wish it talked about, as it is enough to stamp him as a madman." The little man has been pulling down proclamations addressed by the Footae to the foreigners: very proper proclamations in my opinion. He follows Parkes — but at a distance. I disapprove of his tone & conduct entirely; he's a dangerous man, and seems to me to be trying to have a regular embroglio ready by the arrival of Parkes. Now I want to have everything quiet all round, so that Sir Harry may not have any excuse for going beyond his consular & municipal duties. Thank heaven! Gordon is off, and gone to work again.[63]

Ying has been appointed Taoutae, I am glad to record; to [characters for *tai-li*; "to serve as a replacement"] for three months. He's a well-disposed, intelligent man.[64]

[Three blank pages]

MONDAY, 29 FEBRUARY 1864: This morning's shipping list contains the minutes of an "Indignation" meeting, held by the merchants at Hankow, in wh' several resolutions were passed, condemning the Actg. Comr. MacPherson's action in stopping the "Hu Kwang's" shipment & discharge of cargo in consequence of an insult offered the Tidewaiter Gray by 2nd [assist.?] Engineer Petersen. Mssrs. Tyson & Forbes, of Russell and Co.'s, called on me about noon, and placed in my hands copies of the correspondence that passed between Mr. Breck as their agent and as U.S. Consul, and MacPherson, on the subject. They will claim Tls. 10,000 damages. They said they were about to write to Mr. Burlingame on the subject; I, however, remarked that as their doing so would only result in the matter being referred to me, it might be as well for them to defer doing so, until I had myself made enquiries. I, of course, cannot officially give any opinion, until I have recd. a proper official reply to the queries I must put to the Commissioner. Meantime, I think MacPherson has exceeded his powers, and has placed me and the service generally in a disagreeable predicament.[65]

Mr. Seward called this morning, and said Mr. Burlingame had written to him to make enquiries about the Phaeton [?] and another vessel, that had been seized and confiscated by the Chinkiang Customs, when found trading at Eching with the U.S. flag flying; the flags, I think, had been given to them by Mr. Breck, while Consul at Kiukiang. He tells me, too, that Williams is to be hung tomorrow morning.[66]

Adkins and Lee breakfasted with me. Ying paou she made his first call, at 12, as Taoutae. He brought with him a very long letter from Le Footae, about the purchase of land by missionaries and his late proclamations.[67]

Received four despatches [Chinese characters for the 4th day of 1st lunar month; i.e., 11 February 1864] from the Tsung Le Yamun today. Also got a letter dated the 4th Feb. from Sibbald: I wonder how it came.[68]

Russell & Co's Steamship *Huquong* (built 1862, burned 1866).

Cox called today: had a long talk with him about Dr. Wong.
Lord arrived this evening from Canton.[69]

1 MARCH 1864: The convict Williams cut his throat, and in that
way escaped hanging. Pity that the rowdy lot shd. have lost the benefit of an
example!

Attended a meeting today at the Library called for the purpose of reforming the North China Branch of the Royal Asiatic Society.

Recd a well written and sensible letter today from the committee appointed at the Hankow Indignation Meeting, condemning MacPherson's
action. This will be a very difficult case for me to deal with: if I don't support
MacPherson, the service will cry out, and people will say I'm truckling to
the merchants; on the other hand, if I do support him, the mercantile people
will raise a howl—and, in my opinion, would be justified in doing so. It is
very trying for a quiet and peaceably disposed chief, like myself, to have
such fiery and inconsiderate subs as MacPherson.

A note recd from Col. Hough tells me that Murray has written to him to
the effect that the General approves of what Gordon has done.

Still very cold.

2 MARCH 1864: Recd. a letter from Ying Taoutae today telling me that the Tsungleyamun had approved of my action in the case of confiscating Vaucher's goods and in demanding a bond from Remi Schmidt when importing shot.[70]

Cowie, Gilmour, Lord, White, & Wright dined with me in the evening. The Carting Co. is dying—if not quite defunct, and Mr. F. O. B. Twigg is to aid Mr. Wright in his duties as sexton, instead of cantering about the settlement for orders. The coolies will greatly rejoice when the carts disappear.[71]

No mail, as yet.

3 MARCH 1864: Mail arrived today: strange to say, no letters from home, and, on the other hand, a note from Smith Elder & Co. 'dunning' me. The money I sent by the mail of the 9th Nov. last ought to have arrived before the end of December. I see, however, from the papers that the latest Shanghae dates Nov. 9 only reached London, via Marseilles on the 9th Jany.

The papers contain the correspondence relative to the sending home of the Fleet. The 'uniform' is the card played: made any sacrifices, of course, did O. [Osborn] & Co., rather than stain the British name! Were I to append certain facts, as marginal comments, to the papers published, O. and Co.'s cause wd. not look so well.

4 MARCH 1864: Met Parkes on the Bund: he is as lively as ever, and has got the old mark of drawing out others' opinions without giving his own. I told him the cause of the break up of the Fleet: his comments were neither one thing nor the other, but a certain kind of half & half mixture, in which one could scarcely tell what predominated—assent or a 'what next' query.

Sent a note to the Herald pointing out the mistakes in the translation of the Footae's Proclamation about Gordon.

5 MARCH 1864: Today at 1 P.M., a deputation appointed by the Committee of the Chamber of Commerce—Antrobus, Tyson, & Morburn,— called on me, and talked about drawbacks—they want money, instead of paper.[72]

At 2, the Chekeang Leang Tae [grain intendant], Hoo, with Hwang Sun Sang, called. They want me to think out a plan by which the taxing officers in their provinces shall be enabled to collect taxes from the producers of goods, to make up for the loss experienced by the use of Transit Certificates. They say, it wd. not interfere with the Transit System atall; I show them that if they pound [?] today on a man for Ten taels, who has sold 100 taels' worth of goods to a foreigner, the same man will tomorrow ask for 110 taels for the same quantity of goods. Tso Chetai, the gov.-genl. of Fuhkeen & Chekiang— sent them to consult with me, and in doing so remarked that if I could devise a plan it would be 'all up' with the Keen-wuh of the province.[73]

At 3, the two Chins, from the Defense Committee called. The chief at first read the Footae's Proclamation as Mayers & said, to boot, that there had been 'negotiations' for the murder of the Na Wang; after more careful consideration of the sentence,— the [characters for *ch'i-hsien*; "at first"] & the [characters for *ch'i-tao*; "his arrival"] he came round to my view. The sentence certainly by itself can be interpreted in either way; but the context seems to me to show that mine is the right rendering, more especially when one criticizes the placing of the [characters for *li-i*; "negotiations] before the [characters for *ting-ch'i*; "fixing of a time"].[74]

Walked with Meadows on the Bund. Took a hot bath before going to bed, & feel as if a horrid cold were coming on.

SUNDAY, 6 MARCH 1864: Busy today from 10 @ 2, and got through steamer a/c. for Le Footae and the Yamun. Thank heaven! I shall have more leisure now, having got this load off my shoulders.

Talked with Talbot tonight: did not go to evening service, as I feared sitting in such a cold place wd increase the violence of my cough.[75]

It is six months today since I started on the [characters for *cheng-tao*; "the proper path"]: many inward struggles, but no outward giving way, in the direction I most feared. I have felt quite happy during some time back, and have as it were had a season of that 'perfect love which casteth out fear.' But such happy seasons are necessarily ephemeral, and the fight and struggles will have to be gone through afresh. But one must live with armour constantly on: death, when it comes, will bring rest and peace. Strange to say, I like to think about death, and a very favorite place of mine is the cemetery. At night, too, I sometimes prepare myself as if I should like to see, and were about to see, spirits. Last night I had very peculiar dreams which have now fled from my mind; but when I awoke this morning, I almost felt as if I had been conversing with, or listening to spirits. If there be spirits, invisible & that cannot be touched, floating about through the air, may they not get into one — evil spirits especially, in order to invite one to sensual indulgences, and thereupon derive a sort of pleasure, of the kind they most were addicted to when in the flesh?

I feel rather lonely, and I wish very much I had a wife — I don't see how I'm to get such an appendage. Pity I didn't make it all right, say, with M. M. before leaving Ireland: married some years ago, 'twould have done very well; now, unfortunately, the lady is becoming too aged for one to look to her as a bride: all for the best, evidently!

7 MARCH 1864: Dined at Thorne's tonight: present Meadows, Parkes, Gould, Maitland, Reed, & both the Thornes. Pleasant party: I watched Parkes, and noted in him the usual peculiar mode of getting out of the difficulty of ignorance on any subject. He would knit his brows, look up, "Ahem!" "Let me see", and, by the time that was done, some one else would

be sure to break in and <u>he</u> wd. get out of the bottle by saying, "Do you think so? Ah! I see." I wonder how he likes to be Consul. I hear he addressed a <u>Chaou</u> <u>Hwuy</u> [communication between equals], and not a Shin-chin [report from a subordinate] to the Footae: after lording it over Viceroys at Canton, it will scarcely come natural to him to deal gently with Taoutaes and Chehiens [magistrates]. Home at midnight: a nasty wild night — just the night for ghosts to walk, and murders to occur.[76]

Have had a bad cold coming on the last three days, & feel rather stupid.

8 MARCH 1864: Dore, the Naval Storekeeper, who has been coming out 'strong' on the tariff during the last year or two at Shanghae, & who fell into a large fortune some time ago, was shot on the Ma Loo Mun [?] "House" last night about ten o'clock. He was taking a light for his cheroot from a lantern, and while stooping down, someone fired & sent the bullet into his belly. He was picked up by Mr. Cox, & taken to Dr. Henderson's: the wound is a bad one. The man who fired is supposed to be a Cantonese: many 'roughs' from that province are now in Shanghae, and nearly all of them carry revolvers. The Municipal Council offers a reward of $500 for the apprehension of the man. The occurrence is a strange one: Chinese don't take away life without an object. What was the man's object in this instance? not plunder: he did not attempt to rifle Dore's pockets. Had Dore struck him, or hurt him in any way: or did he mistake him for another person?[77]

My cold makes me quite stupid today.

9 MARCH 1864: Poor Dore is dead. Last night, again, on Hongque, a policeman was murdered by a gang of Cantonese: he killed one of them. Foreigners seem likely to have to now reap the results of the covetous desire to become wealthy speedily, which led them to harbor so many Chinese in the settlement.

Poor Dore was about to go home! So it always happens in China: whoever makes money rapidly, or unexpectedly, and delays going home for a season, is somehow or other sure to be cut off. Looking back there are in this category, Dore, Gingell, Richardson, Ryin, Dowman, & many others: many, too, just get home and then 'disappear.'

How necessary to live always ready: but what care and watchfulness does it require to keep the lamp trimmed and burning! My last six months have not been gone through without much struggle: my besetting sin, 'womanizing,' has worried me day after day, but, fortunately, I have been preserved from giving way outwardly. The inner battle, though, has been a hard one: and now what troubles me most is my imagination — I find it almost impossible to refrain from indulging in imagination in those pleasures which I have strength enough to refrain from outwardly. "Wretched man that I am!" Last night, I had an awful battle: the imagination had to be put down — it was put down. Flight, instant flight, and determined wrestling prayer, are the only means of rescue: it does not do to hold a parley with such a treacherous foe. I hope I am now in the right road, and I trust I shall be kept to the end: But what an awful thing it would be after all to be found among those who say "Lord, Lord!" but to whom it shall be said, "I never knew you!" How necessary to be careful in self-examination, so that self-deceit may be avoided.

I don't like, generally speaking, to put down feelings of this kind in my journal; my chief reason for doing so is that, should I be carried off suddenly in this far-from-home land, there may be for those that remain behind something in my journals to give them reason to hope that they will meet me again in the "better," the "heavenly" Country. At present, I have great joy in believing: and I can truly say—for I feel it, and realize it—"In the multitude of my thoughts within me, thy comforts delight my soul!"

10 MARCH 1864: Had a long visit today from Lent, which rather interfered with my work. His object in coming to see me was to ask for the gratuity that he had formerly applied for to Mr. Lay: viz., a year's pay. I told him that insofar as I was concerned, I thought his application a very fair one; but that I had resolved not to pay away such sums of money without having in the first instance mentioned my intention at Peking. He thinks he has been very unjustly treated; and indeed, considering how well Lay took care of himself, and also the reckless way in which he put money into the hands of others—Davies, for instance, who went home on full pay, and to whose widow a present was made of the two years' pay or thereabouts in which, drawn in advance, Davies was indebted, and had undertaken to return in the case of death, to the Chinese—it seems that Lent is right when he says he has not been so lucky as others. People say he wants to get back again into the Customs: he is not, however, to my mind, the right kind of man for our progressing duties, however excellent he may be in some respects.[78]

Meadows, Jamieson, Bowra, and Cliquet, & Dick dined with me tonight.[79]

At the meeting of the Asiatic Society last night, Sir H. Parkes was elected President, Dr. Henderson V. P., and myself one of the Directors.

The "Tsatlee" was carried off yesterday; Jamieson says she may have been retaken.

11 MARCH 1864: Forbes tells me that the "Tsatlee" has not been retaken. He says Jones went off on Saturday last to visit Gordon. When will these months end? I wish Pitman was here that I might put the "Elfin" in commission. I wrote to Le Footai today to ask him to order the "Confucius" and the "Pluto" to anchor at the South Barrier, & to assist our people there in stopping steamers.[80]

Sent off a despatch today No. 7 to Yamun, giving [a] list of Commissioners: & No. 8 acknowledging receipt of despatches (3) of [characters for fourth day of the first lunar month].

Gave Mr. David Reid a note to Brown at Ningpo, telling him to let the "Wm. IVth" run with passengers between that & Yuyaou: a step in the right direction, opening up the river to steam traffic.[81]

Last night Mercer, at the Kung Kwan [office], heard some people moving about during the night. He got up, & found some robbers in the house; he was lucky enough to shoot one of them.[82]

A volunteer concert tonight; my cold keeps me in. Another circus company, Lewis', is putting up its tent on the site of Risley's. Shanghae is gradually coming more & more within the range of distractions of the Western world.

I have been in correspondence with Mr. Seward about Mr. Consul Breck's connexion with certain junks that were confiscated for trading at Eching. I think Mr. Burlingame wishes to put Mr. Breck 'through'; he will not forget in a hurry the "thunder" & "lightening" with which the smuggler threatened him, from Western skies.

No news in from Gordon yet: I wrote to him today to put him on his guard, and to warn him about the "Tsatlee" & the steamer of Pustan's that was sold to the Keahing foo people.[83]

12 MARCH 1864: This morning, one of the Pustan's people called to see me in consequence of a remark he had seen in the morning paper, which had made him very uneasy about his steamer, the "Greta." He said that a silk man from Keahing was desirous of purchasing her, & that on Saturday last (5th) he had allowed her to go away Keahing-wards on a trial trip for four days, and that now he feared, either that she had been taken off by a rebel agent, or been seized by the "Tsatlee." We decided that the other steamer the "Faust" should be sent after her, manned by some 30 of the crew of the Prussian frigate "Gazelle" which is fortunately in harbor. I supplied him with a 'Hoo chaw' [passport]: so I hope we'll get back both the steamers.[84]

13 MARCH 1864: Wet day, did not go to service. In future, rain or no rain, I'll not neglect the means of grace. The appointed means are certainly aids to anyone desirous of leading a godly life, and of growing in the love and fear of God. Reading Whatley's "Errors of Romanism have their origin in human nature." Also dipping into "Dr. Thorne"—a book of which I am very fond. Wrote today to Maxwell & Swinhoe.[85]

14 MARCH 1864: Hurrah! Today the paper contains the news of the capture of the "Tsatlee" by Ching at Keahing foo: and this afternoon, the "Faust" returned, having met the "Greta" on the way back all right, at Minhong. Hurrah, again, say I![86]

Sun came to me this evening with a story about a friend of his, who has been taken on board a boat in the harbor, near the East Gate, where he is held to ransom for Tls. 1500. I shall send tidewaiters tomorrow, and get him out of the scrape.

Very odd the French Mail has not yet arrived. This morning's paper contains my remarks about the cities, 7, that have surrendered since the taking of SooChow. Chapoo, Keashon, Hae yen, Ping-hoo, Tung heang, Hae-ning & Shih mun: all in Chekiang & all sent their delegates to Le Footae, from which I argue that the execution of the Na Wang did not inspire the people with distrust of the Footae.[87]

15 MARCH 1864: Sun came round at 1/2 p. 10, and said that his friend Chang had been taken away from the boat he was confined in yesterday and could not be found. I sent him to Dick, who sent out three tidewaiters, who succeeded in finding Chang confined in another boat. They released him, seized the boat, and made prisoners of four men in it, one of whom, named Wang, is a brother of the blackguard who wanted Tls. 1500 from Chang. Dick sent them into the city to the Taoutae. One tidewaiter, whom Watson left behind in charge of another boat that seemed to be implicated was made prisoner by some of the French police: subsequently Dick sent for him, and the police, on learning that he belonged to the Customs, released him. But these French gentlemen are carrying things with a high hand: they had no right to put him in durance.[88]

Had a call today from the French gentleman, a traveling Inspector, who takes Bertolini's place.[89] Report says that the French mail str., due a week ago, is on shore near Haenan. Ying Taoutae returned today from SooChow: he brings civil messages from the Footae. He consulted me about — 1°. making over Chinese in the settlement to the jurisdiction of the municipal council, 2°. about maintaining a water police out of the Tonnage Dues, 3°. about watchers for the South Barrier, and 4°. about the people seized in the "Tsatlee" & the steamer herself. With reference to 4°. I tell him to take the heads off the Chinese — some 20 Cantonese — and to keep the steamer for the present. He thinks the str. ought to be confiscated; but I don't see how that can be done. He tells me the Chinese vessels, the Footae sent with Hoo to Tso-che-tae [governor-general Tso Tsung-t'ang], were from Hangchow. Gordon took Ehing on the 25th i.e. the 10th instant; and that G. left directions with the Footae not to forward any letters from Peking. How Mayers would swear, were he to hear that![90]

Wrote a note to MacPherson today, telling him how strongly I disapproved of his action in the "Hukwang" case.

A note from Cowie tells me that Davies' debt to the Chinese was over Tls. 9800; & that Lay released Mrs. D. from it on account of the 'important services' (!) rendered to the Chinese Govt. by the deceased.

Some queer facts are coming out about poor Davies death. He went out on the day in question to Laou Ke-chang to see a woman that he once kept:

found two Cantonese there, one of whom he kicked downstairs: they followed him, & he went into the fruiterer's [?] shop, where he stood 1/2 an hour hoping they wd pass on. They shot him when he left the shop! I thought it odd, he made no dying declaration: on the other hand, it seems he told his boy, "Joe," to stick to the "lantern story". Poor fellow!

16 MARCH 1864: Why will merchant-skippers discharge their ill-shapen guns, charged with indifferent powder, badly rammed home, when leaving port; this morning, the "Emily Faithful," leaving Shanghae, at irregular intervals fired her guns; five reports all in all; two came first, then one, & then two. I thought the French & English mail steamers had come in together: ran, & found it was only a morning lark on the part of the commander of the "E. Faithful". Jolly old bloke! Glad, I suppose, to get away from S'Hae.

The freed Chang called this morning to present his thanks: as he ought: & knocked head [kowtowed]. Had I not got him out of limbo yesterday, he'd have suffered 'some' by this time!

Nothing particular to put in my journal today: save that I have been busy at my I.G.'s work. I've — Hilloa! What's up? a wei-yuen [deputy] named [character for *wang*], from the Defense Committee, wanting to see me, at 1/2 p. 9? Aw! Yih-peih Keun-ho [?]: some arms going to Keahing? Send him up to Dick, who, perhaps, will be able to put the thing through. My no savee: no can takee care this small-oo pigeon now: belong "Mr. Commissioner" as Ninqua wd. say.[91]

Letter today from Seward enquiring as to the date, on wh: Breck fitted out junks from Kiukiang. We'll put Mr. B. "up a tree."

Wrote letters today to Woo: Ying: Le Footai: Meritens: Maxwell: Hammond. The Major down from Chinkiang en route for Europe.[92]

17 MARCH 1864: Walked out this evening. My kneecap is not all right yet; felt sore when I came home. Roads awfully muddy: but the walk, after a week in the house, very refreshing.

When the released Chang was being examined by the Cheheen, he named as one of his tormenters Twan San. Ah! sd. the CheHeen, why that's the man we have 'suspended' but who wont confess complicity in the Chow-twan robbery. Wd. you know him?[93]

I rather think I shd., sd, Chang. So they were confronted. "Twan laou yay," sd. Chang. "Chang sun sung. Kew too teih ming [?]," sd. Mr. Twan.[94] Then it came out that three of the four, we seized and sent into the city, are gang robbers: and the authorities are highly delighted to have got hold of them.

Ying Taoutae wrote today to tell me that Gordon took Le Yang on the 9th [characters for the 2nd day of the 2nd lunar month] so he must have opened up communication with Paou Chou at Ningkuo all right: I hope he'll go on.[95]

18 MARCH 1864: Calls today from Mr. de Champs, and Mr. Chichester, a Frenchman and a Yankee: to the latter I have promised employment from the 1st of next quarter. If Meritens allows it, I shall give an appointment to de Champs as well. Holgood & Butler can be weeded out. I shall now gradually get rid of all our "bad hats."[96]

MacPherson's letter of explanation to hand today: so I must now make up my mind as to the Hankow question.

Mayers called today; he's going to pitch into me tomorrow in the "N. C. Herald", in defense of his rendering of the Footae's proclamation about Gordon.

I notice from a word that Ying Taoutae let drop the other day, that he knew I had written to the Footae about the "Confucius" & the "Pluto": a copy of my letter must have been sent to him by Sun, who I have no doubt supplies copies of all my correspondence – the old blackguard! Still what can I do? any other Chinese that I could get hold of wd. require years of drilling before he could do what Sun does, & wd. then play false just in the same way.[97]

Where can the Mail have got to?

Got a letter tonight from Gordon from Leyang about 158 miles from S'hae, dated 11th. He has got E-hing, Le-yang, and a place he calls Ta-poo-keaow: with 35 000 Rebels, among whom is the Shih-wang. He says Kin-tan will come over in a few days. He has not yet seen Paou; but he is in communication with him: NingKwo distant 80 le. He sends me the rebels' surrender petition: and a page from a curious letter of Mayers in which he called Hough an "old beldame," and says that something Gordon quoted expresses his "opinion of my action perfectly." I shd. like to see what Mayers says: now, R. H., let me ask you one question, has not general expediency been what you aimed at in the whole matter? no, by George! there has been a mixture of motives: self, the public, and China, have all been intermixed – perhaps with more weight given to no. 1 than was right. I don't know, though: I thought I was acting, on the whole, for the best. Gordon says Mayers is a "little idiot": I think him a narrow-minded, & somewhat-dangerous youth. Ayah![98]

19 MARCH 1864: Today I sent the Returns for the 11th, 12th and 13th Quarters, by the "Pembroke" via Teentsin, to the Tsung Le Yamun, in Shin ching [report] No. 9.

Also wrote notes to Brett & Brown. With me dined Klezkowsky, Noetzli, White, Smith, and Dick: yet to be asked Hough, Knight, Towell, Gibbs, Sidford, Jaques.[99]

20 MARCH 1864: The N. C. Herald of yesterday, contains Mayers letter, pointing out, or rather 'exposing the fallacy' of my attempt to correct his version of the Footae's "mendacious proclamation". Looking at the one sentence – the Chinese alone – and without being in any way influenced by

what one knows of the Moo Wang's death, perhaps it might be admitted that it could be translated as it has been by Mayers: but taking into consideration, what Gordon says, that even the Na Wang knew nothing of the intention to murder the Moo Wang an hour before the occurence took place, and coupling the two sentences in the paragraph—the [characters for *ch'i-hsien*; "at first"] with the [characters for *ch'i-tao chih shih*; "the time of his arrival"]—I think my rendering is the correct one. I shall write to Le Footai and ask him whether the [characters for *i-i*; "negotiations"] is to be taken as putting each of the following four clauses in the infinitive, "negotiations entered into to surrender, to murder, to give up a gate, to fix a time"; or whether it only governs the [characters for *t'ou-hsiang*; "surrender"]: or whether the [characters for *ch'i-hsien*; "at first"] refers to five things, viz.—of the first occurences, the negotiations, the surrender, the murder, the giving up of the gate, the fixing a time—Gordon was aware. Again the [characters for *tseng-tseng*; "by stages"]: does that phrase refer to things after accomplishment, or while in contemplation? [In the margin Hart has written later: "Both Wan Seang and Le Footai say my translation was the right one."][100]

Now Robert H., allow me to lecture you a little. What you pray for is a tender conscience, and not a quiet one; and what you really wish for is safety in the end rather than a mere sense of security: you don't want to be an ostrich, and merely put your head in the sand at the approach of danger, nor are you desirous of thrusting your head under the blankets, like a child, in the dark: no, what you want is truth—the stake is too awful a one to allow of life being influenced by, or eternity sacrificed, to humbug. So, my dear R. H., I proceed to lecture you: and think of what I say, my boy! In the first place, don't allow yourself to be influenced by merely selfish considerations—or by personal notions—in the advice you give to the Chinese: is it not a fact that you are conscious of having advised some things to be done on some occasions more because they were likely to strengthen the Customs' Inspectorate, than because they seemed right—that you threw the question of right to one side, and went ahead with the view of gaining such ends as would secure the dynasty, and with it keep you and the Customs safe? Have you not in this respect been somewhat jesuitical, in that you paid more attention to the ends than to the means? Thus, with regard to Le Footai's execution of the Wangs, were you not more anxious to prove him right, than to get at the truth? Were you not more anxious to get Gordon to go to work again, than to have the Footae punished? So my advice to you is:—will you take it?—

1°. Aim at truth, first and above all things:

2°. Never back the side that is in the wrong:

3°. Confine yourself as much as possible to the Customs' business:

4°. When the Chinese ask you for your advice in matters not connected with the Customs: see what they want: if they merely want you to devise a plan to get them out of complying with some foreign demand, either tell them it's none of your business, or take the foreign side: don't oppose foreign advice or demands, unless you see it to be a kind likely to prove detrimental to China, or merely through any feeling of jealousy: [sic]

5°. You are paid to collect the revenue: make it your first care to do that well, and don't burn your fingers by meddling with what does not concern you. At the same time, the above rules, though calculated to keep one out of trouble, are of a very selfish kind: how "be a hero in the strife," and act on them? Ah me! Man is mortal and is not infallible: he is very prone to err, and make mistakes. The safe rule is "to love the Lord with all thy strength, and thy neighbor as thyself." You must first do what your conscience, enlightened by study of God's word, says is right: and mixture as you are of good and evil, a bundle of emotions as you are, you must just plod on, doing with all your might whatever you find to do, remembering your accountability, &, knowing, that while God can see in your heart of hearts, He knows your frame that it is but "dust". I'm sure I wish to do what is right: God help me to do so!

"When ranting round in pleasures ring
　　Religion may be blinded!
Or if she gie a random sting,
　　It may be little minded:
But when on life we're tempest driven,
　　A conscience but a canker—
A correspondence fixed w' heaven,
　　Be sure a noble anchor." Say [sic] Burns.

Mr Muirhead preached this evening from "Ever learning but never coming to the knowledge of the truth." As he spoke of the "learning of the lesson", how many thoughts of old times came up: Christian parents, Christian schooling, Christian friends, Christian privileges! "Auld lang syne."

21 MARCH 1864: Heard the Mail Guns about six o'clock this morning; so I presume the letters may make their appearance any moment. I expect a treat in the letters from home, for they ought to be in acknowledgment of the Christmas presents I sent home, and such letters are generally of such an affectionate character as to be much more pleasant in the perusal than others.

What I want to do now is a little analysis: an analysis, in fact, of my doings—motives—conduct—feelings in the case of the execution of the Wangs by Le Footae. To commence from the very commencement:

1°. In what frame of mind was I when the news of the execution reached Shanghae? Osborn and Lay were both here at the time; the former on his way home because he refused to serve under local officials who might wish to act cruelly or who might fail to keep good faith; the latter, too, was on his way home for much the same reasons. On the other hand, I myself had been arguing that, except under the local officials, the fleet could never get along atall, and that they could be so managed as to prevent the occurrence of any of those things dreaded by Lay & Osborn. Such being Lay's views and such being mine, how did the news affect us respectively? To him no doubt it was a confirmation of all he said he feared: he said to himself, no doubt, "Look here, now: not to speak of local officials generally, under whom you Hart say the fleet might be placed without harm, just see what Le Footae, the high officer under whom it was, first of all, to act, does! He uses Gordon to take SooChow: that object effected, he throws him to one side; he gets him to be present at the conference with the Wangs, and uses his presence to give them confidence: the moment they surrender, he takes their heads off! There you are: he wd. do just the same with us, if we put ourselves in his power: he would use us while it suited his purpose to do so, & then he would throw us aside; he wd. break our promises; throw discredit on us, and we would be in the power of a cruel savage incapable of good faith!" No doubt Lay and Osborn looked on the occurrence in that light; and, just as little doubt had I that they will "make capital" of it, to support the views they expressed and the action they had taken. So much for them; now for myself. I had been glorying in the fall of SooChow, delighted that, at the time of the disbanding of the fleet, the Imperialists should gain a point that wd. give them confidence, dispirit the Taepings, and cause outsiders to believe in the possibility of the rebellion being effectually and speedily put down, without further foreign intervention, by the Chinese officials themselves. Glorying in the fall of SooChow, I was too somewhat elated in another respect; for in the letter I wrote to Lay before I heard of the fate of the fleet, I told him not to found his demands on the idea that the govt. was so weak that it must accede to them — that SooChow wd fall in a couple of weeks. Being in such a frame of mind, the news of the execution of the Wangs, produced 1°. a feeling of heartsinking and intense disgust — heartsinking as the thought struck me I had been erroneous in my views & had taken the wrong side, and disgust at the Imperialists for, by that action, playing in such a way into the hands of Lay and Osborn, 2°. the feeling arose in my mind that it could not have been the treacherous act, it was represented to be, and that Le Footae must have had for such conduct good and sufficient reasons, that wd. come out and be recognized as such in due time; 3°. the disgust remained, but it made its object less the Imperialists than the unfortunate contretemps, and, as the conviction gained strength that Le Footae would be able to explain his conduct, the heartsinking left me. Such was the first age: the only thing then to be done was "to wait for the end".

I, however, having got so far as to feel convinced that Le Footae must have had good reason for what he had done, commenced to think and to guess at what those reasons might have been; and having once commenced to guess, the next step was to place in order what seemed to me to be satisfactory reasons for the conduct of H. E.; having once put together what seemed a satisfactory explanation, I could not, for the life of me, help dwelling on the idea that that must be the proper explanation; and the next step in this, the second stage, was to think and talk of Le Footae, as though his action had had for its causes and excuse, the very explanation that I had thought out as a satisfactory one.

At this stage of the analysis, I shall put in a quotation from Whatley's Essay on Pious Frauds: —"There is hardly any evidence which a man may not bring himself to resist, if it come, not before, but after he has fully made up his mind."

Then commenced the third stage, which was, to consider that Gordon in withdrawing from the Footae had taken a step that the execution of the Wangs had not demanded; and the next idea was, of course that he ought, if possible to be got to cooperate with the Footae again. Now this time, besides having for its foundation the opinion or conviction that I had been growing into, of what had led the Footae to execute them, was strengthened, no doubt, by selfish and interested considerations. The customs' service, and my position, I could not help regarding as being to some extent dependent upon the fate of the dynasty; and I hence naturally wished to see any step that imperilled Imperial interests averted, and any step that might aid Imperialism prosecuted without delay. I do not mean to say that such was the only motive in operation; but in the mixture of motives, I cannot but say No. 1, or its traces, is to be detected.

Thus from disgust at such an untimely occurrence, I proceeded 1°. to doubt the treachery, 2°. to weave excuses for the Footae's conduct, 3°. to feel confident that those excuses formed the real explanation of his actions, 4°. to think that Gordon had no sufficient reasons for his wrath and withdrawal, and 5°. to think it wd. be possible to get him to cooperate again with the Footae.

Having got so far, the next thing determined on was to go to SooChow, and get an account, from Le Footae himself, of the causes which had induced him to execute the Wangs. My hope was that he wd. be able to give such explanations as shd. make it possible for me to effect a reconciliation between him and Gordon. In this, I was quite honest in my intentions: my intention was to get the Footae's explanation of his conduct; my hope was that, going on it, I shd be able to induce Gordon to take the field again.

When I called on the Footae, I told him very plainly that the public charged him with a breach of good faith; but that I myself had not formed my judgment, though I had endeavoured to conjecture what causes had led to the execution, basing my conjectures, and the rope of reasoning & explanations which tied them together, on the rumors that were to be met with among the Chinese as to the conduct of the Wangs when at the interview with the Footae. At this interview, I was the chief speaker certainly, but the Footae's occasional remarks and bits of explanation led me to believe that my previous conjectures were near the mark, and the execution was not an act of premeditated treachery.

We then talked of Gordon, & the Footae said how anxious he was to put the execution of the Wangs on one side — not to refer to it atall again — and see Gordon as usual. I advised him strongly for mere honesty's and fairness' sake, to settle all claims against the Force, and to pay all the monies Gordon had asked for for the wounded men, & for those characters of whom it seemed more and more expedient to get rid. I then left him with the determination of explaining to Gordon my view of the execution, and of advising him, for the sake of general interests, and to further the British policy of crushing the rebellion & supporting the Imperialists, to let the past be the past, and again go to work.

Strange to say, I could not find Gordon at any of the places I went to, and after ten days searching, I returned to Quinsan when I met him for the first time. One of the first things he said was "You were near missing me again here, I was near going to SooChow this morning, and I am about to go there tonight. The Footae has paid up all claims, and has behaved so liberally about the wounded men and other matters, that I had made up my mind to see him. You come with me, and your position will be strengthened by your getting the credit of having 'brought back the rebel'." I said I was glad to hear he was going to SooChow; that I shd. gladly go with him, but that the first thing I shd. tell the Footae wd be that Gordon had made up his mind to visit him before I found him; and, when we subsequently met the Footae, I did tell him so, but he seemed to think that I deserved as much of him as though I had induced Gordon to visit him. Gordon and myself had a long disjointed talk: in which I urged him to to go to work again, not attempting to explain or palliate the Footae's conduct, but merely saying that, even though he had acted treacherously, I thought that the action of him as an individual, high in office as he might be, ought not to be allowed to 1. harm the Imperial cause, 2. frustrate the British policy, 3. prolong local troubles, and 4. inspirit the rebels, by being considered as a sufficient reason for preventing Gordon from again cooperating. Gordon seemed to think himself that inactivity was becoming bad for the force, and was likely to give room for the rowdy element to gain strength at Shanghae. At all events he determined to go to work again; and on the following day, I acted as his Interpreter, in explaining that the past need not be again referred to, and that Gordon wd. cooperate just as before.

Thus my desire for seeing the Imperialist cause triumph — grounded on two things: 1°. my honest conviction that Imperialism gives the promise of better things for China than does Taepingism, & 2°. my personal interests, which lead me to wish the Imperialist cause, in which I am a paid employé [sic] with the consent of my government, — led me to wish the execution to be explained, or overlooked, so that Gordon might again go to work. But, strange to say, it was not necessary, and I had indeed no proper opportunity for doing so, for me to attempt to palliate the Footae's conduct: for I found Gordon already determined on visiting the Footae — his visit probably may have originated in the Footae's having taken my advice to settle all just claims without delay, — and also on going to work again, — the reasons for the going to work being unconnected with my opinions or mental processes in regard to the execution of the Wangs.

I did, however, write to Sir. F. Bruce giving my explanation of the Footae's doings.

Here ends my analysis. The question is, have I been to blame atall in this matter? In reviewing all that has taken place, I see plainly that I have been anxious for, and endeavoured to effect, what seemed to be generally speaking most expedient. In my fallibility and weakness, I may, too, have allowed considerations of general expediency [to] absorb my attention to such an extent as to make me careless to the possibility of my taking for granted what had not been proved, or of regarding as true merely what I wished, but did not know, to be true.

Well: in public life, I see there may be temptation to sin that one never wd. have dreamt of, and of a kind more difficult to be guarded against from the greater difficulty of detecting them. O for a tender conscience! Let me remember that the good man is "He that speaketh the truth in his heart."

In this affair it was quite right for me, being convinced on grounds of expediency that it was the proper course to be followed, to wish to induce Gordon again to take the field: what was wrong, was in allowing myself to be carried away as to accept as true an explanation, based on conjecture, merely because I wished it to be true. Fortunately that mistake of mine had nothing to do with inducing Gordon to again take the field: though he cooperates with, he is still as bitter as ever against, the Footae.

*　　*　　*

Got letters today, posted for the mail of 20th Jany, from Father, Mother, Jaimie, Sarah, Maggie, H. McCall, FitzRoy, & Glover. The money I sent home in Nov. arrived safely on the 10th Jany. Strange to say Smith Elder & Co. have not yet acknowledged the receipt of what I sent them: perhaps they have written by the French mail, which is not yet to hand. Odd, too, that Lizzie Lindrum does not write! Cassie is to write by next mail. Father has been very ill. Minnie Harte is to marry a Mr. Glanville & go to Australia: poor dear Minnie! I suppose we shall never meet again! I feel quite a sinking at the heart as I think of my little playmate at Tyrilla. Jaimie's letter says he's sure I'll come out all right, out of the fleet disaster, and that Lay will leave China in disgrace: how odd to have a letter from him, that I left a little chit in petticoats, written so well in such a manly strain. I think he'll do!

Today I lent linguist Ying yuen of the River Steamer office Tls 200. He's going to get married; and I lend this to him to repay the kindness of Mr. Chang to me, who, while I was at Ningpo, and when robbed, lent me $500 without interest or security. "One good turn deserves another."[101]

22 MARCH 1864: Today I called on Parkes. I told him that the "Joint Tribunal" matter was likely to be carried through this year, and promised to let him see the proposals made by the Yamun and my corrections. He said that he had often told Lay that such an arrangement wd. strengthen his hands, — that it was his "trump card," — but that the "little man was sometimes very obstinate." He said he was glad to hear all I told him, as it showed a "willingness to cooperate": and that now interests even of such a conflicting (seemingly) kind, and yet so identical, and, for good results, cooperation was so necessary, that it was requisite people shd. here & there give way. I'm not a match for Sir Harry: but I'm not playing any game. If he is, my openness will make him unsuspectingly show his hand. [In the margin, a question mark][102]

Called on Lecat, & left a card for Knight. Went to the circus this evening: the riding and tight rope dancing were first-rate. The Spanish dance with the Castanets brought back old times wonderfully: how I remember starting to Pablo Fangere's in Belfast: and how well I recollect one night on returning to my lodgings at D. Aickin's. finding the doctor taking off his shoes in the kitchen. He used bad language that night, & though[t] Ben and myself were corrupting his son Bill! Again it brought back one night in Dublin in Sept. 1853, when, my degree examination over, I went for my first fun, & selected the circus. There I met little Johnny White, whom I had not seen for four years; but whom I recognized at once.[103]

Sun tells me <u>SooChow</u> is <u>threatened</u>!

23 MARCH 1864: A note from Col. Hough today stating that E-hing, Kin-tang, and Fuh Shan have again been occupied by the Rebels, and that he is anxious about Gordon, fearing that his rebel prisoners, 30 000, may give him trouble. I think the report of the taking of these cities is not true, but it is evident the rebels are moving about: probably the original garrisons of those places, are now working around by Chang-shoo. I hope there's to be no more trouble. But the reports from SooChow are not good. Sun says, people are allowed to leave, but not to enter the city, and that it is full of rebels—old ones—and spies from outside. What next?[104]

I had a short note from the Footae today about the 2 steamers, "Confucius" & "Pluto", which he says are not at Shanghae! Why they have been in harbor this last month! His note is dated 5 days back: he speaks of no troubles—.

Yen says to White, that SooChow has been retaken! Meanwhile, letters came today from the north: from Brown dated 11th March. He had recd. my letters of the 13 Jany. & 22 Feb: but not mine of the 8th Feb, about Gordon. He says Sir F. was pleased with my letter and has sent it home confidentially to Lord Russell: & that the Yamun were equally delighted with my Chinese letters. Sir F. approves of Gordon's moves.[105]

Mackey still at Teentsin, at which Baker had not on the 14th arrived.

Wrote today to Sutherland, and the Amoy and Swatow Commissioners about arrangements to be made to facilitate movements of steamers on the FooChow line.[106]

I am reading Wilkie Collins' wonderful novel: the "No name." It is a masterpiece of art! But it interferes with my other work not a little.[107]

Called on Col. Hough: hope he'll send out a column to Taetsang, &c.

24 MARCH 1864: Jebb called today to ask about the Rebel news, but I could do nothing more than give him my conjectures; he said that the report, having originated with Mayers, had reached him to the effect that the Footae had written in for help. But this, I think, may be doubted: by the way, Mayers once said he shd. like to hear of Gordon's being well thrashed by the Taepings in the first instance, and of his losing his commission afterwards. Nothing, therefore, wd. please him better than to hear that the Tsung-ching [brigade-general] had got into a fix.[108]

Today recd. a letter by the "Nanzing" from Brown, P'King, who tells me

Sir F. says I ought to send home an account of my share in originating the Fleet scheme, as Lay & Osborn are likely to make me out to have been the cause of the failure of their philanthropic schemes. He also sends down Forest's complaint relative to Brown's action in the case of the "Vivid," which unfortunately we have not yet heard the last of. I must give Brown a severe wigging: I think I shall "circularise" my opinions regarding his & MacPherson's doings.[109]

Hobson arrived today: accompanied by Ma-urh. I fear Jonny Brett is not doing altogether as well as he ought at Peking. My letters of 8th & 9th Feb. had not reached up to the 14th March: where are they, I wonder?

Very likely the Footae delayed the despatch of them, in order to give such a state to his own report of his reconciliation with Gordon, as shd. secure for himself the honors that will follow the report of G's first success! Poor "bellows blower!"

25 MARCH 1864: Good Friday. I met Clements in the street this evening: he says that the news from Le Footae is that he does not want any assistance. I imagine the Taepings who are now between Chang Shoo and Fuhshan are men, who on Gordon's approach from Kintang towards the Grand Canal between Tanyang & ChanChow, crossed it, and marched South East. Some days must elapse before reliable news can come in.

Burgevine has returned from Japan: he cannot, I hope, do damage now. At all events, Mr. Seward has at once had him arrested; such a step as this, on the part of the Consul General from whom he may possibly, from the past have looked for other treatment, will probably discomfit him so much as to make him anxious to have done with "filibustering" in China. Americans, joining in rebellion against the Chinese Govt., are liable to the punishment of death; so Mr. B. had better not try Mr. S. too far.[110]

The mail left for England today; I, however, did not write by it.

26 MARCH 1864: Hobson handed me the missing quarters (Dec. 62) cash a/c of the steam Fleet.

I have got off my circulars No. 3, 4 & 5; and shall now be, comparatively speaking, free for the future. I have only to compare the translations of the a/c which can be done in three days easily, and then the work will have been got through.

All sorts of rumors flying about relative to the defeat of Gordon's force.

Went in the evening with Dick to the circus, taking Ma-urh — now named [characters for *Tĕ-lin*] — with us. He went to Olyphant's while I was at dinner, and was told Hobson's boy was not in; the informant said he would take him to the other, so Urh-kih started. They had only gone a little way, when the guide took him by the hand and asked if he had any dollars or cash, and thereon proceeded to search him: the only thing found was a small knife, which the blackguard carried off. The youngster then broke away and ran back: he thinks the Shanghai people very daring, and is in no small funk about going out. All right: this will keep him in the house.[111]

27 MARCH 1864: Col. Hough sent me to read a letter just recd. from Gordon, in which he says "I am getting on all right again, thank God." From which we of course infer that he has at last been hit. His letter is dated 24th, 5 P.M., and he writes from a place 30 le from Woo Sieh on the Grand Canal. He is just about to start with 1500 men & guns after Chung Wang, who is out in the vicinity of Fuh Shan.[112]

Jebb came in to ask for the news: he tells me Gordon has had a ball through the leg, and that Kirkham has been brought down here badly wounded.

Rather a curious sermon from Mr. Muirhead tonight, the text of which was that much as 'ministers' might be looked down on here, they are 'to rule' in the future.

Noticed Mr. Lewis & one of his girls, from the circus, at church this evening: even Hippodromists have souls to be cared for.

28 MARCH 1864: The 'Recorder' of this morning contains the news of Gordon's failure — not defeat — at Kin-tang: the rebels neither showed themselves, nor replied to the fire of the guns, until the stormers attempted the breach, on which they let at them with a terrific storm of missiles of all kinds. Gordon was early wounded, and had to be taken to the rear: Kirkham then led on the men, & was shot through the shoulder. Major Taite is killed with 13 men: 10 officers and 50 men, besides Gordon & Kirkham, have been wounded. Gordon on finding the attack likely to be more severely contested than he had expected, quietly drew off his men, and started for the Grand Canal. I hope he will succeed in nobbling the Chung Wang.

Called on Ying Taoutae at ten o'clock: arranged about a boat for Hobson, and chatted about various matters. I commence to think that he can "fib" a little; I have caught one or two expressions of his heedlessly let fall, which don't tally with other things he has said in his guarded moments. A man who once fibs — what lies he has to resort to, to save himself afterwards.

The F. of China [Friend of China] of the 26th copies an article from an Indian Paper, entitled Osborn's Failure, which is remarkably well written, & hits the right nail on the head.

30 MARCH 1864: Mayers came round with Bond of the R. N. in a great hurry this morning to ask if I had heard of Gordon's death! He was much excited, and his excitement seemed to me to be that of a man who hoped the news was true! The reports, through every part of the settlement, are that Gordon has died of his wound, and that his men have retired to Quinsan. I never fully realized the value I put on Gordon, until this news

came in; were it true, Mayers would win <u>his</u> game — at all events, temporarily. The Defence Committee had no news, and, so far as can be made out, the report is only to be traced to one of our shoopan, who probably confounds or exaggerates the wound he has heard Gordon to have recd.

Dr. Wong called today: just up from Canton. I tell him that if I were in his place, I shd. be Gov. Genl. of some place in 20 years time. I don't think, however, he has got the "go" in him; he is anxious, too, to make his pile before he commences to do anything for his country. His Chinese nature here "crops" out: an Englishman wd. be an enthusiast in his patriotism at the <u>first</u> go off; here, on the other hand, the Chinaman's first thought is the sensible one of having the "wherewithal" secured first, before he tries his wings. He seems, too, awfully afraid of being seized and 'put through' by the Mandarins. He tells me the Footae wants his services, and has already given him a <u>6th</u> <u>rank</u> Button. He almost blushed, when he admitted it.

Dined with me tonight Brown, R. N., Jebb, Clements (who goes home tomorrow), White, Dick, and Hobson: afterwards we all went to the Volunteer amateur theatricals. Lowder made a lovely girl; and Bowra acted well.[113]

Jebb showed me a letter from Gordon of the 26th, written <u>en</u> <u>route</u> for ChangShoo: he had just come up with the rebels, and was about to fight. The rebels were under the Wang, from whom Dew took Ningpo.[114] So as he was all right on the 26th, I don't doubt but that he is alive and well still.

31 MARCH 1864: Sent today to Mr. Seward, draft of my letter to MacPherson in the "Hukwang" case. He says no claim for the damage can stand, but he thinks M's action was radically wrong. In my letter to the Committee, I hope to put the Hankow clique through their "facings" in a quiet way.

<u>Keahingfoo</u> was actually taken on the 25th [characters for 18th day of the 2nd lunar month] by Genl. Ching. Ching will be awfully cocky; so jealous of Gordon before, and now taking such a <u>Foo</u> [prefectural city] at the time Gordon failed before a <u>Heën</u> [district city]![115]

Mail in from England with letters from Mamma, Cha, and Dr. Jennings [?]: also from Leonard [?] and Pitman, who, save the mark: "remembering the service he was brought up in, and not willing to do anything that wd. make the opinion of Osborn be lowered", refuses the "Elfin"!

11 APRIL 1864: During the last ten days, I have had several letters from Gordon. He moved out from his former encampment above Woosieh to a place he calls WaeSoo between ChangShoo and Keangyin. On the 27th and 28th March, he fell in with the Taepings, some 10 000 strong under Chung Wang's Kan urh tze [adopted son], the Tsze Wang, and two others; he drove them about just as he pleased, but seeing that his movements would force them south of Chang Shoo into comparatively quiet country, he moved round to the East, and on the 30th sent Rhode and Howard with a

thousand men to go at them from the South East, while he himself went in his boat with the artillery to WaeSoo. Not finding the Infantry coming up, he returned to the camp, where were his supplies and resources, and found it in a state of great commotion. A lot of the boats had started for WooSieh, soldiers ran about naked having thrown away arms and clothes, and the European officers were at their wits' end. Every one panic stricken and useless. It appeared that Rhode and Howard had advanced, without either protecting their flanks or keeping any men in reserve. They were soon surrounded by the Rebels, armed only with spears and knives, and, one of the Regts, new recruits from the Le Yang Rebels, became alarmed, & the whole 500 of them broke and ran. These fellows called out to the Taepings: "We are your brethren: we are Tsze Wang's men": the Taepings said "O indeed!" and continued to spear them. The more of these fellows, men that have been rebels, are killed the better: they wd never live quiet lives again. Gordon's mode of recruiting from them, seeing that they follow the leader who pays; instead of from quiet coolies, is not a bad one. The result of the action was a loss of 250 men, and 7 officers: Gibbon, Pratt, Hughes, Dowling, Polkson, and Schinkoff among them. Gordon's letters show the Rebels to have been committing cruelties of all kinds: in one village, little children lay about in all directions with their throats cut, and one girl, who was seen with her hands tied behind her back, her breasts cut off, and her middle slit up. His last note dated 6th, just received, shows him to be in very good spirits, about 5 le from the rebels, & still at Wae Soo. His camp was previously at Le-Yang-Keaou. He states, he "is all right again"; so I hope his wound no longer troubles him. When the 3rd regt. arrives from LeYang, he will go at the Taepings again; but, as he says, it is no easy task attacking so large a body of desperate men with his small force.[116]

My last entry recorded the taking of Keahing Foo; I am now delighted to be able to add that Hang Chow itself fell on the 31st March. The only place now held by the Rebels in Chekiang is Hoo Chow Foo: there is a good fighting Wang there, who says he'll never give in. In KeangSoo, Ching will now be able to assist at Chang Chow, and Gordon too, as soon as he disposes of the expeditionary force which has now but little chance of working its way back again to the Rebel lines. Chang Chow once taken, TanYang, Kintang, & Keiu-yung must give in: Nanking will then be the only place left.[117]

On the 4th I sent Herbert Hobson up to Gordon, to be on his staff as an Interpreter; Leang went with him as far as SooChow, where they saw Le Footae on the 6th. I hope he will make himself useful.[118]

On the 6th I recd a semi-official from the Yamun, informing me that my letters sent through Le Footae early in Feby. arrived on the 18th of March, 2nd m. 11th d.; this letter says they are expecting me every day at Peking, and that if I have not already left Shanghae I must go up by the first steamer. It, too, tells me to carry with me to Peking, whatever surplus money I have in the hand from the Steamer Fund.

On the 10th recd. letters from St. John & Brown. The latter tells me that Sir F. Bruce was much pleased with my long letter about the execution of the

Na Wang, and has sent a copy of it to Earl Russell. My surmises as to what Sir F. was likely to do proved to be correct. Gordon, too, has recd a long despatch and also a private letter from the Chief himself, approving of what he did, and more particularly of his acting before receiving instructions. You know says the Chief that it was on your representation that a decision had to be come to, and instead of throwing the onus of forming and directing that decision on another, you yourself took it and acted. Such gallant conduct commands my respect, and entitles you to my confidence, &c. &c. All of which will, I hope. please Gordon very much. The diplomatist, however, crops out in the letter at the end, where Sir F. says <u>he</u> <u>will</u> <u>give</u> <u>him</u> <u>every</u> <u>support</u>, <u>and</u> <u>approves</u> <u>of</u> <u>what</u> <u>he</u> <u>has</u> <u>done</u>, <u>provided</u> <u>he</u> <u>takes</u> <u>care</u> <u>to</u> <u>see</u> <u>that</u> <u>carried</u> <u>out</u> <u>which</u> <u>he</u> <u>demands</u>, <u>and</u> <u>in</u> <u>the</u> <u>way</u> <u>of</u> <u>humanity</u>, <u>&c</u>.[119]

Yesterday had a letter from Giquel by the French Mail, telling me that he will start on 19th April.[120] The Papers show that the merchants' refutation of Lay's charges has been published: altogether, <u>he</u> will have a hard time of it at home. I wonder has he anything in any of my private letters which he could publish of a kind likely to damage me?

By the "Confucius", today, I send a note to the Yamun giving them the news of the fall of Hang Chow; and a note to Sir F. Bruce.

Last night <u>Nevius</u> preached.[121] Today sent a subscription of Tls. <u>300</u> to Mr. Muirhead; Tls <u>150</u> for his Press, & Tls <u>150</u> for charitable purposes.

Yesterday wrote a long letter to Hoo Taoutae, Tso Chetae's wei yuan, relative to Transit Dues, and Taxation in Chekiang. I intended to have gone to Ningpo today, but as the weather threatens, and the steamer is the "Feima," I put it off till tomorrow, when I shall go down by the "Emperor."

On Saturday last had to dinner Alabaster, White, Wright, Mercer, and Lowder; afterward went to the circus.[122] Madame Cousin's Benefit had a crowded house. Davies' supposed murderer seized yesterday: he fired a shot at his captor.

12 APRIL 1864: About ten o'c. last night I recd. a note from Ying Taoutae, evidently sent out in great haste enclosing two covers from Gordon. No very particular news however. A plan that accompanies his note to Col. Hough shows his position at Pu Kow, between Chang Shoo and Kong-yin: the Imperialist lines and stockades will surely prevent the expeditionary force from getting back again. He commences to think it useless to hunt the rascals, as they can throw up stockade after stockade with ease, and leave one for another as he approaches: besides they select positions inaccessible to his boats, and if he wants to use his guns he must then land them and drag them across the country—a by no means safe thing to do. He was about to go in at them once more on the 9th, and then, in all probability he will go on to Chang-Chow, and assist at the siege of that place. His note contains one piece of good news: Tan-yang has fallen. Thus Chang Chow is now the only place on the Grand Canal held by the Rebels. [In the margin is written: "It appears to have been Keu Yung 25 April." Later, in blue pencil, a question mark.][123]

Wrote a note this morning to Gordon, & forwarded a letter & papers for Hobson. Also wrote to Le Footae, enclosing translation of Gordon's duplicate copy of the Bill sent by the War Office for supplies given to the Sung Keang Force [the Ever-Victorious Army] since June last.

The Chinese Govt. have been so stupid as to write the U.S. Minister promising to prohibit the furnishing of supplies to the "Alabama" &c.: by Jove! what fools they are! Ten to one, [indistinct; Hinnes?] declares war against China, and, joined by Burgevine and immense numbers of rowdies, plays the mischief with the country![124]

Every virtue, sd. Nevius in his sermon the other night, has its counterfeit; every view its disguise. Very good!

Another argument in favor of supporting the Imperialists is that not only has little been done so far by the Rebels to lead one to hope for good from them, but they, in point of fact, could not be expected to form one strong govt. They are not fighting for a cause — nor is it love of Hung seu tseun that pitched so many people into the field. They are all of that class which delights in turmoil and adventure, and were the Manchoos put down, the next thing wd. be fighting among the Wangs for precedence and place: they would not be govd. by Hung seu tseun. Many, many years of civil war, bloodshed, and disorder, would have to be gone through, before the country cd. be quieted, and that wd. not be until one strong govt. appeared.[125]

Wd. it be a good thing to get the Govt. to issue an Edict allowing people to become Christians, at pleasure. Those issued hitherto have been forced from the Govt, and have had but little effect in the provinces. Now were the Govt. of itself to issue such a proclamation, it might have a most excellent effect, more particularly following after the overthrow of the Taepings, from whom "Exeter Hall" expected so much. Besides it wd. in another way strengthen the Chinese: for any departure from proper treatment of converts can now be construed into a breach of treaty, and made a casus belli; it could, too, be worked in such a way as to avert a French protectorate of propagandism.[126]

Started this evening 5 P.M. in the "Emperor" for Ningpo. Some 200 Chinese passengers on board, and no accommodation for foreign passengers whatever. I was shown into a room behind the wheel-house on the Hurricane Deck, and with A. Fang, occupied it during the night. Another passenger, Mr. Jackson of Ningpo on board: a well-educated man; talks well. He is full of some plan having reference to the water communication of Ningpo with the interior. The steamer's comprador, a Mr. Wang, somewhat amused me by his enquiries; his inquisitiveness had no bounds, and I had at last to give way under it, although for a time I battled him after an Irish fashion, by replying to his queries by interrogations. His father, he told me, had been Keou-Kwan [educational official] at Wänchow. He asked me if I had not formerly lived opposite the Yue-lae Hong, and been intimate with Twan Taoutae: from which query, I infer the Ningpo folk have not yet forgotten me. No dinner; but got a cup of tea at two and some ham and eggs from the Captain.[127]

13 APRIL 1864: At 7 a.m. arrived at Ningpo. The harbor crowded with foreign shipping,—some 40 Sailing Vessels and 6 or 8 steamers. What a change has taken place in it since I first entered it in the "Erin" in '54! Then not a dozen foreign rigged vessels were to be seen in it in as many months, and the only way of communicating with civilization was through Luggers of 30 & 40 tons, via Shanghae: now some 200 ships visit it during the year, and some two or three steamers leave it for, or arrive from, Shanghae every day. Each steamer carries from 200 @ 300 Chinese passengers, who pay $2 a head: cheapness, regularity, and celerity will develope an immense passenger traffic along the coast and up the rivers of China, and steamers will find abundant occupation. What is wanted is civility on the part of the captains, and accommodation of some kind for the passengers: as it is now, they are herded together like so many sheep on the deck.

Landed at seven and walked up to the Commissioner's residence, a fine new house built opposite the Yen-tsang-mun or Salt Gate. No one was stirring, so I strolled up by the Consulate and round the pond in front: I felt somewhat affected, as my eyes again rested on the old sights with which I had once been so familiar, and not a little exhilarated did I feel when I compared my position now with what it was when I left Ningpo six years ago.

Found Brown up at my return. His brother is not so much disfigured as I expected to find him: one side of his face is not touched in any way, while the other does not, though badly cut up, present so repulsive an appearance as I had anticipated it would. His neck below the right ear is sadly marked — his jugular vein narrowly escaped, when the piece of the gun that killed Le Breton, struck him sideways. That first wound left him insensible for a fortnight, and kept him unfit for work for some three months. The second wound,—recd. from a cartridge of shot, which had previously passed through a deal-board,—destroyed his right eye and lodged in his cheek, forehead, and head. He has had as many as 52 grains of shot cut out, and pieces of the bone from the skull have from time to time come away; he was reading at the time, so that the eye lid was not hurt. The doctors say he will be able to put in a glass eye, and when his whiskers grow his wound in the neck will be to some extent hid, so that he will not after all look so bad. But it was a terrible accident for the poor boy, not eighteen years of age. The first wound was recd seven days after he joined Le Breton; the second, after he had been with Cooke only five days—[128]

Henkel the German assistant reminded me a little of Lenox Davis: he is very quiet, and has a soft red nose.[129]

Walked with Brown to see the Customs' land: I think the dispute with Kirby & Co. about the piece that firm bought, was unwarranted. Pointed out a mistake in the Returns of Expenditure for the 14th quarter, and gave instructions as to the necessity for making the Confiscations Returns intelligible.

Called on the Taoutae at 2 P.M., and chatted with him for an hour. His Yamun seemed to me to be quite deserted. H. E. [character for *shih*] She is aged 63, and is a native of ChangChow Foo in KeangSoo.[130] He seemed to me very intelligent, and a man that I could get on with: indeed, I don't understand why Brown and he have not hit it off properly, except it be for the reason that he gave, that he cannot make out more than a quarter of what Brown says. I called his attention to various matters, but left the settlement of them for his return visit.

On my returning, found Hwang waiting; but as my head ached violently, I told him to call at 12 tomorrow. Walked up to the Consulate, and called on Holt, whom I found in "buttons and lace": the youth never asked me to sit down.[131] After that walked to the grave-mound behind the Consulate, and then down by the old temple to the Bund. Dined at half past six, and jawed with Brown — what a long-winded fellow he is! — till after nine, my head aching horribly all the time.

14 APRIL 1864: Up at 7 1/2, head still aching. Wrote to Mr. Jackson, in reply to his note, telling him I cd. see the merchants at 11 1/2. At 10 the Taoutae called: his retinue was not an imposing one. A dozen dirty little boys carried flags and title board: ten men marched with muskets, followed by ten who carried rattan shields: one gent carried the chains and another the whip. H. E. was very chatty. I talked into him:

1°. The propriety of being on good terms with the Commissioner, who, in point of fact, is the she-yay [?] for managing Customs' affairs, but who, being a foreigner, ought to be treated with the consideration due a guest;[132]

2°. The Customs' land question, in reference to which I said I shd. advise the authorities to make no more fuss about it, inasmuch as the piece claimed by Brown did not seem to me to have been negotiated for in the first instance, and, if it should be deemed indispensably necessary to procure it, to arrange for its purchase amicably with K. & Co.;

3°. Kirby & Co.'s Shot, which I found to my surprise to be stored in the Customs' go-down, I arranged shd. be delivered up at once on the proper bond being signed;

4°. The "Vivid case": I advised H. E. to act with Brown in local settlement of unimportant cases;

5°. Brown's brother: I said I shd. write to the Prefect, who pays the Yang-tseang-tuiy, and ask him to pay young B. his salary during the time he has been unfit for service in consequence of his wounds, & begged the Taoutae to support my application.[133]

6°. "Wm. IVth": I arranged that the steamer shd. be continued to be allowed to run with passengers to Yuyaou: no cargo to be carried: I am to write a despatch to the Taoutae on the subject.

We parted on good terms.

No sooner had the Taoutae gone than I had to meet the mercantile people: Jackson, Rayner, Smith, Brown, & Cerruti. Cerruti was very polite; Rayner was somewhat violent, if not impertinent; the others said but little. They wished:[134]

1°. That I shd. aid them in doing away with the obstructions to communication with the interior: Mr. Jackson proposed by cutting away the dams over which boats have to be carried at Shaou-hing; Mr. Rayner by laying down rails, and providing means for carrying boats across without unlading them. In reply I said that I shd. require more information before I could move in the matter, and that the information, to be attended with the results they wish for, must be accompanied by something which shall enable me to secure the Chinese against those things which they built the dams to counteract.

2°. A light on the Chao-paou-shan, for the convenience of vessels generally.

3°. One jetty for the examination of goods is insufficient; I sd. you can have three.

4°. Complained that before one boat can leave the jetty, all concerned in the shipment have to be there for examination: I sd. I thought the boats might be moved off as examined.

5°. Mr. Raynor asked why Transit Dues were collected on all their Exports? He thought the system in force ought to be changed and made to resemble that at Shanghae. I agreed, and that the fact of goods being bought at Ningpo ought to free the buyers from payment of Transit Dues, and recommended them to apply through their consul to Sir F. Bruce. As I made this proposition, they all laughed, and looked at me as if they thought I chaffed them, saying that to apply to Sir F. was quite useless — they had done so about other matters, but cd. get no reply. The fact is, the practice of the Ningpo Customs is in opposition to Sir F.'s opinion as to the interpretation of the clause appended to the tariff. Sir F. holds that clause to refer to certificated goods; the Chinese say, it means all goods. Now were I to change the practise, the Chinese will be down on me for taking money out of their pockets; and were I to say to the merchants, the Ningpo Customs are in the right, Sir F. will ask me if I have forgotten his view of the subject.

6°. Mr. Raynor thought examination ought to be done away with, and the merchant's word taken: he himself said he wd. willingly show his invoices. I said it wd. not do —

After talking over an hour, they went away assured by me that my object was to collect as much revenue as possible, and to reduce the delays & trouble given to merchants to the minimum.

Hwang then called on me. He said he had been waiting for me for the last month, told to do so by Hoo Taoutae who had gone on to HangChow. He said he had had orders to provide for my journey to HangChow, & to accompany me if I wished to see Tso Chetae. I then gave him a letter I had written for Hoo, — it had previously been read by She Taoutae, who thought it clear and to the point, — which he sd. he wd. send at once; Tso Chetae he sd., was certain to see it, for Hoo wd. give it to him to show that he had really seen and consulted with me on the Chow-le question.[135]

When Hoo Taoutae returned me the letter, after reading it, he said "I see now why Prince Kung thinks so highly of you."

Hwang has a Bill against the Customs, amounting to about $2000 for things supplied when building the new house: I must tell Brown to tax [fix?] it.

Went down to the office, and looked into various matters. While there General Cooke called on me. "Dressed to the eyes," of course: he seemed a good sort of fellow. He has been 3 or 4 years in the "Ever-Victorious", was in 25 actions, not counting small fights, and was once hit by a spent cannon ball. He told me that once, when She Taoutae refused to pay the troops, he shut the gates, and ordered his men to allow no one to leave the city. She tried to go out with his retinue; but the Chinese sergeant of the guard drew a line on the ground with his bayonet, ordered his men to fall in, and said he shd. shoot any one who crossed the line. The Taoutae's chair thereon went back to the Yamun, and the troops were paid. Cooke's men, 1000 in all with 17 officers, cost $12 000 a month. The French force, under d'Aiguebelle, 1500 strong, costs about 28 000 a month. Cooke is very anxious to get a commission to Peking, so as to be independent of the Taoutae's whims. He is a man who talks pleasantly, and who seems to belong to the chief mate, or burly skipper class of seagoing folk.[136]

Called on M. Verney, a French Engineer who is building gunboats—one launched & 3 on the stocks—and who is also "prenant les fonctions" of French Vice-Consul.[137]

I am astonished at young Brown's light heartedness; his right eye always shut gives him a most comical appearance. His brother, the assistant in charge, is a terrible stick: an impracticable, unyielding, unimaginative person. He'll never have charge again, so long as I hold the reins.[138]

When I return to Shanghae, I have to:

1°. write to She Taoutae about the "Wm. IVth".
2°. '' '' Peen Ta laou yay about young Brown's pay.
3°. '' '' She Taoutae   ''   ''   ''   ''
4°. '' '' Brown about salaries of Westergaard, Fisher, Linguist Leang, & Writer Wong.[139]
5°. '' ''   ''   about Kirby & Co.'s ground.
6°. '' ''   ''   ''   ''   ''   '' shot.
7°. '' ''   ''   '' jetties examination.
8°. '' ''   ''   '' building office.
9°. '' ''   ''   '' Hwang's bill for house.
10°. '' '' Le Footae about Kirby & Co.'s shot.
11°. '' '' Ts. Le Yamun ''   ''   ''   '' ground.

[In left margin, Chinese characters for She Taoutae's name, Shih Chih-o, with blue check marks against nos. 1, 2, 3, 4, 5, 6, 7 and 9.]

Took my passage by, and went on board, the "Wukee" at 10 1/2 p.m.

Brown expatiated upon the impropriety of de Meritens taking upon himself so much of the functions of the I. G. The Baron does good service; but it is a fact that he tries to make out he is number one. To me he is most subservient; when I am not at hand, he is the man.

15 APRIL 1864: A wet, nasty day: half inclined to be seasick. Forest and Hubbard also passengers; both very seedy.[140] Anchored near the Beacon at dark.

The only Chinese I recognized at Ningpo were Meadows' old tailor, and dog-coolie—who has been getting on in the world, a boatman at the Salt Gate Ferry; and the courtyard [?] boy in the shop opposite my old house. By the way, I saw <u>Mo Be</u>, Wadman's old shroff, but he did not recognize me. Called on Davidson yesterday, who said "You're all right now," with a grin.[141]

16 APRIL 1864: Landed at 9. My head-ache still continues: exposure to the sun on Wednesday morning when walking through the paddy fields brought it on, I think, or rather aggrevated the one caused by the discomfort of sleeping above the engine of the "Emperor". Found letters from home: from Mamma, Cassie, Lizzie, Sterne [?] and Miss Davis.

Today's "N. C. Herald" contains the Minutes of another meeting held at Hangkow [sic] with more correspondence in the "Hukwang" case. When my despatch gets up there, there will be a third meeting, and then it too will be published.

17 APRIL 1864: The P. & O. steamer in this morning with the newspapers—among them one from Hugh M'Call: must send him one in return.

Gordon appears to have had two engagements with the expeditionary field force of late, in both of which he was victorious. The body of men ought by this time to be reduced to great straits.

An American preached tonight, taking for his text the account given of the young man whom, seeing Jesus loved [?] but "who went away sorrowing, for he had large possessions." His sermon was unequal—the part that showed morality alone to be useless was lengthy and pretentious, while that portion wh' insisted upon the necessity of <u>religion</u> was neither forcible nor clear. The preacher has a most tremendous voice, but unhappily he cd. not manage it well. He gave out the hymns strangely; "let us sing to the praise of God, <u>in the use</u> of the −th hymn, omitting the −th verse, (turning to the organist) omitting the −th verse." I think preachers, or those who lead in prayer, ought to study their prayers: otherwise, it is difficult to join with them in their petitions in a rational manner.

18 APRIL 1864: Last night, I had a most remarkable dream. I thought I was standing in a verandah with some one looking towards the moon, to the right of which the stars seemed to be clustering strangely; the light they have attracted my attention, and as I gazed the upper and right-side changed into a large cloud shaped mass of light grain colored glass-stone, below that and stretching to the left there appeared another irregular and cloud-shaped mass of the same kind of stone but of a delicate pink color, and then behind and below that again was seen a somewhat opaque, a milky-smoke colored mass of the same kind. Looking at this, and wondering what it might portend, suddenly and with great rapidity a child or babe was seen:

alive but marble-like. Just at that moment, the person with me cried out "The Saviour, by George!"—it was Wm. Swanton who spoke—I shouted "Hurrah", jumped from the veranda, and sped through the air toward the babe,—shouting praises to God, and feeling exultant beyond measure. As I advanced, the phenomenon disappeared gradually, and in its place there seemed to be against the sky a large Gothic window, like the East window of a church, upon which were people kneeling, and through which shone stars; I tried to speak to the people, to tell them the Saviour had come, but I cd. scarcely speak, and they looked at me with blank and disapproving looks, and gradually I sank to the ground. Suddenly two steamers appeared rushing along, evidently racing—the faster of the two passed the other, and seemed jumping up and down at the bow and stern, like the motion of horses in cantering; as she went ahead, she fired a gun, and set off a lot of crackers, to the disgust and astonishment of a Chinaman who stood on the bank, but who rushed off shouting "Wo-po shih-lim-pow [?]!" when I awoke. I felt, however, as if I had really seen a heavenly vision, and since that time, I have had a more vivid sense than I can give expression to of the reality of the fact that the Saviour will again come. May I be ready to go forth and meet him![142]

Of late, I have on several occasions awoke praying, or lain half asleep with most pleasant feelings of that "perfect love which casteth out fear." None but those who serve God can understand the feeling—to none could it be explained: in fact, it is a foretaste of that "peace which passeth understanding."

[At the bottom of the page, added later: "And yet how changed when storms of passion rush over the soul, or clouds of disbelief sicken the heart.' 6 July"]

I have been busy today, putting my accounts in order; I must take care not to let them get into such a mess as were those of my predecessor. My secretary, Man, I am sorry to say, is not working so well as I wished; he is merely "acting," so, if he does not take care, I shall have to try another. My instinct has never been altogether in his favor.

Hough sent me, to read, a note from Gordon dated 11th, on which day he attacked the Rebels who were strongly placed at Waesoo—some 15 000 in number: he had 800 of his own people, and about 8000 Imperialists. Le Footae was there too: he turned their flank, and then they bolted, followed up by the Imperialists who cut them up pretty well. Gordon says they deserve severe treatment, in return for the cruelties they have everywhere been committing during this expeditionary raid.[143]

19 APRIL 1864: Today Major Edwardes of the Engineers called, with Lister.

Occupied chiefly with drawing up a memorandum for Sir F. Bruce, and for the public if necessary, relative to the steam Fleet.

Ying Taoutae called. He tells me Gordon and Le Footae went on to ChangChow Foo on the 15th, i.e. [characters for the 10th day of the 3rd lunar month] (today is the 14th of the moon), and that the expeditionary

Taeping force has been completely cut up and dispersed — 20 000 in all.

Report says that Lew Fantai has been made Footae of Chekeang: Ying thinks it unlikely to be the case, as Tseang Fantai is the man likely to get the post.[144]

The Emperor every 3rd year submits 6 of the most worthy Peking [character for *nei*; "inner," i.e. metropolitan] officials and 5 provincial [character for *wai*; "outer"] whom he praises as having given the greatest satisfaction and as having done the state best service during the 3 years: among the 6 Peking, are <u>Prince</u> <u>Kung</u> [the number *1* written underneath], <u>Wo-jin</u>, <u>Wän</u> <u>Seang</u>, <u>Paou</u> <u>tsun</u>; and the 5 provincial worthies are <u>Kwan</u> <u>Wän</u>, <u>Tsäng</u> <u>Kwo</u> <u>fan</u>, <u>Le</u> <u>Hungchang</u>, <u>Lo</u> <u>ping</u> <u>chang</u>, and <u>Tso</u> <u>Chetae</u>. I know the 1st, 3rd, & 4th of the 6, and 1st, 2nd, & 3d of the 5. This is called "Ping lun," also "Kin-ts'a."[145]

A note from Adkins says that Keu-yung was taken on the 12th instant [Chinese date]. But from Lord, I learn that at Tan Yang (where they said they wished to surrender) the Rebels cut off one body of Imperialists from Chinkiang, and that the other had returned without having captured the place.

Sun says that west of Hoochow the Rebels hold some villages and <u>Tsih-Ke-heen</u>, from which they are likely to cross Ganhwuy, and go into KeangSe again. The KeangSe Footae in a memorial said they had some 20 or more important passes by which they could get into his province, and that he had no troops with which to drive them back. The Imperial Decree in reply calls the attention of Le Footae to the report, and hints that he ought to kill more of the Taepings, instead of allowing so many of them to escape. The Shang Yu [edict] winds up curiously: Le Hung chang yih neng te-leang tsze-e, fow?[146]

Ying told me today Tsäng Kwo Fan and others feel angry with Le Footae for having retaken so many places!

I have made up my mind not to go north for a few weeks more.

20 APRIL 1864: Called today on the Defence Committee. The only one I saw was the <u>Chin</u> last appointed. The former <u>Chin</u> <u>King</u> is now in a difficulty; the Footae sent down a wei-yuen to enquire into some occurrences. The first thing the wei-yuen did was to ask to look at the a/c; these Chin at once provided, on which the wei-yuen had them folded up in a bundle, put his seal on it, and sent them there and then to the Footae, — much to Chin's astonishment, such a procedure being as objectionable as it was unexpected. So I presume his "goose is cooked": I never liked the man, and thought him a dangerous little wretch.[147]

The other Chin, is tung neën ["same year"] with both Le Footae and Shin Footae; he tells me the rebels have been crossing from Tsih-Ke-heen (Ganhwuny) into Kiangsee. Confound them all! The officials of one province don't care a fig what becomes of the other places so long as in their neighborhood there is seeming quiet.[148].

The "Vulcan" and "Ringdove" left today for England.

Recd. another letter from Hankow Committee,—about 1/2 duty deposited on teas: they are right in what they say, so I shall try to free them from the [furthers?].

Dined with me @ 1/2 p. 7, Col. Hough, Sir Harry Parkes, Major Jebb, Captain Murray, and Mr. Comr. Dick—a rather slow party.

Dick said to me this evening that he quite agreed with me as to the policy of advising the Chinese to agree to the proposal for joint tribunals for investigation. He let out, too, that when de Meritens was up here in Jany, he expected to find me distrusted and thrown over by the Chinese—no doubt he was prepared to act accordingly.

21 APRIL 1864: Nothing noteworthy today. It is certain that Genl. Ching is dead. He was the first rebel that submitted: that occurred at Gan-Hing, a few years ago.[149]

Dined tonight with Mongan at the Mess of the 67th.

22 APRIL 1864: English Mail closed today. Mayers and Douglas go home on leave.

Capt. Henderson, who came out by the last mail, called the other day, and handed me a letter he brought from Montgomery Martin, who is anxious, on behalf of the Imperial Bank of China proposed to be established, to get the consent of the govt to make its notes the legal tender in the payment of duties. This matter requires my careful consideration.[150]

Lay was a thoroughly conscientious man. It strikes me, however, that, man being fallible, it is the one who prides himself most on his conscientiousness that is likely to err, and his errors, too, will in all probability be in those matters about which he thinks (as he imagines) conscientiously. One's own personal motives intermingle to such an extent with the desire to be conscientious, that they are sometimes mistaken for conscientiousness itself. In the fleet affair he conscientiously thought that harm wd. be done unless it was placed wholly under his control, and he thence proceeded to add that it must be placed under his control: no doubt the opinion derived force, too, from the policy of power and position that wd. ensue to himself from such an arrangement; and he thus was totally unable to see the force of the objections made by the Chinese to his proposals, as also to see any other way of utilizing the fleet than that which he had previously thought out.

My plan is to yield to everyone: I wd. not turn a beggar off the path; but I in the end always carry my point. I am awfully frank in face [?], and unreserved in conversations; I don't object to tell a lot of things that I don't expect to derive benefit from by concealment; this frankness stands me in good stead, when I have anything that I wish to keep in the background.

Most delightful spring weather during the last few days.

The new French Consul-General M. Godeaux called yesterday with M. Rameau.[151]

27 APRIL 1864: Nothing particular has occurred during the last few days. Yesterday I returned the calls of Braun and Godeaux, and in the evening I walked with Parkes with whom I had a long talk about joint tribunals, and the appointment of a second in command for Gordon's force. As regards tribunals Parkes is willing that investigations shd be held at places other than the Consulate; but he thinks the Taoutae and Consul shd be the persons to form the tribunal. He evidently does not want the Commissioner to sit. Perhaps a good plan for me to follow wd. be to propose that the Taoutae shd sit as Examiner & Judge with as assessors the Commissioner & the Consul of the nation concerned. With reference to the appointment of a second in command for Gordon's force, a letter recd from Brown, now made Assistant Chinese Secretary at Peking, also tells me that Sir. F. Bruce has been urging such an appointment on the F. O., and that the F. O. has written to me on the subject: I don't know how Le Footae will like the idea, but I shall try to put it through — say, for 3 years with £3000 a year: Major Edwards of the R. E. might do well for it. However, as he goes up with me tomorrow to see Gordon, we may manage to make an arrangement there. Parkes talked too about the opening of WänChow, and asked where the third port was to be on the Yangtsze: his idea is, that ports ought not to be open save where there are consular authorities or arrangements for keeping lawless foreigners in order.[152]

Saw Lockhart for a minute at the Consulate, and had a short visit from him this morning.[153]

Dr. Longhead called this morning, having just come up from Ningpo. He says that the $12 000 heretofore paid for Cooke's force, has been ordered to be sent up to HangChow, and that were it not that some Chinese merchants have come forward and guaranteed $6000 a month, the whole force wd. have to be disbanded. As it is, Cooke will have to disband 400 men, and some half dozen officers, and he has had, too, to reduce the pay of the others — Longhead's among the rest. "Evil communications corrupt good manners." I see the truth of this in even Longhead, whose tone has become lowered and coarser — doubtless from associating with Cooke's rough 'uns — They wish me to try to get employment for officers and men with Gordon. More complications! Longhead tells me that the French Admiral sent up some 20 soldiers in uniform to d'Aiguebelle the other day: evidently the French are playing a queer game in Chekiang:[154] Oh! China, China! What is to be done? How Wade will swear, and tear his hair when he comes out again, and hears all these things! I must not send Gicquel [sic] back to Ningpo: that's clear. But "what to do, what to do?" as the Major used to say! By the way, I had a call from little Treves today, who used to be at Teentsin; he tells me the Major's daughter is the most beautiful girl in existence, &c. &c.

Longhead says HooChow has not fallen: that it is very strongly fortified, and that there are 13 Wangs in it.

It is true that Keu Yung has fallen, but Tanyang is still held by the Taepings. Storey, of the 67th, came down from Gordon's last night, and he says

G. is now only some hundred yards from the wall of ChangChow, and that he is waiting for the attack until he gets a storming party. The "braves," however, don't volunteer readily.[155]

A letter just to hand from MacPherson tells me that a meeting took place at Hankow the other day to receive Breck's explanations, and that the feeling is on the whole setting against B. & his noble ally C. D. Williams. Webster seems to be antagonistic to us: these fellows, confound them, all want sops![156]

I am going to Chang Chow tomorrow. With me go White, Man, & Major Edwards. I must see Gordon & the Footae, and endeavour to make some arrangements by which the force may be held together and placed on a safe footing for the future. I hope I may not get shot: at all events, I'll try to keep out of harm's way, as fighting is not in my line.

[The next four lines have been bracketed to show their importance, then almost completely excised. They seem to begin: "If anything happens to me. . . " and later seem to read: "I hereby leave all. . . . "[157]]

Long letter from Meritens yesterday on many subjects; he no longer objects to de Champs' leaving Heard & Co.; so I must find room for him. His office is unable to pay up its share 80 000 taels for Feb. & March.

Today is Race-day, but I don't go: don't care much for the 'noble' sport, first of all, and secondly, I have a lot of work to put through which keeps me in the house.

Schenck breakfasted with me this morning. He is on his way to Teentsin, escorting the wives, family, and corpse of Ke-ling, formerly Gov.-Genl. and Tartar Genl., who on his death-bed begged Meritens to send him safely north. I told him to go to Peking, and spend a week there to see the sights.[158]

Treves, when in, remarked "de Meritens is now your left-hand man." "O, no," sd. I, "a Glover is senior to him."[159]

[Editorial note: Appended to note 159 are Hart's brief and nearly undecipherable loose-leaf remarks on his trip to Ch'ang-chou, dated 28 April–15 May 1864. The journal proper resumes on 1 June 1864. See Chapter 4.]

CHAPTER THREE

Peking 1864: Establishing the I.G.'s Status

Robert Hart arrived in Peking in June 1864 with a considerable reputation. In the foreign view, he had helped Governor Li Hung-chang and Major C. G. Gordon resume their cooperation (which they were going to do in any case). Ch'ing officials gave him credit for preserving British aid in suppressing the Taipings (whom the Ch'ing forces were going to defeat anyway). All this helped the I.G. as he felt his way around the capital once again. Meanwhile, what Hart had learned from his close association with the Shanghai Taotai, Ying Pao-shih, earlier in the year, prepared him well for his daily encounters with members of the Tsungli Yamen. For Ying had taught him not only about the ins and outs of Ch'ing local administration, but also about Chinese techniques of barbarian control. Note, for example, how Hart discovered that his Chinese amanuensis, Sun, was in the habit of sending the Taotai copies of all Hart's correspondence, and deduced that other Chinese writers would surely do the same.

In ·the modern world of surveillance and multiple copies, when "gentlemen" do indeed read each other's mail, we must recall the Victorian esteem for privacy of correspondence in order to appreciate Hart's reaction. (18 March 1864) But the important point is that, after Hart's initial outrage, he reached a typically pragmatic conclusion: In dealing with Ch'ing officials (and their underlings) at all levels, he had to be especially cautious, whether in conversation or in simple dictation. No room remained for his private thoughts, which might be divined in some fashion by his Chinese interlocutors; if he had secrets, they could be consigned only to the safety of his almost illegible journal. By clearing his head of all extraneous notions, Hart could speak frankly to the ministers and secretaries of the Yamen, while they, in turn, revealed their secrets to him.

THE I.G. UNDER THE TSUNGLI YAMEN

Although the new diplomatic requirements of the early 1860s had mandated the Tsungli Yamen's creation, the attitudes, values, and institutions of the T'ung-chih Restoration, operating like a cultural gene pool, determined its nature. If we are amazed at Hart's bicultural flexibility in combining the roles of a minor Ch'ing employee and dictator over the Customs Service, what can we say of his employers, who skated on the thin ice between Chinese hatred of things foreign and foreign contempt for China?

Prior to the establishment of the Yamen, China had nothing close to a foreign ministry for the management of its inter-state relations. Foreign relations were tributary relations and therefore came under the jurisdiction of Peking's Board of Rites—except for the tribes of Inner Asia with whom the Ch'ing dealt through a special office for handling external vassals known as the Court of Colonial Affairs, or Li-fan yuan.[1] For example, as Ch'ing contact with Russia developed on the borders of Mongolia and Central Asia, early Russian relations were conducted by the Li-fan yuan. Meanwhile, contact with the obstreperous European maritime trading powers had generally been handled by the high provincial officials in charge of the sea frontier where the problems arose. In short, China's foreign relations had been frontier relations, not state-to-state relations.

The Western (primarily British) demand for modernization of China's foreign intercourse produced the Tsungli Yamen in 1861 as a proto-foreign ministry. For the next forty years, however, the torpidity of change in Peking was such that no genuine foreign ministry was set up until in 1900, in the aftermath of the Boxer Rebellion, the troops of eight foreign nations invaded and helped to loot the capital. During the 1860s, Hart's bosses were in a peculiarly half-modern, half-traditional position, and this was one of his major problems. The Maritime Customs Service was appended to a still informal and temporary agency, accepted by the Ch'ing bureaucracy only on sufferance.[2]

The hold of the past over China's foreign contact had just been demonstrated in the American treaty of 1858. This egregious document had two facets: It followed British and French precedent in allowing a diplomatic envoy of the United States to visit Peking to "confer with a member of the Privy Council [i.e. the Grand Council]"; but then fell back to acquiesce in the old tribute system by limiting such visits to one each year. According to treaty, the American envoy had to inform the Board of Rites and receive its directions and protection on his journey; while at Peking he was to be "furnished with a suitable residence," his entourage "not [to] exceed twenty persons." All of this was straight out of the traditional rules for tribute bearers.[3] The unfortunate William B. Reed, whose sentimental American-type friendliness toward China allowed him to be conned into these treaty provisions, had been repaid in 1859 with an excruciatingly uncomfortable cart ride to Peking and numerous other appropriate humiliations. Thereafter, the Americans by invoking the most-favored-nation clause were able to disregard their American treaty and follow the Anglo-French practices.

The two sets of wars and treaties in the 1840s and 1850s had induced Peking to centralize its foreign-frontier relations under an imperial commissioner. This official was concurrently a governor general (first at Canton, later at Nanking) who was expected to conduct relations with the Western powers as far away from the capital as possible. Thus, in 1861, at the same time the Tsungli Yamen was set up in Peking, Northern and Southern imperial commissioners for foreign affairs were designated to handle local problems of Western contact within their North China and Central-and-South China territorial jurisdictions. At the treaty ports, in other words, the pre-1860 practices continued at the same time that the Yamen met the persistent foreign demand for a point of contact at Peking.

A specific incentive for setting up the Tsungli Yamen had been the problem of paying the large indemnity of Tls. 16 million (8 million each to Britain and France). The October 1860 Conventions of Peking specified indemnity payments every three months of one-fifth of the gross customs revenue at the treaty ports, so that foreign trade would pay for the foreign invasion. Thomas Wade, Chinese Secretary of the British Legation at Peking, reported early in January 1861 how Prince Kung's chief minister Wen-hsiang declared the Ch'ing government unable to "manage the indemnity questions without foreign assistance in the Customs establishments"—which, moreover, the Chinese were bound by treaty to bring under a uniform system. The indemnities thus provided the immediate occasion for setting up a central government council or committee to handle customs as well as other aspects of foreign affairs. But we must keep in mind that the Yamen's area of jurisdiction was not the overall monopoly of foreign relations normally expected of a Western foreign office. This meant that, even when Hart was backed by the Yamen, he could still not be certain that his writ would run automatically in Canton or Shanghai.

Executives in a Washington administration of today, whose capability may be embarrassingly limited by the separation of powers within the three branches of the federal government as well as between it and the state governments, may appreciate the old China's pervasive division of power between Peking and the provinces. The central administrator had constantly to feel his way. Some Washingtonians may still remember, too, the second-class status accorded the new fly-by-night agencies of wartime — for example, the State Department's smug conviction that the Office of Strategic Services or the Board of Economic Warfare might dabble in policymaking but only temporarily. Yet the State Department in Washington could claim a history of much less than 200 years, while the Six Boards in Peking traced their provenance uninterruptedly for 1,200 years from the T'ang dynasty.

The name Tsungli Yamen itself bears out the point. *Tsung-li* was a fine term connoting general superintendence, the man in charge. As deified head of the Kuomintang after his death Sun Yat-sen would be called Sun Tsung-li. As Prime Minister of the People's Republic the venerated Chou En-lai would be Chou Tsung-li. Later, Teng Hsiao-p'ing (Deng Xiaoping) as Deputy Prime Minister would be Fu-tsung-li. *Ya-men*, however, was a bureaucratic term of no account, meaning merely official quarters.

The full title of the Tsungli Yamen, as it appeared in Prince Kung's initial memorial, was *Tsung-li ko-kuo shih-wu ya-men* or "Office to superintend affairs of the various countries." But the imperial edict in reply, apparently attempting to downgrade the importance of the office, inserted the word "commercial" *t'ung-shang* (lit. "foreign trade") so that the title read *Tsung-li ko-kuo t'ung-shang shih-wu ya-men* or "Office to superintend the commercial affairs of the various countries." This was dirty work indeed — sabotage at the source of authority, quite contrary to the original idea. Prince Kung quickly memorialized again and got *t'ung-shang* taken out of the title. But since edicts were sacrosanct and could not be rescinded, the result was that both edicts and both titles remained in the official record. "Commercial," though left out of the official seal, was sometimes used in the title nevertheless.[4]

A further sign of the Tsungli Yamen's lowly status was its location in a nondescript old building, "the deserted office of the Department of Iron Coins, situated on Tung-t'ang-tzu Lane in the eastern section of Peking. (Iron coinage, we might note, had been used as a last extremity in a time of fiscal crisis.) This edifice when renovated in the style of a government office, perhaps late in 1861, subsequently impressed some of the few foreigners who saw it as in poor repair, "very small and inconvenient," "a dirty, cheerless, barren building."[5] But whether it was outstandingly unprepossessing compared with other Peking offices of the late Ch'ing remains somewhat uncertain.

Judging from appearances today, the quarters of the Grand Council were none too grand — yet it was the most important single metropolitan office in China from the time of its creation in 1729 to the end of the dynasty. Grand Councillors, whose number was not fixed by statute, met with the Emperor in the wee hours of every day to do the imperial business, and were clearly at the center of power.

The Tsungli Yamen, however, was nothing more than an ad hoc subcommittee under the Grand Council. Whatever prestige it enjoyed, therefore, derived almost entirely from the direct participation of Grand Councillors in its affairs. Although in 1861, only one out of a total of six Grand Councillors served in the fledgling Yamen, during the T'ung-chih period as a whole (1862–1874), an average of over three members of the Grand Council (out of an average total size of less than six members) held concurrent positions in the Yamen. Put another way, from 1863 to 1868, at least three Grand Councillors were also ministers of the Tsungli Yamen; and from 1869 to 1874, at least four.[6]

During the 1860s, Prince Kung, Wen-hsiang, and Pao-yun (all Manchus) held concurrent memberships in both agencies, while most other members of the Yamen held concurrent high-level positions in one or another of the Six Boards, the Censorate, or the Grand Secretariat. Moreover, the service of these individuals in the Tsungli Yamen was surprisingly long, given the generally short tenure of most Ch'ing officials. Prince Kung, for instance, served in the Yamen from 1860 to 1884 (and again from 1895 to 1898); Wen-hsiang, from 1860 to 1876; Pao-yun, from 1861 to 1884; Ch'ung-lun, from 1861 to 1875; and Tung Hsun, from 1861 to 1880. The terms of other ministers appointed in the early to mid-1860s were less impressive: Heng-ch'i, from 1861 to 1866; Hsueh Huan, from 1863 to 1866; Hsu Chi-yu, from 1865 to 1869; and T'an T'ing-hsiang, from 1865 to 1870.[7]

By mid-1864, Hart had already formed preliminary opinions about several of these individuals. His journal entry of 14 August, for example, offers an incisive critique of the Yamen's chief ministers based on his growing knowledge of both provincial and metropolitan personnel. In this entry, too, he praises Wen-hsiang for his intelligence, good nature, foresight, and attention to detail, but faults him for a certain lack of fortitude. He wishes Pao-yun would "attend to business," and that Heng-ch'i possessed the self-confidence to "dare speak out." Clearly appreciative of Tung Hsun's erudition, Hart nonetheless looks on him as rather impractical and something of a "bookworm." He has little use for either Ch'ung-lun or Hsueh Huan, preferring to see them replaced by provincial leaders such as Li Hung-chang and

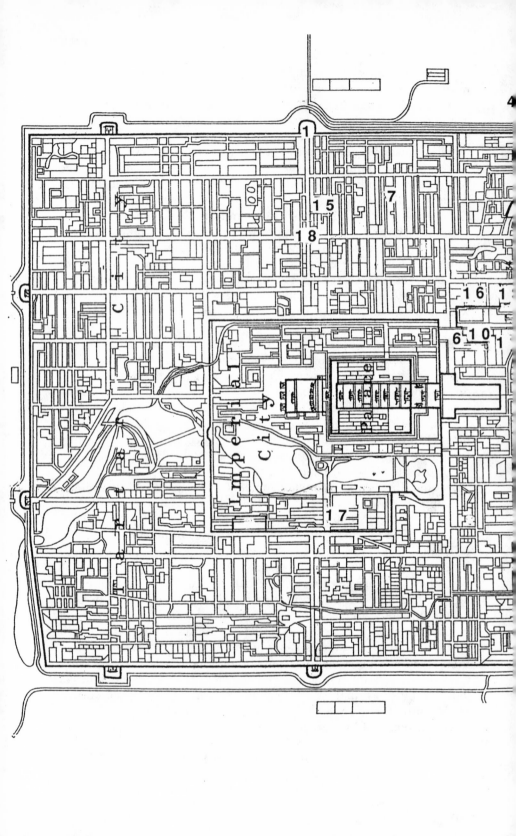

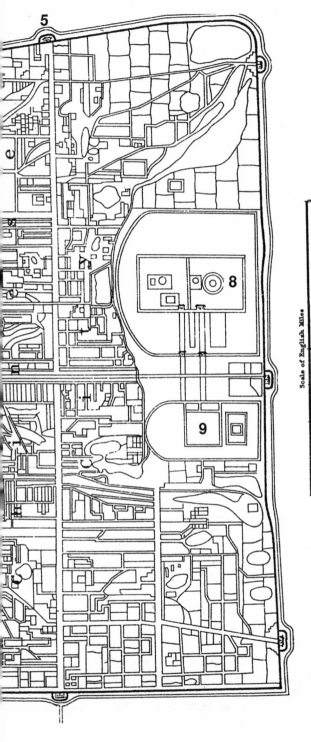

1. Ch'i-hua Gate

2. Hata Gate

3. Ch'ienmen Gate

4. Tungpien Gate

5. Shakuo Gate

6. Hanlin Library

7. Tsungli Yamen

8. Temple of Heaven

9. Temple of Agriculture

10. British Legation

11. Russian Legation

12. American Legation

13. French Legation

14. German Legation

15. Customs Inspectorate andCustoms Students, 1863-1866

16. Customs Inspectorate, 1867–

17. Old Peit'ang

18. Eastern Four Arches

Scale of English Miles

Map 3 Plan of Peking

From Hosea Ballou Morse, *The International Relations of the Chinese Empire,* vol. 3 (London, Longman Green & Co., 1910–1918).

Table 1   Ch'ing Personnel in Office 1863–1864

At Peking

  Grand Council

    I-hsin, the Prince of Kung
    Wen-hsiang
    Pao-yun
    Li T'ang-chieh
    Ts'ao Yü-ying

  Tsungli Yamen

    I-hsin
    Wen-hsiang
    Ch'ung-lun
    Heng-ch'i
    Pao-yun
    Tung Hsun
    Hsueh Huan

    Inpsector General of Maritime Customs
    (at Shanghai 1861–1864)

Lao Ch'ung-kuang. At this point, Hart offers no particular opinion of Prince Kung.

The appraisals of Dr. W. A. P. Martin, the American Presbyterian missionary whom Hart had known in Ningpo, are also worth noting. In 1865 Hart got him to teach at the Interpreters' College (T'ung-wen kuan), of which he served as the head from 1869 to 1895 (see chapter 7). Funded by the Customs, it taught foreign languages to potential diplomats under the aegis of the Yamen. Martin had substantial contact with the ministers, and as a writer in later life was less inhibited than Hart about publishing his impressions.[8]

Martin spoke of Prince Kung as "lank in figure, swart in complexion, and so near-sighted that he appeared to squint." He was, however, possessed of a "kindly and gracious" demeanor and a "rapid and energetic" style of speech. In Martin's view, Prince Kung was extremely cautious: "he never acted without the advice of his subordinates, and his speeches were nothing but a summary of their deliberations."[9] Prince Kung's intelligence, royal connections, and experiences in both domestic politics and Sino-foreign relations made him indispensable to the dynasty and to the Throne throughout the 1860s. Even so, he was never able to establish personal control over the Ch'ing government, and his political career in the 1870s and 1880s was marked by considerable disappointment and occasional humiliation. But during the 1860s, when he held the primary responsibility for the day-to-day management of both the Grand Council and the Tsungli Yamen, he handled his difficult and frequently hazardous tasks with uncommon efficiency and insight.[10]

Much of Prince Kung's administrative success can be attributed to the advice and assistance of his close friend and confident, Wen-hsiang. At the relatively tender age of 47 (15 years older than the Prince), Wen-hsiang was China's premier elder statesman. It was he who had negotiated with the foreign powers in 1860, and had proposed, together with Prince Kung and Kuei-liang, the establishment of the Tsungli Yamen in 1860. His, too, was the bold and innovative proposal to organize a Western-trained Banner contingent known as the Peking Field Force (Shen-chi ying) in 1862.

By all accounts, including Hart's, Wen-hsiang possessed remarkable qualities of mind and character. The British Minister, Frederick Bruce, once remarked that he had "never encountered a more powerful intellect," and Bruce's successor, Rutherford Alcock, considered him to be "by far the most advanced among the leading ministers of the [Tsungli] Yamen and Grand Secretariat [sic]."[11] Martin called Wen-hsiang an "enlightened" statesman, who, although fiercely proud of China and Chinese culture, was also highly receptive to Western influences. "We shall," Wen-hsiang reportedly told Martin, "learn all the good we can from you people of the West."[12]

Although not so well known as either Prince Kung or Wen-hsiang, Pao-yun (1807–1891) performed capably as a minister of the Tsungli Yamen. He, too, was a Manchu Grand Councillor, and like his more distinguished colleagues he was a man of letters with a great deal of practical experience as well. Wen-hsiang and Pao-yun have often been considered together by modern Chinese scholars as among the most capable, conscientious, and uncorrupt Manchu officials of the late Ch'ing era. Martin, however, preferred to compare Pao-yun to Tung Hsun. Both had been school teachers in their early careers and both were extremely gifted in the composition of verse. "Both poets when in their prime," Martin once wrote, "were extremely handsome, and Pao, who was born under the same star with his Chinese compeer [1807], and lived to a greater age, was to the last alike conspicuous for nobleness of aspect and mental vivacity. Both were great jokers. It was a treat to hear them bandy their classic sally and repartee.

Wen-hsiang, about 1872, age 54

From J. Thomson, *Illustrations of China and Its People* (London, Sampson Low, Marston, Low, and Searle, 1874).

In science they stood at the level of Virgil and Horace; but Tung, who took a great interest in the [Interpreters'] college, and carefully read all my books, giving me the benefit of no little verbal criticism, was slowly emerging into broader views. Pao, whose thoughts never strayed beyond the rules of prosody, adhered to the old traditions. I once heard him in the presence of our students ridicule the doctrine of the earth's diurnal revolution, accompanying his jokes by peals of laughter, the students on their part smiling at the ignorance of the great minister."[13]

Among the ethnically Chinese (as opposed to Manchu) ministers of the Tsungli Yamen in the 1860s, Tung Hsun undoubtedly enjoyed the best reputation. Martin describes him as "a model scholar," "a gentleman of perfect polish," and a man clearly sympathetic with the Western notion of progress. Although he chided Tung for a "superstitious" belief in *feng-shui* (an interesting observation in light of Tung's derisive remarks concerning the practice in Hart's journal; 20 August 1864), he credits him with being the man behind Prince Kung's pen. According to Martin, Tung drafted most of the despatches of the Yamen, and served ably as a "regent" of the Interpreters' College. Probably Tung's close association with the College produced a particularly favorable impression on the part of Martin, since he had a substantial stake in the school.[14]

Glimpses of Tung's interest in both poetry and the West can be seen in his collaboration with Thomas Wade on a translation of Longfellow's well-known and oft-quoted "Psalm of Life." According to the modern Chinese novelist and man of letters Ch'ien Chung-shu, Tung recast and made properly poetic Wade's rather opaque and overly literal translation of the work, identified as "Tall Friend's Poem" ("Ch'ang-yu shih"). The double filtration process was a tricky one. For instance, Longfellow's line "Footprints in the sands of time" became "the footprints of a wild goose in snow-mud"—a distinctly Chinese metaphor taken from Su Tung-p'o's famous poem to his brother.[15] We are reminded here of the vast literary and cultural gap between Chinese and Western poetry and, by extension, the formidable communication problem confronting Westerners in their daily contact with Ch'ing officials. Where compradors had used pidgin (business) English, the early Western users of Chinese had to settle for their own rather inelegant form of business Chinese. Although competent enough in the spoken language, Wade, Hart, and others like them could never hope to achieve the sort of literary refinement that was so central to the Ch'ing elite's self-image.

Aside from Tung Hsun, the Tsungli Yamen had little remaining

Chinese talent. Heng-ch'i, a Chinese Bannerman, had been the Hoppo at Canton in 1858–1859 when young Hart was Interpreter to the Allied Commission governing the city. Heng-ch'i had then made friends with Hart, giving him a pony, which probably explains the attention Heng-ch'i receives in Hart's journal. A minister of the Tsungli Yamen from 1861 till his death in 1866, Heng-ch'i evidently had the wealth to be active as a principal glad-hander in entertaining the foreign diplomats in Peking. In this setting he gave Hart a mule cart for going about the city, though it was not very comfortable to ride in. There is no reason to believe, however, that he had any particular importance within the Yamen. Although his Canton background helped him gain a degree of prominence during the Sino-foreign negotiations of 1860, and he continued to negotiate for the Yamen into the mid-1860s, Hart considered Heng-ch'i to be almost completely ineffective. He was likeable to be sure, and "by no means a fool," but Hart's journal depicts him as conservative, narrow-minded, short-sighted, skittish, critical, conniving, and inconsistent.[16]

Hsueh (Hsieh) Huan was no better. A Szechwanese provincial graduate of 1844, Hsueh had been an expectant prefect at Shanghai as early as 1844, and in 1857 he became Shanghai Taotai. He negotiated with Lay in the fall of 1858 to revise the treaty tariff, and served as Governor of Kiangsu from June 1860 to April 1862. In this latter capacity he tried to persuade the British and French not to advance on Peking in 1860, while at the same time trying to secure foreign assistance for the defense of Shanghai. Although he apparently got on fairly well with the brash American founder of the Ever-Victorious Army, Frederick T. Ward, most Westerners had a low opinion of him. So did Hsueh's Chinese contemporaries in Shanghai, who considered him nothing more than Wu Hsu's mouthpiece.[17] In April 1862 Hsueh was appointed Imperial Commissioner for Trade at the Southern Ports, and from May 1863 to mid-1866 he served as a minister of the Tsungli Yamen. In both positions his career was undistinguished. At several points in Hart's journal the I.G. criticizes him severely, and Wen-hsiang's remark on 23 June 1864 that he had "no high opinion of Hsieh" was obviously an understatement.

Ch'ung-lun, like Heng-ch'i, was a Chinese Bannerman. He gained his initial experience in negotiating with foreigners at Tientsin in 1854, when, as a salt controller, he was deputed by Kuei-liang to talk to the British, French, and American envoys who had sailed northward in an effort to secure treaty revision after failing in their attempts to negotiate at Canton and Shanghai. Ch'ung-lun managed to refuse their principal demands, and this limited "success" launched him on a diplomatic career which included negotiating the Prussian treaty at Tientsin in 1861. He was not progress-minded, and by his own admission his memory had begun to fail.[18] His career, like those of Hsueh Huan and Heng-ch'i, reminds us that in China during the early 1860s simply to have had some contact with foreigners in one's early official life might justify an appointment to be a minister of the Tsungli Yamen. On-the-job training was the only diplomatic education available at the time.

In meetings with the Yamen ministers, Hart was the youngest man present. Prince Kung, whom he seldom saw, was only two years his senior, but Wen-hsiang (1818–1876) and Hsueh Huan (1815–1880) were half again as old, Ch'ung-lun (1792–1875) more than twice his age, and Heng-ch'i (1802–1866), Tung Hsun (1807–1892), and Pao-yun (1807–1891) only a decade or so younger than the venerable Ch'ung-lun. In a culture where age and status went hand in hand, Hart plainly knew how to acknowledge his youth in appropriate ways, just as he also knew the value of an apt Confucian quotation (see journal, 21 August 1864). Like the Yamen ministers themselves, the I.G. learned on the job.

The Tsungli Yamen's bureaucratic organization below the ministerial level fluctuated during the first few years of its existence, but by 1864 it had the following features. Under the ministers themselves were a number of subordinate secretaries (*chang-ching*). Eight of these were drawn from the Grand Council staff, the rest from the staffs of the Grand Secretariat (Nei-ko), Six Boards, the Li-fan Yuan and other parts of the Peking bureaucracy. In 1861 there were 28 secretaries, but by 1864 their number had increased to 36 (and much later to 56). Among them, 4 were secretaries general (*tsung-pan*) and 2 were assistant secretaries general (*pang-pan*), who supervised the flow of business.[19]

Hart's journal indicates the substantial role played by the Yamen secretaries, especially the 4 secretaries general and 2 assistants. With them he corresponded by exchanging "official letters" (*kung-han*), which did not require as much formal processing and official decision as official despatches.[20] Hart refers to the secretaries as operating in a "semi-official" capacity. Two useful and influential *tsung-pan* in 1864 were Ching Lin (Ch'eng-lin, who later attained ministerial rank), and Tsae (presumably Ts'ai Shih-chün, whom Hart described in a 4 May 1867 journal entry as "chief of the Tsung Pan"). When Hart arrived in Peking on 1 June 1864, he recorded, "Sent my card at once to the Yamun to report my arrival and say I shd. call on the following day. Ching Lin's came in return." The journal continues: "2nd June. At 11 the cards of the Tsungpan came asking me to go early to the Yamun" to see Prince Kung. "Went immediately . . . had a few minutes talk with Ching and Tsae" before the Yamen ministers and the Prince arrived. Although Hart's substantial contact was with Wen-hsiang, Heng-ch'i and the other ministers, the *tsung-pan* performed important ancillary functions. On 11 June, for instance, "Tsae hinted this morning at Wan Seang's wish to cut down the Customs' grant"—information that allowed Hart to present a strong argument against so doing, almost certainly stronger than he could have presented to his superior Wen-hsiang on the spur of the moment. (As it turned out, the grant was increased.)

The Yamen's flow of business, after some early experimentation, was handled from 1864 by a combined regional-functional system that would have made denizens of Whitehall, the Quai d'Orsay, and the State Department feel immediately at home. Business was divided among four bureaux (lit., "legs," *ku*) named for Russia, England, France, and America. Each bureau, in addition to handling matters concerning its designated country, was then charged with a number of other duties. Thus, in addition to Russian affairs, the Russian Bureau came to handle Japan, overland trade, and boundary disputes. The English Bureau dealt also with Austria-Hungary and with the commercial treaties, tariffs, tonnage dues, and other matters connected with the Maritime Customs. The French Bureau eventually dealt with the affairs of France, Holland, Spain, Brazil, Christian missions, and Chinese emigrants. The American Bureau came to deal with matters concerning the United States, Germany, Peru, Italy, Portugal, Belgium, Scandinavia, and Chinese laborers overseas. This helter-skelter addition of further duties to the regional bureaux resulted, of course, in some inefficiency. The American Bureau had to concern itself with seven European countries. Germany was under it but Austria-Hungary was under the English Bureau, and the Dutch were under the French Bureau. Chinese emigrants and laborers abroad were under two bureaux. Finally, the four bureaux of 1864 were served by three offices that dealt with communications, documents, and finances. It was a comprehensive setup, and probably no more confusing than the outside world as a whole.

As if the complexities of foreign relations were not enough to tax the energy and ingenuity of the Tsungli Yamen, its members also had to contend with deeply entrenched Ch'ing bureaucratic practices and policies. In the first place, since all the Yamen's officials—ministers as well as secretaries—retained their original posts in the offices from which they were selected, their work at the Yamen was an additional and concurrent chore. In the interest of efficiency, the secretaries were divided into two shifts, each of which would function for a 5-day (later 4-day) stretch before being spelled by the other shift; but for the ministers themselves no such surcease was possible. Consequently, they tended to handle their regular jobs in the morning and come to the Yamen in the afternoon, as Hart notes repeatedly in his journal. Sometimes, according to Tung Hsun's autobiography, they found it necessary to work throughout the night.[21]

Chester Holcombe, for many years Interpreter and Secretary of the American Legation in Peking, provides a revealing account of the daily routine of one "senior and responsible minister of the Foreign Office" (most likely Wen-hsiang). An average day, he says, began at 2 in the morning. From 3 to 6 a.m., the official had to be on duty at the Imperial Palace, since audiences normally took place before dawn. Affairs at the Grand Council occupied the hours from 6 to 9, after which additional bureaucratic duties consumed the hours from 9 until 2. The minister then went to the Tsungli Yamen, where he labored from 2 until 5 or 6 in the evening. "These," Holcombe adds, "were his regular daily duties." In addition, "he was frequently appointed upon special commissions, boards of inquiry, or to posts involving additional labor, and these he sandwiched in between the others as well as he could. He stated that he never reached home before 7 or 8 o'clock in the evening."[22] One is reminded of the long-suffering British commanders in World War II who often had to stay up conferring with Winston Churchill till 2 AM, before starting each day with their own usual staff conferences.

Furthermore, like most other bureaucratic offices we have described, the Tsungli Yamen operated within the framework of an elaborate system of checks and balances. Not surprisingly, its composition reflected the well-entrenched principle of Manchu-Chinese dyarchy. During the 1860s, the institution was dominated by Manchus. Some ethnically Chinese ministers, such as Ch'ung-lun and Heng-ch'i, were in fact Han Bannermen and thus more Manchu in identification than Chinese. At several points Hart's journal reveals the sensitivity of the Manchus to their alien origins, as well as to factionalism with the Yamen that sometimes had an ethnic dimension.[23] Yet despite factionalism and unavoidable disagreement, the decisions of the Tsungli Yamen had to be unanimous; separate memorials by ministers of the Yamen expressing individual opinions were expressly prohibited.[24] Under the circumstances, the safest decision was often no decision at all.

Another feature of the dynasty's checks-and-balances system was censorial supervision. Throughout its history, The Tsungli Yamen not only had to endure a barrage of foreign criticism, but also domestic criticism, often launched by censors. Ch'eng-lin once told W. A. P. Martin that "the plans of the Tsungli Yamen sometimes go down before the force of outside antagonism. A clever censor or a powerful viceroy gets the ear of the emperor, and forthwith quashes our wisest schemes."[25] Martin informs us that Prince Kung's strategy for neutralizing his critics was to request that they be appointed to the Tsungli Yamen, where they could see for themselves the difficulties involved. This strategy brought the notorious arch-conservative Wo-jen to the Yamen for a brief period in the late 1860s, but it was not particularly successful in stifling criticism.

Another problem with the Yamen was overlapping jurisdictions. As we have seen, the Tsungli Yamen shared administrative responsibility in foreign matters with several other agencies, including the Li-fan Yuan, the Board of Rites, and the Commissioners for the Northern and Southern Ports. Although these commissioners ostensibly represented branch offices of the Tsungli Yamen, they were not subject to its authority![26] Moreover, despite the Yamen's close connection with the Grand Council, it often could not force its will on provincial officials — especially since the Throne's usual approach during the 1860s was to urge the settlement of foreign affairs locally.[27]

A final and crucial problem faced by the Yamen was the lack of formal training in foreign affairs on the part of its ministers. Most had at least some practical experience in Sino-foreign relations; but, as we have indicated, this experience was usually localized, sporadic, and completely uninformed by any sort of systematic education in Western diplomacy. The ministers of the Yamen, like most other Ch'ing bureaucrats, were Confucian generalists rather than specialists — products of an examination system that powerfully and persistently reinforced outmoded notions of foreign relations. As late as 1880, for example, one topic for the metropolitan examinations was the following quotation from the *Doctrine of the Mean*: "By indulgent treatment of men from afar, they are led to resort to the [Chinese] ruler from all quarters."[28]

The stigma that attached to foreign relations made the tasks of the Yamen all the more difficult. In later years, for example, Li Hung-chang is reported to have continually declined the Tsungli Yamen's requests for recommendations of competent men to serve as foreign envoys for fear of offending the men whom he might recommend. Similarly, the Grand Secretary Yen Ching-ming once answered the question "Who among men of rectitude today excels in foreign affairs?"

with the retort: "Do men of rectitude care to engage in foreign affairs?"—the obvious answer being "no."[29]

This was the situation confronting Hart and his Manchu and Chinese colleagues in the early 1860s. Although his appointment as Inspector General of the Customs administration in Peking allowed Hart to walk the corridors of Ch'ing power, he had to tread lightly. Prince Kung and Wen-hsiang were his patrons, but not really his partners—and, even if they had been, his position would have remained tenuous. He still had much to learn about Chinese politics and bureaucracy. Hart had met the proper time, but he still had to prove himself.

THE I.G. OVER THE MARITIME CUSTOMS SERVICE

All the time that Hart was quietly developing his relations with Ch'ing officials he was also steadily building up his administrative powers as Inspector General. His control of the service began after Lay, from his base in Shanghai, opened offices at Canton and Swatow. Hart opened all the rest: early in 1861 at Chinkiang and Ningpo; in May at Tientsin; in July at Foochow; and in December at Hankow and Kiukiang. Amoy was added in April 1862, Chefoo in March 1863, followed by Tamsui on the north end of Taiwan in May and Takow in the south of the island later in the year. Finally Newchwang was added in May 1864, making 14 in all. Thus, by June 1864, Hart had in fact set up and staffed Maritime Customs offices at 11 ports, compared with Lay's original 3.

Hart began to integrate these branch offices by inaugurating the I.G. circulars that would thenceforth provide the life blood of his administration. For us of a later century, these circulars, like blood samples, yield significant data when analyzed.[30] Circular no. 1 of 1861 set the style of concision, precision, and unequivocally in-line authority:

TSUNG-LI YAMEN.
PEKING, 30th June 1861.

Sir,

1.—In accordance with the commands of H.I.H. the PRINCE OF KUNG, I now transmit, for the information of yourself and the various members of the establishment over which you preside, copy and translation of Instructions issued by H.H. appointing Mr. FITZ-ROY and myself to exercise conjointly the functions of Inspector General of Maritime Customs.

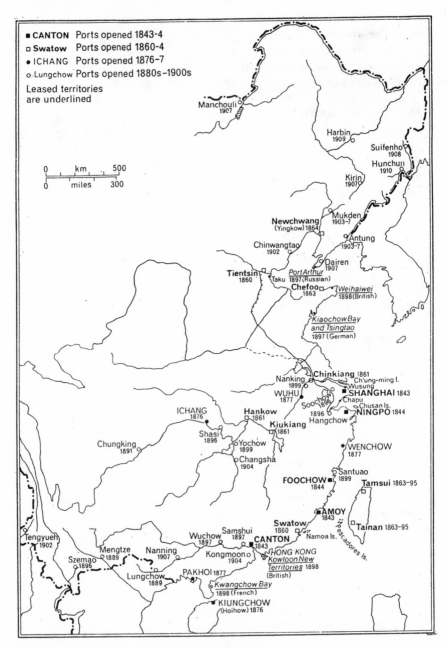

Map 4 Eventual Growth of the Treaty Port System

From *The Cambridge History of China*, Vol. 10, ed. John K. Fairbank (London, New York, Melbourne, Cambridge University Press, 1978), and reprinted with the permission of the Cambridge University Press.

2.—H.H. THE PRINCE has likewise officially communicated the appointment to the Ministers of the Treaty Powers, by whom the various Consuls will be notified of the position of Foreigners employed in the Chinese Customs' Service.

I am &c.,

(signed)   ROBERT HART

Officiating Inspector General of Chinese Maritime Customs

This simple statement has several noteworthy features. First, Hart writes demurely as from the Tsungli Yamen and under the "command" of its head (whom he rightly calls by his title as the Prince of Kung; the Prince's personal name was I-hsin). Hart makes plain the Chinese status of the service by sending both the Chinese original and an English translation of the Prince's instructions and by announcing that Prince Kung (as we call him for convenience) is communicating them also to the treaty-power ministers, asking them to tell their treaty-port consuls in effect that foreigners in the Customs are Chinese officials. Finally, Hart signs alone as "Officiating I.G.". What has happened to the worthy Fitzroy, doing his job in the key post of Shanghai Commissioner? Though he is "conjointly" officiating in the first sentence, he disappears from the signature at the end. Subsequent circulars are signed "Robert Hart, O.I.G. of C.M.C." Hart is in command, velvet glove and all. But not until Circular no. 1 of 1863 does he write as from the "Inspectorate General." *Festina lente*, as he might have said.

Following Circular no. 1 of 1861 which established his authority, Hart wrote individual letters of appointment. For example, Lay had informed Wilzer at Swatow on 13 April, from Hong Kong: "I have appointed you to a Deputy Commissionership" (see letter quoted above). But Hart on 1 July wrote "I have laid your name before His Imperial Highness the Prince of Kung for an appointment as Commissioner." The Prince having approved, "your location while serving the Chinese Government . . . will be determined as the exigencies of the service may seem to the Inspector General to require. . . . You are hereby appointed" to Swatow. Hart left no doubt as to the chain of command.

To accompany his circulars in an unofficial and parallel channel of communication, Hart corresponded directly with each commissioner. Thus he wrote Wilzer in November 1861: "Do you like Swatow? I trust you do not; for in March you will in all probability be moved to a more northerly port". (It turned out to be Tientsin.)[31]

Where the circulars of 1861 begin "I have received the command" of

Prince Kung (see no. 2, no. 3, no. 8, also no. 8 of 1863), or "H.H. the Prince directs" (no. 4, no. 5 of 1861, also no. 13 of 1863), by 1863 the style has changed. Circular no. 10 of 1863 reads simply:

Inspectorate General,
CANTON, 16th February, 1863.

SIR.

I have to request that you will forward to my address, Shanghai, on the first of April next, a return of the names of all the members of your establishment, as composed on that day, in accordance with the form hereto appended.

I am &c.

(signed)   ROBERT HART
O.I.G. of C.M.C.

Directly to the point, with no words wasted. Of course as the Service settled into routines, the commands of the Prince no doubt became less frequent in fact. Meanwhile the "Inspectorate General" still is located wherever Hart happens to be.

The I.G.'s autonomy and his aim to facilitate trade were both made apparent in Circular. no. 5 of 15 February 1863 from "Inspectorate General, Canton." The question had arisen whether re-export of foreign imports could be allowed under drawbacks (if to a foreign country) or exemption certificates (if to another treaty port) in cases where the goods "have passed from the hands of the original importers to either Native or Foreign purchasers," Hart wrote:

In the absence of instructions from the Tsung-li Yamen I can merely acquaint you with my own view of the matter. . . . I am of the opinion that it is *not* necessary, in order to the granting of Drawbacks and Exemption Certificates, that the merchandise should be re-exported by the original importer. . . . I am convinced that a liberal interpretation of such rules, instead of proving detrimental to the interests of the revenue, will, on the contrary, in the end prove beneficial, and that the true principle to be followed is to facilitate, and not fetter, commerce.

I shall lay the matter before the members of the Tsung-li Yamen, in order that instructions may be issued by them in accordance with the views I have above stated.

In short, on this point the I.G. professed to feel that he could deliver the Tsungli Yamen's vote. And why not? The two documents (drawbacks and exemption certificates) had been invented by the foreigners and put into their treaties. The I.G. now sought to make them available to Chinese merchants shipping foreign goods.

As models of clarity, the circulars dispense with formalities. No one ever "has the honor to" or has "to instruct you to." "Please" is quite unnecessary. As the time goes on, the I.G. instructs his commissioners more *ex cathedra*: "You will be careful to . . ." (no. 4 of 1864), "it will be your duty to comply with . . ." (no. 3 of 1865), "you will take note in particular of . . ." (no. 9 of 1865), "you will for the future be careful to . . ." (no. 5 of 1866). The "you will" came from the one person who selected, paid, promoted, and could always fire the recipients. Hart never threw his weight around. After his Circular no. 8 of 21 June 1864, there was no need to, for it summed up Hart's conception of his job in China.

The Maritime Customs' function, as Hart conceived it, was to support the British consular crusade in China, which, as in many other parts of the Victorian empire, aimed to expand the rule of law in the service of trade. Today we might call it the modernization of administrative technology. Consuls of imagination like Rutherford Alcock or John Bowring had backed the Foreign Inspectorate as a means of curbing the retrograde tendency of enterprising British merchants and wily Chinese customs collectors to reduce China's foreign trade to an unpredictable chaos in which the smartest crooks on either side could connive together and be the sole winners.

The reformers had a tough job ahead of them because the high value and illegality of the India-to-China opium trade had brought the normal corruption of the Chinese customs administration to a new height of cynical skulduggery. Our perspective on this lawlessness along the China coast must go back to the Ch'ing anti-opium movement of the 1830s, championed by Lin Tse-hsu, and its signal defeat. Twenty years later this formerly contraband drug was pouring into China under the treaty tariff of 1858. Not only was the Emperor's morality flouted, but during the 1850s Britain maintained neutrality in China's civil war while Western merchants and soldiers of fortune dealt with both sides. After 1856 the British had even begun warfare against the Ch'ing at Canton, where the Anglo-French occupation for a time in 1858 stopped the trade and closed the Customs.[32] Foreign-owned river steamers came and went, smuggling with complete freedom. Canton threatened to become a free port as Shanghai had started to become in 1854.

The task of the Foreign Inspectorate was to make a comeback from this sort of chaos. As it developed, by the early 1860s the Ch'ing crusade to save the dynasty from the Taipings joined with the British crusade to save the China trade. Hart found himself deeply embroiled in both causes. The bedrock function of the Maritime Customs was to ensure equal terms of commercial competition by seeing to the proper payment of the duties due by foreign merchants under the treaty tariff. Included was Chinese produce conveyed on foreign vessels from one treaty port to another. Also included were foreign goods going inland and native goods coming out from the interior for export when covered by transit passes. As the foreign assistant (actually partner) of the Chinese superintendent of customs at each treaty port, the foreign commissioner of customs was to serve as the assessor and accountant of the dues and duties on direct foreign trade and foreign-borne Chinese coastal trade.

In Hart's view, his foreign commissioners were, like Hart himself, servants of the Chinese government. This led quite soon to the propagation of an idealistic ethos, a mystique, about the role of the Foreign Inspectorate in the government of China. Especially in his early years as I.G., Hart spread a gospel of service to China in resounding statements that have been widely quoted. His tone was not unlike that of contemporary missionaries preaching their Christian message. Both gospels of help to China were uttered and widely accepted as proper statements of ideals, although both were sometimes at odds with the socio-political realities of the time. On 7 December 1864, Hart writes of Mr. Thomas of the London Mission, who will soon resign to join the Customs: "A man with a missionary spirit in our service would have a wonderful field before him, and might be very useful."

Was Hart then a secular missionary? Or should we say simply that the impulse to help the Chinese people that generally characterized missionaries also motivated Robert Hart? Given Hart's sincere religious devotion as described at length in his journal, we can assuredly say that he wanted to do good. A first step would to be acknowledge the equality of Westerners and Chinese as human beings—a sure bet in the long run but not a dominant idea among foreign denizens of the treaty ports in the 1860s. In a journal entry of 2 August 1864 he asserts: "Except in that they don't fight, I consider the Chinese, as a people, superior to any other: had they our learning & Christianity, they would be infinitely *beyond* us."

At Peking in the summer of 1864, Hart moved ever closer into the confidence of the ministers of the Tsungli Yamen. The key to his success was a healthy kind of cultural schizophrenia. Although enamored of Western "civilization" and "progress," critical of Chinese administrative practices, and never unaware of his responsibilities and loyalties as a British citizen, Hart nevertheless became to a remarkable degree Sinicized—that is, pro-Chinese in attitude and acutely conscious of the sensibilities of his colleagues and employers in Peking. "I am on the Chinese side," he declared emphatically in his journal in mid-August 1864, "and I will help them to the best of my abilities." Hart remained the perpetual optimist, in contrast to Wade with his gestures of gloom, and Lay with his ultimata for instant reform.

The Customs gospel was enshrined in Hart's very long and famous Circular no. 8 of 21 June 1864. The context of this document was the treaty-port vogue of attacking the Foreign Inspectorate by word of mouth, in print, and in letters to England while simultaneously ostracizing the Customs foreign employees as traitors within the treaty-port society. That society's early isolation on dangerous foreign soil had left a tradition of China-bashing that united the community in suspicion, fear, contempt, and ridicule of all things Chinese, including China's new foreign employees. After all, the denigration of America's and India's people of darker complexion provided a ready model for many foreigners in China. Circular no. 8 therefore led off by demanding the acceptance by the Customs staff of the essentially Chinese character of the Customs service. "It is to be distinctly and constantly kept in mind that the Inspectorate of Customs is a Chinese and not, a foreign, Service, and that as such it is the duty of each of its members to conduct himself towards Chinese, people as well as officials, in such a way as to avoid all cause of offence and ill-feeling. . . . It is to be expected from those who take the pay, and who are the servants of the Chinese Government that they at least will so act as to neither offend sensibilities nor excite jealousies, suspicion, and dislike. . . . The first thing to be remembered by each is that he is the paid agent of the Chinese Government for the performance of specified work, and to do that well should be his chief care."

Hart also wanted to achieve some sort of balanced representation of nationalities in the higher levels of the Chinese Customs Administration. Four days after issuing Circular no. 8, for instance, he wrote a letter to the American Minister, Anson Burlingame, asking for assistance in recruiting U.S. citizens into the service. This letter, which represents the I.G.'s basic attitude toward recruitment, deserves to be quoted at length. It begins, "In a service such as ours, cosmopolitan in nature, and transacting business with people of so many different countries, it would be but natural to expect that, numerically, the United States would be strongly represented. Unfortunately, I have found it quite impossible to recruit in China for our offices. We have no difficulty in procuring seafaring men and others fit to perform the work of out-door departments, and accordingly amongst the tide-waiters, whose pay ranges from £ 240 to £ 600 a year, a great many Americans are to be found. Of the dozen commissioners who preside at the ports, three are American; three are French; one Prussian, and five are English. We have not one American who can interpret, or who can be said to have any knowledge of Chinese, and the few that we have in the offices as clerks are very far indeed from being a superior class of men."

Hart goes on to say: "I should, therefore, consider it a very great favor if you could get for me from America three young gentlemen, above 18 and under 22 years of age, who have received a collegiate education. I should like men of at least fair average abilities, of good standing in society, and of industrious habits. £ 200 sterling (about $900, Mexican) would be paid to each upon his arrival in China, to reimburse him for expenses incurred on his passage out. For the first two years they would be located at Peking, to study Chinese, where they would be provided with rooms, and receive pay at the rate of £ 400 (about $1,800) a year. At the expiration of the second year the pay of each would be raised to £ 600 (about $2,700,) from which it would gradually, as vacancies occurred in the service, and as opportunities for promotion allowed, rise to £ 800, £ 1,000, and £ 1,200. In the course of time they might expect to become commissioners, whose pay is at the rate of £ 1,200, £ 1,400, and £ 2,000 a year. An industrious, hard-working, and able man might fairly expect to be a commissioner in eight or ten years. After five years' service, a year's leave is granted on half pay. In the event of the Chinese government desiring to dispense with any one's services, he would be entitled to either three months' notice or three months' pay. After the second year in Peking, the inspector general would locate each gentleman at the port he might consider the most fitting."[33]

Like Gordon, but with a greater chance, perhaps, of eventual success, Hart envisioned eventually replacing the foreign officers in his organization with Chinese. In November 1864, he wrote: "The Inspectorate, while it does good service for its employer — the Chinese Government — in collecting an increasingly large revenue, is, for the present, a necessity, under the Treaties; a necessity, however, which need not be regarded with dislike, or suspicion, for while the ally of commerce generally in enlisting in its favour the sympathies of the Chinese Government, the Inspectorate will be for a time, and while it exists, a more and more efficient, though extraneous, public servant; it will have finished its work when it shall have produced a native administration, as honest and as efficient to replace it." In truth, however, during Hart's 44 years' service as I.G., no Chinese would ever rise to the post of commissioner. A "native administration" at the top level of command began to appear only after Hart's retirement. The hard facts of treaty-port life torpedoed many an ideal.

There was more. Hart had to deal not only with foreign prejudices but also with the Chinese social system of personal connections (*kuan-hsi*) and its resulting obligations. By the time Hart had accumulated some decades of experience as a close-to observer of the late Ch'ing bureaucracy, he had evidently concluded that to put a Chinese into a Customs commissionership and expect him to live up to the example set by well-paid foreign commissioners who were necessarily outside the Chinese system of *kuan-hsi* would create a precarious and virtually intolerable personal situation. A Chinese commissioner could hardly escape Chinese-type obligations created by his position of local power. Not to honor such responsibilities would compel him to deny Chinese values of friendship, courtesy, and proper decorum. Even the powerful Li Hung-chang found it politically expedient as Governor General of Chihli to shift his funds for navy building in the 1880s to building the Empress Dowager's summer palace. Hart did not want to put Chinese Commissioners of Customs to the test.

Another cultural impediment to Customs work was the Chinese official's own sense of his proper status and dignity. No self-respecting Ch'ing bureaucrat would, after all, compete for promotion by a foreigner in a foreign-run institution. Only a lowly comprador would do that. At the very beginning, in 1861, Hart had appointed a Chinese to the post of Assistant "at the request of Chung How, the San K'ou [Peiyang] Ta Ch'en; he was three months in the Tientsin Office — and he would not work, so I got him withdrawn." Chinese customs assistants, if they were to be on the career ladder leading to commissionership, would have had to be of the official class, not mere clerks; and Chinese officials of the late nineteenth century could not become foreign hirelings and remain in good standing in their own society. The bind against Chinese qualifying to become commissioners thus operated from both sides.[34]

Nevertheless Hart saw the Customs service as a valuable device for modernizing China. In his Circular no. 8 of June 1864 he offered the opinion that the Inspectorate was the "representative of a civilisation of a progressive kind," and that, as such, it was to serve as a medium for the introduction of those appliances that "the experience of the West has shown to be productive of generally beneficient results." At the same time he warned his foreign Commissioners that "those plans and that action which march in the train of progress, . . . to be both beneficial and successful, must be guided by the good sense that patiently awaits its opportunity, that can suggest without affectation of superiority, that labours to convince rather than dictate to, and that can introduce remedies without causing the irritation that attends the exposure of defects."

The tradition of using Customs personnel for modernizing purposes began with Hart's predecessor, H. N. Lay. According to Prosper Giquel, whose career in the Customs Service commenced at Ningpo in 1861, Lay told each of his foreign inspectors to find a way to become indispensable to the Chinese authorities, and to acquire an influence that could later be used for the progressive reform of China. In a document entitled "Inspectorat étranger des douanes de la Chine," written in mid-1863, Giquel recalled Lay's private remarks on the subject: "China, he told me, has need of the assistance of foreigners to pull itself from the state of disorganization in which it is cast. It is we that must render it [China] this assistance. But as we are just beginning we must hold to our titles, at least officially, of customs inspectors."[35] As we have seen in chapter 1, Hart assiduously followed this tradition himself. From 1864 onward he regularly allowed foreign commissioners and other Chinese-speaking Customs personnel to serve as translators, negotiators, and military advisers for the Chinese. At least some independent Western agents of the Ch'ing government, notably Halliday Macartney, felt that the Customs were "too often given to interfere in matters that do not concern them," but the "interference," if such it was, continued.[36]

Hart's Circular no. 8 of 1864 did, however, remind the foreign Commissioners of Customs that any advice given to their immediate superiors, the Chinese Superintendents of Customs, which put the latter "in either an impolitic, inexpedient, or more especially untenable position," would regrettably lead to dismissal. Another warning was to "avoid antagonism to the merchants" in spite of their "deep-rooted dislike for the Inspectorate." Commissioners should strive by all means to facilitate the merchants' business. They should, however, go slow in getting into non-Customs activities at their ports; they should never interfere in matters at another treaty port, nor try to reduce the pay of or to dismiss foreign staff members, nor leave their port area, nor charter a vessel, and so forth without the I. G.'s approval. Hart finally laid it on the line, though a bit speciously. The I.G., he wrote, "is liable to be dismissed from his post at a moment's notice;" ergo (?), with the I.G. "alone rests the right to employ or dismiss, to promote or degrade, or change from one port to another." In other words, no one else could crack the whip. Hart's logic here is simply that, since he could be dismissed in the bat of an eye, so could his employees.

These concluding threats to the Commissioners portray a distinctly Confucian-minded approach. A man of rare talent (*jen-ts'ai*), given complete personal responsibility (*tse-jen*), seeks to be guided by benevolence (*jen*) and to achieve justice (*i*), meanwhile expecting his subordinates' loyalty (*chung*) and devotion (*hsiao*). There is no idea that the I.G. has the right of appeal through due process concerning his own tenure, nor have his Customs employees concerning theirs. For merchants, meanwhile, who may suffer fines or confiscations, there is originally no specified right or procedure of appeal. In short, Hart had joined Western administrative principles with Confucian ideals of government by the superior man (*chün-tzu*). He now hoped that the Western-style behavior of his well-paid and incorruptible Commissioners and other foreign employees would set a somehow contagious example of public probity.

Partly because of its reputation for honesty and efficiency, the Customs Service suffered relentless criticism from Western merchants in the early years. British consuls and American merchant-consuls, as leaders in treaty-port communities, often joined the foreign merchants in regarding the Foreign Inspectorate as an outrageous attack on their vested interests. Particularly at Shanghai, Hart found it advisable to tread cautiously and kept a low profile. To quote anti-Customs diatribes is scarcely necessary when Hart himself did so well at describing the merchants' complaints. His long "Note on the Introduction and Working of the Foreign Inspectorate of Customs," dated November 1864 at Shanghai, helps to explain the hostility. The document had been requested in June by Hart's sponsor and ally Sir. F. Bruce as British Minister, who had it presented to Parliament as a bluebook, "China no. 1 of 1865."[37] The Parliamentary Papers were the legitimate channel through which a British government could state its case in public policy discussions — in this instance to counter the China traders' attacks on the Foreign Inspectorate.

In his summary Hart covered many bases. He first depicted the pre-Inspectorate taxation of China's foreign trade, then the origin and growth of the Inspectorate, its problems with the old Chinese Customs Administration and with foreign merchants — especially concerning fines and confiscations — and finally its many benefits to all concerned. The essay was most vivid in describing the traditional Chinese method of setting rather low revenue quotas for Customs collectorates, demanding no accounts and leaving any surplus to the collecting official. Canton had for centuries seen such revenue quotas required from the Hoppo, who waxed notoriously rich on the above-quota surplus. This tax-farming by officials, without the element of competitive bidding, brought the Ch'ing government only very modest revenues. Native tariff rates in the coast trade were about 2 to 3 percent at ports of shipment and 7 to 8 percent at destination — say, 10 percent overall. But something like half of the duties nominally due by the old native tariff were dissipated in other directions, into a myriad open hands. They were systematically siphoned off to pay customary but unfixed and of course illegal sums to the merchants, their middlemen, the customs examiners, collectors, accountants, and their superiors through successive levels up to the top officials concerned. Thus every customs transaction was a sequence of personal deals and peculations, not predictable with any certainty. The merchants' competition was to see who could effect the greatest corruption. In modern terms, this was not the best way to run a business or a government.

Moreover, in the old China trade of the first half of the century, foreign merchants at Canton had paid their duties through the licensed guild of hong merchants. When that guild was abolished by the treaties, five licensed linguists took their place as fixers for the foreigner. At the new ports customs business had continued to be handled by the foreign merchants' Chinese staff (comprador, shroff, linguist et al.). For him, said Hart, "the custom-house was practically a nonentity." But now the Foreign Inspectorate dealt with each foreign merchant directly, demanding applications and other documents with signatures and moreover delaying examination of goods and clearance of ships if regulations were not complied with. Fines and confiscations could be levied. The good old days were gone, and "paperasserie" took another unrelenting step toward its envelopment of modern business.[38] In retaliation some old China hands spitefully sent "coolies or boatwomen . . . who handed in . . . illegible scrawls on scraps of white paper." Compradors tried to create a deadlock in hopes of resuscitating "that old state of affairs in which they had been masters."

Formerly, according to Hart, examination of goods had been "a mere farce." Now the smuggler was caught, although his counter-accusations against the Inspectorate might make him seem a martyr. Unfortunately, no provision had been made for public airing and adjudication of cases that led to fines and confiscations, which might therefore seem, and in fact be, arbitrary. The problem had been evident and much discussed for several years. All agreed that a way had to be found to give the foreigner a legal avenue for possible redress of his complaints. Lack of a procedure for redress of grievances was a valid source of treaty-port ire.

So also was the initial inexperience, Hart confessed, of the Customs' newly hired foreign staff members. In competition with the opening of treaty ports in Japan and of more foreign consulates in both China and Japan, competent personnel had been hard to find. But Hart maintained in China no. 1 of 1865 that Customs performance was improving, and he concluded his defense with a considerable list of the benefits his Foreign Inspectorate had brought to foreign trade.[39]

The next defensive step was to arrange for "joint tribunals" to handle merchant appeals against the Customs' seizures and confiscations. As early as 1861 the Shanghai Chamber of Commerce had complained to the British Minister that there should be some adjudication of otherwise arbitrary Customs decisions by a joint tribunal. Lord Elgin in 1862 favored some kind of Mixed Court. On 20 April 1864 the Shanghai Customs Commissioner, Thomas Dick, "quite agreed with me" that Hart should advise his superiors to acquiesce. At Peking Hart found Bruce and the other Ministers all supported the joint-tribunal idea.

Still the matter hung fire because Hart could not be sure that the Tsungli Yamen would agree to Chinese administrative actions by the Customs being brought under review and possibly reversed by foreign consuls acting on behalf of foreign merchants. This kind of review seemed demeaning. (One is reminded of the guilty-till-proved-innocent attitude of Chinese police officers who even today say to an arrested person,"We would not have brought you here if you were not guilty.") The nub of the problem was how to avoid a situation where Harry Parkes and other British consuls on behalf of the foreign merchants might dominate the procedure and perhaps unduly countermand the carefully weighed Customs decisions. Sir Frederick Bruce in June 1864 thought that "the tribunal shd. consist of the Taoutae [i.e., superintendent of customs] and the consul" with the commissioner sitting in to assist the former. Finally Hart submitted to the Yamen on 20 July 1864 "four regulations which are to form the basis of the tribunal for the public investigation of confiscation cases."[40]

The first of these regulations provided that, if a vessel or goods were seized at any Chinese port, the matter was to be reported immediately to the Chinese superintendent, who would then direct the foreign commissioner to inform the persons concerned about the reasons for the seizure, and that confiscation would occur on a certain date unless the appropriate foreign consul informed the commissioner that he wished to investigate the matter. Shipowners and merchants could appeal directly to the commissioner, and if the superintendent refused to release the ship or goods, the accused could then appeal to the consul.

The second rule stipulated that courts of investigation in confiscation cases were to be held at the customs house, that the superintendent of customs, as the principle official concerned, was to invite the consul to take a seat on the bench as counsel for the accused, and that the foreign commissioner was to be present to assist the superintendent. The third rule required that a detailed account of the proceedings be signed by both the superintendent and the consul; if the consul disagreed with the superintendent's decision in the matter, appeals could be made to Peking after copies of the proceedings had been forwarded to both the Tsungli Yamen and the appropriate foreign minister. The fourth rule stipulated that the accused could obtain release of the vessel or goods during the appeal process after paying a bond, to be sealed by the consul and deposited with the superintendent.

These regulations were approved by the Tsungli Yamen and sanctioned by both the British Minister and his American counterpart (whose countries accounted for about 90 percent of all foreign trade in China at the time). In a despatch of 23 July 1864 to the Shanghai Commissioner, the I.G. directed that these four regulations be put into force experimentally at Shanghai. They were not at that time sent to all ports in a circular. Their merit was that they would provide a way of publicly establishing the evidential facts of a case, which could be documented and reported to Peking for settlement by negotiation at the diplomatic level between minister and Yamen.

So what was the outcome of this venture into Sino-foreign quasi-judicial cooperation? Until the Joint Investigation Rules were revised in 1868 the joint tribunal remained stillborn. According to Stanley Wright and the Customs archives, not a single confiscation case at Shanghai under these 1864 rules was ever referred to a joint court. The reason, Wright asserts, was that the individuals concerned, rather than appear in a Chinese court and submit to Chinese jurisdiction, "preferred to let things go by the board, or, if need be, demand settlement by the old method of appealing direct to their Consul to have the matter either arranged by him or by the higher authorities at Peking."[41] Even after revision in 1868, the joint tribunal rules had little actual effect. H. B. Morse indicates, for example, that, at the outset, "many judgments, and all those involving any important principle, were dissented from." He does acknowledge, however, that even in these cases "the higher authorities, including the Inspector-General, had the inestimable advantage of no longer having only *ex-parte* statements to rely upon."[42] In the words of the American Minister, Anson Burlingame, the system assured that "the evidence coming up to us will have been agreed to by both sides, and so arranged as to make a decision by us practicable."[43]

This joint-tribunal venture was part of a general effort in the 1860s to create legal institutions to handle Sino-foreign disputes. Another example of the trend was the setting up in May 1864 of a Mixed Court at Shanghai to handle Sino-Western civil and criminal cases.[44] A similar development was the establishment at Shanghai in March 1865 of the British Supreme Court for China and Japan, which removed from the British consul all his previous civil and criminal legal jurisdiction over British subjects in China. In this context the British government in London in January 1866 approved Hart's four Joint Investigation Rules at Shanghai; and in 1867 the Yamen agreed to extend them to all treaty ports. When they were revised in 1868 they were expanded into eight articles to deal with fines as well as confiscations.

For our purposes here—to cast light on Hart's journal from 1863 to 1866—it is enough to note the rising pitch of treaty-port aggressiveness toward China. Anglo-American diplomatic efforts to spread the rule of law over Sino-foreign trade could not keep up with Western enterprise or hold back the foreign merchants' expansion into China's domestic trade. By 1869, unfortunately, the British trading interest in London would secure the rejection of the more egalitarian-minded Alcock Convention of 1867, which had been negotiated in good faith at Peking over many months. Sino-foreign amity was by that time on a downward course.

Between the Tsungli Yamen ministers, the Customs Commissioners and staff and the treaty-port foreign public, Hart had his hands full. His contacts in the summer of 1864, judging by his journal, were all connected with business. They vibrated between the two nodes of the elder statesman of the Tsungli Yamen, Wen-hsiang, and the heads of the British Legation, Bruce or Wade. A polite but astute young man of quick intelligence could perform a vitally needed function as a go-between. On one day he might have extensive conversations in succession with the Russian, French, British, and American Ministers to China. On the next day for five hours he might give Wen-hsiang a much appreciated briefing on China's foreign problems. Already Hart was the man in the middle. British consular despatches for him to read over and discuss piled up on Bruce's desk marked "Wait for Hart." As Chargé in Bruce's absence, Wade seemed frequently at a loose end and rather gloomy; he would often drop in and spend the evening till Hart walked him back to British territory.

While this busy official contact occupied most of the time away from his standing desk, Hart's journal also shows the intensity of his Wesleyan conscience and its concerns about his conduct. From the first pages of his journal emerges a theme that is continually repeated — the struggle between moral duty and sinful lust or, as contrasted by Hart, between God and womanizing. How far the tension between the spiritual and the carnal aspects of behavior was the secret of the Victorians' high level of public performance (or of their psychological quirks and breakdowns) we need not decide. This is a story of a life in China, where the first datum of sexual mores, in the absence of a Western doctrine of original sin, probably was that an orgasm was good if you could get it. Young Hart, however, had brought his own culture with him. In his world, the incompatibility between sex and godliness accentuated the danger of spiritual damnation. Hart confides to his journal on 9 March 1864: "My last six months have not been gone through without much struggle: my besetting sin, 'womanizing,' has worried me day after day. . . . Last night, I had an awful battle: the imagination had to be put down — it was put down." But, he adds, "what an awful thing it would be after all to be found among those who say 'Lord, Lord' but to whom it shall be said, 'I never knew you!'"

This theme is illustrated by what we may call the "episode of the girls next door." After Hart at age 30 arrived in Peking on 1 June 1864 for his annual sessions with his superiors at the Tsungli Yamen, the woman question reappeared on 9 July in the person of two young Chinese ladies of the household next door, daughters of a retired Ch'ing official. "I caught them peeping over the wall and then had a jaw." On 23 July Hart felt he was maturing and losing interest in sex but later he added a marginal note: "O! my eye! Just look at what you say on the 13th and 26th August!" On 27 July he concludes his journal, "A jaw with Miss Le over the wall tonight: what teeth!"

Mr. Li, the retired red-button mandarin next door was over 70; his first wife having died he had three others in their thirties from Canton, Szechwan, and Hunan plus a fourth just arrived aged 16 or 17 and kept indoors. The two daughters by his first wife were 16 and 18; they could read and write and were out for fun.

On 6 August a Yamen minister in connection with Hart's impending receipt of Chinese rank raised the question of Hart's establishing a family. It is plain that acceptance of a Ch'ing official post and a Chinese wife would anchor the foreigner more firmly in the Chinese scheme of things. We may speculate that for the I.G. to accept an arrangement with an educated daughter of his mandarin neighbor Mr. Li may even have been encouraged behind the scenes by Hart's friends in the Yamen. In any case, Hart comments: "The temptation to get a concubine is very strong." He adds, it is "more than a year since I even 'touched' a woman." On 6 August he reports: "Had another talk with one of my fair neighbors over the wall this evening; one of them age 36 asks me to make her Kan-new-erh [an adopted daughter] and another, an elderly undersized rabit-toothed, Hoonan hag, would like to follow me all the world over." 9 August: "Another chat with my fair neighbors," when one of them gave him a scent purse and "threw off much previous shyness."

On the morning of 14 August Hart wrote one of his longest journal entries — on the veracity of the scriptures, the divinity of Jesus, and the moral worth of intention to do right versus that of actual conduct. Putting this long disquisition under date of 13 August, he confessed the next day that it "was actually written this morning: the train of thought had its origin in a moonlight talk I had last night with the ladies next door. Not that we talked either religion or philosophy, but that we pressed each others hands, and that they allowed advances to be made which, in the case of Chinese ladies who are taught not to be familiar with males, shows that they could easily be induced to go the 'whole hog.' They set my blood on fire." Hart wonders whether he is forcing himself to "abstain from what is wrong, or . . . trying to enshroud myself in a cold philosophical discussion of morals which can go hand in hand with immorality."

An only moderately suspicious reader can take this episode as "the attempted seduction of the I.G." But if so, Hart proved surprisingly resistant. He had definitely put behind him a five-year liaison with Ayaou and their three children. He records the hard facts: "I am mad upon the pleasures of the couch. . . . I like to have a girl in the room with me, to fondle when I please." For other indulgences or pleasures "I care nothing; but for women, what wd. I not give." Yet Hart's resolve to be righteous appears equally firm. *"For a whole year,* I have *on principle* abstained from womanizing. I have hardened myself against the temptation. . . day after day passion has implored to be allowed to gratify itself, while principle has set its teeth and with a 'stiff upper lip' has day after day said 'no you don't.'"

This "desperate struggle," Hart says, is a close fight. "Here at last I find passion 'taking the bit between its teeth' and I'm almost off." 17

August: "crossed the wall this evening . . . moonlight chat with Le Tsaey Tseang [the girls' father]. Paid my devoirs to the girls" and got back after 1:30 a.m. Hart's night life took its minor toll. When the French Minister called the next morning, the I.G. was still asleep.

The force of virtue, however, did not give up. 20 August: "Had another 'delicious' fight with myself tonight." He knew the girls were out in their courtyard but he did not go over to see them. "This war of passion and principle is horrible." 21 August: "I wonder what St. Paul's 'thorn of flesh' was? I know what mine is. . . . Seven devils, in fact, come back to take up their station in the quarters from which one has been expelled. Matrimony is the only thing for it. . . . Truly the fates are unkind: or, am I going through a course of mental and moral training, which is fitting for something in the future?

This drama of the girls next door is soon concluded in Hart's journal; no earth-shaking climax. 22 August: Mr. Li's second wife arranges for the girls to come out at 11 p.m., but Hart keeps away.[45] The devils had met their match. For the next 45 years the I.G. would grow increasingly famous for his self-control in all circumstances.

CHAPTER FOUR

Journal

1 JUNE 1864: Left Hosewoo at 4 a.m.; arrived at Chang Kea Wan at 10: started at 12, and arrived at the Kowlan Hootung in Peking at 6 in the evening. The day very hot, and the roads exceptionally dusty. Leang had arrived two hours before with the luggage. Met Fitzpatrick and another priest saying "good-bye" to Brett as I entered. Brett has grown very tall, and is as nice a youngster as ever. Sent my card at once to the Yamun to report my arrival, and say I shd. call on the following day. Ching lin's came in return. When entering the city, we were stopped at both gates and had to produce our passports before entering.[1]

2 JUNE 1864: At 11 the cards of the Tsungpan [secretaries-general] came asking me to go early to the Yamun, as the Prince who would be there early would receive me. Went immediately afterwards; had a few minutes' talk with Ching and Tsae, when Wänseang, Hangke, Tsung lun, and Tung hsun came in. They shook hands with me—Wan Seang never did so before, and received me in the pleasantest and most friendly way. We had only talked five minutes, when the Prince arrived; he went at once to the Whating [conference room], and we were called there to see him. H.M. recd me very kindly, and we talked in a very friendly way for an hour. He told me to set my mind entirely at rest—that I was not to be blamed in any way for what had occurred, and that he was only sorry he had ever taken the affair of the fleet out of my hands. He asked about the amount of duties, about Le Footae & Gordon. The Prussian Minister then arrived, Baron de Rehfues; I took my leave of the Prince and with Häng & Tsung, went to the rooms I used to live in, in 1862, and talked till 3, when Wan Seang came in, having got through with the business that brought the Prussian Minister to the Yamun. He told me that when the Minister came up to Peking, he said that he had not power to interfere in the affair of the seizure of the Danish vessels by the Prussian frigate at Taku; the Prince, therefore, declined to receive him. The Baron then wrote to say that he cd. and would act, on which the Prince appointed a day for an interview. At the interview, the matter was discussed—the Prince holding that the Gulf of Pechele was a <u>mare</u> <u>clausum</u>, supporting his view by the fact that it is on all sides bounded by Chinese territory and that at the mouth (180 le in width) <u>90</u> le are under charge of the Shin King military and the other <u>90</u> under Shantung. The Baron eventually

sd he would settle the affair in a few days. The Prince will not return his visit until the point is settled. I understand the British and the U.S. Ministers, though they refrain from interfering, are of the opinion that the Prince is right. I hope he will carry his point, as it will bring China more and more into contact with, and make it respected (as standing up for its rights and able to get them) by the world.[2]

Wän Seang talked about all sorts of things with me for an hour or two. He cd. not have spoken more kindly, or done more to make me feel at ease.

I then called on Sir. F. Bruce, who received me kindly. He wants the "Elfin" returned spontaneously, and wishes the joint tribunal question to be settled before he goes away — which will be in 10 or 12 days time.[3] He translated and sent a copy of Lay's letter to Lord Russell to WänSeang, with whom he talks about the "Lay school" and the "Hart school". He wanted me to stop for dinner, and told me to call soon on Mr. Burlingame.

3 JUNE 1864: Went to the Yamun at 11: and remained there till after 6: talked about all manner of things, and gave Wan Seang my letter to Le Footae, relative to Gordon's force, to read. He got a copy of it for the Prince, and I think they will act on my suggestions. I mentioned Gordon's commission to get him a couple of Tetuh's [provincial commander-in-chiefs] dress: they snapped at the idea at once, and WanSeang said he wd. get it sent to him by an Imperial Decree: they will also send him a medal (& Moffitt) through the British Minister, through whom they will request the English Govt. to do something for Gordon.[4]

A note just recd. from TsungHow has set the Yamun in a flutter, as he says Alisch had written to him to say that he was about to sell the Danish vessel. T. H. [Tsung How?] wrote to all the other consuls protesting the sale.[5]

4 JUNE 1864: To the Yamun at 12: sat till 3, chiefly occupied with Hsieh who has been appointed [characters for pan-li; "to manage"] the Portuguese Treaty — not to hoo hwan [exchange views]. He is in an awful funk about the matter. I gave him some hints on the way to go to work if he wished to alter the treaty: but I said "It's no concern of mine: if you wish Macao to be considered Chinese territory, the Treaty requires alteration; if you wish it to be looked on as Portuguese, the treaty can stand as it is. All I have to say is that in its present condition, without any Custom's estab. in it, Macao harms the Canton revenue. If you wish to aid the Canton revenue, you must establish an office at Macao: and to establish an office there, you will probably find it necessary to state clearly that Macao is still Chinese territory." I don't wish to be mixed up in this affair atall, but I spoke too frequently about the matter in 1861 & 1862, to escape the reference that they now make to me.[6]

Went at 3 1/2 to call on Sir F. Bruce, who 1. said that there could be no deduction now from the Quarterly Indemnity funds on the steamer a/c, and that it was unnecessary, for Osborn had written out that he had all but arranged for their sale, and that Wade wd. be certain to bring definite instructions, or intelligence, 2. with regard to Siamen duties, he said <u>he</u> wd. not start the questions — so they need not be looked on as liable to the Indemnity deductions, 3. I told him from Wan Seang that the "joint tribunal" may be regarded as conceded, & that the details will be discussed and arranged by & by.[7]

I then called on Watters & Brown: and then on Mrs. and Mr. Burlingame. Mr. B. talked in his usual inflated style: says 1. the "Elfin" ought in equity to be returned, 2. that the "Emma" case ought to be reconsidered, that 3. the "Hukwang" case does not call for compensation, and that 4. he had appointed Mr. Seward to enquire into charges against Mr. Breck, whom he will (if the charges are proved) suspend.[8]

5 JUNE 1864: To the Yamun at 11 and back at 6. Talked about all sorts of matters. We have not got properly to business yet. There is a great deal of talk about in a general way, before we settle down to details. But everything goes on so pleasantly, that I feel jolly and quite at my ease. The house in the Hootung is to be retained, and I may put as many students in it as I like. Gave WanSeang a copy of Aesop's fables today, with which he was much amused. Some of the irons I put in the fire in '61, are becoming workable: in future, as vacancies occur at the Treaty Ports, the Taoutaeships will be filled up from the Sze-kwan [lower officials] of the Yamun, and the Sze-kwan may in it look forward to become Tang Kwan [high officials].[9]

Saw the monthly examination papers for the boys who are learning English and French; some of them give signs of getting on.[10]

6 JUNE 1864: Breakfasted today with Hang-ke: present
the English Minister, 2nd secretary, & Brown & Murray:
'' Russian   ''   , with 1st & 2nd secretaries;
'' French   ''   , with Fontanier
'' American   '' ,   '' Dr. Williams, and old Tsung lun.
Hengke gave us a wonderfully fine entertainment: his house is most tastefully fitted up. He brought out to show us with great glee his little son aged 3 and daughter aged 2. Mrs. Burlingame and Mrs. Williams were guests of Hengke's ladies. Got back at half past 2.[11]

7 JUNE 1864: Wrote up my a/c this morning, and went to the office at noon. WanSeang, Hangke, Tsung lun, Hsieh, and Tung were there. Did no particular work but talked of things in general, until six o'clock.

8 JUNE 1864: Brown breakfasted with us. [characters for the 5th day of the 5th month] holiday.[12]

9 JUNE 1864: Went to the office at one o'clock. Talked chiefly with Wan & Hsieh though the other three came in afterwards. The talk chiefly referred to Macao. I said that if they exchanged treaty ratifications, allowing them to stand as they are at present, they would never again have an opportunity of making alterations; at the same time, the present did not present an opportunity in every respect favourable to making the change, inasmuch as, not only wd. the Portuguese Minister object to the change proposed, but the French, who had so much to do originally with the drawing up of the Treaty, wd. in all likelihood come forward in the matter, and, if not successful in inducing the Chinese to agree to the ratification, wd feel "huffed", and by pushing forward some of their unsettled claims, place the Chinese in great straits. The question, therefore, was whether or not it wd. be advisable for a small gain to risk a great misunderstanding. Supposing the Portuguese yielded everything, the only gain wd. be in the possible good effect it might have on the Canton revenue, and the satisfaction of having it granted at Gaou-mun.[13] Now the gain to the revenue might be secured equally well by stipulating distinctly for the appointment of such an official to reside at Macao who shd. have full control over Chinese vessels coming & going: it is not necessary that he shd. collect duties, or that any reference shd. be made to the territorial question. But in the event of the Chinese receding from their demand that the place be distinctly stated to be Chinese, and contenting themselves with the appointment of an officer of the kind referred to, the Portuguese must on the other hand consent to do away with every phrase or expression contained in the wording of the treaty giving rise to the inference that Macao is Portuguese territory. I advised them to add a clause to the second article to the effect that "Macao being Chinese territory ought not to be without a resident official, but that the Portuguese having lived there long shd. be allowed to continue to rule themselves without any interference." or to do away with the second article altogether, and at the top of that one referring to the treaty ports place "in addition to continuing to reside at Macao, Portuguese shall be allowed to trade at so & so".

The Portuguese Minister has prepared a draft of a despatch to the Chinese asking them for a high officer to Shang-leang pan-le [discuss and manage things], and he makes a curiously vaguely worded general reference to trading at the ports west of Macao, which WanSeang suspects to have for its object an exchange:[14] that is the Portuguese take high ground and say or prepare to say, "if you leave Macao as it is, we will say nothing more about the places to the west". I tell Hsieh to go along quietly and carefully, and, if possible, to lead on the Portuguese Minister to be the first to propose additions or alterations. I tell him, in conclusion, however, that the responsibility rests with himself and that he must balance clearly all the pros and cons.

I alluded to the case of the "Elfin" and "Emma", and said that I thought the punishment too heavy in each case. Wan says he does not object to a revision of the "Emma" decision, but the "Elfin" cannot easily be reconsidered, inasmuch as Shin Footae has twice memorialized on the expense of her keep. I told WanSeang that at the time the Chinese are standing out for their rights vis à vis the Prussians and Portuguese, it might be as well for them in the case of the English and the Americans to let it be seen that they are ready to take into consideration those features of the cases referred to, which make in favor of the merchants. The "Scotland", they tell me, was released, inasmuch as the English Minister begged that it might so be done, the English Consul having been the person from whom the Customs' authorities at Canton had been made aware of the "Scotland's" doings.[15]

I left the Fleet a/c at the office, where I am to go through them, with Tsae and a couple of others, on Saturday. Wan seems in a fix about the additional sums paid to Lay; he looked a little surprised when I told him that I only paid away Tls. 2000 more than the Yamun had authorized. I must put it this way to them: "not only have I exceeded your grant by Tls. 2000 (half of the sum really due on a/c of rent) but I have saved you some Tls 60 000 which he cd. & wd. otherwise have charged as commission."

Today I saw a quantity of the clothing intended for Gordon: they are going to give him four sets of a Tetuh's uniform.

With reference to Lynne — the Legation soldier that was murdered — Wän is anxious to know whether or not a money compensation wd. be taken as a set off against the nonpunishment of the murderers. He is curious, too, to know why Sir F. wishes to see him alone tomorrow.

Wonderfully cool pleasant day: thunderstorm last night & rain.

10 JUNE 1864: WanSeang having to go today to call on Sir. F. Bruce, and Hsieh being engaged with his preparations for proceeding to Teentsin, I did not go to the office. Instead, I called on the French, Russian, and U.S. Ministers. Mr. Berthemy said he could not make the T. L. Yamun understand that I only wanted a Bond in the case of Remi Schmidt's shot, that they always seemed to think he meant to say I have levied a fine, that the Yamun had backed my action by every conceivable kind of argument, and that he had finally dropped the matter. He said that his great difficulty was with the R.C. [Roman Catholic] Missions in the interior, — that with the missionaries at the ports there was no trouble, — but that with those in the back provinces the difficulties were of continual occurrence. He did not consider them always in the right, he said; at the same time, knowing the power of the clerical party in France and in view of what that party had forced the Emperor to do in Syria (M. Berthemy was then in the French F.O.) he had to be very cautious in refraining from taking up their cause, and in carrying out the missionary views. He therefore wished the Chinese authorities to act with him in friendly cooperation for the adjustment of all such questions. He expressed himself well pleased with all that had been done in KweiChow since Laou Tsung kwang had been appointed Yun-kwei

tsung-tuh [Governor General of Yun-Kwei], and he said that once they apprehended T'seen Tetuh (he cd. not do so sooner), he wd. move his govt. to let the affair drop. He also referred to the joint tribunal, and said that he had been the first to propose it, but that the Chinese had addressed him a very strongly worded reply, stating that he was trying to take away their keuen [authority]: his proposition was that, after examination, a third party—a consul—shd. be called in to decide debated points. I informed him that the matter had been at length settled, and promised to get a despatch written to him of a kind similar to the one addressed to the English & U.S. Ministers.[16]

At the Russian Legation, I talked for about half an hour with Mr. Vangali [sic]; he spoke in French, I in English. Our talk was of a general kind; he however referred to the French Missionary question, and remarked that it was fortunate for the Chinese the French representative was so little of a fanatic and so well disposed toward the present administration. He asked a question about the Portuguese, and said he supposed the Macao question was a difficulty that still remained to be got over.

I then called on Mr. Burlingame, who talked a great deal about affairs generally; he read one draft of a despatch he is now writing to the Consuls, which will be a most important document, as it gives his views, supported by scattered decisions, on a great many questions that are not well understood except at Peking. He also told me about the way it came to pass that Lay was dismissed and myself appointed, and said that not only had I the confidence and good will of the Chinese, but the support of all the foreign ministers, who approved of my style of acting, and wished "logic" to triumph and not force. He has a curious way to talking about the "poetry," meaning the details, of any occurrence.

I then called at the British Legation, and had a few minutes talk with Sir. F. I also saw Brown, Saurin, Walker, Solby and Allen. St. John gave me some papers to read,—despatches from Consuls—on which Sir. F. has marked "wait for Hart."[17]

11 JUNE 1864: Went to the office at 10; compared the translation of Osborn's a/c; and at 2 WanSeang came in with whom I talked till near seven o'clock. I told him what the French and Russian Ministers had yesterday said, and he was not atall slow to allow that the present representation [sic] of France was a great improvement on his predecessor. He is, however, very wroth with the Roman Catholic missionaries throughout the interior, and, I believe, justly so. They do not give themselves up to their work wholly, but interfere in various ways with the local officials. Shd. a convert commit a crime, to attempt to arrest him is at once styled "persecution, on account of his faith"; such interference irritates the officials, and causes bad characters to style themselves Christians in order to secure interference on their behalf when they get into trouble. WanSeang says he does not like to meet [and] argue with the Minister until the Kweichow affair shall have been settled;

but that so soon as that is ended, he will then be on equal terms with the Minister, on whom he will call to act with him in putting a stop to the airs given themselves by the Missionaries, and the doings of the soi-disant converts. The original of the French treaty was produced,, and the 11th article of the convention was seen to have, in the original French, no reference whatever to the right of Missionaries to "buy and build" in the interior. Wan-Seang will take advantage of this at some future period, when a fitting opportunity presents itself. The great trouble with him is that he has no French Interpreter, and that he completely distrusts F. [Fontanier].

The question of establishing a Transit Office at Newchwang is one which Wan is anxious to have settled; but he is not provided with such specific information relative to the place as wd. enable him to bring it forward in proper shape.[18]

I told him the way in which Tarrant writes in the "F. of China." He says, the matter must yet be attended to.[19]

He is much afraid Burgevine will again cause trouble, and says that so long as he is in the vicinity of China, he will be unable to set his mind at rest. I tell him, Burgevine or no Buregvine, the Japanese will give him trouble some day or other.[20]

Sir F. is soon to leave, and the Prince is to give him a breakfast; Wan wishes it to be done with all honors, and asks whether all the other Ministers ought to be invited too.

Tsae hinted this morning at Wan Seang's wish to cut down the Customs' grant; I told him that, with the grant, I cd. keep up some cruisers, which without it could not be done: that without cruisers, duties must in some respects fall off. They would not cut down the grant more than Tls 100 000; now with that amount, I can secure Tls. 300 000 to the revenue, — a balance in favour of the govt. of Tls 200 000 which wd. otherwise be lost. We cannot do with less than the following: Canton Tls. 8000; Swatow Tls. 2000; Amoy Tls. 3000; Foochow Tls. 4500; Formosa Tls. 2000; Ningpo Tls. 2000; Shanghae Tls. 13 000; Chinkiang Tls. 2000; Kiukiang Tls. 3000; Hankow Tls. 3000; Chefoo Tls. 2000; Teentsin Tls. 2000; Newchwang Tls. 2000: i.e. monthly Tls. 48 500: yearly, Tls. 582 000 and Tls. 40 000 for Inspectorate General Tls. 630 000, say. The additional amount will keep two or three steam cruisers.

12 JUNE 1864: Went to the office at noon and remained until six. Wän, Tung, Häng, & Tsung were there. Our conversation was rather general than otherwise, and commenced with a talk about religion and morality. Wan says, when he has money enough, he will send a Buddhist Priest to Chueen Keaou [preach] in France![21]

Häng told me that he had seen a Rm Catholic book, in which, in explanation of the text, "Do unto others as you would that others shd. do unto you", the writer said it was the Christian's duty to treat the parents of others as his own parents, their children as his children, and — their wives as his wives! He also said that the book explained how it came to pass that unmarried girls sometimes produced children: these christian maids, sd the writer, are affected by a divine influence which impregnates them; they bring forth, and still remain pure as virgins—just as a bottle of water on a stand on which the sun shines, the glimmer of light comes in one side passes away the other, and leaves bottle and water as it was before—"not the same kind of Ping k'ow [bottle mouth] though!" remarked Tung.[22]

It struck me, it wd. be a good thing in revising the Portuguese and drawing up the Spanish treaty to insert a clause relative to the Missionaries which shall withdraw them from French protection. I imagine the French Minister wd. not be sorry were such to take place; it would save him a good deal of trouble, and wd. do away with the chance of war on a religious difficulty.

Brown dined with me this evening, and stayed until midnight. We had a long and pleasant talk about home. It is quite refreshing to me to have a chat with any one who can talk about the old place.[23]

13 JUNE 1864: [characters for the 10th day of the 5th lunar month] Did not go to the Yamun today; remained at home writing letters. addressed a despatch to Meritens, telling him he must confine himself to Custom's business properly speaking, and not actions outside of the waters of Fuhkeen. Also had a slap at Hughes for saying "he could not be always considering mercantile interests, and would not truckle to them at Amoy as people did in some other ports he could name."[24]

Father Fitzpatrick, called this afternoon from the Pih Tang. He is now Rector of the College there, in which he has forty or fifty boys. He is opposed to any attempt to denationalize the boys, and thinks that the more Chinese priests resemble their own countrymen the better. He says they are quite devoid of gratitude, and that numbers of them become converts from interested motives. He told me that when Laou went to Kweichow, he got on good terms with the Bishop there, and induced him to write up to the Tsung-le Yamun asking that Te'en Tetuh's life might be spared, and the letter arrived at the time M. Berthemy was pushing with all his might for his execution in the name of the French Govt. He said, too, that the pretensions of the French Missionaries were extravagent, and in every way calculated to cause difficulties. He hinted at some great difficulty that the French legation is now in, and then went on to say that as the priests were chiefly Italians and Germans, there was, perhaps, a way out of it: I wonder what the affair can be.[25]

14 JUNE 1864: The weather cool, still wearing cloth clothes.

I remained in the house today, writing a few letters. Sent Dick's "Bonded" despatch to Sir. F. Bruce for perusal, and legal terms in re Customs to Mr. Burlingame.

Tonight had a terrible mental conflict, after reading some portion of

"Westminster Review". "Lord, to whom shall we go? Thou hast the words for Eternal Life!" The moment an evil doubt is entertained, a thousand evil passions spring up clamours for indulgence, and giving to that doubt a ten-fold power. The early days of the other religious faiths are lost in mystery and in distance, and such faiths naturally point and appeal, in support of their authenticity, to something miraculous or mysterious about their commencement and origin. The argument is then directed against Christianity, and the skeptic says: you say these religious faiths are all false, and that the strange stories handed down relative to any unexplainable facts connected with their origin must be without support, or authority, and therefore to be rejected; and he goes on to infer, that inasmuch as there are strange facts connected with the origin of Christianity, therefore Christianity is to be rejected! A strange syllogism certainly, bad enough in itself; but perhaps the best way to meet [it] is, — not to point out its fallacy, so much as, — to insist upon the fact that all we know about Christ has come down to us, not — from a barbarous people, not from an early stage of society, shrouded in doubts and away in the past beyond history, but — from highly civilized people in the very day of their waning [?] greatness, and from a time in which history was daily being written, and literature flourishing. Truly, "if Christ has not risen from the dead, we are, of all men, the most miserable." The only thing to do is to cling to this anchor: without it there is none to hold by.

15 JUNE 1864: Went to the Office about one o'clock. Found the Prince there with the others, waiting for Sir. F. Bruce, whom they had invited to a farewell repast, on the occasion of his speedy return to England. I saw the Prince for a few minutes, but had no particular conversation with him.

After Sir F. went away, I sat with WanSeang and the others until six. He showed me the Edict just issued conferring on Gordon the Hwang Ma-kwa [yellow riding-jacket], and presenting him with Sse-tao E-fuh [four sets of official dress].[26] The Edict is very complimentary, and recounts all the services in which Gordon has been engaged; it gives him full credit for everything he has done, and to foreign eyes will prove a fuller recognition of his services than anything that has ever appeared. They also showed me, for my opinion, the despatch written to Sir. F., in which they ask him to move the British govt. to confer some mark of its approbation on Gordon, stating that he now holds the highest military rank it is possible to confer on anyone. The despatch was well worded, and I did not attempt to correct it.

I handed Wan my suggested article relative to missionaries, for the Portuguese and Spanish Treaties. If they can induce those Govts. to take charge of missionaries who are their subjects, the French may be scared [?] off and the excuse or necessity for their interference be done away with. Wan said that he had the highest respect for any one who was a real convert or a guileless missionary, but that for any one who was not so he has the deepest detestation.

The 1/2 duty on Hankow Teas was referred to, but Hängke again brought forward his stupid account of what used to be done at Canton by importers of Fuhkeen teas, and the affair was not settled.

At the office I found waiting for me a large parcel of letters, &c., just recd. from Teentsin. They came by the "Gund," which vessel passed the "Osprey" with Wade on board at Chefoo. Dick's letters tell me that Parkes and the Foo-tae are on not the best of terms relative to Gordon's force, which has been disbanded; — some letter of his is, however, missing — probably on board the "Osprey", so that I do not know all the details. The Footae does not want Gordon to go to Nanking, and refers to the letter he had promised me he would write. Gordon will, however, go, and Dick has sent for the "Elfin" to take him up. I hope Parkes will not go with him.[27]

One letter from Wm. Furneur [?]; but none from home. A thunder storm this evening.

16 JUNE 1864: Put on white trousers today.

Sir Frederick approves of Dick's Bonded Warehouse Plan.[28] I have also sent H. E. my Investigation Memo, about which, however, he wishes to talk to me, so I shall go down and breakfast with him tomorrow morning.

In the house all day, doing nothing in particular. Wrote a long letter to Dick.

17 JUNE 1864: Breakfasted this morning with Sir. F. Bruce, and afterwards had a long talk with him about various matters.

Joint tribunal. — He thinks the tribunal shd. consist of the Taoutae and the Consul, the Commissioner sitting merely as an assessor or assistant of the former's. In fact, the Taoutae wd. sit to investigate and decide the case: while the Commissioner wd. bring forward the evidence on which he wished the Taoutae to decide: and the Consul wd. "watch proceedings," and cross-question. The Consul ought not to express any opinion as to the proving or not proving of the charge: to ask him to do so wd. be to give up some of the Chinese right of adjudication. Expenses to be borne by the appellant. The great object in view, says Sir F., is to do away with the ad captandum defense now made, that there has been no investigation, and that the merchant has no opportunity of bringing forward extenuating circumstances.[29]

Le Footae. — He wishes me to give him a Memo, which he will quote as information derived from a trustworthy source relative to the actual occurrences at SooChow. He thinks means shd. be devised for publishing in the papers anything done, of a progressive kind, by Le, and seems to consider Le's desire to be spoken well of by the papers as a wholesome sign.

Missionaries. — He will not use his official influence in their behalf as Missionaries; but will give them just such protection as British subjects are entitled to. With me, he thinks that China, if again at war, will be so in consequence of some missionary complication in the interior.

Dynasty. — He tells me WanSeang talked to him in a very confidential way the other day, letting out an anxiety to strengthen the Manchoo, and showing that the Manchoos feel that a war with the foreigner will always endanger them by strengthening the Chinese or native party. This feeling forms an additional safeguard of peace. I remarked that the Manchoo now acquires influence, and gains security by assimilating himself to the Chinese, and that on the other hand the Chinese absorb the authority which wd. otherwise more properly belong to the dynasty: in course of time, the assimilation and absorption process will make the ruling family a popular one.[30]

"Elfin"—The only way seemingly to meet Sir F.'s views is to resell her at a nominal price to the original owners. In that way, we shall be able to put on a heavy fine, and save our own 'faces', seeing that we pronounced her confiscated more than a year ago.

After leaving Sir. F., at one o'clock, I went to the Yamun, where I talked with Wan and the others till six. Häng was particularly friendly; is going to give me a mule, and also a "bloke". Wan talked generally; he fears Wade will make work, and cause trouble; and he enlarges on the number of cases which, brought before the ministers at the suggestion of local authorities, remain unredressed. I talked to him about WänChow; he agreed with me that for officials at non-treaty places to charter foreign vessels, is objectionable; and he seemed to think that if the Wän Chow people wished to have the place opened, and Le Footae backed the request, there wd. be no difficulty. About WanChow, in my opinion, there need be no hurry.[31] I read through the NewChwang statement, and arranged that the matter shd. lie over for me to enquire into in September, when I hope to visit that port.

Hänke gave me a curious proverb, or saying today. "Kih Keaou, tsue heur" "to put on the boot after cutting off the foot", corresponding to our "to shut the door when the horse is stolen".[32] He brought it out apropos of Kleczkowski's argument for giving Macao to the Portuguese: "Hongkong is as a center of smuggling more formidable than Macao; why then attempt at Macao what you didn't do at Hongkong. Better place Macao in the same position as H'Kong, i.e. make it a foreign place where you cannot establish a Customs' office, and then adopt at Hongkong the measures which you may find it possible [?] to carry into effect at Macao." He talked to me as if I were a child, sd. Häng.

A curious report is going about the city to the effect that foreigners buy children to eat them, and use their eyes in compounding photographic drugs. It seems that some kind of kidnapping is going on, as children have been disappearing. Tsung lun was talking about a man able to practise some kind of seang-fu [?] which enables him to force his K'e [life-force] to any part of his body, except the bridge of his nose, thereby making the part in question insensible to pain, &c. Some men charged with kidnapping have been arrested, and people say they give the children [indistinct word] by them as food [?] some kind of Hwang-leu-tang to drink.[33]

Brett awfully sleepy this evening after dinner.

Wade arrived.

18 JUNE 1864: In the house all day writing letters and despatches.

19 JUNE 1864: Brown came up from the legation this morning, with a quiet pony which he has succeeded in getting for me. He tells me the Rev. W. Barnes, the Amoy missionary, who dresses in Chinese style, and who has been so much in the interior, has been pestering Sir. F. with claims and petitions to own land in the interior, basing his demands on the English version, translated from the Chinese, of the VIth article of the French convention of 1860. W. B. was tremendously taken aback, when the French — original — version was shown to him. No wonder! seeing that it does <u>not</u> give the right to own land in the interior.[34]

Hanke sent for me at 3; I went and found he wanted to introduce me to the man he and Tsung Lun recommend as a writer. He is aged, 62; has been some 20 years in office as Chihëen in Keangse; and he is now a How-poo-taou [expectant taotai].[35] I shd. much rather get a man who had not been an official, but I suppose I must make the best of what comes to hand. The old gentleman cannot be badly off for money, for he keeps a small cart and a mounted servant.

20 JUNE 1864: Went to the British Legation at 11 by Sir. F.'s request: found that the mail had just arrived, and that the China debate had come off — Mr. Layard replied to Mr. Liddell's motion chiefly by quotations from Mr. Burlingame's despatches; and the affair ended in a 'count out'.[36] Burgevine is back again in China, and is squatting somewhere near Ningpo; won't the Yamun be in a flutter? They'll be sorry now, they did not take my advice as to the folly of acting precipitously.[37] Sir F. wishes me to write out a Memo. for him on the Foreign Inspectorate, showing:

1.° what the Chinese idea of administration of revenue was before,

2.° the difficulties thereby put in the way of the Inspectorate,

3.° the growth of the inspectorate,

4.° the fact that with treaties, and more especially treaties of such a kind, such an inspectorate was a necessary supplement; that the Chinese wd. of themselves have failed to understand and carry out Treaty stipulations.

5.° that though the effect has been great financial benefit to the country, the attempt has been to make the Chinese learn and understand their duties under treaties, in that way prevent trouble, and cause them gradually to learn and understand their own business.

6.° that during the run of the inspectorate, ameliorations have been made: Yangtsze Regls., Bean Cake, Formosa, Canton Steamers, Drawbacks, or Exn. certificates, intimacy with officials, and generally to show how the system has been useful rather than otherwise to all parties.[38]

H. E. also wishes it impressed on the Chinese Govt. that they must try to act as to command and retain the moral support of England, and to let them know that they must commence to act for themselves. More especially on the Yangtsze, where the French have just proposed a conjoint system of search and protectorate.

Bade Sir F. good bye, who "wished me every success."

Called on Mr. Burlingame who was drafting a reply to Mr. Berthemy's letter, objecting to conjoint action in search, &c. on the Yangtsze. He also read me his circular to the Consuls: he is, I think, wrong in one point—he says the Chinese Govt. cannot in any way sue an American in a Consular Court. He is very anxious about Ward's affairs, and does not know how to get them settled. He will write again about the "Anna"; but I fear the news of Burgevine's return will hurt his advocacy of the steamer's case.[39]

Saw Mr. Wade, who looks much improved. Also met the Russian Minister, at both the British and U.S. Legations.

The writer, Ping Laou Yay, called today at 3: I wish much he had never been a Laou Yay.[40]

Put on light summer clothes today.

I sounded the Chief as to the possibility of taking advantage of the arrival of Portuguese and Spanish Minister to have clauses put in their Treaties on the missionary question. He did not seem to like to say anything, but he continually remarked that in any new treaty the Chinese might try to make a specific arrangement commencing it with a preamble: "When Missionaries have been found to interfere in local matters to the detriment of order, &c., it is agreed that while they should be allowed to go into the interior, they must do so as private persons, and shall not interfere with the local action of the officials &c."

TUESDAY, 21 JUNE 1864: Up before 4: beautiful morning: air cool and pleasant: no wonder the Emperor holds his court at daylight.

Got through my first draft of circular to commissioners, on their position and duties, and pointing out the principles by which they shd. be guided, &c.: I think it will be useful, and will be welcomed by most, if not all of them.[41]

Mail arrived: a note from Lay telling me all the ships had reached England and that the Govt. wd. probably buy them all. His supplementary a/c will arrive in a month or so.

Note from Brazier congratulating me. No letters from home yet, strange to say. My last letters were dated 18th Feb.!

Emma S. sent me her likeness: dear little girl.

Wade called yesterday evening: he sd. he did not wonder that Lay had come to grief, and that it must be attributed to the absurd position he took up, forgetting he was a subordinate, and attempting to dictate, and that too in a bad-tempered way. He does not approve of an attempt to introduce such a clause as I was thinking of about missionaries in the Spanish treaty: the Roman Catholic world wd. be savage, and the French, 'the eldest son of the Church,' wd. look upon it as a bad sign. He thinks, though, that a circular despatch, temperately written, to all the Ministers might be productive of good results. He agrees with me that my quiet way of dealing with the Chinese, though slow, is in the end likely to be sure; he evidently regards Lay as superior to me in vigor and elasticity [?] which he no doubt is.

Danish depart at Düppal.[42] Note from Seward; awfully disgusted at Burgevine's reappearance. Dick writes that he has had to discharge Sun senior. Gordon gone to Nanking. Long and interesting letter from Maxwell.[43] Cholera at S'hae. Man rather seedy.

Edkins called: savage with Sir F. for allowing Romish [?] misconduct to influence him in his attitude toward Protestant missionaries. The Rmn. Catholic converts, it seems, are exempted from having to contribute to idolatrous festivals, &c.: he thinks Protestants ought to have the same privilege. Missionary question a very difficult one.[44]

WEDNESDAY, 22 JUNE 1864: Up again at 4. At 11 1/2 went to the office having been sent for by WanSeang. I found him and all the others in the best of good tempers, and had a very pleasant business talk for three or four hours. They first showed me the Portuguese Minister's despatch to Hsieh, enclosing a protest, addressed to the Tsung Le Yamun, against the non-ratification of the Treaty: he bases his protest on the allegation that the Treaty having in point of fact been made in Peking, and with the knowledge of the Yamun, cannot be said to contain anything that had not been fully agreed to, and further that, no notice having been given by the Chinese of intention to reopen negotiations, it is too late now to talk of non-ratification. Somewhat amusingly he says "How can I have the presumption to alter that which the King has agreed to? Ratify the Treaty, however, and as I have full powers, we can make changes, &c. afterwards." He thus 1. admits that he has the power to make changes, and 2. does not see how absurd it is to say that he would not presume to change what one sovereign had agreed to do, in the face of the statement that follows to the effect that he wd. not hesitate to make changes after both had agreed to it. He of course wd. like to have the ratifications exchanged, and then tell the Chinese to whistle for changes. A despatch in reply was written in which they pointed out that last year when acknowledging the receipt of his despatch announcing his arrival in China, the Prince wrote to say that the Treaty wd. not be ratified. He threatens to return to Macao. The first part of Hsieh's reply was good; but the end was bad, — it rebuked him for attributed motives, and asked him did he not think the great Emperor's commands of importance? The conclusion was in the worst style of a pig-headed anti-foreigner: but no one, save a pig-headed man like Hsieh, with his experience with foreigners, wd. have written such an asinine despatch.

Three despatches left behind him, to be forwarded after he had started, written by the Prussian Minister, were then shewn to me. One about one of the ships seized last year at Wän Chow—stating that she put in there through stress of weather, and disposed of some cargo in order to make repairs, and quoting a garbled extract from the 31st article of the Treaty; a second relative to a claim against some Chinese who were partners with a Prussian in the charter of 2 steamers to convoy wood junks; and the third calling for punishment &c. of wreckers on Formosa. These despatches are evidently intended to <u>meet</u> the Chinese demands in the 'Danish seizure case'. The Minister says "Look here! what a number of unredressed grievances I have to call to your attention!" They said they would not answer him, as they had not recognized him as Kin Chae [imperial commissioner; i.e. resident minister]. I advised them to tell the Comr Le Footae to write to the Prussian Consul General. The despatches were very lame, and we all had a good laugh at them.[45]

I then let them know that Burgevine had returned.

Wan Seang at once became furious; asked what sort of <u>Kin chae</u> Mr. Burlingame was — had he not the power to send him [Burgevine] to his own country in the first instance? He said that it was on Mr. B's assurance that he wd. not return to China, that the Yamun had memorialized to the effect that he might be let off at the time after Le Footae and others had pressed for his execution: that if B. caused any trouble now, they must look to the U.S. Govt. for damages, and that he, <u>W.</u>, would have them. They think Mr. B. has treated them very badly, and indeed it <u>is</u> scandalous that he shd. not have taken the proper precautions to guard against the man's return: what was the use of sending him to Japan? It merely enabled him to recruit his health, and bide his time.

Came away at 5: dined alone, and had a good read afterwards.

My cook arrived today from S'hae; he was seized at the City Gate and brought to the Yamun. I got him away in time to cook my dinner, which I had the satisfaction of finding wonderfully better than anything the Peking chef cd. turn out.

23 JUNE 1864: Up again at 4. WänSeang came and called on me at half past eight. He sat for an hour, and let out that he had no high opinion of Hsieh, & that Häng had not proved of much use in 1860. He sd. he wished he had known as much of foreigners as he does now in 1858, when he cd. have put things on such a footing as wd. have saved much trouble afterwards.

Just when smoking after breakfast, when [sic] my writer came bringing his son with him; and then came Glinka who told me the Portuguese Minister had left Teentsin.[46] I asked what the result wd. be: he sd. he did not know, that the Portuguese govt. must determine on that, but that he imagined the matter wd. drop, and that a new treaty wd. be tried in a few years more.

I then went to the office, and read over the letter just recd. from Hsieh. Made a change in the draft of the Yamun's reply to the Minister, in which they say that as he has the power to make alterations in the Treaty after ratification, he surely ought to be able to do so, beforehand as well. Advised them to send the 'protest' and the reply in a circular letter to the Ministers at Peking.

Went and called on Wade at one. He looked rather gloomy: hopes the Spaniards will get a good treaty as it wd. be dangerous to irritate all the Catholic Powers, and Spain has a base of operations too close to China to be pleasant: wishes the Chinese wd bestir themselves to meet Berthemy and settle missionary questions and reclamations: thinks that the Portuguese Treaty was very favourable to China, for the 6th article arranges that each shall abide by his own text which the 9th says that the Emperor [character for *jeng*; "still," or "as before"] appoints officers, &c.[47]

Called on Mr. & Mrs. Edkin and intended to have called on Mr. Burlingame, but seeing a lot of mules at his gate I inferred Hangke was there and did not go in.

Very hot.

24 JUNE 1864: Up again at 4; wrote a note to Emma S.: I wonder what she will be like if we live to meet in '67. Was called on by Fontanier at 10, relative to Tonnage Dues. The French wish vessels to be allowed to go to Japan and Saigon with a 4-mos. Special Tonnage Certificate, and it is hinted that if that be conceded, they will give up the clause which enables them to hire Chinese junks without paying Tonnage Dues. The ground on which F. [Fontanier] put the desire to have Saigon made a 4-mo. was that as the English had Hongkong, the French ought to have Saigon.[48]

Went to the office at 11. Found Tung there alone. One of the Rm. Catholic "restitution" cases settled in KeangSe. Letter from Keangse Footae about indemnities v. drawbacks was shewn to me: Hammond is right, the Taoutae wrong. WanSeang then came in. I sd. I thought Hsieh had been in too great a hurry, and that he had not played with the Portuguese Minister as he might have done: his faith in the treatment of 'the barbarian' knows but two modes of action: to 'p'o' and to 'tsih-fei'.[49] Got them to write a note to Teentsin at once, asking Tsung How to be very polite to the Spanish Minister, to ask him to dinner, &c., & explaining what Wade sd. yesterday about the three Catholic powers. Wan seems inclined to concede residence at Peking, and will probably allow Manilla [*sic*] to be put on the 4-mo. list; I advise them to conclude the Treaty with the clause "if within twelve months no notice has been given of any wish to alter the treaty, it shall be exchanged afterward at a certain time the Ministers set [?] without further question."

Murray came in with a present for Wan Seang from Mr. Bowra: his old glasses; and one for the Prince, a silver case containing candle &c.[50]

Went to the paradeground and saw drilled men of the Shin-ke ying [lit. Divine-Mechanism Battalion] — Shin ke miaou swin [?] — under Foo Tsiang Keun [Tartar General Fu].[51] H.E. is a tall man of 49, but younger looking: he was wounded at KewChow in Chekiang in '58, when the Taipings entered the province, and the ball is still in his right leg. It does not seem to inconvenience him much, although the wound is still open: on a yin te'en [cloudy day] he feels it painful, so that it acts like a 'Han-shoo peaow' [thermometer]. The troops were drilled by an adjutant on horseback—English horse and English saddle—who gave the words first in English and then in Manchoo. The men went through their evolutions wonderfully well; they had Gordon's men in staffing together, and, on the whole, present a smarter and more soldierly appearance. The thousand men of the eight thousand commanded by the Tseih Yay [Seventh Prince], who exercise in the Nan Yuan, are under drill. The govt. I am happy to say is likely to go ahead. Foo Tsiang Keun sd., "What a stupid [*sic*] I am, and how deficient in politeness: to think that you and I shd. live in the same street, and that I shd. not yet have called on you!"⁵²

Old Hängke has had the civility to go to Cart shop, and select a cart for me: he arranged for one of two—one yellow the other reddish-brown; they ardently want me to drive in the yellow one, but will not object to the red. If I bring the red, I must mount my Ting chai [office attendant].⁵³ It's very civil of the old man.

SATURDAY, 25 JUNE 1864: Up again at 4. Engaged in the house in various ways during the day. Had a call from Tung Tajin [characters for Tung *ta-jen*]. Wrote a note to Fontainier relative to the mutual action or effect on each other of those clauses of the English & French treaties, which open the Yangtsze, provide for provisional regulations, & lay down what junks shall, and shall not, pay Tonnage Dues. Also wrote to the U.S. Minister, Mr. Burlingame, asking him to get me out three young Americans for the service.⁵⁴ A thunderstorm with rain cleared & cooled the air in the middle of the day. A Call from S. Wells Williams in the evening: he has a wonderful stock of information in his head about every place, has that man. When I meet such a one, my own superficiality disgusts me exceedingly. He thinks the effects of missionary teaching will not be much seen until a few truly Christian Chinese commence to influence each other. He tells a curious story of a man at Amoy who committed adultery, and who afterwards at one of the meetings got up and said he felt so unhappy, on account of having met with some verse in Proverbs, that he could not but confess it, and begged to be punished. Also of a boy, who said to his mother, 'I must take back that book which you made me steal, for God has seen the act, & I fear he will punish it.' And of a boy at Macao who went to his brother's shop to buy paper: sd. he would let him have it for 75 cents, but that he must charge his master 100; the boy refused to cheat his master, & for days after his brother wd. not speak to him. He also tells of the arrival of the troops for the first time at Amoy: the Chinamen said—"they came and battered down our forts, took our town, would not talk to us, were of a kind we had never seen before, & then left the town, and took up their quarters at Koo lang soo: why did they come, where from & what did they want? What odd people they must be!" He thinks the most difficult part of Chinese idolatry to be conquered by Christianity will be their ancestral worship.⁵⁵

Egypt produced priesthood: Greece, imagination, & literature: Rome, arms: India asceticism: China, 'this world-ishness' [?].

SUNDAY, 26 JUNE 1864: Again up early. Hangke called on me after breakfast. As he usually does, he launched into an account of his doings and sufferings, and of the shortcomings and imbecility of everyone else, at the time the Allies were marching on Peking. He then commenced to talk in a very low tone, and in a very confidential manner, prefacing his remarks by saying that he was about to talk to me in a way which he wd. not adopt save towards a most intimate Chinese friend. Sd. that Hsieh wd. ruin everything: that although Tung is a safe man in the office, yet WanSeang has now commenced to listen to only half of what he says, while he takes in 9/10th of Hsieh's views and advice: that Hsieh, however much he may smile before our faces, regularly talks of us as <u>Kwei</u> <u>tsze</u> [devils] behind our backs, and does so too with expressions of hatred and resentment. If Häng says a word in opposition to Hsieh's policy, he is at once attacked as being in league with the foreigner: just as before the Allies reached Peking, the Prince sd. to Häng that if he wd. stop their march &c., his merits wd. be very inadequately rewarded with even a Dukeship; when he did stop them, and matters were arranged, the Prince took whatever glory there was to himself, and it was all the cry that Hang had acted in concert with the foreigner. At the Le-Yang-Tang, Hsieh insists on collecting duty on things taken to it for private use, alleging that the priests there cannot be supposed to be entitled to the same privileges as Ministers: Hangke very wisely says that to examine the priest's boxes and collect duty on their dutiable contents will, while it can add but little to the revenue, cause much ill feeling, and that too at a time when there are <u>internecine</u> [?] troubles in China, and when it wd. be very imprudent to cause a row with any foreign power. I told him that I understood him to mean <u>Macao</u> too, when he spoke of the Le Yang Tang. The old man's eyes filled with tears repeatedly, and once they came welling out, when pulling off his spectacles, he struck his breast, and said that although he was awfully fond of his life and his money, he wd. give up all for his "Kwo" [dynasty]. He then went on to say, that the present Taipings were trying to drive the Tartars out of the country, and that the more successful the Taipings were in any place the more respectable were the class of people that joined them: that at the bottom of every Chinaman's heart there was a feeling of elation when he thought of the possibility of driving out the present dynasty: that <u>Chinese</u> advisers of the crown wd. therefore not unwillingly give such advice as wd. lead to troubles between the <u>Govt.</u> and foreign powers—that every blow given to the govt. weakened <u>it</u>, and doubled the chances of the Chinese party: that therefore it must be the policy of the Govt. to keep on the best terms with foreigners, and avoid everything, even to making great sacrifices, rather than cause trouble.[56] I was surprised to hear WanSeang's opinions—confidentially expressed the other day to Sir Frederick—coming out in such a way from Hängke, and I infer therefrom that he must mean what he says. But he is a very slippery old gentleman—can lie as no one else ever could—and he may be playing a game. I'll keep my eye on him and act cautiously for the next few months. He sd. that when the fleet smash occurred, their reason for treating Osborn so handsomely was this fear of offending the foreigner: they executed their punishment on Lay for exceeding his orders, and they, at the same time, 'saved their bacon' with foreigners by paying Osborn handsomely. 'Let it be 5000,' sd. Wan Seang: 'It must be 10,' sd. Hang. 'Tsun-wan puh Ko ta na-Ko siaou swan pan.' I don't know whether Hang's object is to damage Hsieh, or to make me suspicious of WanSeang: or to save himself, he having been the man that originally drew up the Portuguese Treaty, about portions of which questions are now raised. When going away, he told me to keep in mind what he had been saying. I arranged with him that my cart shd. be tsze-seih-teih.[57]

A few minutes after Häng left, Wan Seang sent for me. At the office I found they only wanted me to correct the drafts of a few despatches, one to Le Footae about the three Prussian cases, and one to Mr. Burlingame about the "Anna." I made some additions in the despatch to Le; and they decided on withholding the "Anna" despatch until they have recd. a Shin ching [report] from me.[58] They had told Mr. B that as he had heretofore been just, they therefore, out of pity for the merchant, now consented to lessen the Anna's punishment. I sd. they ought not eternally to be sticking in the Minister's justice, &c. as a reason for their commuting punishments &c.: that such expressions were sickening to the foreigner, and excite the contempt of their own people outside; that the "Anna" case was capable of certain explanations, & that they ought to ground the change of sentence on those explanations, and on nothing else.

Talked till six about various matters, Tung taking notes about our budget & revenue. Häng advised me in a quiet way to beware of "tsun and seih [?]," for, sd. he "I don't see to what position business may not carry you, and you ought to take care of both body and mind.[59] Look at me at 63," sd. he, "with a couple of babies in the house!" And indeed, I don't see to what I may not look forward: last year, Lay sd. they ought to consult him on every subject, & insisted on the point, but they wd. not do so; here I try to fight shy of everything but Customs' matters, and they ask my opinion in all matters, and allow me to criticize & correct despatches on all subjects. "Quietly does it, Bob!"

Murray dined with me this evening. Man going to be laid up, I fear.

MONDAY, 27 JUNE 1864: At home today, drafting a Shin-ching relative to the Foo Chow Opium Case.[60] Ping laou yay takes in one's meaning very quickly. Had a call from old Tsung-lun today: he says his memory commences to fail. A curious report in circulation among the Chinese to the effect that foreigners are buying up little children, whose flesh they eat, and whose eyes they use for photographic purposes.

TUESDAY, 28 JUNE 1864: Quite cool this morning when I got up: so much so that I cd. not walk about in my sleeping dress in the courtyard. Man very seedy.

Worked hard with my writer till 2 p.m.; finishing the FooChow Opium despatch and drafting one relative to the "Anna."

Went to the office at 2 1/2, talked with Wän, Tung, Hang & Tsung, about matters in general. The joint tribunal for confiscation cases, Wan wishes arranged in such a way as to keep merchant consuls from forming [indistinct word] on any occasion. While at the Office recd. my April magazines, with a letter from Pyne [?], and notes from Dick, 21st, Kopsch, & Jameson.[61] Hobson also writes from Nanking, where Gordon has gone, and been politely recd. by Tsäng Kwo tseun: the Imperialists number 60 000, and have only 2000 stand of arms; some of their stockages are within 200 yards of the walls, but having arrived there, they have got into the "Rest and be thankful" rut. Operations for mining and blowing up part of the wall are going on. Gordon wants to start on the 18th to visit Tsang Chung Tang at Ganking. They don't show any inclination to do the work with foreign assistance.[62]

Wade came in after dinner, talked til 1/2 p 10, when I walked down to the legation with him getting back at midnight. Tiresome walk on a warm night, through such dusty streets. He asks 1. do the Manchoos fear a Chinese party? 2. What Manchoo is there of ability besides WänSeang? 3. Wd. it be to the interest of the British govt. to support the dynasty at all hazards against a strong native party—a party such as Tsang Kwo fan's, who could rule? 4. Wd. not the French go in for the support of the Manchoos and make their own terms? 5. He thinks we ought to get up a police force at Ningpo, and put it under Giquel's care. 6. Lay's want of consideration for others, his inability to reason logically, his impatience of details, and his high-handed slang were quite reasons enough for making him unable to hit it off with the Chinese, able as he was in other respects, and pure as were his motives.

Awfully hot this afternoon.

WEDNESDAY, 29 JUNE 1864: Awfully hot morning: do. afternoon.

Did not do very much work. Called on W. A. P. Martin in the evening: he lives in the Tsing Poo Hoo tung, and has got very good quarters. He looks older and thinner, as does his wife too; but he talks in the same schoolmaster like style.[63]

THURSDAY, 30 JUNE 1864: The last day of the quarter: very hot indeed. Went to the office at 2, but as WanSeang was away at the Tih-shing mun, reviewing troops with Tseih Yay, no business was gone into. I had an hour's talk with Tung & Häng, to whom I read off in Chinese a piece from M'Cullough's Com'l Dicty. giving the Receipts & Expenditures in England in 1857.[64] An edict was issued yesterday granting an Amnesty to Rebels.

FRIDAY, 1 JULY 1864: Tung Che, 3d y. 5th m. 27th d. [27th day of the 5th month of the 3rd year of the T'ung-chih reign]

Wrote today to Sir Rutherford Alcock, Col. Pym, Capt. Forbes, Con. Gen. Seward, Barrister Owen, and Editor Jamieson,—also Commissioner Hannen: saying <u>no</u> to each <u>in re</u> applications for employment for selves or friends in the Customs.[65] They have no consciences, these acquaintances of mine: they think I have an unlimited stock of appointments in my gift, and they look upon the customs as a "Refuge for the destitute". I am getting into the habit of saying <u>no</u> pretty well, now. In private life, I find it the hardest word to say: to refuse a request or to blame or scold for a mistake, privately, as R. H., is what goes tremendously against my grain; in public life however, as Inspector General, I say <u>no</u> without hesitation, and "pitch into" people right and left when they go wrong.

Drafted Nos. 17 and No. 18, and sent in Nos. 13, 14, 15, & 16 [characters for *shen-ch'eng*; "reports"] to the Tsung le Yamun. My secretary, <u>Ping</u>, takes to the work very readily, and I can draft with his aid with the greatest ease.

Rain this evening: air a little cooler. New cart came today.

SATURDAY, 2 JULY 1864: WanSeang sent for me at one: so I went to the office, and staid till six. He thinks the "Anna" ought to be fined tls. 2000. The French Minister's reply to the letter relative to the Portuguese Treaty was shewn to me: Fonter. [Fontainier] makes it, "I thank you for your communication, but I must plainly tell you that I must bring the matter to the notice of my govt." The original French reads: "I take advantage of the opportunity of thanking you for your communication to inform you that it will be my duty to send a copy of it to my govt." Confound F.! There's mischief in that man, be its origin intention or inability! Talked <u>Taou-le</u> [morality] to a great extent with Wan.[66] He says if I had read Chinese books, I shd. be able to say more on the subject than most people. I note four points in the history of the week:

1. The Emperor has commenced the study of ancient history.
2. An amnesty has been proclaimed.
3. Tsang Kwo fan has memorialized to have Le Footae ordered to Nanking.
4. The Tseih Yeh, hostile to foreigners and <u>drill</u>, went with WanSeang to review the Yang-tsiang tuy [foreign-arms corps] on Thursday: he was delighted with what he saw. and asked for the <u>drill-book</u>. Hurrah! He'll be the Duke of Cambridge of China, and now for military reform and organization.[67] Again I shout Hurrah!! Hurrah!! Hurrah!!!

We unfortunates who were thrust into affairs and forced to work the moment we landed in China, have in studying Chinese worked from the top downwards, instead of laying a solid foundation, and building thereon. Is it too late to commence the other way? I have half a mind to try what an hour a day for the next three years will produce in the shape of learning the four books by heart. If I live long, I might make good use of such knowledge afterwards.[68]

Wade, St. John, and Savrin came up after dinner, and sat till ten.[69] Wade was delighted with my four items of intelligence. He talked chiefly of the waste that attends the way in which the missionaries go about their work.

WanSeang, I told today, that I am about to devote the surplus of the customs money to the getting up of a small fleet, if the Hoo Poo [Board of Revenue] did not interfere. He said, "Go ahead, and according to your own plans!"[70]

SUNDAY, 3 JULY 1864: Wade called this morning chiefly to talk about the possibility of getting the Yamun to consent to the Spanish Minister's coming up to Peking. The Minister writes a circular memorandum to all the Resident Ministers, complaining chiefly of Hsieh's hardness. It is proposed that the English, French, and Russian Interpreters shall call together, and ask on what day WanSeang will give them the Prince's answer to the Ministerial request.[71]

Talked too about the Rules drawn up to facilitate coming and going of steamers at Nuhkow [?]: Wade thinks they ought to be communicated through the Ministers.

Brown from the Legation came up and dined with us.

Had a long argument about the possibility of the recurrence of civil war in England at some future time: Man maintaining such a thing to be impossible, while Brown and myself thought that it might be possible and that it wd. originate in some religious movement, such as a crusade of free thought against the Church establishment.

MONDAY, 4 JULY 1864: [characters for the 1st day of the 6th lunar month] The first of the sixth moon, and the "4th of July"—grand day in the U.S. Went to the office at 1/2 p. 11, sent for by WanSeang, and came away at 3 1/2. He had heard that Gordon had been carried off by the Rebels, with Adkins, a steamer and tls. 80 000. I reassured him. This rumor, which seems to have come up through Tsung How to whom Baker communicated it in a note, must be the one current at S'Hae about the 15th June, when Dick got the 'Confucius' sent out to make enquiries, and everything found quiet. No news from Teentsin, except the Spanish Minister, writing for a copy of the Danish Treaty had not seen Hsieh for some days. The Chun-Keun Wang [Prince Ch'un], i.e. Ts'eih yay, is becoming quite ardent in his military fervour: powder was being burnt at the Office today, but the inferiority of the Chinese made as compared with some foreign powder that Hängke produced was only too conspicuous. Hängke had a rather curious breach-loading rifle with him, one I shd. not like to discharge and which I wd. advise Tseih Yay, for whom it seems to be intended [,] to be careful about. Camel's hair or wool, they tell me, is used in the manufacture of rope, felt mattresses, &c.[72]

WanSeang looked rather seedy. I got him to talk confidentially and he displayed no feeling, whether hostile or suspicious, as a Manchoo against the Chinese: he said that if it were the will of the <u>Chinese</u>, the Manchoos would not stand a day: that the only way to secure their allegiance was for the dynasty to treat them better than Manchoos. Still all he said would go to prove the desirability of making the Manchoos strong. Wan says the Manchoos are too slothful, too luxurious, and too quick tempered. They cannot <u>chih</u> <u>sin-Koo</u> [endure hardship].[73] He says that during the troubles of the last 15 years, the Chinese people, as a body, have stood by the Tartar Dynasty, & that such support is owing to the justice of the Emperors who, though conquerors, made no distinction, but treated all their subjects as their children.[74]

The 48 Manchoos for S'Hae are officers: they take with them 12 servants: 4 1st class, tls. 320; 56 second c., $\frac{\text{tls. 1600}}{\text{tls. 1720}}$.[75]

Working with my Writer Ping at various letters: he gets on very well, and begins to understand matters.

TUESDAY, 15 [*sic* as written. Should be the 5th] JULY 1864: [Large star in red pencil written over this date]

Are the Chinese going to move? Lay wd. say: "they'll never move, they'll never do anything!" He is right to a great extent in his opinion: they will not do anything suddenly, or in such a way as to attract much attention, but inovations will creep in gradually, just as they become more necessary, and as the people and govt. become more ready to take them in hand. Hot house formed [?] fruits are ever insipid: put them in the open, & they fade: better much have a healthy plant, which having battled with the elements, has attained its maturity, & brings forth fruit on its own button! [?]

For the last five years, during which I have been in the Chinese Service, I have been constantly racking my brains to hit upon or devise some line of action which, if carried out, wd. eventually enable one to think that my life had not been wholly thrown away or useless, and which in particular would enable me to leave China with the conviction that I had done something for the country. The performance of my duties as a Customs official, and the effort to give efficiency to the Inspectorate, by aiding the govt. to collect a large revenue and by forwarding the legitimate interests of commerce, as well as to endeavour to induce the govt. to expend properly, and not squander its funds, are objects at which I have to aim in the mere discharge of the duties for which I am paid. Accordingly, I have, night and day, planned and thought, with these objects in view. But I want to <u>do</u> something more. A little I have attempted in preaching military reform, and in bringing the govt. to eye with favor the establishment of a fleet which shall protect the revenue, put down piracy, and give security on the waters and rivers of China. I now today thought of a plan, which if persevered in must do good. I have at my disposal the monies of the confiscation funds and I now propose to apply them partly in carrying out the following projects:

1. to pay for the translation and printing of a complete set of Chambers'

Educational Series:[76]
2. to put, myself, into Chinese Senior's Political Economy:
3. to get Mr. Martin to translate Mill's Pl. Economy:
4. to get a library of books on International Law, Political Economy, Jurisprudence &c.: and,
5. eventually to induce the govt. to memorialize and obtain an Edict making the study of such books incumbent on all who compete for degrees.
Le Footae and Wan Seang will surely appreciate this, and help me to put it through. Such an undertaking must do good: and will fill the ground, and pave the way for the operations of missionaries. Before leaving China for good, I hope too to publish an introduction to and history of Christianity which coming from a layman may take up the subject in a way the Missionary does not think of, and which with a heathen people, of such morality and civilization as the Chinese, may prove more beneficial than other means. What I want is health, industry, and God's blessing.

Finished a long circular addressed to all Commissioners explaining sundry principles by which I wish them to be guided. I must now try and give shape, consistency, and efficiency to the Service.

At 5 was sent for by WanSeang, and just when about to start met Wade, who was coming to see me. He says the three notes from the Ministers had been sent in asking the Yamun to allow the Spanish Minister to come up to Peking. He is in a state of mind, too, about the French, who, he thinks, will give trouble about the Customs' business, for they hold to a peculiar reading of their 4th article — viz. that whatever privileges are in future granted to any country are to be by them enjoyed in their <u>entirety</u>, <u>without</u> <u>any</u> <u>of</u> <u>the</u> <u>obligations</u> <u>attached</u> <u>to</u> <u>them</u>! I wish he would not fret or worry himself so much.

When I went to the office, I found they first of all wished to show me Gordon's dresses. They are very splendid, and no expense has been spared to make them the proper thing. Wan then showed me the three notes about the Spaniard. I said that if the request was one that could be complied with, it wd. be best for them to yield, and asked if it was quite impossible to concede the point: they said, it was quite impossible without sacrificing Hsieh: for, sd. they, the Spaniard first wrote that he was at T'tsin, and that he begged for ministers to meet him; without delay. Hsieh and Tsung were appointed; Hsieh when going away reported his departure [characters for *ch'ing-hsun*; to request approval (for leave)] almost a month ago; he has been a long time at Teentsin, and he has only had, its seems, one interview with <u>De Mas</u>. Why then does de Mas wish to come up? Is it that he has had a row with Hsieh, or is it that he treats the Chinese Ministers disrespectfully? Or, if his interpreter is not up to the work, why not let a legation send one down? Why did he not in the first instance ask to come up to Peking? His wish cd. have been met then. Did it not occur to him that he ought to make sure of his interpreter beforehand? and, sd. Wan, "I know you foreigners look upon the matter as very easily arranged: but, with us, it is just one of the hardest things we could be asked to do." He sd. too, that supposing De Mas were to come up, he wd. demand the 'reciprocity' basis, &c. &c. &c. I am to go and see Wade tomorrow: meanwhile, I have got them to delay their reply.

WEDNESDAY, 6 JULY 1864: Hot again this morning; after three pleasantly cool days.

Called on Wade and talked for a couple of hours. His idea now is that the best plan wd. be for de Mas to arrange with Hsieh and Tung about coming to Peking, and that the Yamun ought to reply to the Ministerial notes, by recounting their difficulties, pointing to Hsieh as the proper person, & promising their support.

From Wade's went to the office: WanSeang listened quietly to all I had to say, and having taken in my meaning thoroughly—to the effect that the coming to Peking of the Spanish Minister cd. not possibly harm China, while the refusal to allow him to come wd. irritate the French Minister, & make their work difficult—he promised to speak to the Prince & do what I advised.

Rode in my new cart—a sze-leu chang—today, and found it very comfortable.[77]

THURSDAY, 7 JULY 1864: In the house at despatches all day: slept from 1 @ 5, though. very hot.

FRIDAY, 8 JULY 1864: Brett and myself breakfasted at the Yamun today. Present Hang, Tung, and Wän. They were all very pleasant and treated Brett very kindly. Wan said he took a great interest in youths so far from home. Afterwards, when Brett left, went at the reply to the Ministers, which gave a couple of hours' work [characters for *ju-ch'ieh ju-ts'o ju-cho ju-mo* "as you cut and file, carve and polish."][78] I hope it will do. It tells them "to go to Teentsin": I hope they'll not look on it as equivalent to saying "go to Hongkong."

Hsieh's new microscope arrived today. It is too complicated for my knowledge however. With it came a box addressed to the Emperor of China from Day & Son. No one dared open it for awhile, but Hangke's curiosity got the better of him at last, and he had it opened. It was found to contain two pictures of the Osborn Fleet! Insult added to injury in this way is hard to bear! I suppose some disappointed officer sent it out: surely not Osborn! Bad taste, and impertinence—whoever it was!

Thunder storm which cooled the air much.

SATURDAY, 9 JULY 1864: My liver feels queer this morning; so I must stop my Beer for a while. Some time ago Le Footae wrote up, asking that Walter Lay might not be removed from Kiukiang: it surprised me much, for W. was no favorite with either Chinese or foreigners. Now has arrived a despatch from the Gov. of Keangse asking that <u>Hammond</u> may be refused, and Lay appointed in his stead: they complain of Hammond's <u>absences</u>,—his trips to Hankow and Shanghae, general inattention to business, and ignoring of Tsae Taoutai. I don't understand how Lay has become so '<u>good</u>': he has probably been quietly putting a 'spoke' in Hammond's wheel. This, however, supports me in writing my strong circular.[79]

Had a talk with the young ladies next door the day before yesterday: I caught them peeping over the wall and then had a jaw.

The Mail of the 10th May arrived today. I had one letter from home, from Mamma. Poor Mary is not recovering rapidly after her second confinement, which brought her a little daughter. Minnie Hart has been married to W. Glanville. Sam McCullough dead.

A letter from Wilzer, resigning his appointment. Brown from Ningpo tells me that Gicquel [sic] has been appointed by Tso Chetae to go with D'Aiguebelle. A tremendous number of letters from the ports.[80]

Danish fleet thrashed the Austrians off Helgoland.

SUNDAY, 10 JULY 1864: Doing nothing particular. Had headache and though they sent for me, I did not go to the Yamun. Forbes and Knight called in this morning <u>en route</u> for the hills to see Mr. Burlingame.[81]

MONDAY, 11 JULY 1864: Went to the Yamun at one o'clock. Gave them all the Shanghae news. Found another letter—long and unintelligible—from the Portuguese Minister: he writes from S'hae and says he is willing to exchange ratifications, and will discuss changes <u>afterwards</u>. Hsieh has written him a capital reply: I wonder who composed it—certainly not Hsieh, possibly <u>Chin</u> of whom Martin spoke so highly the other day.[82]

Tchang-hsing in Chekiang taken by the Imperialists; Bailey made the breach, and the men went in gallantly, losing heavily though: it is said, no rebels escaped—so much the better—I'm sorry to say![83]

Forbes and Knight came in and dined and slept, <u>en route</u> to NewChwang. Forbes expressed himself very much surprised and disgusted with all the news about Breck. Knight wants a light-ship and the point lit [?] at NewChwang.

Up from before 4 till midnight: rather done up.

TUESDAY, 12 JULY 1864: [characters for 9th day of the 6th month]
Got off my circulars 9, 10, & 11, today with a host of letters, and copies of the Trade Returns for 1863 to each of the Chinese newspapers, and Mr. Lobscheid.[84]

I feel a little seedy: a touch of liver, I imagine. Had a walk on the Wall.

WEDNESDAY, 13 JULY 1864: Drew up a list of the members of the service. Worked at the joint tribunal regulations.

Creation! How the attempt to account for existence presses down the mind! Deny a God, and the difficulty is greater than ever; recognize him, and to then try and ask His How, Where, and Whence — it is as it were a mental effort to raise a weight that the strength cannot move!

THURSDAY, 14 JULY 1864: Man very seedy this morning. Last night had a <u>caterwall</u> with a Ya-too [?][85]

Wade has sent me for perusal a despatch from Osborn from which it seems that there is not the least likelihood of the fleet being disposed of. The tone in which Osborn writes is very aggravating, he seems delighted at having got the Chinese in a fix.

Went down to the French Legation, and left cards on Fontainier, Du Chelsny [?], and Pichon.[86] Then went round to Wade, with whom I had a long talk. He says the next best thing to sending Ministers to Europe that the Chinese can do is to write circular despatches to the Ministers at Peking. He says we must hold by the [characters for *jeng-tzu*; "the 'still' character"] in the Portuguese Treaty. Osborn's letter has bothered him exceedingly. He is about to write in relation to camel's wool and the 1/2 duties on Teas.

Went to the office, and sat with Hang, Wan, Tung, & Tsung, from 2 1/2 till 6. Talked about the joint tribunal investigation, and handed WanSeang my re-revised rules. We must take care how we move in this matter, for Parkes will try to make the Consul the Chief man in the Tribunal; we must make it a Chinese tribunal, at which the Consul will by country have a seat, where he can hear the evidence, and ask queries. I explained the chances of a war in Europe, and the nature it wd. likely be of, and told them that while in Europe, people would be too busy to attend to affairs in China, the Chinese govt. ought to be actively engaged in <u>setting its house in order</u>.

I proposed to Wade to let us have back the 'Thule,' 'Kwangtung,' and 'Amoy', and to allow one quarter to pass without payment of indemnity. No go, though![87]

FRIDAY, 15 JULY 1864: Yesterday was our first really hot day, the first two of the <u>San fuh</u> [three hot periods], which last 30 days, being 10 each.[88] The heat though great is not unpleasant, for it is proper summer heat.

In the house all day, not working very hard. Put into Chinese a reply to the despatch relative to the confiscn. [confiscation] of the Prussian vessel "Amoy Trader". Showed the writer the wonders of the microscope.

SATURDAY, 16 JULY 1864: Drafted a shin chin relative to the complaints made against Hammond, and then went to the office, where I arranged that camels' wool, which is to be called <u>Lo To Sung-mao</u> [loose camel hair] and not Lo To Jiang [?] shd. be allowed to be exported for a year on payments of m3. c.5 per pecul.[89] Went through the Confiscation Rules with Wän & Tung, and chatted about things in general, showing them "Punch", &c. until 5 when I came away. The idea of presenting the King of Prussia with the Order of the [?] struck them as "too rich".

After dinner Wade came up, evidently hipped and out of sorts.[90] He sat till near 11, when I walked part of the way home with him. He is awfully savage with Lay & Osborn; and he allows that Parkes tries to make too much of the Consular position. He [Wade] talks fairly, and is the best friend in thought that China has got. Deliciously cool breeze during the night with moon.

SUNDAY, 17 JULY 1864: Photographed this morning by Brett in pajamas. Awfully lazy, with no heart for work atall. Very hot indeed; slept most of the day, and in fact did nothing whatsoever.

It strikes me, judging from my own experience, that at the root of infidelity lies the desire not, or to believe, and that that again is based upon the wish to be free from the feeling of necessity to obey the moral law in order to give way to the peculiar inclinations of the individual. "The law of liberty" is more exacting than mere ceremonial law; and there is abundant room left for the exercise of it in the necessity for conscientious action in the many cases in which the Scripture teaching may seem open to a double interpretation. "Who believed not the truth, but had pleasure in unrighteousness" 2nd Thess. II.12.

MONDAY, 18 JULY 1864: Last night was very hot, and the sun has come out this morning in a way that looks as if he were determined not merely to bake us, but to toast us too, before night.

At the Yamun today, found everyone crying out against the heat: Tsae looked as if he were about, meltingly, to disappear, and all the Sze-kwan were enjoying themselves in pajamas and boots. Wän & Tung, when they came out to me, had evidently put on their dresses to meet me, & they sd. they were very hot, and so, I know, was I. They shewed me letters from Wade & Berthemy,—the former asking for a copy of the French lease of ground at Yentae, the latter about Tonnage dues, proposing to assimilate the French to the English Treaty, provided the Chinese wd. consent to put Saigon and Japan on the same footing,—payment once in four months,—as Hongkong. Wän when talking about ming-gan [murder cases] told me the Kount had caused murder: he employed a pimp who made a good thing of it; another man, jealous of the first's games, took to pimping too, and spoiled the market for the original rascal, whereon they had a fight, and death ensued. An Enquiry took place, the facts came out, and the Kount paid hush-money. So much for our superior civilization, and the representatives of the West![91]

TUESDAY, 19 JULY 1864: Hot and close all morning. Thunderstorm and rain in the late afternoon. Man very seedy: Brett rode down to ask Dudgeon to come up, but that Christian doctor said that, as he thought the rain wd. hold up for a little, he wd. avail himself of it to make the best of his way to the hills! Man, I think, is an awful old woman when sick; he gives way completely, and likes to make himself interesting.

I have started an ice-box in our office, & find it cools the air somewhat. I have been eating sequa [watermelon], and find boils appearing.[92]

Here ends this volume of my journal. R. H. [End of Vol. 5]

[New volume; inside reads: Vol. 6 — Robert Hart Journal 20th July 1864 (at Peking) @ 21 Feb 1865. Vol. 6]

WEDNESDAY, 20 JULY 1864: [characters for the 17th day of the 6th month the 3rd year of the T'ung-chih reign]

Wrote a shin chin today proposing that Opium intended for the northern ports shd. not be called on to pay duty when being taken from the Receiving Ships at Shanghae, and another containing four regulations which are to form the basis of the tribunal for the public investigation of confiscation cases. It was originally wished that a joint tribunal should be formed not merely for the investigation, but also for the settlement, of all disputed cases; to have yielded such a point wd. have made the Consuls practically the judges, and it was therefore thought that the proceedings of the tribunal shd. be confined to investigations merely. Another modification has now been made of a kind which will meet all the ends proposed, although it may not prove altogether acceptable to the Consuls: it is that the Supt. will, in any case for which the Consul demands enquiry, in open court investigate fully and take all the evidence, pro and con, and that, while he will be assisted by the Commissioner, he will invite the Consul — as each case occurs — to meet with him at the Customs, and sit with him while he investigates the case, the Consul being allowed to cross question as much as he pleases. My reason for introducing this additional modification is because I see Parkes at Shanghae has already formed a set of regulations of a kind which wd. make the Consul everything, and the Superintendent nothing — and the Commissioner less than nothing — in the matter; and as we are giving up some of our rights — wisely, I grant — we must be careful that we do not of our own accord place ourselves in a fix.[93]

Was at the office today from 3 @ 7, with Wän and Tung; we went through the letters to the Footae about the public investigation, and drew up a reply to M. Berthemy relative to Tonnage Dues. The Tls. 375,000 for the fleet was likewise talked about, and W. said that no part of it ought to go to Lay, although I explained that he and Osborn might either be forced to sell the ships at a loss, or might wash their hands of the whole affair. I tried to get them to write a circular desptach to the foreign ministers, informing them that China had no objection to the presence of Ministers of treaty powers at Peking, provided they procured their own residences: I said that after two years, they will have Ministers here, whether they [the Chinese] like it or not, and that they might as well make what capital they could in the meanwhile. W. replied that he understood the suggestion, but feared outside Chinese wd. find fault with such a move.

Wade came up this morning and told me that to his invitation to use the British Legation, de Mas had made no reply, and that, in answer to the French invitation, he said he would rather rent a place of his own where, after completing the treaty, he might at his leisure indulge in some philological investigations. Wade "smells a rat," and thinks the Spaniard wishes to use the Foreign Ministers to get him up to Peking, and that, once there he will refuse to move away again; so M. de Mas is not likely to get much countenance from the John Bull section of the ministerial community: what a rascally trick it wd. be, were he to act in such a way!

If I can get Wan to write the letter stating all may reside at Peking, it will be a grand coup. By the way, the Chinese papers just recd. from Shanghae at the Yamun publish Dent's notification of his appointment as Portuguese Consul General: the Yamun will, of course, avail itself of this fact in its fight.[94]

THURSDAY, 21 JULY 1864: Cool morning. Looked at the stamen of a tiger lily with the microscope; never saw anything so wonderful! The Emperor goes to the Ta Kung paou [great temple] today to pray for rain.[95]

FRIDAY, 22 JULY 1864: Heavy rain in the morning, and rain falling without any intermission all day long. In answer to the prayers addressed by the Emperor to the Unknown God? There is something quite touching in the idea of a little boy—now nine years old—the father and chief of his people, prostrating himself before Heaven, and entreating it to send down rain.

[In red pencil over this paragraph is written: Nanking completely in the hands of the Imperialists.]

Some months ago, Prince Kung was ordered to pray for rain; while he was doing so, the Rev. W. Collins at Church prayed that God would not hear him, and thereby give him a signal proof of his errors—that he would not send down rain lest he shd. thereby confirm the Prince in his idolatry.[96]

SATURDAY, 23 JULY 1864: Brett's 19th birthday.

I notice a gradual change—I don't know whether it is a physical or a psychological one—stealing over me. I used to revel in reveries about women; hour after hour could I spend without the slightest sense of weariness or satiety, in picturing to myself the delights and concomitants of female society. Now, however, when I attempt such a reverie, I soon lapse from it into something much more serious, and cannot keep it up. Again, when thinking of matrimony, I see myself inclined to dwell more on its cares and troubles than on its pleasures; formerly, I used only to think of its delights,—now I commence to see its disagreeables, and fancy they are not compensated for by the agreeables. What is this significant of? Merely, I presume, that I have gotten through the "love-fever," 20 @ 30, term of life, and that for the future some thing other than woman will chiefly attract me. I wonder what folly it will be: will it be love of money, ambition, or what? Quite possibly, some egregious stupidity: not impossibly some worthy pursuit. Meanwhile, I record the change.

[Over this paragraph is written boldly in blue pencil: "O! my eye! Just look at what you say on 13th and 21st August!"]

When I was a youngster, before I left home, I used often to feel savage with my father for things I saw him do: they were chiefly <u>inconsiderate</u> actions. Thinking of them calmly, it struck me that so to act was quite in accordance with the current of thought of a man of his age: that of course did not make them the less unpleasant, but it suggested itself to me often to note down what I objected to, and how I felt in regard to it, in order that when I attained a similar age my conduct might evince greater consideration for others. Unfortunately I never jotted down my ideas as proposed: and thus I have kept no history of my psychological changes.

Rain during the night: the sun, however, out again this morning.

Employed in drawing up a plan for promotion in the service, retiring allowances, formation of grades and classes: all of which will tend to regularize the customs, and, making individuals like it better, give the service greater coherence and consistency.

"When I was in my teens, I loved sweet Margaretta: I wonder how it is, But I now quite forget her!"

"Noble aim is more than fame, and truth surpasses glory."

Went to the office at three, made two or three corrections in the French Tonnage Dues Despatch, handed in my <u>shin ching</u> relative to camels' wool and joint tribunal, gossiped a little with Tung, ate some Sequa and came away again at 5. Hängke appeared again, his five days' leave having expired. WänSeang has not been able to go out for the last two days,—paou t'oo-tsze [stomach ache];[97] were anything to happen to him, it would be a terrible calamity—that is, it would 'spoke' certain plans and thwart the hopes of those who build their imaginings on his longevity. Personally, and so far as I can understand the wants of China, I shd. lament his disappearance most deeply; but, as France has it, "Il n'y a point d'homme necessaire."

SUNDAY, 24 JULY 1864: Pretty hot. Did not go out atall today. Drafted two despatches to Dick about Tribunal and Opium Duties. As regards the tribunal, we must keep it purely Chinese, and just give the Consul a seat at it and allow him to cross-question by courtesy, so that the truth may be fully elicited, and the merchants for the future be unable to insinuate that they have not had a fair hearing. [Hand drawn in the margin: Macaulay's Minutes on Education in India: Macmillan, [indistinct word]]][98]

MONDAY, 25 JULY 1864: This day ten years I landed at Hongkong from the old "Pottinger". How thankful I ought to be for the health I have had and the success in life that has attended me! Only one sickness during the ten years, and now — although I feel occasionally nervous after a smoke — my health is excellent, and my strength unimpaired; besides I am now at the top of the service!

The Mail of the 20th May arrived this morning: it was on the same day that the mail of the same date arrived last year. Letters from FitzRoy, Klezckowsky, & Wilzer; but none from home.

Went to the office at 1 1/2. Found that news had yesterday arrived of the successful attack on Nanking on the 19th: after a week's fighting, the Imperialists had established themselves in the city. The rebels still hold an inner city; but there is no doubt now but that the knell of Taepingdom has been rung. The news arrived yesterday morning just as the Emperor had returned from thanking Heaven for the rain that fell a few days ago; only 4 1/2 days en route from Nanking, 800 le a day.[99]

WänSeang looks seedy, but says he is all right. They showed us three letters just recd. from Meritens — one about drilling and loans, — the next about the "Volunteer" and WänChow, — and the last about Taewan. I must remind Meritens that I am the Chief. Wan asked whether I thought the Treaty Powers would exchange NewChwang for Wäan Chow. Also was shewn three Chinese despatches: one about Kiukiang office issuing transit certificates for Hoopih; another reporting the seizure of the "Alert"; and the third relative to a vessel that had been wrecked at WänChow. They asked me, would I have a Commissioner ready for Nanking in a few months?[100]

TUESDAY, 26 JULY 1864: Man & Brett went to the hills this morning.

Le Footae writes up that he has directed the Kiukiang Keentuh [superintendent of customs] to dismiss Hammond: and says that it is on record that, although the I.G. may move them from one port to another, the local Keentuh may dismiss them. This is a fix, certainly: if this principle be allowed, the Customs' Service must fall through as a service. The tendency in China everywhere is evidently to localise responsibility, and as regards the public service to do away with, or not to allow the existence of vested rights, E.G. or I.E. when a man enters a service at home, he looks upon it as employment for life, whereas in China an appointment is only for three years, and the occupant may at any time, whether at the caprice or whim of his superiors, or at an unexpected turn in the wheel of fortune, be ejected from his berth. Such a state of affairs has two direct & opposite tendencies: 1.° to make man feel exceedingly careful to keep right — but such an excessive care must produce a fear of responsibility of a kind that will clog all action; & 2.° to make people—perhaps careless of other results—lay hold of every means of securing money. I don't see exactly whether the system tends to develope the virtuous or the vicious—the public-spirited or the selfish part—of human nature: it is a natural system looking at it from the Chinese standing point, "jin pun shën" ["man's nature is basically good"], and if all men were good, working on a good soil, such a system ought to develop the better part of nature, and be attended with beneficial results; but looking at it from our point of view—that human nature is bad—the system is the wrong one, and the one most likely to lead to mischief: and experience, I think, and history shows that the word <u>mandarin</u> is almost convertible [?] with "all that is bad"—veniality, inability, rottenness, &c. All the teachings of the Chinese go to foster the system. [characters for *tao-chih i-te ch'i-chih i-li yu-ch'ih ch'ieh ko*; "if [the people are] led by virtue and given uniformity by means of ritual, they will have a sense of shame, and become good."][101]

The localizing of responsibility is a tendency towards individualism: individualism in matters of religion and daily life wd. be the proper thing in a more perfect state of society. But such a state of society wd. assume as its tendency the tendency of doing away with all government whatever: is such a tendency justified by history? There have been attempts at it in all ages—republicanism is such an approach—but no success has as yet been seen commensurate with the grandness of the underlying idea.

I must again try and get the Keen-tuh disassociated from local offices, & appointed direct by the Tsung-li Yamun: at all events, I <u>must</u> have it clearly understood, that no <u>Keen-tuh</u> is to dismiss or procure or an Impl. court to dismiss a shwuy-wuh-sze without reference to the Inspector General.[102] [In margin red pencil: Settled 20th Aug."]

"Official Life in China: its nature—its theory—its practice", wd. not be a bad subject for a <u>first</u> <u>class</u> paper for the N. C. Branch of the R. Asiatic Society.

WEDNESDAY, 27 JULY 1864: Went to the office today at 2 o'c. I first had a long chat with Hangke alone, who told me they had just recd. letters from Le Footae, who informed them that he had retained Gordon at Shanghai to "leën ping" [train troops]. H. then went on to say, that if I had not arranged the difference between Le and Gordon after the fall of Soochow, the Chinese wd. not have been able now to congratulate themselves on the happy state of affairs that exists: that at the Yamun they all wondered that at my age I was <u>chih-tih-choo</u> [?], and that my elevation had not made any change in me—that in China they could not find any people under 30 who could control themselves so perfectly, and not be spoiled by prosperity, &c. God help him! If he only knew the fighting that goes on in my inner man, and the intensely strong desire I have to "break out", he wd. scarcely think me so "good".[103]

Tung then came in, and reading over Le F.'s despatch about Hammond, said "here's a pretty go: matters brought to a deadlock". He then suggested that the Yamun shd. give me a <u>Cha-tsze</u> [instruction], authorizing H's retention at K'Kiang; and that, with it, I shd. reply to the Footae. He pointed out a passage in the despatch where, says Tsae Taoutae, "men's dispositions crooked and dictatorial [character for *che*; referring to the above-mentioned characteristics] are in the majority; complaisant and virtuous <u>che</u> are in the minority". The characters [*fan-jen*; all men] had evidently not been the ones in the original, which were probably [characters for *yang-jen*, foreigners] or something worse; Le had changed the disagreeable expression to <u>fan-jen</u> [all men] but I pointed out that such a remark was not in accordance with the Chinese <u>Taou-le</u> [moral principles] atall.[104]

Wän & Ching then came in, and we talked about various matters. Wän asked again about NewChwang: I said I had yesterday spoken to Wade about it; that he thought there were difficulties in the way, that he cd. not act without the sanction of the govt. and that he wd. first of all have to get the opinion of the Chambers of Commerce on the subject. Wan says he must, nevertheless, try and put the matter through.

Wade is in a pleasant [?] state of mind about the murder at Hankow, of which I gave him the news yesterday. Webster fined Dr. Cross, who had shot an old man, $500! and deported him. The Chinese, of course, protest against such a proceeding. They don't know of it yet at the Yamun.[105]

Legation Brown has been seedy, but is better somewhat. Like the rest of them, he has fled to the hills.

Despatches in from English & French asking for a change in the Yangtze Regulations. The French, by writing this despatch, <u>commit themselves to a recognition of the Regulations</u>. Hängke, of course, opposes the change: he says [characters for *wu-i yü Chung-kuo*; "no change on the part of China"]

Another letter from the French asking for indemnity in the case of a vessel wrecked & plundered on the <u>Pratas</u>. What is the meaning of this? Do they wish the Chinese to say the Pratas don't belong to China?[106]

A jaw with Miss Le over the Wall tonight: what teeth!

THURSDAY, 28 JULY 1864: Two things suggest themselves: 1st, to ask for an Edict permitting Chinese merchants to own foreign built ships to trade to Treaty Ports, & pay the same duties as foreign vessels, & to be under Customs: flag [sketch]: where ought the Dragon to be?[107]

2.° to put up a college at Peking, with six professors: the professors to be our <u>students</u> for a couple of years & then to go to work: Chemistry; Modern Languages; Fortification & Engineering; Artillery; Natural Philosophy &c. &c. &c. Caine President, Thomas Modn. lang. with officers from <u>foreign</u> countries for some branches.[108]

Rain again: weather moderately cool. Engaged in putting into Chinese my rules for the service.

FRIDAY, 29 JULY 1864: Spent a very pleasant afternoon at the office. Some Frenchman wishes to convey goods from Teentsin to Kiachtcka, and applies for a Certificate to enable him to do so, as though he were Russian; Tsung How asks for instructions: I say that the French, having the "most-favored-nation" clause can claim as a right what the man asks for, and that the only people who could effectually stop such action would be the Russians, who, unless they had a treaty to the contrary, could stop goods crossing their frontier. Hangke objects to a transfer of the <u>Keuen</u> <u>Ping</u> [authority] to the Russ. WänSeang then produced the letter that had been written to the Yamun by Count Kleizkovsky, asking for special permission for govt. agents to convey silkworms by the route in question, and stating that it was asked as a favor, the treaty not entitling the French to demand it as a right; he also showed me a letter from M. Berthemy, not worded so quietly as the count's, but in quite the same spirit, notwithstanding. So I told them that if they did not agree with me in what I said about "the most-favored-nation" clause, they had better tell Tsung How to refuse the Certificate, and then, in the event of any discussion, support their action by quoting letters of the Count & M.B. I shall be curious to know the <u>issue</u> [sic] <u>result</u> of this case.[109]

Read over the Yamun's reply to the French letter relative to the ship that was wrecked and plundered on the Pratas. They say the Pratas are within the jurisdiction of <u>Keung</u> <u>Chow</u> <u>Foo</u>, and that the Treaty provides that the Chinese shall not be called on to "pay damages".[110]

They make difficulties about taking the half-duty off tea at the river-ports — thanks to my dear old female friend Hängke, bother him!

Had a long jaw with Tung & Wan about <u>Taou-le</u> [morality]: its points of difference & resemblance as talked of by Chinese & foreigners, & its results in each case. Wan said: "if with your sing-tsing [disposition], you foreigners had only our taou-le, how you wd. go ahead!" I said that taou-le was at the root of sing-tsing — that it taught, informed, and guided it, and that accordingly our Sing-tsing was the result or child of our taou-le, just as the hollowness of the Chinese sing-tsing was the result of theirs: that if they adopted our taou-le they wd. soon find the sing-tsing follow. Wan said he thought the reason for our differences lay in the fact that China knew & practiced taou-le long before we did: that taou-le came to us later, & that we were still in the first flush of it, & that right wd. yet overtake us too. I said the differences between the Chinese & ourselves were to be traced to a radical starting point: the Chinese say man's nature is good; we say it is bad. The Chinese accordingly appeal to principles, and rule by <u>Keaou</u> or instruction: we make laws & rules by <u>Ching</u>, <u>governing</u> or punishment of infractions. As human nature is imperfect, the result must be a meeting of the two systems at a half-way house. The ethics of the Chinese books, I granted, was very fine: but the conduct of the Chinese, they allowed, differed very much from what the books taught. The gossip wound up by their regretting I had not been born a Chinaman, as I wd. have been able to discuss Taou-le.[111]

Proposed a college at Peking.

SATURDAY, 30 JULY 1864: Deliciously cool morning. We are now at the 7th m. I think of the 2nd fuh, and in a few days more autumn will commence lih tsew [the beginning of autumn].[112] The summer may then be looked on as ended.

I wonder does [characters for *chu miao chang-i*; "to help sprouts grow"] correspond to "to bring coals to Newcastle".

Kleinwächter and Des Champs arrived this morning. The Prefect at Tung-Chow was very kind to them, and supplied them with ponies to ride up to Peking. The Chinese name for the latter will be [characters for Te-shan]: for the former Kih-lan-fa Kea-ta: settled that it shd be [characters for K'ang Fa-te]

Brett in from the Hills in the evening [character for Po Lai-te][113]

SUNDAY, 31 JULY 1864: The last of the month. Fine weather: the early morning quite cool.

MONDAY, 1 AUGUST 1864: Drafted replies this morning to Le Foo-tae's despatches relative to Lay and Hammond. I wonder what H.E. means by directing me to ascertain the date of Gordon's return to Shanghae: the more especially as Gordon seems to have been at Soochow on the day the despatch was written 6th m. 9th d.[114]

Went to the office at two: Wan was not there. He was at the Keun-Ke-choo [Grand Council] drawing up the Edict relative to the fall of Nanking. The news arrived this morning in a Memorial from Tsang Kwo fan, from Gan-King: to the effect that the city which was entered on the 16th of the 6th moon was entirely in the hands of the Imperialists on the 19th. Hung Siu tseuen put an end to himself during the 5th month, and his son destroyed himself in the palace by setting the place on fire. Not a rebel escaped, and Le Seu-ching, the Chung Wang, has been taken alive. The success is complete, and it has been effected without foreign aid: this is a capital thing for the Chinese government, and Sir F. Bruce will now be proud to have done the right thing when he advised the British to support the dynasty.[115]

HooChow is still in the hands of the rebels, and may possibly give trouble: but, thank heaven, the Taeping affair may now be regarded as ended! I trust the country has before it long years of peace & prosperity.[116]

I showed them my Rules for the service in Chinese, and they seemed very much pleased with them. Hangke said that they ought to be sent to me by the Yamun, as though for my direction, in order to supply me with the proper Keuen [authority].[117]

Häng, when talking of Nanking, remarked: "Lay's fleet was not required, after all: he'll be rather surprised to hear of the fall of the place: his regrets, however, will come too late!"

Tung put forward in a very clear & masterly manner the idea by which they ought to be actuated in consideration of the proposal to do away with the half duty deposit on Teas: "the rule," sd. he, "was originally enforced in order to provide against certain irregularities, which, under the circumstances, seemed likely to crop out: now do the circumstances still continue the same? If they do, then the irregularities referred to are still possible, and must be guarded against. Are they changed, and the irregularities impossible? Then the half duty may be reconsidered." He hit the nail on the head — the rationale of the question — in a way that even WänSeang wd. scarcely have thought of.

Yin-Keen [introductory audience] is for officers of the 7th rank & upwards, Che-heen, & Show-fei: Chaou-keen [court audience] differs from Yin-Keen in that in it the Emperor admits the person into the room, & talks with him, while in the Yin-Keen the individual kneels in the court yard about 20 paces from the Emperor — who sits in the tang [hall] — and repeats his name, age, &c.: this is called [blank in diary]. Some people break down, forgetting even their own names. Thus in the Yin-Keen ceremony, a man to some extent shows the stuff he is made of by the tone of voice, manner, and accuracy with which he introduces himself.[118]

Kih-t'ow differs from P'ing t'ow: the first is merely to bend the head towards the ground, while the second is literally to "knock head".[119]

TUESDAY, 2 AUGUST 1864: [characters for 1st day of the 7th month]

When finishing dinner this evening, it suddenly came into my head to send a Ting Chae [office attendant] down to the Legation to inquire if Mr. Wade had returned from the hills: Ma-urh came back saying that one of the Ting Chae had been at the legation in the morning, & that Mr. Wade had returned. Said I to him: "Well just let us see if Mr. Wade will not be up here shortly; the idea of him came into my head so suddenly that I should not be surprised if he were just now ordering his horse to come up." Twenty minutes afterwards, Wade really made his appearance: rather curious, this?[120]

He is delighted with the Nanking success, of course; the French & Russians, he thinks, are not delighted; and he thinks the Chinese shd. go in at once for making political capital vis-à-vis foreign powers, 1. by abolishing ling che [death by slicing], & 2. by letting it be known that they do not object to the coming of ministers to Peking. He says de Mas wrote to Hsieh at Teentsin, & that Hsieh had written back to tell him that he had misunderstood the proper purpose of the last clause of the note written by the Yamun to the Ministers when they wished de Mas to be allowed to come up to Peking: I wonder has Hsieh written so stupidly?[121]

I had a long jaw with my writer about Cycles this morning. A Cycle is a period of sixty years; and three Cycles form a complete 'Period'— there being a Shang-yuen [upper cycle], chung-yuen [middle cycle], and hia-yuen [lower cycle] Kea-tsze.[122] In the 180 years thus made up, the first sixty are generally years in which the prosperity of the country increases year after year; the middle cycle is always a time of tranquillity & happiness; the third Cycle is, however, one in which troubles always crop out, & in such a way, too, that affairs become worse year after year. The <u>Hia-yuen</u> <u>Kea-tsze</u> commenced in 1803 and ended last year; during that time,—the reigns of Kea King, Taou Kwang, & Heen Fung,—affairs become worse year after year: in Kea King's time, were the rebellions of the Pih-leen Keaou [White Lotus Teaching] and of the female leader in Sze Chuen Tseih wih Kwafoo.[123] Taoukwang was initiated into the pleasure of foreign hostilities, and his unfortunate son, Hëen Fung, had the Taeping Rebellion raging all through his reign, and had the foreign wars between 1854 [*sic*] & 1860 too. Things could not have been worse, in fact. This is the first year of the Shang-yuen Kea tsze, and an improvement is already perceptible, and the future is full of promise. During the Chung-yuen Kea tse, from 1743 @ 1803, Keen-lung was on the throne; his reign was one of unexampled prosperity & peace. The <u>Shang-yuen</u> <u>Kea</u> <u>tse</u> from 1683 @ 1743 had Kang-he and Yung-ching on the throne: it commenced badly, but improvements took place year after year, and Yung Ching's reign was an exceedingly prosperous one. He must have been a most able Emperor; the decrees of his reign form the most important set of authorities on all questions that the Chinese have got. The preceding Hia-yuen Kea tsee, 1623 @ 1683, saw the downfall of the Ming Dynasty, and the disturbances which accompanied the establishment of the Tartars. The Hia-yuen Kea tsee [*sic*] that preceded—1443 @ 1503—was one in which great troubles took place. The young grandson of the first Ming Emperor was dethroned by his uncle, Yung luh, who put to death many high officials, and whose actions led to great disorders. [Over this last sentence is written in blue pencil: Ping-ting Kwei-keen (Yuen chaou).][124]All this seems very strange: but history shows the facts to have been thus during the last 600 years, at all events—and the idea seems to have been in existence long before that. Can it be that national life has its regularly recurring <u>seasons</u>? I certainly think that China is now going to improve daily, and I am confident that during the first half of the 20th century, she will be the mightiest & most prosperous of Kingdoms. Except in that they don't fight, I consider the Chinese, as a people, superior to any other: had they our learning & Christianity, they would be infinitely <u>beyond</u> us. [large question mark in margin]

Tsäng Kwo fan has been made a Hou-tsëo—or Marquis: Kwan Wen Tsang Kwo Tseuen, & Le Hung Chang have each got Pih-tsëo,—Earldoms: honors of all kinds have been profusely scattered about to mark the Imperial satisfaction at the capture of Nanking. The captured chiefs, the Chang Wang & the Kan Wang, have been ordered to be sent to Peking. Tsang Kwo fan reports as killed 100,000 Rebels & 3000 of their leaders: this is all nonsense—there were not 10,000 fighting men in the city. I wonder what has become of all the women and children?[125]

WEDNESDAY, 3 AUGUST 1864: Went this morning to call on Ching Taoutae: "the way was long" and the road was bad, & when I got there, he was out, so I had to come back again.[126] My continued squatting, 2 1/2 hours, in the cart tired me horribly.

My writer brought the teachers for Kleinwächter and Des Champs today: his own son, a soft faced lubber who says <u>She-she</u> ["yes, yes"] to everything, and that too in a way that gives one a curious idea of combined solidity and softness of sound — as if it were a <u>fat</u> <u>substance</u> blown out from an indian rubber ball; and a man named <u>Ke-lin</u>, who is a <u>Keu jin</u> [provincial degree-holder] & whose father was a Taoutae in Chekiang — rather mercurial & impertinent, I shd. say, but seemingly fond of talking, & therefore likely to be a good teacher.[127]

Thunderstorms and heavy rain in the afternoon, which, as usual, made me sleepy.

THURSDAY, 4 AUGUST 1864: Almost cold when I tumbled out at five this morning. The summer may be regarded as over.

Went to the office at 2: found everybody very busy, and did not therefore get through any work. I left my draft of regulations with WänSeang, who smiled when he saw the words "after 20 years' service", but he seemed pleased with them on the whole; I also gave him to peruse my letters to Le Footae about Hammond & Lay. Wan has been made a Tae tsze tae-paou [grand Guardian of the Heir Apparent]; honors have been conferred on the Prince, Paou, and other Keun-Ke [Grand Councillors]. By the way, my writer did not come till late this morning, having been sent for by Hängke, who, he said, was again unwell: he then went on to say that Hängke had been talking to him about my <u>Kung-laou</u> [merit], & had stated that, if it had not been for my <u>Teaou-ting</u> [mediation] in Gordon's affair, matters wd. now be of a very different kind, and that the Govt. ought to do something for me. It struck me that the writer had been asked to find out what would content me, and that they intended to give me some honor or other: so I told him that I had <u>already</u> got what I hoped to get, i.e., that my action had been taken up with a view to the adoption of such measures as might lead to a speedy putting down of the rebellion, and that, after what I did, every step in that direction, every success was an honor, as it were, conferred on me, — that these were my rewards, and that I wanted nothing else: [characters for *Chao Meng chih so-kuei Chao Meng neng chien-chih*; lit. "That which Chao Meng exalts he can also debase; i.e., take lightly."], said I. I however explained to him that, as regards honors, it was with me, "Aut Caesar, aut nulles" — that I would rather have nothing than something middling kind, and that if they gave me a button atall, the only one I wd. have wd. be one of the <u>first</u> class.[128] "Wd. not a second or third class do?" asked he. This query made me think the matter had certainly been talked over. When at the office, Hängke made hints in that direction: but he of course, wd. wait to hear the writer's report before doing anything more. The writer thinks, the generals at Nanking ought to be called upon for the money they found in the place.

While at the office, the letters by the "City of Nantes" and "Nanzing", with portion of Mail of 4th June, arrived. At S'Hae, Parkes is busying himself about the joint tribunal: he will find himself completely checkmated on the arrival of the instructions. No letter yet from de Meritens: I shall have to suspend him yet I fear. Hammond applies for a year's leave: he is sick at last: I think I shall send White there. Williams writes from Swatow that trade & duties increase there. At Canton the opium smuggling still goes on: Glover is [infuriated] with the Hoppo for keeping him waiting at the gate, & seems to have come back from his leave in much the same frame of mind, as did Lay, i.e. forgetful of what he had previously learned about the Chinese. Lay has sent me some supplementary fleet a/c; but as yet I hear nothing of the sale of the ships: I must cut my connexion with the business as quickly as possible.

I find, on calculating, that in addition to the amounts paid as Inspector General's balance to my credit, the offices have balances amounting to tls. 30 000, and that the Confiscation Fund also amounts to over tls. 30 000. I shall make them pay all this money to me: it will enable me to get two steamers at once, and to build.

A letter from Maggie dated June 1st. Minnie Hart was married on the 29th March.

FRIDAY, 5 AUGUST 1864: In the house all day reading my letters from ports, &c.

SATURDAY, 6 AUGUST 1864: A somewhat sultry morning: I saw a most wonderful meteor cross the sky in the South-east about 3 1/2 A.M. It appeared all at once in the mid heavens, then burst, and as regarded the star, disappeared: it had however already formed a line, like this [a line with an arrow parallel to it ↙], which faded & reappeared, faded and reappeared several times — the last time it was like this. [two wavy, elongated "s" shaped lines ∬] I never before saw such a curious appearance in the heavens.

Put into Chinese today a Memo, asking for some compensation from the Chekiang authorities for the young Brown: also wrote a letter to Ying Taoutae, and drafted a couple of shin chings to the Yamun sending in the Returns for first quarter.

Wade came in about 9 o'clock, and talked for an hour. He was in good spirits, and the only thing he spoke out about was a despatch written by Hsieh to De Mas, relative to the wish of the latter to come to Peking — in which he tells him that the Prince has nothing to do with it, & that an Edict is an Edict. Wade is wroth, & so will be all the Ministers, who will feel that the Yamun's polite letter was merely humbugging them. Wade has had a letter from the F.O. informing him that the Govt. will take charge of the sale of "the fleet," and that care will be taken to prevent the Chinese being losers to any great extent.

SUNDAY, 6 AUGUST 1864: My old writer surprised me by coming in today, although I told him yesterday not to come. He gradually let out that he had been with Hängke, who had informed him yesterday he & Tung had spoken to Wan Seang about me, and that today they were to see the Prince: the old man said he'd come to "make the preliminary congratulation". I wonder what they'll give me: I hope not a miserable button of the 3rd or 4th rank! He went on to talk about what might be done after the expected event of tomorrow: in way of,—having changed dress and donned the button,—for instance, establishing a family, and comforting my loneliness with a tsëe [concubine].¹²⁹ The temptation to get a concubine is very strong, I must confess: nothing bothers me so much, as my liking for women. It is, however, more than a year since I even touched one!

Had another talk with my fair neighbors over the wall this evening; one of them aged 36 asks me to make her Kan-new-urh [adopted daughter], and another, an elderly undersized rabbit-toothed, Hoonan hag, would like to follow me all the world over.¹³⁰

MONDAY, 8 AUGUST 1864: Man & Brett returned this morning from the hills.

WanSeang sent for me at eleven: and I found only himself and Tung there. They wanted nominally to talk about Ships' stores, & then showed me, too, a despatch from the FuhKeen Seun foo [Governor] relative to merchant-consuls. Wän then told me of his visit to the French legation on Saturday, and said that M. Berthemy had been discussing the Tonnage Dues question, and the reply relative to the coming of the Spanish Minister to Peking: that they had in fact promised the four months clause, in a kind of way, to both Spain and Saegon, and that as long as it merely hurt the Kwo-Kea [country or state] (revenue, in this case, I presume) without damaging the Te-che [prestige] of people he was inclined to give way—from which I infer that M. Berthemy has frightened him about something, probably Teen Tetuh; and he then went on to say that M. Berthemy had misunderstood his reply about de Mas—that the reply said in a circuitous way that it (the coming to Peking) could not be managed, while the interpretation put upon it was that, though the Yamun could not do it, yet Hsieh might. This interpretation said Wan, was quite wrong; and he fortified the assertion—which was a lie—by pointing to the [ai?] character and [ju; "as," "like," etc.] characters and by petty dissection of the style.¹³¹ (And he went further, Wade tells me: he said that I had been consulted about the letter.) Wan then commenced to talk about stars and buttons evidently trying to ascertain what I would like to have. Wade was then announced, so I was left alone with Tung, and afterwards with Häng—with whom I had a talk about the button, of which I don't now think anything will come — and Häng told me that Wade was also complaining about having been 'done' by the letter: all the other ministers thought it meant that Hsieh could put the affair through, & they led de Mas to apply to Hsieh, and thereon Hsieh told him bluntly that the Edict could not be altered. Wan & the others stuck out for it, that the letter told them in a circuitous way that the thing could not be done atall, and he said that I had not seen the letter until it was finished — which was a lie. Wade kept his temper, and merely expressed his opinion quietly: and that fact will probably alarm them somewhat. When he went away, Wan came back and talked with me about the matter: I said that if the Ministers had interpreted the letter incorrectly, I too had misunderstood everything that had been said at the Yamun, for I remembered distinctly that my impression was that what the Yamun meant to say was that it could not get the edict changed, and that Hsieh was the only person that could, and further that Hsieh and Tsung had been written to to devise some way of arranging the matter. [last three lines marked in margin with red pencil] For Wan now to turn round in this way, and lying like a trooper and letting in his best friends is really too bad: what is to be hoped for for or from them?

Camel's Wool, they tell me, Tsung How objects to: duty on tea, they have sent to Le Footae to make enquiries: Formosa, they have sent to FooChow to see about it. Everything looks unsatisfactory: it will be "from pillar to post" with a vengeance. What is to be done for them, or with them?

Wade called in just as I was about to sit down to dinner, so he staid and dined. He is disgusted that WanSeang should have endorsed such a trick, and he is not likely to allow himself to be taken in again. Nor will I, by Jove! Wade says Tsäng Kwo fan is the man for emperor: the man who will take heads off, and dare to rule. WänSeang has no pluck, and the Prince has become fond of money. I say that the Chinese leaders show themselves faithful to the dynasty: and that I do not anticipate any violent upsetting. Hitherto the Tartar rulers have been assimilating more and more to the Chinese: for the future a process of absorption is likely to go on, until a homogeneous state of things arrives, and government & everything will be Chinese without trouble: in fact it is almost so already, and we may wake up any [?] morning with a full consciousness of the fact that though the Hwang-te [emperor] is a descendant of Shun-chi, the govt. is formed of Chinese.[132]

Sent Wade home in my cart: in a thunderstorm, with tremendous rain pouring down.

TUESDAY, 9 AUGUST 1864: Nothing particular to note down for today, except that, having Man back, I got through the answers to a bundle of despatches that have been lying over for some time.

A deliciously cool breeze sprang up about ten o'c. Oh, by the way, I had another chat with my fair neighbors, when one of them gave me a scent [?] purse and threw off much previous shyness.

WEDNESDAY, 10 AUGUST 1864: My writer told me this morning that they think of giving me "T'ou-urh-pin ting taë" [upper 2nd class hat button] and a "hwaling" [peacock feather]: if they do, I suppose they'll throw in a "paou-sing" ["precious-star" decoration], and that'll be all. An addition to one's "fung luh" [salary] wd. be more substantial.[133]

Went to the Office at 2: sat with Wan, Tung, & Häng for a while: said that, as regards the misunderstanding with the ministers about the Spanish note, perhaps I myself was to blame for having, mistaking their meaning, advised the writing of the note in the terms in which it stands: I said that if I had understood the matter to be absolutely impossible of arrangement, I shd. never have advised them to do otherwise than say so plainly but politely: and that for the future, I shd. not interfere with anything outside of Customs' matters. I told WanSeang that I had heard Ch'in at Teentsin had told the Spaniards that as the Chinese wd. not allow the Prussians, who have a residence clause, to reside at Peking, there was not use atall in discussing the introduction of such a clause in the Spanish Treaty! Wän said it was quite impossible: that Ch'in could never have said such a thing.[134]

Wän then went out to meet Mr. Burlingame, with whom Ward's estate was the subject discussed. Mr. B wishes the Yamun to say that the old man's claim is just: the Yamun refuses to do so until it is proved to be so.[135] Dr. Williams, said Wan, made a remark which cd. not be understood, to the effect that the four ministers were about to write to the Yamun pointing out its she and the Spaniard's puh-she.[136] Wan probably reversed this speech.

Meantime, Murray came up to give a message from Wade, relative to the residence-clause, and the demand the Chinese make for trade with Manila on a 5% tariff. Murray only saw Hängke; but, as Wade told me when he came up this evening, Häng said that Chin was quite right—that residence had only been granted to the English and the French under compulsion, and that it was, too, to some degree, reparation, but the Prussians wd. not be allowed to reside at Peking, and that no other treaties wd. be made having the residence clause! Is it possible that the old man could have said so? What could he mean? Perhaps to make a row in the hope of smashing Hsieh: but his statement does not tally with Wan's. But then, whom is one to believe?

Had a long talk with old Tung, while Wan & Hang were doing Burlingame & Murray: chiefly about literary matters. We, however, went through my service rules, and made the proper corrections, and arrangements: so that that affair looks like settlement. Camels' Wool, Tea, & Taewan, still remain unsettled. Otherwise, my work is done: a/c excepted, which can always wait.

Letters of 2nd, from S'Hae by "Guard". Lord writes that there was no slaughter—no fighting at Nanking atall.[137]

Wade & St. John came up in the evening to ask me to dinner on Friday. Wade is in an awful stew about the fate of China! I wish he and the other ministers would mind their own business: too many cooks spoil the broth.

THURSDAY, 11 AUGUST 1864: Notified the Yamun, Le Footae, & Tsae Taoutae of White's appointment to Kiukiang.[138] Saw Murray this afternoon, and asked him whether or not Hängke had said it was a fact that Ch'in told the Spaniard that the Prussians would not be allowed to reside at Peking, and that therefore the Spaniard need not ask for a residence article? Murray did not answer very clearly, but I did get it out from him that Hängke had not made any such statement, although he had, in a private way, expressed his opinion to the effect that ministers might become too numerous if they came.

Wade's excitement was therefore, to a great extent, unfounded: I come reluctantly, in one sense, but gladly in another, to the belief that he must be styled an alarmist.

Brett gave a great spread tonight to his student friends of the French, British, and Russian Legations, who mustered to the number of nine to give him "goodbye" with all honors. The number was thus 13: so Man left the table, and dined alone. I wonder is the number actually an unlucky one, or is it that out of any thirteen who sit down to dinner the chances are that one will die during the year? Songs were sung, and the fun kept up till eleven. I did not join the party: I have lost my youthful elasticity.

FRIDAY, 12 AUGUST 1864: An extract of a letter from Lord to Dick says that there was no slaughter at Nanking, and that there were no dead bodies about, on the day after the capture, to give evidence of fighting: no loot, no women, no rebels. The fact, I fear, is that during the last four months they have been allowed gradually to pass through the Imperial lines with their goods and chattels. The last to leave was seemingly the Chung Wang, and as the Imperialists were then sure of the city, they appear to have thought it a good thing to nobble him too; or possibly Chinese-like, it was bargained that, for the city & Chung Wang, the others would be allowed to pass.

Dined with Wade. He quite dampened my ardor and spirits by the dismal way in which he crooned over the stupidity and ignorance of the Chinese: their puerility in not giving people what it will not hurt them to give, and in asking for things that will be of no benefit to them. England and America are the only nations that have any real interests in China: they ask for nothing but what is fair. At the same time, their reciprocity is a very defensive kind, for though they get angry with China when anything asked is refused, they don't hesitate to refuse what China asks for in the coolest and most unsympathetic manner. France in pursuit of la gloire thought fit to join in the operations against China, and the game has been kept up of supporting propagandism in a most iniquitous manner, damn them! — to please the clerical party in France: the missionaries and their converts from all one can hear of them are a curse to this country. Then come the other nations: Prussia & Denmark have a little interest in the coasting trade; Portugal has interests connected with Macao, and here comes Spain to make a treaty—

merely because other nations have made treaties. I say, it argues as much, it is as much, and perhaps more blameworthy, puerility, for nations to come rushing in this way to make treaties with a country like China which they affect to despise. Wade thinks every thing is going to the deuce, and he talks in a way that makes me awfully uncomfortable. If each country wd. mind its own business, I think matters wd. go on more pleasantly.

Heavy rain tonight.

SATURDAY, 13 AUGUST 1864: What is religion? Is it feeling, or is it doing? Is it enough to have a conscientious desire to do right? Will such conscientious, i.e., real & truthful & conscious, desire to do right, be nullified by the fact that what is done is wrong? Will a right action done by chance or by mistake by a man be a score in his favor? The measure of the value of a man's conscientious desire to do right — is it his knowledge of what is right? But again what is his knowledge but his belief? His belief cannot be a satisfactory one unless he knows why he entertains it & can give a reason for it: is it worthy of being styled belief, or knowledge, and consequently of being taken as the measure of the value of the conscientious desire to do right, if it be a belief, the result merely of association — a belief which the individual has never investigated, and which, as an intelligent creature, he ought to have a reason for? Will it suffice as a reason for a belief to say that "everyone says so"? Surely not in all cases: will it then in the most important of all? Will if suffice to say that "so-and-so teaches it"? Surely not, considering the fallibility of man. Where then are we to look for a solid starting point in morals? This man conscientiously eats [sic] his father: that man conscientiously keeps half a dozen wives: can we then in the customs of the country, at large, find a standing point? I doubt it very much: and I doubt too whether it will do to appeal to our own inner consciousness, inasmuch as its deposits and its ways of looking at things are the results of the teachings to which the individual has been exposed. The question, however, with which I set out is this: what is the safe thing — the desire to be right in what one does, although one may thereby conscientiously go astray, or the doing, perhaps ignorantly, of what is really right? In the one case, will not the wrongness of the action nullify its conscientious element? In the other, will not the difficulty arise of giving a reason for what is pronounced on any occasion to be right, for opinions are very diversified?

Will a man's lifetime suffice for the examination of the grounds on which he rests his belief? If not, what is the value of the belief of the young man, who is taken from this world before he has made any examination? Does not the question, taken from this point, resolve itself into one of feeling — heart rather than intellect? Will it do to say, "I feel safe"? You may say, you "feel happy", because that is a state or condition of your own mind; but to say, you "feel safe", involves another party — and what know you of that party, your belief being without intellectually tested grounds, save through the mirage of imaginitive feeling?

In short; is it the <u>truthfulness</u> of the man in himself, or the extreme properness of the actions, by which a judgment is to be guided and formed? If the man's truthfulness, or honesty, then why or what matters a diversity of creeds? If the external rightness of the act, the simple doing of it is enough: why then bother one's self with weary enquiries?

Perhaps a mixture of the two elements is the basis of the safety: "if you make a conscientious use of the means at your disposal, or knowing and doing what is right, your good actions will be noted and your mistakes pass unrecorded: but your measure of conscientiousness will be the measure of the forgiveness that follows conduct."

The Christian doctrine seems to meet this intellectual difficulty: shall I say, it thoroughly does so, or merely that it appears to do so?

It says: "your imperfections are fully recognized, and your difficulty to do what is right: but atonement has been made for your misdoings, and you have only to accept that atonement, and obey the words of the saviour by whom it was made."

Then comes up the query, is it an actual fact that atonement was made? The Scriptures say so.

But what are the scriptures; are the books given in the Old & New Testaments <u>all</u> scriptures? Do those that have been thrown out, really form no part of <u>the</u> Scriptures? Do those that are kept contain nothing but what is true, and are they all <u>divine</u> revelation? If they are <u>all</u> divine revelation, are they without contradictions, and are there not many things, which were done in them by <u>men</u> <u>after</u> <u>God's</u> <u>own</u> <u>heart</u>, placed under a ban as wicked and inadmissable, at the present day—E.G., plurality of wives? If all <u>cannot</u> be said to be divine revelation, what parts are correct? and to find what parts are correct, on what principle of criticism is one to proceed? Is the New Testament to be entirely taken? Is part of the Old to be rejected? In short, on what is it that we base our acceptance of the Scriptures as God's word—the English version, for instance?

Again, in criticizing the Scriptures, is it admissable to argue that because such and such teachings do not seem to us—to <u>our</u> <u>minds</u>—to be reconcileable with the idea which we form (perhaps from other parts of the same books, perhaps from abstract reasoning) of what the character of the Deity is, or ought to be, they are therefore to be rejected? Is it allowable for us to judge in such a way? And if it is not, why so, and how escape the necessity for allowing an <u>infallible</u> <u>church</u>, or, at all events, an infallible rendering of the Scriptures—and where is that infallibility—and in what version—to be found?

The reasoning above followed out resolves itself into this as a way of escape: is it the right one?

A. Is it a fact that Christ lived? Now, that about 1800 years ago a great teacher did appear in Judea, known as Jesus Christ, is as well established by historical evidence, as that Napoleon died in St. Helena.

B. Is it a fact that he taught what he is said to have taught, and what we find in the evangelists? There seems to be no reason for doubting that he did;

enquiry shows that the Gospels were written and accepted before the end of the first century: they did not exist before that time, and they have not been altered since: there is a continuity, and a one-ness of principle, let alone a loftiness of morality, which proclaim the teachings to be the product of one mind, and that a very superior one. The Teacher claimed, too, for his teachings that they were of God.

C. Are the teachings to be regarded as of divine origin? They were accepted as such by the disciples and promulgators of them; they were said to be of God, by the Teacher himself; they were given forth while the Teacher was still a young man, a man of about thirty years of age, and were not the product of a ripe old age which (free from passions and with the grave before it) could vent its experiences, and in fact discover principles, and from the heart of things tear the rule of conduct; in their purity and highness of tone, they go beyond the teachings of all sages in all parts of the world; and in that they make the rule or measure of virtue obedience to God's will, & support it by offers of mercy and threats of punishment, they form a connecting link between the Creator and the creature, and show a knowledge of the wants and peculiarities of human nature, which we do not find—and the want of which is the actual <u>working</u> defect—in any system of philosophy or morals that has ever elsewhere been given to the world; they were uttered by a youth who was born of humble parents, who consorted with the lowly, and who does not seem to have had the advantages of studying in the schools of philosophers; thus in themselves intrinsically, in their surroundings, in their peculiarities, in the Man from whom they came, in the effect they had on those taught, they <u>do</u> seem to be what the Teacher claimed for them, <u>of</u> <u>God</u>.

D. Did the Teacher perform the acts & work the miracles recounted, and did he rise from the dead? Granting that the Teachings are what we allow them to be (c) of God, there is proof presumptive that the miracles recorded as having accompanied them actually did occur; and if the teachings were of God, and if we allow one miracle to have been wrought, there need be no hesitation in accepting the <u>last</u> statement as a fact—that Christ did rise from the dead, and that he ascended into heaven. Further, the histories of those acts were in circulation soon after they were said to have occurred; is there any contradiction of them? Did concurrent history rebut them? on the contrary, it rather supported them.

E. Was then Christ God? He claimed to be so: and looking at the purity of this life, the sublimity and adaptation of his teaching, and granting that he worked miracles, and rose from the dead, His claim cannot be questioned.

F. Allowing then Christ to have been God, and the Gospel teachings to have been his, and of God, what then? Simply, that we are bound to study them, to hold them in reverence, to shape our conduct by his example, and to rule our lives in accordance with His commands.

G. <u>But</u>: does such acceptance of the Scriptures—does such acknowledgement of the fact that they contain teachings <u>of God</u>—preclude all criticism? Does it mean that every word is to be accepted? If we assert this, what would

177

we mean? That the translations are to be accepted, or that the originals are to be held as genuine? If the translations, what of <u>marginal</u> readings? If the originals where are they, and what of textual differences? <u>No</u>: it seems that criticism is allowable, and even necessary: the words must be winnowed — the spirit is what is to be got at. But to get at the spirit what principle, in our criticisms, is chiefly to be kept in view? I should say, what is to be kept in view was what we consider to have been the <u>intention</u> of the Deity in making the Revelation. Now that 'intention' would seem to have reference to the future rather than to the past: it was not to teach us the history of the past that Christ appeared; it was to teach us simply what kind of lives we, as the creatures of the creator, should live, and to give food to that hungry part of our nature which gropes for the invisible — "bread of life" in fact, to our spiritual starvation. The principle shd. be to separate from the unimportant the important, to disintegrate the substance, and to eliminate the accidental portions.

H. Allowing then the propriety of criticism, and fixing for its grand principle a right understanding of the objects of Christ's teachings, what may be looked forward to as the end likely to be attained, the goal to be reached finally, by criticism conducted freely but without hostility, fearlessly but yet reverentially? I should say, the result will be, in the first place, the fixing of the <u>relative</u> values of the Book that at present confers the scriptures of the old testament and new, that will lead to a proper understanding of the mutual connexion, and intelligible ideas of their bearing and influence on each other. In the second place, such criticism ought to lead to a settlement of the best authenticated text, and truthful rendering of the same. In the third place, a commentary will grow up by which the real meanings of the <u>understood</u> parts of the scripture will be fixed, and by which the doctrines of the Christian religion will be established for all churches and for all times.

I should say then on the Scriptures that, — while criticism may show they contain something which cannot be reconciled with our ideas of the Divine Nature, and other things which seem contradicted by history and by scientific investigation, — yet they <u>do</u> contain teachings of God, and <u>do</u> contain all that is necessary for our salvation.

SUNDAY, 14 AUGUST 1864: What precedes, put under yesterday's date, was actually written this morning; the train of thought had its origin in a moonlight talk I had last night with the ladies next door. Not that we talked either religion or philosophy, but that we pressed each others hands, and that they allowed advances to be made, which, in the case of Chinese ladies who are taught not to be familiar with males, shows that they could easily be induced to go the "whole hog". They set my blood on fire, and I am doubtful whether I am arguing with the object of cooling myself and forcing myself to abstain from what is wrong, or whether I am trying to enshroud myself in a cold philosophical discussion of morals, which <u>can</u> go hand in hand with immorality — and prove that <u>feeling</u>, in matters of religion, is nonsense—"feeling," mind you, being much akin to a tender conscience, and feeling, hurt at what it feels to be wrong.

My most immoral tendency is in the direction of "the sex." There's no doubt, of that: for other indulgences, or pleasures, I care nothing; but for woman, what wd. I not give?

Now, for a whole year, I have on principle abstained from womanizing; I have hardened myself against the temptation, and I have victoriously, as regards outer action, fought a continued fight, in which for twelve months, day after day, passion has implored to be allowed to gratify itself, while principle has set its teeth, and with a "stiff upper lip" has, day after day, said "no, you don't!" Here, at last, I find passion "taking the bit between its teeth", and I'm almost off: is this desperate struggle—this gnawing of the heart, this keeping down of fiery and natural impulses to go on? As I sit calmly at my table and write, or as I walk with hands behind my back and head bent down with overladen brow, trying to work out schemes for the good of this country, how little would a looker on think that my heart was on fire, and that a continual struggle was in the background being fought against womanizing!

It wd. be a wonderfully good thing for me if I were married: I would then be actually at peace. I have outlived the riotous tastes of youth; neither gaming, drinking, nor social dissipation have any hold on me: I am a hard working, earnest man, delighting (after my necessary outside work is done) remaining quietly in the house, with my books, and simple indoor pleasures,—liking to see my friends at my table occasionally, but not caring much to go out or present myself at the tables of others: but, I am mad upon the pleasures of the couch. O Woman, lovely woman! And yet it is sexual desire—it is, I fear, more brute passion, than desire for the society of women. I like to have a girl in the room with me, to fondle when I please: and I like to have something to be affectionate with, for I have got a great stock of love in my nature. So I say it again, it wd. be a good thing for me if I could get married. But, confound it, I can't! I shall not be able to get home till 1867; so I must wait three years more for a wife, unless I send home and ask them to choose one for me. Such a thing wd. be rather hazardous: heaven only knows what she might turn out to be! Were I to send home, I only can think of four to ask for: Marian Moorhead, Norah Shillington, Henrietta Shillington, and Miss Clendening. I should like most to get out the third, and yet I have a sneaking fondness for them all. At home polygamy would not do; and indeed, with English girls it would not pay; they wd. tear each others' eyes out, run off with outsiders, and weary the life out of their common lord. In China & with Chinese, in a house surrounded with high walls, and in the Chinese style of keeping the women in the back apartments, polygamy does get on—though it does carry with it rows, &c.: and were I always to remain in China, I might do as the Chinese do—for though socially I consider polygamy inexpedient in the west, I do not think it inexpedient in China, nor do I consider it morally wrong in itself.

The two young ladies who come out to talk with me over the wall next door are aged 16 and 18; they talk well, are amusing, had have received some education, being able to read and write. Their father is over <u>70</u> years of age, and is a 'red-button,' having held high office in the provinces; his first wife, their mother, is dead, and he had, until ten days ago, three other wives, each about 35 years of age, — one Cantonese, one from SzeChuan, and one from Hoonan; ten days ago he invested in another, a girl of 16 or 17! What a game old gentleman, to be sure! His three wives — the "thirtys" — come out and gossip freely, and I should say from their pranks, that he does not render them "due benevolence"; the young ladies, his daughters, are skittish, and, being badly supplied with pocket money, seem inclined for fun, combining, if it did and as it would, "fire" and "tin". The last-taken young wife has not showed herself yet: the old gentleman keeps her close to him, and, I dare say, his fondness or partiality for her, has tended to decrease the respect of his daughters for himself, as well as to lead the other wives to feel fonder of outdoor sport. I hear that the old gentleman gave a dozen pandies to one of the girls, and kept her on her knees for half a day, for coming out into the yard to gossip with some of my people.[139] Last night, they cribbed the key of the back door and stayed out till half-past nine! Going ahead, indeed!

If I don't take care, passion will be off with me — confound it!

[Below, a row of crosses and stars]

* * *

Yesterday I talked well into Ping laou-yay who will retail it to Hangke, the weakness of the Chinese, and the impolicy of offending foreigners. They must give the French justice in the Te'en tetuh case: is it that they cannot or that they will not? It must be either the one or the other: if the former, then the Govt. has no authority, and may collapse any day: if the latter then the French have just cause of offense. If the French take action, the Portuguese, unable to ratify their treaty, will be in the row too, and will get more than Macao out of it. The Russians, too, wd. secure more ground in the north. The French wd. seize ground as a material guarantee; and England, seeing other countries seize territory, wd. have to take some, in support of British interests. There are the Spaniards, too; if they are irritated, — if the Spaniard breaks off negotiations, Manila is close at hand, and forms a capital base of operations. China could not stand atall! And yet the policy of Chinese officials seems to be: "we'll not give you except what you take; what you ask for, we'll not give, simply because we can refuse it." They give when they ought not; they hold back when they ought to give. They do everything at the wrong time, and with a bad grace.

If the Tsung le Yamun — which is now, and will for the future be, the most important office in China — had better men in it: if it had Le Footae, and had not Hsieh; if Paou wd. attend to business and either Häng or Tsung keep away; and if, too, it had Laou Tsung Kwang in it — what a capital thing it would be![140]

If WanSeang had Le Footae's courage: if Le Footae had WanSeang's care for minutiae, and could look before he leaped; if Tung were more practical

and less of a bookworm; if Häng dare speak out, and were sure of backers; if Tsung's old age were made an excuse to allow of his going into private life; if Hsieh were smashed — or if at all events, he had Häng's cleanliness, Tung's literature, WanSeang's good nature and intelligence, Le Footae's pluck, Laou's steadiness, and Tsäng Kwo fan's influence, why then he might do!
[A line of crosses and stars below]

*　　　*　　　*

Went to the office at 2 P.M and had four hours conversation with Wan and Tung, during which I explained to them freely and earnestly the impolicy of causing ill feeling by quibbling and making small difficulties while the govt. is weak, which it would not condescend to stoop to if strong. I gave them my idea of Hsieh, and they asked me where a man was to be found combining all such qualifications: Wan went on to enquire whether I would feel satisfied if the people I had alluded to were attached to the Yamun. I answered that I rather should: that the Yamun, having to transact foreign affairs, was the most important office in the country, and that in it ought to be found the ablest men.

They sanction a thousand taels for young Brown: they cannot do more, as they only gave tls. 1400 in the case of the Frenchman, Tardif, who was killed.[141]

Told them that I feared the Nanking success when scrutinised would show that, although they had got the city, the "birds had flown" — in fact, that the mons. (mountain) had brought forth a ridiculous mus: "Tae Shan yew zün, säng hia sho ko k'o seaou tih haou-tsz, ["In all of exalted Mt. T'ai there are (only) ten ludicrous mice."]][142]

MONDAY, 15 AUGUST 1864: Louis Napoleon's fête day. Wrote a couple of savage notes to Wade today, — an explosion which he styled "refreshing," — and which brought him up to jaw in the evening. I said that hitherto I had been giving my advice at the Yamun, on the understanding that no reference was to be made to me, and that I consequently, being always cautious and reticent, had been constantly in a position of one who must feel that being a secret adviser his position, though honorable enough, has certain homogeneity with that of a spy: that Wän Seang had been letting it out that my opinions had been asked for, and that, no doubt, people wd. suppose or suspect that I was making a "sneaking" attempt at becoming what the 'China Mail' when writing of Lay, styled "the pivot." So I said that I had determined that for the future I shd give information and advice to the Chinese, with the full conviction that it wd. be some day "fathered" upon me, and that, just as I would not make any underhand attempt in the direction of the pivot, so I would not hesitate to own and acknowledge whatever had really dropped from me. And such is my determination: I shall not thrust information, or force my views on the Chinese; but when they ask for one or the other they shall have them freely. I am on the Chinese side, and I will help them to the best of my abilities: and I don't care who knows what

I do or what I say. I shall for the future ever hold myself in readiness of publicity—and shall not attempt secrecy or mystery atall.

Did not go out atall today.

TUESDAY, 16 AUGUST 1864: Doing nothing in particular.

Received a couple of despatches from the Yamun, one about "Dock Stores", and the other relative to "Funds for the NewChwang Estabt."

Gave Mr. Edkins tls. <u>100</u>, one half for his school, the other for charitable purposes.

Rode out for an hour this evening, and enjoyed the ride greatly. My pony, though, nearly came down when galloping, and hurt me slightly by throwing me on the pommel of the saddle.

WEDNESDAY, 17 AUGUST 1864: A visit from Mr. Martin, this morning, with whom I had a pleasant talk about prospects of progress in China. He made use of a good analogy: heavy bodies though moving as quickly—and of course more difficult to set in motion—do not seem to do so much as light or small ones: the earth does not seem to us to move, but compare it with planets, &c., and we see it does: compare China with Turkey, &c. He showed me the first page of his translation of "Wheaton": I told him, if he wanted more than tls. 500, I could get it for him, and that I should move the Govt. to grant him some money for his Mission, in recognition of his services. He seemed gratified: I dare say, <u>all</u> men have a little self love, and even Christians can indulge in vanity—why shouldn't they? Talked about Mormonism—freedom of discussion—voluntary societies—established churches, &c. &c. &c.

The West is not <u>imitating</u> China; but acting on its own experiences, it is doing many things which assimilate it to China. Thus, we might point to <u>competitive</u> <u>examinations</u>; the tendency to endow all sects: the principle in civil govt.—daily more insisted on—that what the people can do for themselves, the govt. ought not to do for them, &c. &c. &c. It would be worth while to work this out into a "C'est moi" for the "Herald".

Went to the office by appointment at 2 1/2, and came away at 5. Nothing particular said, or done; Wän Seang went through the Commissioner's Regulations with me, and we decided definitely on their form. I notice he asks regularly whether or not I have seen any of the Kin-chae [here meaning foreign ministers]: I suppose he is becoming sensitive and wishes to know their opinions on his conduct. I told him and Tung—the only other present, Tsung and Häng having gone on Chae-she [official duty] to the Imperial tombs—that I had had a correspondence with Wade on Monday, and that in future they must understand that I had no objection to their pointing to me as the giver of any information or advice I may actually have given.[143]

Crossed the wall this evening, and had a moonlight chat with Le Tsaey Tseay: it is amusing to see how the urh-moo-tsin squeezed herself out of a hole near the roof, let herself down to the ground, gave a sop to the dog, then tied him up, and stood by him in the shade while I paid my devoirs to the girls. One of them handed me a note with some of her poetry in it — something like the Widow Bêdott's, I imagine — the last line of which is "Why don't the Ta-jin [great man] come across the wall?" It was half past one and more by the time I got back to my rooms.[144]

THURSDAY, 18 AUGUST 1864: The French Minister called this morning at eight, but I was fast asleep at the time and did not see him.

Rode down to see Brown in the evening; he is better, he says, but looks much pulled down and seems to me quite feverish. Had a short talk with Wade: he now thinks that the Spanish Minister has himself chiefly to blame for all the delays and disagreeables of Teentsin; he has made up his mind to communicate Lord Russell's letter about the fleet to the Yamun. Three years according to Chinese reckoning since Hëen Fung the Wän tsung heen Hwang te — on 7th m. 17th d. — died! "Resquiescat in pace."[145]

FRIDAY, 19 AUGUST 1864: Rode out to the Gan-ting Mun tonight; the Yuë ching [courtyard] there is very spacious, the walls high, the gate well preserved, and the little red temple in the enclosure quite picturesque. What a pity it is that foreigners resident in Peking are not established in that quarter, or near the West Wall![146]

Ping pointed out to me today a curious coincidence: the first Emperor of the present dynasty entered the city by the <u>Shun-che</u> mun, — the most Western one, on the south face; the <u>Kwo-haou</u> [reign name] he subsequently took was also Shun-Che — selected accidentally, it is said, and not because he entered by that gate. In Nanking, too, one of the gates is named the <u>Hung-wo</u> Mun: the first Emperor of the Mings was known as Hung Wo, — the gate had its name before the Emperor established himself.[147]

Talking of cycles, Ping said that in the Yuen chaou [Yuan dynasty] a book was written, to which an addition was made towards the close of the Ming dynasty — Ming mô — named the Ping Kwei-Keen, showing that the Ping wu and Ting wei years of each cycle from time immemorial have been unlucky ones.[148]

SATURDAY, 20 AUGUST 1864: Went to the Yamun at 2, having been sent for by Wan Seang. Wade's despatch relative to the fleet had arrived, and the last two words of the quotation from Earl Russell's letter had attracted their attention: the Earl says the Govt. will take care that the Chinese do not eventually lose <u>the value</u> of the ships. Wan asks, what 'value'? what we paid for them, what they are worth now, or what they may sell for in five years' time? He does not show the slightest ill temper, but he seems to feel that the affair may put him and others in a fix — they may be called on by successors in office to "make up" the deficiency. We arranged that a despatch in reply should be written to Wade arguing the matter fully, and that a note should be addressed to Sir. F. Bruce requesting his good offices to bring the matter to a speedy settlement in England.[149]

A note from Tsung-How was handed to me proposing to value camel's wool at tls. 14 per pec. & charge 5 per cent; also relative to the Siamese ship that was talked about last year, and which, having returned to Teentsin, he says ought to pay duties, &c., to the Laou Kwan [old customs establishment].[150]

Tung went out to receive Fontainier, who came up to get a correction made in a letter, in which the Yamun tells the French Minister that for him to appoint merchants to be consuls is a violation of the treaty, meaning thereby a violation of the written promise made by Baron Gros, after negotiating the Treaty.

They handed me the despatch, slightly altered, but approving of my rules for the guidance of Commissioners: also a despatch directing the payment of Tls. 500, from the Yamun's 3/10 of Tonnage Dues, to W. Martin, to print his translation of Wheaton's International Law.

Had a long gossip about yün-ke [luck], Fung-shwuy [geomancy], swanming [fortune-telling], &c. &c. &c. Tung said he would not allow books on such subjects in his library: to tell a man that he will be lucky, is to make him trust his luck and not work: to tell him he'll be unlucky, has precisely the same result. Therefore, says Tung, such books and such ideas are to be kept from young people: he is evidently no fatalist. Wan told us an amusing story of a diviner who lately was telling the fortune of a friend of his: "Yes," went on the man, "and before the end of the year, you'll have a son, too!" The friend blushed, Wan laughed, and said the former, "O come now, you're humbugging me, Walker!" [?] or something to that effect. Then came the explanation, that the friend's wife had gone to her home months before, not in an interesting condition, and that his concubine had but just been taken to himself, and it only wanted a few months of the end of the year.[151]

Tsäng Kwo fan, they say, is devoted to astronomy.[152]

Had another "delicious" fight with myself tonight: I knew that the girls were out in the Yuen-tsze [courtyard], and I wanted to go to them, but eventually did not do so.[153] This war of passion and principle is horrible: in fact, it is almost wearing me out! Confound it all! merely, I presume, the last kicks of a fiery youth—the last flare up of the candle before it goes out—before the quiet of middle age comes on, and nature turns in some other direction.

SUNDAY, 21 AUGUST 1864: I could not get asleep last night; so I got ahold of Legge's Classics, and 'repeated' the first two chapters of the Confucian Analects: is it worth while going on day after day, committing to memory the words of Confucious? If I remain long in China, and devote any time into putting English works into Chinese, I may find it useful, and it supplies an apt and clinching quotation for conversations, now and then.[154] To be mastered, though, the work has to be gone at regularly every day.

[Asterisks across the page]

* * *

The Scriptures must be either true or untrue: if the latter, the sooner they are proved so, the better; if the former, they have nothing to fear from hostile criticism. It strikes me that Christians, generally speaking, have a very <u>superstitious</u> belief in the Scriptures, and that their ideas of their duties and positions as Christians, are of the vaguest and most irrational kind. Few, indeed, they, who can "give a reason for the hope that is in them!" Still if they have quiet and mental satisfaction, may it not be "the peace that passeth understanding"? It is hard to say which ought to please the Deity most, Logic or Love!

I wonder what St. Paul's "thorn of flesh" was? I know what <u>mine</u> is: praying & fighting free from it for a time, but it comes back with redoubled force. Seven devils, in fact, come back to take up their station in the quarters from which one has been expelled. Matrimony is the only thing for it, and horrible to say, with money and the means to support a wife comfortably, here am I, the very one that is unable to provide himself with a partner! Truly the fates are unkind: or, am I going through a course of mental & moral training, which is fitting for something in the future, for which I shd. never have been fitted were it not for the exercitations [sic] consequent on the working of my "thorn".

[Asterisks across the page]

* * *

John XIV.15. "If ye love me, <u>keep</u> my commandments".

This day last year, I left Peking to return to Shanghae. Changes!

MONDAY, 22 AUGUST 1864: Last night, at all events, principle had its triumph. Ma-urh had arranged with the girls to come out and talk over the wall at 11 P.M., and, though they did come out, <u>I</u> <u>kept</u> <u>away</u>. I was quite right to keep away, but it was not easy to do so. Action is the thing: passive impressions by being often repeated, says Butler, become weakened; it does not do to rush day after day into temptation, with one's eyes open, and then pray to be delivered from it.[155]

Up and dressed this morning soon after six: had two good hours' work at my "Memo. on the working of the Foreign Inspectorate", through which I now begin to see my way pretty clearly, and of which I hope to make a good job. It is much easier to think out a subject well with a pen in one's hand than by mere rumination.

Dined at the French Legation, and got back about ten o'c.

TUESDAY, 23 AUGUST 1864: Went to the Yamun at 2; Häng and Tsung back from the Imperial cemetery. Read through a moderate despatch to Wade about the fleet, and talked about sundry unimportant matters.

WEDNESDAY, 24 AUGUST 1864: Had a long gossip with my writer about the duties of the several provincial officials; what I learnt from him, I shall embody in a paper for the Asiatic Society.

THURSDAY, 25 AUGUST 1864: My papers of the 10th June came in today, as did also my mail of the 20th. The papers had been mis-sent to Japan. No letters from home. The "Alabama" sunk by the "Kearsage" near Cherbourg. Letters from Hammond show clearly that Walter Lay has been scheming at Kiukiang. Piry has given Lay a thrashing.[156]

A letter from H. N. Lay has appeared in the 'Times' commenting on Sir. F. Bruce's despatch approving of Gordon's having again taken to the field. It is not conceived in a good spirit, and it is written in very indifferent English. A note came from him by the mail, but it contains no particular news.

Rev. W. Martin called this morning, and read to me his proposal for establishing a school: it will in the 1° place give Chinese a good native classical education; 2°. will teach them science; 3°. medicine & surgery; and 4°. theology. I undertake to promote him, so long as I am at the head of the Customs, with tls. 1000 annually from the Customs (Confiscation Fund), and have promised him tls. 500 annually as a private subscription. He must keep me incog., however, to avoid complications.[157]

Had a jaw with Le tseay tseay [elder sister] in the evening.[158]

FRIDAY, 26 AUGUST 1864: Working at my memo. Had a pleasant ride in the evening. A call from Wade.

SATURDAY, 27 AUGUST 1864: Finished the corrected draft of my Memo today: I think it will do; but it is somewhat voluminous. Rode out with Man. Le tseay tseay sent for me about 10 o'c; but I begged to be excused.

SUNDAY, 28 AUGUST 1864: Took Man to the Shing-ke Ying [Peking Field Force] this morning to see the troops drilled. They improve daily; their drill this morning was excellent, and embraced some difficult manoeuvers — marching off the square; changing face; retiring by fours through the skirmishers, &c.[159]

MONDAY, 29 AUGUST 1864: Went to the Yamun at three, having been sent for by WänSeang; he wanted to talk about the "Mercury" case, but, just as he commenced, Wade was announced, and the matter dropped. I afterwards saw Wade for a few minutes, and he said that in his talk with Wän, the latter had insisted strongly upon the fact that the Chinese did <u>not</u> wish to keep De Mas the Spanish Minister out of Peking—and that as soon as he made his treaty he might take up his residence at once, but that he must provide his own quarters. Wade evidently thinks now that the Spaniard himself has been making "a mess of it" at Teentsin.

Hangke called on me this morning: I don't know with what object, for, as old Ping came into the room, we could not talk freely. However, when I pitched into Hsieh, he pulled me up by remarking, that in 1861 when Tsung Lun returned from Teentsin, after negotiating the Prussian treaty, he said that Tsung How had told him to warn Hängke against me, as I had been making disparaging remarks, &c. I now see one defect in myself; I find I have been too free in my criticisms, for I know that I have never hesitated to point out to the "heads" the failings of people I have met. I always did it, thinking to benefit China thereby: but I now see, I have been making a mistake. My words have had no other effect than to make people either afraid or suspicious of me. So, for the future, I shall take more care; and, instead of pointing out the failings of <u>individuals</u>, shall criticise general policy. What I said of old Häng was that he had brought a great deal of money from Canton; he did so, & he got it dishonestly, i.e. by making false reports of the duties collected; and what I think of him is that (in that respect not worse than others) he is a man of a certain smartness in small matters, but without the brains for a large policy. However, "'Ware hawk'! my boy!"

TUESDAY, 30 AUGUST 1864: Put into Chinese today a couple of Shin-chin, one about the Pootung Point, and the other about Passengers' Luggage. Paid Dr. Martin tls 500 for the printing of his translation of Wheaton's International Law.[160]

At two went to the Lung fuh-tze, where "fung kew, fung shih", the people congregate to buy and sell, and Kwang-meaou ["visit temples"]. Saw nothing very fine; great crowd of people, very orderly but not over-clean; innumberable stalls, laden with curios of more or less value; one story-teller; and a set of 'ta-pa she-teh' [?], whose doings were somewhat curious. A boy was put into a most extraordinary position [sketch], with his feet resting on two stools, & kept there—he cried—until the lookers on subscribed a certain number of cash to free him; he shouldered one of his legs, too, just as if it were a fire-lock, and made a curtsey—bending the other. Saw a rather good picture, in which there was a little Chinese sarcasm,—a lot of soldiers charging most furiously at Pa-le-keaow and an old woman hobbling off, while a little boy scuttled under the arch to hide himself.[161]

Had a pleasant ride under the walls in the evening. Quite cold after dinner.

WEDNESDAY, 31 AUGUST 1864: The last of the month; how 'sixty-four does slip away!

"Kih-Keaou chuen heueh": to pull a boot on a leg that has no foot i.e. "to shut the door when the horse is stolen."[162]

"Tow-shoo che-chē": to break the plate in catching the rat — or something of the sort — Look before you leap, or, to cut off your nose to spite your face.[163]

Went to the office at 2, went away about five; showed them my drafts about "luggage" & "Pootung point".[164] Nothing particular talked about or said.

THURSDAY, 1 SEPTEMBER 1864: [characters for the 1st day of the 8th lunar month; in the margin] Paid the August wages, &c., to the establishment.

Rode in the afternoon past the Tsün Mun to the Shun chi mun, where I saw a fine Roman Catholic Cathedral. They certainly do things in style: very different from the Protestant Missionaries. Then went up by the Se Sze Pae Low, and turned eastwards near the Hoo Kwo she, getting home after a three hours' ride about eight.[165] Man "pot-lucked" with me.

FRIDAY, 2 SEPTEMBER 1864: Dispatched Leang today to Teentsin with Gordon's uniforms.

Put into Chinese proposition relative to seizure of contraband goods on board foreign ships, or in foreign godowns, without waiting for Consul warrants; also a proposition making the limited Siamese vessels pay duty at the Teentsin Hoo-Kwan [old Tientsin customs house], at the same time taking out permits at the Sin-Kwan [new customs house], and making the others — i.e. those in excess of the limited number — pay duties at the Sin Kwan.[166]

When riding out, passed some archers near the Chaou-yang mun: stopped to watch them: no one hit the target. The bystanders looked disgusted with them and said, "Puh tso leen" ["they don't practice."][167]

SATURDAY, 3 SEPTEMBER 1864: An uncomfortably warm morning.

Hänke called at 9 1/2 & sat for an hour. He told me that the camels' wool difficulties originated with Hsieh: so to checkmate that worthy, Wade had better come down with his 5 per cent declaration. He said too that they have written to Hsieh to endeavour to put the Spanish Treaty through more quickly.

The fact is, Hsieh likes to give himself out among the Chinese as being hostile to, and knowing how to manage foreigners: when he went to Teentsin about the Portuguese & Spanish Treaties, he accordingly gave out that he would change matters; if the Yamun interferes with him, he will say to the others, who expect great things from him, "Of course, I could have done it,

Gordon in Chinese Dress

From Demetrius C. Boulger, *The Life of Gordon*, 1896.

but the Yamun interfered: blame them, not me." This will ensure his reputation, and will damage the Yamun — and the Yamun seeing this does not like to interfere; he, on the other hand, <u>must</u> see the impossibility of gaining <u>his</u> points, and he knows that sooner than allow a row, the Yamun will interfere. His game is a good one, and he has hedged cleverly: or rather, made his best book to win on either event.

Wade called yesterday morning, and told me that he had again written to the Yamun about the fleet. O dear! Oh dear! When will this wretched business be settled? He left with me a memo about the duty troubles at S'Hae in 1853-54, and the establishment of the inspectorate.

SUNDAY, 4 SEPTEMBER 1864: A wet morning. Started with Afang for Teentsin at noon: slept at Chang Kea Wan. The roads heavy, and the mules bad.[168]

MONDAY, 5 SEPTEMBER 1864: Fine day, but heavy roads. Afang's cart capsized. Never before have I been so utterly disgusted with carts as a means of traveling. Slept at Yangtsun.

TUESDAY, 6 SEPTEMBER 1864: Arrived at Teentsin about noon: went on to the new building at the fort, Leang Kea Yuen, where Baker and the others have taken up their quarters.[169]

WEDNESDAY, 7 SEPTEMBER 1864: Arranged with Alisch for the str. Ying-tsze-fei to take me to NewChwang, and to call for me on the way back from Shanghae. Paid Shanghae taels 1575.

THURSDAY, 8 SEPTEMBER 1864: Called on Tsung How, Hsieh, and Senor de Mas, the Spanish Minister. Tsung told me that with the exception of the "residence" article, all else had been settled with the Spaniards. It, he said, would probably be arranged as to admit of the minister's residing at Peking after the lapse of three years. The Spaniard is a little, unkempt man, somewhat of the Robertson style — and smells disagreeably. Dined with Hanna.[170]

FRIDAY, 9 SEPTEMBER 1864: Return calls from Tsung and de Mas.

SATURDAY, 10 SEPTEMBER 1864: Left on the "Ying tsze fei" at 10 a.m. The only other foreign passenger was the Rev. Mr. Thomas, — who has got on wonderfully with his Chinese, having made as much progress in two months as the majority of people make in as many years. He has, too, been acquiring Mongolian and Thibetan. Remained at Takoo for the night, where I saw Payne: looking rather used up, poor old boy![171]

SUNDAY, 11 SEPTEMBER 1864: Up anchor, and off soon after ten. A blowy day on the whole. The steamer's purser by the way, is a Mr. Blow from Belfast: I remember his sisters quite well. Two of them I met every morning, near Albion Place, when going up to College lectures at Belfast. I afterwards made their acquaintance at the Hardy's. Had some pleasant talk with Blow: he had, however, been in Australia, gold digging, 1852 @ 63.

MONDAY, 12 SEPTEMBER 1864: About noon off the Shing King Coast: ought to have been at New Chwang.[172] Saw some boats coming out; supposed to be pilot boats at first; but the Captain thought he must still be to the south of the port, and, not being able to get the sun, kept off to the northwest. Every appearance of a nasty night: — anchored — don't know where — at 4 P.M.

TUESDAY, 13 SEPTEMBER 1864: Was awake soon after midnight: thought the vessel was merely turning the screws occasionally to ride easily: found we were under way — is it "way" or "weigh"? — blowing horribly. Soon came a tremendous bump: rushed up on deck, and found we had struck: another bump, and then bump after bump: nasty sea, raining heavily, with thunder: the poor steamer looked forlorn as each flash of lightning showed her staggering through the water, bumping continually, and laboring through the nasty muddy sea, which with its angry white-capped waves, looked frightful. The Mate told us to go below as the mast would soon go; and Blow cried out, "Lord, Lord, to have come so far, and to finish here!" Mr. Thomas secured a buoy; I followed suite [*sic*]; and a China boy secured the third. Still bump, bump, bump. Went below. After about an hour and a half, got over the shoal, and anchored in 9 fathoms. The ship making no water: how staunch and tight she must be! Before securing the buoy, Mr. Thomas went down to get a piece of rope from his cabin: when inside, the door closed, and he could not open it! What a fix to be in! He had to knock it out by main force.

As soon as the first shock of the prospect of immediate death was over, I grew quite cold, callous, and resigned: my chief wonder was as to who wd. be appointed to succeed me as Inspector General! How empty, trivial, and worthless seemed everything that had previously been thought worth striving for; and how necessary to be always prepared!

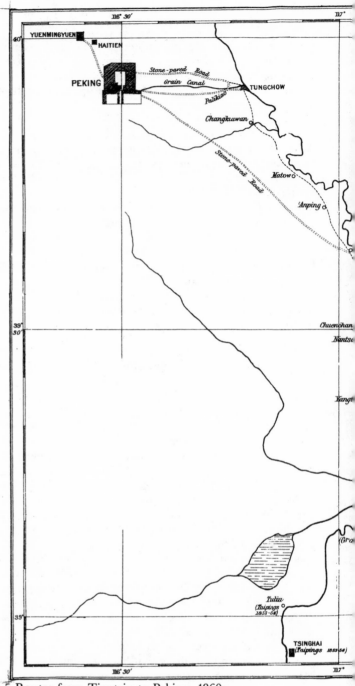

Map 5 Routes from Tientsin to Peking, 1860s

From W. F. Mayers, N. B. Dennys, and Charles King, *The Treaty Ports of China and Japan:*
plete Guide to the Open Ports of Those Countries, together with Peking, Yedo, Hong Kong, and Macao (L
Trubner and Co., Hong Kong, A Shortrede and Co., 1867).

A Peking Cart
From *Old Photos of Beijing,* by Fu Gongyue

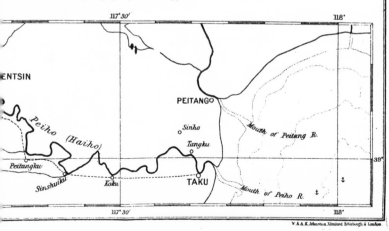

WEDNESDAY, 13 SEPTEMBER 1864 [*sic*]: Capt. Stocks takes great blame to himself for being so rash as to get under 'way' in the dark! Staggering along towards the port with the wind in our teeth and a high sea, I was sick last night; and today I smoke at the stern although to sit there is like being on a 'see-saw', with a rising and falling, and twisting from side to side fulcrum. Anchored near the bar in the afternoon: the chain soon went, and we had again to go ahead until another anchor could be got ready.

THURSDAY, 14 SEPTEMBER 1864 [*sic*]: With difficulty got across the bar, there being no pilot outside. Landed at Yingtsze at noon: found the place very muddy. It lies low, but there is a fine range of hills seemingly a score of miles off. Found Mackey living in an amazingly comfortable house, but he has made no attempt to furnish it: he has nothing save mere necessities. In the evening went with him to Meadows "Wednesday at home": drank coffee and smoked cigars until ten. Mackey is in an awful bunk of robbers: shut all the doors securely, but could not sleep.[173]

Remained at New Chwang, or rather Muh-kow-ying until Sunday the 2nd day of October, when I left it at noon in the "Yingtsze fei."[174]

[Several blank pages]

TUESDAY, 4 OCTOBER 1864: Arrived at Teentsin at noon. Rather a warm day.

WEDNESDAY, 5 OCTOBER 1864: Called on Tsung How and Hsieh. Found that the Spanish Treaty had been settled, and that it would be signed in a few days. Tsung agrees to the proposition that camel's wool shall pay a 5% ad. val. duty. Hsieh says the Yamun cannot get on without me, and is more civil than when I passed through on my way to NewChwang.

Find the Japanese affair is settled, and the Inland Sea opened.

Application from L. N. Pedder for an appointment replied to in the negative.[175]

THURSDAY, 6 OCTOBER 1864: Races commence at Teentsin. Not being able to spare time to see them, I started for Peking. Slept at Hosewoo.

FRIDAY, 7 OCTOBER 1864: Arrived at the Sha-Kwo-mên at 4 p.m. and made a row at the gate, refusing to give up my Passport until some one properly charged should come out for it. Arrived at the Hoo-tung at 5 p.m. all well, thank God![176]

SATURDAY, 8 OCTOBER 1864: Went early to the Yamun, and had a long talk with WänSeang, to whom I explained some of the "ins and outs" of the state of affairs at NewChwang.

SUNDAY, 9 OCTOBER 1864: Busy all day reading the despatches and letters that arrived by the last three steamers from the south.

Dick has turned Mercer out of Hwashing—very properly—for ill treating a coolie; and had threatened to suspend the Harbor Master Hockly for owning a share in a tug. Letters at last from Meritens: but as some fifteen are missing, I don't know where he was in June and July.[177]

MONDAY, 10 OCTOBER 1864: Breakfasted at the Yamun, and had a long day, going into official business of various kinds with Wän and Tung. Wän seems to have aged considerably during the last month: his moustache is getting white.

Introduced to the new Canton Hoppo, She-tsän,—who called at the Yamun to see me. He is an able looking man, of character: but he has only one tooth, and that not only crooked but black, so that he articulates rather indistinctly. Call from Johnson & Rawson.[178]

Brown dined with me.

TUESDAY, 11 OCTOBER 1864: In the house working on my report for the Yamun on NewChwang. In the afternoon rode out and left cards on Johnson and Rawson at the Kaou-ch'ieh [?] Meaow. Called on Mr. W. Martin, when I was introduced to Rev. Mr. Burns, who soon asked me if I could do a bit [?] for him.[179]

WEDNESDAY, 12 OCTOBER 1864: Still at my report. Rode out in the afternoon. Warmer than it was a couple of days ago.

THURSDAY, 13 OCTOBER 1864: A grand rifle-match today, at which all the Legation people assist. Hangke, Tsung-Lun, some of the disciplined troops, and a good many bebuttoned individuals were present. The whole wound up with a grand dinner at the British Legation. I had my own work to do—a good many letters to answer, &c.—so I remained at home, and got a load of arrears off my shoulders.

In the evening recd. a mail by the "Nanzing". Edwards from Mongolia; he found it too cold to be pleasant.

FRIDAY, 14 OCTOBER 1864: Lovely morning. Got off a mail by the "Nanzing".

Went to the Yamun at 2 and remained till 5. The chief objects for consideration were:

1. The "Mercury" case, in which I advise the steamer's confiscation.

2. Siamese ships, in reference to which the arrangement to be made for the three northern ports is that they shall pay duties at the old or new customs according as they have Chinese or foreign papers.

3. ships' stores — or copper sheathing, rather, in regard to which they have amusingly consulted Dick on my proposal; and

4. building of foreign-styled craft by Chinese.

As regards the last subject, I am happy to say that WanSeang commences to show pluck. He sees that sooner or later, such must come to pass, and he thinks it better at once to make the permission to own and build such ships public, and place that permission under such regulations as shall prevent the privilege from being abused.

Long despatches from Meritens relative to Formosa, and Brown's doings with reference to the "Volunteer". Ships now load, &c., at Tae Wan foo, but the Taoutae opposes the opening of an office there.[180]

SATURDAY, 15 OCTOBER 1864: Mr. Martin called this morning, & handed me a book published in Peking on vaccination. It is an original Chinese work, but founded on some missionary tract, to which it makes reference. This shows that on useful subjects, the Chinese themselves will take hold of and apply whatever information we place within their reach.

She Tsäng, the newly appointed Hoppo for Canton, called on me this morning. I impressed upon him the desirability of getting the Salt Commissioner, and local officials, to cooperate with him, in preventive measures in order that the opium revenue might be collected. I also advised him to ask Chin Chaou Ting to remain a few months at Canton, in order that the new comers might be put up to the work of the place before the departure of the old set. He seems to be a man of more force of character than either Yu or Häng, and possibly he may effect something.[181]

SUNDAY, 16 OCTOBER 1864: Yesterday and today, I received no less than eight despatches from the Yamun.

A call this morning from the Commandant of the drilled troops, who told me that Tsung Lun is by no means a cordial supporter of the innovation, but that Wan Seang and Foo Tseang-keun are.

A call from Wade, who asked Edwards and myself to dinner. He has been pitching heavily into T.T.M. and thinks NewChwang is too small a place for a Consul. Morrison, he says, must leave Chefoo, to which Hughes goes as viceconsul.[182]

Very fine weather.

Dined with Wade; found Mr. C. Murray and Mr. Mercer [?] & wife with Col. Yonge [?] (67th) and the commander of the "Manila" there.[183]

MONDAY, 17 OCTOBER 1864: Went to the Yamun about noon and came away at five. Had a chat with Hangke alone, who is anxious about the Portuguese Treaty, and who is now wishing to be repaid some tls. 20 000 which he says he expended out of his own purse when the Inspectorate was first started at Canton. He then went on to say that they wished to give me a button, and hinted at one of the third rank. WanSeang then came in, and the conversation soon again turned to the button. Wan said "So & so have all got honors: but there is one person as yet who has not received any." I at once said that I would not affect to misunderstand him; that I knew he meant myself: that I did not wish for a button: that it was quite the same to me whether I got it or not: that in Customs' matters, I had already got my reward — which was that things were going smoothly and that the revenue was increasing: that in regard to my other doings in connexion with Gordon, &c., I too had already got my reward — that the rebellion might be said to be over, and that tranquility was returning to the country — that was my reward: — in fact it was a case of "She-she joo-e" [everything according to one's wishes], and I did not want anything else: that he was mistaken (and had pained me) by supposing I wanted money: that I had an objection to a button of a low rank — though I admitted all to be respectable — inasmuch as it wd. expose me to comparison with others to whom buttons had been given: that people outside placed me & Ward or Macartney, for instance in a different category, and that to give me a 3d class button, while they had 2d class, would be very inconvenient: and that I begged they wd. let the matter drop. Wän said "I understand"; but nodded his head in a way that said, the matter is not yet finished.[184]

We then corrected the letters about Camel's Wool, Siamese Ships: and talked about allowing Chinese to own foreign-shaped craft. The letter to Sir F. Bruce about Osborn's fleet was then carefully read and corrected — and I think that was all.

TUESDAY, 18 OCTOBER 1864: Ping came this morning with his semiofficial hat on: I suspected something. He then went on to say that he had been asked to talk to me about yesterday's conversation, and went on to explain that a military and a civil button were two very different things, and that the Yamun cd. not begin by giving me a high button at once: that they wished to ask for a Wän che (civil Edict) and give me "Judge's title" Nee-tai-heën with a 3d rank button & feather: that after that, when an opportunity offered, it wd. be advanced to one of 2nd rank, & so on: & he, fung keuen or begged to advise me to not refuse (tuy-tsze). He also went on to talk about changing my dress, fuh-suh, marrying, and settling in China, &c. &c. &c. I'm sure I don't know what to do. Nous verrons: but I must think it well over for a day or two.[185]

Got through all my Shin-chin today. I have asked for 1/10 of Tonnage dues to enable me to lay down buoys, &c.; and have added a rule to my 27 making Harbor-masters, &c., appointable and removable by me, &c. Also wrote about Taewan & about the land at New Chwang.[186]

Rode in the evening: and walked in the courtyard after dinner: beautiful night.

Ping's 6th son read with me an hour this morning: he did not know where Tae Wan was!

WEDNESDAY, 19 OCTOBER 1864: Cold again this morning.

Paid Ping Tls. 70 for Shin Ching's Choo Tieh [?] volumes: & Tls. 6.5.0.0 for the Shang-yü of the same admirable Emperor.[187]

Went to the Yamun: only Tsung & Häng there: came away after half an hour's gossip.

Tea'd with Mr. Martin. His youngest son, Claude, when about to go to bed, kissed me as he passed, and that spontaneous salute affected me so much as to make me feel quite tender. Such a thing has not occurred to me for the last ten years, and it brought Jaimie (when about 7 years of age) before me most vividly. Mr. Martin thinks of calling his school the Tsing-Shih Kwan: taking the words from the line [blank where Hart meant to write in characters but didn't].[188] The name will do well.

I hear the "Yingtsze fei" is expected back at Teentsin, & that she will have immediate despatch. In all probability, therefore, I shall have to leave this on the 23d.

THURSDAY, 20 OCTOBER 1864: Vide Evening Mail 22 @ 25 May 1863, for "Slave Trade in Cuba".

Called on Wade this morning; he says his instincts are against the 'button', but on the whole he thinks I ought not to refuse it. It will be a useful thing to have vis à vis the Chinese at the ports; and as it gives civil rank, will show to the public an appreciation of services on the part of the Government. He says, I must not forget that I am Ying-min, or a Britisher; and that the Govt. must be prepared to give buttons to others, once they do so for me.[189]

Then called on Mr. Burlingame who kept me talking for three hours. He professes to be greatly pleased with my Customs Memorandum, & says he will send home a copy to the U.S. Secretary of State; he thinks with regard to the Tribunal Rules that the words 'merchant consuls' ought to be left out, as he got instructions from his Govt. not to yield to the Chinese in their demand that merchant consuls shall not be appointed; and as regards railways and telegraph lines, he thinks that they must be given time, and that it wd. be best for the govt. itself to take the initiative. By the way, the "fung-shway" supersition [geomancy] is our greatest obstacle as regards telegraph and railways:[190] their construction, too, ought on the other hand to prove a death blow to the supersition. As regards merchant consuls, I advised Mr. B. not to move in the matter, for it wd. have the effect of causing the Chinese to retire from their present position, and do away with the little element of con-joint-ness that it professes: he agrees with me. He is wonderfully well disposed toward us, and if he remains here as minister for another four years, our American difficulties will entirely disappear. I said it was very well for people, where no interests were at stake, to be ultra-liberals, but that as in most countries there was vested interests to be met with, perhaps a liberal conservatism wd. be the best policy. Yes, said he, "courageous moderation"— a capital expression.

Called at the Yamun, but found the Ta-jin [high officials] had all gone. Gave my despatches to Hia Liaou Yay, and also a note, to be sent to Baker at once, to secure passage by the "Ying-tsze-fei".[191]

Alisch called this morning: I read him my despatch, about his claim, written to Klezkowsky in 1861; he now sees it in a new light. I advised him to work it in a gentle and reasonable manner through the Prussian authorities.

Have been awfully busy today; and feel quite done up. The Pa-yay married today: to a che-chuh lai tuh: Häng's wife did the Tsen foo-jin part.[192]

FRIDAY, 21 OCTOBER 1864: Went to the Yamun at 2, and handed in my despatches. They agree to give me 1/10 Tonnage Dues, and say that they will put Formosa right without delay.

SATURDAY, 22 OCTOBER 1864: Left cards on the French and Russian Ministers, and dined with Mr. Burlingame, who likes the "Memo" and "No. 8."

SUNDAY, 23 OCTOBER 1864: Left a card on She Tsäng, the newly appointed Hoppo.

Dined with Wade.

MONDAY, 24 OCTOBER 1864: Took Kleinwachter to the Yamen, to breakfast, and introduced him to the Ta-jin as the student selected to take charge of the Kung Kwan [office] during my absence.[193] Spent the whole day at the Yamun; gave the microscope to Hsieh, who is delighted with it; bade them good-bye at 5.

My visit this year to Peking has in every respect been a pleasant and satisfactory one.

TUESDAY, 25 OCTOBER 1864: Left Peking at 7 a.m. Slept at Hosewoo.

CHAPTER FIVE

Hart at Work: Facets of Administration

F ROM LATE OCTOBER 1864 to late June 1865, Hart was away from Peking. For part of the time he managed affairs in familiar surroundings at Shanghai; during much of it, he toured the other treaty ports. Both these experiences gave the I.G. a better understanding of provincial administration and a new appreciation of the problems and potentialities of his position as head of the Customs Service. They also allowed him to put across his own point of view as Inspector General. At Shanghai he met the dynamic reforming Taotai Ting Jih-ch'ang and renewed his ties with Ting's patron, Li Hung-chang. He also took the opportunity to promote the Feng-huang-shan military training program that he had helped to establish in the Shanghai area during mid-1864.

On his tour of the treaty ports, Hart came to see that, despite the fall of Nanking in July 1864, rebel remnants still posed a serious threat to several ports, including Swatow, Amoy, and Hankow. These dangers buttressed his effort to support defense-oriented foreign-training programs in treaty-port areas. During his travels, he met with a wide range of scholars and officials in various port cities — both Manchus, such as the newly-appointed Hoppo at Canton, Shih-tseng, and the Tartar General, Jui-lin — and Chinese, including Mao Hung-pin and Li Hung-chang's elder brother, Han-chang. He also chatted informally with local scholars who provided him with all sorts of off-the-record information. Everywhere he went, Hart heard political gossip, and learned about the Ch'ing system of government from inside sources. In the course of such formal and informal conversations, he also managed to establish his personal authority and credibility with taotais and other local Chinese officials in port areas.

FINANCING THE GROWTH OF THE SERVICE

The Foreign Inspectorate commended itself to Peking by greatly augmenting its revenue from foreign trade. But in this process, how was the Inspectorate paid for? Although the details have not yet been

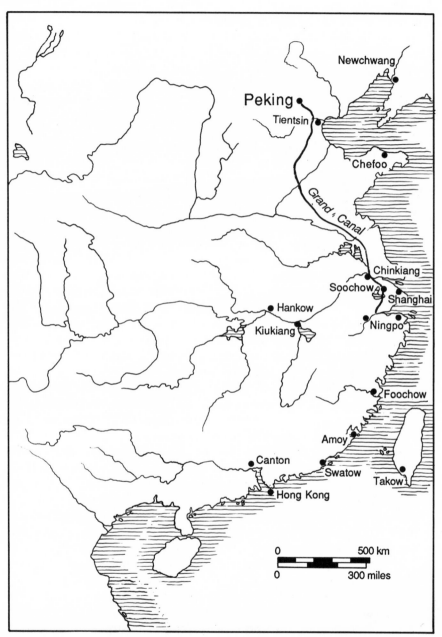

Map 6 Cities Visited by Hart during His Tour of the Treaty Ports, 1864–
1865

worked out, Hart's journals keep referring to several aspects of finance that we can at least begin to define and unscramble: such matters as the indemnity payments during 1861–1865, the Tsungli Yamen's annual grants or "allowance" to maintain the Service, the opium duties, funds from confiscations and fines, tonnage dues, the I.G.'s three bank accounts, and the growth of the Customs functions and staff structure. Looking at these briefly in turn, we begin to see how the Service not only survived but prospered. The key to its success was that it avoided encroaching upon vested interests of the Ch'ing bureaucratic behemoth. Rather, it lived off the new growth of foreign trade.

To begin with, though we still lack precise summaries, we know that the growing foreign trade gave the Chinese provincial as well as central authorities an unexpectedly large source of revenue in a time of dire need. For example, Customs duties at Canton had been set at a quota of Tls. 900,000 for all the foreign trade of China before 1842. In 1861 the actual receipts were Tls. 1,230,000 — 35 percent higher for the single port of Canton alone. At Foochow, the first year under the new system produced Tls. 1.5 million, while Shanghai took in Tls. 2.5 million.[1] The deep-lying tension between Peking and the provinces was evident in the tradition that 6/10 of customs collections were retained for provincial use and only 4/10 were to be remitted to Peking. This was the pre-treaty balance, and it continued for a time to be the arrangement under the treaties.[2]

One immediate reason for the installation of the Foreign Inspectorate at the ports open to foreign trade had been China's obligation to pay the indemnity required by the 1860 Convention of Peking. Tls. 16 million were to be paid in quarterly installments derived from 1/5 of the Customs receipts. By the beginning of January 1866, Hart could announce the completion of the indemnity payments (half to Great Britain, half to France). At the same time, he reported that an imperial edict had instructed each treaty-port customs office to transmit to Peking "four-tenths of the Import, Export and Opium Duties." Since the indemnity payments had used 2/10 of Customs gross revenue, this meant that Peking had been receiving only 2/10 for itself, while 6/10 of Customs revenue had been left in the provinces. In effect, the Tsungli Yamen's Customs revenue doubled in 1866.

This was helpful because, in June of 1864, Wen-hsiang had pressed Hart to accept a reduction of say Tls. 100,000 in the annual grant or allowance to maintain the Service. In reply Hart argued that, if Tls. 100,000 were spent on a preventive service, it would bring in Tls. 300,000 more revenue. A reduction therefore would be penny wise, pound foolish. Furthermore, Hart had always argued that the Ch'ing government, by paying only nominal salaries to its officials, had made corruption unavoidable. He thus tried hard to hold the line. "We cannot do with less than the following," he noted in his journal of 11 June 1864: "Canton Tls. 8,000; Swatow Tls. 2000; Amoy Tls. 3000; Foochow Tls. 4500; Formosa Tls. 2000; Ningpo Tls. 2000; Shanghae Tls. 13 000; Chinkiang Tls. 2000; Kiukiang Tls. 3000; Hankow Tls. 3000; Chefoo Tls. 2000; Teentsin Tls. 2000; Newchwang Tls. 2000; i.e. monthly Tls. 48 500: yearly, Tls. 582 000 and Tls. 40 000 for Inspectorate General Tls. 630 000, say." Here was evidently Hart's bedrock estimate. We are told by the Customs historian, S. F. Wright, that on 30 November 1863, the maintenance allowance for the Service "stood at Tls. 700,000 but was shortly afterwards increased to Tls. 748,200 at which figure it remained till the 1st January, 1876."[3]

In order to keep both himself informed and the Yamen impressed with the Customs' fiscal progress, Hart had from the first arranged to receive quarterly returns of revenue. The returns presented a complex picture worth our attention.

Opium duties were reported as a distinct category. Despite continued smuggling from the free port of Hong Kong, Wright estimates that in 1868 the Maritime Customs collected Tls. 1.6 million from its opium import duty of Tls. 30 per picul (of which Peking received 4/10) while the provincial authorities collected about Tls. 2.6 million, partly by taxing opium more heavily after importation. These local charges varied from Tls. 14 at Hankow and Tls. 17 at Tientsin to Tls. 44 at Shanghai, Tls. 84 at Foochow, and Tls. 90 at Amoy (in addition to the original Tls. 30 import duty).[4] Such wide variations in domestic tax rates bore witness to the extreme variety of circumstances in the opium market. Fortunately for Hart, the Customs was not concerned.

Confiscations and fines made up another revenue source, sometimes in contention between Customs and merchants as indicated in chapter 3. In January 1863, the I.G. asked for precise details from each port every month. Since smuggling was an inherently joint Sino-foreign activity, the reports were to include names in Chinese — even in the English version — as well as copies of all correspondence in both English and Chinese. We can see why a commissioner's office, like a consulate, always had a big job of hand-copying to do.[5]

In February 1863, the Yamen asked for reports of "Seizures, Fines and Confiscations" henceforth on a quarterly basis, and also, retrospectively, for all the nine quarters since 1860. The prescribed report-

RETURNS FOR THE QUARTER ENDING ....

	Ta.	*m.*	*c.*	*c.*

A.—1. Entered ....Foreign Vessels; Tonnage ....Tons, ...
2. Cleared................ „   „   „   .... „   ....

B.—1. Import Duties collected: [exclusive of Opium,]........................
2. Opium   „   „   ....
3. Export   „   „   ....
    4. Total liable to Indemnity Charges,.........................
      5. Payable to British on Indemnity account,........................
      6.   „   „ French „   „   „   ....
      7. Total payable „   „   „   ....

C.—1. Tonnage Dues collected,............................
2. Coast Trade Duty „   ....
3. Transit Dues   „   ....

D.—1. Chinese Craft [   ] Import   Duties   collected, ...
2.   „   „   Export   „   „   ....
3.   „   „   Coast Trade Duties „   ....
4.   „   „   Tonnage Dues   „   ....
    5. Chinese Craft : total amount collected,........................

E.—1. Sum total of Duties, &c., collected by the Commissioner's Office, during the quarter,.......

F.—1. Amount of Fines and Confiscations during quarter, ...

G.—1. Total expenditure in Commissioner's Office during quarter : *exclusive* of sum remitted to Inspector General, (Harbour Master's Office, and South Barrier Station,) ....

II.—OFFICE EXPENDITURE.

1. Salary of Commissioner,..........................
2.   „   „   ....Assistants,..........................
3.   „   „   ....Foreign Tidewaiters,..........................
4.   „   „   ....Chinese Linguists,..........................
5.   „   „   ....Shupan and Writers, ...
6.   „   „   ....Examiners, Weighers and Watchers,..........................
7.   „   „   ....Office Boys, Runners, and Boatmen, ...
8. Office Expenditure : Stationery, &c., ...
9. Miscellaneous and Extraordinary Expenditure, ...
10. Preventive Service Expenditure, ...
11. Rent of.........Buildings and.........Chops, ...
12. Sum total expended in Commissioner's Office,..........................
13. Amount remitted to Inspector General, ...
14. Balance in hand at end of quarter, ...
15. Amount received during quarter from Superintendent, ...
16. Balance from *preceding*, in hand at beginning of present, quarter, ...

I.—CONFISCATION FUND.

1. Balance from preceding quarter, ...
2. Proceeds of goods confiscated, ...
3. Amount of Fines, ...
4. Sum handed to Superintendent, ...
5.   „   „   „   „   for transmission to Peking,..........................
6.   „ expended by Commissioner,..........................
7. Balance in hand at end of quarter, ...

N.B.—All the above amounts are to be reported in Haikuan [關 平] currency.

(*J.*—1. Expended in Harbour Master's department during the quarter, ...
2. Amount received from the Superintendent for Harbour Master's department during the quarter, ...

K.—1. Expended for the South Barrier Station during the quarter,..........................
2. Received from the Superintendent for the South Barrier Station, during quarter,..........................

N.B. - Amounts under headings *J.* and *K.* are to be reported in the currency, in which the monies concerned are drawn and paid [Tsaon-ping, I believe].)

Table 2 Quarterly Returns, Reporting Form, ca. 1864, Shanghai Version

ing form had an entry for "Portions paid to Spies and Seizing Officers". The struggle was real, and the Customs minions, like the smugglers, had to be motivated by greed for gain. By March 1864, the Yamen requested three Chinese copies of the quarterly report of Confiscations and Fines. After deducting all expenses for spies, hire of boats, and so forth, the net proceeds were to be divided 3/10 to the local Superintendent of Customs, 3/10 to the Superintendent to transmit to Peking and 4/10 to be retained by the Customs Commissioner. Table 2 shows the various categories of Customs income and outgo.[6]

Tonnage dues had special significance for the Customs because they became in large part earmarked for its use. As in other countries, tonnage was calculated according to the cubic capacity of different categories of vessels. The dues were to pay for their use of port facilities. In China these duties had behind them the old Canton trade practice of exacting arbitrary fees from foreign ships, especially according to "measurement" but also as gratuities on entering and leaving port and as fees for weighing, meltage, and exchange — for example, the conversion of funds to silver ingots (sycee), and so forth. In time these fees were consolidated into a gratuity of Tls. 1950. Much was made at Canton of this sizable present to the Hoppo.[7]

The treaties abolished this ancient accumulation of various levies. Instead, Caleb Cushing in the American treaty of 1844 arranged that tonnage dues (at a lower rate for vessels of 150 tons or under) should take the place of "the former charges of measurement and other fees, which are wholly abolished." In 1858 H. N. Lay specified in drawing up the rules of trade that the tonnage dues were to be used to maintain "lights, buoys, beacons and the like"— facilities in which Chinese ports were woefully deficient. As foreign vessels entered more fully into the coastal trade of China (from Hong Kong and from treaty port to treaty port), it was agreed in the autumn of 1861 that such vessels need pay tonnage dues only once every four months. In February 1863 this privilege was extended to French vessels plying between ports in China and in Indo-China. Later it was extended also to vessels plying between Chinese ports and Japan, and later still to Russian ports in Northeast Asia.

To support the Interpreters' College (T'ung-wen kuan) that Hart had set up under the wing of the Tsungli Yamen in 1862, it had been agreed that the Superintendents of Customs should send Peking 3/10 of the tonnage dues. In August 1863 this transmission overland was stopped and the 3/10 were to be handed to the Commissioners for them to send to the I.G. In January 1865 Hart got the Yamen's agreement to the stipulation that the Superintendents were to hand over to the Commissioners another 1/10 of the tonnage dues to be deposited to the I.G.'s account, for him to use for "harbour improvements . . . as I may deem expedient."

In this way Hart established, in addition to the Customs Office allowance, control over 4/10 of the confiscation receipts and 1/10 of the tonnage dues. And, since the remaining 3/10 of tonnage dues received at Peking had been allotted to the upkeep of the Interpreters' College, which was under Hart's care, the result was that he now received in effect 4/10 of the tonnage dues. Looking ahead, we can see that, by early 1868, as harbor improvements, coastal lights, and other facilities were being developed, the Customs would henceforth receive monthly, and would report quarterly, 7/10 of the tonnage dues.[8]

At the beginning of 1865, Hart was able to summarize how his Commissioners were to pay various funds into the I.G.'s accounts in the Oriental Bank Corporation at Shanghai or Hong Kong. First, any remainder from the Customs allowance for office expenditure drawn monthly from the Superintendent was to be paid into "my account A." The net proceeds of confiscations were to be paid into "my account B," and the recent tonnage dues one-tenth into "my account C." These I.G. accounts were all of course quite separate from Hart's personal bank account, of which we get only fleeting glimpses.[9]

Thus fortified, Hart pressed ahead with the further establishment of the Customs' various branches. One was a Customs Printing Office in Shanghai to publish the Returns of Trade received by the Shanghai Commissioner directly from all the ports. There followed the gradual proliferation of Customs publications in a number of different series and on a great variety of topics.[10]

The first modern surveys of the China coast had been carried out by the British navy. The military invasion of China required technology to come with it, but commercial harbor facilities were a different matter. The Foreign Inspectorate's first order of business had been to help vessels enter the up-river port of Shanghai without going aground or suffering some other mishap after they entered the estuary of the Whangpu River, 12 miles downstream at Wusung. H. N. Lay in 1855 had installed "the first harbour facilities for mariners . . . on the approaches to Shanghai," although his jealous critic, the British Consul, remarked that "the survey work itself and the positioning of the first buoys were carried out by an American naval vessel."[11] A harbor master had early become a regular part of the Shanghai Customs staff. In April 1867, after Hart's return from his 1866 leave in England, still another topic for quarterly and annual returns would be the harbor master's salary, pay of boatmen, "support of lightship," and so on. Also in April 1867 pilotage regulations would bring under closer Customs control yet another element essential to shipping.[12]

Finally, in September 1867, the I.G. would be able to systematize the distribution and treatment of the 233 foreign members of the Out-Door Staff: tide surveyors, examiners, tidewaiters, and so forth. Tide surveyors, as general supervisors of port activities, usually did the work of harbor masters (except at Shanghai). Foreign examiners in the 1860s dealt mainly with staple goods. They needed to be honest above all, not necessarily highly sophisticated. Tidewaiters had to keep watch over ships' cargoes everywhere within the ports' limits.

In 1868 also came the establishment of the Marine Department, which would eventually have specialized staffs for engineering, harbors, and lights. It would dredge channels, particularly at Shanghai, and maintain buoys, beacons, lightships, and lighthouses. Soon also the Coast Staff would be separately set up to handle the cruisers and patrols of the preventive service. A Statistical Department, and Postal Department would appear in due time. The tables of organization and terms of service of all these branches, together with all their Chinese staff members, form a significant slice of the modern world's administrative history.[13]

Eventually, in 1874, Hart called for S/O correspondence, that is, fortnightly semi-official letters, from all his Commissioners, to be addressed to him personally. Such communications were to appraise informally the major problems of the post, its ongoing needs and projects, and the writer's major concerns, personal and otherwise. This channel of personal contact, once one learned how to read the idiosyncratic handwriting in Hart's holograph replies, was a great morale booster for the Commissioners. And for the I.G. it created the best intelligence network in China.[14] By keeping constantly alert at his standing desk in Peking, Hart often probably knew more of local situations over the empire than either the British Minister or the Grand Council. The Yung-cheng Emperor, that administrative genius of the eighteenth century who invented the early Ch'ing secret, eyes-alone channel of correspondence with selected informants, would have been impressed with Robert Hart's approach.

TOURING THE SOUTHERN PORTS

Hart also had to see things for himself. Like his contemporaries, the missionaries, he felt it essential to itinerate. His first time around had been in 1861, when he established offices in Chinkiang, Ningpo, Tientsin, Foochow, Kiukiang, and Hankow. Since then, 5 more treaty ports had been opened (see chapter 3). By 1865, it was time to go around and check up. As we travel with the young I.G. over the terrain of his nascent Customs Service, two things will strike us forcibly — the crucial role of steamships and the extraordinarily small size of the foreign settlements they connected. The rapid growth of the treaty ports in later years should not mislead our imaginations in retrospect.

America's semi-colonial experience in China was a pale substitute for the British experience in India, but it did have certain noteworthy features. The conquest of nature in the American westward movement had stressed the overcoming of distance both by water and by land. Since South China was a country of well-developed waterways that would long obviate the need for railways, it became a fruitful area for the steamboat. Just as the Americans in the 1850s had taken the lead in developing the clipper ship using wind power, so they had pioneered the use of steam power in steamboats on the Hudson. The steamers that proved their worth in China were of the eastern American-Hudson River type, not of the Mark Twain-Mississippi River type. (Presumably this meant that the stern paddle-wheels of the Mississippi were less useful on the Yangtze than the side-wheelers of the east coast, but this has not been explored systematically.)

After Russell & Co. put together the Shanghai Steam Navigation Co. in 1862, using mainly local capital from foreign and Chinese merchants, they enjoyed a decade of dominance on the Yangtze from Shanghai to Hankow. British observers at Shanghai reported how "the huge, white, two-storied 'Yang-tz' steamer, built on the American plan, passes swiftly by on its way to Hankow."[15] All the Russell & Co. ships seem to have been side-wheelers. Of the 16 steamboats operating on the Yangtze in 1864, 10 were owned by 3 American companies and 6 by 4 British companies. Russell & Co.'s 5 vessels, each of 1,000 to 1,350 gross tonnage, stole the show because they maintained a steadily reliable twice-weekly service each way between Shanghai and Hankow. This involved, say, 3 days en route and a 4-day layover at each end while handling cargo.[16]

The steamship was already the main distributor of opium cargoes. As early as 1858 steamers plying between Canton, Macao, and Hong

Wellington Street, Hong Kong, ca. 1870

From John Warner, *Hong Kong 100 Years Ago* (Hong Kong: City Museum and Art Gallery, 1970).

Kong had been the chief medium for smuggling all sorts of goods. By 1864–1865 the Peninsular & Oriental Co. and the local firm of Douglas Lapraik & Co. each operated 3 steamers on the coastal route to Shanghai. These vessels made successive days' runs of 175 miles to Swatow, 150 miles further to Amoy, and 185 miles thence to Foochow. From Foochow to Shanghai was 410 miles, so that these coastal steamers reached Shanghai usually in 5 days. The direct Hong Kong to Shanghai run could be made in 3. Over this network the I.G. toured the ports.

Hart left Peking on 25 October for his southern tour, arriving in Shanghai on 4 November after short, uneventful stops at Tientsin and Chefoo. During his month-long stay in Shanghai, he conducted Customs business, socialized with the Shanghai foreign community (including merchants and missionaries who lobbied for special favors, as well as several attractive young women who "captured my heart"), met the new Taotai, Ting Jih-ch'ang, and renewed his acquaintance with Governor Li Hung-chang. He also had the opportunity to chat with a number of local Chinese scholars, who filled him in on political and military developments in the provinces and fed him rumors regarding Li and Tso Tsung-t'ang. The rivalry between Li and Tso, both protégés of Tseng Kuo-fan, was always a hot topic and would remain one until Tso's death in 1885. Chinese scholars invariably discussed their relative merits and usually took sides. So did Hart. As we have seen in chapter 1, Li made his military reputation in Kiangsu during the Taiping Rebellion, while fighting together with the Ever-Victorious Army. A native of Anhwei province, he was eminently pragmatic, reportedly corrupt, and a strong advocate of the reform of China's land-based forces during the 1860s. Tso, originally from Hunan, established his military reputation in Chekiang, relying in part on the French-led Ever-Triumphant Army. He was in Tseng's mold: more rigid than Li and apparently less greedy. During the late 1860s he became increasingly interested in naval reform. Both men had their merits, but Hart, who knew Li personally, sided with the Kiangsu Governor, making the I.G., almost by definition, a critic of Tso.

After leaving Shanghai, Hart went on to Canton, also familiar turf. He arrived on 12 December exhausted after over 70 hours of travel by steamer. Again, he plunged almost immediately into Customs affairs, but did little socializing. Rather, he spent a good deal of time during the next several weeks negotiating with Ch'ing officials, renewing old friendships, and talking with local scholars as he had done in Shanghai. Hart's journal descriptions of his search for a Chinese writer indicate that he had an excellent knowledge of documentary Chinese, but quite naturally he found it easier to read Chinese than to write it — hence the need for an amanuensis. Hart's calligraphy, like that of most foreign writers of Chinese, is rather cramped and unattractive, and he occasionally miswrites even simple characters in his journal.

In conversation, Hart felt perfectly comfortable, although by some accounts his colloquial Chinese betrayed a foreign, "even Hibernian," origin. His talks at Canton with local officials, scholars, and yamen underlings were not only fruitful from the standpoint of handling specific Customs problems, but also useful in expanding Hart's general base of knowledge. Informal reports on the backgrounds, activities and appointments of Ch'ing bureaucrats kept the I.G. *au courant* of personnel changes in the provinces (although he was sometimes misinformed) and highlighted his awareness of regional differences, local identifications, and north-south rivalries in Chinese politics. Similarly, the many stories he heard of irregularities in the examination system, bureaucratic corruption, official caprice, and fiscal mismanagement helped fashion his views on Ch'ing government. Even trivial conversations could prove instructive. Descriptions of Shih-tseng's blunders in matters of protocol, for instance — like the story he heard on 14 December about the problem of procuring sedan chairs for the Kwangtung Governor and his wife — reinforced Hart's sense of the enormous importance of ritual and status distinctions in Chinese society.

While at Canton, Hart spent a couple of days in Hong Kong, a city he clearly did not enjoy visiting. After over two decades as a crown colony, it still had only about 1,000 European males and half as many females, not counting children. There were estimated also to be 80,000 Chinese residents and a "new foreign population" of Europeans, Americans, Goanese, Manilamen, and the like, totaling 3,500 Although Hong Kong was the military bastion of the Western advance on China, the chief news in its press was of piracy on the water and burglary by land. The colony's function as a free port, and thus as the distribution center for Indian opium, had attracted Chinese cutthroats; no effective Chinese government control could be established over them. The high incidence of piracy and general lawlessness faced by the British at Hong Kong was no doubt a consequence of their inability to govern the Chinese population.

In late February 1865 Hart left Canton for Swatow, the next leg on his treaty-port tour. He decided to travel light, sending his secretarial assistant Man with two Chinese, Liang Su and Ma Erh, to Shanghai.

211

"I shall make the rest of the rounds alone," he remarked in his journal of 21 February. "It is too much bother with so many changes as I shall have, to have a half a dozen people, and so much luggage to look after." By this time Hart had received official word that Li Hung-chang's request for him to be given brevet rank as a provincial judge had been granted by the Throne. This, of course, only enhanced his growing prestige.[17]

One of Swatow's most distinctive features as a treaty port was its long previous experience as an entrepot for the illegal opium trade. In the mid-eighteenth century, the Ch'ing dynasty had confined all foreign trade to Canton and permitted none on the seacoast of Kwangtung province where Swatow was the principal port. But, once the illegal opium trade had been driven out of the Canton estuary in 1821, it began to seek points of ingress to the China mainland. In addition to Hong Kong, a principal post was the island of Nan-ao (Namoa) east and a bit north of Swatow. This famous island extends 12 miles east to west and is 5.5 miles wide at its broadest eastern part, separated from the mainland by a 3.5 mile-wide channel. Two peaks, rising some 2,000 feet above the sea, make Namoa a landmark. From the 1820s to 1850s, the opium captains of the duopolist firms of Jardine and Dent built up rather sumptuous if illegal establishments there. Though it was quite populous and had a walled town with a Chinese magistrate, Namoa was on the coastal periphery of Ch'ing administration.[18]

At first the Chinese local officials who connived in the opium trade preferred to keep it out of sight. But after the opening of the first treaty ports in the mid-1840s, the opium-receiving stations had become established points of foreign presence. Gradually the opium merchants succeeded in acquiring establishments on shore while their receiving ships lay openly at anchor just off shore. Foreign merchants built residences on Double Island some 4 miles below Swatow.

This small city at the estuary of the Han River was the port for the prefectural city of Chaochow, 35 miles upstream. In the late 1850s, the chief foreign activity at Swatow had been the coolie trade. The enterprising successors to the Atlantic slave traders as suppliers of cheap labor, together with their Chinese crimps and their baracoons of indentured coolies for shipment abroad, had become a world scandal — so much so that popular Chinese feeling was sufficiently strong against all foreigners to keep them out of the city of Chaochow until 1866.[19] By the time a Customs House was opened at Swatow by H. N. Lay in January 1860, the opium trade was legalized and could come ashore. But the new Customs House at Swatow had to confront the fact that foreign trade had grown up there for some decades past as a matter of informal collusion between foreign merchants and Chinese officials.

Aside from opium, however, Swatow had played little part in Sino-Western commerce. The trade in sugar by Chinese junks to Manchuria, returning with soybean cake, had well-established channels into which the foreign opium import had been inserted. Few foreigners were needed to manage the new foreign trade, which could be better handled by Chinese from Singapore and Canton on behalf of principals in Hong Kong. There was therefore only a handful of foreign residents; the Customs Commissioner and the British Consul had few merchants to deal with.

The walled city of Swatow was on the north bank of the Han River estuary, but the British Consul and foreign missionaries found their best sites for habitation across a mile of water on the south bank. After arriving at Swatow in the evening of 28 February, Hart went out the next day with Commissioner Williams and soon selected "a site for Commissioner's residence on the South side, near the [British] Consulate." Significantly, however, the I.G. observed that there may be "some difficulty in obtaining possession of it, as it affects the fung-shwuy [*feng-shui*; i.e., geomantic fortunes] of some families whose tombs are there situated." This journal entry, like a number of others (2 July 1863, 23 January 1864, 25 January 1865, etc.) suggests the pervasiveness and power of traditional Chinese beliefs regarding auspicious and inauspicious times and locations.

Another of Hart's observations at Swatow was about the building of walls by pounding "a mixture of clay and lime between boards, which subsequently becomes as hard as granite and dreads nothing but water." This description of a form of pounded earth (*hang-t'u*) construction, so widely used in North China, reminds us that Hart for all his ten years in China had been a city dweller not close to the soil and moreover a skilled user of written records, not of building tools.

Fortunately for Hart, neither *feng-shui* considerations nor problems with building materials complicated his decision to locate the Swatow Customs Office on the north side of the river, near the city. Eventually, the office would maintain access to the shipping by way of a jetty that projected at low tide for 200 yards across the mud flat of the shallow foreshore.[20] During his brief stay at Swatow, the I.G. also called on the British and American Consuls, smoothed over some Customs-Consulate friction, made Customs staff changes, and went on his way to Amoy. No time wasted; a good day's work.

In contrast to Swatow, the port of Amoy rivaled Canton as an historic center for Chinese oceangoing shipping. Its junk fleets had long traded with the small ports of Malaya down to the Straits of Malacca as well as northward to Manchuria. The rather small island of Amoy with a circumference of about 40 miles had a population somewhere between a quarter and a half million Chinese, although the local Ch'ing military establishment had its headquarters on the larger island of Quemoy, farther from the coast. Portuguese, Dutch, and British contact with Amoy had been extensive, though sporadic, since the sixteenth century. Amoy's inner harbor was half a mile across between the city and the small rocky island of Kulangsu, roughly a square mile in size. The foreigners had made Kulangsu the site of their settlement; by the end of 1865, there were about 115 foreign residents but very few women among them. Here again the Westerners resided apart on their own small island while the Customs Office functioned on the main island next to the crowded native shipping. The fact that the large prefectural city of Chang-chou was 35 miles up river on the mainland illustrated a general rule: Major Chinese cities avoided the coast and the marauding naval power of pirates and/or foreigners that might endanger a coastal location.

At Amoy (2–7 March), Hart discovered that "the great topic of conversation is the rebels"—specifically, Taiping remnants under Li Shih-hsien, whose forces had occupied nearby Chang-chou in October of 1864. Li had enlisted well over a dozen foreign mercenaries in his cause, and the Ch'ing authorities at Amoy were in a panic—particularly since they believed erroneously that the British Consul (Pedder) was somehow in collusion with the insurgents. Hart clarified the situation for the bright but timid Taotai, emphasizing Great Britain's solidly anti-rebel stance and indicating that, if foreigners in the Taiping service were killed in battle, "no one wd. complain, & that wd. be the best way to dispose of them: but that, if they [the Chinese authorities] took them [foreign mercenaries] prisoners, they must hand them over to the consuls."

The case of Henry Burgevine, former commander of the Ever-Victorious Army, soon illustrated the point. He had become a Chinese subject, then joined the Taipings after an altercation with the Ch'ing authorities. Finally, he was arrested by Hart's foreign Customs officials at Amoy in May for illegally returning to China after having been banished to Japan for various crimes against the Ch'ing government. Eventually, while being transported by Chinese officials from Foochow to Soochow, Burgevine drowned in a boating accident, but not before his extraterritoriality case had captured the attention of Ch'ing and Western diplomats at the highest levels.[21]

During Hart's week-long stay at Amoy, he made a 24-hour side trip with his Commissioner there (George Hughes) to the port village of Takow, later called Kao-hsiung, on the island of Taiwan. The two treaty ports on the island—Takow and Tamsui—were on a Chinese as well as a Western frontier. Historically the non-seafaring Manchus had regarded Taiwan with distaste as a refuge for pirates and uncontrollable renegades. By the 1860s, the entire Chinese population was only about 3 million. Their gradual expansion of rice culture pressed the Malay-type aborigines into the mountain spine on the east. The southern port of Takow was about 20 miles from the prefectural capital, Taiwanfu, now Tainan, near which the Dutch had once had their Fort Zelandia. The port of Tamsui in the north (both these ports were on the west side of the island) saw some exports of camphor and tea, but it was by no means an ancient Chinese trading center. Foreign residents were few, north or south. Hart noted that "the place seemed a curious mixture of the Chinese harshness and Malay richness." The Takow Customs officer, Maxwell, "resides with McPhail & Co. and at their place I spent the night: the house very rough and the walls rich with chirping lizards." It was agreed that Maxwell would visit Taiwanfu when he wished and keep some tidewaiters there. But for part of the year its open roadstead was unsafe for shipping.

When the I.G. sailed on the *Cadiz* from Amoy for Foochow, the steamer became fog-bound for 24 hours at the White Dogs below the entrance to the Min River. (In 1872 the Customs would erect a lighthouse on Middle Dog Island.) Thus delayed, the *Cadiz* at the mouth of the river met the Chinese government steamer *Volunteer* on which the provincial authorities were sending Eugene de Meritens, Commissioner of Customs, from Foochow to Amoy to stop supplies being sent to the rebels at Chang-chou and to root out the foreign mercenaries there. De Meritens had established at Foochow in 1864 a program for training Chinese troops in Western drill similar to the one Hart, Gordon, and Parkes had set up at Feng-huang-shan during the same year.[22]

The foreigners' circumstances at Foochow were reminiscent of earlier times at Canton. This capital city of the two provinces of Chekiang and Fukien was situated 34 miles up the Min River. European travelers often compared this long passage up from the sea with the Rhine. The route went through defensible narrows before reaching Pagoda anchorage, which, like Whampoa inside the Boca Tigris, was still 10 miles below the city. At Foochow also the foreign merchants had found it most convenient to settle on the south bank and on the small island of Chung-chou in the middle of the Min River next to shipping but some 3 miles south of the walled city. As at Canton, entrance to this important provincial capital had been opposed by official as well as popular feeling. When the British Consulate was finally allowed inside the walls, it was inconveniently far from the shipping.

Because of the great expansion of tea exports since the mid-1850s, there were now about 50 foreign merchants at Foochow. Measured by value, imports were half opium, exports 9/10 teas. The foreign community — although it had a billiards club, a fives court, a bowling alley, and a reading room — had not yet been able to organize them into a club. Meanwhile, strong contingents of several different denominations of missionaries had agitated for years and finally become established inside the walls.[23] There was no single foreign community. The Commissioner of Customs, de Meritens, was ambitious and obviously able; in fact he had an eye on Hart's job (see journal entries for 14 and 20 April; also 23 July 1864). Hart noted: "The Customs are now well lodged: the Commissioner and May live together in a fine house, on the site purchased when I was last at Foochow. . . . Meritens deserves great credit." The young I.G. also remarked, "In the F'chow office I saw an amusing letter from Meritens to the authorities complaining that while they had praised Hughes' doings in Memorials, they had left his own name unmentioned!"

While at Foochow Hart called on the Tartar General who was in charge of the Maritime Customs and the Fukien Governor, noting with satisfaction that "in both cases the central gates were opened and tiffins laid out." In short, Hart had public prestige or "face." He found the Governor, Hsu Chi-yü, a "fine looking old man with placid countenance and magnificent white beard." Hart would see him again as a minister of the Tsungli Yamen.

After his 3-day visit, the I.G. left Foochow in the *Cadiz* on 18 March and returned to Hong Kong on 22 March (after brief stopovers at Amoy and Swatow). Four days later he left again in the *Cadiz* for Shanghai and —"after a narrow escape from shipwreck on the 27th when we touched on a shoal off Amoy"— arrived on 31 March.

ADMINISTRATIVE PROBLEMS AT SHANGHAI

Almost immediately upon his return to Shanghai, Hart found himself in the midst of a sticky situation that had already attracted his attention in November of the previous year. It involved the polite corruption among the Shanghai linguists who were licensed to help merchants with their Customs business and who received scheduled fees for their services. They had built up the racket of receiving large "presents" in addition. When the reforming Taotai, Ting Jih-ch'ang, took over at Shanghai, he sought to change this state of affairs. Hart was much impressed with the new Taotai, whom he described as honest, courageous, progressive, and resolute, with "no fear of responsibility." Ting, by his own account, had been "censuring" left and right at Shanghai, and had "beheaded some officials for extortion." In conversation with Hart, Ting observed that he had recently received a note from Li Hung-chang remarking, anent Ting's censuring 13 persons, that "such measures will leave the public service without men." Ting claimed, however, that the people approved of his actions — which seems to have been the case.[24]

One of Ting's targets was the linguist Tong Achik, who had received presents as large as Tls. 500 from one man and evidently spread the story that such sums were "for division between the Taoutae and the Commissioner!" At first (8 November 1864), Hart says such "doings must be punished as heavily as the laws admit; the times necessitate extreme severity; and it is a comfort to have a man like Ting to put people through." Obviously he is concerned with the reputation of the Customs Service. Then, on 19 November, Ting informs Hart that the jailers have been told "not to molest him [Tong] in any way," and that he will be dealt with as leniently as "the law will permit of." Three days later Tong's brother tells Hart that, despite the Taotai's orders, Achik is in great discomfort and that "to save him from torture &c. his friends will be squeezed of very farthing they possess." The I.G.'s humanitarian spirit now got the better of him, and he concluded, "I must try and get him out." His best course of action, he thought, was to point out to Ting that corruption, in the two forms of gift-giving and outright extortion ("flowers and thistles"), goes on everywhere in China, and that, if "the object of punishment is to deter others," the end had been achieved and Tong had already been punished enough.

In the meantime, Li Hung-chang had become involved. He referred Tong Achik's case to Peking, and wrote to the Hoppo asking if Canton linguists were allowed to accept merchants' presents. By early January 1865, having decided that Tong was guilty, Li memorialized the Throne, requesting that Tong's hat button, denoting official rank, be stripped away "in order that he may be dealt with most severely." This preliminary step was necessary because of the special legal immunities enjoyed by individuals possessing official rank; to impose penalties appropriate to a commoner on a member of the Chinese scholar-official class would be to demean the elite status. Such were the requirements of Ch'ing law.

In May the I.G. wrote Governor Li, asking that Tong be set free and claiming that he has "suffered horribly." Later in the month (24 May), Hart again raised the issue of release with Li, this time in face-to-face conversation. When Li heard that the jailers have "already got most of [Tong's] money out of him," Li simply laughed. He promised, however, to do what he could for the unfortunate linguist. Apparently he succeeded — probably by allowing Tong to buy his way free — for we hear no more about the case. Hart concluded: "I'll take care not to let anyone fall into the hands of the authorities again who does not deserve the harshest treatment." The episode taught the I.G. two important lessons: one, that corruption was easier to rail against than to eradicate, since even he had had to compromise his original standards; the other, that extortion may be greater under the criminal justice system than in trade.

When we hear of foreigners' crimes against the Chinese, Hart tells a different story. Take, for example, his account of a return trip from Hong Kong to Canton in mid-January 1865 on the steamer *Plymouth Rock* (3,017 tons). He writes: "In steaming through the harbor, a boat with a woman and three or four children in it got under our one side-wheel and as far as I could judge all with the exception of one boy who sprang into the water in time to get clear were smashed to pieces." Although Hart believed that the boat was run over with no effort to avoid it, he records nothing more about the incident. On another occasion (24 May 1865) Li Hung-chang "asked about the junk the 'Hukwang' had run down." Hart replied that, until Tseng Kuo-fan would consent to send the Chinese witnesses to appear in court, the case could not be pursued. In neither event did the I.G. intervene to seek redress. A cultural-political gap existed between Chinese and Western legal systems that impeded justice and usually favored foreigners. To rectify such kinds of injustice was beyond Hart's capability, and perhaps even beyond his imagination, except in the course of Customs administration.

Hart could and did, however, exert influence in matters related to treaty-port security, since the protection and promotion of trade at the ports was one of his primary duties. He took a particular interest in the development of foreign-training programs such as Gordon's camp of instruction at Feng-huang-shan — a small town about 25 miles southwest of Shanghai. Although Hart had helped to establish the British-sponsored camp after the Ever-Victorious Army had been disbanded in May of 1864 (see chapter 1), its principal architect was the ever-aggressive British Consul, Harry Parkes. Hart, always sensitive to "foreign rivalries," correctly perceived that the retention of a force "officered by Englishmen—whether you style them Military instructors or commanding officers" would promote rivalry among the other Western powers—but local British officials at Shanghai considered the move justifiable in the light of growing French influence in foreign-training programs. On 29 July 1864, for example, Parkes reported to Wade with dismay that there were "probably" more French than British subjects serving the Ch'ing government in a military capacity.[25]

Anglo-French competition had of course been a feature of Western military assistance to the Ch'ing government from the very beginning. Ironically, one of Hart's own Customs employees, Prosper Giquel, proved most active in promoting French interests against the British. In the summer of 1862, for instance, Giquel urged the French Consul General at Shanghai, Benoit Eden, to support the establishment of a Sino-French contingent to serve as a counterweight to the Anglo-Chinese Ever-Victorious Army. He argued: "In rendering the Chinese the immense service of our help in battling the rebels, we [the French] augment our influence and create new obligations from Peking. The formation of these troops permits the convenient placement of some young compatriots currently without position. In sending these carefully chosen officers, France gives herself agents who will penetrate to the court of the country [China] and be of great service to its [France's] future politics." Significantly, he went on to say that this was precisely the approach used by Great Britain with individuals such as Hart.[26]

Giquel eventually succeeded in raising a French-led Chinese force, the Ever-Triumphant Army. This Sino-foreign contingent achieved for Tso Tsung-t'ang in Chekiang almost precisely what the Ever-Victorious Army did for Li Hung-chang in Kiangsu. Like the EVA, it was sustained primarily by Customs revenue and assisted by Customs personnel; it protected foreign treaty-port interests and helped to recover a provincial capital (Hangchow); it brought similar rewards to its foreign commanders; and introduced similar problems of security and administrative control. Indeed, one of its leaders, Paul d'Aiguebelle, once held a city ransom in order to force the Chinese authorities at Ningpo to support his contingent.

After the disbandment of the Ever-Triumphant Army in 1864, Giquel continued to promote French foreign-training programs in the Shanghai area and elsewhere, at least in part because Great Britain remained actively involved in the Feng-huang-shan project. Giquel's activities—like those of de Meritens at Foochow, and H. Octavius Brown, who on Hart's recommendation began training Ch'ing cavalry forces in late 1865 — could be tolerated by the I.G. as long as the individuals involved remained under the aegis of the Imperial Maritime Customs Administration. When, however, Giquel informed the Inspector General that he planned to leave the Customs Service to help Tso Tsung-t'ang found the Foochow Shipyard, Hart was outraged. (See his journal entry for 13 November 1865.) Later journal entries reflect the I.G.'s unremitting antipathy toward, and competition with, Giquel (18 May 1867; 5 August 1867; etc.)

Originally, Hart believed that the Feng-huang-shan training program was merely a "sop" to the British; but his journal entry of 9 November 1864 indicates that Li Hung-chang "supported the movement thoroughly, and that 3,000 men and 60 gunboats, in all a force of 4,500 men, are to be regularized, under Pwan Fantae [P'an Ting-hsin]," one of Li's Anhwei Army officers. The problem at this stage was that Li greatly resented British meddling in the Feng-huang-shan program — particularly after Gordon's resignation as head of the camp in mid-1864. Li, knowing only too well from his experience with the Ever-Victorious Army that foreign assistance invited foreign interference, perceived in Western demands for the expansion of foreign training an attempt to "seize our military authority and squander our financial resources."[27]

But Li could not ignore British pressure. On 12 November, therefore, after extended and not always cordial negotiations, he and Consul Parkes reached an agreement whereby a British officer would be appointed head drillmaster (Lieutenant Jebb of the 67th Regiment), but all other matters of promotion, dismissal, camp discipline, payment, rations, and other aspects of military administration would be left in the hands of P'an Ting-hsin. Soon after assuming command of Feng-huang-shan, P'an, under Li Hung-chang's direct orders, led troops from the camp to help recover Chang-chou in Fukien — at the same time that Tso Tsung-t'ang ordered the Commissioner of Customs at Foochow, de Meritens, to do the same with the foreign-trained force under his sponsorship.

When Hart visited Feng-huang-shan on 22 May 1865, he found the program in good shape. The Chinese soldiers under Yü Tsai-pang and Yuan Chiu-kao of the Anhwei Army "drilled remarkably well," and Jebb told him that "he could not complain of anything done by the Chinese, or left undone with regard to the Camp." Aside from "propositions of a distasteful kind brought forward by Parkes," there had been "no trouble whatsoever." Jebb was of the opinion that "Parkes' interference has done harm, and has been the only thing that has tended to make the camp more inefficient than it wd. have been, if left alone;" but other observers — Chinese as well as Westerners — felt that Jebb's performance as head drillmaster left much to be desired. There were apparently few regrets, therefore, when in June he received his transfer back to England.

On the other hand, Jebb's departure raised the troublesome issue of who should succeed him. Local British officials were convinced that the new British Commander-in-Chief, General Guy, should name a successor, but Ting Jih-ch'ang, perhaps with Hart's assistance (and assuredly with his approval), cleverly bypassed regular channels to secure the appointment of William Winstanley, a former British officer who had also served in the Ever-Victorious Army. In justifying this move to his superiors, Ting emphasized that Gordon had recommended Winstanley in a letter from home, and he took pains to point out that Winstanley's lack of official connections with the British government would be an advantage. British officials at Shanghai protested Ting's coup vociferously, but to no avail. At Peking, Thomas Wade affirmed China's right to appoint a successor to Jebb, asking only that the Chinese inform him of their final selection.

Following his visit to Feng-huang-shan, Hart met with Li Hung-chang at Soochow on 24 May. At that long and productive meeting, the Kiangsu Governor expressed admiration for Parkes's ability but denounced him for interfering "too much" in matters that did not concern him. Li and Hart went on to chat at length about diplomatic and study missions to Europe, iron and coal mining, foreign steamers, weapons and arsenals, as well as Customs matters. No further discussions were possible, however, for, within days of their conversation, Li was transferred to Nanking as Acting Governor General of Liang-Kiang, and Hart began the final leg of his treaty-port tour.

THE YANGTZE PORTS AND HART'S RETURN TO PEKING

On 31 May, Hart boarded the *Fire Queen* for Hankow. At 3,801 gross tonnage, she was twice the size of the other foreign steamships in China. Her British owners were Lindsay & Co. Of the big steamship he observed: "The 'Fire Queen' is fast but her state rooms are badly arranged: food indifferent: cabin noisy: boys insolent and dirty: shall not travel by her again."

When Hart journeyed up the Yangtze, he was on historic ground more than he realized. The great river served China in some degree as the Mediterranean served Europe — as a 1,000-mile waterway providing transportation east and west. The "Long River," as it was (and is) commonly known, had in fact been the scene of inland naval action during earlier civil wars that intervened between dynasties. For example, the rebel chieftain Chu Yuan-chang, who in 1368 became the Hung-wu Emperor and founder of the Ming dynasty, had used fleets of war junks successfully both upstream and downstream from his original base at Nanking. Similarly, during the Taiping Rebellion, one strategic advantage was naval control of the Yangtze. The Chinese Commander-in-Chief, Tseng Kuo-fan, had developed a naval force along with his Hunan Army, and victory on the water went eventually to the Ch'ing forces who took advantage of steamships for transport and even attack. Thus, in the opening of the Yangtze ports, the Maritime Customs represented an incursion of civil government and tax gathering supported by sea power, moving into China up the Yangtze. The Customs, in short, followed the steamship.

During the 1860s and 1870s, American towns in the prairie states lived or died in proportion as the railroad came to them. The contemporary Anglo-Saxon expansion in China saw a comparable dependence on the arrival of the steamship. Particularly was this true in the opening of the Yangtze River to foreign trade. On the southeast China coast the opium trade had pioneered the way and created the first foreign settlements outside of Swatow. But up the Yangtze such pioneering had not preceded the treaties. Lacking the benefit of experience, the treaty makers selected some ports that did not turn out well. Chinkiang, for example, because it marked the Grand Canal's crossing of the Yangtze, had been the choke-point used by the British in 1842 to stop rice shipments to Peking and thus throttle the Ch'ing Court. By 1860, however, the Grand Canal was no longer a vital artery; rice shipments were going by sea, and the selection of Chinkiang as a treaty port proved ineffective. There was no hinterland for produce to exit from and no great market to be supplied from the outside. Its salt trade remained in Chinese hands, out of bounds for foreigners except as they invested in it through Chinese merchants. Being 150 miles from Shanghai, Chinkiang suited the technology of the time as a stopping point for steamers, but as a treaty port it had little significance otherwise. By 1865, the city had only about 20 foreign residents including those of the Customs. Not only did it have no anchorage, but the current on the south bank of the Yangtze at Chinkiang was so strong that the foreigners' hulks were moored preferably on the north bank where many residents still lived afloat.[28]

On 1 June Hart "saw Lord at Chinkiang: the Custom house there is rapidly approaching completion. It is a rough structure but will house three bachelors comfortably." A day later, still on the *Fire Queen*, Hart "saw White for a few minutes at Kiukiang." Here again, foreign judgment seems to have been questionable in the selection of a treaty port. Kiukiang, 495 miles from Shanghai and 137 from Hankow, near the outlet of P'o-yang Lake, commended itself as an outlet for tea exports. In point of fact, however, it was a limited commercial facility because the P'o-yang Lake junk traffic came out to the Yangtze 15 miles downstream at Hu-k'ou ("lake mouth"). This necessitated Chinese vessels reaching Kiukiang by going upstream 15 miles against the current, most uneconomically. In fact, Chinese merchants found it best to pursue a land route 11 miles from the trade center on the P'o-yang Lake exit at Ta-ku-tang, 14 miles in from Hu-k'ou, and 30 miles by water from Kiukiang. This overland route was much preferred.

In setting up the foreigners' port, the British Consul secured a site of 500 yards along the south bank of the Yangtze, and lots were leased to foreign firms. But, by 1866, there were still only 8 British firms and 3 American ones with a single missionary, making a foreign population of about 25 persons. Trade was carried mainly by the foreign steamers that brought opium imports and took out tea. Access to the steamers was by long wooden jetties staked out from the Bund. The Chinese junk traffic on P'o-yang Lake, which was forbidden to foreign steamers, continued much as before. The city of Nan-ch'ang had its big junk anchorage inside a breakwater but this had little connection with the foreign trade. Nor did the fact that the lake gave access to the ceramic industry at Ching-te-chen. The junks of the established Chinese firms continued to handle 3/4 of the trade at Kiukiang; Yangtze steamers were superficial to it.

Hart reached Hankow on 3 June and spent a week. The foreign settlements on the Yangtze north shore at Hankow faced the walled capital city of Wu-ch'ang one mile across on the south, while the third city, Han-yang, occupied the upstream peninsula between the Yangtze and its big tributary, the Han. About the central commercial importance of Hankow in the Chinese economy there was never any doubt; the opening of the port for foreign trade coincided with the arrival of the steamship, which increasingly carried the portion of the port's cargo that traveled in foreign bottoms. (Foreign sailing ships going 600 miles up the Yangtze risked many dangers of rock and shoal.) The major export of teas through Hankow powered the trade; steamers of 14-foot draft could arrive from Shanghai in 3 to 5 days and return in 40 to 50 hours.[29]

The British concession at Hankow built its Bund 800 yards along the shore and soon had a Municipal Council which was working on all the problems encountered at Shanghai. At Hankow the principal problem annually was the tendency of the river to rise 50 feet in the flood season. The Bund had to be built up accordingly; but even so, the entire foreign settlement with all its buildings was sometimes inundated along with the surrounding countryside. The foreign population by the end of 1863 was about 150 and big installations were made by them. But the idea began to come through that the handling of the trade was really dominated by the Chinese with their knack of competing in groups instead of individual enterprise. As *The Treaty Ports of China and Japan* (1867) declared: "three years had not elapsed after the opening of . . . [Hankow] before a large proportion of the mercantile houses in China would gladly have withdrawn their branches from this port, in favor of the continuance of the system of trade formerly in vogue." Steadily "rejecting the principle of competition as the basis of trade, the Chinese by combining among themselves secure continually a firmer hold on all its principal operations and tend more and more to reduce the European mercantile community to the position of a mere agency for carrying on transactions conducted on native account."[30] The fact that a foreign firm's comprador could handle its business equally well if not better led to the withdrawal of some of the foreign employees of the big firms from smaller ports like Kiukiang. While some sailing vessels loaded direct for London, the great bulk of the tea trade went down by steamer for transshipment at Shanghai.

Hart recorded with satisfaction, as he had at Foochow, the proper recognition (face) given him by the local Chinese authorities. "On Saturday, 3rd, arrived at Hankow; when walking down the Bund in the evening met the Taoutae, who got out of his chair to speak. On the 4th, the Taotae called on me on board the steamer; I returned his call in the afternoon. On the 5th, I called on the viceroy [i.e. Governor General of Hu-Kwang], who was very polite, & gave me a seat this time on the raised dais." The viceroy in question, Kuan-wen, a Manchu Bannerman, clearly knew how to appeal to Hart's Chinese sense of status as well as to his personal feeling of self-importance. The Governor General's remarks on the need for closer Sino-foreign cooperation and his condemnation of consular interference in trivial matters were well calculated to fall on sympathetic ears, as was his shrewd statement that "the ministers, both Chinese & foreign, wd. be the better for an annual run round the ports to see things with their own eyes: you, sd. he, are the only one who knows the people & the affairs of each place." In Kuan-wen's memorials to the Throne, however, he presented a less accommodating point of view, and a less positive image of both the West in general and Hart in particular.

After dealing with various items of contact and business at Hankow, Hart arrived back in Shanghai 12 June. When Hart sailed north from Shanghai on 20 June, it was by his old friend the *Ying tsze fei*. Though its gross tonnage was only 422 compared with the *Fire Queen's* 3,801, it was under the civilized management of the British firm of Trautmann & Co. Hart's first stop was Chefoo, where he was quite content to remain only during the steamer's usual 24-hour stopover. The new Shantung treaty port mentioned in the treaties was the prefectural city of Teng-chou. The name Chih-fu or Chefoo was derived from a peak and cape near the harbor of Yen-t'ai, a rather ordinary Chinese coastal village with a population of 10 or 12 thousand, off which the French fleet had anchored in 1860. The boundaries of a settlement or concession area not having been marked out, foreign houses were built indiscriminately. By 1865, the foreign residents were about 25 or 30 individuals including the Customs establishment plus a British Consul. Chefoo, which commended itself by having the best climate in China, was soon used as a place for vacations and convalescence. The growth of trade, on the other hand, was not phenomenal, even though in 1861 the British Minister had succeeded in getting a prohibition removed so that foreigners could engage in the beancake trade. This cake or pulse, made from soybeans, was used in South China for fertilizer. Opium was, as usual, the chief import. Significantly, Chefoo's harbor was the only one accessible in North China during the months of December, January, February, and early March when the river at Tientsin remained frozen.

Hart recorded that en route to Tientsin, before crossing the Taku bar off the mouth of the Peiho, "the thermometer stood at 75°; half an hour afterwards, it was 105°. We seemed to have been thrust into a burning fiery furnace." The Customs jetty was on the north side of the inner anchorage. A British Vice-Consul resided some 2 miles upriver, but at Taku itself the foreign community consisted mainly of Customs men, among whom a tide surveyor had taken over a temple and pagoda. There were also European pilots and a hotel keeper. It was purely a way station. The city of Tientsin was 60 to 67 miles up river, although it could be reached by road at a distance of only about 40 miles. Chinese junks came in such numbers that they were moored at times 12 abreast. They found it hard to navigate the river, however, and the steamers from Shanghai carried much trade and many passengers, including Chinese officials.

Crossing the bar at about 1:30, the *Ying tsze fei* anchored at Tientsin at 8 p.m. The foreign settlement had grown up about 2 miles below the walled city on the south bank of the river. Along the British concession area at Tzu-chu-lin foundations of houses were raised 5 to 8 feet to avoid floods. A fine Bund had been constructed with a jetty at which steamers could unload. A French area upstream and an American area downstream both remained undeveloped in 1865. The Customs' Commissioner's residence was set up in the old south fort about a quarter of a mile downstream from the British settlement.

The chief foreign recreation at Tientsin was riding, including hunting and coursing, with races in May and October. In the settlement several stores catered to foreigners, and missionaries had made a beginning. The French Consulate and Roman Catholic mission with schools were on the bank of the river opposite the town at the junction with the Grand Canal, formerly one of the imperial resting places. Trade through Tientsin was derived from all the northwest of China, including Inner Mongolia, in a great variety of products for export. Opium again was a big import. The chief phenomenon met by the foreign merchants was the gradual taking over of the carriage of cargo in steamers by the Chinese merchant community.

Travel from Tientsin to Peking was most comfortable but slowest by the waterway which formed an extension of the Grand Canal to the town of T'ung-chou, 13 miles east of Peking. The 80 miles or so to be traveled on this waterway required usually two boats for a single foreigner or a couple, and perhaps a third for extra baggage—one boat for the foreigners and the second for the Chinese cook and servants. On this route the trip took about 4 days. The first day's journey from Tientsin usually stopped "near a village called Yang-tsun [Yang-ts'un]. The second at Ho-si-wu [Ho-hsi-wu]; thence to T'ung-chow [T'ung-chou] takes about a day and a half, the time occupied in all cases depending on the wind, the number of trackers employed, and the strength of the current. . . . If the coolies are kept tracking all night (which they are generally very unwilling to do) T'ung-chow may be reached within three days." At T'ung-chou, the usual place of accommodation for foreigners was the Ta-wang-miao, a temple in the suburbs, "situated on the riverbank just opposite the landing place."[31] Boat travelers could then travel from T'ung-chou to Peking by cart or on horseback on a road paved with enormous stone blocks —hard on both the wheels and the occupant of any cart. The point of entry to the Inner (Manchu) City was the gate called Ch'i-hua men.[32]

In 1865, Hart traveled by cart all the way from Tientsin, despite the rough riding. The overland route followed much the same basic northwesterly path as the water route, but with additional stops, hazards, and hardships. Hart's record of his trip (25 and 26 June) suggests some of the difficulties: "At 1 P.M. on Sunday, I left Teentsin with Three carts: Leang-soo & Man remaining behind to bring the luggage, some 80 pckgs, as soon as carts, hidden in the country through fear of being pressed into military service, cd. be obtained. At 6 p.m. I was at Yangtsun, where we awaited the mules; again on the road at 9, traveled all night, passed Ho-see-woo about 4 on the following morning, and arrived at Matow [Ma-t'ou] at 7 1/2 where we stayed till near ten." Hart arrived at Chang-chia-wan about noon, bypassed T'ung-chou entirely, and entered Peking before 4 p.m. by way of the Sha-wo Gate on the east side of the Outer (Chinese) City. From there he entered the Ha-ta Gate on the south side of the Inner City, where he "got such a shaking over the stones that I gave way entirely, & my head began to ache fearfully." Apparently, bypassing the route from T'ung-chou to Peking did not make the journey any less uncomfortable. We can imagine that, no matter how cramped his quarters may have been, the sight of Kou-lan Lane's dull grey walls must have appeared inviting.

CHAPTER SIX

Journal

[Ed. note: The Journal here covers the period 26 October 1864 to 18 June 1865 when Hart was *away from Peking.* He arrived back in Peking on 26 June 1865, but did not write up his Journal account of late June until 2 July.]

WEDNESDAY, 26 OCTOBER 1864: Left Hosewoo at 4 a.m., but did not arrive at Teentsin until 9 p.m. It rained most of the day.

FRIDAY, 28 OCTOBER 1864: A call from Tsung How.[1]

SATURDAY, 29 OCTOBER 1864: Called on Tsung How. After dinner went on board the "Ying tsze fei."

SUNDAY, 30 OCTOBER 1864: Left Teentsin at 7 a.m.
Cabin crowded with passengers. Alisch, Livingston, Man, Lent, Schmidt, Marshall, Murtagh, Davidson, Major and Mrs. Wood. The company of the 67th, so long at Takoo, also formed no inconsiderable part of the passengers.[2]

MONDAY, 31 OCTOBER 1864: Left Takoo about 3 p.m. and crossed the bar safely. The pilot Connor says that placing of buoys on the bar will do away with piloting: in view of which contingency, he would gladly take service with us.

TUESDAY, 1 NOVEMBER 1864: At Chefoo. Pwan Tajin tiresomely civil. Morrison begged hard for an appointment for Pignatel, chiefly on the score of his wife! Got away from Chefoo about midnight. Promised Hannen an increase of pay. Poor Hewlett going to the dogs fast: so, by the way, is Payne at Takoo.[3]
The soldiers enjoy themselves in the forecastle every evening, singing songs. They sing well, and their patriotism and military ardor seem unquestionable.

FRIDAY, 4 NOVEMBER 1864: Anchored at Shanghae at 2 p.m. Glad to get back again.

TUESDAY, 8 NOVEMBER 1864: Called on Ting Taoutae. He is a little thin man with a bad mouth but very intelligent eye which when he is in earnest flashes with meaning. From Chaou Chow, his language is not at once intelligible. He impressed me very favorably: his views are good: he is progressive, and resolute, — he is besides clean-handed, and he has no fear of responsibility. He told me that he had been "censuring" right and left: he had just tsan'd [impeached] Tsan-seang [lieutenant-colonel], on the ground that he never went the rounds at night, and neglected his duties generally: that he had beheaded some officials for extortion; and he showed me a note just received from the Footae [Governor], relative to some thirteen "censured" people, in which Le says that such measures will leave the public service without men. The people, however, says Ting, like it. About Gordon's business, he says we must now shang-leang [discuss], and put everything straight: I tell him to take care — that too many cooks spoil the broth: that we must consider for whom the "broth" is being prepared — his tastes and his necessities — and not allow any "helper" to drop in an ingredient which might spoil the mixture. About Achik, I said that he must put the matter through: that for linguists who are well paid to accept presents regularly, and to such an amount as Tls. 500 from a man, is intolerable, and savors of extortion. He told me that some of the taxed said the money was for division between the Taoutae and the Commissioner! I am sorry for Achik; but his doings must be punished as heavily as the laws admit: the times necessitate extreme severity; and it is a comfort to have a man like Ting to put people through.[4]

From the south, the news is that Chang Chow has been taken by the rebels — a body which left Hoo Chow, and went through Keangsi and crossed the Kwangtung frontier into Fuhkien: at Amoy, the people had been in great alarm, but some gunboats were sent up from Hongkong, and it is now safe. Meritens, too, has sent down a hundred men, a couple of guns, and his French officers. Chaou Chou foo is likewise said to be in danger, and Swatow people are alarmed. I wonder what the results will be: is the rebellion about to make head there, or is it merely the run-aways from the north are pillaging on the way home, or brought to bay?[5]

Hobson down from Gordon who wishes me to go up, as he has resigned the command of the camp. The men drilled are not picked men, but consist chiefly of the Le Yang rebels taken on by Gordon long ago; from this I infer that the camp is a mere "sop" thrown at us by the Footae, and that he takes no great interest in the movement, and has but a low opinion of its utility. I must ask Ting about this. The Footae was greatly enraged at the receipt of a despatch from Parkes, saying that he must ask for six British Officers, &c.: the matter requires to be carefully thought over. My long letter to Sir Fred. Bruce about Gordon's taking the field again has been published in the Blue-book, and the "China Mail" supports me bravely.[6]

Gas on the Bund at the Club for the first time: the brilliancy of the light, compared with the oil lamps, is astonishing.

My house not yet finished. Parkes today wounded by a stag.

WEDNESDAY, 9 NOVEMBER 1864: Ting Taoutae called on me this morning. I repeated my caution against there being so many cooks as to "spoil the broth", and told him that what we wanted was the shih — the reality — and that the ming — or name — might be yielded to others. He told me that Fung Wang Shan camp was in the first instance started merely to keang-kew [placate] foreign officials — just as I suspected, — but that Le Footae supported the movement thoroughly, and that 3000 men and 60 gunboats, in all a force of 4500 men, are to be regularised, under Pwan Fantae. Le would rather have put in command or in charge a man to be nominated by Gordon than the nominee of any foreign officials: and I think he is right there. The great difficulty is "funds." Ting is anxious about the men thrown out of employment by the permission accorded to foreign ships to carry beans, &c, from NewChwang, and he says that he proposes to establish a Chuen-chang [shipyard] to enable Chinese to build ships after the foreign model. Bravo! I think we shall be able to move. I wish we had a dozen such men as Ting: he is of the right kind.[7]

Went to the races, and won a cigar case from Mrs. Patridge. One beautiful race between 'Exeter,' 'Traveller,' and 'Pathfinder.' Hodge won two races; Cock's stable carried off four firsts out of six, and it deserves its luck for it does racing in a quiet, unpretentious, gentlemanly style.[8]

Albert Heard asked me were Wan Chou and Chinchew to be opened soon as dependencies of FooChow?[9]

In the evening went to hear the Christy's Minstrels: singing and dancing good. The violin playing was exquisite.

What a jolly little girl is Miss Roberts: and what a pleasant-looking lass is Miss Wainwright — not unlike Teressa Cox —

THURSDAY, 10 NOVEMBER 1864: Last night went to hear the "Christy Minstrels". Today went to the races in the afternoon. Cock again winning everything. In the evening again went to hear the Minstrels: of whom I now think I have had enough.

FRIDAY, 11 NOVEMBER 1864: Called on Sir H. Parkes and Mr. Seward in the morning. Went to the races again: Cock still victorious, and most deservedly so. Introduced to Mrs. Norton [?], whom I found to be an exceedingly nice person; made the acquaintance of a Miss Cooper, and was also introduced by Mr. Seward to Mrs. Eames. Rather like Miss Cooper: pity she's not ten years younger. I have quite lost my heart to three or four young ladies: Miss Billsland, a Miss Delano, Miss Roberts, and another young girl whom I saw for the first time, but about whom I cannot learn anything. The fourth is, in so far, the favorite. I intend to go more into society now than I have been wont to do.[10]

[A star in the margin against the girl about whom he could learn nothing: "Turned out to be a married woman who dropped her 'aitches'!" June 1865]

MONDAY, 14 NOVEMBER 1864: Gordon came down from the Camp yesterday, en route for England. He had been succeeded by Jebb of the 67th, for whose appointment Parkes made the arrangements with Ting & Pwan on Saturday: the particulars, I have not yet heard.[11]

Hoo Kwang-ting and Hwang Seën Sang called yesterday: I don't know with what object. They said that the escape of the rebels from Hoo Chow [was] owing to Le Footae's doing, and they praised to the skies Tso Kung-paou inasmuch as he Gae-min, yung ping, and only sends home 300 taels annually.[12]

Went to the theatre on Saturday night, but found it rather tiresome.

News from Chefoo of the loss of the "RaceHorse," despatch boat: only seven people saved! Letters from Kleinwächter and De Champs, who, confound them have been quarreling![13]

Doughty, from what I have just been told, may prove a bad bargain: can't be helped now. [Against this is written: "Dismissed Augt. 1865."][14]

TUESDAY, 15 NOVEMBER 1864: Yesterday evening Gordon told me that Mayers, when on his way home, wrote up from Hongkong claiming some money-return for the services he had rendered the force, & that Parkes asked for Tls. 1500 for him. The Footae consented to a disbursement of $1000, but said half ought to go to Alabaster. Parkes then withdrew the claim. I am very sorry Mayers' demand was not complied with. It is rather amusing to find <u>him</u> anxious to get a little money out of the affair. Gordon told him to hand all his papers to his brother, and objected to his making use of them to write a history of the campaign. This I think is to be regretted: Mayers could have produced a very readable book, although it must be confessed his dislike of Le footae, and his opinions regarding Gordon's resuming operations after the occurrences at SooChow, might have tinged his descriptions, &c.[15]

Most charming weather.

Had a long talk with Hwang Seen Säng today.

[Written at bottom of page: "Gordon has placed his journals, &c. in the hands of A. Wilson, formerly of "The China Mail," so we'll have a fine book. Oct. 1865"][16]

FRIDAY, 18 NOVEMBER 1864: The mail of Sept. 20th came in yesterday. In Europe, the great news is that Florence is to be the capital of Italy, and that in two years' time the French troops are to be withdrawn from Rome. From U.S., that McClellan has declared for "the Union," and that Atalanta [*sic*] has fallen.

I have a note from Maggie; as usual it contains no news — though, by the way, it does tell me that Mrs. Hazelton has a little daughter: "my wife" of 27 years ago a mother at last!

Le Footae appointed Acting Che Tae [Governor General], and Woo Tang acting Footae [Governor]. Tsäng Kuo Fan ordered into Hoo Pih with troops — much to his disgust: the old gentleman after ten years of anxiety and hard work, when about to settle down to enjoying himself, has again to take the field.[17]

No additional news from Amoy; but from Keang Si came intelligence of a fight in which the Imperialists defeated a large body of rebels, killing one & capturing another Wang ["king"].

Lord down from Chinkiang; I have "pitched into him": rated him soundly for inattention to Circular No. 9.[18]

Giquel up from Ningpo.[19]

SATURDAY, 19 NOVEMBER 1864: Called on the Taoutae today.

A. Yangtsze steamers: told him that I am about to propose that they be permitted to call for passengers at Wuhu, Tatung, and Ganking; he did not say much, but seems to favor the idea.[20]

B. Heard & Co.'s claim for drawback: he yields the point, but wishes a rule for the future.

C. Tong Achik: he has given special orders to the gaolers not to molest him in any way, and he promises to deal as leniently with him as the law will admit of.[21]

I must be cautious with Ting in future, for I find he acts on my opinion the moment I express it.

Went to the Theater in the evening. A full house, but very indifferent acting. One of the actresses was married this morning: she notwithstanding appeared on the boards!

The news of the Rebels Defeat in KeangSe is confirmed. One of the Wangs killed is the real Kan Wang. Chung Wang's companion was not, it now appears, the Kan Wang, but another of the same sing [surname].[22]

TUESDAY, 22 NOVEMBER 1864: Yesterday Tong Akue called to see me about his brother Achik, whom the gaolers are treating very badly notwithstanding the Taoutae's orders. This case somewhat puzzles me. The curse of China is the small and insufficient pay of the officials, and from that root has sprung forth a crop of what may be styled "flowers and thistles"— the thistles being downright extortion and peculation, the flowers being presents to people in office. The linguists, it appears, have for years been in the habit of receiving gifts from Chinese merchants on term-days: the gifts, says every one, are given freely, and without being demanded: — so say the donors themselves; but I cannot look upon the receipt of them in any other light than as being extortion of the "flower" pattern. The merchants think, — whether consciously or not it operates as a reason, I know not, — that if they do not make the presents, their business will be neglected, and no doubt among the linguists are some who make differences in their treatment of those who give liberally & those whom they think "mean". I therefore regard the receipt of presents by our linguists, all of whom are well paid, as being simply a form of extortion, and as such to be put a stop to, and punished. The system has been in vogue for years; but it was not until the Ting Taou-tae came into office that it was actually detected as a system, although last year Le Kipbü [?] was discharged at Amoy for precisely the same kind of things. When Ting first discovered that the linguists on term days received gifts from Chinese merchants, which were calculated on the number of pack-ages passed (according to a regular tariff, in fact) he thought it would be a good thing to turn the collection into the public purse, and make it a legal tax. After some consideration he decided not to do so. It was a month after that that Achik received the gifts for the Eighth Moon. He was seized and imprisoned, and the matter was officialised by the Taoutae on learning my opinion, — which was that he ought to be punished, — and the case referred to the Footae. Achik was then thrown into the common prison, like any other offender, and in it he now suffers the hardships incidental to prison life in China. A friend went into see him on Sunday, and found his head fas-tened by the tail to a nail in the wall: a spike projected so as to stick into the back of the head in the event of his leaning back; from his hands, — confined by the smallest and tightly fitting handcuffs — projected two iron bars, one to the throat, which prevents his head from moving forwards, and the other to the belly which keeps his hands constantly stretched out. His feet too are pulled away from him, and his discomfort is extreme. Poor fellow! I am very sorry for him, but he has brought it all on himself. The Footae may order him to be beheaded: but the legal punishment is, it seems, transportation; if not released at once, he will be utterly ruined, and to save him from tor-ture, &c., his friends will be squeezed of every farthing they possess. Akue proposes that he be let off with a fine, or at all events that he be kept a pri-soner at S'Hae. [In the margin in a different ink: Ja san Keh'rh.][23]

I am now about to write to the Taoutae to say: the extortion under its two forms goes on every where in China: that, although that fact does not make the practice less objectionable it does give me a reason for begging Achik's release; that the object of punishment is to deter others and that Achik being a linguist, the object of his punishment is to deter the other linguists from malpractices; that the punishment he has already received is quite enough for his offence, and that, it with my orders to all the offices, will be sure to prevent linguists from acting so for the future; that in other respects, so far as I know he has been a good and valuable servent, &c. &c. &c. I must try and get him out.

FRIDAY, 25 NOVEMBER 1864: A letter last night from Cowrie, stating that they have ceased to torture Achik; I have not yet attempted to obtain his release, and am in doubts still as to whether or not I ought to interfere.

Gordon left this morning by the "Cadiz" en route for England. All good go with him, for a noble disinterested man! He is rash and hasty, and disconnected in talk and reasoning; but he has great ability, abnegation of self, honesty, pluck, modesty, and is the soul of honor. The mercantile community have written a most handsome letter to him — of which I am quite glad. He was not, by any means, the man for such a quiet thing as a small camp of instruction.[24]

A letter today from Maxwell: difficulties not yet ended on Formosa. No hurry: they cannot live out another year.

Through Kingsmill, Maude R. E. threatens to sue Brett for Tls. 292 entrusted to him in 1862. Brett cannot be got to pay up or show accounts. I am disappointed in him; what I saw at Peking led me to think him selfish, unreasonable, inconsiderate, and cruel. At the same time I have a great liking personally for the young brat![25]

Applications without number come in every day for employment. Many mercantile men of standing in China call on me: they tell me — how judiciously they speak, to be sure — that they have tried everything and everywhere, and now they turn to the Customs! Very kind: we are not a "Refuge for the destitute," my friends!

Dined with [characters for Pa ta-jen, "his excellency," Parkes] on Wednesday last: shammed a cold & would not talk. Ha! Ha! Ha!

TUESDAY, 29 NOVEMBER 1864: 11th moon, 1st day. Ting Taoutae called yesterday morning; he had no particular business, and talked in a general way about his efforts to right matters. I wish we had more mandarins of his stamp: honest and courageous; such men China stands greatly in need of. He has a side-door by which he goes out at night in private dress, and then he chops down most unexpectedly on 'sleeping sentinels' and evil-doers. He was quite savage with the people in the district jail for having tortured Achik after he had for the second time given orders to refrain from molesting him: the gaoler got a thousand blows and said what was done was done by the Munshang [deputies] of the Pootung [warden]; the Pootung, ordered to do so, produced the mun-shang who today is to be examined by the Taoutae himself: Heaven help him! Won't he catch it? Ten to one, he will criminate [sic] the Pootung himself, and Ting will at least tsan [impeach] him. The Footae has referred Achik's case to Peking, but whether to the Yamun or to the Hing Poo [Board of Punishments] I don't know. Ting says Le Footae will soon return to Soo Chow, and wd. like to see me: I hope this will not interfere with my intended departure on the 10th for Canton.[26]

An amicable letter, 22nd, from Meritens, who had recd. my long one of the 7th which had put him in a good humor again. ChangChow, he says, if not quietly retaken may prove a second SooChow: rowdies are already joining the rebels there, and at both Amoy and Foo Chow queer looking foreigners of the 'Micawber' type, in so far as they seem to be waiting for something to turn up. Report has it that WänChow is taken too, but that I cannot readily believe.[27]

Davidson of the "Hyson" is dead: "a native of Ireland!" Strange what a fatality has attended the foreigners who led the Imperialists against the rebels! Scarcely one of them escapes.

Brown dined with me last night; and we had a pleasant chat about College professors and Q.C. [Queen's College] students.[28]

Letters from Hankow show the Hu Pei [area of Hupeh province] is now somewhat more tranquil than it was a month ago. If the Imperialists do not organise, and keep together a small but effective flying column, they will never be able to put down the troubles that are springing up in different parts as fast as they are put down.

THURSDAY, 1 DECEMBER 1864: Dick and myself breakfasted with Ting Taoutae this morning; met there Wong Ashing, who seems a nice sort of man, and the Taoutae's own linguist, also named Wong, a native of Penang.[29]

WEDNESDAY, 7 DECEMBER 1864: Mr. Thomas of the London mission called this morning and told me that he had a difference of opinion with Mr. Muirhead, the chief of the Mission. Mr. M. wishes him to follow a certain plan of study, and to preach: Mr. T. refuses to follow that plan and also refuses to preach until he has been two years in the country. Mr. M. threatens not only to report him to the Directors, but to stop his salary. Mr. T. thinks the best plan is to resign, but is afraid to do so until he sees some way of supporting himself. In this position he comes to me, explains the matter, and asks if I can assist him.[30]

I say that I am disinclined to say anything, as I don't wish to be brought into conflict with either Mr. Muirhead or the Mission: that I do not wish to say anything, before he has decided, to influence his decision: that the matter is a serious one, and that, before taking so grave a step as that of leaving the society, he ought to think the matter well over.

I further said I could quite understand his position, and that I was too of the opinion that a missionary ought not to begin his work too hastily, or without preparation, in this country, & that further dictation by one man as to the course to be pursued by an other [sic], when that other saw a better way before him, was likely to defeat the common object: that I did not wish it to be said that I had been encouraging insubordination in a young missionary, in supporting him against the chief of the mission: that he ought to consider the matter, and make up his mind, apart from anything that I could promise him in the way of certain support in the event of his leaving the mission: but

235

that if he had fully decided, and carried his decision of resigning into execution, I shd. take care to get him employment.

He went away, with the distinct understanding that he was to tell Mr. Muirhead all that had passed.

His ability in the way of picking up languages — though Mr. M. hinted the other day he was but a smatterer in all — is very remarkable, and he would be a very valuable acquisition to us. We shall see. It is a very serious fix for a man to be in: in China, however, a man, with a missionary spirit, in our service would have a wonderful field before him, & might be very useful.

On the 9th, I leave by the "Aden" for Hongkong.

Raining here during the last two days.

If Mr. Thomas does join us, I imagine Chefoo will be the best place to which to send him.

THURSDAY, 8 DECEMBER 1864: Mr. Thomas appointed to Chefoo as Fourth Class Clerk! He called a meeting of the Committee yesterday evening, and tendered his resignation which was accepted.

MONDAY, 12 DECEMBER 1864: [characters for the 14th day of the 11th lunar month] Arrived at Hongkong in the morning after a rough, uncomfortable, but quick passage by the "Aden", at seven o'clock; altogether 69 hours under steam. Came up to Canton by the "Hankow", and found Glover well.[31]

TUESDAY, 13 DECEMBER 1864: Calls from Chang, Luh, writer Chin, Sha.[32]

WEDNESDAY, 14 DECEMBER 1864: Call from Mingqua who told me the whole story of Kwo Footae's family troubles. At the taking of some city, two very beautiful girls were found in a brothel of the superior kind: Tsäng Kwo fan appropriated one of them, and Kwo — who had already lost his first wife — laid hands on the other. In process of time, they both had children — the one a boy, the other a girl. The children were then betrothed to each other, and the Kwo and Tsäng families became in that way connected. Kwo for a time was titular taoutae in charge of some tax offices in Keang Soo, and got the reputation of ability in that department shen-yu-chow-le [?]; Canton being thought rich, and not sufficiently productive, Tsäng Kwo fan procured his nomination as Footae, in the hope of 'raising the wind'.[33] At Shanghai there was a [characters for Ch'ien chia; Ch'ien family], the head of which had formerly been a Footae somewhere; and a busybody, knowing that Kwo was appointed to Kwangtung, and that he had no 'chief' wife, as [sic] also that the Tseën Kea [Ch'ien family] had an eligible and unmarried daughter, got up a match. The marriage took place, to the great disgust of the lady seized on in the wars, and Kwo and family came to Canton by sea via Hongkong. On arrival at Canton the usual 8-bearer chair was sent by the Kwang Chow foo [Canton prefect] to carry the Footae to his yamun, and another with as many bearers for the Taetae [wife]. The Footae went off first, and then, before the Taetae had time to get into the chair provided for her Urhfoojin [the "second wife"] took possession of it and, with her children, was carried into the city. The Taetae thereon asked for another 8-bearer chair; the Kwang Chowfoo refused to get it for her, and said that there were only three such chairs in all Canton. After some time, the Taetae got into a 4-bearer chair, and was carried to the Yamun. No sooner was the chair put down in the grand hall, where all the officials were collected, than [the] Taetae burst out into a torrent of abuse, and behaved in a most unseemly manner. Thereforward, she and her good man quarreled every day: — Robertson heard him whipping her on one occasion; and eventually, after having vainly tried to provide for her return home through the Foo and Nanhae, she got into a steamer, went to Hongkong, and thence to S'Hae. A plucky little woman, one wd. say. I recollect seeing the occurrence in the papers at the time; in the Chinese issue, it said that she was a daughter of Hsieh's.[34]

Mingqua said that in 1863 he had seen a man named Fung (Ting-yew) who had been one of Tsängkwofan's Suin Poo [followers] when I called on him in Nov. or rather January 1863; who had told him that the old gentleman after my departure had remarked:

"Na-jin shih tsae sha pang-tsoo wo-min-teih ["That man is really helpful to us"].[35]

SUNDAY, 18 DECEMBER 1864: Called on Rameau & Robinson.[36]

MONDAY, 19 DECEMBER 1864: Call from Perry: about Tea transshipped at Hongkong, arrived at FooChow without Duty Paid Certificate. Told him, FooChow ought to treat them as of foreign origin, and collect full import duty, returnable by drawback in the event of the goods going again to a foreign country.[37]

Think of DeGrijs for a Commissionership; have arranged my plan of action as regards steamers.[38]

TUESDAY, 20 DECEMBER 1864: Theatricals. "Birth [?] at the Swan," Canton Minstrels, and "Taming of the Tiger". Acting very poor, and the theatre bitterly cold and full of draughts.

Recd. letters from Shanghae, and my box of clothes from England.

Tsäng Kwo fan ordered back to Nanking and Le Footae to SooChow.

This shows that either the bandit-doings in Hoopih are checked, or the Peking authorities cannot move the laou-ta-jin ["old gentleman"] against his will.[39]

FitzRoy has resigned, and Wilzer refuses to come out again.[40]

Mama writes of a Miss Breadon, and speaks of £5000; by the time I go home, I shall be able to lay down £4 for each £1. The desire for a pleasant fireside increases; but that for matrimony wanes.[41]

Old Mossman has written me a letter too, in which he asks for c'est moi's literary aid towards a book narrating the decline of Taepingdom. He met Miss Hessie Chapman [?]—who desired him to say <u>she</u> is now <u>Miss</u> Chapman—at the British Association.[42]

21 DECEMBER 1864: Races. only went to see a couple; dreadfully cold, excessively stupid. Man eats—the ponies [looked?]

Letter from Peking. Cartwright sends a pleasant note; Wade wishes I was <u>there</u>, as the yamun people are going astray about 3-per cent tax on opium at New Chwang, and tells me Farger's [?] wife found <u>enceinte</u>, and that people wd. like him to have a berth in the Customs; Meadows says Baker's fever and ague was really D.T. Amy writes for 'consideration'; I don't think Dick was right altogether in dumping him. I must make a rule, that any Tide-waiter who has served say three years shall not be dismissed without reference to me.[43]

22 DECEMBER 1864: [characters for 24th day of the 11th lunar month] Glover has written to Vanderhavin to inquire for De Grijs' where-abouts. I must try and get hold of a couple of people: perhaps the Spanish consul at Shanghae, and Adkins. I am puzzled about our staff, as none of our young men are yet fit to take charge.[44]

23 DECEMBER 1864: Called yesterday on Mao Chetae and Kwo Footae. The former, Mao Hung Ping, is a native of Tse Nan foo in Shantung, aged 59. He resided in Peking as a Yu-she [censor] for some 17 years, and then was appointed to Hoonan, where he was Footae [Governor] when I stayed at WooChang in the summer of 1862. Appointed to Canton a little more than a year ago. He is a nice old man, with a good head and a pleasant face. I talked to him about 1. Emigration, 2. Canton Revenue, 3. Shelter, and some other matters and found him sufficiently intelligent. From his place, I went to the Footae's[,] who is a younger man, not more than 2 or 3 and 40, a native of Hoonan, for whose appointment (known to him in that province) Mao applied when made Tsung-tuh [Governor General]. He has a white, bad-colored face; cunning eye, and underbred look; but he seemed sharp, inquisitive, and practical. I put forward my idea of remitting import duties for a year, & he seemed to nibble a little. His Hoonan Kwan-hwa

["Mandarin" dialect] I found it somewhat difficult to understand.[45]

Today Mao Tajin returned my call. I asked him what he thought of the foreign drill: he said honestly, "it was good so long as the foreign instructors remained with the men, but the moment they left it wd. be useless." I did not attempt to argue the point, but went straight at the question of the Canton Revenue, and talked well into him my reasons for proposing to collect no import duties for a year or so; he coincided in my views, and said that he & the Footae & Hoppo wd. join in carrying them into effect, provided it were merely she-pan [on a trial basis] for a year.[46]

24 DECEMBER 1864: A card from Kwo Footae this morning saying that he intended to have called with the Chetae yesterday but was ill: will call in a few days. A visit from the Hoppo, who was in a terrible state of snuff: poor old boy! I went at him, too, very patiently, anent the remission of Import Duties, and he says he'll join the others in carrying it into effect, but that the new Hoppo ought to join too: quite right! His remarks showed that he understood me at all events.

Chang Seaou-tang brought a candidate for the writership today K'ow-teen Woo [character for Wu]: a very ugly Cantonese Sew-tsae [lowest degree holder], who for leading braves into KwangSe in 1857, has been paou-keu'd [recommended] as a Keaou-kwan [educational officer]. He is intensely ugly, & talks badly, but he wrote off a letter I asked him to write in a style I have rarely seen matched. I am to see several other candidates, and then I shall make my choice.[47]

CHRISTMAS DAY, 25 DECEMBER 1864: Busy at work most of the day writing necessary letters. I have offered a Commissionership, with Tls. 4800 a year, to Adkins, and a General Interpretership with Tls 3600, to Brown, and I have written to Wade to allow them to join me. I hope he will do so. If he does not, I must fall back upon some of our young men: probably Bowra & Des Champs.

Wrote to the [indistinct word] Bank, Shanghae, asking them to debit my private a/c with Tls. 19,000, which I wish to place in the Bank as a permanent, interest-bearing, deposit; it will give me Tls. 950 a year, which it is better to have than to let the money lie idle.[48]

26 DECEMBER 1864: The Shanghae Mail in today; it brings me my home letters from Mary and Sarah, dated 17th Oct.: all well and no news.

FitzRoy's official resignation also came, with a private note, offering if necessary, to refund his half pay for the last six months.

Ting Taoutae writes to congratulate me on my coming Nee-tae ship [brevet rank as a provincial judicial commissioner]: Le memorialized on the 5th of the 11th m. [month, lunar calendar][49]

27 DECEMBER 1864: Another candidate for the writership came today, by name Tang, a native of ChangChow in Keangsoo. He has evidently more experience of official documents than Woo, but he is not so ready with his pen. He was five years with Morrison and Parkes, but left them in 1857, when the troubles in Canton came to a head.[50]

30 DECEMBER 1864: Had a long jaw with old Chang yesterday, who retailed some amusing items of local gossip. Kwo Footae, he says, has been tsan'd [impeached] by some censor on various grounds: — in one case, he called on a Keujin [provincial degree holder] named Lin to contribute Tls. 10 000 to the military chest; Lin's family is fairly wealthy, and has some hundred thousand taels or more, but there are several brothers to share it. The Keujin at once promised to pay the subscription, intending to take the amount from the general fund; his brothers, however, objected, & he himself, unable or unwilling to pay out such a sum from his own share, bolted; Kwo Footae thereon seal'd (fung) his houses and property: Lin then got a friend of his, a Censor, to memorialize; Kwo replies to the accusation, that he has not been acting harshly, that the Lin Kea [Lin family] is very wealthy, and that the Keujin, to avoid payment of a subscription in aid of provincial wants, had, shamefully, taken refuge in Hongkong. Whichever is in the right, Kwo has certainly got the ship-hand, in that Lin did actually hide in Hongkong; and nothing will displease the Govt. so much as to hear that a literary man has hid in a foreign settlement.[51]

Again, at the late military examinations all the men who made Woo-keujin [military provincial degree holder] belonged to the Kwang chow foo: suspicious, says the public. Hitherto it has been customary to give two or three of the degrees to the candidates from the Hia-sze-foo, and some three hundred candidates generally come from that quarter; the expenses of the journey are considerable, and it has been a custom for the successful man to pay the travelling expenses for their unsuccessful competitors. At the last examination, not only did no one belonging to Hia-sze-foo get a degree, but some of the Kwang-chow-foo candidates, who had only struck the target nine times out of thirteen shots, were successful, whereas the Hia-sze-foo men struck it thirteen times. When the names of the successful candidates were made public, the Hia Sze foo people were much discontented, and they sent in a statement of their grievances to the Footae & Chetae in petitions; the petitions were not received, and the consequence was there threatened to be trouble. The Hia sze foo men said that they had been to great expense in coming to Canton, & that through the Footae's injustice they were unable to pay their way back, & refused to return. At length the Footae sent them some hundreds of Taels to pay their expense, & the matter to a great extent ended. Threats of appealing to Peking were, however, muttered, and thereon the Footae issued a proclamation stating that he had given the degrees in accordance with an Edict of the 13th year of Taoukwang, which directed degrees to be given not merely for success in archery, but for ability to wield the sword, lift the stone, and "general appearance." The proclamation remained on the wall one day, and was then removed by the Footae's own orders. The Footae is a hasty man, and, when he takes an idea in his head, he acts without further thought, and thus, having on this occasion made himself somewhat ridiculous by an unnecessary appeal to the people in justification of his action, he gave cause for further laughter by the haste with which he withdrew his proclamation.[52]

At the literary Keujin examinations, H. E. got into trouble too. He gave, as a Te-muh [topic], a line from the Books, which a few years ago had produced some celebrated wän chang [essays] in Chekeang. The candidates successful were about 90 in number out of [number never filled in] competitors. When their wän chang were published in the usual way, the public made haste to read them, and it was at once detected that the first 30 were exact transcripts of the Chekiang essays,—the first of the lot being the essay that had figured as 19th in the Chekiang series, sent in by a sewtsae, aged 17, of the Shimtih Heen, a friend of Chang's. As soon as the Choo-kaou [examiners] heard what had occurred, they sent for the 30 candidates, and made them in great haste write new essays, and as some of them were very poor, the trouble the Chookaou had to go to to correct them & fit them for public scrutiny was wonderful, especially as they were limited to time, the essays and the official report having to be sent off on a given day to Peking. The same theme may be given twice or oftener, but the examiners ought to take care that the wänchang are original.[53]

Speaking of young men getting degrees, Chang referred to the present Hio-tai [Provincial Director of Education] of Fuhkeen, who at 16 became sewtsae, at 17 Keujin, at 18 Han lin [member of the Hantin Academy], and is now Hio-tae at the age of 21. His father was a teacher in Howqua's (Wu-tsung-yaou) family, & taught his own son, with his master's children. Howqua took a fancy to the boy, and offered to give him a niece of his, a Miss Woo, as wife: the boy said yes readily, but the father thought the match unfit, as his family was poor while Howqua's was very wealthy. It then came out that the girl was blind, her eyes having never been open since her birth! The boy was again asked his idea: and he, not 15, said a blind girl wd. suit him as well as any other. So the match was made & now, lo and behold! he is Hio-tae of Fuhkeen, & his Tae-tae [wife] is blind![54]

Howqua's name then brought out another story. The local authorities were very hard up some time ago, and through Howqua got a loan of Tls. 170 000 from Russell & Co. The time for payment arrived, and Howqua got Russell & Co. to claim through the U.S. Consul, not only the Tls. 170 000, but also some other sums which Howqua had advanced to the authorities from his own funds at the same time. Lo Tun-yen, of Lo-Lung-Soo notoriety, now the Hoo Poo Shang Shoo [President of the Board of Revenue], got wind of the affair, and being an enemy of Howqua's, memorialized: his memorial drew forth an angry edict, & the Kwangtung authorities have been ordered not to pay Russell & Co. Howqua meanwhile has died, & his son, on hearing of the Edict, was excessively alarmed; he at once petitioned the Chetae [Governor General], & made a statement of the real facts, from which it appears that Howqua has subscribed for government use, during the last 24 years, Tls. 10,500,500 or £3,500.00 stg [sterling]![55]

Immensely rich some Chinese families must be! Circumstances are gradually leading me to think that on me yet devolves the task of re-modelling the Chinese finance system throughout the whole Empire; the great, and indeed only difficulty, wd. be the want of honest native agents. In private life, no man is honester than a Chinaman; give him an official position or connexion, & he is the greatest nojin [?] [perhaps *niu-jen* (bad man)?] going.

1865

3 JANUARY 1865: New Years day come and gone, and now we are fairly launched into 1865! My Xmas and New Years day have both been as dull, as dull days could well be, and the season has inspired but little sentiment. The weariness and listlessness which so often oppress me are quite unaccountable: is it that I am getting old? Is it that I have no object to live for? Or is it that I have no wife? Whatever the cause, there it is: very successful as regards advancement in life, but yet discontented! The tree I have been climbing has been ascended too quickly, or else it has not been a very tall one; I have half a mind to throw it up, and commence some other career just for the sake of having an object to aim at, and a battle to fight. The chase is certainly more pleasant than the prey: the pursuit is the great thing, but what we run for, when got, is generally of no more value intrinsically than the fox's brush.

It's all very well for writers who have sprung from the people to dilate on the excellence of the gentleman by nature: the gentleman by birth is far better. That is: in society, the man who is only a gentleman by nature will avoid giving offense,—he will be tolerated but not welcomed; on the other hand, the gentleman, by birth, carries with him a consciousness of his position, or rather an unconsciousness that only accompanies what has never been striven for or questioned, and he is welcomed. To the one is accorded a positive recognition, to the other a merely negative one. And yet, as Emerson says, a man may always have what he takes: but there is a distinction, for the man who has never had any doubts about what he has as being his property and right will act naturally, whereas the other who may have, buried at the bottom of his heart, a consciousness of assuming something, to which he has not been always accustomed, will not act naturally, and will see slights where they are not intended, and defeat his own object by what he cannot altogether hide, a fight for the portion which he strives at consciously, but which thus [?] wd. give him more readily if he less evidently strove for it. I am discovering my own moral secretions, as Dick says. In point of fact, I am just ripe for running into excess: drink or debauchery. I am not happy, and I almost fear to ask why. I have every reason to feel satisfied and thankful, and yet I am horribly miserable. I wonder is my brain softening, or is my liver growing [?]: what can it be?

Last night dined with the Hoppo: in gratuities to his servants, spent $20. The dinners are absurdities: civility in abundance, but none of that familiar cordiality which wd. make the thing thoroughly agreeable.

Went to the theatre, and saw "Love's Devil" & "Toodles." The latter play brought out, as Toodles, Master Mush, a boy of 15; he acted wonderfully well, and we'll doubtless, hereafter, find him a stage notability. The girls were very captivating.

Le Footae has written to the Hoppo to find whether the linguists here do anything in the way of accepting presents &c. from merchants, and says that he has memorialized to take away Tong Achik's button, in order that he may be dealt with most severely.[56]

10 JANUARY 1865: A letter from Hughes, recd. yesterday tells me that on the 1st instant the ChangChow rebels came out to attack Kaou and Hwang Tetuh but were repulsed. This is good news.[57]

Chin brought me today the K'ow-Kung ["confession"] of the Chung Wang. I see that with regard to the execution of the Wangs by Le Footae, he styles it sha-hae [slaughter], and says that on account of it the other Wangs would not tow-heang [surrender]. This somewhat contradicts the opinion I have held, that Le's act did not frighten other leaders from coming over; but I note that Tsëng [sic] Kwo fan's comment on the K'ow Kung is that it contains much that is false, but that he publishes it entire, to present what of truth there is in it.[58]

The export of Tea through Macao does not seem to be quite so great as I had calculated. Acheen said 200 chops, and, with from 300 to 400 peculs a chop, the amount ought to have been over 70 000 peculs. Deacon now says that about 2,000,000 lbs went through Amoy: that is say 15 000 peculs.[59]

Tseang Taeyay's brother has got into disgrace. He has spent the last fifty days in a brothel, and has had to pawn everything to pay his way out. He moreover fell in love with a girl there, and finding that he could not purchase her wished her to die with him; she, however, rejected the cup of tea opium-drugged, and said that, though she liked him not a little, she did not like him quite enough to die with him. He then in the course of the night tried to poison himself by swallowing opium; the girl, however, foiled him, & made him vomit. He then tried to throw himself into the river, but the watchman got hold of him; and, subsequently, towards morning, he took off the girl's garters and suspended himself to a beam intending to hang himself, but the girl woke up & cut him down. He was then sent to the Tsze How Kung [prison], near the Hoppo's Yamun.[60]

In 1854, Lo Ping-chang, then Hoonan Seun foo [Governor], wrote to Yeh Ming-shen to put his son to death. The youth had been behaving badly, & Lo feared he wd. ruin the family. Yeh called for Lo's Taetae [wife], and made enquiries, which resulted in his bringing the old lady and her son to Canton, where he gave them in charge to the Nanhae heen [magistrate], who provided a teacher for the gentleman & kept him in strict surveillance. That saved him, it appears, from joining the rebels, who would have made him a t'ow-tsze [leader]. Strange to say, Hwa-yuan is the native place of both Lo and Hung Siu tseuen: an able officer & the rebel chief.[61]

A letter from Dr. Happer today accepts my offer to provide for Andrew's education. He is a good boy, & I don't grudge the money; it will amount to $2500, as I promised him $500 a year for four [sic] years.[62]

I intend to go down to Hongkong tomorrow to make sundry arrangements before leaving the south.

She-tsang is coming through Keangse. He left Peking with a chair, 5 waggons [sic], & 74 carts; and he has already spent Tls. 30,000! Chin and I calculated yesterday that during the first year to meet all his expenses, he must peculate to the extent of Tls. 100 000![63]

SUNDAY, 15 JANUARY 1865: I returned from Hongkong yesterday by the "Plymouth Rock": The English Mail arrived just as we started: in steaming through the harbor, a boat with a woman and three or four children in it got under our one side wheel, and as far as I could judge all with the exception of one boy who sprang into the water in time to get clear, were smashed to pieces. The boat in my opinion was run over — there was room enough to have kept to the right more, and even had the steersman not been to blame the officer by the wheel might have stopped the engine, and thereby done less damage.

While at Hongkong, I tried to arrange with Lapraik to allow his steamer at the end of next month, to call at Takao on the way to FooChow: he feared that such a detour might inconvenience passengers and vitiate insurance, but promised to see into the matter & send me an answer.[64]

Arranged my a/c with the Bank.

Did not succeed in seeing Lobschied, so that I had to leave undone the private business I was most anxious to have got arranged.[65]

Called on Sutherland, Delano, and Neilson. Put my name on Lady Robinson's Visiting Book. Met Swinhoe, who had just come down by the "Swallow"; the last time we walked together in Hongkong was in 1854, September: changes since then not a few![66]

A letter from Maxwell tells me that the Tae Wan difficulty has at length been arranged and that tidewaiters are not located there. So far, so good.[67]

Recd. a letter from J.McL.Brown, who seems pleased with the offer I made him, but naturally wishes to think over the matter well before taking a step, which wd. affect so seriously all his future prospects.

Hongkong is not a pleasant place for any one to be at, who has no business to do, and the two days that I spent there thoroughly wearied me. Lawrence was at the Club, waiting impatiently for the arrival of his fiancée. Sir R. Alcock arrived en route for England; I caught a glimpse of him in the street, but did not speak to him.[68]

Among the arrivals by the French Mail were Mr. Aug. Heard, and Mr. Ward, formerly U.S. Minister to China.[69]

The weather continues changeable, and today it is almost oppressively hot. My industrious moments seem to come by fits and starts. I think if I were to exercise my reason more, and give less reign to my foolish imagination I might become a wiser and more contented man: but, really, living so unsettled a life, it is difficult to settle down to any line of study seriously and vigorously.

A note from Dick says that the Hupih Rebels have surrendered: in that case, the troubles on the Keang-pih [north of the Yangtze River] may be said to be ended. And as Hughes writes that on the 1st instant, the ChangChow Rebels failed in an attack they made on the camp of Kaou & Hwang Tetuh, the tide seems to turn against them too. Kwo Sunglin is on his way to Fuhkeen, & when he arrives affairs will doubtless go right, vigorously. Old Mossman wants to raise a government loan for China; and Surgeon Lockhead wants a medal—how mad some people are after decorations.[70]

FRIDAY, 20 JANUARY 1865: Really it is difficult to determine by mere abstract reasoning which of the two systems is the better, ours or that of the Chinese. With us, taxation is fixed, and no one dare ask for a cent beyond that allowed by the laws, made and agreed to by the representatives of the people; our national expenditure is very large,—ludicrously large compared with that of China, and our taxation is likewise of a stricter kind than any known in China. With the Chinese, on the other hand, taxation is light, national expenditure (as publicly accounted for) is a trifle, and while they seldom get half the taxes the laws allow them, the officials continually pocket money which they draw from the people locally in various ways, and which custom at all events, seems to have now formed [?] into a matter of right. With us, the representatives of the people settle the taxation, and then enforce it: with the Chinese the officials & their followers, in direct contact with the people, have ways and means of procuring whatever monies are required for public works, or necessitated for local protection. With us the Parliament discusses the question of supply; with the Chinese, the people in the locality interested provide funds on the spot. We recognize, and start from, the "original sin" doctrine; we accordingly rule and coerce; the Chinese start from the "sin-pun-shen" [man's nature is basically good] side, and appeal to a man's ideas of what is right or wrong. We keep people right by impressing upon them the inexpediency of going astray; in China, people are taught to make sacrifices, because it is for the right. At the same time, one system seems the correct one, for it provides equality of rights for all concerned, and prevents private outrages. At the same time with us, the percentage of crime is greater, & the criminal has less chance of reforming.[71]

This chain of thought is not a new one, but it is suggested today by what Mr. Albert Heard said when he called: to the effect that China ought now to get up a foreign loan. Why, I—as a Chinaman—ask? For what purpose shall we borrow foreign money; and in my other capacity, as a foreigner,— and anxious to introduce our emblems of civilization—railroads, &c.: though

I might ask, why are they wanted—I again enquire, supposing we had the loans who would superintend the appropriation of the funds. [Four asterisks below]

       *   *   *   *

Yesterday the Tsae Lou-chan's garden, had a theatrical entertainment given by Chan and Luh: present Chang, with Man, Glover & myself. Very tiresome.[72]

MONDAY, 23 JANUARY 1865: Wrote to Cane of the Artillery today offering him a Commissionership with Tls. 3600 a year. If not too cranky, he would suit us well, and, at Newchwang, where I intend to place him, he will do good service by getting up a body of mounted police, say fifty or so, and by patrolling in winter.[73]

WEDNESDAY, 25 JANUARY 1865: On Monday last, the new Hoppo [characters for Shih-tseng] arrived: with about 220 followers. He got into his boats from the "White Cloud" and went on to Fa-te, where he remained till this morning; he passed down the river about half past nine, & landed at the Te'en tsze Matow [Imperial wharf], on his way to Kungkwan [office] at noon. At the jetty he was received by all the officials who went through the "kneeling" & "knock-head" ceremony, Kwei-shing-gen, of enquiring after the Emperor's repose.[74] When the old Hoppo starts for Peking, he will also embark at the Teen-tsze jetty, and all the officials will then kneel, and send their good wishes to the Emperor.

The office closed today for the New Year Holidays, and it is not to open again for a week or more. Glover wanted to open it on Monday: that, said the Deputies, was an unlucky day in the Calendar; On Tuesday? That, said they, is an unlucky day in the present Hoppo's nativity-cast. On Wednesday? That, said they, is equally unlucky for the new man. Funny, this idea of lucky & unlucky days, with all its following of Fung-shwuy [geomancy], &c. &c.![75]

Called this morning on Mrs. Chalmers, Mrs. Condit, Mrs. Sampson, & Mrs. Happer; and had a very pleasant gossip at each place.[76]

I have just read Macauly's Essay on Lord Clive. It suggests strange reflections: the idea has not been mooted for the first time. Many have feared that China would become another India; now for the first time the idea strikes into me, that some such fate may be in store for this country. Who is to be its Clive?[77]

Two things are certain: the people will accept any government that is strong enough to eject the existing one; and the existing government, if it does not initiate radical changes, will not, in the presence of the men from the west, be able to go on. To exist, the govt. must do this: it must acquire strength, and it must centralise. It, however, objects to centralisation; & it is too rotten to do that which wd. give it strength—i.e. to get strength, it must have money, & to procure money it must remodel its taxation; and to make any remodelling of taxation useful, it must place its officials above want, by giving them high salaries. At present, their salaries are quite inadequate, & indeed few of them draw their pay. What they live on, and enrich themselves with is the money that they squeeze from the people. The theory of this govt., and the "architectural plan" are very fine; but carried into effect, its whole course is downwards, and its rottenness becomes daily more perceptible: even to me, whose close contact with it ought to have the effect of blinding my eyes! So many countries, however, have now to do with China, & news flies so fast, & the people at home are so averse to another "India" that affairs will not follow the turn given to them in that country a hundred years ago by Clive — China in her weakness is strong in the protection she has in the jealousies of the foreign powers who deal with her: her greatest safety lies in making many treaties, and in having many representatives in Peking. At the same time, any great commotion in the West might uproot everything out here. Either the country must change now, or it must divide into several states, or it must be subjected to foreigners.

By the "Tyneminster" [?] I received a despatch from the Tsung le Yamun, forwarding the Edict that gives the Nee-tae-ship: it merely says: [characters for *shih-chiu-jih pen-jih feng-chih Ho-te cho shang-chia an-ch'a-shih hsien ch'in-tz'u*: "19th day. On this day was received an imperial decree: Let Ho-te [Hart] be rewarded with the brevet rank of provincial judicial commissioner. Reverently received."][78]

Does [characters for *pen-jih*; "this day"] in a despatch, where a date has just been referred to, mean "the same day", or "today"—the date referred to or the date on which the despatch is written?[79]

26 JANUARY 1865: The new Hoppo, She ta-jin called on me today at 3 p.m. He talked about business matters in a way that promises well. He said it was quite evident that the increase in the Revenue in the past five years was entirely owing to the aid given by the Inspectorate; that at Canton, the difficulties that exist must be recognized,—that great improvement could not be expected in a day,—that it would be satisfactory if things did not become worse,—that after a time a small & gradual progress would do,— that every tael gained was a tael to the good,—and that, at Hongkong, where the flourishing business surprised him, every additional ship that discharged or loaded, was a loss to the Canton Revenue. His clearness encourages me, and, if he only works with me, I can promise him a successful term of office. I said to him that the people at the T.l. Yamun had told me they expected much from him: he said, "You are complimentary". "Not atall", said I, "I merely say what I was told, and if you do not transact business with success, you will return north with 'loss of face'". By this remark I surprised him not a little. His anxiety, <u>teen</u> <u>Ke</u> [?], to come out & see me so soon, shows him to be in earnest. I merely talked to him in a general way; I hope I shall get him to do what I want.[80]

Robertson called today: I told him, I hoped to get the Import Duties taken off, and to a certain extent, Bonded Warehouses established. He is delighted, & says it will "make Canton".

From Acheen I learnt that during the last year 200 chops of Congou had gone to Macao each chop averaging 600 1/2 chests of 7 catties each: i.e. in all 84000 Peculs; and that other teas to the extent of another 16 000 Peculs had gone there too. We must put the stopper on Macao, & make Export Duties by their increase make up for the Imports that we forego.[81]

I have purchased the "Willex" [?] for the Customs for $11,000.

The English Mail in today: Gordon made a C.B. [Companion of the Bath] for which I say Hurrah!

The "Dumbarton" with troops left Hongkong on the 24th; so that my letter to Cane did not reach him in time. I wish Brown and Adkins wd. make up their minds, so that I may know what to do.

In Macaulay's Essay on Warren Hastings, the 1st Gov. Genl. of India (1773), I notice he lays stress on the curious state of the country, in which the nominal was disassociated from the real power. In China that anomaly is doubled: not only does <u>nominal</u> seem disassociated from <u>real</u> power, but the one refers you to the other in a "from pillar to post" style which makes <u>all</u> action impossible.

The "Beach House" at Amoy offered to me for $9000. Very cheap, I think. I must now make our people comfortable, and the offices respected. The Customs' Service is bound to be a <u>great</u> service yet: respected & useful.

FRIDAY, 27 JANUARY 1865: This is the Chinese New Year's day [characters for 1st day of the 1st lunar month of the 4th year of the T'ung-chih reign]

SUNDAY, 29 JANUARY 1865: With regard to the Holy Scriptures, I am inclined to be of the opinion that the doctrine of "plenary inspiration" must be given up. The anathema which John in Revelations, pronounces against those who "add to or take from" the words of the book, cannot be held to apply to all the parts of '<u>the</u> Book', arranged as we have it; nor can the words "Holy men of old spoke as they were moved by the Holy Spirit" be taken to mean more than that those who really were prophets prophesied as moved by the Spirit. All that we find in the new testament bearing on the inspiration of the Scriptures refers to the scriptures of the <u>Old</u> Test[t].; "the more [?] sure word of prophecy." I should therefore say that with regard to the Gospels, they were written by men who had a Knowledge of what they wrote about, and who wished to leave a record of it for the future: that, in writing those histories, they were, while anxious to put in them nought but the truth, subject to the failings and infirmities of other men, and that they may possibly have transposed facts and conversations, and made mistakes of more or less importance — important if we hold to "plenary inspiration", but unimportant if we give up that dogma. With regard to the Epistles, I should look upon them just as upon sermons of the present day; only that they were written by men of a more earnest faith and of greater ability, and who perhaps had enjoyed nearer access to the Teacher than men of later ages. The pith of all the teachings is "love to God" and "love to one's neighbours"; on these two commandments hang all the law, the prophets, and the teachings of Christ himself. Of course, if we give up "plenary inspiration", we then make the scriptures the subject of criticism just as though they were other books & referred to other subjects, and criticism may go a length that will shock all who, with their mothers' milk, have drunk in the <u>mystical</u> interpretations that a superstitious reverence has put upon what is styled Holy Writ. I always fear to approach this subject — though it has great attractions for me; for I am in dread lest, through my desire to do sundry things which early teaching has made me regard with an amount of dislike that is superstitious, I may be led to view the truth through other than neutral glasses: lest I should be one of those who, having "pleasure in unrightousness", "believed not the truth".

What agonizing anguish, what secret trouble, what doubts and fears, has not the Christian faith called forth in men! How little do we know of the terrible moments which we each have, and how "exercised" our minds are on this subject! Well: our frames are but "dust" and the Lord knoweth <u>that</u>.

*   *   *

Lucy and Lillie made me a present of a pair of slippers the other day which they themselves worked for me. Lucy's letter is very poor for a girl of her age: <u>14</u> on the 19th of July next. Lillie will be 12 on the 13th August. I sent them each a piece of gauze as a return present.

The new Hoppo has done nothing but make a series of mistakes, I hear, since his arrival. The Che-tae [Governor General] refused to "Kwei shing gan", saying that She's rank was not sufficiently high, and, though he promised to receive him at the jetty, he came an hour or two late. She then went at him about the 300 000 Tls. required for the Kwang-chow-sze, and Mao, very much riled, replied to him with a tart irony that does not bode well for the future. The next day, the last of the year, the new Hiotae [provincial director of education], who left Peking <u>before</u> She, being expected to arrive, Mao sent to She, and said he wd. expect him to "Kwei shing gan" at the jetty, when the Hiotai appeared, and by the same messenger notified him that they would <u>pae pae</u> [pay respects] at the Birth Day Temple: She, instead of excusing himself on the ground of not having taken over the seals, said, "all right". On the following morning, he went to the Wan Show Kung, in full court dress: it is the etiquette at Canton to go there in ordinary attire, and await the Chetae's arrival to whom all pay their respect in that first instance, and that done, to don the Chao-e [court dress], which they take off when the ceremony in honor of the Emperor is over. She did not know the etiquette, & so he looked as foolish as a man in a shooting coat would at an evening party when all are in dress. In the afternoon, too, he had to "Kwei shing gan" to a man who left Peking before him, that honor having a day before been refused himself. It appears he got a despatch from the Board directing the Chetae to "tsow tsan" [memorialize to impeach] in the event of there being anything wrong in the a/c of the Hoppo when handing over charge; at this, as well as at neglect of three or more memorials on the subject of the Kwangtung finances, Chetae Maou is enraged. He must mind himself, or Mao will put him through.[82]

Chin told me the other day that the Hoppo will only have some Tls. 50 000 to settle down with after arrival at Peking, and that his Taetae may have half as much more which she must take care of in order to get the daughters married off. The peculations seem to have been: Hoppo Tls. 600 000: Chin & Luh Tls. 200 000: the others in the Yamun Tls. 400 000 or so: —I suppose about a million and a half of Taels in five years; not bad by any means. I must get the particulars from Chin, & keep them as a curio for future purposes.

Had a letter 25 Dec. from Gordon from Aden: he says he'll come out for $500 a month, & $5000 when finished.

TUESDAY, 31 JANUARY 1865: Sze ta-jin returned the call I made him on Sunday: he had nothing particular to say, but I frightened him a little about Swatow. His eye is restless and his manner somewhat brusque.[83]

WEDNESDAY, 1 FEBRUARY 1865: Yu ta-jin called. We had a pleasant chat. I made him feel interested in the Swatow matter, & he promises to go with me to the Che-tae's tomorrow.[84]

I today have at last succeeded in getting off my long [characters for shen-ch'eng; "report"] to Maou chetae proposing a temporary abolition of import duties at Canton. I propose to take them off for eighteen months: that step will break the back of the smuggling organization, and will drive trade back to Canton. On the expiration of the term, my revenue fleet will be in readiness and we shall be able to prevent any return to old practices.

THURSDAY, 2 FEBRUARY 1865: Called today on the Chetae.

Yu-Tsing was also there, and he explained very clearly and well all that I told him yesterday about Swatow. I simply put the matter before the Chetae in this way: by treaty we have the right to enter Chaou Chow, but, as yet, the Consul has been unable to enter it; should it continue impossible for him to enter it, and rebels appear there, you will one future day have foreigners making a casus belli out of it; should rebels take the city, he will have the Consul willingly coming to terms with them for the protection of the merchants—he will simply say to them "don't interfere with us, and we'll not prohibit trade with you". I therefore advised the Chetae to look sharp and, before the Rebels appear at ChaouChowfoo, get the authorities there to receive the Consul, so that, shd. rebels take the place, the authorities may be able to get the Consuls to act <u>with</u> them in preventing trade with the rebels.[85]

Relative to my proposition for an abolition of Import Duties, Maou said it wd. <u>not</u> do for with the demands that come south for funds, the Peking people wd. be sure to find fault with a scheme, which, on the face of it, has the voluntarily giving away of Tls. 300 000. I said "If I pay you down Tls. 300 000 in ready money, to be refunded during three years, will you agree?" Maou said, "if the new Hoppo agrees with you, I'll assist him in his representations to Peking." From all I see, I fear the thing will not be carried, and so have lost my labor: I'm sorry for it, for no <u>preventive</u> measures will bring back trade to Canton for many a long day. Confound the Board! It's always in the way. It is evident that Maou and Sze are not friends.

FRIDAY, 3 FEBRUARY 1865: Mr. Stuart of the Oriental Bank Corp[n]., just from England, called today. He is anxious about a mint, and will act with me in everything I propose. The payment of monies to the fleet after it was disbanded have raised the credit of the Chinese govt. wonderfully at home, he says. I talked my ideas of China into him; and showed him that I hoped for success from patient & systematic sapping, rather than from taking them by surprise.[86]

Major Edwards R.E. came up from H'Kong yesterday to stay with us till Monday.[87]

The French Mail arrived yesterday. I see Lay has got a son, and FitzRoy is about to be married to a Miss Eugenia Chapman.

Today I wrote note to Sir F. Bruce, sending him my "Memo on the working of the Inspectorate."

SATURDAY, 4 FEBRUARY 1865: Edwards went down to Whampoa today with Man & Luson: he is fidgeting about the command of the camp, and I tell him my opinion is that it would be folly for him to throw up his commission to take command under a provincial governor, who may be changed at any time, whose successors need not carry out his plans, and who, too, may change his own mind, and that for a man to join the camp who holds a commission in a foreign service would only put the Chinese against him, and cause international jealousies that would do more harm than the good affected in the camp.[88]

Price & Lister came up today: fortunate that the others have gone to Whampoa, as I shd. not have know [sic] where to put the new-comers. Rather cool of Lister, the way he walked in: but he is a big quiet fellow, so it doesn't matter.[89]

This evening, I don't know for what reason, the idea came into my mind to take a run home in October next, stay there a couple of months, come out in March or April, and then remain in China till '69. The more I think of it, the more am I in favor of it. Leave Peking at the end of Sept[r]. and, then, instead of going round the ports during the winter, go straight home. Capital idea!

SUNDAY, 5 FEBRUARY 1865: The idea of going home in Oct. grows stronger. I really think I'll do it. I can easily get away, and as neither Forbes nor his vessels will be ready for work before June 1866, I can be out before him: and at home can make some useful arrangements for the future. Perhaps, too, I may have a chance of getting married, or something of the sort!

TUESDAY, 14 FEBRUARY 1865: The first five of the last ten days were delightfully warm, and the nights so hot as to make blankets useless. The last five have been proportionately cold — so cold it is almost impossible to get warm.

I have got through all the work that requires me to be at Canton, and I now only await the Chetae's reply to my 'Emigration Despatch,' and old Chang to finish copying my drafts into the books, to start homewards.[90]

Yesterday the 'Deputies' or mun-shang, of the new Hoppo called. Leang is the elder of the two; he was in Canton with Hoppo Yu-Kwan in the 23rd year of Taoukwang's reign; the other man Chang is seemingly not so bright as Leang, and both of them seem to me to be of a low class. They said that with the demands made on the Hoppo for funds, more especially by the Nuy-woo-foo [Imperial Household Department] for the Imperial Household, it would be quite impossible for H.E. to propose a scheme which, however advantageous for the future, might be attended with loss during the first year, and greater anxiety is felt for money during the first than is likely to be shewn during the second year. The Hoppo will keep the scheme in mind, and will if necessary reconsider it and act upon it next year.[91]

The Chetae's reply to my despatch proposing to do away with duties on Imports, says that there is much truth in all I have said, but scouts the idea of being afraid lest energetic repressive measures shd. cause local disturbances; he too says that present receipts cannot be forgone for the uncertainty of future gains: and he thinks the schema not altogether a proper one. He is certainly right; but looking facts in the face, no other scheme — no other action — will prove so effectual in bringing trade to Canton, & increasing the revenue, as the one I proposed. I must now go at the Chinese Boats; that will walk into the private perquisites of the Hoppo with a vengeance.

Relative to Emigration, I adopted Laou's old rules, simply making a few alterations: but I proposed that the Yamun shd. write to the Plenipos calling on them to make four regulations: 1°. providing for registration of migrants in the countries to which they go; 2°. providing that the forfeiture of 3 months' pay shd. pay in full all debts into which, during the term of servitude, the master gets the man by advances, &c.; 3°. that China shd. from time to time send officials to inspect the conditions of the Coolies; & 4°. making provision for the extradition of criminals, who, by changing their names, had emigrated.[92]

My mind is still bent on going home; and I hope really to start by the French Mail in October next. The idea makes me feel so jolly!

MONDAY, 20 FEBRUARY 1865: [characters for 25th day of the 1st lunar month of the 4th year of the T'ung-chih reign.]

Ai-ya! Today I am thirty years old! The first half of the "Three Score Years" gone by! And to be no longer able to say "Twenty and odd," makes me feel that that years grow apace. Thirty and still unmarried: the sooner I plunge into the connubial state, the better! If I don't do it during the next four or five years, I must for ever leave it alone. I fear my ten weeks' stay at home at the end of this year will scarcely suffice for inspiring—though an hour is enough for me to fall in—love.

Today I called on the Tseung-Keun [Tartar General], Juy-lin, the Chetae, Fantae [Provincial Financial Commissioner] (Le Han chang), Yen-tae [Salt Intendant] (Fang), and two Hoppos. Juy-lin is in person a very fine-looking man, with a clear intelligent eye: I shd. imagine his ability is far beyond that required in his present position,—and in fact that he has been a [characters for chung-t'ang; Grand Secretary] shows such to be the case. He lamented want of funds, and showed that if he had money he wd. "work". Le is like the Footae, but fatter & shorter: his language is not very intelligible. Fang is a pleasant man, but his eyes are not straight in his head, and it is impossible to say with which he looks at one. I was dreadfully cold when I got home. By the way, Yu-tsing asked me to destroy Office Records prior to the payment of Indemnity, and to substitute others in accordance with the reports made by him to the Board! I told him to keep his own, and we would keep our records: I shall send back by Chin those he sent out some days back.[93]

21 FEBRUARY 1865: The Chetae returned my call today. Both yesterday and today, he was extremely pleasant and affable.

Man with LeangSoo & Ma-urh are to go to Shanghae by the "Nanzing" on Saturday: I shall make the rest of the rounds alone. It is too much bother with so many changes as I shall have, to have half a dozen people, and so much luggage to look after.

Call from Mr. Tyson, objecting to the moving of the Customs Offices at Hankow.

[Hart writes: "Vol 7° Robert Hart Vol: 7 25th February, 1865; @ 2nd March, 1866." Second date in different ink; journal begins with entry for May 7, 1865]

SUNDAY, 7 MAY 1865: [characters for 13th day of the 4th lunar month of the 4th year of the T'ung-chih reign]

In commencing this new volume of my journal, I have a good deal to write up, inasmuch as my last entry was made some months ago at Canton. First of all, let me record my dates of departure from and arrival at the various places visited, and then proceed to put down whatever may occur to me as worthy of remembrance.

Man with Leangsoo and Ma-urh having been sent on in the "Nanzing" direct to SHae, I myself, on the same day 25th February, left Canton and went to Hongkong, from which, per "Peking", I went up the coast, on the 27th, as far as Amoy; having previously touched at Swatow, where we arrived on the night of the 28th, leaving again on the afternoon of the next day. At Amoy we arrived on the 2nd March, and there I remained with Hughes until the 7th March, Tuesday, when we went together in the "Vindex" to Takow, having left Amoy at 3 p.m. and arriving the next day at 11 a.m. At Takow I spent twenty-four hours, and leaving it about noon on the 9th, arrived again at Amoy on the 10th at 5 p.m. There I remained until the 13th when I left in the "Cadiz" at 1/4 to 4 for Foo Chow, where I arrived, after 24 hours detention through fog at the White Dogs, on Wednesday the 15th at 2 p.m. I left FooChow on the 18th in the "Cadiz"; was at Amoy on the 19th & 20th, at Swatow on the 21st, and arrived again at Hongkong on the 22nd March. On 26th left Hongkong in the "Cadiz", and — after a narrow escape from shipwreck on the 27th when we touched on a shoal off Amoy — arrived at Shanghae on the 31st. From the 1st of April to the 25th I was busily occupied with service arrangements, and answering despatches; from the 26th to the 30th, I did no work, but took holiday at the races; and, having taken a house for three years on the 1st of May, I commenced to flit; and now Sunday the 7th, feeling somewhat at home in my new quarters, and, having got over the idleness produced by the demoralizing and upsetting effects of races & flitting, I again begin to feel fit & inclined for work.

Swatow. — I went up to Swatow, & with Williams looked at both sides of the river; selected a site for Commissioner's residence on the South side, near the Consulate, but fear there will be some difficulty in obtaining possession of it, as it affects the fung-shwuy [geomantic fortunes] of some families whose tombs are there situated; the office ought to be on the North side, and I have commenced negotiations with Dircks & Co. for the purchase of their house ($16 000), and only refrain from purchasing it because I dread the approach of rebels. Got Preston to write a civil note to Caine, to the effect that he did not mean any insult in the letter about which Caine had complained, & thus settled that matter. Dismissed the head Shoopan [accountant] Wong-Kwan; he has not done any office work of late, & was insolent when I spoke to him about the matter. Decided on transferring Preston to another port. Trade is steadily on the increase, &, with it, duties. Double Island looks quite deserted now, and, with the exception of pilots, ours are the only people on it, all the merchants have moved up to Swatow; and the south shore, opposite the village, has quite a number of foreign houses on it. The buildings are very good-looking, but the construction of the walls struck me as being strange; they do not use bricks or stones, but pound a mixture of clay and lime between boards, which subsequently becomes as hard as granite and dreads nothing but water. Called on Mrs. Caine, Mrs. Richardson; the former has a fine family growing around her, & Caine himself grows fat & jolly; the latter reminded me strangely of Janet Russell. I also called on the U.S. Consul, Mr. [left blank], who impressed me very favorably. The only question that remains to be settled connected with S'tow is that of Opium; the Footae had written to me to say that, in addition to the duty, a tax must be collected, & that the Customs' deputy must collect it. I have not yet replied to his despatch.[94]

FooChow. — I arrived at Foo Chow on Wednesday afternoon and left it on Friday afternoon for the anchorage. While going in on Wednesday morning, we met, between the White Dogs and Sha' Peak, the "Volunteer" going out, and on board of her was de Meritens: I therefore did not feel inclined to prolong my stay at F'Chow. Thursday I spent at the office, and on Friday I called on Ying Tseang-keun, and Seu Footae, in both cases, the central gates were opened, and tiffins laid out. Ying is a sharp little fellow; Seu is a fine-looking old man, with placid countenance & magnificent white beard. My visit to Seu was attended with amusing circumstances, but these must be penned on some future occasion. The Customs are now well lodged: the Commissioner & May live together in a fine house, on the site purchased when I was last at FooChow, and the other clerks live in a new house a little to the back of the office premises. Meritens deserves great credit for having got them thus housed. The "Spartan" was in good order too, and the men on board very comfortable. May is about to get married, and Meade also. The Prefect, Ting, a native of Peking, seemed to me a very sharp little fellow but devoid of any portion of veraciousness. The Haekwan Chang Hooling, still the same, with his hat on one side, his feather awry, and as pleasant and as intelligent as ever. From March @ October, the Foo Chow office sent $13 000 to my a/c from office funds; since October '64, it has sent nothing — the "Vindix" costs about from $1000 to $1200 a month. The expenses of the Foo-Chow office are about $5000 a month, leaving $5860; Tls. 6000 = $8860: so that I may simply [?] call on FooChow for Tls. 2000, and leave them still tls. 500 or 600 for contingencies. The authorities told me that they had sent Meritens to Amoy to stop supplies from being sent to the rebels, and to try and get Rhode and Co. to come away from ChangChow. They have purchased the "Volunteer" for some Tls. 32 000, and have sent to Amoy a special delegate who was formerly Taoutae there, a man named Tsäng, and also the Prefect Chin who was at F'Chow when I first visited it. The Gov. Genl. Tso is still at Yen-Ping-Foo where he has some 30 000 troops. May was busy with Hewlett in making arrangements for drilling troops: 700 Chinese to be drilled by Frenchmen, & 300 Tartars by English. I imagine we must build at the Pagoda Anchorage, but I am not sure as to which wd. be the best side. Meritens says the Nan-tae, i.e. south side, for to it he hopes to bring his road. Neither the telegraph nor the road have as yet succeeded. In the F'Chow office, I saw an amusing letter from Meritens to the authorities complaining that, while they had praised Hughes' doings in Memorials, they had left his own name unmentioned! Wm. Lay is decidedly improving in temper, &c.: I think I took the right way to utilise him, when I took him from Kiukiang, and gave him promotion at FooChow. The younger Howell is, they say, a good man: Schencke & Ingelhardt only fair.[95]

I asked Chang Hu-ling to write to Kwang at Amoy and remind him that it is the Commissioner he is to act with & support, and not the Consul.[96]

Takow. — I had been seasick when crossing in the "Vindix", and my head ached all the time I was at Takow. The coast is bold & rocky; high hills coming down to the water's edge; a little cleft in the rocks admits to the harbor or lagoon on the left which stretches out a verdant country, while on the right is a long sea wall of sand of the softest kind; the hills are coral, & the vegetation tropical. The place seemed a curious mixture of the Chinese harshness and Malay richness, in point of scenery & production. Not more than a dozen foreigners, all told, resident; and some six or eight vessels in port. Maxwell resides with McPhail & Co., and, at their place, I spent the night: the house very rough, and the walls rich with chirping lizards. Maxwell is to reside at Takow, and to visit Taewan when he chooses; at the latter place he is to station two or three tidewaiters, and in that way the difficulties are got over. At Tamsuy our office opened on the 1st Oct. 1863, and at Takow on the 6th May 1864. The Takow allotment is Tls. 1000 a month = $1470. At Takow they have been spending $1000 & at Taewan $336, leaving monthly balance, $130. The only difficult question is that connected with the prohibitions of export of rice, enforced occasionally against foreign vessels: the grievance lies chiefly in the fact that, while the foreign vessel is not allowed to ship rice, Chinese junks continue, under the very eyes of the officials, to ship it as before. The Formosan ports may now, I think, be removed from their position of subordination to FooChow. Called on Mrs. Swinhoe, a frightened-looking little lady, with wondrous jet-black eyes; they live in the queerest hole one can well imagine, & S's attention is said to be given much more to his pursuits in connexion with natural history than to his wife. Off Takow, when leaving, saw a fine school of whales: they seemed to be 60 feet long, and disported themselves in the water in an extraordinary manner.[97]

Amoy. — At Amoy, the great topic of conversation is the rebels. The local authorities, I found, looked with suspicion on Pedder, the Consul, and represented him as acting in collusion with the Taepings; for, sd. they, he paid a visit to the chief at ChangChow, brought down a rebel to Amoy, and under his office is a store kept by Gerard who is a well-known agent of the rebels. The "store" part of the charge is easily explained: Pedder rents the upper part of the premises from the owner as offices, while Gerard rents the lower portion for godowns & store, and such was their position long before the appearance of the rebels in the neighborhood. The visit to ChangChow & the bringing of the rebel to Amoy, the authorities have only themselves to thank for: Pedder, since the fall of ChangChow, had been urging them in every way to act strenuously, but all to no purpose, and English ships of war secured the safety of Amoy itself: the She-wang [Li Shih-hsien] sent letters Pedder thought were for himself, but which the authorities intercepted (beheading Chin Kin-lung); they never sent them to Pedder for perusal, & he was consequently irate. Having British interests to guard, he was not a little anxious to know the intentions of the rebels, & what it was that they tried to communicate with him about; so he resolved to pay a visit to Chang-

Chow & ascertain their intentions. The senior naval officer, Capt. Kingston, of the "Perseus", gave him a gunboat, &c., to go up the river, but wd. not accompany him; he sent an officer, however, and a letter to the rebel chief, telling him that, if he had aught important to communicate, he cd. send down one of his people to Amoy, who wd. be safely sent back again. Thus it came to pass, that Pedder returned accompanied by one of the Taepings: the man had nothing of importance to say, & the She-Wang, in sending him down, merely did so to show his faith in English honesty. Pedder, I conceive, was right in going to ChangChow, but wrong in bringing to Amoy a man who had really no business, & whose presence only tended to alarm the Imperialists & give hopes to the Taepings. To that effect, I wrote to Sir F. Bruce from Amoy.[98]

The HaeKwan [Customs taotai] at Amoy is the man who was formerly there [character for Kuang], a man who knows nothing about business, & cannot be got to talk sensibly about any matter. The Taoutae is named Täng Shwang-poo: he was formerly in the Kung-poo [Board of Works] with Wän Seang (Po-tseuen), and with whom he interchanged cards. He is a timid man, but very intelligent. He and the others, doing nothing, were only too glad to divert attention from themselves to what they considered the evil doings of Pedder; & Meritens at FooChow hurried the report along to Peking. I called on the Taoutae, and made him write down:[99]

1°. that as to the foreigners with the rebels, if they cd. be killed in fight, every one wd. be pleased, no one wd. complain, & that that wd. be the best way to dispose of them: but that, if they took them prisoners, they must hand them over to the consuls.

2°. that as to foreigners who attempted to join the rebels, that the military must prevent either by shooting those who attempted to force their way past the lines, or by seizing or turning back those who approached them: &

3°. that the only persons to pass the rebel lines shd. be such as had a pass from the Taoutae himself.

He wrote all down,— the first & second readily enough,— but the third he cd. not see, & wd. not do: I told him that it was the proper course to pursue, & that he wd. get into trouble if he did not take my advice. By despatches from the Footae [Governor] & Tsiang Kuen [Tartar General], Meritens & Hughes were appointed to act with the local authorities in cutting off supplies of both men & arms: the last day I was at Amoy, the preparations were made for blockading the port or rather the river that leads to ChangChow; the "Volunteer" was to be used for that purpose, & the blockade had been notified to all the Consuls. A special messenger too was about to go up & try to get Rhode out: I have since heard from Meritens that Rhode's first answer was an indignant refusal, that he then sent a message to say he & his men wd. be happy to come, that Meritens then sent up his messenger again with protection, but that the man with his papers fell into the hands of the rebels & has not since been heard of, & the result has been to destroy whatever confidence the Taepings had in Rhode & Co. Since I left Amoy, some foreigners have been caught & sent back to S'Hae: on the way up, the man in charge shot the well known <u>Butler</u>, who died, as the local press says, "respected & lamented by all who knew him." The "Poohing" [?] a steamer which (having heard from the "Janus" that she had been seen at anchor in Hoi-tae Bay, near TongShan) I sent "Vindix" out to cruise for, has been seized in Amoy, &, on the evidence of the commander of the "Janus", confiscated. A lorcha too has been seized with 400 stands of muskets, and the people are doing what they can to blockade the Coast.[100]

It was impossible to get good information, but I think the Taepings in Fuhkeen have not more than <u>15 000</u> fighting men. Yang & Kwo Tetuh have gone down with their well-armed semi-disciplined veterans, & on the 11th April, Martin & Kirkham commanding the left wing, Kwo the center, and Kaou the right, gave a good thrashing to the rebels, who, led by three foreigners made a sortie in force from ChangChow. I shd. think the place will fall before the end of September.[101]

Customs business goes on smoothly; the only question is the old & long-standing one relative to stores for the Docks; as, however, the profits last year were something like 30 p. cent, and a dividend of 12 p. cent was declared, I don't think the dock is much hurt by present arrangements. Britishers like to have a grievance, and a spot that itches they are sure to scratch until it becomes a sore. Porter is as light-headed as ever: Hughes thinks highly of Jones: Cable does his work very well: and an examiner named Julius C. Porter is also valuable.[102]

At Amoy, I saw a good deal of the officers of the "Perseus," and found the marine, Allen, a particularly good fellow. Cane [?], who commands the "Vindix", is a good <u>sailor</u>, but, perhaps not just the man — not the right sort to act independently, or to be left to his own discretion. Hughes almost keeps open house, but he says the expense is nothing. Spent a pleasant evening with Mrs. Pedder, and another with Mrs. Jones; both of them charming women.

"Beach House" offered to me for $9,000; & the Doctor's bungalow for $6,000. Tait's house on Amoy side: upper story for 5 years for $2000, or, with godowns, $3500, or to purchase $25 000.[103]

Hughes' Returns Books, made by Shortrede & Co.; very neat indeed. I don't altogether like Hughes' office management: he seems to me fussy and uncertain, & cannot take things coolly. He has got a man named Lin Kin as his factotum: I think he places quite too much confidence in him, and his antecedents, I learned, are anything but good.

The last day I was at Amoy, Tsäng and Chin called: so did Kwang, to whom I gave a little talking, telling him that I did not like the way in which he refrained from supporting the Commissioner, &c.[104]

What is written above will serve as a record of the state of affairs at the ports. I need only add to it, the improvement &c. at Hongkong during the last two years surprised me much: new houses in every direction — gas — telegraph — bund — roads, &c. &c. &c. I shd. like to live at H'Kong much.

Called on Mrs. Delano, Vaucher, Pauncefoot, Misson, Miesar, and dined with Edwards, Tarry, and Lamond.[105]

In the "Cadiz" coming up the coast, were Mrs. & Miss Brown, wife & sister of the Capt. Miss B. wd. not suit me atall. I almost lost my heart to a young girl (Marie Wilde) who, one of Pedro Laurno's protegés, traveled as Miss Brown too; a pretty little girl.

Between the 1st & 25th of April, I made all my Service arrangements. Mackey has resigned, and the appointments are: Teentsin, Dick. Newchwang, MacPherson. Chefoo, Hughes. S'Hae, FitzRoy. C'kiang, White. Kiukiang, Hannen. H'Kow, Giquel. N po, Leonard. F'Chow, de Meritens. Amoy, Klezkowsky. Takow, Maxwell. Tamsuy, _____. S'tow, Williams. C'ton, Glover. and Brown to S'Hae as Deputy Com^r.[106]

At the Races, I lost a lot of bets to ladies & to pay them I have expended Tls. 111.40. [sic]

I have called on Mrs. Lowrien, Markham, Jones, Fahis [?], Hazion, Laurence, Grew, Tyson, Coghill, Wright: and have yet to call on Mrs. Eames, Jennie, Macintosh, Essex, Cuthbertson, & one or two others.[107]

My last despatch from Peking was one in which I was directed to return to Meritens certain letters that he had sent direct to the Yamun; I have done so officially; he complains of my official letter; says he was insulted by Wänseang, and that his letters were not official but private.

Everyone taken by surprise on the appearance of an Edict degrading Prince Kung. It came out on the 2nd April. Another has since appeared in which he is appointed to the Yamun, and allowed the entrée of the Palace.[108]

Dick started yesterday for England, & by the same mail left Mr. Burlingame & Gen. Pinzer. Sir F. Bruce has been appointed to Washington, & rumor says Alcock will come to China.

My last letter from Lay brought me the cheering news that Govt. has decided to take over the fleet, paying some £165,000. That is a great load off my mind.

On the 3rd, I moved into my new house, which, for a bachelor, is comfortable enough. My establishment consists of the following lot:

Tls. 100	Writer		Copyist	
Tls. 30	Kan Pan: Liang Su		Butler: Chih Hui	$
	Boy: Ch'en Huang	$	Boy: Ma Erh	$
	Cook: Hsü Yü-sheng	$	Gatekeeper: Yen Wen-sheng	$10
	Coolie: Ku A-wu	$	House Coolie:	
			Huang Shih-yüan	$[109]

I have written to Le footae to endeavor to do something towards getting Tong Achik set free. He has suffered horribly: I'll take care not to let anyone fall into the hands of the authorities again who does not deserve the harshest treatment.

What is written down brings matters up to date: anything omitted can be put in hereafter.

MONDAY, 8 MAY 1865: Engaged Lin Kwang tsoo & a copyist. Tls 100 a month.

SUNDAY, 14 MAY 1865: "Learn what you are not fit for, and give up wishing for it; learn what you can do, and do it with the energy of a man." Thus, and well, speaks Robertson in his sermon on "the irreparable past." Give up bubbles, and do your work: "trust no future, howe'er pleasant; let the dead past bury its dead; work, work in the living present, heart within and God o'erhead."

During the past week, I have been hard at work, and I have now almost got through my arrears of Chinese correspondence. My new Writer is not a very elegant composer; but I get through the work quickly with him. It takes quite a load off my mind to have a man of my own, well up in the questions that arise, and always at hand.

The mail of the 20th March arrived on the 12th. My letters from Geoffrey & Lizzie were very amusing: they seem clever children, and original. I am very glad I sent money to Aunt Mary; it was no loss to me, and has made them so happy!

Andrew Happer goes by the mail, under Mr. Burlingame's care: hope he and Jamie may meet.

Sir Rutherford Alcock appointed to Peking: he intends to travel through Russia.

Sir Harry Parkes elected Commandant of the S'Hae Volunteers. What self-assertion that man has got, & how much fortune favors him!

No particular news as yet from Fuhkeen; at Hankow the troops have mutinied in consequence of the non-issue of arrears of pay, and they are said to be ravaging the tea-districts.

On Friday some 20 men carried off the Taoutae's steamer the "Hyson" from alongside Customs' hulk; the chief of the gang, a pilot named Johnson, is now in the Consular jail. He said, he had a claim against her. Measures are being taken for the arrest of the others concerned.[110]

THURSDAY, 18 MAY 1865: Bought a pair of carriage horses & harness for Tls. 450.

FRIDAY, 19 MAY 1865: Dined with Mrs. Coutts.[111]

SATURDAY, 20 MAY 1865: Left S'Hae for S'Chow [Soochow].

MONDAY, 22 MAY 1865: 8 a.m. arrived at Fung Hwang Shan, and spent the day with Jebb, tiffening & dining with his Mess, composed of himself, Winstanley, Cardew 67th, Lempriese 67th, Hall, and Hobson. The house they inhabit is on a hill with a fine southern frontage from which on a clear day one can see the islands in Hangchow Bay in one direction, the Consular flags at S'Hai in another, and SooChow in a third, with Quinsan, Tsingpoo, and Sung Keang, and at least a dozen pagodas.[112]

In the evening saw the men drilled. In all there are about 900; 600 under Yu Footsaeng, and 300 under Yuen. They drilled remarkably well, the instructors interfering but little, and the words of command given in Chinese. I did not see the artillery, who were busy moving ammunition. The men are still unable to step together. Jebb told me that he could not complain of anything done by the Chinese, or left undone with regard to the Camp, & said that, apart from propositions of a distasteful kind brought forward by Parkes, there had been no trouble whatsoever. Pwan the Genl. with 10 000 men at Sung Keang, used formerly to visit the camp very frequently, & did several things that Jebb suggested, such as making a road to his first stockades about 2 1/2 miles from the hill & then on to Sung Keang, 6 1/2 miles further, and he sent his people occasionally to be instructed; Parkes however went up & "scolded"; asked for a road to S'Hae &c.; & the result has been that Pwan has ever since kept out of the way, & looks upon Jebb as if he had asked Parkes to "talk at him". Jebb is of the opinion that Parkes' interference has done harm, and has been the only thing that has tended to make the camp more inefficient than it wd. have been, if left alone.[113]

Yu is from Lung Chow-foo in GanHwuy, near Le Footae's place; he showed me a wound in the right arm recd. when fighting in Keang Pih; he does not appear very brilliant, but he is no doubt as good as half our colonels.[114]

Hobson has the drill finished, and is busy arranging the sheets: he will be able to leave at the end of the month.

The use of which the camp will be is this: it will have placed in the hands of the Chinese, a translation of the words of command, and it will have supplied Chinese soldiers, acquainted with not merely the words but their meaning & consequent movements, to instruct as many troops as the govt. may wish to keep up.

At 1/2 p. 10 bade Jebb good-bye. We'll probably not meet again for years, as his regt goes to the Cape in a month.

WEDNESDAY, 24 MAY 1865: Queen's birthday. [characters for 30th day of the 4th lunar month] 4 p.m. arrived at SooChow. Sent in Leang to Le Footae to ask for an interview early tomorrow, as I wish to leave at 4 p.m. He came back with a message to the effect that tomorrow being the 1st of the moon, the Footae wd. be too busy to receive me, but requested me to go in at once and see him. I accordingly went in accompanied by Man who wore his Order: the Footae sent out chairs for us. I remained with him from 1/2 past 5 to 1/4 to 8. My talk was not so satisfactory as it might have been, for, not having intended to go so soon, I had not arranged my ideas. I spoke to him about the camp; told him what I said to Parkes when he called on me before starting for SooChow; he said I was quite right — that he himself took a great interest in the camp, and that foreign drill, on French & English models, was being taught to all the soldiers, but that he could not increase the number of the men at the camp on account of Parkes' interference — that the officers do not like to go there lest they shd. come into contact with him. He praised Parkes' ability, &c., but said he interfered too much with things that concerned him not.[115]

B.   He enquired about the possibility of sending people to Europe to learn to make guns, &c., & said that it wd. be necessary to send a <u>Kin Chae</u> [imperial envoy] with them, a man who could talk with our Tsae Seang [Prime Minister], and who cd. make the learners apply themselves, & keep them, generally speaking, in good order; I told him that if the men committed any crime they would be punished by the English authorities — an idea that he did not quite like, "for" sd. he, "your criminals in China are punished by their own authorities". I explained the treaty, and told him of the position in Turkey, assigning the difference of creed, &c., as the reason for such peculiar stipulations. {N.B. By the way, this strikes me as an argument to be used with officials in support of Missionaries; you complain that the punishment of foreigners by their own authorities interferes with you locally: become Christians, & you can then do it yourselves.}[116]

I however told him that to send a <u>Kin Chae</u> wd. be of great use in other ways: & explained, in reply to his enquiries, how well he wd. be recd. and treated. In this, I see an opening for working out what I have long aimed at — the sending of a Chinese embassy to Europe. I shall have the trouble of carrying it through, & Sir Rutherford Alcock will get all the credit.

C.   He sd. that the iron & coal used at SooChow, if native, wd. not do; that foreign had to be purchased, &c.: I am delighted to hear him make such a remark, for it opens the way to coal & iron mines in the interior.

D.   He talked at great length about the <u>Sha Chuen</u> [coastal junks], and asked me to devise some means for renewing the prohibition on foreign ships carrying Beans &c. from Newchwang. I explained to him that the people who use the foreign ships are Chinese & not foreigners — that to prevent ships (which cd. not be done now in face of the Danish Treaty) wd. be to come back to junks, & I asked how he, knowing the use of guns and shells, wd. like to have to come back to bows & arrows. I sd. the only thing to be done was for the Sha-Chuen Hangkia [business firms] to invest slowly in foreign ships. He begged me to think over the matter, and devise a <u>fa tsze</u> [method (for handling it)].[117]

{When I come back from Peking, I shall try & get up the coast Company that I have long thought about.}

E.   He sd. that now that the <u>Sha Chuen</u> decrease in numbers, the sending of rice to Peking becomes difficult, & asked how it cd. be sent by foreign craft. I asked him did not that proposition look like cutting off another support from the Sha-Chuen, but explained that foreign ships wd. do it more quickly, more cheaply, & more securely. He was anxious to know, if they cd.

be made to pay for short delivery, and I then explained Bills of Lading, and Insurance, &c., with all of which he seemed much pleased.

F. He spoke highly of Dick, & sd. he had met Giquel who had done good service in the field.

G. He said Le san ta-jin was keeping out of the way—that too many officials were in their family.[118]

H. He did not like to send his guns to Fuh Keen, for Tso Chetae did not value such things, they might be lost; he knew they were paou-pei [precious things].[119]

I. Achik's affair, he wd. do his best in; I suggested that he might memorialize again. He sd, that as soon as the tsung was fixed, they cd. determine whether Achik cd. buy it off or not, & that meantime he wd. not be maltreated. He laughed, though, when I said that the gaolers had already got most of his money out of him.[120]

J. I told him trade was everywhere bad, & that the duties this year wd. not be very flourishing.

K. He asked me to write to Dick to find out what the expense wd. be of sending 20 men to a gun factory.

He asked me to remain & dine with him on the following day, but thinking he was merely talking politely I sd. no. We then took our leave, & when he was seeing me to my chair, he asked about the junk the "Hukwang" had run down, and I said old Tsang chung-tang wd. not send down the witnesses: I told him that without the witnesses nothing cd. be done, & that until they were provided there cd. not be any examination into the case; & that even if provided, the decision wd. be determined by the circumstances as explained by them. Tsemmo-hao-ne? ["How could it be OK?"] sd. he.[121]

He looks thin & consumptive.

25 MAY 1865: Left SooChow at daylight.

27 MAY 1865: Arrived at Shanghae at noon; an hour after the mail came in, & with it the following items of news: Lee's army surrendered; Lincoln & Seward assassinated; Parkes appointed to Japan; Winchester to S'Hae; ChangChow evacuated on the night of the 15th May; Burgevine seized on the night of the 14th.[122]

SUNDAY, 28 MAY 1865: Called on Ting Taoutae. He consents to let steamers go into the river waters, but will not put his consent in writing: with each steamer, he will send a Wei-yuen [deputy], & if too many steamers wish to go he will stop all. I told him not to do anything unauthorizedly.

Giquel's order is, I see, [characters for *erh-teng*; "second class"].[123]

MONDAY, 29 MAY 1865: This morning the Taoutai went to Soo-Chow, being summoned there in haste by the Footae, who has just been appointed to act as Che-tae [Governor General]. Tsäng Kwo-fan has to take the field against the Nien-fei, vice the celebrated Tsäng Wang, Säng Ko lin sin, who was killed the other day at Yün-ching-Hsian. Lew Fantae is to act as Footae.[124]

Tsäng Wang's death will be felt at the capital; he was about the only warrior of Mongol or Manchu extraction on whom the Ta-tsing [great Ch'ing] dynasty cd. rely, and he was really an able, hard-working man, who kept his soldiers well in hand, paid his way, & won the respect of the people. In appointing Tsäng Kwo fan to take Tsang Wang yay's place, the Govt. acts astutely: if he is successful, more honors will be heaped on him and he will have rid the govt. of a great source of internal disorder; if unsuccessful, every honor that he has already won will be taken from him, and the govt. will see its way to putting aside a man whose rise, pretentions, and influence must occasionally be felt as obstacles.

Lew the Acting Footae was Shanghai Hsien [District Magistrate] a few years ago: he is a stupid, stick in the mud, sort of man.[125]

TUESDAY, 30 MAY 1865: Letters from FooChow today.

Meritens put May in charge on the 18th May, & left Foochow on the 24th. May tells me Burgevine had been sent across the country to Yen Ping foo, and that although seven or eight days had elapsed since his departure for ChangChow he had not up to that time been heard of; also that the Gov. Genl. is determined to have his head off. I am highly glad that there is at last a chance of his being put out of the way: his friend Butler has already preceded him; but I fear his disappearance will give rise to an investigation and a newspaper entry that will give trouble to the Govt.[126]

Drew pay today to the end of the June quarter. I hope the Peking folk will authorise the amount I have been drawing.

Yesterday a letter from Mossman arrived, forwarding a printed prospectus of a railway line from S'hae to Woo Sung. Such a line wd. pay well, and it wd. be a capital beginning.[127]

The work I have before me in China is as follows:

1°. to get the Customs into good working order, so that the transaction of business shall be efficient towards the Govt., and expeditious for the merchants;

2°. to induce the govt. to maintain a small fleet of steamers for the suppression of piracy, officered by Englishmen & manned by Chinese, and to be conducted on such a plan as to teach the Chinese troops & form the nucleus of a navy;

3°. to induce the Yamun at Peking to keep four bodies (2500) each of soldiers, drilled by for[n]. officers, & under one for[n]. inspector, in contradistinction to local forces, & more immediately under the Yamun for service at the ports. On such a force the govt. cd. always rely, &, even if provincial authorities allowed their men to sink to coolies in the streets, in emergencies the other four cd. be relied upon.

4th. [*sic*] to induce the govt. to send a minister to Europe, & thereby commit the Chinese to an entrance into the comity of nations;

5th. to secure an opening in China for drawing out the resources of the country, for working coal & other mines, & for improving the means of communication;

6th. to get Chinese merchants to have done with junks & trade in ships and steamers.

[There follow two blank pages, on which Hart has written diagonally:]

These pages were left blank quite unintentionally; seemingly, the fates mean to say "L'Homme propose, mais Dieu dispose": [Chinese characters for *jen-shuo ju-tz'u ju-tz'u T'ien-yen wei-jan wei-jan;* "Man says like this, like this; Heaven's words are not so, not so."] Work that I have never dreamt of probably lies before me; and work that I propose to myself may never be done by me. 22 Sept. R.H.[128]

7th. to translate into Chinese useful works of a <u>largely</u> <u>practical</u> kind;

8th. to attempt to get all officers salaried, beginning with the Customs, & thereby put a stop to extortion, and secure good govt.

I see openings toward all that I propose, and I shall try to work out my own views; time and patience, with an eye ever open & ready to take advantage as chances [are] offered, will carry me through. Meanwhile, I have to try and <u>prepare</u> myself for the more important work that any success may open up for me.

WEDNESDAY, 31 MAY 1865: Went on board the "Fire Queen" after dinner & started for Hankow. On the 1st June, saw Lord at Chinkiang: the Custom-house there is rapidly approaching completion. It is a rough structure, but will house three bachelors comfortably. On Friday night, 2 June, saw White for a few minutes at Kiukiang; the new Taoutae had arrived but had gone on to Nan ChangFoo. On Saturday, 3rd, arrived at Hankow; when walking down the Bund in the evening met the Taoutae, who got out of his chair to speak. On the 4th, the Taoutae called on me on board the steamer; I returned his call in the afternoon. On the 5th, I called on the Viceroy, who was very polite, & gave me a seat this time on the raised dais; talked about nothing in particular. He said that in international affairs he objected to our action in that we made too much of trifles; we ought to be ready to smooth away difficulties instead of aggravating them, & when real troubles appeared we ought to act strenuously & harmoniously to solve them. The consuls, he thought, looked out for difficulties, & were delighted to get hold of anything that cd. be styled a grievance. He said he was sorry Dick had been taken away & that MacPherson had been sent to another port; as for Giquel, sd.

he, you appoint him, but he does not come, & his <u>locum</u> <u>tenens</u> does not speak Chinese. He thought the ministers, both Chinese & foreign, wd. be the better of an annual run round the ports to see things with their own eyes: you, sd. he, are the only one who knows the people & the affairs of each place. It took me two hours to get to his place: the tide or current not running strong down, & the wind—what there was of it—being upstream.[129]

On the 6th, Wetmore [?], Mackenzie, Gordon, and Francis called to talk about grievances: permits for treasure, stamping tea chests; sycee [silver] goes too. They were polite enough, thanked me for getting half-duties done away with, &c. Dined with Evans on Monday evening: with Halkett on 3rd, 4th & 6th: with the steamer people on the 7th, & with Hallam on the 8th. Called on the Taoutae on the 7th; he says he will do away with the stamping of tea at the end of the month: that having written to all the ports, to tell them of the new rule, he cannot do away with it at once, but at the end of the 5th moon he will again write to say the practice, found too troublesome, is discontinued. The sycee question I cannot quite understand: the merchants say Tls 108.4.7.1 = HaeKwan Tls 100, while the Taoutae's calculation is Tls. 109.0.2.0. Halkett tells me the treasure-permit affair has never given trouble, & it is evidently one of the smallest grievances, one of a kind that, there being nothing to complain of, the B.N. [British Navy] must noise abroad. Dinner at Hallam's passed off very pleasantly: all the people were more than civil, & I had a pleasant talk with both Wadman & Mackenzie.[130]

Brett explained his difficulties: Mande's [?] money he had lost in payment of his race bets, & he is greatly involved besides. I shall pay Mande for him: original Tls. 292 & interest @ 10% for 3 years = Tls. 470 = $540. He looks seedy: poor boy; but he has evidently been womanizing. He has promised faithfully to give up racing & betting for the future, & womanizing for one year.[131]

Halkett's wife is a pleasant little body.

Left Hankow with the "Silver Eagle" in tow on Friday evening 9th June. a little below Hankow saw a tug-boat at anchor: Mail apparently in, & some important news.

At Kiukiang on Saturday morning: took breakfast with White; looked at Smith's house, which wd. not suit us; called on Hughes, & saw [indistinct word] who looks well. White is the leading man at Kiukiang. The main news is: Lincoln dead; Czarewitch dead; Seward recovering [?]; Lee surrendered. Pd off Ian. The new Taoutae is local Taoutae; the former acting man Tsae is <u>Keen</u> <u>Tuh</u>; and the preceding man Ting is to look after affairs connected with foreigners, & converts: a curious arrangement.

Passed through Chinkiang on Sunday. Went ashore & saw the office & new house: called on Hannen, whose boy sd, "<u>Ta-laou-yay</u> <u>shwo</u> <u>Shwuy Keaou</u>." Master says he's asleep.[132]

Arrived at Shanghae about noon on Monday, the 12th. The "Fire Queen" is fast, but her state rooms are badly arranged: food indifferent: cabin noisy: boys insolent & dirty: shall not travel by her again.

SUNDAY, 18 JUNE 1865: During the last week I have been dreadfully busy, getting through arrears of work & packing up for Peking. Memo: don't leave packing, &c., to the last moment in future.

On the 13th I found awaiting me letters from the Yamun telling me to go to Peking at once: the Russian Overland Rules are to be reconsidered: the rebels are out in the north, & ChiLi finances are in such a state that they want the aid of me, who am acquainted with the affairs of each port; they also enquire about the pistols & binoculars WanSeang asked me to get for him: strange to say, the very things came here on the same day!

By the mail I have letters from Forbes dated Havanna [?] 30 March, & from FitzRoy 14 April.

On the 16th dined with Mrs. Jenkins: her sister "no can." On the 17th with Giquel: French party.

Tomorrow night, I start by the "Ying-tze-fei" for Teentsin: so my journal, good bye for ten days, & we'll chat again when we rest in PeKing after the hot jolting we are in for from Teentsin up. R.H.

CHAPTER SEVEN

Anglo-Ch'ing Reform Measures

HART RESPONDED QUICKLY to his on-the-spot observations at the ports. No sooner had he returned from his arduous tour than he began to advocate an ambitious and wide-ranging reform program. Experience gained from the tour not only provided him with a clearer vision of the need for change but also built in him a greater confidence in his power to initiate some of it.

On the domestic front, Hart's travels could only reinforce his already well developed sense of the limitations of the Ch'ing government. Although local officials such as Li Hung-chang and Ting Jih-ch'ang were undeniably impressive individuals—tough, smart, and savvy—they were always in the minority. The reasons were rooted deep in traditional Chinese values and inherited institutions. Thus, although their activities were laudable, they were also limited, and not at all well coordinated with those of the metropolitan bureaucracy. At the capital, Tz'u-hsi's temporary dismissal of Prince Kung in April of 1865, and her appointment of the conservative scholar Li Hung-tsao to the Grand Council later in the year, marked the consolidation of the Empress Dowager's political power, and reflected, perhaps, a certain complacency bred by the defeat of the Taipings—even though the Nien Rebellion was still out of control in the north. The status of the Tsungli Yamen remained uncertain, though Hart continued to consider it "the most important office in China."[1]

In foreign relations, the Western powers still chafed over the Middle Kingdom's persistent failure to live up to European standards of diplomatic behavior—especially the Ch'ing government's reluctance to grant the foreign ministers an audience with the Emperor on terms of equality. But at least the powers were willing to consider the Tsungli Yamen a bona fide Foreign Office, and to work together within the framework of the so-called Cooperative Policy. By mid-1864 this policy had come to mean cooperation on the part of the Ch'ing government and the major foreign powers—Great Britain, Russia, France, and the United States—in securing the peaceful resolution of disputes and the gradual reform of China. It was, in the words of its prin-

The Front Gate of the City Walls of the Tartar City of Peking, 1870s

From *Old Photos of Peking*, by Fu Gongyue (Beijing: National Publications, 1989).

cipal architect, the American Minister, Anson Burlingame, "an effort to substitute fair diplomatic action in China for force."[2]

"Reform" was an ambiguous term. On the material level of firearms and steamships, all could agree that reform meant technological innovation. But on the level of institutional behavior and the ideas guiding it, China and the West had very different assumptions. Western "progress" implied constant improvement, both spiritual and material, while Confucian reformism sought primarily to revive the moral excellence of times past. As it turned out, agreement was easiest at the level of firearms and steamships, science and technology; administrative innovations like the adequate salaries under the Maritime Customs were much harder to achieve. Even more difficult to carry out were fundamental institutional changes. In the background, largely unknown to Hart's generation of foreigners, remained the perennial Chinese issue of bureaucratic centralization (*chün-hsien*) versus a less centralized or "feudal" (*feng-chien*) localism.

THE RESTORATION REFORM PROGRAM

The reform efforts of the T'ung-chih Restoration have occasioned much lively debate. Some studies, notably Mary Wright's pioneering "portrait of the age," *The Last Stand of Chinese Conservatism*, have emphasized the noble aims of Restoration leaders, giving more attention to what they tried to do than to what they actually did. Others, such as James Polachek's case study of Restoration policy in Kiangsu, have concentrated on the limitations of reform, stressing instead the way local elites protected their own interests at the expense of the peasantry. If Wright's portrait is too idealistic, Polacheck's conclusions are possibly too cynical. As had often been the case in Chinese history, Confucian altruism during the T'ung-chih period found itself periodically at odds with particularistic loyalties and vested interests. Ch'ing scholar-officials found themselves forced into compromises that sometimes bordered on hypocrisy. Still, there can be no doubt that, during the 1860s and 1870s, a great number of officials, both at Peking and in the provinces, genuinely desired reform, and tried hard to achieve it in the face of powerful resistance.[3]

To such individuals reform meant mainly "adjustment" (*pien-t'ung*) and "ordering" (*cheng-tun* or *cheng-li*), not basic change (*pien-keng*). T'ung-chih reformers had in mind neither the abandonment of traditional Confucian values, nor a fundamental restructuring of "established institutions" (*ch'eng-fa*). To correct abuses within the inherited system was the aim, not to change the system itself. For most Restoration officials the primary goals in the 1860s were the rectification of government, the suppression of rebellion, the reestablishment of local control, the rehabilitation of the economy, and military "self-strengthening."

Rectification of government presupposed the reassertion of virtuous rule by Confucian-educated scholar-officials. In the words of Ch'en Li (1810–1882): "Government depends on human talent, while human talent depends on scholarship." Restoration leaders therefore earnestly sought to reinvigorate the traditional civil-examination system, with its emphasis on moral knowledge derived from the Confucian Classics and amplified by orthodox commentaries. Provincial and county-level examinations that had been suspended because of rebellion were made up immediately after recovery, and most of the newly established academies of the T'ung-chih era devoted themselves wholeheartedly to the goal of producing successful examination candidates.[4]

But there was also a counter-trend at work. Under acute financial pressure since the early 1850s, the Ch'ing dynasty increasingly resorted to the sale of rank and office in order to raise precious revenues. The result was a demonstrable decline in the quality of Confucian government, especially at local levels. More and more county magistracies were purchased after 1850 — the majority apparently bought by profit-seeking urban merchants. Clerks and runners proliferated in local yamens, almost invariably outlasting the regular civil officials they served. And even the most idealistic officials had to close an eye at least occasionally to the pecuniary interest of their subordinates.[5] Nonetheless, Restoration leaders tried their best to eradicate corruption and other forms of malpractice. A number criticized not only the sale of rank and office but also the usurpation of power by unscrupulous clerks and runners. A few even went so far as to assail long-standing features of the Ming-Ch'ing system of checks and balances, such as the "rule of avoidance" and frequent transfer. There was, however, no basic reform proposed in either the structure of government or the system of law, and no attempt made to centralize administrative responsibility. Rather, old-style, quasi-official bureaus (*chü*), often staffed by gentry members and officials awaiting appointment, tended to assume new functions.

In economic affairs, reform meant a general commitment to the promotion of "state finance and the people's livelihood." No responsible official, however, advocated fundamental reorganization of either the national economy or local fiscal practices. The Ch'ing government saw as its basic goal an austere and stable agrarian society, to be

A Peking *hu-t'ung*

From L. Carrington Goodrich and Nigel Cameron, *The Face of China as Seen by Photographers & Travelers, 1860–1912* (Millerton, NY, An Aperture Book, 1978), photographer unknown.

achieved primarily through the expansion of agricultural production — this, by means of resettlement, land reclamation, and water control. Some genuine reforms were attempted — including the reduction of land taxes in various areas (notably in Kiangsu in 1863), and the implementation of rehabilitation and welfare programs for those inhabitants of areas ravaged by fighting and destruction. But rent reduction — a critical problem in the rural sector — received no attention whatsoever. Lower land taxes were in the interest of landowners; only lower rents would have helped the cultivators.

Similarly, although the Ch'ing government appreciated the administrative efficiency and revenue-generating capabilities of the Imperial Maritime Customs Administration, it had no concept of promoting foreign trade as a vital engine of economic development. Even less would it have considered revamping other Chinese fiscal institutions to follow the model of the Inspectorate. Most officials saw foreign trade as harmful to Chinese manufactures and the source of Sino-Western conflict. Wen-hsiang put the matter this way to Hart: "We would gladly pay you all the increased revenue you have brought us, if you foreigners would go back to your own country and leave us in peace as we were before you came."[6]

Predictably, no one was in a mood to propose basic reforms in the traditional Chinese salt monopoly, or in the realms of central government finance, minting, or banking. Nor was any Ch'ing bureaucrat inclined to advocate the use of telegraphs and railways to facilitate economic growth. By 1867, certain small innovations were visible; for instance Chinese merchants were finally allowed to own steamships legally in order to compete with Western merchants. But few Ch'ing officials at any level displayed an interest in using other forms of Western technology for economic purposes until the 1870s and 1880s.

Military affairs proved to be another matter. The Ch'ing authorities were quick to see the advantages to be gained in adopting Western military methods and technology for the purpose of "self-strengthening." Thus, during the 1860s, in addition to raising foreign-officered contingents such as the Ever-Victorious and Ever-Triumphant Armies, China began to purchase foreign weapons and steamers for use against the Taipings, and to employ Western drillmasters in training programs. Other innovations crept in. Foreign instructors, technicians, and translators came to be hired at centers of progress such as the Kiangnan Arsenal in Kiangsu and Foochow Shipyard in Fukien.[7] Along with these early modernizing efforts went an attempt to reduce the size of Ch'ing military and naval forces — not only the "temporary" imperial armies known as *yung-ying*, but also the traditional

Banner and Green Standard troops. The Peking Field Force, established in 1862, and various provincially based "retrained armies" (*lien-chün*) organized later in the decade, represented the Ch'ing government's best effort to upgrade its regular forces in the fashion of *yung-ying*. This limited attempt at military reorganization was not at all well coordinated, however, with the result that arms, training, and even the language of foreign instruction differed from place to place and time to time. Nonetheless, the use of Western weapons by Ch'ing armies enabled the dynasty to maintain domestic control in China throughout the remainder of the nineteenth century.[8]

It was no accident that Hart's Manchu and Chinese colleagues—both in Peking and in the provinces—took the lead in advocating Western-inspired reforms during the T'ung-chih era. At the capital, the Tsungli Yamen stood solidly for moderate but meaningful change. Despite its precarious institutional position, and the general stigma attached to foreign affairs during the T'ung-chih period, the Yamen proved more willing than any other metropolitan agency to advocate reforms along Western lines. Prince Kung's memorials—written on behalf of the Yamen and in the spirit of consensus—are a case in point. For all their compromising and equivocation, they suggest a genuine appreciation of the need for Western-inspired military and technological innovation.

Prince Kung's private thoughts are, however, more difficult to gauge. Neither Hart's journal nor any other contemporary Western source gives us a clue to his innermost feelings (although we know that he was fond of flowers and T'ang poetry). Fortunately we have access to the Prince's collected essays, entitled *Lo-tao-t'ang wen-ch'ao* (Essays from the Hall of Delighting in the Way; published without revision in 1867). Although these short tracts—well over a hundred of them in five Chinese chapters (*chüan*)—are short on practical statecraft and long on traditional values, they accurately and eloquently reflect the main currents of morally grounded Ch'ing Restoration thought. They are, moreover, revealingly consistent with other such writings of the period.[9]

Most of the essays were probably composed in the early 1860s. The striking feature of the collection as a whole is its avoidance of issues such as the introduction of Western science and technology—even though it is clear from Prince Kung's memorials and from other sources (including Hart's journal) that he dealt with such matters on a daily basis. The timing of publication suggests that the Prince was particularly intent on establishing his orthodox intellectual credentials in the midst of the Tsungli Yamen's effort to promote radical and controversial reforms—including institutional support for the pursuit of Western learning by traditional degree-holders and members of the prestigious Hanlin Academy.[10]

A few themes are worth noting. The first is that, like virtually all orthodox scholars of his time, the Prince considers literature to be "a vehicle for transmitting the [moral] Way"; he esteems the Confucian Classics above all, and believes passionately in their enduring value. Thus, except in emphasis, he differs little from either his colleagues or his critics, including the arch-conservative Mongol scholar, Wo-jen. Most of Prince Kung's essay titles are based on allusions to historical events discussed in the Classics or to famous Confucian personalities and sayings. One representative title is "On the Priority of Using Human Talent to Govern"—a conventional Restoration theme. A number of essays deal with the relationship between the moral "Way" (*tao*) of Heaven and the responsibilities of human beings—both rulers and subjects. Others focus on the importance of ritual (*li*) and moral education (*chiao*) in maintaining proper social and political order.

Although each of Prince Kung's essays is conspicuously and self-consciously framed by orthodox Confucian ethical principles, he is not content with mere moralizing. Sandwiched between his lofty discussions of exemplary rule and proper behavior according to status we can also find some concrete discussions of administrative statecraft. He analyzes taxation and addresses other concrete economic issues, including land distribution and relief for the poor and infirm. Somewhat surprisingly, he writes about the encouragement of commerce in a manner quite uncharacteristic of most Restoration thinkers. On the other hand, nowhere in his essays do we see the argument that Western-style machinery might contribute to China's economic development.[11]

One may, of course, view Prince Kung's writings cynically. He was, after all, surrounded by corruption and egregious maladministration; and he had recently been humiliated by an Empress Dowager who displayed few, if any, of the virtues he extolled. Was the Prince's appeal for a return to benevolent rule by sage kings, then, nothing more than posturing? Or did his essays represent a genuine if necessarily veiled critique of the Throne? Did he really believe in the transformative power of ritual and morality? On balance, he appears to have been as deeply committed to Confucian ethical principles as he was genuinely convinced of the need to acquire knowledge about Western science and technology; the two convictions were not, as is often assumed, fundamentally incompatible. It is ironic,

Prince Kung after Formally Offering the Ch'ing Dynasty's Surrender to the
Allies, 4 November 1860

From *Imperial China: Photographs 1850–1912* (A Pennwick/Crown Book, 1978). Photo by Felix
Beato.

however, that Prince Kung's essays on traditional values were published at a time when, in the name of Western learning, the Prince and his colleagues in the Tsungli Yamen were forced to argue publicly that it was not a good policy simply "to consider loyalty and faithfulness (*chung-hsin*) as armor, and ritual and right behavior (*li-i*) as a shield."[12]

Like Prince Kung's, Wen-hsiang's record of support for Western-inspired reform is well documented. Hart represents him as an individual who did not fear, as did some of his colleagues, the rise of a so-called "Chinese party" in opposition to the Manchus (see his journal entries for 17 June, 28 June, 4 July, and 8 August 1864; also 2 January 1866). Nonetheless, it is evident that Wen-hsiang and others in the Tsungli Yamen had reservations about placing Western weapons in the hands of Chinese troops. One of the Yamen's earliest memorials on the subject, written in mid-1863, expresses the view that knowledge concerning the production and use of Western weapons should be confined to Banner forces. Similarly, Frederick Bruce notified Lord Russell in June of 1864 that Wen-hsiang in particular was "desireous to hold . . . [strategic] places with Manchoos and that he did not wish to see the Chinese population initiated in foreign discipline and the use of foreign arms."[13]

Unlike his superior, Prince Kung, Wen-hsiang left no extant collection of Confucian essays on statecraft. He did, however, write a brief autobiography of about 150 pages, distinguished primarily by its modest tone and straightforwardness. In the sections that cover the period from 1863 to 1866 he says virtually nothing about Western science and technology (except for foreign rifles), and very little about either foreign affairs generally or the Tsungli Yamen in particular. The bulk of Wen-hsiang's autobiographical writing at this time focuses on the suppression of rebellion in North China (the Nien uprising) and local banditry in Manchuria—undoubtedly because he personally commanded the Peking Field Force in several campaigns against insurgents during 1865 and 1866. By this time, of course, the confinement of Western weapons to Banner forces was clearly impossible.[14]

Wen-hsiang's writings reflect his obvious concern with the restoration of Confucian moral values, the rectification of popular customs, and the need for performing proper public and private rituals. Significantly, he also mentions the widespread theory of three 60-year cycles (*yuan*)—which Hart touches upon in his journal entry of 2 August 1864. According to this longstanding Chinese belief, the year 1864 (*chia-tzu*, by traditional reckoning), not only marked the auspicious start of a new 60-year cycle, but also a new phase in a larger cycle of 120 years. Wen-hsiang's awareness of auspicious and inauspicious dates and times, we might add, was not at all unusual for Ch'ing officials, whose daily activities were often dictated by the annual State Calendar.[15]

Among the ethnically Chinese ministers of the Tsungli Yamen, Tung Hsun was undoubtedly the most progressive thinker and by far the most prolific scholar. His travels throughout China, together with his vast administrative experience, provided him with the material for a great many treatises and monographs, ranging in subject matter from studies of grain transport to a brief history of Western intervention in the Ch'ing-Taiping War. In his lifetime Tung published at least 4 volumes of poetry, and somehow, in the midst of his official responsibilities, he managed to write a substantial autobiography. This work, though more detailed than Wen-hsiang's autobiography, is less philosophically revealing than Prince Kung's essays.[16]

Like Wen-hsiang, Tung Hsun dutifully records his bureaucratic, ritual, and personal activities, as well as the special honors and gifts he has received from the Throne. He also discusses important domestic developments, from economic affairs such as likin management to the suppression of rebellion. He is, however, far more scrupulous than Wen-hsiang in recording—and sometimes in analyzing in detail—events related to Sino-foreign relations. For instance, he discusses at considerable length the founding, structure, personnel, and functions of the Tsungli Yamen—not to mention his own close involvement with the Interpreters' College (T'ung-wen kuan). Through his eyes we see how the principle of Manchu-Chinese dyarchy operated within the Yamen, affecting the appointment of secretaries as well as ministers. Tung also remarks on Western-related events such as the establishment of the Peking Field Force, the Lay-Osborn fiasco, the dismissal of Lay, the appointment of his replacement as I.G., Ho Lo-pin (i.e. Robert Hart), the awards granted to Gordon, and Tung's own specific diplomatic assignments. Unfortunately, he simply records without comment the Tsungli Yamen's memorial of late March 1866, discussing Hart's "Bystander's View" and Wade's "New Proposals" (see below).[17]

A comparison of the private writings of Prince Kung, Wen-hsiang, and Tung Hsun is difficult. On the basis of their essays and/or autobiographies alone, Tung stands out as by far the most personally interested in the particulars of foreign affairs. But he was, after all, an especially prolific writer; and, although his administrative and ritual responsibilities were extremely heavy, they do not seem to have been as burdensome and time-consuming as those of either Prince Kung or Wen-hsiang. Perhaps he simply had more time than his Manchu counterparts for recording Western-related events. On the other hand, his close personal relationship with W. A. P. Martin may have given him a special appreciation of foreign affairs.

This much is certain: Prince Kung, Wen-hsiang, and Tung Hsun were far more attuned to the need for foreign-inspired change than any other members of the Tsungli Yamen in the mid-1860s. One might suppose that the appointment of Hsu Chi-yü to the Yamen in 1865 would have brought additional knowledge of the West to the capital. As an official in Fukien during the 1840s, Hsu had acquired a good deal of experience with foreigners; he had even written a popular geography of the world entitled *Ying-huan chih-lueh* (A brief account of the maritime circuit; 1848). In truth, however, the aging scholar had long been out of touch with foreign affairs, and had not even seen a Westerner since he had been dismissed as Governor of Fukien in 1851 for his overly close relations with the hated barbarian.[18]

The provincial counterparts to Prince Kung, Wen-hsiang, and Tung Hsun were Tso Tsung-t'ang, Tseng Kuo-fan, and Li Hung-chang. All three stood as self-confident champions of Western-inspired innovation, despite the hostility engendered by their "regional" power and foreign contacts. Of the three, Li deserves special mention, not only because of his longstanding and close relationship with Hart, but also because of his pivotal position in the history of China's self-strengthening movement from 1860 to 1895. For over three decades, Li stood as the foremost exponent of the quest for "wealth and power." He was a good deal more progressive than Tseng, and more generally flexible than Tso. Hart's journal entry of 24 May 1865, which recounts his long conversation with Li at Soochow, provides one early indication of the Kiangsu Governor's progressive views. Hart would later refer to Li as his "ally" in reform (journal, 16 February 1867).

Li's comparatively progressive outlook can be traced to two main sources: (1) his early contact at Shanghai with foreigners such as Ward, Gordon, Macartney, and Hart; and (2) several talented and foresighted Chinese members of his own staff, including Kuo Sung-t'ao and Feng Kuei-fen. By virtue of their instructive experience with foreigners and foreign relations in the late 1850s and early 1860s, Kuo and Feng understood better than most Ch'ing scholars of their time the need to learn from the West. In 1860, just prior to the Anglo-French assault on Peking, Kuo scandalized the guests at a social gathering by declaring that China's "barbarian problem" could be solved only by diplomacy, not by war; and, in a forceful essay written at about the same time, Feng went so far as to assert: "When methods are faulty, we should reject them even if they are of ancient [Chinese] origins; when methods are good, we should benefit from them even though they are those of the barbarians."[19]

This essay was one of several dozen written by Feng while at Shanghai during the Taiping occupation of southeastern Kiangsu. Brought together in late 1861 under the title *Chiao-pin-lu k'ang-i* (Protests from the Chiao-pin Studio), these short polemics covered a wide range of territory. Most dealt with domestic reform and reflected an obsession with administrative and military efficiency. Like many reformers of the T'ung-chih era, Feng railed against familiar evils: corruption; the complexity and inefficiency of Ch'ing administration; the sale of rank; inequities in tax assessment; and the abuse of power by yamen clerks and runners. He advocated land-tax reform, the strengthening of local control systems, the regularization of local gentry rule, and the reduction, rearming, and retraining of Chinese troops along Western lines.[20]

But Feng's proposals went further than those of most other advocates of reform in the T'ung-chih period — in part, no doubt, because in 1860–1861 he did not have to bear responsibility for acting upon them. He urged, for example, in the realm of administration: the replacement of clerks by regularly appointed civil-service degree-holders; the popular election of salaried village headmen by means of paper ballots; a system of public accounting for all public funds; a national land survey and a graduated land tax; and even the reduction of land rents (although in practice Feng seems to have protected the financial interests of local landlords, including his own family). In the realm of self-strengthening, he explicitly acknowledged China's technological inferiority to the West, and advocated the use of Western technology, not only for military purposes, but also for agricultural development. Furthermore, he believed that both the civil-service and military examination systems should be reformed, and he went so far as to claim that "Western learning" should be included as a new examination category (*k'o*).[21]

Such ideas were too radical for most of Feng's Chinese contemporaries. When the Soochow scholar sent a copy of his unpublished book to Tseng Kuo-fan, Tseng remarked after perusing a dozen or so essays that the ideas were "mostly difficult to put into practice." Tseng did arrange for some of the essays to be forwarded to his friend Li T'ang-chieh, then a Grand Councillor, but Li brought only one of Feng's proposals to the attention of his colleagues in the Grand Council — on the desirability of replacing clerks with regular degree-holders. We may safely speculate that he held little hope that even this change would be approved.[22]

Among high-ranking Ch'ing officials, only Li Hung-chang took Feng's ideas seriously in the 1860s — and even he backed off from the most radical of them. He had no qualms about endorsing the use of Western arms and drill for the Anhwei Army and other Chinese military forces — although he resented and resisted foreign meddling in the training programs under his control. Li argued successfully for the opening of foreign-language schools at Shanghai and Canton on the model of the Peking T'ung-wen kuan; and he sponsored the establishment of several arsenals in Kiangsu province. He even wrote a letter to the Tsungli Yamen in 1864, proposing that a new category on technology be created for the civil-service examinations — although he stopped short of specifying "Western learning" for the content. As it was, the Yamen considered Li's proposal too bold, and merely appended his letter to one of its memorials to the Throne.[23]

Hart understood only too well the obstacles Li faced. His journal entries for 1864–1865 identify virtually all of the major institutional impediments to meaningful change. Just to list them gives some idea of their complexity and stubborn persistence. There was first the stultifying effect of the Chinese civil and military examination system; then the corruption encouraged by inadequate payment for officials and the widespread practice of "tax-farming"; next, the inveterate "localism" of Ch'ing administration, which stood in the way of centralized, unified reform; and finally the short tenure and frequent transfer of officials that stifled initiative and deprived modernizing programs of sustained leadership. Behind all these evils were deeply embedded political and economic interests that stood in the way of progressive change.

Hart perceived such obstacles clearly. He came to see, for instance, the conservative implications of Manchu rule, and the power enjoyed by a number of rabidly anti-foreign officials close to the Throne — including Li Hung-tsao, Lo Tun-yen, and Wo-jen. All were bitter factional enemies of Prince Kung and Wen-hsiang, whom they accused of "truckling" to the Westerners. Hart also recognized that China's cumbersome and corrupt fiscal system had to be "remodeled" in order to provide the dynasty with adequate revenues for modernizing purposes. And increasingly he came to believe that he was the man for the job. His journal entry of 30 May 1865, which lays out "the work I have before me in China," suggests Hart's growing sense of mission: "I see openings toward all that I propose, and I shall try to work out my own views; time and patience, with an eye ever open

& ready to take advantage as chances [are] offered, will carry me through. Meanwhile, I have to try and prepare myself for the more important work that any success may open up for me."[24]

HART'S "BYSTANDER'S VIEW" AND THE CHINESE RESPONSE

Prior to late 1865, Hart seems to have kept most of his ideas on fundamental institutional reform to himself. In part, his reticence may have arisen from a certain ambivalence concerning the nature of Ch'ing administration. In a letter to Gordon, for example, he once described China's governmental policy as "the strangest imaginable mixture of liberalism and conservatism, of despotism and radicalism, of emperor-ism and republicanism, and of centralization and the opposite. The conservatism is like an Indian-rubber string; it stretches when pulled upon, & then flies back to its original position; the despotism cuts off heads . . . but the radicalism prevents that from being carried too far; the emperor is a god, only so long as he goes with the popular current; centralization is blended, judiciously in some respects, and unhappily in others, with independent localism."[25] His journal entries also reflect similarly ambivalent feelings about Ch'ing administrative assumptions and practices (see, for example, 20 January 1865).

In any case, Hart began promoting his reform ideas in the ad hoc spirit of the T'ung-chih era, suggesting improvements as he found them needed. His journal of 15 July 1864, acknowledges that the Chinese "will not do anything suddenly, or in such a way as to attract much attention, but innovations will creep in gradually, just as they become more necessary, and as the people and govt. become more ready to take them in hand." So it was in the early 1860s. We have already seen the willingness of Ch'ing officials both in the provinces and at the capital to embrace innovative Western arms and military techniques, and to devote large amounts of Customs revenue to the establishment of foreign-officered contingents, foreign-training programs, arsenals, and dockyards. Later in the 1860s, Customs revenue would also be used to support two pioneering missions of exploration to the West, as well as extensive programs of lighthouse building and harbor improvements in the treaty ports.[26]

Of the foreign things that could be helpful to China, Hart early saw the utility of international law. The unequal treaties — though technically not part of international law, because each was bilateral between China and one foreign state — became in effect a single document through the operation of the most-favored-nation clause included in every treaty. Ch'ing officials soon found that, when consuls quoted the treaties as law, they were invoking them as a charter of rights, but by the same token they could be taken as a set of limitations. What was not in the treaties, they reasoned, could not be demanded.

From a Western standpoint, international law provided the ground rules for state-to-state intercourse, the rules of the diplomatic game. But Ch'ing officials resisted learning its principles, since they neither shared its assumptions nor wanted in fact to play the game. The I.G. to the rescue. As early as 15 July 1863, he had begun working on a précis of part 3 of Henry Wheaton's *Elements of International Law* "for translation into Chinese." Less than two weeks later, Hart presented to the Tsungli Yamen his own rendering of some 20 sections of Wheaton's book relating to "Rights of Legation," together with a few "introductory remarks" on the work as a whole. Both the translation and the introduction were well received by the Yamen.

During the next month, Hart continued to translate Wheaton, as well as sections from the British naval regulations and the "U.S. Consuls Manual." His journal for 7 August 1863 records with undisguised pleasure that he "went to the Yamun at 3, taking with me the translations of Wheaton's chapter about treaties. Tung had no difficulty in understanding them atall." This success paved the way for Hart's friend, the missionary-translator W. A. P. Martin, to gain an introduction to the Tsungli Yamen in November.

Martin had begun his own translation of Wheaton in Shanghai in 1862, quite independent of Hart. Martin at first thought of translating Vattel's *Le droit de gens* — a portion of which Dr. Peter Parker had summarized for Lin Tse-hsu at Canton in 1839 — but the U.S. Commissioner, John E. Ward, suggested Wheaton "as being more modern." When Martin came north in 1863, he called at Tientsin on Ch'ung-hou, who had escorted the Ward party to Peking in 1859. Ch'ung-hou perused Martin's translation and promised to write a letter to Wen-hsiang on his behalf. Hart, meanwhile, assured Martin that the Tsungli Yamen would welcome his manuscript. By the time Martin had been introduced by Burlingame to the Yamen in November, Hart had already left Peking for Shanghai — but his recent work on Wheaton was still very much on the minds of the Yamen ministers. Wen-hsiang, for one, asked Martin pointedly on their first meeting whether his translation contained the "important passages made for them by Mr. Hart."[27]

From that point onward, Martin became Hart's staunch ally in the struggle to introduce Western law and learning to China. Hart got the Tsungli Yamen to approve 500 taels from its tonnage dues for publication of Martin's translation of Wheaton — which was then widely distributed throughout China, although apparently seldom used by Ch'ing officials.[28] He also promised Martin 1,000 taels a year from the Customs' "confiscation fund" to support a missionary school called the "Ching-shih Kwan," designed to "give Chinese a good native classical education," while teaching them Western science, medicine, and theology. Hart even contributed 500 taels from his own funds to help sustain the school. Eventually (as his journal entry of 15 July 1864 indicates), the eternally optimistic I.G. hoped that he could somehow induce the Ch'ing government to make the study of Western works on international law and political economy "incumbent on all who compete for [regular civil-service-examination] degrees."[29]

In late 1865, Hart abandoned his strategy of urging piecemeal reforms in favor of a more comprehensive approach. Perhaps he had simply grown tired of the slow pace of change in China (see his journal entry of 22 September 1865), and felt that the time was right to prod the Ch'ing government into immediate and dramatic action. Presumably he now felt both knowledgeable enough and self-confident enough to do so. His vehicle for advocating institutional reform was a detailed memorandum disarmingly entitled "A Bystander's View."

According to Prince Kung and his associates, Hart presented the memorandum to the Tsungli Yamen on 6 November 1865 — a day when his journal indicates that he was, in fact, in Chefoo, far from Peking.[30] This may have been the formal date of submission, but we know that, at least a month before, the ever-cautious Inspector General had already run the main ideas and arguments of the document by at least a few members of the Tsungli Yamen, including Tung Hsun and Pao-yun. His journal entry for 11 October states, for instance: "I talked into Tung my 'Bystander's View': Paou sat listening, & he had an opportunity of hearing matters handled in a way that he had never met with before." On 13 October, Hart notes that he showed an actual draft of the memorandum to Tung, "who seemed much struck by it." Tung told the I.G. prophetically that the document would offend some people and excite suspicion, but he advised Hart "to hand it in notwithstanding."

On 28 October, Hart's journal indicates that the Tsungli Yamen returned his *lun* (essay or discussion; i.e., memorandum), asking him to make a few changes in it because the document was about to be sent to various provincial officials "for their edification & criticism." Thomas Wade's confidential letter to Lord Russell, dated 2 November, confirms this. He writes that both Wen-hsiang and Prince Kung considered Hart's language "too blunt," and that they had told him to "revise the form, retaining the substance of his memorandum." The document would then "be laid before the throne, and . . . a decree issued directing that copies be sent to all the provincial governments." The required changes were made, and on 1 April 1866, an imperial edict directed ten leading provincial officials to offer their opinions on Hart's memorandum—distinguishing what could be done right away from what could be done by degrees, and what was utterly harmful and unacceptable.[31]

The memorandum was called in Chinese *Chü-wai p'ang-kuan chih lun*—a title evidently drawn from two traditional Chinese phrases: *Chü-wai chih jen* ("People on the outside [are impartial]") and *P'ang-kuan-che ch'ing* ("Bystanders possess clarity [of vision]"). Hart begins his memorandum by observing that a short person standing on the shoulders of a tall person can see farther than the taller person, and that the true face of Mount Lu can only be seen in its entirety by someone standing outside, at a distance. With a nod to conventional Chinese-style self-deprecation, Hart goes on to offer his straightforward opinions on China's governmental needs and present dangers. Wade described the document as "a paper much in the style of the memorials laid before the Throne by Censors."[32]

Hart's rather disjointed memo, which spans about 18 pages of Chinese text, attempts to weave together time-worn themes of internal disorder and external calamity. His basic position is that Sino-Western relations during the past several decades have introduced several new problems for which the ancient Middle Kingdom is simply unprepared. These problems are interconnected, and they require immediate attention. Although initially China's difficulties in foreign relations can be said to have arisen from her domestic condition, Hart argues that a failure to contend effectively with foreign-policy problems in the future will create further domestic difficulties.

The reform of China's domestic administration gets first attention. Hart denounces nepotism, corruption, red tape, and self-interest at all levels of government, with a rebuke in passing to the Ch'ing censorial system for "failing to hear the grievances of the people." Although censors were supposed to be the "ears and eyes" of the Emperor—charged with the responsibility of encouraging administrative rectitude on the part of both the Throne and the bureaucracy—their vast powers were often abused. The "ears and eyes" are on the wrong people, Hart maintains. He goes on to say that Ch'ing administrators are rotated too often, overburdened, and hindered by too much official interference from above and arrogation of responsibility from below.

Military reform comes next. Hart castigates the Chinese army for its lack of adequate pay, its padded rosters, and the poor quality of its arms and training. Only one out of every ten soldiers is reliable, he asserts; most are old, weak, lazy, or stupid. In peacetime the men try to eke out a living rather than devoting themselves to drill; and, when they train, they merely go through the motions of drawing bows and lifting stones. Called into battle, they act as if they were townspeople "treating weapons like farm implements;" and upon encountering enemy forces they will advance only if the enemy happens to retreat. He writes scornfully of military officials reporting a great victory against the Taipings after slaughtering one or two innocent villagers who had deserted rebel-held areas but not yet shaved their foreheads in the Manchu style.

Hart then returns to civil administration. The original purpose of mastering the Confucian classics, he affirms, was for practical use. But Chinese scholars of the present seem to know nothing of everyday affairs. Although thoroughly versed in traditional poetry and prose, they are quite ignorant and ineffective as administrators. Here, he boldly launches an assault on the hallowed notion of moral government by Confucian generalists — a cornerstone of Restoration ideology. He also criticizes the Ch'ing government's "rule of avoidance" and points out once again the absurdity of transferring officials so frequently. In his view, these policies served only to decrease administrative efficiency and to place inordinate power in the hands of solidly entrenched yamen clerks and runners.

Hart believed that many of China's internal problems could be traced to misguided fiscal policies. The Ch'ing central government was, he felt, an extraordinarily weak financial instrument. Although China had abundant resources, little wealth actually found its way to Peking. Irregularity and inefficiency prevailed in the administration of taxes; low official salaries and the widespread practice of tax-farming encouraged corruption at all levels; and the arbitrary system of forced "contributions" by officials caused the people to say that they were being "skinned alive." Such malpractices, the I.G. maintains, cause people who are normally docile and compliant to become unsubmissive and rebellious.

Equally straightforward is Hart's discussion of China's external problems. He extols the mutual benefits of Sino-Western trade, and condemns the tendency of Ch'ing officials in the past "to view foreigners as barbarians and to treat them like dogs." Further, he argues that observance of the so-called unequal treaties is necessary for the smooth conduct of Sino-foreign relations. Hart pulls no punches. He grants that the treaties were imposed on China by force, against China's will, and concedes that they were motivated by several different purposes. Some countries coveted China's land (Russia); some nations desired missionary privileges in particular (France); and all wanted trade (Great Britain's stake was, he acknowledged, the most substantial in this respect). Significantly, Hart distinguishes between Protestant missionaries—who, he claims, do not act out of any sort of national interest—and French Catholic missionaries—who, he says, are "under the general direction of the Pope." His point is, of course, to show that Catholicism poses a more serious political threat than Protestantism; and his purpose, at least judging from a journal entry of 12 April 1864, is to "avert a French *protectorate* of propagandism."

Naturally enough, Hart wants China to abide more faithfully by the treaties (although his journal of 9 July 1865 suggests, that he is fundamentally satisfied with China's performance). He points out that nations establish treaties in the same way that people conclude contracts (*ho-t'ung*); and that, just as a breach of contract might well invite bureaucratic resolution, a breach of treaty will surely entail recourse to international law—including the possibility of military action as a means of redress. Hart underscores at several points the unpleasant consequences of non-compliance with the treaties, including additional indemnities and further demands. He later softens his remarks somewhat by indicating that the foreign powers have no desire to harm the dynasty; and he reminds the Tsungli Yamen that the West has honored its treaty obligations and has helped the Ch'ing government to suppress the Taipings. But the ominous tone of his argument, whether intended or not, persists. Fully half his memorandum consists of warnings over the dire consequences of China's failure to puts its house in order. (One wonders how Hart's earlier version must have sounded!)

In a genuine spirit of helpfulness, and in line with the stated goals of the Cooperative Policy, Hart does make several concrete and positive suggestions. Most of these proposals appear in his journal entries for the period from 1864 to 1865. He wants to see a graduated land tax, an overhaul of the salt monopoly, and the eradication of corruption in both coastal and inland customs administration (presumably the likin tax on internal trade in particular). He also advocates the restructuring of China' official salary system, so that bureaucrats will not have to resort to irregular methods such as "squeeze" in order to make administrative ends meet. In military affairs, he argues for drastic troop reductions, and the establishment of modern, Western-trained defense forces of 5,000 soldiers in each province. The capital, he says, could support an additional 10,000 men who might be paid from Customs revenues. Implicit in all of these recommendations is his view that the Ch'ing central government must take an active leadership role in fiscal and military reform.

Finally, Hart urges closer ties between China and the West — to be achieved not only by sending Chinese envoys abroad, but also by joint, Sino-foreign efforts to develop China's communications and economy. "The convenient methods of the foreign countries," he emphasizes, "can all be learned and acquired by [the Chinese] people." China should investigate and adopt Western steamships, locomotives, factory machinery, telegraphs, and modern minting practices. If such "ingenious" (*ching-miao*) devices of the West can be incorporated, benefits will redound to both the Chinese people and the Chinese state; if not, China can only continue to experience difficulties with the West. Hart ends his memo with a plea for resolving immediate diplomatic difficulties: the audience issue, the matter of entering the city of Chaochow (see chapter 5), and the arrest of the Kweichow provincial Commander-in-Chief, T'ien Hsing-shu, whose troops had killed a French missionary.[33]

How realistic were Hart's proposals? Hart himself was optimistic. On 14 October, for example, he recorded in his journal that Tung Hsun talked to Pao-yun "in a way that leads me to think they commence to <u>realize</u> their position. <u>This in itself is an immense step</u>." The next day he wrote: "I commence to see that what I have been saying and writing for years back is taking effect, & that the sluggish minds of the big men are being stirred up." And on 28 October he exclaimed joyfully: "here <u>I</u> am being made use of to aid the progressionists in China!"

But Hart faced numerous obstacles. In the first place, as Tung Hsun had predicted, a number of Ch'ing officials proved to be both suspicious of and offended by his memorandum. Another problem was timing. As it developed, Hart's memorandum was presented to the Throne together with a similar set of proposals by Thomas Wade, who, unlike Hart, was a British official.[34] Hart had a premonition that Wade's memo could well cause trouble. In his journal entry for 2 March 1866, for example, he notes that Wade's work might "frighten [the Tsungli Yamen] to such an extent that they will not let me go [on leave]."

An examination of Wade's "Brief Discussion of New Proposals" ("Hsin-i lueh-lun") suggests that Hart's fears were justified. Although a brilliant scholar, Wade was not tactful. As Chinese Secretary and Secretary of the British Legation, he had a deep knowledge of Chinese history and culture; but the pessimism he felt regarding China, abundantly revealed in Hart's journal entries, is reflected also in his memorandum. Although studded with erudite references to China's illustrious past, and informed by an in-depth analysis of contemporary Ch'ing documents—including memorials from Chinese officials in the *Peking Gazette*—Wade's "New Proposals" seemed to the Chinese even more threatening than Hart's "Bystander's View."[35]

In some respects the two memoranda are similar. Like Hart, Wade emphasizes that a new situation faces China, that an inextricable link exists between domestic and foreign affairs, and that the Ch'ing government needs to undertake immediate reforms in the realms of civil and military administration, education, and foreign relations. The two men not only identify many of the same problems in Ch'ing government and fiscal policy, but also propose many of the same solutions. But to an even greater extent than Hart, and at greater length ("New Proposals" occupies more than 26 pages of Chinese text), Wade dwells on the dangers facing China. Moreover, it is clear from his opening remarks that he is speaking not as an impartial observer, but on behalf of the new British Minister, Rutherford Alcock, who wishes to know about the prospects for both domestic administrative reform in China and friendly Sino-foreign relations.

In addressing the relationship between China's internal and external situation, Wade emphasizes the Ch'ing government's double jeopardy. Domestic unrest, he asserts, has been more than simply a matter of pillage and banditry; Chinese rebels want nothing less than to found a new dynasty. Furthermore, even if rebellions are suppressed, China's failure to cooperate with the West and to undertake reforms that will "eliminate corruption and give rise to profits," might still invite foreign domination. The history of the Anglo-French occupation of Peking in 1860 and the record of foreign assistance against the Taipings demonstrated England's good will and lack of territorial ambition, but Wade emphasizes repeatedly the threat to China's sovereignty (*tzu-chu*) posed by the Ch'ing government's inability to contend with its internal and external problems. He underscores this theme not only by reference to China's recent difficulties with Britain, France, and Russia, but also to the colonial activity of these three foreign powers on the periphery of China—specifically, in Burma, Indo-China, and Central Asia.

China's fundamental problem, according to Wade, is its "love of the old and hatred of the new" (*hao-ku o-hsin*). Yet the adoption of "new methods" is obviously essential both to China's present and future well-being. He adduces the Imperial Maritime Customs Administration as an example of meaningful institutional reform which, although Western-inspired and undertaken in part by foreigners, remained under Chinese control and proved to be of great advantage to the Chinese. Wade winds up his memorandum in a fashion similar to Hart's. The latter had remarked: "If China makes changes in administration, it will not be difficult for her to be the leader of all nations. If changes are not made, within a few years China will certainly be the servant of all nations." In the same vein, Wade declares: "If China advances she can prosper and again become strong. If she stands still, it will certainly lead to irredeemable decline."[36]

Quite naturally, what Hart and Wade phrased as unattractive possibilities the Tsungli Yamen took to be threats. In their memorial to the Throne of 1 April 1866, Prince Kung and his associates acknowledged the need to "borrow [new] methods for self-strengthening" and the fact that time was certainly of the essence; but it is clear that the Yamen itself had serious reservations about the proposals. Although "outsiders," as the title of Hart's memo indicated, Hart and Wade were not truly impartial, and, although their suggestions were worthy of consideration, their motives were suspect.[37] The Throne held a similar view.[38] The Grand Council, for its part, recommended that some of the proposals by Hart and Wade might be accepted in order to pacify them, but not the whole package.[39] Basic institutional change was simply not on the Ch'ing central government's agenda.

Nor, as we have seen, was it foremost in the minds of high-ranking provincial officials. About a dozen prominent leaders eventually memorialized the Throne concerning the issues raised by Hart and Wade. Although all favored the principle of self-strengthening, none advocated more fundamental changes. Nor did anyone challenge directly the principle of government by classically educated "men of ability" rather than specialists. All feared, to a greater or less degree, the disruptive potential of devices such as telegraphs and railways. Their resistance was based on three primary arguments: (1) China would lose control of strategic areas; (2) graves would be disturbed and the principles of geomancy (*feng-shui*) violated; and (3) the welfare of the people would be endangered.[40]

Several officials took special pains to point out what all of them knew: that domestic reform, at least on paper, was well under way, and that efforts to modify the land tax, to curb the power of yamen underlings, to increase official salaries, and to both reduce and upgrade the army should be continued. Tung Hsun himself told Hart on 13 October 1865 that his proposals were "much the same kind" as those of the Soochow scholar-reformer, Feng Kuei-fen—which indeed they were.

Hart did have some supporters among high-level provincial officials. Ch'ung-hou, for instance, felt that the success of arsenals, foreign-training programs, and the Imperial Maritime Customs administration under Hart offered tangible proof that foreign methods could be "extremely advantageous" to China. Tso Tsung-t'ang, for his part, readily acknowledged the value of foreign steamers, since he had just begun to establish the Foochow Shipyard with Prosper Giquel's assistance. On the other hand, several Ch'ing officials, notably the Governor General of Hu-Kwang, Kuan-wen, believed that Western reform proposals and offers of assistance were nothing more than the expressions of naked self-interest. The logic of adopting foreign methods demanded the use of foreign personnel, and the use of foreign personnel merely enhanced the wealth of foreigners. (It may be added that, shortly after writing his self-righteous memorial, Kuan-wen was cashiered for corruption.)[41]

Liu K'un-i, Governor of Kiangsi, championed military reform—including the acquisition of Western weapons—but he railed against Hart's contention that Chinese scholars were "well-read yet ignorant about [practical] affairs" (*tu-shu erh pu hsiao-shih*). On the contrary, he argued, if scholars are ignorant, it is precisely because they do not read books (i.e. the Classics and the Histories). Further, like many of his provincial colleagues, including Tseng Kuo-fan and Li Hung-chang, Liu rejected proposals for fiscal changes such as the abolition of the likin tax. Other officials argued with equal vehemence, and at some length, against abandoning time-honored administrative practices such as frequent transfer and the "rule of avoidance."[42]

In the realm of foreign relations there was a rough consensus. Most provincial officials recognized the inevitability and advisability of abiding by the treaties, and many assumed that an audience would eventually be granted to the resident ministers in Peking. Most also felt that China should eventually send Chinese envoys abroad—although a few expressed concern over China's shortage of qualified personnel. But, even among those individuals who saw the need for changes in China's system of foreign relations, few found it easy to break out of their traditional habits of discourse and thought. Most continued to emphasize ritual, moral suasion and classical education as the means by which to "transform men's minds"; just as most employed traditional terms of imperial condescension—such as "indulgent treatment of men from afar" (*huai-jou yuan-jen*), "controlling by loose rein" (*chi-mi*), and "using barbarians to attack barbarians" (*i-i kung i*) — in discussing ways to accommodate foreign requests.[43]

Finally, there was the problem of rising Chinese anti-foreignism in the 1860s. This phenomenon, which has been extensively documented in relation to missionary affairs in China, had its counterpart in the Western-inspired reforms of the T'ung-chih era. As with Chinese resistance to foreign missionary activity, opposition to Western-style modernization had both a practical and an ideological side.[44] The practical problem can be seen in one of Hart's pet projects, the foreign-training program at Feng-huang-shan, which fell victim to the disruptive influence of Western officers within the camp as well as to the persistent meddling of local British officials from without (a double-edged problem that was not unique to Feng-huang-shan).[45] Ideological opposition to Western-style reform is epitomized in the history of another of Hart's favorite enterprises, the Peking T'ung-wen kuan, which in 1867 was fiercely attacked for teaching occult "computational arts" (*shu-shu*) and for "honoring barbarians as teachers" (*feng-i wei shih*). The stigma of learning barbarian skills from alien teachers, like Chinese fears over foreign intervention in China's military affairs, made Western-inspired change of any sort extremely difficult to initiate, much less to sustain.[46]

Thus, while Hart maintained that from a distance he could see the entire face of Lu Mountain, it appeared to at least some Ch'ing officials (for example, Jui-lin, Governor General of Liang-Kwang, and Chiang I-li, Governor of Kwangtung) that he had the point of view of a person who "sits in a well to look at the sky" (*tso-ching kuan-t'ien*).[47] From a Restoration perspective, most of Hart's proposals for basic institutional change and closer Sino-foreign cooperation were either ill-informed or unrealistic. Whereas Hart felt that domestic unrest and continued foreign-policy problems highlighted the deficiencies and limitations of imperial administration, Ch'ing officials felt that the suppression of the rebellion and the lack of foreign wars after 1860 testified to the validity of the dynasty's conservative reform program.

In short, China signally failed to achieve a breakthrough into modernity such as Japan's leaders would soon accomplish in the Meiji Restoration of 1868. But few would have guessed the outcome in the mid-1860s. At that time, Japan was still gripped by the turmoil preceding civil war against the Tokugawa Shogunate; the dramatic victory of Satsuma, Chōshū, and Tosa domains was still years away. China, meanwhile, seemed far ahead of the Japanese in its cooperation with the Western powers and in its mastery of domestic rebellion. The cruel irony is that China's very success over the short haul kept the Ch'ing government from undertaking more fundamental and ultimately necessary reforms. The Tsungli Yamen neatly summarized China's ad hoc approach to reform: "When something happens, we hurriedly plan to make up our deficiencies; but after the incident, we again indulge in pleasure and amusements."[48] In foreign relations, the Cooperative Policy of the 1860s masked the true nature of China's external threat, while internally the suppression of rebellion enabled the Chinese elite not only to reassert but also to enhance its traditional power and privileges. Both the Chinese elite and the Manchu Throne enjoyed a false sense of security.[49]

Japan, by contrast, was chronically insecure and ripe for revolutionary change. The breakdown of feudalism, the rise of the Japanese merchant class, and the unchecked invasion of the foreign powers rapidly eroded samurai support for the Shogun's central authority. At the same time, Japan's long tradition of foreign borrowing, together with the absence of either a centralized, Chinese-style bureaucracy or a civil-service-examination system that encouraged orthodoxy, gave members of the disgruntled Japanese elite in various feudal domains the freedom and incentive to learn about Western science and technology, as well as new ideas and institutions. Thus, following the overthrow of the Tokugawa Shogunate in 1868, the Meiji oligarchs, in the name of the newly "restored" Japanese Emperor, rapidly applied the lessons they had learned from the West in a centralized, systematic, and sustained way.[50] By 1895, Japan had become an imperialist power, and China, its hapless victim.

Hart saw it all happen, but he could do little about it. Although he never abandoned his effort to promote meaningful reform, he found to his frustration that he could only tinker with the system, never transform it. The value of foreign technical knowledge became increasingly obvious to Ch'ing officials over time, but the need for fundamental change was not obvious until it was too late. One doubts that Hart gained much satisfaction hearing from the Empress Dowager in 1902 that she regretted not taking more of the advice he had offered in his "Bystander's View" during the 1860s, for events had shown him to be correct.[51]

CHAPTER EIGHT

Journal

2 JULY 1865–2 MARCH 1866

SUNDAY, 2 JULY 1865: I left S'hae in the "Ying tsze fei" on Tuesday evening, the 20th June, at 8 a.m., steamed through a sea as smooth as glass until Thursday about noon, soon after which we reached Chefoo; there we remained until 4 p.m. the following day, when we again made a start, in company with the "Glengyle", and arriving at Lan Keang Sha about 1 1/2 anchored at T'tsin at 8 p.m. on Saturday evening. Before crossing the bar, the Thermometer stood at 75°; half an hour afterwards, it was 105°! We seemed to have been thrust into a burning fiery furnace; at all events we were fairly in the middle of the dry northern summer. On Sunday morning at 8, I met Chow Ta-jen at the Tsze-chuh-lin office, & the Taoutae [characters for Li T'ung-wen] also called on me there; I advised them to hire the steam-barge, and get the troops ashore as quickly as possible from the "Glengyle", "Viola", "Fusiyama" and "Phoenix": these four steamers, with as many ships, bring up the detachment that was at Sung Keang under Pwan Tajen, when I visited Fung-Hwang-shan — about 7000 men in all, to assist in putting down the Honan, & Shantung Too-fei [local bandits]. I also told them to take care, and issue pay regularly, for that the troops, though useful when paid, might give greater trouble than other people if any one played tricks with their wages in Chili.[1]

At 1 P.M. on Sunday, I left Teentsin with Three carts: Leang-soo & Man remaining behind to bring in the luggage, some 80 pckgs; as soon as carts, hidden in the country through fear of being pressed into military service, cd. be obtained. At 6 p.m. I was at Yangtsun, where we awaited the mules; again on the road at 9, traveled all night, passed Ho-see-woo about 4 on the following morning, and arrived at Matow at 7 1/2 where we stayed till near ten; passed Chang-Kia Wan at 12, Yu Kea Wei at 2, and got to the Sha-hoo-men before 4, and to the Kow-lin Hoo-tung about 4 1/2. The night part of the journey was cold in the extreme, and the day part as hot in proportion; I was thoroughly tired when I got to the city gate, when, having to wait while my pass was being copied & stamped, I was literally baked by the setting sun; entering the Ha-ta-men, I got such a shaking over the stones that I gave way entirely, & my head began to ache fearfully.[2]

The Students all welcomed me at once, & with them I dined. Followed up the dinner by two Corkle's pills, which I found an agreeable medicine. I sent my card to the Yamen to the Sze-kwan [lower officials], and asked how they were; in return the cards of Wän, Häng, Tsung, & Tung came back.[3]

Tuesday, 27th, went to the Yamun and was recd. kindly by them all. Before I went, Tsae called, & told me that Hsüeh had gone back to SzeChuen, to see his old mother", but, in all probability to get out of the way of the Han lin Peen-Shoo [Han-lin Academy compiler], Tsae Show-Ke: I think he will no longer interfere in foreign affairs, and that Wan had taken the measure of his foot.[4]

I remained at the Yamen till five, talking about general matters: the only subject of interest referred to was the sending of people to Europe to learn; Wan says the time now approaches for taking that step. He remarked that if it had been done in 1861, it wd. have caused great suspicion & dissatisfaction, but that, inasmuch as, since 1861, Chinese have seen the use of foreign arms, steamers, & drill, while at SooChow the attempt to make an arsenal was but a partial success, now has come the time when it will cause no remark to send men to learn such things where they are best taught.[5]

In the evening about 8 p.m. I was just about going to bed when it came on to rain: as I stretched myself, I said, "If Wade were to come out tonight, he would be caught in the wet": no sooner had I made the remark to myself than he actually came into my own court! He sat & talked till 11 in the usual way: expects nothing from the Dynasty, thinks that everything depends on himself and me, and hopes to get away from diplomatic into philological employment.[6]

On the 28th, in the house all day resting; my trip up completely knocks me up. At dinner in the evening, I turned around and asked Ma-urh suddenly how long the carts drawn by five horses ought to be on the road; the words were no sooner out of my mouth than Man's foot was heard, and the carts about which I was thinking arrived! Two curious cases of suggestion of ideas which cannot easily be accounted for; save that by allowing that an accomplished fact can in some way inspire in the person to whom it is relative, but who is absent, a thought about it at the exact time. The Hoppo also arrived at Hwang-tsun, 40 le distant.[7]

29th. Went to the Yamen and handed them the Revolvers & Binoculars: presented Tung Ta-jen with the small opera glass I had secured [?] for myself: having forgotten a burning [?] glass for which he had asked me. Saw Foo Tseang Keun there.[8] Wade up in the evening for some hours.

30th. dined with Wade: present the Russian Minister & Secretary; after dinner the French chargé came in, de Billonet. I had been employed all day in examining my young men, giving them questions political, geographical, literary, &c. De Champs had been down to tell de Billonet, & he had rushed round to Wade to express his approval &c. Wade said I had magnetized my students.[9]

July 1st. Went to the Yamen at 1: talked chiefly with Häng about the Portuguese question. The French have proposed that there be a custom-house there, & that at Canton there be a Portuguese Commissioner; that 3/4 of the duties of the two places be paid to China, & 1/4 to Portugal: another proposition is to do away with the 9th (objectionable) article. HangKe shewed me his counter-propositions; feeble & aggravating in the extreme! He mentioned Sir R. A.'s [Rutherford Alcock's] name; I took occasion to remark that China wd. never again have at Peking four such considerate ministers as Bruce, Berthemy, Burlingame, & Vlangali, and that it had better clear away all questions that might contain the germs of discussion before Sir R. A.'s arrival: I meant presentation and ChaoChow.[10]

Wade arrived about 4, so I came away early, having done nothing in particular, save that I put a spoke in the wheel of Mr. Menzies, whom Baker was so foolish as to take with him on Tsung How's staff to Tung Chang foo.[11]

Today I have been arranging my papers quietly, & taking it easy in the house.

MONDAY, 3 JULY 1865: Today, having been sent for, I went to the Yamun; where I first met WanSeang, who, on various pretences, kept sending HangKe out of the room. He talked chiefly about my propositions relative to the temporary suspension of the collection of import duties at Canton,— wanting to know what arrangements I could make for funds for bonded warehouses, whether merchants wd. not make an outcry, &c. &c. Paou Ta-jin, whom I had not seen for two years, then came in, and at once began to talk about the proposal; WanSeang interrupted him in a nasty, fidgetty [sic] way, saying "O, we have put that all right; he has explained all the difficulties that I foresaw," to which, Paou rather sternly replied, "and what, pray, may have been the difficulties that you foresaw?" On the whole, & throughout the conversation, WanSeang did not shine, and was evidently not at ease before Paou. The fact, however, is that my proposal is viewed very favorably: they say, they like it, not so much for the increase it will cause in the duty collections, as for the good it will do the locality to have such lawless & violent smuggling quietly repressed. I don't know what they are really animated by: I conceive it to be one of three things: either the desire to take the wind out of Hong Kong's sails, or a desire for the money increases, or because they think that, if successful, the coup will be a feather in the Yamën's cap.[12]

TUESDAY, 4 JULY 1865: Today all my students, with myself, Brown & Murray from the Legation, breakfasted at the Yamen at 9 1/2: broke up about 12.[13]

After breakfast, I talked quietly with Wan & Tung for a couple of hours. The Canton scheme is now to be laid before the Chinese President of the Hoo Poo [Board of Revenue], Lo Tun-yen, and, if he approves it, it will be carried out.[14]

Said good-bye to Wän, who tomorrow is to start for Tung-ling [the Eastern Tombs], to inspect the vault that has been prepared as the last resting place for Heën Fung's remains, & on which some 3 millions of taels have been expended. Before starting, W. said that he wished me to send for MacPherson in order to talk about Newchwang, & also that he wanted 900 revolvers in addition to the 100 already purchased.[15]

WEDNESDAY, 5 JULY 1865: Heard all the students talk today. Cartwright is the readiest.[16]

THURSDAY, 6 JULY 1865: A call from Hangke, who talked for a couple of hours. He is anxious about the Portuguese Treaty, with the responsibility of everything growing out of which he is saddled. He says he envied me my "equanimity", & my calmness and unchangeableness under all circumstances. He's right there: I seldom "fash" myself; while I work hard, I take results quietly, hoping on, &, for the time being, trying to learn to be content in the state in which I find myself.[17]

Called today on M.M. de Billonet, Fontainier [*sic*], & Blancheton; with the two former talked French, & managed to get along. M. de Billonet talked slowly, so that I cd. keep up with him; he expressed himself pleased with my plan with my students, sd. I ought to increase the number & procure men of another stamp, engineers, &c. &c., & advised me not to give appointments to any French who had not left the French service.[18]

Fontainier's collection of coins first rate.

I afterwards called on Wade with whom I talked for an hour & a half. He took down notes about the state of the ports, & read me a long, & able, private letter that he had hurriedly written to Lord Russell about "the fleet". The instructions from the Govt. are that, when the fleet is sold, the British will make up to the Chinese the difference between the proceeds & £152,000. While with him the mail came in, & he read me his letter from Hammond, Under secy. It sd. Alcock wd start on the 2nd aft. mail, & that one of the new students for China is the unemployed Lowder in Japan: thank heaven! he'll not try to put him on my list.[19]

FRIDAY, 7 JULY 1865: [characters for the 15th day of the 5th intercalary month][20]

Recd. my mail today: letters from Gordon & Forbes. The latter comes out by the French mail of the 19th May, & ought now to be in China.[21]

Perry sends me the plans, &c., for the railway, projected from Canton to Fatshan by Sir Macd Stephenson: doesn't he wish he may get it! I certainly wish them "Godspeed", but many are the difficulties they have in their way.[22]

My students stand thus: highest attainable mark 200: 1st, Cartwright, 162; 2nd, Bowra, 126; 3rd, Kleinwächter, 99; 4th, De Champs, 94; Hamilton, 21; Doughty, 14.[23]

I went in to ask Doughty to dine with me today, & found him in bed; he sd., he had been so unfortunate as to have a woman some time ago: I thought he said "wound": hinc ille lachrimae.[24]

Wade came up this evening & talked for an hour; he is always frightened about China. Of course he is quite right; danger is on the cards, but mutual fears, suspicions &c., will prevent anything that is not joint action, unless the British take a lead — as they may possibly do under Sir R. Alcock.

Weather is hot in the daytime, but cool at night; especially pleasant just now, with such fine moonlight.

SATURDAY, 8 JULY 1865: Called at the Yamên for a few minutes: gave Che my despatch for Ching, calling MacPherson to Peking. Saw Häng; told him Le Taoutae had better write to Mongan about the powder the Yamên wishes to buy from the military at Takoo. Anent the Portuguese Treaty, he remarked that he had <u>knowingly</u> consented to the semi-contradictoriness of the 9th article for, sd. he, "although the Portuguese, now the stronger, may, for the time being, enforce the stipulation according to the latter half, we, at some future day, with increased strength, shall be able to come to an issue with them in support of the upper half of the sentence." I mark this with !! & ?[25]

Left a card on Williams, with a copy of the Returns '64; called at Edkins, who is in an anxious state about the sum to be paid for his furniture, & whom I told I cd. not take back any, but must await the receipt of the pieces agreed on by purchasers with the Legation. Then went in to see Wade, to whom I also gave a copy of the Returns, & with whom I talked for half an hour. Left a card on Hewlett: introduced to Mitford: call from Jamieson: Cartwright dined with me.[26]

SUNDAY, 9 JULY 1865: Brown breakfasted with me this morning. We mutually expressed our longing for the quiet way of living to which we had been accustomed at home, & our disgust at our increasing slothfulness & incapacity for work. I have not half the go in me that I had ten years ago.[27]

Wade gave me a long report he had addressed to Lord Russell in March last to read: he takes the gloomiest view possible of affairs in China. He says that the dynasty only exists by the forbearance of foreign powers, & that it may at any moment fall to pieces before the anger of any one. He charges it generally with [a.] infractions, or [b.] unfulfilment of treaties, & says that it must go to the wall unless it [a.] developes its wealth & resources, [b.] employs its own men & mean ., and [c.] conciliates foreign powers.

He writes very powerfully, but in general terms, and does not refer to any individual cases. I confess that the govt. moves very slowly, but I cannot see how it could move more quickly except under pressure; but that it is moving, I am convinced. I do not know of any infraction of treaties, or of any disposition to break them; and with the <u>Chaou Chow</u> exception, & non-receipt of the Ministers by the Emperor, I know of no non-fulfilment. As to the non-conciliation of foreign powers, it must be remembered that we are but breaking ground in this country, & that the bulk—in fact, we may say all, with <u>one</u> or <u>two</u> exceptions—of the officials, ignorant & suspicious, are against us; so that it is not to be wondered at if those with whom we come into more familiar contact are shy and backward. Official correspondence may be styled interminable; but I don't know that it is more so here than in other countries, E.G. the Indian Army Rights question, corn law league, &c. The post moves slowly, the country is large, & official information & opinion have to be collected sifted & weighed.

The fact is that we have forced treaties on them, allowing but little, if atall, for the modes in which such treaties, in respect of individual stipulations, might affect them; we insisted on bringing them into the comity of nations — lugging them in by the ears, with no very far-sighted arrangements for their comfort, — and solacing ourselves with the conviction that to act thus was, in the long run, at all events, to secure progress. Now, however, the treaties have been in operation for some years, & the points in which individual stipulations pinch show themselves. The Chinese are at their wits' end to devise means by which either the shoe may be cut or removed: we say, you must wear the shoe, & "be damned to your corns": we won't even allow the shoe to be taken off for a moment to ease the foot; hence excessive irritation on their side.

Wade speaks of the forbearance of foreign powers and that too in a way as if the Chinese ought to be obliged to them for it. Now I grant that good fortune brought at first to Peking half a dozen considerate men as ministers: also that an inconsiderate man might have picked up a cause of quarrel. But I assert that it is our duty, as just & Christian nations, to be forbearing: and, too, that to be so is politic. The Chinese need not thank us for that; we have forced ourselves into their house, & unless we mean to turn them out, we ought really, as men, to allow the "give and take" principle to operate.

Further, to say that during the last few years we have done nothing wrong is out of the question; we have acted in a very high handed way, & have refused redress in certain matters, thereby placing the central govt., to whom the local authorities (in following out the policy which we wished inaugurated) had refused them [sic]: we left despatches unanswered, or we said we were very sorry, & there the thing ended; all of which tended to place the people whom we wished to be in the right — the Yamen — in a wrong position, & weakening the power, jeopardizing the position of the very men we wished to see strong.

I think facts must be met as facts, & that any sentimental view of either faults or difficulties ought to be kept in the background, for it prevents a proper view from being obtained & impedes action.

We think we have a right to the thanks of the Chinese for the assistance we have given them in putting down the rebels: but it must be remembered that a. in so far as we have aided them governmentally, we have done so because we thought it our interest to do so, and b. that a great deal of individual aid has sprung from the desire of individuals (& their competition) to distinguish themselves, and for which they have been handsomely paid: further, c. we have so often reminded the Chinese of what we have done for them that the obligation on that score may be considered cancelled.

I deny that the Chinese are not moving: their military affairs are on an infinitely better footing now than they were; officials of a better stamp have, in opposition to rule & precedent, been brought forward; attempts are being made to learn foreign languages & arts, under govt. patronage, & thus to initiate measures which shall promote a good understanding between Chinese & foreigners; at S'Hae, a dock has been bought; the Chinese people are investing largely in foreign vessels, & the govt. is prepared to legalise such doings; we live in Peking in peace & quietness, & I can't see any attempt to thrust us aside atall. On the contrary, I think they wish to observe the treaties, & to act justly & fairly. But they rightly demand that we shd. observe treaties, too, & act justly & fairly also. They can't see the benefit of one-sidedness in such respects. As Mill says, — "though it is to the interest of each that nobody shd. rob or cheat, it is not anyone's interest to refrain from robbing & cheating others when all others are permitted to rob & cheat him".

We talk to them about the good faith of foreigners, &c.: & they point to the French Convention, & to the many places in which the Chinese text of the treaties differs from the foreign, & also to the fact, that when it is possible to seine out of the text any hidden meaning which wd. benefit the foreigner, that is declared to be the meaning & interpretation![28]

No: Wade takes too black — may I say too unfair? — a view of the state of affairs.

As to his apprehension in respect of the possible trouble that some new minister might stir up, I can only say, that while a man may go out as to pick a quarrel any day, that the possibilities are on the side of his trying to prevent one; & there is something always turning up in the flow of events, by which one man's power of causing trouble is being limited, & controlled — explicable at the time, but unexpected beforehand.

We need not be too sanguine, & we need not be too apprehensive as regards the future; let us, with calm minds, take each day's work, and do it well — acting fairly & justly, honestly & uprightly, and leave the issue to Providence.

*   *   *   *

Dined at the French Legation, & had a pleasant talk with Mr. de Bellonnet.

MONDAY, 10 JULY 1865: Dined with Wade.

THURSDAY, 13 JULY 1865: The body of the Säng Wang — the renowned Sang Kolin Sin — was brought into the city today. By law, it is forbidden to bring a corpse into Peking, but, on special occasions, to do homage to some highly deserving man, the regulation is relaxed. The funeral cortège entered by the Ping tsih mën; before the coffin carried by 124 bearers was led the deceased's horse, and behind it came his son as chief mourner, followed by the chairs and carts in use while alive; some 60 or 80 Wan-min-san [honorific umbrellas] were also carried in the procession. The students all went to see the sight; but my curiosity was not great enough to induce me to submit to so much discomfort.[29]

Went to the Yamen about two o.c., & had a couple of hours' talk with Paou, Häng, & Tsung. I tried to drop a few bits of information in a casual [?] way into Paou, and get hold of his attention about one or two matters; but the conversation was on the whole amusing rather than edifying, and trifling more than promising.

I have promised to do something for HängKe in the way of drawing up my proposition anent the Portuguese treaty; I don't quite understand what he wants me to do, though.

The highly sentimental view of the position and duties of a foreigner in the employ of, or in official relations with, the Chinese Govt. is that, in addition to the performance of his own paid-for duties, he shall look upon the country as rotten to the core, and shall so act as though its salvation and regeneration depended on his exertions alone. I myself, in my most helpful moments, have been for holding this obviously sentimental view; I now commence — wearied and frustrated — to lay it aside, and content myself with, in the first place, trying to do, to the best of my ability, the work I am paid for, and, secondly, outside the work, to originate or assist in carrying out any plan that may seem to be of a useful kind, and for the working of which the time seems ripe and circumstances favorable.

SATURDAY, 15 JULY 1865: Chin Chaou-ting called.[30]

SUNDAY, 16 JULY 1865: Luh ming-sung called.[31] Went to the Ya-mên at two; saw Häng & Tsung. Gave the former my proposition for a special article to be added to the Portuguese Treaty, and talked with the latter about the defects of China. The old man's eyes are being opened as he grows older, — but he is 74, his <u>wei</u> <u>fen</u> [reputation] is nothing, and he cannot carry out any reform. He says Sang Wang was <u>yung</u> but <u>Puh-tsuh-mow</u>, — "brave but ignorant of strategy".[32]

Yesterday it rained some hours, and the return of cool weather may now be looked for.

Wan Seang back yesterday from the Tung Ling [Eastern Tombs].[33]

WEDNESDAY, 19 JULY 1865: I am awfully lazy, and feel but little inclined to put forth my strength in any direction. The having nothing particular to do for the moment, and, at the same time, being charged with the responsibility attending general management, go hand in hand to keep me idle and miserable. At S'Hae, I cd. fix my own hours for every kind of work; but here not knowing at what minute I may be called off, I hesitate to commence any useful course of reading or study.

When the Tartars seated themselves on the throne of China, the first Emperor Sun-chih created eight T'sin Wang [imperial princes], making the title hereditary: the gazette of the 24th, — today is the 27th, — confiscates the Foo, or Palace and Grounds of Hwa Fung, the Suh-ts'in-wang [Prince of Su], the descendant of one of the eight Wangs alluded to. WänSeang & the others wished to use a portion of his grounds in which there is a water-power for powder-manufactury, but the Wang-yay [prince] refused to allow it; they thereon reported the matter to the Emperor, who tells him in an Edict that he has no manners (or, rather puh che ta te [he is ignorant of basic principles]), and confiscates the whole property concerned; Wan is to make use of the part originally wished for, and the rents, &c. of the rest are to be appropriated; as <u>King-fei</u> [expenses], for the support of the factory.[34]

This is, to me, a most unjust spoliation; Wade is horrified at it on other grounds, regarding it as evincing a split in the family.

Yesterday, the Emperor visited the residence of Säng Ko-Lin-Sin, and did honor to his remains by filling three cups of wine — tsze-teen — in front of the coffin. Hängke wanted me to let it be known at the legations that the emperor was going out, and request people not to cross the streets held by the military: "we used to write letters," sd. he, "but we have given that up, as it looks like a prohibition on their going out. So if you will just mention, &c." I sd. that I shd. not object to tell my own people at the Hoo-tung [lane], but that I cd. not convey the message to the others in Peking.[35] He thereon said snappishly, spitting it out like a cat, "It's necessary to take such precautions, for some of <u>your</u> people rode into the funeral procession the other day, when near my house, and struck the bearers of the corpse with their whips." I was certain he lied, while he spoke, and that he said it merely out of spite; so I had much satisfaction in telling him that <u>all</u> my people went to see the sights by the wall, and returned in carts, and not on horseback.

Yesterday I returned the calls of Chin and Luh; & Vidal; chatted for an hour with Brown, & do. with Wade.[36]

Last night & this morning very warm; the clouds are now gathering, & we'll probably have a fall of rain — for which Yutsing is still praying at the Nan Hae.[37]

THURSDAY, 20 JULY 1865: I was at the office today from two to six, with Wan, Häng, and Tsung. We had a little talk about Ching-lin and Meadows, — about the Coolie emigration rules, — about foreigners purchasing houses in the treaty-port cities [characters for *ch'eng-k'ou*; lit., "city ports"], &c. &c. &c; but we actually did no work. We talked ethics to a great extent, Wan enlarging on the superiority of a man who does right because 'tis right, while I endeavored to show that man being what he is the holding out the hope of reward or fear of punishment need not be regarded as making virtuous acts less virtuous, &c.[38]

Out of the 100 revolvers I got for them lately, one was given to Prince Kung's brother, the Tseih-yay [Seventh Prince]; he loaded it with powder, pulled the trigger, and off went the whole six barrels together! How odd that he shd. have been blessed with this experience![39]

Wade came up and talked for a couple of hours in the evening; he is down upon T. T. M. & thinks, taking them all on the whole, that <u>Hewlett</u> is the best man in the consular Service now.[40]

Dampish heat, with rainy and towards-cool-weather, tendencies. The first I think of the San-Fuh [three decades of hottest summer weather], which the Intercalary 5th moon has somewhat misplaced this year.[41]

SUNDAY, 23 JULY 1865: [characters for the 1st day of the 6th lunar month]

Wade dropped in to breakfast this morning, and sat with me to 12 o.c. He still groans over China: China does move, he grants, but not quickly enough, and WanSeang, the only man on whom the safety of the ship depends, is daily becoming more timid; he fears the ship will go down in the night, &c. &c. &c. He hinted that he commences to find the thought occasionally in his mind that a change of treatment — a show of more determination on the part of the minister — Sir R. A., E.G. — may prove beneficial; I think so myself. He explained to me his plan for the elementary works for Chinese students, on which he is at present engaged: it is a capital plan, & succeeding generations of students will rise up to call him "blessed".

Went to the office at 2, and remained there till after 6; during most of the time I was alone with W.Seang. He seemed dispirited; his cry is, "give us face; if you don't give us face, we can do nothing." The Yamen, at the suggestion of foreign ministers, is constantly rebuking provincial officials for one thing or another; the said officials thereon forward the complaints that they have to make against the foreigner, and ask the Yamen to procure redress; thereon the Yamen addresses the minister, and there, seemingly, the matter ends; the local officials, meanwhile, finding themselves blamed and interfered with by the Yamen, and, too, finding the Yamen unable to procure the redress that they have asked for, naturally learn to regard the Yamen with dislike, and with either suspicion or contempt. "Give us face," cries WanSeang: "You want us to carry out your railroad scheme, telegraphs, &c.; we once tried a steamer scheme, and disgraced ourselves by the same!"[42]

He shewed me a despatch they had written to Wade about the Kiukiang "right to purchase houses in the city" question; I said to him it wd. be better to state plainly that the Yamen agreed with the interpretation Wade puts upon the words [characters for *ch'eng-k'ou,* lit. "city port"], and he, thereon, modified it, by an addition, curiously worded so as merely to give room for an inference.[43]

The arrest of British subjects in the interior was alluded to; Wade, it seems, proposes that before attempting the arrest, the official shall always fortify himself with a Consular Warrant. That wd. take some time to procure, however!

Sir R. A.'s probable policy was also alluded to; W [Wen-hsiang] is fidgetty and evidently feels ill at ease in respect of the change. He tries, however, to brazen it out in words, and says, "Let him do what he likes, what has China to fear?"

The pistol which the Tsieh-yay [Seventh Prince] was amusing himself with, was brought to me to inspect. Häng Ke took it to pieces readily, and cleaned it: it was very dirty; and we then tried it with Ting's powder, and with caps made at Peking. The barrels went off separately, and thereby proved that the pistol itself is, in no way, defective.[44]

Hurried home, dressed, and then went to the French Legation to dinner; had a horrible headache all evening; sat still & said nothing. Home at 1/2 p. ten. Cool night, with rain coming on.

TUESDAY, 24 JULY 1865: [*sic*] At the Yamun today from 2 @ 6: most of the time, alone with Wanseang. I at once pressed him with two points, an ambassador, and the Woosung railway. As regards the first, he says it will not do to attempt anything until every matter has been so arranged as to ensure the success of the experiment; he does not fear that any of those sent to England will commit any <u>crime</u>, but he does fear that, in respect of women, they might in some instances so act as to disgrace China; further, it is important that a proper arrangement shd. be come to relative to audiences with crowned heads, &c. I imagine what he is driving at in the latter respect, is to arrange that, as Chinese officials will not seek for an audience in any country, so, too, will foreign ministers at Peking refrain from demanding to be recd. by the Emperor of China. As regards the Woosung Railway, he says he has no objections to railways, &c., provided the names that appear in connection with them are Chinese: the Chinese, he says, may borrow foreign capital if they like, but he distinctly objects to allow foreigners to commence undertakings, which might give grounds for foreign interference, in various ways, in the interior: ? [*sic*] — wd. foreign capitalists consent to risk their money in undertakings of such a kind — in which the Govt. of China might, without possibility of having to account for it, act capriciously, &c.?[45]

THURSDAY, 26 JULY 1865: [*sic*] Called on Señor de Mas, the Spanish Minister, and his attachés. The Govt. has not yet sent back to him the Treaty for exchange of ratifications, and he does not know what to think of the matter.[46]

The Hing-poo [(prison of the] Board of Punishments] is in a wretched condition: I could not help smiling at Parkes' "dread portals!" The walls are low, and covered with prickly thorns to prevent the escape of its inmates, and the filth of the interior oozes out into the street. The lanes in the neighborhood are in very bad condition, and of the houses around but few appear to be occupied. Afterwards called on Mr. McClatchey, Parkes' brother in law, an Irishman with a very blue eye and a very red beard; then on Mr. Collins, a milk & water individual, with a chatty and sarcastic wife, who came out from her early dinner, with her mouth very full.[47]

I next went to the French Legation, where I had a long talk with M. de Bellonnet. He says, in a few years the govts. are sure to insist upon seeing the Emperor — that, in his opinion, the Chinese will not consent to it, — and that then force must be again resorted to; also, that in his opinion, the Chinese are perfectly in the right, and the Portuguese as much in the wrong, in respect of Macao, but that the French Legation cannot do nothing [*sic*] in the matter, inasmuch as it was its action, through K.[?], that put the Portuguese in their present untenable position.[48]

Then called on Wade, with whom I had been but a few minutes when Wan Seang arrived. I then saw Brown, had a chat, and came home.

In the evening, Wade came up: I had a fit of the blues, while he, on the contrary, was cheery. His interview with Wän was, on the whole, satisfactory; he told him about the flotilla, and of the arrival of the Belgian Minister, both of which questions Wan took to without showing any alarm or concern.[49]

SUNDAY, 30 JULY 1865: [*sic*] Yesterday I was again at the Yamên all the afternoon. Tung has reappeared, but Häng was not there. Wan told me of his visit to Wade, & stated that he had been boiling with rage all the time he was there; he let out most furiously against Meadows, and on the various P'ei-poo [?] questions. He then spoke about the fleet, and said Wade had asked him whether he wd. consent to any loss, to which he had replied, "Put it in writing, & it will be passed on to the Hoo Poo [Board of Revenue]." I sd. I thought he must be mistaken, as what the govt intended to do was to sell the vessels, and of itself make up the difference between the sum fetched by them and the valuation [or original price?] [*sic*]. He sd., he had lost his confidence in Wade, &c. &c. &c.; Tung came in as mediator, & Wan then cooled down, & became pleasant.[50]

I tried to settle the Tonnage Question, i.e. exemption of Boiler space, &c., in steamers, and the repackage rule; but nothing definitive was arrived at.

I also brought up my Canton Scheme, and from the interest they take in it, as well as the way they talk about it, I entertain hopes of being able to carry it.

Wan spoke of the proposed Town-Dues at S'Hae: he does not quite understand the question, and, so far, he does not favor the scheme.[51]

He says, "I wish I were Kin-chae [Minister], and your Kin-chae myself for a month." So say I, too.[52]

They asked particularly, in the event of aught happening to me — death or going away (perhaps including dismissal too) — whether there was any one who cd. succeed me. Honestly, although I don't believe there is any necessary man, I think that I have qualities for my present post which none of my subs have got: the others may be more clever & more able; but there is none of them in whom I have as much confidence as in myself — rather a queer explanation. I proposed Meritens, and they all laughed: I then said seriously that Dick, Giquel, & MacPherson were the best men — that they all had excellent qualities, &c. &c. What does it mean?[53]

On Wednesday last, I examined the boys at the T'ung-wän-kwan [Interpreters' College]: Fung-yih I put first, but Ping-Ho seemed the most promising: Tih-ming second.[54]

TUESDAY, 1 AUGUST 1865: [characters for 10th day of the 6th lunar month]

MacPherson arrived this morning from Newchwang. He came across in a small pilot-boat! Four days from his port in Takoo, and two days from that to Teentsin. From what he says, Ching-lin is seemingly not the important man at Newchwang, but a she-yang of his, Lin [Liu?], a friend of Wänseang's; the God of War, as Wade calls Ching, has taken to opium smoking most energetically, and has been calling on his imaginary powers largely in his accounts of the great things he has done since he got to his post. We are to go to the office at 1/2 p. 1 tomorrow. Mac looks wonderfully well, and three years younger than when I last saw him three months ago at S'hae. He likes Newchwang, & thinks it a very healthy place to live at.[55]

WEDNESDAY, 2 AUGUST 1865: Before the hour fixed on yesterday, the Ta-jin, being all at the Yamên, sent for MacPherson and myself. At first we talked in the back-room with Häng—who immediately launched into his stale moralizing, his ideas of national intercourse, and the story of Parkes—and Wän. Soon one of the Soo-la [secretaries] came & said in a low voice to Häng, "The prince is in the reception room, & asks Mr. Hart to step across", on which Häng beckoned me out of the room mysteriously, whispering that he had something to say to me, although I had heard the man and knew perfectly well what it was; when we got outside, the told me, what I already knew, in a round-about manner, & said he wd. present me; "but," asked I, "won't he see Mac-Pherson?" The Wang-yay [Prince] came to the door to receive me, and smiled pleasantly enough, congratulating me on my Neë-sze-heën [brevet rank as provincial judicial commissioner]; he asked about the state of the southern provinces, Le Footae, the duties, and displayed some anxiety relative to Le She-heën, the She-Wang.[56] MacPherson was then brought in, and after a quar-ter of an hour's desultory talk (in which the Prince said the "right state of affairs is when the Consuls have nothing to do, & the Commissioners have no time to themselves",—meaning that it was then that the one set of officials gave no trou-ble, while the other brought in lots of money). The Prussian chargé was announced, & we took leave of the Prince. From that till six, we talked with WänSeang about the state of affairs, but of course did not settle anything; W. is anxious to collect Transit Dues on produce in such a way as to make the car-goes in foreign bottoms pay more than those in native, & the final idea at which we arrived was to collect T^t.D. from all & sundry in the first place, and then to supply each junk with a Drawback Certificate entitling her to be freed at S'Hae from the same sum when paying the junk-tax there; as to opium, he seems anxious to substitute a Transit Due for the levies of the Hang-teen [busi-ness establishments]. But it's useless following the conversation through all its windings; when we get at something definite, it can be recorded.[57]

The Prince looks very well,—stouter & healthier than when I last saw him. Wän sd. to me that the Hoo-Poo Tang-Kwan [high official of the Board of Reve-nue] had just put in writing some remarks on my Canton scheme, to which he wished me to write a rejoinder: there is evidently some chance of its success.[58]

A mail in in the "Ying-tze fei" from south: Steamers "Corea" & "Chanti-cleer" lost in a typhoon, & the "Lalla Rhook" & "Johns"[?] in a fog near Ningpo.

THURSDAY, 3 AUGUST 1865: Wän Seang sent for me today about noon, and I was with him at the office from one to five. We had a good deal of general talk, in the course of which openings presented themselves for questioning some of his antiquated ideas & suggesting new ones: but the work of a regeneration is slow! "What's the use," sd. he, "of convincing me? What's the use of my taking in hand your projects? Who is there outside to cooperate with us? Puh-hing [It can't be done]!"[59]

One idea I tried to drive well into his head, with its concomitants, & that was the primary object in the establishment of Custom Houses is to collect revenue,—and not to interfere with the operations of trade: hence the rules ought to be as little restrictive, & mercantile requirements ought to be studied and complied with as much, as possible.

1°. Repackage at Shanghae. There is a tendency to fall in with my ideas, but I must explain the matter fully, in order that Le may again be communicated with.

2°. The action of Consul Hughes & the gunboat carrying off the junk, flying D & Co.'s flag, detained at the WuSueh barrier, for want of papers. My advice is to demand that she be taken back there by a gunboat and handed over to the deputy. The right is clearly on the Chinese side; & the object to be aimed at is to prevent the recurrence of such doings. Now if a gunboat has once to tow back a junk, the Captain will be generally laughed at, & the Admiral will be furious: the result will be that the Commanders of ships of war, when called on by the Consul to act, will be afraid, or unwilling to do so—if not positively forbidden—until either full enquiry shall have been made, or the orders of their superiors have been recd. Wän's idea is to demand nothing but merely point out that this fresh act of violence is not a fulfilment of the promises made, when similar ones were formerly complained of.[60]

3°. My Canton scheme. Wo Chung-tang has written his [character for p'i; comments] on my propositions: he merely says, are merchants to be informed that after a year & a half duties will again be collected? If so, will they not take measures to make it more advantageous to trade at Hongkong during that period, & will not smuggling go on as briskly as ever afterwards? If not told, will it not be like a breach of faith? On these, & similar points about which Wan had already questioned me, I am to write out some further explanations: Wan & Tung seem both convinced that my plan is a good one, but, before acting, they wish others to be convinced as well.[61]

4°. New Chwang Transit Dues, &c. The most likely way to benefit Chinese shipping is to take off the excessive taxes at S'Hae: even that, I say, will have no result, for Chinese will still prefer foreign ships. If they wish to collect some 30 000 taels addition at N'Chwang, they can easily do so, but the tax will really fall on Chinese, & will not in any degree damage foreign shipping.[62]

Opium must be treated of separately.

5°. [characters for hai-yun, sea transport] Wän looked horrified when I sd. Le Footae thought of using for[n]. ships to bring grain to Teentsin, and spoke of yih Kae twan [?], &c. &c. I am sure it cd. be done more economically, certainly, expeditiously, &c. by foreign craft than by the sha-chuen [junks], & it must come to that. Wan says for[n]. ships wd. never submit to the delays, &c. &c. of examination of Teentsin: let them change their examination system, say I.[63]

FRIDAY, 4 AUGUST 1865: By appointment, MacPherson and myself went to the Yamen at nine a.m., and breakfasted there. After that business was discussed, and dispatched in that clever way for which the Yamen is so remarkable, and which is as admirable for the smallness of the result as for the terrible look of industry with which it appears to have been attained.

Opium.—It is proposed that [a.] the San Woo Poo-Keuen [3.5 supplementary tax] remain untouched: it is a kind of income tax, being 3 1/2 per thousand, on sales of all descriptions; [b.] the Yang-yoh Keuen [opium tax], Tls. 11 per chest, to be done away with; [c.] the Ya-teë-heang [opium stamp levy],—Tls. 15 p. chest, of which the govt. gets Tls. 5, while the collectors retain Tls. 10 for the expenses of collection!—to be also done away with; [d.] for the Tls. 26 thus paid by the merchants, and the Tls. 16 that ought to be recd. by the govt., a tax of Tls. 15 to be levied on each chest at the time of import. For this arrangement, it will be necessary to get the consent of the English Legation, &c.[64]

Transit Dues.—The main object according to WanSeang, in deciding on the levying of Transit Dues is to place such a tax upon Teas, &c., carried in foreign bottoms as shall enable Chinese junks—Sha chuen—particularly, to engage in the trade profitably. I have over and over demonstrated that, even if that tax cd. be imposed on foreign bottoms alone, it wd. not in the slightest degree affect the question, and, that to be successfully collected on them, it must be put upon Chinese as well: that the result arrived at will be nought save the imposition of a fresh tax, and the collection of some tls. 30 000 additional at Newchwang. It has, for a moment, entered into his proposition to return, by a diminishing of the ship-duties at S'Hae, the sum paid as transit dues by Chinese cargoes; but, on this occasion, he seems to have given up that idea, for, evidently, where the sole result wd. be a slight increase of collection at Newchwang, the Keang Soo authorities wd. not, without a fight for it, give up an equal amount from the Chuen Keuen [junk tax] at S'Hae. Two or three plans will be drawn up on paper, & submitted to the KeangSoo and Sha chuen people, and the work to be done will be determined by the reply made by them.[65]

Canton.—I showed Tung the remarks made by Maou Chetae on my Canton scheme. He said it was all "Kwan hwa"—'red tape'—and putting his thumbnail on the word Keen-tuh [Superintendant of Customs], with whom, Maou sd., it wd. be necessary to consult, remarked "it would not do at all to take them into the discussion".[66]

Dined with Wade in the evening, and was introduced to the Belgian Minister, Mr. t'Kint de Roodenbeck, who has come to negotiate a treaty. The King objects to that, in four articles, taken home by Mr. Bols, made with Hsieh at S'hae; and Mr. Vlangaly, also at dinner.[67]

Wan sd. today that with respect to the Belgian, Wade had at once blown them up for the four articles and sd. that, if it were his affair, he wd. suggest that Belgium & all the other small states to unite & arrange their treaties backed by ships of war: at which Wan was very much enraged. I sd. he must have misunderstood Wade; that what the latter meant was evidently that to irritate the Belgian needlessly might produce such an effect, & that he spoke of himself as a "Pe-fang-tih-jin [devil's advocate]," &c. It would not do: it was all

"Puh pei-fuh [?]."[68] Wade does seem to have an awkward facility—while being their best friend—for rubbing them against the grain and irritating them at every point.

Apropos of the despatch in which Adml. Hope told Kwan Wan he wd. put him in irons & take him to Peking, I sd. that Europeans generally have been in the habit of regarding China as an uncivilized country, and the people as semi-barbarians: that therefore they wd. merely dictate to, and not reason with them: and that much of what China objected to, was done because the Europeans had mistaken ideas—in fact, resulted from [characters for *wu-chih*; ignorance].[69]

SATURDAY, 5 AUGUST 1865: English Mail of 4 June arrived.

Letter from Cha: all at home well, but, I am sorry to say, she tells me Uncle Richard died on the 26th May. Thus since I left home, five have died whom I should like to have met again: Grandma Hart, Aunt & Uncle Cox, Aunt Charlotte, and now Uncle Edgar. The old people have been commencing to disappear; if I don't get home soon, some others may go, and not to see some of them—father & mother, for instance—again would weigh upon my mind all my life.[70]

MacPherson & the other students have all gone to the hills. Strange to say the northern hills have snow on them this morning,—a thing almost unheard of at this time of the year. Very cool yesterday & today.

SUNDAY, 6 AUGUST 1865: Thinking to have a quiet day in the house, I was mistaken. Häng Ke came to call on MacPherson at one o/c & Wan-Seang sent for me to the Yamen. Häng amused me by saying that it was good policy for a man in the second place to be content to hold his tongue & play second fiddle, "show-kow juh-ping" [keep the mouth closed like a bottle],— evidently a slap at me for neglecting him & talking so much to WanSeang.[71]

Macao.—Last time Häng & Lemaire met, Lemaire asked "Will you not exchange the ratifications?" "Of course, we will," sd Hang Ke. "Then what more remains to be sd.?" asked L. "Nothing," sd. H. "save tsun puh tsun?" "Tsun then [we] will shih kwan, pu tsun, then we need not ratify." The old boy has managed to put the affair in a nutshell. I don't think the Portuguese will come forward about the matter anymore. de Bellonnet advises them to be quiet, I believe.[72]

At the office with Wan, Hang, Tung and Tsung, did nothing particular: arranged the

1. "HuKwang" Tonnage Dues affair—the refund will be made:[73] 2. saw that the opium despatch setting aside the orders to impose no more Exemp[tn] certificates was ready to be issued: 3. brought away a couple of memos drawn up by Wan about opium and transit Dues at Newchwang. I enlarged on my [characters for *wu-chih*, ignorance] text, and added that whatever benefit they give to a foreigner, they ought to secure to the Chinese. I have thus three texts to

go upon for a while: in trade, facilitate business, & you'll increase your revenues; in foreign relations, remember that ignorance of each others' ways mutually tends to differences, &c.; and, if you find the foreigner cutting out the Chinaman, what you ought to do is to give the Chinaman the same privileges which treaties, &c. secure to the foreigner.

On returning home found Mr. Kint [t'Kint de Roodenbeke]: he had been waiting for an hour, & was just about leaving. He sat for a few minutes, and asked me to look through the Danish treaty, & let him know if any changes had taken place since it was drawn up.

The hot weather is decidedly over: the nights are cool, the mornings fresh, and in another week I expect we shall have to put on woollen clothing. I fix the summer heat at the 15th July; and the commencement of cool weather about three weeks later — say 5th Augt.

MONDAY, 7 AUGUST 1865: Macpherson & the others in from the hills at 7 1/2 this morning.

Among the papers recd. by the mail is a memo. from Forbes of a very interesting kind. He proposes nothing new, but all he says is good, and might work well. The Chinese, however, have not the money, & wd. not at present consent; in a couple or three years, when their increasing confidence in me developes [sic] itself, something perhaps may be done; for the present we must be content to move mildly, slowly & imperceptibly.[74]

I have also a note from Sir F. Bruce; he urges "self-strengthening", & says it wd. be well to have some one to furnish truthful information to the public on Chinese matters. Wade holds the same idea; & I believe in it, too. But where is the right sort of man to be got?

Beginning of fall [characters for 16th day of the 6th lunar month]. Warm day, but cold in the morning & cool toward night. A call from the Spanish Minister, Señor Sinibaldo de Mas. He wonders [why] our Returns of Trade give no information about H'Kong & M'Cao.

TUESDAY, 8 AUGUST 1865: At the yamên from 2 @ 5 1/2: the chief business attended to was that concerning NewChwang, and the point at which we arrived is this: — collection of Transit Dues is settled on as far as regards the Yamen, but the mode of collection, &c. is to be decided upon by the people most interested; opium question is to be referred to Wade, & the Yamen will propose to do away with the Eleven Tael Tax and Fifteen Tael License, provided he agrees to a collection of Tls. 15 by the Customs as a kind of Lo-te [unloading fee] or P'an Shwuy ["half tax"] — [75]

As to my Canton scheme, two new queries were put into my hand: 1°. will not merchants bring in four or five years goods during the year & a half; and 2°. what wd. become of the scheme were ought to befall me in the meantime? To the first, the reply is that the supply of the chief article, opium, is limited, and that, generally, the duty being so small on all goods — 5% — while the rate of interest is from 12 @ 18%, it wd. not pay any merchant to buy & store up his goods so long: to the second, the reply is that all the records are in order and ready to be handed over to my successor, for whom they have only to look among the Commissioners, three or four of whom are very promising men.

THURSDAY, 10 AUGUST 1865: Macpherson left this morning to return to Newchwang. He has been fortunate in seeing the Prince, and in being brought into contact with Wan Seang and the others, in the discussion of affairs in which they take considerable interest. As Häng Ke,—who came to say goodbye (but too late to see him) with a dozen miniature cheese cakes in his hands, remarked to me: "It's a good thing he has been here; it's well to have another P'ang Show [helping hand]." Of course to introduce my subs to the Yamen, will make them see that they are independent of me; but I don't mind that. So long as I do my work well, they'll retain me: if I do it badly, the sooner they send me to the right about, the better. The interests at stake are of too important a nature to admit of bad handling.[76]

Hang Ke is by no means a fool: in a "peddling" way, he is excessively sharp. He does not see far, nor can he take broad views; but within the limits of his vision, he can see clearly and act generously. If he were anywhere but in the Yamen, I shd. rather like him; in the Yamen, however, he really, in relation to grave affairs, is a "stick".

[In margin, hand pointing to this sentence] Left off white trousers and put on fall clothes today.

SUNDAY, 13 AUGUST 1865: For the last three days, at dinner time I have drunk water instead of milk or champagne, and have limited my daily amount of sherry to two glasses: I find wine has not taken any hold upon me, & that my will is still strong enough to enable me to dispense with it, & [with] smoking whenever I wish. Last night took a couple of Corkle's pills, & now I trust my liver is good for the remainder of the summer.

Wade came up on Friday morning, and talked for three or four hours: he pitches into the Chinese for the poor despatches which he says are not fit to be laid before diplomatists at home, & which if shewn to them [would] only cause them to be of Lay's opinion that the only plan to make these people move, is to punch their heads; & he says that let only England move a finger, & every other country will follow suit. Turned the conversation, & made his face shine by talking about his books; he says that if the home govt. does not do the proper thing by him, he will come to me! For the printing, it wd. be necessary to lodge Tls. 15,000 in the Bank. Fancy Wade in the Customs again![77]

Yesterday I went to the Yamen, & handed in my draft relative to the junk D. no. 3, which simply calls for the rendition of the vessel in the first instance. The Coolie Emigration Rules were also looked through, & the one proposed by Wan, to the effect that offending Chinese shd. be sent back to China for punishment was thrown out, Tung saying, that if I thought it very unlikely the Ministers wd. agree to it, it wd. be much better to refrain from raising the point. I also handed in my <u>Shin-chin</u> [report] reporting the capture of a Tung Kwan [Eastern Customs] Guard Boat, with opium & salt on board.[78]

*   *   *

Alas, alas! Ma-urh has left me: he refused to "knock the head" to De Champs whom he had offended, and the only alternative left to him was to go home. It's a tremendous nuisance, losing a really good servant in this way![79]

*   *   *

Had a curious dream last night,—vivid enough while it lasted, but now all but vanished,—in which I saw <u>Dick</u> going up the "small walk" at Solitary Lodge. I shd. not be surprised to hear that he had been to pay a visit to my people at Ravarnette.[80]

MONDAY, 14 AUGUST 1865: Again dreaming: but on this occasion I found myself in Church with Mr. Crossley and a lot of clergymen in their robes, all of them seemed reading the magazines and papers: I had great difficulty in finding a card, with which to announce my arrival, but when at length I did get speech of Mr. C. he asked me wd. I not go in and "see his little <u>May</u>". I wonder what the name of the remaining Miss Crossley is, about whom Mrs. Twinem wrote to me some time ago; & I wonder what this dream portends.[81]

*   *   *   *

Dined with the Spanish Minister, Señor de Mas, tonight: bad dinner, bad wines, stupid evening, and tiresome ride there and back.

TUESDAY, 15 AUGUST 1865: Issued Gazette No. 3 today: made Cartwright my secretary: de Champs highly pleased with his promotion, but Bowra and Kleinwachter are much disappointed that they leave Peking as they came to it, 3^d C.C. [3rd class clerk].[82]

Two of the new Americans, Taintor and Woodruff arrived today; promising looking men, thank Heavens![83]

Ma-urh back again.

WEDNESDAY, 16 AUGUST 1865: Wade came up and dined with me tonight: we had a pleasant talk about all sorts of things, and, keeping clear of Chinese officials, we kept clear of excitement. He had been under the idea that the ships cost £300,000 and was much relieved when I told him they had only cost £150,000.

THURSDAY, 17 AUGUST 1865: At the Yamên all the afternoon. Handed in my additional explanations regarding the Canton scheme, to which I may now say I have the consent of the Yamen. Talked about a variety of matters, but did very little business.

312

Wan always cries out: "Ask me nothing about the occurrences of the 3rd & 4th moons! I forget everything". That was when Prince Kung was in difficulty.[84]

Saw a draft of the despatch from the French about Tonnage Dues: cd. not make out head or tail of it! What interpreters to be sure!

Spoke about de Mas, [who] wrote that Spanish ships shd be permitted to go up the Yangtze. Saw Hsieh's letter on the subject. It sd. plainly enough that we cd. go: another piece of translating — F's [Fontanier] I suppose — which is quite wrong.[85]

FRIDAY, 18 AUGUST 1865: Wrote to Senor de Mas; told him Spanish ships cd. go up the Yangtze, and also trade at all the other Treaty ports; also in reply to his letter about a Spaniard he wants me to take on, sd. I objected for three reasons — 1st no vacancy; 2nd. over 23 years of age; & 3rd. I cannot accept the nominee of any foreign official. He'll probably be "riled".[86]

*   *   *   *   *

I have not been myself atall this summer: I'm dreadfully languid — not to say lazy.

SATURDAY, 19 AUGUST 1865: A funny dream about Minnie Edgar last night.[87]

SUNDAY, 20 AUGUST 1865: Dreaming again: in Dr. Aickin's shop at the Corner; Bill behind the counter, just as I left him, & Jane Smith, too, but grown up & pretty![88]

Up at daylight this morning, & translated Hsieh's letter to de Mas. Sent for to go to the Yamun at once; went & found Wade had sent in Osborn's a/c. which they wished to hand to me; they also shewed me a letter from Sir F. Bruce in which he advised them to take back 3 or 4 of the steamers, and a despatch from Wade who said that Govt. wd. pay £152,500 for the six. WanSeang was in a great rage, and sd. that he was being humbugged; he calmed down a little when I told him that Sir F's letter had been written before the govt. had decided what to do. The War Office had also had to pay some £13 000 for stores, so that China will get back [characters for *wu-shih-wan liang*; 500,000 taels]. I shall only be too delighted when the affair is finished and done with.

Dined with the students.

MONDAY, 21 AUGUST 1865: [characters for 1st day of the week]

Up again at daylight, & commenced Fawatt. I intend to "go in" for useful reading & regular study for the future.

Hängke came in at ten to say good bye to Bowra and the others who are to leave tomorrow. He sat with me a few minutes, and gave me some new details respecting the affairs of 1860. It appears that Parkes & he had arranged for an interview with the Emperor, but that the E-Wang [Prince Kung] refused to memorialise. Wän, he sd. was much given to details, & has no courage [characters for *chüeh-tuan;* decisiveness]. I asked him what he really thought of my Canton project; he sd. that possibly it might be useful, but it did not seem to have struck him as particularly promising from a revenue point of view.[89]

Called on de Mas, & handed him my translation of Hsieh's letter: he was very stiff: I told him that if he ever had <u>serious</u> business to transact, that with such an interpreter (he sd. it was Fontainier) he cd. not get on.

Then called on Wade who will not consent to the Newchwang opium half-duty, unless other concessions are made: he is savage that the French shd. get the Japan Tonnage Dues Concession: he looks excessively seedy.[90]

THURSDAY, 24 AUGUST 1865: Bowra, Kleinwächter, and De Champs have now left Peking, and gone to their respective ports, Canton, Swatow, & Chefoo.

The last two days have been abominably warm,—close & sultry.

It has today occurred to me, that, instead of bringing Jamie out to China, the best thing I can do for him wd. be to get him into one of the large manufactories in the north of England, and in a few years let him have £5000 or something of the sort to enable him to get a share in the concern. I do not like the idea of bringing him out here to serve under myself.[91]

Yesterday, I put into Chinese the plan I had ex-cogitated for the improvement of the Chinese mercantile marine: to do away with junks and substitute seagoing ships and steamers. The main points on which I insist are that the Tsung Le Yamun shall take the control through our offices, and that duties shall be charged on the cargoes of such ships according to the foreign tariff.

Ping sd. yesterday they think of asking for an Edict to present me with Neë-tae's clothes. I object, because Hängke wd. have to pay for them, and say that preferable to changing my "fu seih" [clothing] wd. be their changing the <u>neë-tae</u> [provincial judicial commissioner] to <u>Fan-tae</u> [provincial financial commissioner].[92]

FRIDAY, 25 AUGUST 1865: Went to the Yamen today to ask after WanSeang's health; he came out to see me, & sd. he had a sharp attack of diarrheea [*sic*], but is now better. He looked rather pulled down, but seemed as game for work as ever. Looked through the Coolie Emigration despatch.

Wade came up to see me in the morning; he said the damages done by braves, & the ChaouChow question <u>must</u> be settled.[93] He looks excessively ill; aged; aguish, he says.

SATURDAY, 26 AUGUST 1865: The mail of the 20th June arrived today: the same mail last year arrived on the 25th Augt. Letters from Mary & Sarah: Uncle Harte has again got married, but this time, it is to one of his servant girls, a Roman Catholic! A letter from Willie Hart, who tells me his father is dead, Agnes married, & Annie soon to be. From the Ports, Jones writes Maxwell is not likely to recover, & Scharferort has resigned:— so far this year two Englishmen have resigned, one has been dismissed, one German has resigned & one been dismissed, one American has resigned, & two have been dismissed—i.e.: our numbers are decreased by Eight: on the other side, we have added 3 Americans, 3 Germans, & 1 Englishman, seven in all.[94]

Robertson says: "It is the price which all, who are possessors of influence, must pay—that their acts must be measured, not in themselves, but according to their influence on others."[95]

THURSDAY, 1 SEPTEMBER 1865: [characters for 11th day of the 7th lunar month of the 4th year of the T'ung-chih reign. Date incorrect. Should be Friday, 1st September. Hart corrects it after 17 September.]

I was at the Yamen for a couple of hours today, but did nothing particular. Tung Ta-jin has been named tseuen-keuen ta-chin [great minister with full authority] for the arrangement of the Treaty with Belgium. A dispatch has been sent to the French conceding the Japan & Saigon 4 months' clause in respect of tonnage dues: it is a badly worded one. Wade tells me he spoke to Bellonet about the difficulty at the Yamen, and that B. had put all the papers in his hands. He showed them to me, and the affair seemed simple enough. O these interpreters, these Interpreters! No wonder we are constantly about to get into hot water. I think it wd. be well for the Yamen to write a circular to the ministers, saying that so many ministers now come to Peking, & that interpreters are so young that, to avoid mistakes, when it has a controversy with any one minister, it will forward copies of the dispatches to all.[96]

SATURDAY, 3 SEPTEMBER 1865: [2 September] Refused de Mas' invitation for dinner on Monday.

English Mail of 4th July in. Letters from Maggie & Robbie Moorhead.

Poor Henderson, doctor at S'hae, dead. The same low typhoid fever that I had in 1862 carried him off.[97]

TUESDAY, 6 SEPTEMBER 1865: [5 September] Weather somewhat cooler.

I am plodding wearily, with many groans, through the Flotilla a/c. I cannot yet unravel the skeins, so as to put them intelligibly before the Chinese.

Working every morning before breakfast at Political Economy, which I commence to like: I took up the study to fit myself for future work in

China—to guide me in my taxation schemes, & enable me to put something on the subject into Chinese. I see, though, that it will be useless to attempt to translate any book; I shall have to read all, saturate myself thoroughly with the subject, and then steam.

WEDNESDAY, 7 SEPTEMBER 1865: [6 September] Went to the Ya-men, and found the prince was there receiving the first visit of the Prussian Minister, Baron de Rehfues [characters for Li ta-jen]. After the Baron went away, the Prince came into the back room and talked pleasantly for some twenty minutes; I handed to him the album of crowned heads which Gordon sent out, and which he seemed much pleased with. He asked me why my own likeness was not among them, and said I must have it painted: in Chinese dress too. He made a funny face at Wan, when going away; they are evidently on most intimate terms. The Prince looks happier, and certainly grows fatter.[98]

Afterwards talked with Wän and the others till 5 p.m. Gave them back the Coolie Emigration Rules, now ready for issue; and advised them in respect of future regulations to always fix a day—a few months ahead—for their coming into operation, so as to avoid reclamations, discrepancies, &c.

Asked for six months' leave to visit home in 1866. Have arranged to come north by the first steamer next spring, & then if nothing has occurred or seems likely to occur to make it expedient for me to stay, I shall at once go home. Hurrah! "Many a slip", of course; but this is a step nearer going. The Yamên will send off one of its smartest clerks with me, to take notes, &c: this, too, is a first-step towards sending an Embassy. [Hart has drawn later a hand in the margin pointing to his time of leave, with exclamation mark.] Hurrah! Further, in the letter that forwards the Coolie Rules, the Yamên officially notifies the ministers that it expects good treatment for any officer it may send to the places towards which coolies go, to enquire into their condition. This is the first notice, voluntarily given, of any intention of sending Chinese officials to other countries. So, I again write Hurrah, with three !!![99]

The Yamen wants to drill 500 horses at once and asks me for my man: I name O. Brown. Glad to see they are "getting their backs up" somewhat, & grow impatient of national jealousies in respect of the people they employ: a first sign of returning vigor.[100]

On Saturday, the prince calls on all the ministries, and goes to the Russian Embassy to see the telegraph.[101]

Recd. 4 dispatches from the Yamen authorizing funds for building at Newchwang, Chefoo, Swatow, Takao, & Tamsuy.

In Flotilla a/c have got the Tael, Dollar, & Rupee conversions all right: the £ stg. are still in a muddle. I cannot help thinking Collins & the others wished to give me trouble in sending out the a/c in so disordered a condition.

THURSDAY, 8 SEPTEMBER 1865: [7 September] Note from Tsung How asking about "my nominees" for cavalry-drill.

Had a jolly gallop outside the Tung Chih mên this evening.[102]

Weather still hot: I have now been <u>three</u> <u>months</u> in white clothes!

TUESDAY, 13 SEPTEMBER 1865: [12 September] Went to the Yamên today by appointment, but found that what I was chiefly wanted for was to go over the collection of pictures that I some time ago gave to Tung, and explain them to him. Brown from the Legation came in while I was there, and had a little <u>pan-tsung</u> [?] with WänSeang, who let out in the usual way against Meadows of Newchwang. When Brown went away, we did, or rather talked a little business: in the First Tonnage Dues question, they sent off two despatches without showing them to me, and they are both incomplete, and unsatisfactory. The Prince says I can have my leave if there is a good man to take my place; the Canton scheme seems to be hanging fire somewhere in the Hoo poo [Board of Revenue]. I really don't feel very anxious about it now: it wd. give me an immense deal of additional work.

WEDNESDAY, 14 SEPTEMBER 1865: [13 September] Wade came up in the morning, and we had a talk about his Elementary Works for Chinese Students. He wd. like to give up diplomacy and take to philology—in which line, he says, he has work cut out for the next <u>twenty</u> years! But what he wants is that the Chinese Govt. shd. invite him 'officially' to undertake the work, and secure funds for putting it through; he does not want any salary himself.[103]

I have almost got to the bottom of Osborn's a/c; but there are sundry double-entries in them, which I cannot completely trace, and the consequence is that to make his & Lay's versions completely agree I am obliged to take liberty with £200 and put it to one side without being able to point out the precise authority for treating it so. I shall explain the fact to the Yamen, and make no further attempt to unravel threads.

THURSDAY, 15 SEPTEMBER 1865: [characters for 25th day of the lunar month] [14 September]

Still in white dress. The summer, this year, lasts long.

FRIDAY, 16 SEPTEMBER 1865: [15 September] "Le libre echange des personnes n'est pas moins utile que celui des marchandiers."[104]

SATURDAY, 17 SEPTEMBER 1865: [16 September] It rained heavily and continuously all last night, & a drizzle has lasted most of today. The heat has disappeared, & the cold very effective in making itself felt. I have had to change clothes twice, and still feel cold.

SUNDAY, 17 SEPTEMBER 1865: [Finally, the correct date] I find I have been dating the days incorrectly since the 5th.

Yesterday Luh Tae Yay called, and I had some talk with him about Land-tenure in China. He owns some 1500 mow, for which he paid at the rate of 5 taels a mow. The land is let to several people, who pay him one per cent on the purchase money per month, as rent: they ought thus to pay 12% per ann., but the custom is to let the year be counted as ten months, so that the rent is really 10% on the purchase money. He himself, if he wished to do so, cd. enter on the personal occupation of the ground, & cultivate it himself; but, so long as he does not wish to cultivate it himself, he cannot dispossess the people who hold it under him, and the only thing that wd. entitle him to make over the ground to other tenants wd. be the non-payment of rent for three years by the present cultivators.[105]

This system seems very fair; it insures that land shall pay its fair rent according to its real value, and also that the tenants shall continue in possession as long as they pay their rent.

How wd. Ricardo's theory apply in such a case as this? Is there a margin of cultivation? Is there land which just pays expenses, & pays no rent?

Luh says the taxes are paid by himself.

The eldest son of the late Hoppo Yu-tsing died a few days ago; it was to his wedding I was invited at C'ton a couple of years ago, when he married a daughter of the Tetuh Kwän Show, now appointed Tseang-Keun [Tartar General] at HangChow.[106]

Rain falling all day. Very chilly—that raw cold that goes into the bones.

My magazines for June just arrived. Strange to say, letters, &c. are not yet up.

Häng Ke appointed Foo Keen Tuh [Assistant Superintendent] of the Tsung Kän Mên [Peking Octroi]. Yu Tsing is looking after the [characters for San-k'ou ta-ch'en; Commissioner of the Three (Northern) Ports] ship.[107]

WEDNESDAY, 20 SEPTEMBER 1865: Up early, and worked hard on Pol. Economy. [Exclamation in the margin, and a hand drawn pointing to the next:] Found myself, while smoking after breakfast, unconsciously meditating on the advisability, in seeking for a wife, of looking for one with money. This is the first time I have noticed myself connecting a fortune with a wife as a matter of personal expediency. Hitherto, my ideas of matrimony, without being of the "love in a cottage" style altogether, have been of the romantic order: that is, I wd. not marry unless able to support a wife, and my desire has been for a girl without, in preference to one with, money. Today, for the first time, I again say, I have been connecting the idea of a fortune with matrimony. Does not this show a change in my nature—that there has been the transition appropriate to my age?

*　　　*　　　*

What I chiefly find fault with in the letters I receive from home is that there is no interchange of thoughts; they are not sufficiently conversational, so to speak. They never take up what I said in mine, and contain no expression of opinion on the matters about which I may have gossiped.

*　　　*　　　*

Had an exceedingly pleasant dream last night about the Crosslie family: seemed to see them again in church.

*　　　*　　　*　　　*

The Gazette said yesterday [characters for Wen-hsiang *ch'ing-hsun*]: i.e. notified his departure ("asked for instructions"). He is Kung Poo Shang-shoo [President of the Board of Works], & has, nominally, gone to inspect Heën Fung's tomb at Tung ling. In point of fact, he has gone out after some mounted bandits, who have just appeared in that neighborhood. Strange![108]

*　　　*　　　*

Wade came in yesterday for half-an-hour. He said Hängke had "sung po-po" [sent gifts of cakes] the day before, from which the French inferred something was up.[109] His policy he says is this: to sit by in China, and see it [sic] chaos, without putting forth our hands, our interests forbid us to do [sic]; the only choice is between coercion and patience, for foreign repartition must also be laid aside as out of the question; if we coerce, we excite ill-feeling toward us among the people we want to benefit, and we set an *example* which other countries with no interest, or with merely a sentimental idea acted up to as if an interest, wd. too quickly follow, and bring about the chaos or repartition which England's interests clash with. Therefore, we must be patient, but we must be importunate; we must not coerce, but we must never let them alone.

With this, I on the whole agree; but I doubt the utility of being importunate, save after a well considered fashion.

For such importunacy may affect nothing save cause disgust. Apart from active coercive measures, we must trust to time and events; & it is a fact that a concatenation of circumstances has been, is, and will be, at work to produce a change.

FRIDAY, 22 SEPTEMBER 1865: It's a great shame, but the fact is, I feel this evening discontented and peevish to a degree that is absolutely disgraceful.

Discontented: for I see so little progress — so little chance of progress, and peevish because doomed to fight an uphill fight.

Personally, I have every reason to be grateful to God. I have had excellent health, and wonderful prosperity, since I came to this country; but, work as I may, — with the greatest care, & with the least selfish aims, — I see so little accomplished, that I feel utterly miserable, and down-hearted. I know it takes "seven men to pin, and not a man too much," and my philosophy has ever been one of the "still pursuing, learn to wait" kind; but nevertheless, I am "down" tonight. When will these people "step out", and when will the men who control the destinies of this country cease to play as children with soap-bubbles?

SATURDAY, 23 SEPTEMBER 1865: Today I sent in the last despatch I had to write relative to the Steam Fleet a/c., and I confess, I am heartily delighted to have finished the work.

At one o.c. I went to the yamen and remained there a few hours with Häng, & Tung, the former of whom appeared to feel the change in the weather: his disposition to vomit suggested that his liver was affected by the damp chilliness the last few days' rain had caused. I found they wanted to talk about the French Tonnage Dues question, and they appeared to be somewhat alarmed at the tone of M. de Bellonet's last letters. The Prince's despatches to him were in both instances sent off without having been shown to me, and, as I felt certain they wd., they produced anything but a feeling of satisfaction. Mr. de B: writes to say that the concession must come into operation at once, & that, if his wish is not attended to, he will re-claim tonnage dues collected during the last three years,—"in violation"—as he puts it—"of the 22nd Article of the French Treaty." There is nothing for it but to give way to him; he has force at his disposal, and, as he sd. in his note to me yesterday, he is quite ready to be "mechant". Tung asked what was to be done; I sd. they had better write me a despatch asking when the rule cd. be brought into force; the despatch was at once written, and I brought it away with me. On my return, they wrote to M. de B: asking him if the 15th Oct. wd. do for Shanghae, and the 1st Nov. for the southern ports. He has replied to the effect that he will be quite satisfied with my arrangements, & hopes the Yamen will not write to him again on the subject—for it is quite capable of making things worse by another "sottise". I am sorry to say I think so too.[110]

O, these Chinese! these Chinese! When will they learn to do the right thing, in the right way, and at the right time?

From the Yamen, I also brought home M. de B's reply relative to the Coolie Emigration Rules, but I have not yet perused it.

WänSeang, they say, may not be back for a fortnight; so I fear, I shall not get away from Peking before the end of October. Really, I think it wd. be the best plan for me to make up my mind to stay here continually. I cd. keep them out of many a mess if they wd. only be frank with me on all occasions. But then, all the Legations wd. look on me with immense suspicion, and, while gaining in some ways, I might lose much in others.

Rain falling: very cold.

SUNDAY, 24 SEPTEMBER 1865: [characters for 5th day of the 8th lunar month]

This morning I wrote my reply to the Yamen's despatch anent Tonnage

Dues, and also drafted a civil, explanatory, note to be sent to M. de Bellonnet, asking him if the 15th Oct. & 1st Nov. wd. suit his views, as the days on which the change should take effect. These letters I took in person to the Yamen, and handed to Tung; I said I felt ashamed to have to draft such letters,—that it was humiliating in such a way to have to bend to dictation,—but that facts must be accepted as facts,—and that we must not for a moment forget [characters for *fen ssu nan* "when angry, think of the difficulties that follow".] However angry we may be, we must meet the difficulty, and not cause greater difficulties by inexpedient opposition—however galling might be the action that roused that feeling of opposition. One of the sze-kwan [lower officials] presented a draft that he & his mates had drawn up; Tung wd. not even look at it, but directed my draft to be accepted & copied; he was evidently determined to quash the difficulty at once—on a point already conceded, there was no use, & no good could be gained, in widening the breach that already threatened by, stickling for forms, & prolonging a discussion in which we shd. after all have to yield. Häng & Paou read the note. Paou treated the matter as of no importance; he did not understand its gravity. I told him that he & the others, in foreign questions, were like so many children playing with a tiger: you stroke him with the grain & he purrs,—rub against it, when up he jumps, & you may have to give him something to coax him to lie down again. I roused Tung & Häng to something like a display of emotion, in reference to Swatow, by saying that if the right of entry into Chaou Chow were not speedily settled, foreigners wd. take up the question & settle it themselves; & that they have only to give the foreigner cause to resort to arms <u>once</u> more, to bring the house down about their ears. What roused them apropos of this, was my saying that I have now become so much of a Chinaman myself that any disgrace of this sort affects me as much as it does them.[111]

When I came back, I wrote a note to M. de B begging him to accept the Yamen's proposition.

Heard at the Yamen that Foo Tseang Keun has been ordered to take the field against the <u>Ke-ma-tsieh</u> [mounted bandits] who have been coming into the province from Manchuria. This will relieve WänSeang, who may now be expected back in ten days; the <u>bureau</u> is like a watch,—it is run down, doesn't go, & Wän is wanted back again to wind it up. Old Tsung Lin sd. "The idea of sending Wän, a literary man, out in command of troops: what they want is a man who can wield a sword, & bend a bow!" Ha! Ha!! Ha!!!

In the evening wrote a long screed to Wade apropros of his remark the other day,—that he does not believe in any one possessing influence in China.

Thunder in the afternoon, and a few drops of rain. Possibly this may clear the atmosphere, which, though cold & raw, has been heavy and muggy for some days back.

MONDAY, 25 SEPTEMBER 1865: A beautiful day: fine bracing air, with glorious blue sky.

Called on Dr. Williams, Mr. Vlangaly, M. de Rehfues: U.S., Russ:, & Pruss. Ministers. Mr. Vlangaly has been pushing the telegraph propositions, & as the prince has not only gone to see it, but has also written for some further explanations, I think he will soon carry his point: I am cosmopolitan enough to say, I sincerely wish him success![112]

TUESDAY, 26 SEPTEMBER 1865: Another fine day. Went to the Yamén with my despatch about the "St. Jean", which I handed to Tung, to whom I also hinted that it might not be a bad move to extend Four months' Tonnage Dues Rule to the Amoor and Manilla. Fung or rather Foo Tootung came to the Yamen before I cd. talk the thing out, however. I then spent an hour with Häng in the backroom: he is really a funny, chatty, pleasant old man, with a good deal of humor about him. Sung Kwän, he says, he picked up off the streets when a little boy of ten years of age; he gave him a couple of po-po [cakes] to eat, but, on the following day, he saw they remained uneaten; he asked why, and the boy replied that he was waiting for an opportunity to take them to his "Ma-ma". This showed the boy's stuff; & Häng kept him by him. At Canton Sung discovered his father after nearly twenty years of separation, caused originally by the old gentleman's taking a second wife whose children & self became the pets; the old man was in some yamen as a writer, & had got on in the world. When Canton was bombarded, Sung had stood by Häng's effects in the Yamen, & was assisted by the [characters for *Ch'ing-ping*; Ch'ing troops] whose wives & families Hang had for days been feeding (so says H.); & got everything safely placed. Then when Häng was kept in durance, in the Footae's Yamên, Sung did not run away like the others, but stood by his master, who consequently swore eternal gratitude & "put it on paper". Sung wd. never go to the flower-boats or to any of the places of dissipation. He now manages at the Tsung Wän mên, and his father is in charge of one of Häng's pawn-shops. Such is the history of a good-boy, in China.[113]

Häng is anxious about two things: Chaouchow, & Teen tetuh, who still is at large in SzeChen, & does what he likes. The English, he fears, will take up the one, & the French the other question. He thinks that if he were Leang Kwang Tsung-tuh [Governor General of Liang Kwang], or Sze cheun Chetae [Governor General of Szechwan] he cd. settle either question, for, as Tung tells him, he has a "nice discrimination" (che King-chung).[114]

The Prince says I must not think of going away yet: & they all evidently wish me to prolong my stay as long as [*sic*] A-tajin's arrival as may possibly be done. I think I shall have to take up my quarters here for good, & Wade tells me that the feeling towards me at all the Legations is so good that he thinks I can do so without endangering any interests. Nous verrons![115]

Why not send one of the Keang Soo drilled brigades to garrison ChaouChow foo, and another to Sze Chuen to make Teen tetuh move on?[116]

THURSDAY, 28 SEPTEMBER 1865: Col. Kirkham called this afternoon. He is on his way to the Great Wall, to get a brick sent home! He was wounded in the Crimea, was shut up for four months in Lucknow, has a bullet in the head, a hole through the right shoulder blade, & has been in 61 engagements! He has been offered $200 a month to drill troops for Tsung How at Takoo, but objects to his pay being cut down. He says he drew Tls 400 a month for 4 years. He certainly behaved well under Gordon, & deserves well of the govt.; but with such an ungrateful set as Chinese officials are, I fear he can expect nothing. He talks freely, and means well; still, brave as he is, he has neither education nor knowledge. I advise him if hard up to close with Tsung How; he says he's not hard up, & can settle in New Zealand — I advise him to do so. I'll try Wänseang about him when he comes back.[117]

Rain again, but not so cold.

SUNDAY, 1 OCTOBER 1865: [characters for 12th day of the 8th lunar month]

Cold & raw.

MONDAY, 2 OCTOBER 1865: Tsae Laou-Yay called this morning; to all I said he replied, "Don't be frightening me! What are we to do? We have sent off despatch after despatch, and Edict after Edict has been signed!" All I cd. say was, that what he said only made it more apparent that the central govt., however willing to observe good faith towards foreigners, has not the power to compel officials in the provinces to observe the treaties. He tells me a despatch was yesterday recd. from Mr. Wade about Crane, the man seized with Burgevine, demanded unsuccessfully by Hewlett at Foo-Chow, & (said to have been) drowned in Chekiang: in this, says Tsae, our great man Tso tsung-tang is the offender![118]

The Newchwang Wei yuen [deputy] Chang, with his taels 15000, has not yet arrived, although he started two months ago; it is feared the Ke-ma-tseih [mounted bandits] have made him their prey.[119]

Mr. Wade has read my "Fleet scheme; Memo" & says all, whose opinions I value, hold me quite blameless, and innocent of scheming against Lay, &c. &c. &c.

TUESDAY, 3 OCTOBER 1865: M. de Kindt, the Belgian Envoy, called this morning. He hopes to leave Peking in a fortnight with or without a treaty; the only point about which he has any difficulty is the Consular Article; the Chinese don't want mercantile consuls, & he had special instructions on his head, — the 'Bols Treaty' having been rejected inasmuch as he had bound the govt. to appoint paid consuls. I tell him that on the general question my opinion is that of the Chinese; further, 1°. that in 1858, before I joined the Customs, the Chinese had written to Lord Elgin, Baron Gros, and Mr. Reed on this very point, and that Mr. Reed had promised on the part of his govt. that no mercantile consuls shd. be appointed — a promise never carried out, & pronounced by another Minister Mr. Burlingame to be valueless; 2°. that in the Portuguese Treaty, Mr. Guimares promised to appoint paid consuls, &c., and that the first thing he did was, as soon as the treaty was signed, to appoint Hanna at Teentsin, while a few months afterwards a Royal Decree appointed Henry Dent Consul General: again I explained the reasons which led the Chinese to object to mercantile consuls, which are 1°. that, in view of the exterritorial concession, the Consular office carries with it great power, &c., but that none of the mercantile consuls have the powers requisite, and 2°. that officials in China give an official status to all connected with or employed by them of a kind which makes such connections or employees able to do many things that it wd. be better they did not do — instancing compradoric interpreting, &c.[120]

WEDNESDAY, 4 OCTOBER 1865: [characters for 15th day of the 8th lunar month]
Call from Mr. Vlangaly.
Chinese jugglers; the ventriloquist's imitation of insects very good.

THURSDAY, 5 OCTOBER 1865: Called at the Yamên, & had an hour's talk with Tung, to whom I handed my shin-chin [report] proposing that the Chinese be allowed to own vessels of the foreign class. I also suggested to him to yield the "mercantile consul" point in the Belgian Treaty, and to stipulate for the right to buy arms, &c.[121]
WänSeang got back yesterday, but, news of the death of his wife at Moukden having arrived, he will take a few days mourning-leave before he can be again seen. Mails of 28 July & 4 August arrived. Andrew Happer was at Ravarnette when Capri [?] wrote.
Dined at the Russian legation, where I met all the ministers: some 16 or 18 sat down.
Very fine weather.

SUNDAY, 8 OCTOBER 1865: Dined with Wade; found Mongan & his wife there. In time, she'll be a chubby red-cheeked old love of a lady!
A curious rumor here; that under Guierry's teaching I became a Roman Catholic at Ningpo, & was afterwards influenced to "revert" by Mr. Gray at Canton![122]
Kopsch arrived this evening, & with him came Dep. Com. Brown, who is taking his months' leave.[123]

WEDNESDAY, 11 OCTOBER 1865: Went to the Yamen at one, having received a message to say that I was wanted. Found Tung, who wished me to look through a bundle of despatches recd. from Wade having reference to A/. damage occasioned to property at Hankow and Kiukiang by Braves, B/. non-surrender of Crane, when demanded by the Consul, C/. "Vivid" case, D/. ships not allowed to land at Taewan, E/. Baldwin, & F/. last murder at Chinkiang. Wade's demand for compensation must, I said, be attended to, as the damage had been done by employees of govt. whose duty it was to protect, & not to injure, British property.

I talkd into Tung my 'Bystander's View': Paou sat listening, & he had an opportunity of hearing matters handled in a way that he had never met with before. I hope I did him good. He said, "O for an Emperor like Kang He, & for such statesmen as Le teen, &c. &c. He also said that the Prince must be for many years to come at the hand of the young Emperor to talk matters into him, & to keep things straight; that WänSeang has not the pluck he used to have, &c. Referring to my Canton Memo, they said it ought to be acted upon; it seems nine out of ten are in favor it it, but they think the Prince will "funk" the non-approval of the tenth. Tung, however, says it is time to act. The old T. really seems to be getting out of his bookish chrysallis, & is taking a more determined tone than he used to; I shd. not be surprised were he to become the leading man in foreign matters soon.[124]

THURSDAY, 12 OCTOBER 1865: Boyd from Amoy took breakfast with me.[125]

FRIDAY, 13 OCTOBER 1865: Tung called, & left the "Crane" despatch with me; I think I can improve portions of it. I showed him my "P'ang-Kwan che Lun" [Bystander's View] in draft; he seemed much struck with it. He said it wd. offend some, & wd. excite suspicion; but he advised me to hand it in notwithstanding. In it I preach, on the foreign question, Audience, Embassies, & free permission for investment of foreign capital — going on the text that what ought to be yielded, ought to be yielded at once, & that what people will ask for & demand ought to be dealt with initiatively.

In Chinese matters, I advise more determination at the head of affairs, & doing away with obsolete rules; the payment of officials, & general reorganization.

Tung said a Soo Chow man named Fung has been making suggestions of much the same kind lately.

Called on Le Main, de Billagnet, and Bismark: chatted with Wade and Brown.[126]

SATURDAY, 14 OCTOBER 1865: Strolled into the Yamen after four, & found the place in a bustle, M. de Kindt being there "negotiating" his treaty, & fighting the consular section!

Tung came out & I handed him the Crane despatch, & a letter from Tsung How with the translation of Brown's Cavalry Memo. He then left me,

& Paou took his place: Tung had evidently been telling him of the memo I showed him yesterday, & he talked in a way that leads me to think they commence to realize their position. This in itself is an immense step.

SUNDAY, 15 OCTOBER 1865: [characters for the 26th day of the 8th lunar month]

How the time flies past! I have now been sixteen weeks here, and the day of my departure still seems uncertain. I don't think my time has been wasted, for I commence to see that what I have been saying & writing for years back is taking effect, & that the sluggish minds of the big men are being stirred up. If they can only be got to act!—but as Paou said last night, there are so many difficulties on all sides! Well: we'll see; but I do think we are on the eve of a change in China.

China is a veritable Lough Neagh. At the outset its rules, formulae, morality, &c. &c. &c., were of a kind to which the most flourishing of modern states only arrived a few tens of years ago; but everything became petrified, and, now to mend, one must break. Other countries have been going ahead, & China has been going back; if we can only get a fresh start out of the old dame, what may she not be among the nations![127]

MONDAY, 16 OCTOBER 1865: The "fat is on the fire" with a vengeance!

Man dined last night at the French Legation, where news had just arrived of the murder of the Roman Catholic Vicar-general of SzeChuen. De Bellonnet is furious, & swears, if the Chinese don't come down to terms within so many days, he will put the affair in the hands of the Admiral, and blow the town to pieces, cost what it may![128]

They'll believe my Memo now: that's evident.

*   *   *

Last night dreamt about the Crosslie family again. Very odd this!

*   *   *

TUESDAY, 17 OCTOBER 1865: Took my [characters for *Chü-wai p'ang-kuan chih lun*; "Bystander's View"] to the Yamen today, & handed it to Paou. It is evidently likely to create a sensation. He & Tung will be affected by it, I hope.

THURSDAY, 18 OCTOBER 1865: [*sic*] Sent for; on going to the Yamen, found that Häng & Tung wanted me to show me [*sic*] a couple of Edicts just issued, the one ordering the Szechuen authorities to go into the last murder case without delay; the other directing Juy Ling, gov. genl. of the Two Kwang, to proceed in person to Swatow (ChaouChow) and settle the right of entry question.[129]

So far, so good; but they want to cure sores and refrain from physic. I noticed Häng had made a note of one sentence from my Memo, "What you ought to do, or what you are asked to do, twd. be much better for you to act at once without waiting until compelled to act."

SUNDAY, 22 OCTOBER 1865: [characters for the 3rd day of the 9th lunar month]

I have finished my reports on the Yamen of what I think ought to be done in the "Vivid" & "Mercury" cases. WänSeang has not come out yet; but indeed, just now, he is not atall missed, & affairs go on well enough — if not better — without him.

Hängke sent Senor de Mas a dinner some days ago; the senor thought it was an invitation to dinner, & at the time he supposed indicated went with Fontainer to Häng's house, where, of course, he found no dinner prepared, and was merely handed a cup of tea. Häng's son & heir was then produced, who, the moment he saw de Mas, cried out "Kwei-tsze [devil]!" De Mas then asked for a female kitten, attempting himself to speak Chinese, but Häng looked as if he thought he was being asked for his new-urh [daughter]! Delightful all through! Especially that in the house of the Foreign Minister, who tries to do the "soothing" the Treaty powers with his presents of fruits & cakes, the children shd. learn to speak of foreigners as 'devils': it is too good![130]

Yesterday Detring arrived, covered with boils; he seems a pleasant, intelligent young fellow; but he lisps somewhat, & will always speak Chinese with an accent.[131]

I walked down to Wade's yesterday evening, & went through the Coolie Regulations with him. Came back quite weak & faint.

Brown left yesterday for S'hai: Dep. Com.

Very fine weather, bracing & not too cold.

MONDAY, 23 OCTOBER 1865: Went to the Yamen at two, and found that Wänseang had just gone to the Shin-ke ying [characters for Shen-chi ying; Peking Field Force]. Sat with Tung & Paou till half past four. Handed in my despatches relative to Joint Tribunal. "Vivid," & "Mercury": the latter two, — the last more especially, — pleased old Tung: I myself think it a very telling argument. Paou commences to take more interest in foreign matters than he did before, and always comes out now when I am at the Yamen. I told him the story of de Mas' visit to Hängke, which amused him highly. I did so, because I wanted to remark on the impropriety of children being taught to call foreigners "Kwei-tsze [devils]". Sd. old Paou: "Every one must submit to be nick-named: the Chinese call us 'Saou ta tsze' (stinking Tartars), we call them 'Han Man tsze' [space but no characters; southern barbarians of Han] and you in turn —" "are Yang Kwei-tze [foreign devils]" said I, bowing.[132]

Proposed to send Cartwright to Swatow to be at hand to act as Interpreter for Juy Chung-tang, when seeing & dealing with the Consuls: they approve of the suggestion: I also proposed that White shd. be sent from Kiu-keang to Kang-chou-foo to escort Mansfield to the former place: about this they will think.[133]

Wang Chaou-Ke, the Censor, is likely to come to grief; he has been too officious of late, & they have found a weak point in his armour,—so, now he'll get it![134]

TUESDAY, 24 OCTOBER 1865: WanSeang wishes to "Kaou-Kea" [ask for a leave of absence] to see his mother, etc. Paou says 'What shall we do to retain him?' I say, 'Better let him go for a while; he'll come back refreshed; otherwise you'll do him up in a few years.'[135]

The Kung Poo [Board of Works] is busily occupied with the repair of the roads: it is quite uncertain by what route His Majesty will leave the city when proceeding to complete the funeral ceremonies for his father on the 5th Nov. The repairs are all for show; they are merely throw[ing] soft stuff into the holes, so as to make all look flat: O for a Chinese Mac Adam![136]

Wan Seang does not go out with the Emperor this time; he is retained at P'king to attend to business. Tung says it's an excessively wearisome job to receive visits of condolence, for the visitor kneels & knocks head thrice, and the visited must do likewise. A host of visitors must therefore try a man's loins [?] considerably.

I cannot make up my mind as to whether I ought, or ought not, to take up my quarters permanently in Peking. Personally if all went well, I shd. be a gainer: and fitting [?] if all went well, public affairs wd. too; but if aught shd. go wrong, personally I might suffer; and with me the Service might suffer too—although public affairs cd. not receive special damage. A residence at S'hae with the obligation to come to P'King each summer, has its inconveniences; at the same time, to reside constantly at Peking wd. be dull enough too. Wade is in favour of my staying here: I myself don't like to stay, and I shd. like to stay—so the best thing I can do is to say nothing, & just leave it to the Yamên to decide.

Detring arrived on Saturday: he seems an intelligent man, but as he lisps, I doubt he will speak Chinese very clearly. Letters from Porter at Amoy are very satisfactory: what a pity he has not learnt Chinese! Lord & Kleczkowsky are squabbling: the latter put public funds out to interest, & now takes Lord to task for not placing the interest to audit of his private account![137]

Wrote to Mr. Martin today promising to subscribe for three years more to the Chung-Shih Kwan; if the school seems promising then, I shall continue the subscription; if it does not hold out promise of future success, I shall withdraw my support.[138]

Dull morning: & thanks to a bit of a cheroot after breakfast, I have an incipient headache!

WEDNESDAY, 25 OCTOBER 1865: Raining and blowing. Went to the Yamen at 3, and remained there till 5 with WänSeang. He looks thin and worn and his features have sharpened in a peculiar way. He is anxious about the following matters: Transit Dues at Newchwang, Cavalry Drill at Teentsin, and Embassy-affairs. He grows more conservative daily, or, rather, he shows a disinclination to try any experiments, and he is elaborately minute about trifles.

The only important decisions arrived at are that White shall be sent to Kanchow to escort Mansfield to Kiukiang, Cartwright to Canton to accompany Juy-lin to ChaouChow as interpreter, and myself to make Peking my home.

Wade's reply in the "St. Jean" case has come in; he does not sustain the appellant, & thus decides in our favor; he made a mistake, however, in pitching into Kwang at such length, & has rather interested the Yamen in the lout's behalf than otherwise.

About the right to own ships of a foreign class, Wan agrees to arrange matter: they are to pay duties at our offices, but in accordance with the Chinese tariff, and in this way, as Wän said, we shall quietly do away with the old offices and their dishonesty.

THURSDAY, 26 OCTOBER 1865: A tremendous gale last night; I at times thought it would have carried the house away: shouldn't like to have been steaming up the coast! This morning, the sun shines but the wind still blows, and the cold is sharp and keen.

Calls today from Brown, Glinka, Wade. Glinka is appointed to Lisbon. With Wade I walked out; I told him I considered the Chinese Shipping business almost settled—that I am desired to remain during the winter to prepare for the Chinese who are to go to Europe in the spring, &c. &c. With all of which news, he is immoderately delighted.[139]

The Yamen's despatch directing Act^g Com. White to go to KanChow to bring Mansfield to KiuKiang, came in: as did also, the note of introduction which Cartwright is to take with him to Juy Chung-tang.

FRIDAY, 27 OCTOBER 1865: Invested today in a pair of Chinese Boots, lined with flannel chih-jung, and wolf-skin, and lang-p'e: I find my feet much warmer. Strange to say, while my feet & hands are cold I perspire among the roots of my hair, as though I had been eating Cayenne Pepper![140]

Wade came up to dinner. He likes my lun [essay], & has made it the subject of a laudatory despatch to Lord Russell: when Mitford copied the despatch, he said to Wade, "one ought to take service under him"—meaning me—which Wade retailed to me as being a compliment. Provided I can do the work I have in view, I don't care whether I'm praised or not.[141]

SATURDAY, 28 OCTOBER 1865: Again a success: at the Yamên today, they returned to me my lun asking me to make a few changes in it, where it is not quite intelligible; the reason for doing this is that it is about to be sent to the people outside—i.e. the Tuh Foo [Governors General and Governors], &c. &c. &c., for their edification & criticism—the object in view being to let the outsiders see that the Yamen has great responsibilities on its shoulders, & that while it does not shrink, they must not make its tasks more difficult by interference, &c. Hurrah! I presume it will go out by Edict: at all events, here I am being made use of to aid the progressionists in China! I hope they may not astutely make me their dupe![142]

I had to look through a lot of despatches today: the Confirmation investigation rules, Coolie Emigration regulations, & Chinese Shipping arrangements bid fair to be put through satisfactorily.

It is decided that I am to make Peking my head-quarters, & with the Prince's devoted approbation. Lay asked to be allowed to reside here; he did not get on well, & I am ordered to stay at S'Hae: they have now had two years experience of me & my ways, & they have ordered me—somewhat against my will—to take up my residence here! I must not be cock-ahoop. The fact is, the greater my success, the more humble & the more careful I become, lest it shd. be found out how weak & stupid I really am!

SUNDAY, 29 OCTOBER 1865: Went to the Yamen at 1 and remained there till 3. Wan is quite 'daft' in respect of Transit Dues at Newchwang: I show him that to impose them will give no advantages to junks & that they will always be paid by Chinese, but he says "no matter, he is bent upon their collection." Corrected Vivid, Mercury & Investigation despatches.

Called on Glinka & the Prussian students: talked half an hour with Wade, who is mad for philology, but, at the same time, naturally does not like the idea of giving up the reins to another man at the moment affairs seem likely to take a turn for the better. We both fear that Sir Ruth[d] will try to help me; I shd. much rather he went dead against me instead.[143]

O. Brown arrived from Teentsin this evening.

MONDAY, 30 OCTOBER 1865: At the Yamen from 4 @ 5 1/2; took O. Brown there and introduced him to Wan, Tung, & Chung. Handed back de B.'s Loan memorandum & also notes on Coolie Rules: gave Wan the Macao tax memo: read over & corrected the Newchwang [characters for tzu-k'ou; sub-station] arrangement. Glad to say, Wän gives up the idea of pressing for Opium 1/2 duty at time of payment of [characters for cheng-shui; regular duty]. Noticed a general flutter round the table when I said that the [characters for tzu-k'ou pan-fa; management of sub-station] wd. not affect foreigners atall, & that it was only putting an additional tax on Junks &c.[144]

Found Wade waiting for me; he has taken back his Wusueh despatch & Investigative Rules for correction. He is savage with the Yamen for demanding the sending back of the Junk: I told him, I had advised it. He thinks my advice wrong. God help China! When others do wrong, they say it matters not for China is not in a position to enforce her rights; and when China seems to be wrong, no allowance is made for her many difficulties.[145]

TUESDAY, 31 OCTOBER 1865: [characters for the 12th day of the 9th lunar month]

Called on Morrison, de Billagnet [sic], Williams, Vlangaly, de Rehfues, & Wade. Did not see V., but de B. & de R. professed to be glad that I am to winter here.[146]

Tomorrow I start for S'hae. My journal must remain as it is till I come back. Goodbye "Stoopid"! R.H.

Resumed 1st Dec. [characters for the 14th day of the 10th lunar month]

1 NOVEMBER 1865: Left Peking by cart at noon: slept at Chang Kea Wan.

2 NOVEMBER 1865: Slept at Yangtsun.

3 NOVEMBER 1865: Arrived at Teentsin at 11; called on Tsung How at 2 and asked him to write to the Yamen to chaou-huang [communicate with] Wade relative to O. Brown & Lovatt as instructors for the cavalry. Went on board the "Nanzing" at 9 P.M. Arranged for Thornton's lot.[147]

4 NOVEMBER 1865: Left at daylight.

5 NOVEMBER 1865: At Chefoo at noon. Went to Larson's. Saw Drew (Edward B.); he seems a sharp fellow, but is not so polished as Taintor & Woodruff.

After dinner Pwan Ta-jin came in, but he had nothing important to say.[148]

6 NOVEMBER 1865: Blowing a gale: business impossible: had to get up steam & cross to the other side to take shelter; landed there with Tallock & Russell, & walked to the top of the hill.

7 NOVEMBER 1865: Left Chefoo at 10 1/2: Wm. Lay passenger with Cartwright & myself. A Chinese merchant from Newchwang, Tihshing, who called on me when there last year, told me he had loaded over 70 ships & paid 50,000 Tls. duty this year.[149]

8 NOVEMBER 1865: Blowing hard.

9 NOVEMBER 1865: Noon. Arrived at S'hae: put up Lay at my house which, with new furniture &c. looks uncommonly smart. Astonishing apparition of Simpson & Shee (who seems a bright smart youth) in white hats.[150]

10, 11, 12, 13 NOVEMBER 1865: Very busy packing: not a moment to spare. Have arranged with Forbes that he is to be my agent in England with £1000 a year for three years.

On the afternoon of the 13th, Monday, I found that I shd. have to start on the 14th by the 'Gerard': made arrangements to do so. Giquel then said he must now tell me in haste what he had intended to talk about at leisure: he wanted to know when I could accept his resignation, as he wished to take service with Tso Chetae, in company with d'Aiguebille, to superintend a Naval School, Dockyard, Foundry, & Mint: he showed me their proposed rules, sd. all employed were to be French, & that the Emperor had told d'Aiguebille to go ahead and assured him of support. I was rather taken aback, & said that I thought he had been wanting in his duty to me to keep me in the dark so long, and stated that it wd. be better for him to carry out his views in connexion with, than apart from, the Customs. He said he objected to being checked & trammeled by me and evidently wished to start on an independent career. He, however, remarked that he did not object to a position under me, but that d'Aiguebille would be sure to do so. Matters are not yet settled, he says: Tso is determined to carry out his plans, & if not through Giquel, then through another person; Giquel wants of course to get the thing into his own hands, but will not accept employment except under an Edict.[151]

From this must date a new phase in the Customs, and I must have all my wits about me to retain my hold of the reins: more care, more anxiety!

I promised to write from Teentsin. The only settlement we arrived at was that Giquel wd. not think of leaving us until March next, & that he wd. withdraw from the project & leave d'Aiguebille to carry it out alone if I did not consent to act with them. We can only await the upshot. If Tso memorializes, Wan & the others may throw me over.[152]

The Customs' Volunteer Artillery turns out very well, but its drill is far from what it ought to be. Introduced to Sir E. Hornby at the Review: he seems a fine manly sort of person. Old Winchester, as fat as, but looking healthier than, ever. Saw Miss Billsland in one of the streets looking uncommonly fresh & pretty. Call from Mr. Bremier who said he quite understood my position, & that M. Lefevour, "poor young man", wd. not trouble me long, being unwell.[153]

TUESDAY, 14 NOVEMBER 1865: Left, S'hae in the "Gerard" bound for Newchwang & then Teentsin: four Dutch priests, a lay brother, and three other passengers.

From S'Hae I sent a loan (or present) of £1000 to Mary, with £250 to father, £100 to Jamie, & £100 to Geoffrey for the girls: also £200 on my private a/c (N°. 1) to Smith Elder & Co. & £3000 on public a/c (N°. 2) to the same firm.[154]

SATURDAY, 18 NOVEMBER 1865: [*sic*] After a tremendous blow, and a horrible attack of seasickness arrived at Chefoo and found the 'Nanzing' just about to start to Teentsin: at once transshipped, & started in her. How clean & comfortable she is in comparison with the "Gerard", & what a splendid table they keep!

SUNDAY, 19 NOVEMBER 1865: [characters for 1st day of the 10th lunar month]
Arrived at Takoo, meeting the "Ying tsze-fei" (with M. Kindt, Blackmon, & May) on the bar going out. The wei-yuan [deputy], Kwan, came on board to see me.[155]

MONDAY, 20 NOVEMBER 1865: From Takoo to Teentsin by cart, arriving at six P.M. My driver seemed half mad, & did each stage (20 miles) in three hours: I never got such a jolting, & never was conscious before of so many bones in my body.

TUESDAY, 21 NOVEMBER 1865: Called on Meadows, & Mongan: saw Sir R. Alcock & family. Miss, not so pretty as I expected to find her, but sprightly & unaffected; madame very pompous, and H.E. not quite so strong I think as he used to be. They were both very anxious about their dear George (to whom, by the way, I lent Tls. 800 to keep him out of Court at Shanghae & for which he said he <u>need</u> not think of applying to his own friends), asking why he had not recd. an increase in pay, &c. &c. &c., and rather bothering me about him before a lot of other people. Sir R.'s first question was: why is not George promoted? second, why do you not bring him to Peking? third (my answers to first & second not having been satisfactory) how do you get on with the Chinese? and (when I said satisfactorily) he ended by warning me that I must remember "the system is still on its trial yet". Not an easy game to play, I see: but I must keep my temper & go along quietly & cautiously.[156]
At 4 had a call from Tsung How, in return for my visit when on my way to Shanghae. He sat for an hour, but had nothing particular to say.
Dined at Mongan's & took Miss L. in to dinner.[157]

WEDNESDAY, 22 NOVEMBER 1865: Walked up to town, joining Sir R. A. on the road, and found [word unclear] Mackey living in a Chinese inn opposite an old house. He looked very miserable, & was pegging [?] into Morrison's dictionary & Wade's books. I asked him, wd. he take the Tung-Wän-Kuan mastership for £100 a year, but he declined.[158]

THURSDAY, 23 NOVEMBER 1865: Left Teentsin about noon, on my new pony "Gobi" a capital mount, for which I have paid only $60. Light rain. Slept at Yangtsun.

FRIDAY, 24 NOVEMBER 1865: Started at 1/2 p. 4 a.m.; cold blowy day: slept at Chang Kea Wan. Met a Russian Engineer Officer (Col. Brown at Hosewoo).

SATURDAY, 25 NOVEMBER 1865: [characters for the 7th day of the 10th lunar month] Arrived at my house at 1/2 past nine: very early from Chang Kea Wan.
Went to the Yamen at 2, & saw Tung, Tsung, and the new Minister, Seu Ke-yu (formerly Gov. of Fuhkeen, degraded for making a geography & now 71 years of age), who was then to receive a visit from Dr. Williams whom I also sat [saw?] with Martin, and whose Chinese is execrable.[159]

SUNDAY, 26 NOVEMBER 1865: Sent for by Wan. Tung called & then Wade at noon. Wade is furious about my advice in the 'Vivid' case. When I went to the Yamen, I found Wade there with Wan; soon after he left, Brown came in about a servant at the Legation whom the Yamen wished to arrest for a row at a Bank. I thus did not get much talk with Wan. Late in the evening, Brown came to my place, & I talked over Giquel's present position with him.[160]

MONDAY, 27 NOVEMBER 1865: Writing despatches relative to service arrangements, & trying to collect my wits, which have been almost shaken out of me by the hurry-skurry of this month.

TUESDAY, 28 NOVEMBER 1865: A call from Häng Ke, who told me with great glee that his daughter is at last betrothed to one of the Teih-mao-wang [Iron-Capped Princes] — the young Shun-ching Keun-wang: the lady is 24, the groom is 22 & has been once married but is now a widower without children. "They will not be rich," says Hang, "but she will not be troubled with a mother-in-law, or step-children, or sisters-in-law; & his position will keep him from dissipation & all disgraceful conduct." He then asked me to go to the Yamen at once where I was wanted to be at the examination of the boys. At noon I went; he was not there, and the others said they did not require me.[161]

WEDNESDAY, 29 NOVEMBER 1865: Occupied all day, writing & copying my letter to Giquel. Sir R. Alcock arrived.

THURSDAY, 30 NOVEMBER 1865: Last night, without wind, fell two inches of snow: not atall cold. Busy with my letters, &c., which I despatched in the afternoon: the last batch I intend to send by sea to Teentsin this year. Sir R. Alcock arrived at Peking.

FRIDAY, 1 DECEMBER 1865: [characters for the 14th day of the 10th lunar month]
Breakfasted at the Yamen by invitation: took Kopsch with me. Looked at the translations of the English Class, & selected n°s. 1, 2, and 3; but we don't yet know their names. My head aches, & my face burns.

SATURDAY, 2 DECEMBER 1865: Such beautiful weather, as we have had during the last three days I have never before known. The snow swept off the paths still remains unthawed; the air is motionless; by day the sun shines warmly down from a high blue sky, & by night the moon (now full) sails through an equally quiet, & one-tinted heaven. It is not atall cold, & it is a pleasure to breathe the air. The drawback is, that the stenches along all the roads are more disgustingly strong than in summer.
Wade came in this afternoon, and I walked out with him. I told him about Giquel, &c., and hinted at an Inspectorship of Literary Establishments: he does not view it unfavorably, but it is a difficult thing for me to ask an ex-charge d'affairs to take service under me. But we understand each other, & I hope good will come of it.[162]
Note from Baker this morning, telling me the "Corea" arrived at Takoo (on Thursday).

SUNDAY, 17 DECEMBER 1865: During the past fortnight, nothing of importance has occurred. I have had visits from Tung, Häng, & Tsung, and have been twice to the Yamen; no work has been done, & matters seem to be going along pleasantly.
A couple of days after Sir. R. Alcock's arrival, the news came that Caine, the Consul, had been to ChaouChow foo, and had there passed three days in the Taoutae's Yamen as an official guest: thus the right of entry question

335

is in a fair way of being settled, & England, at all events, is not likely to find reason for pitching again into China. I have met Sir R. twice at dinner, & he has personally been exceedingly kind, and, as regards public matters, seems well-disposed.

I don't know what to think of the young lady. She is very pretty, & frank in manner; but whether there is anything in her or not, I cannot yet say, although I have thrice taken her in to dinner. I have half inclined, however, to look in that direction for a wife.

A few days ago had calls from H. H. Vlangaly, de Rehfues, & Sir Rutherford: all came in together, and, for the moment, the meeting of ministers seemed quite portentous.

WanSeang has got three months' leave, & is about to go to Moukden to bring his mother to Peking. I am sorry he goes away now, for he is not likely to be back before I start for home, and, in his absence, many things that might otherwise have been attended to, must, I fear, be left alone.

I have been working at Chinese during the last fortnight, &, though at first I found the <u>tonic</u> exercises difficult, I now commence to see my way. My teacher Hwang does not talk much unfortunately. How sad that at my age, and after having done so much work in China, I shd. have to begin, in this way, at the beginning! Unfortunately I made a wrong start at Ningpo, & that has ever been against me; I must now try to make up for it "by toiling upwards in the night".[163]

Häng Ke's brother has got the acting appointment of Keentuh [Superintendent] at Sha-hoo-kwan. Quite in luck in his old age![164]

Took the 20th quarter's a/c to the Yamen yesterday, where I saw Tung & Hang. The Russian Tonnage Dues' despatch is still unanswered: I advise them to yield without further asking.

Splendid weather! The thermometer has been down to 18° Fahrenheit, &, strange to say, the cold has not affected me late. I never felt in better health!

Brown is now in charge at Teentsin, Baker having gone for 3 mos. leave to Ceylon. He acted on the Baron de Rehfues' request for the Prussian Consul the other day, & settled the matter satisfactorily.[165]

FRIDAY, 22 DECEMBER 1865: [characters for the 5th day of the 11th lunar month] <u>Tung-chih</u> Yesterday I breakfasted at the Yamen, where I was busily employed from 10 @ 6., Wan, Pao, Tung, & Chung being present.

A. Chinese are to be allowed to own ships of the foreign class, but the rules must come from without.

B. Coolie Emigration Rules to be settled.

C. Tls. 1500 to be allowed monthly for Niuchuang.

D. Tls 7500 . . . for building at Tientsing.

E. T'ung Wen Kuan: 3 or 4 teachers to be employed by me, to be paid from Customs, & to be provided quarters by the Yamen.[166]

F. Uniforms to be fixed for the service.

G. No acting Inspector General to be appointed during my absence: Commissioners in S'hae & T'tsing to manage the two divisions [characters for *Pei-nan ko-yang*; north-south, each sea][167] Giquel ⎫
H. Commissioners recommended in following order Dick ⎬ MackPherson & de Meritens. ⎭

 I. Embassy & Audience: people will be sent to Europe without delay, & if audience can be arranged so as to meet Chinese views, it will be granted.

 J. At home I am to make all sorts of enquiries about manufacturing apparatus, & people [word unclear] to superintend such establishments.

K. If I marry my wife may go about in a chair.

L. Paou wants to borrow tls 20.000.000: The Hu Pu [Board of Revenue] will memorialise to request the Yamen to be directed to consult with me, & the Edict will then appoint me to manage the Loan, &c. Paou is very anxious about this matter: he says affairs in Kansuh & Yun-Kwei can scarcely go on much longer without fresh funds. Tsang Kwo fan & Yang are to be asked if they have <u>pa-wuh</u> [a grip on things]: i.e. if they can finish matters with the amounts stated. They returned to me to be again read de Bellonet's loan-memo, and are evidently most desirous of putting the matter through. I say, if they'll use the money well, I shall be glad to help them: otherwise, I'd rather have nothing to do with it, for, if they use it badly, worse than their now will be their then condition. If they act, it secures [?] our Institution and increases my influence, &c: I'll work a <u>She-lang</u> [Board vice-presidency] ship out of it, at the first go off.[168]

M. Juy Chung-tang memorialized on the spread of piracy: this puts the sea-police work into my hands.

N. Tso Chetae has asked for a Tsung-ping heen [brevet rank as brigade-general] for Giquel, & buttons for others, &c. &c. &c.[169]

O. The winding up of the indemnity a/c to be in accordance with my proposal: S'Hae, C'ton, F'Chow, & H'Kow to pay tls. 250 000 by the end of June 1866; the balance, if any, to be paid by S'Hae by the 30th Sept. The other ports to cease payments with this quarter.

P. Wän is very anxious about the steam-fleet money.

Q. ″ desires to send O. Brown & others to take the field against the Ke-ma-tseih [mounted bandits]. Will the British Minister allow it?[170]

R. Four months' Tonnage Dues clause: extended to ports south of Nicolaieffskey.[171]

From what precedes, it is evident that my hands are going to be very full. "Still achieving, still pursuing." The loan rather puzzles me, and, in fact, on every side I must be circumspect in an extraordinary degree.

Dined with the British students on the 19th, & at 9 P.M. went to Sir. R. Alcock. I spent a pleasant hour there, & came away somewhat smitten with Miss Amy: I <u>think</u> I like her better each time I see her — an alarming symptom.[172]

Hängke sick. To the Yamen they have added Seu-Ke-yu [blank space for characters he forgot to add], former gov. of Fuhkeen, author of the Geography;

& Tan ting hsiang [characters for T'an T'ing-hsiang] formerly, in 1858, Gov. Genl. of Chih li—both Chinese.[173]

Wade says the Spaniards will not ratify: they object to the Chinese phrase used for the Queen of Spain, & also the allowing of Chinese to go to Manilla.[174]

Sze-Chuen matters, sd. Häng the other day, look better; Ken [?] is a priest at the Capital Ching-too who speaks reasonably, and has explained matters in such a way, as to make business more easy of transaction for the future. He called him Hang.[175]

Poor FitzPatrick is dead. Died all alone in an inn near Shan-Hai-Kwan.[176]

CHRISTMAS DAY, 25 DECEMBER 1865: [characters for 8th day of the 11th lunar month]

A most lovely day. The air calm & still, the sun shining brightly out of a wondrous blue sky; the thermometer low, but the cold not penetrating.

Yesterday was at the Yamen for an hour & sent a letter through it to S'hae, asking Stewart for information about loans: ought to have an answer before the end of January. Pao is anxious about the matter, and, if they go into the scheme, I think by acting judiciously I can make it a lever to aid me in lifting other matters.

Saw a letter from de Bellonnet, which was not very intelligible but served to imply action threatened.

Dined at the French Legation last night where U.S. excepted, all the Ministers were assembled to meet Sir Rutherford. Sir R. seems aged & weary; he is not the man he was eight years ago; he's inclined to be gentle with China, thank Heaven!

M. Vlangaly tells me, his Interpreter quoted the 12th article of the Teent-sin Treaty erroneously, & that he has written to the Yamen to say that their interpretation of the "most-favored nation clause" is quite correct. That's a point in my favor.

Wade breakfasted with me yesterday morning, & I electrified him by telling him what I have in the fire with prospects of success.

Tonight I dine at the British Legation: I have been busy all morning at an English Memo for Pao of the loan scheme, in which matter I gain increasing light.

Häng Ke has taken five days' leave: poor fellow, they think he is really ill. His absence from the Yamen is, however, desirable rather than otherwise. I wish he & Chung lun were removed to make way for better men.

Heaven help me with wisdom to act aright; my responsibilities increase, and my cares too: my prayer is to be unworldly, unselfish,—to be useful to others,—to do my work honestly, well, & with all my might,—to be a model Christian, & a good man. God grant it for Christ's sake! Robert Hart.

26 DECEMBER 1865: Dined last night at the Legation. The young lady in reply to my "Many happy returns—in China" sd. "O! I hope not." Murray seems awfully smitten: I never saw a man so love-sick before. Miss L. called attention to him at dinner, & I asked how it was he was getting so thin: "O! We know!" sd. Lady A. "don't we, Amy?"[177]

28 DECEMBER 1865: Staid in till nearly five expecting Wan Seang to make his farewell visit: went out for an hour's stroll: on my return, found to my regret, that he had called during my absence.

29 DECEMBER 1865: Sent for to the Yamen today: found Pao wanted to take my idea relative to the Russian propositions respecting trade at Chang Kia Kow: looked through some correspondence. I then said I had never paid any attention to the matter & that I was not prepared, without thinking it over carefully, to say anything,—the more especially as the Land trade regulations did not concern me and I had never been to Kalgan. To Tung I pointed out that the Russian, in assigning one cause for the decrease in the trade of the Chinese merchants in a quarter, was quite right: Viz. that the bulk of the teas now went by sea & not by land. To which he replied: "There it is; we did not know that: that you can say so is one thing, shows that we are right to consult you: carefully think over the rest." I sd. to Pao: "What you want me to think out for you is a way how not to do it?" "Precisely so," replied he, "a way not to do it."[178]

As to the loan: Pao said they must borrow "either large sums or small—small ones like the tls. 300 000 loan got ready for Pwan Taoutae," sd. he, thus showing that a matter which I had only touched lightly with Wan-Seang, had got to his ears & been remembered. They are to write at once to Tsäng Kwo fan & Yang Yao-ping, & ask them if they, supplied with so much money, can bring matters to a conclusion.[179]

Seu Ke Yu was present, looking better & brighter than when I first saw him. T'an ting hsiang also there; a little dark man with black beady eyes, black moustache, black head, black dress black cap, & black looks: he resembles Ting She chang somewhat, but is somewhat bigger across. He scarcely spoke atall; but seemed all eyes & ears. What he did say was uttered very sententiously; he belched four times successively while I was talking to Pao; & I really cd. not keep my face, so laughter-provoking was the noise he made; Pao's eyes twinkled, & his grin gradually broadened.[180]

Häng & Tsung were unusually civil: the former now married: Tung had a bad cold: just made Tso-too Yu-she [Senior President of the Censorate]. His place at the Hu Pu [Board of Revenue] is filled by lately appointed Gov. of Hoopih, who is succeeded by Le Ho-neen, Fantae of Chili. Three Les now governors. A Keun Ke [Grand Councillor] Le has just died, & he too is succeeded by a Le, the Emperor's tutor, a clever man not yet forty.[181]

On the 26th the Yamen made me a present of an official costume: I intend to don it one of these days, hat & all.

31 DECEMBER 1865: [characters for 14th day of the 11th lunar month]

The last day of 1865: Went to Wan Seang's to say good-bye: he was not at home, so I left a goodbye letter, with a pipe & a pencil as farewell presents. His house seems a very small one & is in a very small lane, indeed.

Most glorious weather: blue sky & no wind. In 1854 the 31st Dec. was also on a Sunday.

My Loan Memo for Pao has been put into Chinese; if they negotiate a foreign loan, it will bind China to foreign countries very effectually.

Have just read through the Russian Land Route despatches: I think them just. Unfortunately, China & Russia are such near neighbours, & Russian projects have so long been looked on suspiciously, that one cannot divine what second step may follow a first in any direction. The Russian can take what the Chinese refuse to grant? Will a refusal provoke him to take it? Is the matter really worth arguing about — worth refusing?

MONDAY, 1 JANUARY 1866: [characters for 15th day of the 11th month of the 4th year of the T'ung-chih reign]

Had a message last night from WanSeang asking me not to go out today, as he intended to call: staid in all day, & thus paid no New Year's visits. Wan did not come, but sent a kind letter & some presents.

Last night saw the old year out and the new one in, at Sir Rutherford's. Cannot make up my mind about the young lady: Everytime I see her, I like her better. But I doubt whether we wd. suit each other, and I must therefore avoid haste & be prudent.

2 JANUARY 1866: A call from Häng Ke, who pitched into Wan-Seang, who he says goes to Manchuria to put down the Ke-ma-tsieh, and did not like to tell [?] the Legations. He says the new Keun Ke [Grand Counciller], Le Hung Tsaou, the Emperor's tutor, is one of the Hans [Chinese] who think the Man [Manchus] truckle to the Yang [foreigners]; that the Han have regular Hwuy [associations] in the Chinese city, when they discuss govt. affairs, and that Le, an influence in these meetings, is dragged into the Keun Ke in order that he may, & others through him, understand the importance & difficulties of the foreign question.[182]

WEDNESDAY, 3 JANUARY 1866: At the Yamen with T'an alone, & then with Pao, & Häng.

T'an is retrograde decidedly: he is of the old school: says we must have a "heen che" or limit, — thinks foreigners have not benefited by the increase in ports, — and will evidently prove a stick-in-the-mud, if not worse. The Russian question, & the Loan were the principal matters brought forward: but really they don't seem in earnest about anything.[183]

4 JANUARY 1866: Call from Luh meng seng, who says T'an is a great talker, & a poor doer. Dined with Wade who is going in for diplomacy, & who has made up his mind to be content with subsidiary usefulness as a philologist: then went to Lady Alcock's "at home", & came away thinking Miss Amy lovelier than ever.[184]

5 JANUARY 1866: Call from Tung Ta-jen.

6 JANUARY 1866: Call from Thomas, who has just arrived from Corea where he has been wandering about along the coast the last three months. The people, he says, knew all about English doings at Takoo & Peking. He came via Newchwang, & Shan Hai Kuan, & says Manchuria is in a state of insurrection. MacPherson's letter (22 Dec) says a formidable body of mounted men, 1400 or so, is moving about & causing great alarm. Ching lin has written to Tsung How for Yang Tseang tuy [foreign-trained troops].[185]

7 JANUARY 1866: Call from Kuan Koo, the Takoo Wei Yuen [deputy]. He says 500 Yang tseang tuy, led by Pwan, start today from T'tsin for N'chwang. The disciplined troops commence to be appreciated.[186]

21 JANUARY 1866: [characters for 5th day of the 12th lunar month] During the fortnight I have been excessively busy, and have not visited the Yamen atall. Pao & Seu called on me a few days ago; and Tsae laou yay has been twice with me sitting & talking for hours. I am getting through my work, & hope to have everything clear for a start on the 1st March. The only thing to be recorded is that my writer Ping is not likely to go with me to England: that 'history', however, I shall reserve for entry on the day things are settled. At Lady Alcock's on Monday last, M. Vlangaly spoke to me about the telegraph, & asked my advice as to what I thought he ought to do: I sd. I was "for progress, but a Chinese agent"; I promised to take the matter up for him 'seriously' at the Yamen.[187]

As for Miss L. [Lowder] I don't know what to say: is it do I, or do I not? shall I, or shall I not? I am to dine at the Legation tonight; I shd. not be atall surprised if I were to speak in such a way, as to elicit a 'clincher' of one sort or other. I am of a "cold heart & fond [?] imagination," and could live happily with any one that did not disgust me.

Recd. my mails & letters from S'hae desp^d. 27 Dec. on the 15 inst.: despatched one mail on the 5th and another yesterday.

WEDNESDAY, 24 JANUARY 1866: [characters for 8th day of the 12th lunar month]

Today I dressed as a <u>Nee-tae</u> [provincial judicial commissioner] & went to the Yamen. The Ta-jen [high officials] put on their hats & buttons, and we drank many cups of "Hae-tsin [?]" together. All the Yamen people crowded about to see me, and respect was paid to the 'button' of a kind that showed its value.[188]

Dined at Dr. Williams': cut completely by Miss L!

SUNDAY, 28 JANUARY 1866: Went to Church this morning for the first time in Peking! Mr. Collins called a few days ago, asked why he never saw me at Church, & said that, whether I personally could do without the means of grace or not, I scarcely did my duty by others in staying away from Church, for, while I failed to set a good example, I laid myself open to misconstruction, &, if escaping that, might lead others to argue wrongly & regard attendance as unnecessary. I shall go regularly in future: God knows I am not <u>too</u> good, and I am anxious to avail myself of every means of grace! It does not do to be flippant or fallacious in what concerns one's own soul. If people, in respect of their souls, were only as practical & as much guided by common sense as they are in regard to the concerns of every day life, how differently they wd. act! But they cannot 'see' & they fail to realize the unseen. I do see a certain way, & I do to a certain extent realise the unseen: that is my faith in it is so strong, my anticipation of it so hopeful, and my attempts to prepare for it so constant (feeble though they may be), that— through Christ I look forward to a participation in "what hath not entered into heart of man to conceive" with such a feeling of certainty, that I can to a certain extent correctly say, I realize the unseen. I am conscious of innumerable imperfections, & inexplicable weaknesses: but I am also conscious of the constant desire to please God, of the continued attempt to do so, and of a growing freedom from sins which formerly held me fast; but I know well I have yet "attained", & I am determined to run as one who is "still in the race". Therefore, for the future, I shall not fail to avail myself of such aids as God has provided for me—the means of Grace which all Christians find so useful to them. In fact, my position is such that I have to be careful what example I set; for I am not only 'high up', but young, and others cannot fail to be influenced by my doings or non-doings. I pray for purity of thought, honesty of speech, uprightness of conduct: for the Christian life, both in the heart, & in the outward man; I pray to do, my duty well, industriously & with all my might, in the position of life in which Providence has placed me; and I pray, too, that my influence on others, exercised whether directly or indirectly, may be for good. God grant it!

[curlicue here]

Whether or not Pin will go with me to England has not yet been arranged; Paou is confined to the house, & until he comes out, nothing will be settled. The old man revels in the anticipation of what he'll see!

342

My report for the 5 years has been drawn up: Imports valued at tls. 240.000.000, Exports tls. 360.000.000, Balance of Trade in favor of China tls. 120.000.000: Duties of every kind from Oct 1860 @ 30 June 1865 tls. 32.260.000.

The Yamen has memorialized for the continuance of the Inspectorate, & the Emperor has sanctioned the measure.

From Kleczkowsky's letters, I hear that d'Aiguebille is the man who visited Tso Che-tae. Tso is very angry with me for sending the "Hae Ching" to Canton.[189]

Received another Mail from Shanghae on the 22nd with Shanghae Dates 5 Jan, & home no. 30 Oct. Poor Wm. Swanton died on his way to Australia, having been ordered to take a [word unclear] for his health.

The 4/10th of the duties heretofore linked [?] to the Indemnity Deduction are in future to be brought to Peking. This increase [?] will interest the central govt. in the continuance of the Inspectorate to such an extent that we may safely speculate on 50 years of existence.[190] During that time, God grant that we may do something for China! What I aim at is to open the country to access of whatever Christian civilization has added to the comforts or well being, materially or morally, of man: to give the people a just & wise govt. & to teach them to live in peace & amity with others.

The weather is astonishingly mild: people don't like it: an unhealthy spring is prognosticated.

THURSDAY, 1 FEBRUARY 1866: [characters for 16th day of the 12th lunar month]

Went to the Yamen today and handed in my Quinquennial Report. T'an attempted to compliment me on my Knowledge of Finance &c.

On the 29th arrived at Peking Stewart's reply to the letter I wrote to him about Loans on the 24th Dec. My letter left Peking on the 25th Dec. & reached Shanghae on the 3rd Jany. i.e., 9th day; his left S'hae on the 11th Jany. & arrived at Peking on the 29th. He thinks we could get money at par for 5 or 5 1/2%.

FRIDAY, 2 FEBRUARY 1866: Went to the Yamen & saw Paou, Tung, Häng, Chung, T'an, and Seu. Talked about Kiachta Telegraph, Woosung Railway, and Embassies. My visit was a special one; of late I have had to talk to them so seriously that they—the newcomers especially—might think I was in foreign & not in Chinese pay; so today I repeated all I had said before, & explained to them that as a 'middle-man' I lay myself open to misconception & illwill, whether I do a thing or don't do it, &, that I cannot do my duty by my employers satisfactorily to myself unless I say many things that must be unpalatable to them. Having said my say, I told them I shd. not again refer to the matters about which I had spoken, & shd. keep to my Customs works. I pointed to one of the [Confucian] analects, & said, "that meets my case"; "Oh no," sd. Tung "do the first half, 'faithfully admonish', but don't be guided by the second; 'if they are impracticable, stop'."[191] From today then, I can take a fresh departure, & in the future I really must be careful how I put things before them. One thing is certain: to slight one, irritates all, & strengthens the individual; to be friendly with one, please all. Hard to set [?] up to, though, more especially for an Englishman.

The Kiachta Telegraph line will I think soon be conceded; Häng said to me: <u>Ta-Ka</u> <u>puh</u> <u>näng</u> <u>puh-pan</u> [probably it cannot be avoided] — which shows a great difference in tone. I hope the Woo Sung Railway will follow suit.[192]

On Thursday night, I went to Lady Alcock's at home, & had a long talk with M. Vlangaly. ["Dined there too." written above this line]

The Repackage Regulations have got off at last.

SATURDAY, 3 FEBRUARY 1866: French Mail arrived today. From the south the news is bad; Kea-ying Chow & several places in the vicinity have been taken by the Rebels.[193]

SUNDAY, 4 FEBRUARY 1866: Went to Church today, & took the sacrament. I am determined, with God's help, <u>not</u> to go back into my old ways, and I must fortify myself against the temptations I am so soon to meet by availing myself of those means of grace which Christians use.

*   *   *

At four o'clock I went to the Yamen having been sent for by Hang. I saw Hang, Tung, Ching, & T'an. They wanted to tell me that they have arranged with the Prince that Pin shall go with me; they will make him either a <u>P'ang-pan</u> [assistant secretary] or <u>Foo-tsung pan</u> [assistant secretary-general] in the Yamen, & the Prince as chief of the F.O. will officially instruct him to proceed to Europe. The details have yet to be settled, but, step by step, the thing shakes itself into shape.[194]

T'an was pleasanter than usual; he said 'how can you expect us to consent to everything the moment you ask for it? These things are all new to us; for two or three thousand years we have been going along in China never having, never dreaming of, what now comes before us every day. You must give us time to reflect. We don't know where we are being carried; we must see our way: we must not drift. Don't take our refusal as ill nature: it is not that, — it is the novelty & difficulty of the position. You must give us time, &c. &c. &c.' All this he said very pleasantly.

Tung said that there are some <u>He-she</u> [?] in contemplation; so I presume they are going to give me the Fantae heën [brevet rank as provincial financial commissioner]. He said Paou is the originator of the idea, & that they think of calling me the tsung-le <u>shwuy-loo</u> shwuy-wuh sze [inspector-general of sea and land customs], as they think of making an arrangement by which <u>Kiakta</u> will be the land-port of Russia, & they want me to select a Commissioner for that place. More work coming evidently.[195]

344

MONDAY, 5 FEBRUARY 1866: Putting into new shape the Chinese Shipping Rules. Dined with Wade, & then went to the Students' Amateur Theatricals: "Our Wife" & "To Paris for £5": very good.

20 FEBRUARY 1866: Thirty-one today! [characters for the 6th day of the 1st lunar month] The Yamen has memorialized, & Pin & the others are appointed by Edict to go with me "to travel" You-le.[196]

FRIDAY, 2 MARCH 1866: [characters for the 16th day of the 1st lunar month]

The River has been open for some time at T'tsing, but no steamer has appeared as yet. I have not got through my work, & a hard three weeks I have had of it. A/c are all squared up, & all the Chinese & English Despatches required have been written. I have been busy literally from morning to night, & have not had a moment to spare. A sore foot has confined me to the house for ten days & more: it now gets better.

Pin has been made a Foo-tsung-pan, & has got a San pin heen [brevet third rank]: his son, with Tih-ming & Fung-yi, have got white buttons, & Yen-hwuy has got 7th rank. Hing-chwang Ying (outfit) has been found. Tls. 300 to Pin, & taels 200 to each of the others. When the Ministers called to pay the Prince the usual New Year's visit a week ago, H.E. presented Pin to each, & subsequently Häng took him round to call at the Legations. They take six servants with them; so that counting Afang, twelve Chinese, altogether, will travel with me. Bowra & De Champs will join the party at Chefoo & H'Kong.[197]

The Loan is not to go on. Le Footae says that his work cd. not be done under 4 or 5 years.[198]

Shipping Rules sent out again for re-consideration.

The Yamen proposes to place a Com[r.] [commissioner] at Kiachta, and Macpherson has been selected: sealed orders for him have been Deposited at the Yamen. Shd. they decide on the step, they will send on the despatch; M. will come to Peking for orders, & Man will go & take charge at N'Chwang. [character for E, Russia doubly underlined] has withdrawn the [characters for Chang-chia k'ou] propositions.][199]

Mdse [?] Despatch gone to the Yamen. Com[r.] S'hae [characters for tai-chih tai-?]: Com[rs]. at S'hae & T'tsing to superintend the two divisions of ports during my absence. Shd. anything happen to the FitzRoy, Giquel to go to S'hae; Man in the same way goes to T'tsing, shd. aught hap. to Baker. Vernimb resigned: vacancy given to J. Twinem. Coolidge's vacancy given to G. G. Lowder.[200]

Coolie Emigration Rules take the form of a "Convention" signed by English & French Ministers. Everything settled now, but not til after much trouble.

Pinchon under orders to accompany Pin to Paris![201]

Rennie's "Peking & the Pekingese", full of indiscreet revelations. Had I known he was taking notes, I had never talked as I did in his presence in 1861.[202]

Häng Ke called a few days ago to say that <u>Foo</u> <u>Chitae</u> has memorialized proposing that <u>Yue</u> <u>Hae</u> <u>Kwan</u> [Canton Customs] be done away with, & that it be put under local officials as Hang Chow, &c: <u>H'</u> is <u>anxious</u> that it <u>shd.</u> remain <u>as</u> it <u>is</u>. I sd. foreigners wd object to anything approaching <u>Chow</u> <u>le</u> [?].[203]

On the 24th Feb. paid my new year visit to Prince Kung, who was gracious as usual. He gets fatter. His eyes got quite red & filled with tears, when I alluded to the Macao Kidnapping; I don't know whether it was <u>sympathy,</u> or a <u>yawn</u> <u>suppressed</u> that caused the suffusion.

On the 28th Feb. breakfasted: 'farewell' at the Yamen & had a few hours [word unclear].

Last night went to the Legation. Miss Amy more beautiful than ever, but she is evidently of the opinion that I am a "bore", for she always avoids me. I am glad, I escaped heart-free, and free in every way.

I have learnt one thing, & will act upon it for the future: <u>that</u> is <u>to</u> <u>be</u> <u>more</u> <u>discreet</u> <u>&</u> <u>to</u> <u>talk</u> <u>less.</u> I am generally speaking silent enough, but sometimes I talk too much, & say what I ought not to say. Of this fault I shall take care not to be accused in future.

Steam Fleet Funds: not yet forthcoming. The Yamen wants to say that the money is to be paid to me in England.

Kleinwachter has taken charge at C'Kiang; Lord at K'Kiang; & White goes to Formosa.

Wade is busy at a Memo on the State of China which he laid before Sir Rutherford, & which he now translates for the benefit of the Yamen. My leave has not yet been granted on paper, & it wd. not surprise me were Wade's <u>Memo</u> to frighten them to such an extent that they will not let me go.[204] I have however made all my arrangements, & nothing occurring to prevent me, I shall leave them on Tuesday or Wednesday the 5th or 6th instant.

Robert Hart
Friday, 2 March, 1866
Peking

CHAPTER NINE

Travels to Europe 1866

O<small>N THE FIRST</small> of the two home leaves that Robert Hart took during his fifty-four years in China, he had several purposes in mind. One was to touch home base, to see his ailing parents, who indeed would both be dead by the time he set foot on British soil again. A second was equally personal: to find a bride and set up a household in keeping with his status, a task that not only suited his inclination, but had also become something expected of him, even by his colleagues in the Tsungli Yamen. The third was less personal: to bring with him to Europe some Chinese observers on a mission of investigation, an opening wedge to the setting up of China's diplomatic representation in the Western world. At the same time, he planned to recruit a few Europeans to bring back to China as teachers of science and mathematics in the T'ung-wen kuan.

Hart had long championed the idea of sending Chinese representatives abroad. As early as 29 July 1863, for example, he told Wen-hsiang that "for the management of foreign intercourse, they [the Chinese] wd never get on satisfactorily until they sent Ministers to Europe."[1] He went on to make the point repeatedly, both in private conversations with the Tsungli Yamen and in his memorandum to the Ch'ing government. Wade, as we have seen, did the same. But the ministers of the Yamen balked, reluctant to make a commitment because of the cost, the lack of qualified Chinese personnel, and certain potential problems of protocol. At the heart of the matter was China's sense of "state dignity" (*t'i-chih*), which resisted the idea of an exchange of envoys on the basis of diplomatic equality. This had been, of course, the reason the Ch'ing government resisted so vehemently the idea of granting an audience to the foreign ministers on Western terms — in other words, to give them an interview without the traditional kowtow required of tributary envoys.[2]

But Hart's impending home leave provided the Tsungli Yamen with a convenient pretext for advocating an exploratory mission to Europe, and the Customs Administration provided a ready source of funds. On 20 February 1866, Prince Kung memorialized successfully on behalf of the Yamen, requesting that several Chinese scholars and students be allowed to accompany Hart on his trip back to England in order to investigate conditions in Europe and then report back to China. This, he argued, would give China a chance to learn about the West in the same way that Westerners had for some time been learning about China. He was especially careful to point out that the informal nature of the mission and its association with the Inspector General's home leave would minimize diplomatic complications.[3]

THE PIN-CH'UN MISSION

The individuals recommended by the Tsungli Yamen to accompany Hart were his Chinese writer, Pin-ch'un, a former magistrate and also a brevet officer in the Banner organization; Pin-ch'un's son, Kuang-ying, a clerk; and three students from the T'ung-wen kuan, all Bannermen: Feng-i, a Mongol and a student in the English Department; Chang Te-i (also known as Te-ming), likewise a student of English; and Yen-hui, a student in the French Department. In order to enhance Pin-ch'un's prestige as the senior member of the mission (he was 63 sui; 62 years of age by Western reckoning), he was given brevet rank as a 3rd-degree civil official (the same rank Hart had recently received) and also designated an Assistant Secretary General of the Tsungli Yamen (*fu tsung-pan,* rather then *pang-pan*). His cohorts were accorded lesser but still significant official status.[4]

Hart tells us comparatively little about Pin-ch'un and almost nothing about the other Chinese members of the mission. We know from his journal that "Pin Laou Yay" was quick and capable as a writer, and that he served Hart not only as a valuable source of information but also as an informal mediator between the I.G. and the ministers of the Tsungli Yamen. (see, for example, journal, 14 August 1864; 18 October 1864; 24 August 1865). On the other hand, A. B. Freeman-Mitford, a British attaché at the time, describes Pin-ch'un as "a shocking twaddle," whose primary qualification for heading the mission was his personal acquaintance with Prince Kung and his relationship by marriage to another minister of the Tsungli Yamen (presumably Heng-ch'i). "He and his son," Freeman-Mitford wrote, "are from what I have seen and heard of them quite incapable of forming just appreciations of what they will see [in Europe]." Nonetheless, the young diplomat remarked charitably that Pin-ch'in "is said to be very popular in Pekingese society," and acknowledged that his mission was "the first step toward permanent missions in Europe and better relations here."[5]

As late as 21 January 1866, Hart thought that Pin-ch'un was "not likely to go with me to England," but within a month, for some reason, the situation had changed. Meanwhile, Edward C. Bowra, an Englishman, and Emile de Champs, a Frenchman, were chosen from the Customs staff to serve as interpreters and tour managers. Six Chinese servants also accompanied the group.[6]

The so-called Pin-ch'un Mission was in fact an appendage of Robert Hart as I.G., since it included two secretarial assistants from his own office and three language students from the College supported by the Customs. The Tsungli Yamen had hardly stuck its neck out. While the Yamen recommended the appointments, its members were not directly involved or responsible, and the Emperor of course even less so. Pin-ch'un's rank had been inflated to match Hart's, but he was still a neophyte traveler and a diplomatic small fry. When such an inconspicuous mandarin met Queen Victoria before any foreign envoys had been received at the Court of Peking, it no doubt showed Hart's high standing in British government circles but a lamentable disregard for diplomatic reciprocity.

Despite its lowly status, the Pin-ch'un Mission received a good deal of attention from the press, both at home and abroad. Furthermore, several of its members kept diaries of their experiences. Although these personal accounts differ somewhat in format and emphasis, and do not always agree on particulars, even dates, they grant us intriguing angles from which to view the pioneering mission.

From the Chinese side, Prince Kung's memorial of 20 February expressly stipulated that the members of the mission in traditional fashion were to record their impressions and experiences; hence there are at least three substantial Chinese versions of the trip: two by Pin-ch'un and one by Chang Te-i. Pin-ch'un's *Ch'eng-ch'a pi-chi* (Notes on a mission of investigation) is a day-by-day account of places visited, together with some geographical and historical notes. The Queen's Library at Belfast has a copy of this diary, although the dates of the prefaces by Li Shan-lan and others indicate that it could not be the edition presented to Hart personally by Pin-ch'un on 21 February 1867. According to W. A. P. Martin, the *Ch'eng-ch'a pi-chi* represents only "a meager selection from his official reports," most of which Martin claims were negative in tone. Pin-ch'un also produced a poetic work entitled *Hai-kuo sheng-yu ts'ao* (Draft notes on a fine trip to the maritime countries) to which Tung Hsun added a preface. The third work, *Hang-hai shu-ch'i* (Narrative of odd things seen on a sea voyage), written by Chang Te-i, is the most full and interesting of the three accounts, although somewhat garbled. On the Western side, young

Edward Bowra (not yet 25) put his own version of the trip into writing. Bowra, who had had his first Customs post in Tientsin in early 1863, grew increasingly hostile to Pin-ch'un as the mission progressed; as a result, his account of the proceedings is often critical and sometimes cynical in tone.[7]

Hart, as usual, is comparatively detached. As far back as January 1866, he tells us of the uncertainties, delays, and final arrangements for the mission. What he does not discuss is the number of calls he must have paid on Western diplomats in Peking, and the number of reminders, memoranda, and the like that must have been necessary to set up the elaborate schedule of appointments, diplomatic calls, and contacts with statesmen in more than half a dozen foreign countries. Though far from an accredited diplomatic mission, Pin-ch'un and his group were accorded formal treatment and even meetings with the crowned heads of various countries on their tour.

Pin-ch'un's diary begins with a reiteration of his official orders to travel to foreign countries and to record his observations of the land, people, and customs of the places he visits. He notes that prior to departure, on 25 February, Hsu Chi-yü gave him a personal copy of his *Ying-huan chih-lueh* (A brief account of the maritime circuit; see chapter 7) — a work to which Pin-ch'un subsequently refers at least twice in his narrative. Pin-ch'un also describes the exhausting land journey from Peking to Tientsin that Hart had made going in the other direction less than a year before, and which the I.G. now found himself enduring once again.[8]

We first encounter the Pin-ch'un party together in Hart's journal on 14 March 1866, as they embarked on a small coastal steamer at Tientsin after visits with Ch'ung-hou, Commissioner of Trade for the Northern Ports. It was Pin-ch'un's first experience in a Western vessel, or indeed at sea. After "narrowly escaping shipwreak" in the north, the group arrived safely at Shanghai on 19 March, where they spent four days before transshipping to the French liner *Labourdonnais*. Pin-ch'un's diary describes the ship's dimensions, accommodations, appointments, services, and crew in considerable detail. "In each cabin," he observed, for example, "two glass lamps are inserted beside a large toilet glass, in which the lights are gorgeously reflected. Entering this apartment, one is dazzled with the radiance and bewildered as though lost in a palatial maze." He also found interesting the ship's catering and fresh water supply, "obtained through the agency of fire."

But Pin-ch'un reserved for poetry his description of the foreign ladies of Shanghai:

No artist's pencil can do them justice,
Those fair ones of the West
Slender and graceful their waists;
Long and trailing their skirts.
When they pass you to the windward,
A strange fragrance is wafted to your nostrils.
I have taken them by the hand,
And together ascended a lacquered chariot.
Their whiteness comes not from starch,
Nor their blush from cinnibar,
For nature's colors spurn the aid of art.
The twittering words are hard to comprehend,
But I do not yield to Minghuang in interpreting the language
of flowers.[9]

The *North China Herald*, soon after Pin-ch'un's arrival at the treaty port, grandly editorialized on 31 March 1866 that the mission was a tribute to China's recognition of "the superiority of European nations in the arts of peace [as well as "War and its accessories"], and to the indominable energy which has enabled the great powers of the west to extend their commerce to the utmost ends of the earth." The paper went on to state: "The embassy, or more properly commission, which accompanies Mr. Hart to Europe, by both its composition and the instructions it has received, testifies to the gradual but sure development of enlightened ideas." Other contemporary observers were far less sanguine. Many Chinese found Pin-ch'un undistinguished and his promotions cheaply earned, while Western merchants, hostile to the Customs in general and to Hart in particular for stooping so low as to work in a Chinese organization, feared damage to Western prestige. Foreign ministers had still not been granted audience by the Emperor, and here was a relative nonentity, a private traveler, about to be received with respect by the crowned heads of Europe. Fortunately, the diatribes of newspapers like the *China Mail* probably remained unknown to Pin-ch'un.

During the early stages of his voyage, Pin-ch'un played the affable voyageur, experiencing and enjoying new and strange sights, as all travelers do. If later he became to Bowra fractious and unpredictable, it may have been because, untrained for the diplomatic circuit, he found it overwhelmingly oppressive — and not very interesting. His party arrived in Hong Kong on 27 March and transshipped to the *Camboge,* whereupon Bowra joined them. He was the only member of the group who had not been attacked by the hostile treaty-port press — partly because of his youth, and partly because his expertise in the

Chinese language made him an obvious choice for the mission. (The *Ch'eng-ch'a pi-chi*, incidentally, also acknowledges his language ability, as well as that of de Champs.) Hart had written in February to Bowra, then Acting Interpreter at Canton, to be in Hong Kong no later than 24 March. Bowra, with two years to go before normal home leave, was delighted with his good fortune, and, like Hart, would return to China at the end of the summer with a bride after a similar whirlwind courtship.

After staying only a few hours in Hong Kong, the group sailed in late afternoon. It was "awfully silly," Hart recorded, "to be putting away from H'K in this direction." The next two weeks, during which they stopped at Saigon and then Singapore, were mainly uneventful. Pin-ch'un called on the Governor at Saigon, and was himself called on in Singapore by an official with a blue button of the 3rd class. At both Singapore and Galle, Ceylon, they took on numbers of new passengers. Pin-ch'un and Hart alike described the odd tonsorial styles of the men, and Pin-ch'un the diversity of the Asians. "There are a total of twenty-seven nationalities on board," Pin-ch'un wrote on 10 April, "speaking seventeen different languages." Everyone differed, both in physical appearance and clothing: Some were tall and lanky, others enormously stout; some had huge beards and long hair that dangled loose in the wind. Hart summed it up with the observation, "Some men shave and others grow all that will grow."

The Europeans who came on board the *Camboge* amazed Pin-ch'un not only with "their elegance and refinement," but also with their strange customs. The women walked arm-in-arm upon the deck, or rested on couches made of rattan while their husbands waited upon them. The noise of conversation, he says, was "like that of the twittering of swallows in the eaves, or like mandarin ducks folding their wings." Before the party left Galle, a steamer from Calcutta arrived, bringing a number of Indian military men, and a few women and children.

As they traveled, Pin-ch'un wrote poetry and in general settled down to the simple pleasures of shipboard life. Hart described the Chinese as quite at home on board. Meanwhile, unknown to Pin-ch'un, a complaint had been lodged with the agent in Singapore to the effect that "the Chinese were *as well treated* as the other passengers." Hart records this blatantly racist remark without comment; but when the complaint was again lodged by passengers on the *Camboge*, he remarked (15 April 1866): "the complaint ought to have been 'are not better treated than.'"

Finally, on 24 April, twenty-nine days from Hong Kong, they

reached Suez and disembarked to await the afternoon train to Cairo. Pin-ch'un was then able, "after a sea voyage of a month's duration . . . to take off my clothes." The ride to Cairo was Pin-ch'un's first experience with the railroad, and he was entranced: "Buildings, trees, hills and roads to the side of the tracks fly by like lightning," he rhapsodized. On the trip to Alexandria "the sensation was precisely that of flying through the air." Subsequent train rides invariably occasioned comment, and sometimes inspired poetry. Later in the trip, Pin-ch'un even arranged for a Chinese merchant living in Paris to buy him a working model of a train so that he could take it back to China.[10] His group stayed in Cairo for two days, during the second of which Hart relaxed at his hotel; Bowra and de Champs, on the contrary, bursting with energy after the long voyage, escorted the rest of the mission to see the pyramids, the first of many such sightseeing trips for Pin-ch'un. As he would do at every major stop, he dutifully recorded noteworthy physical features and historical facts.

At last, on 2 May, the party arrived at Marseilles, where, according to plan, Hart left the group and went on his own way to Paris and home. The others began their sightseeing in earnest, following the well-trod route of most foreign travelers who visited Europe in the 1860s. Here they felt the full impact of Western material civilization as manifested in city life: wide paved streets ("it rained but there was no mud"); buildings 6 and 7 stories high; street lighting by gas lamps; a hotel elevator; cold and hot water faucets; and flush toilets. On the morning of 4 May they were taken to the Messageries Imperiales shipyard; the next morning to see the new Palais de Justice; and that afternoon for an 8-hour train trip to Lyons, where they spent the following day at a silk factory—conceivably the first activity that had true personal interest for them, though they made few purchases, finding the colors not to their liking.

On the 6th, Pin-ch'un flatly went on strike—a foretoken of what was to become frequent. The occasion was a Grand Military Fete held under the auspices of the Lyons garrison, which, Bowra records, "we felt compelled to decline, as Pin-ta-jen could not be persuaded to wear his official hat and costume, although informed that all the authorities of the place would be 'en grande tenue' and were anxious to be presented to him." Charles Drage hypothesizes in his account of Bowra's assignment that Pin-ch'un was by this time both bored and fatigued, and that now, "to be asked to don his round black mandarin's hat with its newly acquired and greatly cherished sapphire button" to benefit men of the despised military profession was simply too much. "His wrath exploded, and it was perhaps fortunate that they left for

Paris by the night train." Pin-ch'un may well have had the traditional Chinese scholar's contempt for the military profession, but it did not keep him from recording in his diary information about the armies of Europe, including a comparison of British and French defense needs.[11]

Paris proved to be the most impressive of all the capitals the Chinese would see in Europe. They loved the beauty of its parks, its streets, its amusements, and its women. They enjoyed French food and admired the impartiality of French policemen. But their visit began rather inauspiciously with an open quarrel between de Champs and Baron Eugene de Meritens. The latter—whose bent toward what he considered to be a senior's authority in the Customs Service was already familiar to Hart—was on home leave; and he immediately claimed to have charge of the Pin-ch'un Mission while it was in France. The storm seems to have burst over the question of which man would present Pin-ch'un to the French Foreign Minister. It came to the point where de Meritens vowed, if thwarted, to issue a statement to the effect that the visit was unauthorized and irregular— "dirty words," as Drage observes, in diplomatic circles. Though Hart (who had just left Paris on the evening of the 7th) does not mention the incident in his journal, we are told that frantic express letters were addressed to him demanding a ruling. Drage credits Bowra's "tact" with calming the situation.

Until this problem of protocol was settled, matters were at an impasse, since calls of other diplomats (who had left cards) could not be returned until after the interview at the Foreign Office. But Pin-ch'un could still go sightseeing. He was driven along the Champs Elysees and the Bois de Boulogne, and taken to see a glass building being erected for the Exposition of 1867. At last, on the 9th, the problem of protocol was solved by a presentation made simultaneously by both de Champs and de Meritens, after which Pin-ch'un was expected to attend an official reception in the evening. The occasion served to sharpen his ingenuity, however, for he managed to slip away from the diplomatic function to visit the Theatre de l'Ambigu. Of the occasion Bowra observed merely that they were seated opposite the Emperor, Napoleon III. But Pin-ch'un wrote of the grandeur of the performance with its elaborate staging, special effects, and huge cast. "During the progress of the play natural scenery accompanied by cascades, with the sun and moon alternately shining and obscured, was represented," while "figures of the gods, or clouds of fairies were seen descending from on high amidst a dazzling halo of light, forming an inconceivably marvellous spectacle. . . . Fifty or sixty females, actresses, made their appearance on the stage, of whom one-half were notice-able for good looks, the great majority being nude to the extent of half their persons, and [they] took part in the performance as dancers."[12]

The next day the daily round, dreary to the Chinese, continued. They made calls and received calls; they received promises that Lord Clarendon was preparing sightseeing in England; they called on the American Ambassador, the Russian Ambassador, the Swedish Minis-ter. Finally, on 11 May Pin-ch'un issued an ultimatum to the effect that he and his entourage wished to visit as many theatres as possible, and that these engagements were to have priority over all others. That night they took in two such entertainments, at the Opera Comique and the Theatre du Chatelet.

The next morning Pin-ch'un was indisposed—the first of many such episodes—though reading the schedules from which he escaped, one can understand why. It was an exhausting round expected of him, both then and later in England. He went so far, in fact, as to announce himself unfit to proceed to London as planned, and in-sisted that, except for his son, the rest of the mission must go on with-out him. On being telegraphed, Hart agreed to the plan, insisting only that de Champs should remain in Paris with father and son, in case their interest in the cultural beauties of that city prolonged their stay indefinitely.

Bowra and the others arrived in London on 15 May, Pin-ch'un on 17 May. Once again Pin-ch'un's health was precarious by day but mended miraculously by evening, in time for theatrical perfor-mances. Hart was in London himself during this period, and Pin-ch'un's diary records a visit from the I.G. on 18 May (although Hart's journal says nothing about it). He also received calls from three Com-missioners of Customs—Thomas Dick, George Hughes, and Charles Hannen—all on leave from China. On 23 May Hart accompanied Pin-ch'un and his associates to call on the British Foreign Secretary, Lord Clarendon, and the next day he left for home in Ireland.

During the two weeks of Pin-ch'un's stay in the vicinity of London, he and his colleagues visited museums, churches, parks, Parliament, and other tourist sights, as well as a hospital (where they observed two operations) a military camp, a large newspaper office, a prison, a mint, and several factories. Pin-ch'un records on 28 May a visit from Charles "Chinese" Gordon, whom he meticulously identifies as having been "rewarded by the Throne with the Chinese rank of pro-vincial commander-in-chief for having trained and led the Ever-Victorious Army against bandits [i.e., the Taipings]." According to

Pin-ch'un, Gordon was quite refined and rather submissive, without the "gallant air" of a soldier.[13]

The prospect of a personal presentation to Queen Victoria brought exhilaration to Pin-ch'un and commensurate anxiety to Bowra. He quickly referred the matter to Hart, who wrote on 2 June, "should the Prince [Edward] wish Pin to attend a levee,, let him go . . . but don't let him take his flute!"[14] The next day the Pin-ch'un Mission left for Eton and Windsor Castle, being furnished with royal carriages for the trip. This adventure Pin-ch'un understandably found exciting. Among the treasures in the public apartments, he recognized stanzas from an ancient Chinese poem painted on a fan, and in the greenhouses a wonderfully symmetrical specimen of a japonica plant. What delighted him most, however, were the "eight small carriage ponies," resembling the ponies of Szechwan, "which are driven by the Queen herself." On 5 June, Pin-ch'un and his associates attended a State Ball given by the Prince and Princess, and here Pin-ch'un responded genuinely to the dignity and elegance of the occasion. After presentation to his host and hostess, he spoke a few gracious words of his own. "Envoys from China have never as yet reached your honourable country; and now, having been ordained to travel abroad, I have learnt for the first time that such beautiful lands exist beyond our seas." He was at his best again on the following day, when he was received in private audience by Queen Victoria herself.[15]

Nothing could have sustained such a pitch of excitement and interest. The next day the party left for a tour of the industrial north of England — plate factories, pin factories, button factories, tool factories, in all of which they were shown the complete process from raw material to finished product. At first Pin-ch'un, buoyed by his recent experiences, bore it well. The descent into a coal mine, however, during which he had to submit to donning the garb of a common miner, seems to have been the last straw. Under the pretext of getting back to China in the prescribed time, he proposed now to cancel the rest of the trip. Small wonder, for he was exhausted, bored, and acutely homesick. Once again Bowra, at wit's end, appealed to Hart.

Hart's letter of 13 June from Ravarnet attempts to calm the troubled waters, although he does not mention it in his journal. He does mention on 15 June a further desperate telegram from Bowra to the effect that Pin-ch'un would not leave England without seeing him. On the 18th, therefore, he traveled to London and spent the 19th ironing out the itinerary for the rest of the trip. Washington was scrapped; six European capitals remained; and the party would sail for China on August 19 instead of in September. After doing some other errands, Hart left for Dublin on the night of the 20th, and de Champs went on vacation. Bowra's parents, who had hardly had a chance to glimpse their son, gave a garden party at their house near Croyden, at which Thirza Woodward, Edward Bowra's soon-to-be bride, was present. Meanwhile, Prussia had invaded Hanover, Saxony, and Hesse, and the Seven Weeks' War had begun. The Pin-ch'un party nevertheless sailed on 24 June for Antwerp, their five-week stay in England finally over.

Holland proved interesting to the Chinese primarily because of its canals, dykes, and land reclamation projects. Coming from a country in which water control was one of the chief responsibilities of government, Pin-ch'un and his colleagues marveled over how elaborate and well-ordered the Dutch system was, and how steam machinery was used to such excellent effect in land reclamation projects. In Copenhagen Pin-ch'un enjoyed the Tivoli Gardens but little else. Stockholm was tedious, but the simple friendliness of the whole royal family won his heart.

On 13 July Hart received notes from Bowra and de Champs, indicating that they were "heartily tired of Pin and his ways." Hart now faced a serious dilemma: to support them or him? Knowing that Heng-ch'i and others at Peking would favor Pin-ch'un, Hart made a typically pragmatic decision: "my plan is to keep Pin in good temper, to make him as powerful as possible, & to keep him as a friend in power. . . . I must keep an eye on B. & De C. for the future, however: I don't think they'll do for places where either the plainest common sense or tact are required; they can't look around corners, & they won't make allowances."[16]

Through July the mission continued on its way, now with the added strain of interminable train rides. The trip from Stockholm to St. Petersburg, for instance, took three and a half days. Some of the sojourns went relatively well, others not. In St. Petersburg Pin-ch'un was awed and enchanted by the sheer beauty and grandeur of the cathedrals and palaces; and, wonder of wonders, the Russians left his party to their own devices for a large part of each day. After four days they entrained for Berlin, where hostilities had already been ended by an armistice, and the Germans were so absorbed in their own celebrations that, beyond formal courtesy calls, they took little notice of the visitors.

Berlin was the last capital to be visited officially. It had been suggested, however, that they should see something of the industrial region of the Ruhr, so when they left Berlin on July 24 it was for Essen. De Champs having now returned from his leave, Bowra at last

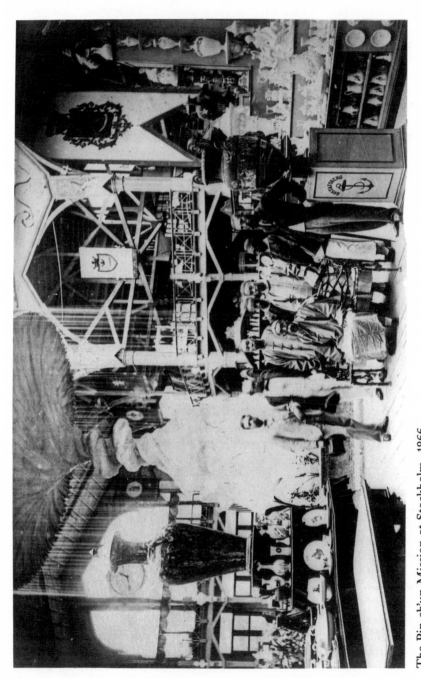

The Pin-ch'un Mission at Stockholm, 1866

From the Bowra Collection, School of Oriental and African Studies, London University.

on 27 July left the group for his own three weeks of furlough before joining them at Paris for the trip to Marseilles and on to China. He obviously made good use of his time, for when he did reappear it was with his bride of two days, the former Thirza Woodward. The party returned to Paris on schedule, there to spend their last free time before proceeding to Marseilles. Hart joined Pin-ch'un and his colleagues for a few days in early August, but stayed only long enough to conduct some business related to the T'ung-wen kuan. By 11 August he was back in Dublin to see his fiancée.

The Pin-ch'un Mission departed for China on the 19th, retracing its original route. While Bowra's bride succumbed to sea sickness during a monsoon, he morosely occupied himself with reading the diatribes of the English-language newspapers that awaited him at each port. The press, remaining consistently hostile during the months since they had left, branded the mission "Mr. Hart's protégés" and finally "Hart's pets." Hart himself was accused of dishonest intrigue on behalf of "his pig-tailed employers" at the expense of a "sell" to the Foreign Office and the Queen herself. The fact that the Queen should have granted an audience was the climax of disgrace. "Every foreigner is sneering at the English," declared the *China Mail*, "content to eat humble pie in Pekin, unrecognized by the Court, snubbed by the Mandarins and laughed at by the people, while half a dozen Pekin parvenus are treated as if they were princes of the Royal Blood."[17]

The mission reached Hong Kong on 28 September, at which point the party broke up and its members went their separate ways. Pin-ch'un visited friends in South China for several weeks, though by this time he must have been utterly exhausted. From Marseilles to Peking, where he finally arrived on 13 November, most of Pin-ch'un's diary entries consist of only a line or two. His concluding remarks consist of a perfunctory listing of the major places he visited (13), the number of steamers and trains he rode (19 and 42 respectively), the distance he traveled (over 90,000 *li*; about 30,000 miles), and the general conditions he observed. In late December the Tsungli Yamen produced a similar summary for the Throne based on information supplied personally by Pin-ch'un. This memorial, received on 27 December 1866, emphasized the value of the mission for China's foreign relations, despite its superficial nature, and indicated that a copy of Pin-ch'un's diary would be sent for imperial scrutiny.[18]

So what of Hart's high hopes for representation abroad for China? As late as 15 July he outlined his aims for the mission in his journal: "1. to get the Chinese govt. to send officials to Europe . . . ; 2. to get European govts to receive & kindly treat such officials . . . ; 3. to cause the Chinese officials to carry away with them pleasant (their time is too short to admit of their beings instructed) memories of foreign lands . . . ; 5. having Pin made a t'ang kwan or Minister for Foreign Affairs, on return to China; 6. getting the [Ch'ing] govt., by his aid to look kindly on some of the arts and sciences of the West; 7. inducing China to appoint Embassies abroad; and 8. establishing a sensible & rational kind of friendship between China and other countries."

Hart believed that he had achieved the first four of the eight goals (we may wonder about the fourth), but the others proved elusive.[19] In short, the Pin-ch'un mission was more form than substance, more public relations than diplomacy. (In the 1860s they were still separable endeavors.) Pin-ch'un never became a minister of the Tsungli Yamen, and, although he enjoyed some political influence in Peking, he seems to have done little if anything to broaden the Ch'ing government's outlook toward Western learning.[20] According to Hart's journal (9 January 1867), Pin-ch'un was made the T'ung-wen kuan's "Director of Western Studies" in early 1867, but his appointment appears to have been only nominal, and in any case he died in 1871. His son, who received an appointment in the English bureau there, also exerted no lasting influence.

Neither the Tsungli Yamen nor the Western powers considered Pin-ch'un to be a regular diplomatic envoy; and, although his visit to Europe may well have eased the way for another mission of investigation in 1868 (the so-called Burlingame Mission, also sponsored by Hart), this venture, like Pin-ch'un's, was tied to the home leave of a foreigner and was by design more of a public relations gesture than a true diplomatic effort.[21] Far from inducing the Ch'ing government to send permanent envoys abroad, the Pin-ch'un Mission encouraged a number of officials to argue that short-term ventures of this sort were all that China really needed.[22] In fact, China's first permanent mission abroad was established only in 1877, and it was related directly to a mission of apology sent to Great Britain after the murder of a British consular official (Augustus Margary) in 1875 near the Sino-Burmese border.

Yet significantly we can hear distant echoes from the Pin-ch'un Mission in this event, ten years later. In the first place, we are told that the newly appointed Chinese Minister to England, Kuo Sung-t'ao, almost certainly read the diaries of Pin-ch'un and Chang Te-i. Moreover, Chang himself accompanied the Margary Mission, wrote another diary, and eventually, in 1901, became Chinese Minister to England. After a similarly long waiting period, a number of Chinese members of the Burlingame Mission had distinguished diplomatic careers abroad.[23]

HART'S MARRIAGE

The Pin-ch'un Mission had been the focus of Hart's attention before he left China; once home, his attention shifted to personal affairs. Indeed, his journal for a Sunday, 15 July, records at length his disquiet at having been ten weeks at home without spending his leave "as advantageously, as pleasantly, or as wisely, as time and opportunities would have allowed." By this he meant that he had ignored the personal advancement that might have been his if — as was possible — he had courted the great men, made himself visible to the world, used his influence in connection with the Pin-ch'un Mission, sought contacts useful for his future. But he meant too that he had not done the necessary chores for the Customs to be checked off before his return to China. So what *had* he been doing?

His journal tells us. He first arrived home on 7 May, but left on 11 May to taste the long-forgone pleasures of London and to accompany Pin-ch'un on his call to Lord Clarendon. Yet the pleasures of the big city, so alluring in exile, seemed somehow less satisfying in actuality. His two weeks there were a busy and turbulent interval. He breakfasted with friends, and dined with other friends; he took a box at the theater; he "fell in with" some girls at the Crystal Palace, and got home late. Wherever he went, he unconsciously ranked the girls he saw. He went to call on an old friend, and found his sisters "not so nice as I expected." On the way to the Derby (which he thought "very slow"), he saw "lovely girls along the road." All in all, London wasn't showing him what he wanted to see. He felt disgruntled. "I hate the life here," he wrote on 17 May, "it is too exciting in some ways; not enough so in others; and it is a bore altogether." He ended with a significant sentence: "I must get up a virtuous affection somewhere, or I shall be miserable."

And so back to Ireland. From 24 May, when he left London, to 24 July, when he left home for visits to Aberdeen and Rugby and for business in London and Paris, he was preoccupied with his family and with the young woman who quickly became his fiancée. He had come home with the definite intention to search out a bride, at 31 both eager and wary. He could offer a wife a good position in China's foreign colony; but she must know how to value it, and to play her role in it. London had proved to be an unlikely setting for his search; so he took the most obvious route. He returned home.

Lady Hart, c. 1895

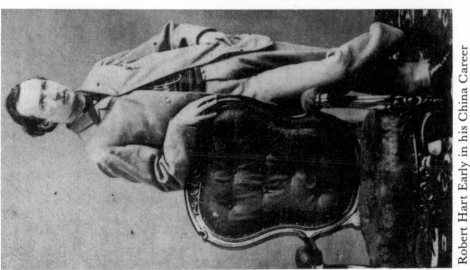

Robert Hart Early in his China Career

From the Irons Collection of The Queen's University of Belfast Library, reproduced here with the

Hester Jane Hart, c. 1866

We must also note the seriousness of his intent as demonstrated in one of his last acts in China. We know from his later letters to James Duncan Campbell that he sent his three children by Ayaou, "a Chinese girl kept by me," to England to be brought up by the wife of a bookkeeper in a firm with which he did business. By the standards of the day such behavior was generous in the extreme, almost quixotic; many Westerners simply ignored and abandoned such children. In the eyes of a later day, exiling three children from their native culture, even with the consent of their mother (who later married a Chinese), raises perplexing questions. But it was done with high intent, and for Hart it cleared the way, as honorably as he could, for a British marriage.[24]

He thus came home to Ireland with narrowed intent. It had become the most obvious route for his search. Years before, soon after his birth in Portadown, we are told by his niece, Juliet Bredon, that he was lying in his aunt's lap while she braided a watch-chain. The family doctor, Juliet's grandfather, Dr. Alexander Bredon, paused on his way out from a visit with the baby's mother and teasingly inquired if she was making a keepsake for her sweetheart. "No indeed," she replied gaily, "I'm making a wedding present for this new nephew of mine when he marries your daughter."[25]

Doubtless this was an old story in the Hart family and Robert himself must have heard it more than once. What could be more natural than to begin his search with a visit to the Bredon family? Sadly, the doctor himself had died less than a month before, on 15 May, but his wife and daughter, Hester Jane, were still living in Portadown. It was Hester Jane's picture that had been sent to Hart by "Aunt Brady" just as he was packing to leave China.

Hart paid his first call on Mrs. Bredon on a Thursday, 31 May, and, significantly, he "liked Miss B. very much." They found they had something in common; she liked the make of piano he had just had sent to Peking. He called again on Saturday (when he also called on Aunt Brady, who must have encouraged his present course of action), and on Monday, though not on Sunday. On Tuesday, when he called again — their fourth meeting — he proposed, and was instantly accepted (subject to the pro forma approval of her older brother).

It seems a somewhat hasty arrangement, but on the other hand not rash. They were not then, or ever, deeply in love. For Hart, Hessie had virtues that he had missed elsewhere, and that he now knew were important to him. She was a known quantity; she came from a family like his, with similar background and similar standards. For her, the same was true, with the crucial addition that he represented a path out of Ireland into the great world. A spirited girl, she was eager for new horizons. She always would be; witness her extensive travels in later years. What would normally have fallen to her lot in Portadown would have been a "good" marriage to a local resident, leading to a life like her mother's. It was not enough. Robert Hart surely stood out in the region as a local boy who had made good in a big way in far-off, glamorous, little-known China. What an opportunity for a girl of her temperament!

Both she and her mother were obviously ready for it. Mrs. Bredon would have preferred a conventional engagement lasting several months, or, if an early marriage seemed necessary because of Hart's impending return to China, she would have liked Hessie to stay at home for some time afterward. But Hart, who read his Hessie realistically from the start, knew better. "Hessie herself," he wrote, "would willingly come to me tomorrow, will also willingly do what I shd. best like, i.e., marry me the day I have to start for China." So they set the date for 15 September, and even that date had to be pushed up to 22 August, for they sailed from Marseilles on 13 September. Meanwhile, the weeks between early June and 24 July Hart spent in getting to know his bride, introducing her to his family, having simple, enjoyable times with his sisters and friends in Dublin, Portadown, and Ravarnet.

One other psychological chore remained for him, which he agonized over in his journal on 13 June. Should he tell Hessie about his Chinese liaison and the three children he had just sent to London? His journal does not tell us here how he resolved the question, but just before this volume went to press we were privileged to receive, from certain Hart family archives, a series of eight letters that Hart wrote to Hester Bredon at the time of their whirlwind courtship and marriage in the summer of 1866, included in Appendix C. They show us a consistent and persuasive advocate of his cause who deftly develops his case in writing—evidently not in conversation. In his letters to Hessie between 17 June and 18 August, he refers to his past only in letter no. 7 of 15 August. In it he confesses to an impetuous engagement in 1856 to an English young lady at Ningpo that was quickly broken up by her father's refusal to accept as son-in-law a young consular employee so lacking in material goods and worldly prospects. This is followed by a further but vague confession of having been in a Byronic state of "dissipation" for some years thereafter. The I.G. says, "My dear! I conceal nothing but I make no unnecessary revelations!" So he does not speak of a long relationship that produced a family of three children. The letter moves on quickly to Hart's abstention from womanizing for two years past. Hart's last letter in this remarkable get-acquainted series thanks Hessie for her "sensible, loving" letter; like her, he now looks to the future. In a letter to Campbell many years later, when his older son by Ayaou was trying to blackmail him, Hart wrote, "I proffered the information in 1866, but was told the past was past, and the future the future, so I said no more."[26]

Given the male tendencies, the Victorian mores of both Ireland and the China coast in the 1860s, and the color line still in place in those days, a prudent counsellor would certainly have advised Hessie to forget the past and welcome the future, as she did. The warmth and sincerity of Hart's letters to her after their marriage bespeak a firm and affectionate relationship.

Meanwhile in the summer of 1866, his leave was slipping past. On 18 June, as we have seen, he had to go to London to settle Pin-ch'un's itinerary. He stayed only long enough to reach agreement on the rest of the European tour, to look at furniture for his new house in Peking, to consult his bank about investments, and to have his photograph taken. He was back in Portadown for Hessie's 19th birthday on 21 June. In that neighborhood he stayed for the next month, absorbed in the activities of family and friends, whom he had missed during his twelve years in China.

But gradually, as the fatigue of those years diminished and his personal life seemed on a satisfactory trend, his thoughts turned more often to China. When Bowra wrote in exasperation at Pin-ch'un's uncooperative ways, Hart was forced to begin to think out his long-range policy on that score, and to contemplate the next stage of his career in China. On 15 July he wrote in his journal a lengthy resumé of his state of mind, his brain having "gradually been clearing" from the "whirl of excitement" of the last months. His basic theme was that he did not need the recognition he might have gained through more aggressive self-promotion; his were the goals of those who strove for fulfilment, not for public rewards. "Don't bother yourself with C.B.'s or 'presentation,'" he urged himself, although he also admitted that "to have C.B. or K.C.B. wd. please me." One is reminded instantly that H. N. Lay had come back to China in 1863 with a C.B. (Companion of the Bath). Hard work, common sense; that was to be Hart's story; no "pursuit of butterflies" for the Inspector General.

So he got back to the subject of China—the Pin-ch'un Mission in particular. Although Hart went for ten more days of seeing Hessie, having tea with his sister Mary, eating strawberries at a fruiterer's (and noticing gradually that what he "had so long wished for proved to be less agreeable than the reminiscences of the past had caused me to expect"), he also began answering the letters that had piled up, and giving instructions to solicitors regarding his affairs. The world was asserting its pull; no longer was he, or could he pretend to be, the country boy content with an effortless routine.

On 24 July he left for visits in Scotland, and five days later was in London. With J. D. Campbell, who was to go to China as his secretary (and later become non-resident secretary at the head of the London Office), he did a round of Customs business. He went to Trinity House about lights for Chefoo Harbor; he arranged for the purchase of presents for Chinese friends; he had interviews with people who wanted posts in the Customs; he had meals with old acquaintances from China. Finally, on 4 August he and Campbell were off to Paris for another round of interviews, mainly for posts in the T'ung-wen kuan, which he was insistent on expanding, as part of his "international" promotion. Though he could resist Paris as little as most visitors, then or now, he found himself after a few days longing to be home.

That entry of 7 August was the last he wrote in his journal for five months, until he was back in Peking and characteristically started a new volume with a new year. The two weeks after his departure from Paris must have been busy ones, beginning with his sister Charlotte's wedding to Wesley Guard, and ending with his own on 22 August to Hessie in Dublin. The honeymoon, Juliet Bredon tells us, was "spent at the romantic lakes of Killarney." For how long she does not say, but, on 13 September, James Duncan Campbell's mother wrote in her diary, "Dearest James left this morning . . . [and] I feel wretched." So they were all on their way—Robert Hart, his new bride, Campbell, and Johannes von Gumpach, the new instructor in mathematics and astronomy.[27] They arrived in China in November.

Hart's marriage lasted forty-five years, during twenty-four of which the partners did not once see each other. In this way it was an odd arrangement, but not an unhappy one, on either side. Lady Hart (as she duly became) did her duty as a Victorian wife. She loyally stayed in what increasingly became for her a dull and constricting life, until she had contributed her part in raising three healthy children, after a harrowing first pregnancy that culminated in four days of labor and the loss of the child. Hart increasingly gave his attention and even devotion to the demands of his career; it is doubtful if ever again Hessie had his full attention as she had done in the summer of 1866. His journal entry for 22 August 1867 — their first anniversary — is revealing on this score. "No one," he wrote, "could have a better wife than I have got & so far, we have got on well." Then he added: "At the same time, matrimony <u>does</u> interfere with a man's work at times." Later journal entries indicate that there were other complications in Hart's personal life. On 2 July 1870, he confides to his diary that he is "startled by a letter from Ayaou: must look into this business: what trouble from first to last!" And again, on 20 May 1872, after receiving two letters from Ayaou, he asks: "Will this ever end?"[28]

Lady Hart left China in 1882, not to return until 1906. Hart purchased for her a comfortable house on Cadogan Square in London, provided her with ample funds for entertaining and travel (both of which she enjoyed, but not to China), and gave her costly presents of jewelry, furs, and silks. They corresponded regularly and politely, even affectionately. Hessie outlived her husband by some years, and was remembered by her grandchildren as a good conversationalist and a fine hostess. For her, life fulfilled the promise she glimpsed as she sailed on that September day of 1866. Robert Hart too had what he wanted: a solidly respectable household in which he was free to devote himself wholeheartedly to his first and overpowering love, the Chinese Customs Service.

CHAPTER TEN

Journal

7 MARCH 1866–7 AUGUST 1866

[Various flourishes of "R.H." or "Mr. Robert Hart"]

Hart's volume 8: 7 March 1866–7 August 1866

Did not take up journal work again till January 1867: in the meantime got married 22 August 1866 and returned to China by the H.M.S. "Alpha" in September: with T'ung Wen Kwan Professors von Gumpach and [blank, followed by two sets of parentheses, each with two indistinct words] de Meritens also with us and Kilsch.[1]

WEDNESDAY, 7 MARCH 1866: [characters for 14th day of the 1st lunar month]
Left Peking at one o'clock en route for home. When all my traps were in the carts, I suddenly realized the fact that I was going home, &, while my throat swelled and my eyes filled with tears, I found it for a while quite impossible to meet the students to say goodbye.
At the Ha-ta-mên, Saurin accompanied by Mitford & the Legation people passed me. Slept at Chang Kia Wan, where, the snow still on the ground, the night was very cold.[2]

THURSDAY, 8 MARCH 1866: Slept at Yangtsun. Foot much better, but not quite right yet. The river is still frozen over; the country does not show a blade or a leaf of any kind, and a cold wind blows. Got a capital Chinese dinner.

FRIDAY, 10 MARCH 1866: Arrived at T'tsing at noon, & found that Baker had just returned from Ceylon, having come up from S'hae by the "Nanzing", which with the "Yingtszfei" & "Japan", now wait for the ice to break up.

SATURDAY, 11 MARCH 1866: Had a call from Tsung How. He spoke of the likelihood of his being the first minister sent to reside in Europe, & said that, if he cd. get six months' leave, he shd. much like to accompany Pin & party. He had prepared quarters for the party, & sent a Wei-yuen [deputy] as far as Yangtsun to meet us, and another outside the fortifications to conduct Pin to the Kung kwan [office].[3]

SUNDAY, 11 MARCH 1866: [*sic*] Occupied all day writing in [*sic*] reading home letters. Some one sent a telegram to England stating that the "Inspector General had been suddenly dismissed without cause assigned." Dick and the others are much alarmed; Dick especially who, the day before, had proposed to & been accepted by a Miss Laurie. Gordon has written me a very kind letter of condolence, & they all think the worst has come to pass: strange this, that such news shd. meet me at the moment when I am going on leave & accompanied by a party which shows how little the Chinese intend to jump over the traces.[4]

A letter from Aunt Brady sends me the photo of Miss Hester Jane Bredon; she is a nice-looking girl, and were I not going home, where I can choose for myself, I shd. willingly send my photo in return, & conclude the "arrangement".[5]

MONDAY, 12 MARCH 1866: Called on Tsung How. Henderson's [indistinct word] are to be returned to him, as they have been only reported & passed at S'hae on first arrival. Tls. 150 a month to be issued by Tsung How on a/c of monies rendered by Brown & Lovett, the sum to remain in the safe and somehow returned. H.E. says that a large city like Kirin has been taken by the <u>Ke-ma-tseih</u> [mounted bandits], and that Wan Seang, having had the assembling of 3000 men for its relief, has had difficult work to get through.[6]

TUESDAY, 13 MARCH 1866: Packing, &c.

WEDNESDAY, 14 MARCH 1866: Left T'tsing on the "Yingtszfei" accompanied by Pin, Kwang, Fung, Tih, Yen, & 7 servants. Pin & the others express themselves highly delighted with the steamer, & are quite at home on board. At dinner, the moment they saw the carvers commence operations, they, Pin & Yaou,—sitting opposite each other,—made a rush with a knife & fork at a couple of roast fowl which happened to be between them, &, as if their lives depended on it, began to hack away in the endeavour to make sure of something to eat: the sight was for the moment most amusing, but they soon subsided into a quieter mood, &, on the whole, get on much better than had been anticipated. Got aground after dark and remained there all night.[7]

THURSDAY, 15 MARCH 1866: Crossed the Bar in the afternoon.

FRIDAY, 16 MARCH 1866: At daybreak narrowly escaped shipwreck. Some <u>500</u> baskets of steel in the cargo had affected the compasses, & consequently we found ourselves 20 or 30 miles out of our course, being too much to the westward. We shoaled [?] the water very rapidly, & had actually commenced to "go astern" when the ship struck. Fortunately there was no wind, & the sea was placid as a lake; had there been a sea on, we must have been damaged by the hard bottom; and had we gone ahead for a couple of minutes longer than we did, the ship would have gone high & dry, & never have got off. I asked Pin how he had felt, & he said: "I thought the crew knew their own work best, & that, as long as they showed no alarm, there was no call for us to be frightened."

Arrived at Chefoo about 2 P.M. & left it again in a dense fog at eight: accompanied by De Champs. On shore saw Luson & Drew; also called on Lay & his wife: the Taoutae came to call on me, giving me his portrait & some articles of dress with 2 pieces of silk for my mother.[8]

The Tidesurveyor, <u>Stent</u>, is an inferior kind of man, & not atall what I hoped to find him.[9]

MONDAY, 19 MARCH 1866: Arrived at S'Hae at 1 1/2 P.M. The passage down was rough, & the boys were very sick; Pin, however, did not suffer atall.

Put up at FitzRoy's; his wife is not very pretty, but she has a fresh pleasant-looking face, & seems to be a charming person. At dinner met Howell, and Capt. Boyse.[10]

TUESDAY, 25 MARCH 1866: Made arrangements for passages to Marseilles: for myself I paid tls. 573, securing a one-bedded cabin. Messageries wd. not allow me to pay more, & even wanted to make a deduction of 30 P.Cent for the party—but to that I objected. For De Champs, with the five 1st class Chinese & 7 servants paid tls. 4029. Paid off my a/c at Hall & Holtz, tls. 600.4.0.0 and at Watson's tls. 163.7.0.0. Got a draft on Marseilles for tls. 1000 = francs 7875.[11]

From a/c B transferred to a/c Z London tls. 20,150 = £6485 @ 6 [indistinct word] and also got £118.2.6 at tls. 600.

While at T'tsing, noticed that <u>Baker</u> was drunk most of the time; I cannot now make any change in the direction of that office, but I have lost all confidence in him, & shall recommend him to resign on my return.[12]

I have also a letter from May, in which he says that the <u>tls.</u> <u>4000</u> applied for by the Foo Chow office were not for the Commissioner, but for the Hae Kwan [customs taotai]! I shall at once [indistinct word] him, & on my return must take not only him but also de Meritens to task for his complicity with official dishonesty. Nothing but truthfulness, honesty, & integrity, will enable us to hold our own with the Chinese.[13]

FRIDAY, 23 MARCH 1866: [characters for 7th day of the 2nd lunar month]

FitzRoy came to me at the last moment, & said he was hurt at his position, &c. I at once wrote to the Yamen asking that he might be appointed Acting I.G.; in this way, I take Baker's superintendance of the three northern ports from him, &, with Brown appointed to Foo chow via May, can go away to some extent unembarrassed but not in a happy frame of mind.[14]

At 4 P.M. started in the "Labourdonais", a magnificent steamer. The Capt. unfortunately is deaf; & a native of Marseilles: Conversation with him is therefore almost impossible.

TUESDAY, 27 MARCH 1866: 8 A.M. arrived at H'Kong: we had a pleasant passage, with a strong breeze however, and I enjoyed myself on the whole. Pin was not sick, but the boys were. The "Labourdonais" is a magnificent ship, & vastly superior in every respect to any vessel of the P. & O. that I ever travelled in.

Remained only a few hours in H'Kong, where, however, I had time enough to do all I wanted. I got £53.10.0 in [indistinct word] for $250, Francs 544 for $100, $133 in cash, & transferred $25 000 to a/c A London and $2200 to a/c Z.

Left at 4 P.M. in the "Cambodge", a fine vessel in point of size: but without the finish of the "Labourdonais" [the name of this ship is spelled differently every time; this time "Liboudais"] Awfully silly to be putting away from H'Kong in this direction. Hurrah!

FRIDAY, 30 MARCH 1866: Arrived at Saigon at 5 P.M. The passage has been fine in point of speed; the cooking not very good, & the servants not well drilled. From H'Kong to S'gon is 915 miles; we did it in 72 hours. From the sea to the settlement seems to be about 40 miles; the river winding through a jungle. The houses are not numerous, but they look well, & the roads are well arranged.[15]

SATURDAY, 31 MARCH 1866: Called with Pin & De Champs on the Governor, Admiral de la Grandier: a mere visit of ceremony.

SUNDAY, 1 APRIL 1866: Started at 3 1/2 a.m.

TUESDAY, 3 APRIL 1866: 8 A.M. at Singapore; from S'gon to S'pore is 637 miles; the "Cambodge" is a fast boat. I am comfortable enough, but the others complain of the attendance. Fittock wanted me to sign a certificate anent the discomforts of Mrs. F's cabin; I refused 1st, because it would be impolitic as I.G. to sign such a document for an English Consul, 2nd, because he had not spoken to the Captain, & 3rdly, because a/ the certificate was matter of fact in regard to the position of the rooms, b/ it made a wrong use of the words "First-class accommodation", and c/ I could not certify that Mrs. F's sickness was to be attributed to the rooms occupied by her, & which had originally been selected [?] by Fittock & herself, both of them old voyagers.[16]

Changed $95 for £20; paid away £3 & $2.50 in various ways. The town grows and the place seems a very charming one. Monkeys & parrots and boys who dance and dive form the chief sights alongside the steamer.

Pin & the others called on [word unclear] but did not see him; he returned the call when they were out. Vrim, a Fuh Keen man named Ching, with a blue button came to the steamer & chatted awhile with Pin, who is by way of being very grand as Pae-d [sent] by Chung Kwo [China].[17]

WEDNESDAY, 4 APRIL 1866: Left Singapore at 9 a.m. We had taken on board many additional passengers, who are chiefly from Batavia, — comic yellow looking women, & some white children. Commenced today to read French with M. Champion; if I kept it up for a month, I ought to be able to speak with some facility when we arrive at Marseilles.[18]

A squall about 7 P.M. with a heavy shower cooled the air very much, & the evening afterwards was fresh and pleasant.

THURSDAY, 5 APRIL 1866: [characters for 20th day of the 2nd lunar month]

At noon today we had run 323 miles; to Galle we have still to go 1181 miles; we ought to be there at noon on Monday next.

Among the objects striven for during the last five years, the most important have been to induce the Emperor to grant an audience to foreign ministers, and to appoint representatives to reside at the various European Courts. Until China shall have taken both these steps, her independence will be in danger; but the moment she takes them, she will be one of the most important powers in the comity of nations. The Western appliances in which we have the precedence, will never be willingly adopted or get fair play in China, until the Govt. practically recognizes the existence of other independent states; nor can we be certain of the continuance of pacific relations, unless China moves from her present position, for she keeps herself out of Court by remaining without the pale of civilised nations.[19]

After having been twelve years in the country, now that I leave it for the first time, it is with considerable gratification that I find myself accompanied by the few Chinese who are with me; I have succeeded in carrying through a great many useful measures,— some of more, some of less importance. This last measure, I look on as being the "finis" which [word unclear]; it ends my first period in China, & it will form the starting point for the second. It is a good winding up of twelve years' labor; it is equally valuable in being full of promise for the future.

After having worked for the point for some years, I had at last given it up in despair; the very day afterwards, Pin came to me, & said that the Yamen had proposed that he shd. accompany me, & asked me would I be willing to take him. He had previously suggested his third son, as being a fitting person to go with me to take notes, & for a couple of years they had all spoken in favor of the appointment of embassies. When therefore his name came forward, he himself could not draw back, for people wd. then say to him that he had not been in earnest in the advice he had previously been given [sic], and they would also say that he was unwilling to expose himself to risks to which he had proposed to expose his son. I at once expressed my willingness, & from that moment the matter was virtually settled. The details only remained to be arranged.[20]

{Here I must stop; the "Cambodge" commences to feel the roll of the Indian Ocean, & I feel in consequence a seasick inclination.}

FRIDAY, 6 APRIL 1866: From daylight till noon we coasted in a westerly direction close to Sumatra, leaving Pulo way on the right.[21]

The hills are wonderfully well wooded in some places, & bare & brown [?] in others; Off Pulo way saw a large school of fish — of a very large kind — which went along as fast as the steamer, making wonderful springs from the water.

Last night it was stiflingly hot; I felt quite feverish, but perspired profusely.

Captain Boris told me this morning that a "complaint in pretty good English had been seen by his own eyes, which had been presented to the agent at Singapore (Saegon?) [sic] complaining that the Chinese were as well treated as the other passengers!"

Among the passengers who joined us at Singapore, are the Chief or President of the Batavia company, and an old Belgian (69 years of age) who has been 48 years in Java, & who now goes to Europe for the first time since he first left it in 1818. There are some ladies and some children,— the ladies yellow & skinny, the children white but lively. There is one very pretty girl of 15 or thereabouts, but I don't think her blood is quite pure; her hair eyes & forehead are very good, & the expression of her face is pleasant. Some men shave & others grow all that will grow. One Spaniard has a line of rough gray hairs from lip to chin which gives him quite a queer look, & another has whiskers, moustache & the same central chin-appendage: why the latter shaves both sides of his chin, & why the former retains such an odd material, are equally inexplicable. [Sketches after "chin" and "chin-appendage"]

From 12 yesterday till noon today, our run was only <u>280</u> miles: very good, though, compared with the general rate of the P & O.

How Pin came to be fixed on was thus: a daughter of the Hwang-tsin-Wang (brother of Taoukwang) was about to be married to a brother of Chang-shen (who by marriage with Kwei Leang's daughter is a brother in law of Prince Kung's) some years ago; the father of the groom died and the marriage was put off for 27 months; just when the mourning was ended, the Wang [Prince] died, & thus the young lady had to mourn for 9 months; thus it was not till <u>February</u> <u>1866</u> that the marriage could take place. Pin was elected to bring the bride home, but he cried [?] off that honorary office, & went simply to the wedding; there he met Prince Kung, with whom he had some talk, & from that it came about that he was fixed upon for nomination to the tour of duty for which I had been wanting some one.[22]

I acceded to his being the man at once: partly because he is sufficiently intelligent, & partly because having talked much with me during the last two years, his faculty of <u>receptivity</u> has been developed, partly because he is well known to all the chief people at Peking, & will therefore be believed by them, & partly because his manners will make a good impression, and he is likely on his return to be "one of the Yamen." What I urged on the attention of all was the propriety of "giving him as much face" as possible.[23]

SATURDAY, 7 APRIL 1866: Last night was an abominably hot one; I perspired most profusely, slept little, & got up today with aching head, and rheumatic limbs.

The run today, at noon, was 296 miles; we are now <u>605</u> miles from Galle.

SUNDAY, 8 APRIL 1866: Distance run 297 miles.

MONDAY, 9 APRIL 1866: Distance run 265 miles. Arrived at Galle at 3 1/2 P.M.[24] By telegraph from [Hart left empty space] we learned that the Calcutta steamer will be in tomorrow morning; the "Cambodge" is advertised to sail at 5 P.M.

Galle seems to me (from the ship) to be much as I recollect it. The prevailing feeling in my mind, as I think of the twelve years that have gone by since I passed through on my way to China, on my first start in life, is one of intense gratitude: a gratitude that is composed of thankfulness for the blessings that have fallen to my lot — health & success — and of sorrow & shame for all the ill that I have done & all the good I have left undone. I wind up my first period with much humiliation of spirit, under circumstances which to others appear of a kind that ought to make one proud and elated: God grant that I may be saved from the self deceit of "the pride that apes [?] humility."

Desultory thought is like desultory reading; it weakens the machine, &

produces nothing. I have been too fond of indulging in reverie; my thought-work has been mere bubble-blowing, and, now that the froth sinks & disappears, I find my mind a blank. I must change all this: I must read, I must think, and I must write. I must <u>prove</u> myself. I am horribly superficial in all respects, and, though I may have done more than others in the way of work that will influence men, I seem to myself an impostor, when I compare myself with ninety nine per cent of educated men, I don't know whether it wd. be right, or not, to attempt to console myself with the idea, that Education has two ends to work out: one to fill with knowledge of facts, & the other to develop the faculties; I fancy that my faculties are in good working order, i.e. that I have been educated in the sense of development, but the point in which I see my weakness is my want of knowledge of facts — not that I have not read much, but that I have read so much & so hastily that facts have formed my mind & opinions, but have disappeared from my memory, & do not come when called. Thus I converse badly, & fail in any attempt to illustrate my opinions. "Discovering my moral secretions", as Dick wd. say.[25]

TUESDAY, 10 APRIL 1866: Went ashore this morning with M. Champion; looked into a few shops, and drove to the Cinnamon Gardens. I did not see anything particularly nice in the shops, & the few articles we priced were excessively dear. The drive, nearly all the way having the sea on the left hand, was a very pleasant one; the roads good & well shaded by cocoa nut trees. The Cinnamon Gardens are a name rather than a reality; there are Cinnamon trees in them of course, & little boys rush at one from all directions to sell Cinnamon walking sticks; these boys plague visitors dreadfully, & they are one and all — though having articles for sale — little beggars; they cry "Save," "Save," most lugubriously, & all but whine if one drives off without giving them anything. I felt the sun a little, & dare say I shall have a headache in consequence.

The Calcutta Steamer, "Erynauthe," came in at 8 a.m.; her passengers some 70 or more joined us during the course of the day; several fit and elderly women, a lot of Indian military men & civilians, and a dozen children.

We left Galle about 8 P.M. On shore I spent half a sovereign and a rupee; Champion repaid me three rupees as his share.

WEDNESDAY, 11 APRIL 1866: Very hot: head aching all day.

THURSDAY, 12 APRIL 1866: Distance run at noon, since starting on Tuesday night, 412 miles.

Read an article in the "Quarterly" on the Extension of the Franchise; it condemns the proposed "Reform," & says it will but open the tide gates for the entry of a flood of Radicalism of the lowest sort.[26]

FRIDAY, 13 APRIL 1866: Distance run 262 miles.

Read an article in the "Edinburgh", on the Extension of the Franchise; it is in favor of the extension, & says that if Radical representatives come in as a consequence, they are not likely to muster very strong, and those who do enter Parliament are more likely to join the Conservative party, so as to oppose the measures, &c. of the employers of labor, who are chiefly in the Liberal ranks. It is strange how much can be said on each side of any subject offered for discussion.

SATURDAY, 14 APRIL 1866: Distance run 290 miles.

Spent the whole morning gossiping with the children on board; three of the more advanced lads, about ten years of age each, are very interesting boys — especially one little lad, Charley, from Tasmania.

In the "London Quarterly" in an article on Lord Palmerston, I saw that in one of his speeches he explained Canning's liberalism by saying that he looked upon those who opposed reform through fear of innovation as likely to have to consent ultimately to innovations when they would no longer be looked upon as reforms. In that remark there is great wisdom.[27]

A review of Palgrave's travels speaks of him as cosmopolitan enough to please all, but not enough of a politician to see the tendency of the political influences set agoing by such cosmopolitanism. Mark that: it ought to be borne in mind in China.[28]

SUNDAY, 15 APRIL 1866: [characters for 1st day of the 3rd lunar month]

Fine weather we have had all along: the last three days what wind there has been — very little of [word unclear] — has been northerly, & the weather cools somewhat. This voyage is an excessively tiresome one; I shall be very glad when we arrive at Suez.

The "Cambodge" is a fine vessel, large & fast, but the cooking is not good, and the servants are neither civil nor well drilled. We have two breakfasts & two dinners, & our Chinese passengers who breakfast second and dine second come in for hot atmosphere, cold victuals, steaming waiters [?] & crusty tempers.

Champion wishes he was at Marseilles, as he cannot stand the "amour" which a lady, English, with a "sympathique" face, inspires him with; he asks me don't I think she is "taken" too? I answer she is an Englishwoman & married. He sighs: then he says "She has smiled at me!"

At Ceylon, I found waiting for me a nice long letter from Andrew Happer.[29]

The Chinese quite at home on board; they don't give any trouble to anyone and, although they don't take to our food kindly yet, they are not likely to starve. Some passengers, says the Capt., complained that the Chinese are

as well treated on board as other people; the complaint ought to have been "are not better treated than."
Run, 280.

MONDAY, 16 APRIL 1866: Run, 303.

TUESDAY, 17 APRIL 1866: Run, 307.

WEDNESDAY, 18 APRIL 1866: Arrived at Aden about 17 minutes past twelve.[30] I lost a lottery of £12 by being two minutes slow, and one of £6 by being two minutes fast. The place has changed its appearance since I was here last; the harbour is buoyed and lighted, and the P & O & Messageries have fine houses, and coal yards, under the peak, which supports the flag staff. The day was very hot, &, fearing the sun, I did not go ashore. The hills opposite Aden looked wonderfully fine at sunset; their jagged peaks resemble very closely the jaw & teeth of a huge fish.

Left Aden at 10 P.M.: the "Norris" P & O left from [word unclear] at 2 P.M. Our captain said he "proposed to follow that vessel." The Bombay Steamer ("Nubia") arrived from Aden at 8 P.M.[31]

THURSDAY, 19 APRIL 1866: Very hot. Head aching.

FRIDAY, 20 APRIL 1866: Distance run since we started 449 miles. At 2 P.M. "Lorna" in sight ahead; passed her about 8 P.M.

SATURDAY, 21 APRIL 1866: Last night a strong northerly wind blew, & a heavy head sea got up. Our run has thus been but a poor one: we only made 226 miles. This will delay our arrival at Suez a day.[32] I was inclined to be seasick in the morning & could not come out to breakfast.

SUNDAY, 22 APRIL 1866: A nice cool day; the sea has gone down, and we are going along well. Distance run, 244 miles; Lat. 24.29 W Lon. 34.01 E at noon. We hope to be in Suez on Tuesday morning.

MONDAY, 23 APRIL 1866: Fine morning: sensibly colder. The shower bath this morning was almost as cold as one could wish it to be. Tendency toward diarrhea; in going north, one cannot be too careful in dressing warmly; when going south, one may dress lightly without fear.

377

At eight a.m. we entered Strait of Jubal; we ought to be at Suez at midnight, provided the moonlight admits of our going on.

Fittock said to Howell "the next few years will be interesting ones in the East; I shall sit by quietly [?], & watch the course of events; I shall not interfere!" This is superb! He & Schmidt have signed a complaint about the bread & salt. Certes, there are not enough salt-cellars, but the bread is the best I have had since I left Europe in 1854. Some other passengers have got up a counter-document, in praise of Captain & crew; that is too much of a good thing. From all such testimonials I keep apart.[33]

The proximity of Mts. Sinai & Horib tend to solemnize one's feelings much. "Write all these thy laws on our hearts, we beseech Thee!" [34]

Distance run [left blank]

Arrived at Suez at 11 1/2 P.M.

TUESDAY, 24 APRIL 1866: Up at 3 1/2 & Landed at 8 a.m. Music on shore at breakfast time at the hotel; the music was enchanting; the hotel greatly improved. Telegraphed home telling them to expect me on the 8th May: paid £4.16.0.

Left Suez about 3 1/2 P.M., and arrived at Cairo at half past eight; put up at the "Hotel des Aurbrofondeurs [?]", where they keep a good table, but have neither baths nor look-out. Salute fired: was it for Pin?

WEDNESDAY, 25 APRIL 1866: At Cairo all day. Very tired. Pin, Kwang, & Tih with DeChamps & Spooner visited the Pyramids. On the north face some 200 feet up on a stone over the doorway, Pin recognized some characters as being those known & in use in China 4000 years ago: the [characters for *chin-shih wen-tzu;* metal and stone writings] also called [characters for *chung-ting wen;* bell and vessel inscriptions]. Very curious & interesting. They got back at noon having lost [indistinct word] when on doubling-back: & then visited the Citadel, &c.[35]

A bad day to be at Cairo, as, being a feast day (Mahomet's birthday?), all the Bazaars were closed.

THURSDAY, 26 APRIL 1866: Left Cairo at 9 a.m., &, arriving at Alexandria about 2 1/2, went on board the tug at once & were taken to the "Said" in which we started at 5 P.M. The sea on the bar thinned the dinner-table at once, and, with others, I was horribly seasick.

Saw M. de Lesseps: an old white bearded gentleman with stern red face & gray moustache. On board with us are two sons of Abdelkader[;] they are poor-looking "critters"; where is their fathers fire?[36]

SUNDAY, 29 APRIL 1866: After dinner in sight of the high Calabrian coast.

MONDAY, 30 APRIL 1866: Last night I walked the deck from 10 1/2 till 2 1/2 when we arrived at Messina: remained there a couple of hours. The town is prettily situated: Reggio opposite. Pity we had not daylight. In the morning missed Scylla & Charibdis: came on deck after we had passed them: wonderful cutting wind blowing — regularly taking a slice off the waters.[37]

TUESDAY, 1 MAY 1866: About noon passed through the Straits of Bonifacio: Sardinia to the left, & Corsica to the East or right. Noted the Bear hill opposite Magdalena and afterwards saw Garibaldi's residence on Le Cafrena.[38] Closed my letters home telling them to expect me on Sunday the 6th.

I send two trunks, one clothes bag, & Brown's box direct to London, & take with me only one trunk & one valise.

We hope to be in Marseilles about noon tomorrow at the latest.

WEDNESDAY, 2 MAY 1866: Arrived at Marseilles at noon; luggage passed "en ambassadeur"; wonderful horses & curious harnesses. Left Grand Hotel about 9 and with Spooner & Champion took a coupé.

THURSDAY, 3 MAY 1866: Capital breakfast at Dijon. Arrived at Paris at 6 1/2; met by Meritens who took me to the Grand Hotel.

FRIDAY, 4 MAY 1866: Called at the French F.O. and saw the Baron Devrée; he did not appear to know Meritens or aught about him, altho M. had previously said they were "so" intimate, &c. &c. &c.

Left Paris at 7.

SATURDAY, 5 MAY 1866: At Dover about daylight, & the Albion Hotel, London, about 7. Saw Dick, Hughes, Gordon & Hannen; left London at 7.[39]

SUNDAY, 6 MAY 1866: At Kingstown & in Dublin before 7 a.m.; put up at Morrison's in Dawson St.; went to the Centenary, but Cassie was not there; dined with the Booths, a nice family, & then saw Cassie who has just recovered from the measles.[40]

MONDAY, 7 MAY 1866: Called at the Connexional & on Mr. Wallace. Took Cassie home by the 2 o'c train. Saw Mary in Lisburne, where Jamie & Geoffrey met me at the train. Got home — dear home again — about 7. Thank God for all his mercies![41]

TUESDAY, 8 MAY 1866: Quietly at home. It rains, & I don't like the climate; I have already got a cold. Call from Mrs. & Misses Brown.

WEDNESDAY, 9 MAY 1866: Went to Belfast and saw Greene, Smith, Andrews, Hill, &c. &c. &c. Recognized by one of the porters. Tired of the town very soon.[42]

THURSDAY, 10 MAY 1866: Went to the Distillery. Saw my old master Mr. Parkinson; Mrs. McKnight; Lenox; Miss & Mrs. David; the Miss Moorheads, &c. Marian looks a little old & "wiszened" as though she had had bad health & was stunted in growth; notwithstanding, I found my heart warming towards her.[43]

FRIDAY, 11 MAY 1866: Left home at 12; crossed from Kingstown to Holyhead.

SATURDAY, 12 MAY 1866: In London at 7 a.m. put up at the Waterloo Hotel in Jermyn St. Went with Hughes to the Crystal palace; great crush: introduced to Miss Annie Taylor, & Miss Florence Churchill & their Mamas: saw H. Dent, Lewis, Gould, Webster, Waller &c. &c. &c. and other "Chinamen". In the evening went to the Strand & saw "Paris". Then to the Argyle Room.[44]

SUNDAY, 13 MAY 1866: Called on the Payne's: Miss P. a nice girl: poor Payne cd. not see me; I fear he is done for.[45]

MONDAY, 14 MAY 1866: Called on the Kings; the girls not so nice as I expected, & the elder the prettier of the two. Went to the Alhambra and Somers'.[46]

TUESDAY, 15 MAY 1866: Chiwen arrived from Paris; Pin is poorly & has not come; took Tih Ming to the Crystal Palace; went to the Adelphi & saw Sothern & Buckstone in the Favorite of Fortune.

WEDNESDAY, 16 MAY 1866: Took Dick and Wheeler [?] to the Derby; started at 9 3/4, got back at 8 3/4. Thought it very slow, but saw lovely girls along the road. Went to Cremorne at 10 & came back at 1. Saw one lovely little girl; I restrain myself so far, & hope to continue to do so, but it is difficult to go near the fire without getting burned. Saw O. B. C. Webster, Chambers, & other Chinamen there. Call from Bonnie.[47]

THURSDAY, 17 MAY 1866: Left cards & letters at the Athenaeum for Oliphant & Crawford, at the Reform for Lay; saw Hammond & Alston at the F.O. & called on Sir W. Ferguson.[48]

Call from Forbes. Paid Bowra £300. Wrote to Wilzer, Kahn, Steward, Chatfield, & Miss Taylor.[49]

I hate the life here; it is too exciting in some ways; not enough so in others; and it is a bore altogether; I must get up a virtuous affection somewhere, or I shall be miserable.

To the Crystal Palace; fun with a couple of girls; home at 1 1/2. Very tired.

FRIDAY, 18 MAY 1866: Lord Clarendon will see Pin tomorrow at 4 P.M., Hammond writes; Pin, however, who arrived last night from Paris is suffering from Piles & cannot go out.[50]

Went & saw the Macafres, at 11 Cattecant [?] West Brompton; brought one of the girls into the city with me. David much changed, and looking older than myself.

Went to the annual China Company dinner at Willis' Rooms; Sir John Davis in the chair. Dinner indifferent; wine inferior; speaking poor.[51]

SATURDAY, 19 MAY 1866: Breakfasted with De Meritens meeting Hughes and Hannen; took the Baron to the Crystal Palace; saw there the ladies Hughes introduced me to; Miss C. blushed charmingly as I came up, but I don't think hers is the face towards which my heart cd. ever warm.[52]

Dined at the R.I.Y.C. [?] & then saw the Baron safely back to the Charing Cross Hotel.

SUNDAY, 20 MAY 1866: Introduced Hughes to Pin. Went to see Payne; found him able to be up, but looking seedy; a very nice girl is his sister.

In the evening after dinner at the Club picked up a couple of acquaintances in the Park and walked with them to Weymouth St.

MONDAY, 21 MAY 1866: Breakfasted with Oliphant at 35 Half Moon St.; he tells me my name has been put up at the Athenaeum, & that I can have the run of the Club for a month or so.

Yesterday sent a "condolence" card to Mrs. Budin, whose husband is dead; also sent £50 to the Zion Hill Sunday School. Wrote to Cassie, & to Campbell; and also to Mr. Chapman, promising to go to Rockhampton on Wednesday.[53]

Nefretti [?] & Zambra tell me they can make for me a Barometer which will show difference in elevation from 5 to 500 feet.

Have taken a box at H. M.'s Theatre for the evening {No. 81, £5.15.6}; Hughes, Dick & Forbes are to dine with me, and then go there.

The sun shines, but the air is cold, and the streets are dusty.

Went to the H. M. Theatre; saw the "Huguenots". Very fine music, fine house, &c. &c. &c.

Called on Mr. Hammond to enquire when Lord Clarendon cd. receive Pin.

TUESDAY, 22 MAY 1866: Hannen breakfasted with me this morning; he said nothing as to his dislike of KiuKiang; I told him I shd. expect him to be there before the 15th Nov.[54]

A letter from Mr. Hammond says, Lord C. will receive Pin tomorrow at 4 P.M.

WEDNESDAY, 23 MAY 1866: Went with Pin & Chinese to call on Lord Clarendon; he recd. us kindly. Went to Rockhampton & slept there.

THURSDAY, 24 MAY 1866: Left London for home.

FRIDAY, 25 MAY 1866: Arrived at Ravarnette.[55]

THURSDAY, 31 MAY 1866: After a quiet week at Ravarnette went to Portadown & called on Mrs. Bredon; sat there from 3.10 to 5.30; liked Miss B. very much; passed the house first of all, but fancied the face in the window. She likes Erand's Pianos: strange enough, that is the name of the maker of the one sent to Peking.[56] Did not call on anyone else at Portadown.

SATURDAY, 2 JUNE 1866: With Jamie went to P'down, & put up at Hall's. Called on Mr. Masaroon, & Mrs. B., & tea'd with Aunt Brady.[57]

SUNDAY, 3 JUNE 1866: Went to the Guinness's in the morning, but only saw Aunt Mary: to the love-feast [church] where Dr. Appleton gave out "Now I have found", "How happy every child of grace", and "Oh what are all our sufferings here"; dined with Aunt Edgar; to the preaching in the evening.[58]

MONDAY, 4 JUNE 1866: Called at Mrs. Bredon's; drove out to Mr. Croans, saw him & John MacAdam: tea'd at Mr. Thos. Shillington's.[59]

TUESDAY, 5 JUNE 1866: Tea'd & spent the evening at Mrs. Bredon's: asked Miss B. while at the piano "could she find it in her heart to come to China with me?" and afterwards asked her Mother: both say "yes", but say the eldest brother must be consulted.[60]

WEDNESDAY, 6 JUNE 1866: Called on the Shillingtons & then spent an hour and a half pleasantly with Hessie, Returned to Ravarnette.

THURSDAY, 7 JUNE 1866: Went to Belfast, & tea'd with Willy Aicken.[61]

FRIDAY, 8 JUNE 1866: Got a piano for the girls, some things for Hessie, dined with Carlisle; went to the Q.C. [Queen's College] Lit. Society; met Catherine Parkinson.

SATURDAY, 9 JUNE 1866: Back to Ravarnette, and thence to Portadown: tea'd with Mrs. B.: the eldest son Robert says "yes", so Hessie is to be my wife.

SUNDAY, 10 JUNE 1866: From the Preaching House walked up with the Shillingtons, & then sat an hour with Aunt Brady: after that went to Mrs. B's, where I dined & spent the evening with Hessie: met Mr. Fitzgerald at dinner.

MONDAY, 11 JUNE 1866: Dined at Mrs. B.'s & met there Mr. Woodhouse, who came out into the hall to ask me to Omeath Park. Had an invite from Mrs. Shillington to tea. Mrs. B. would like Hessie to spend some time with her after she is a wife; but Hessie herself, who wd. willingly come to me tomorrow, will also willingly do what I shd. best like, i.e., marry me the day I have to start for China. Hessie tells me on Valentine's Day last, a friend sent her a piece of Wedding cake on which (for the first time) she dreamt, & that in her dream she saw a man she supposed to be me, walking with his brother down Carleton Place. Strange to say, the name of the girl I admired in Chapel & whom I supposed to be a daughter of Dr. Applebee's, is also Hester Jane!

Came back from P'down, and tea'd with Mary.

TUESDAY, 12 JUNE 1866: Wet morning, but clearing up towards noon.

The Chinese have been handsomely treated in England; they visited Windsor, were asked to the Queen's Ball, & were also privately presented to the Queen, before she held her Court at Buckingham Palace.

Time is slipping past very rapidly; I scarcely know to what to turn my attention first, I seem to have so much to do before returning to China. I have scarcely been able to collect my thoughts since I came home.

Hughes writes to say he has his fears about the <u>Oriental Bank</u>: I must look into this.

WEDNESDAY, 13 JUNE 1866: Took Lizzie today to Portadown, where I spent the day at Mrs. Bredon's. Met there Mrs. Buchanan, Mrs. Waddell, & Mrs. Black. Hessie and myself had a talk about "<u>the</u> day" and she agrees with me in my proposal that it shall be Saturday, the 15th September. Spent a pleasant afternoon, and felt quiet & happy with Hessie beside me; I don't feel the chain when she is at hand; it is only when away from her that I am sensible of a feeling of loss of freedom. But she is an intelligent, lively, unaffected, & <u>wide-awake</u> young lassie — by 'wide-awake' I mean able to hold her own against most comers. I just wish I was quietly back in Peking with her; I shall do all I can to make her happy and comfortable, and — if the past could only be blotted out — I could almost feel certain of unalloyed happiness for the future. O the past! the past! with its ghosts of dead sins, & its living results of manhood's first errors. "Let the dead past bury its dead:"— <u>that</u> is easy enough: what is not so easy is to keep the future free from instrusiveness on the part of the products of the past. Does complete confidence mean "to have no secrets for the future", or "to reveal all that has been done in the past"?[62]

On returning found a telegram from Bowra stating that Pin refuses to leave England without seeing me; he is either pleased with English treatment, frightened by rumors of war on the Continent, or distrustful of Bowra. So I must go to London.

THURSDAY, 14 JUNE 1866: Dr. Bredon dead a month today; myself and Hessie acquainted a fortnight today.

I have written Bowra to wait for me in London: I shall go there on Monday next; one morning with Pin will settle the <u>route</u>, and an afternoon at the Bank will suffice to arrange my money-matters.

Hessie's birthday will be on the 21st; she will then be 19; I must get something for her: I think a dressing case and a watch. I must be back in Portadown on that day to wish her many happy returns, the dear girl!

Walked a little today before dinner; the sky overcast, & rain threatening: in point of weather, I have been quite unlucky since I came home, i.e., in Ireland, nothing but rain, and in London cold easterly winds. I must arrange the manner in which I am to spend the next three months, so as to get through whatever there is that ought to be done before going to China again.

FRIDAY, 15 JUNE 1866: Went to Lisburn today, but was too late for Mary's dinner; dined thankfully and agreeably off a fresh herring & some bread & butter; then met Mrs. & Miss Bredon at the train at 4.53; took them to Mary's where they remained for tea, & after that accompanied them as far as Levogren [?] by the 7.40 train. Hessie looked charming: the girls, father, & Mrs. Maze are all delighted with her. In the train going back, she took off her gloves, & fidgeted most amusingly with her hands: I fancy she wd. have given a deal for a hug at that moment. She is a darling girl, and I love her with all my heart.

Walked home from Kishem [?] with Sarah.

Recd. a telegram from Bowra, to whom I have sent orders to "go or stay as he pleases."

SATURDAY, 16 JUNE 1866: Very cold; rain, hail, snow, and wind.

A telegram from Bowra says Pin will not go to Washington; will await my arrival in London.

By the 10.50 train went to Newry, and thence to Omeath Park; the drive from Newry to Mr. Woodhouse's residence occupies only half-an-hour (quick driving); was there from 2 P.M. to 6 1/2; the young ladies are agreeable girls, but not striking in any way. Miss Saurin was also there. The eldest son seems a shocking lout. Got back to Lisburn at 9 P.M.; father staid at P'down; frightfully cold. Down home with Sarah.

SUNDAY, 17 JUNE 1866: Still cold & shivery. In the morning heard Mr. Knox preach; a short & not brilliant sermon. Wrote to Hessie.

MONDAY, 18 JUNE 1866: Went to London.

TUESDAY, 19 JUNE 1866: Arranged with Pin his route through Europe; he does not wish to visit the U.S., and I shall not therefore attempt any compulsion. He is to go to Amsterdam, Copenhagen, Stockholm, St. Petersburg, Brussels, Paris, and back to China by the mail of the 19th Augt.

Bought a dressing case for Hessie at Howell James & Co.'s, and selected a watch &c. for her at Harry Emmanuel's, each costing £55.

WEDNESDAY, 20 JUNE 1866: Went with Hughes to look at furniture in Druse's in Baker St.

Went to the Bank & saw both Stuart & Campbell; they told me I might set my mind at rest, that the Bank is quite safe, & that should matters look atall threatening, they have an arrangement with Govt. which wd. pull them through. They also advised me as to the way in which I ought to invest my money, & I have authorized them (vide letter 21 June from Dublin) to invest as follows:

£2.000	of E. J. Co.'s 5% Rupee Paper	£100.
£1.000	of New Zealand 6% Loan	£60.
£1.000	of Portuguese Govt. Loan	£50.
£1.000	of Madras Railway Stock	£50.
£2.000	of North Staffordshire Railway Stock	£100.
£3.500	of Oriental Bank Corporation Shares	
	say 100 @ £35	£250.
		£610.

Annual interest, at least £610. The dividends & interest on the £10.500 invested will thus be over £600 a year, & the stock (Banking and Railway) will improve during the next two years.

Went to Mayall's & was photographed. Left [for?] Dublin by the mail train at 8$\frac{25}{}$.

Sir Macdonald Stephenson called in the morning, & so did Genl. & Mrs. Griffith, Rawlinson's mother. A Mr. Bishop also called to see me, who said de Meritens had promised him an appointment; he seemed somewhat put out when I said I did not know his name, & had heard nothing about him; he was accompanied by a young Viscount, & he asked if it would be of any use for three or four M.P.s to apply in his behalf. I said "No".[63]

THURSDAY, 21 JUNE 1866: [A huge red star in the margin] Stopped in Dublin till 2 P.M.

Wrote to the O.B.C. [Oriental Bank Corporation] authorising the purchase of securities, to be debited to a/c "Z."

Hessie's Birthday. Nineteen today. [Written in, diagonally, apparently as an afterthought.]

Got to P'down after 6, & spent the evening with Hessie; found Maggie & Cassie still there.

FRIDAY, 22 JUNE 1866: Spent the day with Hessie, and arranged that as I shall be free after the 15th Augt. our wedding shd. take place between the 9th & 26th.

Called on Mr. Irwin, Aunt Mary, & Aunt Brady; also on Mr. Masaroon. Came home by the 5.45 train.

SATURDAY, 23 JUNE 1866: A warm day; played croquet all morning with the girls. In the evening went to the Distillery with the girls; called at Olge's [?] grave.

SUNDAY, 24 JUNE 1866: Went to the Hillsborough Church in the morning: walked there & sat with Miss Davis. Came out & went home with the Miss Moorheads, who, with Robby & Henry, afterwards walked most of the way home with me. In the evening, drove with Dada & Jeanne to Mr. Brown's; his son died this morning at 2 1/2. One of the girls,—the youngest, I think,—rather good looking.

MONDAY, 25 JUNE 1866: Mary out today [i.e., out to Ravarnette]: talked with her all morning.

TUESDAY, 26 JUNE 1866: Went to Dublin by the first train. Spent an hour at the "Winter Place"; then V.C. Gallery: very interesting. Went to 4 Upper Buckingham St., & was with Hessie from 3 to 5 1/4; introduced to her aunts (her mother's sisters) Miss Breadon, & Mrs. Browning [?] In the evening went to the Centenary, & attended the Ordination Services; Guard & three others ordained.[64]

WEDNESDAY, 27 JUNE 1866: Spent the afternoon with my darling Hessie.

THURSDAY, 28 JUNE 1866: Went to Galway by the 8 a.m. train 22/. arrived at noon; drove about for a couple of hours, & then went to the College, where I found Lufton, who dined with me. After dinner, I spent the evening with him & his wife and Professor Moffatt. D'Arcy Thompson a dreamer, not a practical man: says Lufton. Galway College a finer building than that in Belfast. Galway small: a big [indistinct word] but no one in it; the county from Athlone west depopulated; turf, pasturage, & stones, Galway milk fine, salmon fishing excellent.[65]

FRIDAY, 29 JUNE 1866: Came back to Dublin by the noon train: went to Doblin's entertainment at the Rotunda. Very hot.

SATURDAY, 30 JUNE 1866: Returned to Ravarnette by the 8.00 train. Poor Cassie not very well. Raining again; weather cold. Professor Craik dead & buried.[66]

SUNDAY, 1 JULY 1866: To preaching. Dada officiated. Hymns "Lo God is here", "Jesus lover of my soul" "A charge to keep".
Heavy showers in the afternoon. Wrote to Hessie, who seems from her yesterday's letter in low spirits.

MONDAY, 2 JULY 1866: Went to D'lin accompanied by Sarah & Jamie; spent the evening with Hessie.

TUESDAY, 3 JULY 1866: In the morning with Hessie; I then went to the "break-up" of the connexional, heard part of the recitation, made a speech, & saw the prizes distributed. In the evening took Hessie and Sarah to Doblin's.

WEDNESDAY, 4 JULY 1866: Could not go to Miss Wood's concert. Spent most of the day with Hessie.

THURSDAY, 5 JULY 1866: Took Hessie & Sarah for a walk in the morning; & had tea with them, meeting two Miss Bredins [sic] in the evening.

FRIDAY, 6 JULY 1866: To the Anatomical Museum. Very cold day; had to set fires. Spent the evening with Hessie who, with Sarah, accompanied me to the Winter Palace. Robert Bredon arrived.

SATURDAY, 7 JULY 1866: Spent the morning with Hessie; & then returned, with Jamie, to Ravarnette, taking tea at Mary's. Found letters from China awaiting me.

SUNDAY, 8 JULY 1866: A cold rainy day; staid quietly at home reading letters, writing, collecting my scattered thoughts and reflecting.

MONDAY, 9 JULY 1866: Mr. & Mrs. Hughes dined here. Mary & James out to tea.[67]

TUESDAY, 10 JULY 1866: Had my berth taken and my box packed to go to Aberdeen today, but just at the last moment, 5 P.M., changed my mind, & remained at home. Why shd. I, with so little time at my disposal, be the one to run about, & waste that time? Spending days of travelling to have minutes of meeting, & seconds of conversation? Walked to Corry's Glen.

WEDNESDAY, 11 JULY 1866: Doing nothing particular. China letters by French Mail just read. No letter from FitzRoy. Newchwang was taken by the K'e-ma tsieh [mounted bandits], but given up soon; Ying-tze not visited by them. The tsieh cannot be called Rebels, & for them to seek such a place as Newchwang is of no moment whatever.[68]

Letters from Bowra describe Pin as being quite unmanageable: with me, he is reasonable & mild; with the others—unreasonable & savage: whose fault—? Think of this: for it will not do, to let the old man bolt with the bit in his teeth. Be cool, & think it out carefully: or, you'll be in a fix. [Curlicue design at end of sentence]

THURSDAY, 12 JULY 1866: Today walked into Lisburn with Maggie, Cha, Geoff, & "Doty" Hughes; saw the Orangemen,—a stupid loutish looking crowd of disorderly half-drunk, sweaty, half sun struck fellows: the women were thrice as numerous as the men. They had no idea of a procession, & their music was barbarous in the extreme: a little care wd. make such a turnout—I mean so numerous a turnout—a course of much enjoyment; & the practise of the fife & drum if turned into proper channels wd. produce good country bands.[69] Write a note to one of the Belfast Papers anent it.

Came home in time for 3 o.c. dinner, & spent the afternoon quietly in the house. Mr. Guard came in in the evening.

FRIDAY, 13 JULY 1866: Letter from Hessie today: also notes from Bowra & DeChamps, who are heartily tired of Pin & his ways. What ought one to do—to support him or to support them? Häng & the others at P'king will support Pin, will get him into office: could I prevent their doing so? No reason that I cd. bring forward wd. be sufficient. But will he, once in office, turn around on me & treat me as he does Bowra & De Champs? I don't think he dare—don't think he wd. Well; wd. he be more useful in office than out? Decidedly. Wd. he be more useful as my friend? Most decidedly. Ergo: This train of reasoning points to giving the decision in favor of his wishes.

Today executed nine deeds of transfer O.B.C. [Oriental Bank Corporation] shares, 4 do. North Staffordshire Rwy stock, & 2 do. Madras Rwy stock: James Maze witnessed my signature. Wrote letter, & sent deeds of transfer to the O.B.C.[70]

Warm weather for the last three days; looks like rain today.

SATURDAY, 14 JULY 1866: Accompanied by Baby & Sonnie, went to D'lin by 7^{16} train, & returned by the 5. While in D'lin, Sarah took the children to the Zoological Gardens & the Winter Palace; I sat with Hessie.

A Capt. Phelps, Adjutant of the Scots' Greys, had the impudence to follow Sarah & Hessie the other day, and, after they got home, he walked before the house for a while, & then knocked & asked for the young ladies! Mrs. B. asked him his name &, strange to say, he gave it without hesitation! Dinah, however, sd. she wd. call down the master, & he then made off. It is better to take no notice of this now, but if he goes there again, he must be looked after.

Took tea at Mary's, & got home about half past ten.

SUNDAY, 15 JULY 1866: The brevity of the entries that precede this forms an almost sufficient record of the state of mind in which I have been for the last three months or more: I have been in a whirl of excitement, & have felt it almost impossible to think: I cd. neither criticise the past, nor plan the future, & I experienced an equal impossibility in respect of a conscious process of thought in the present. I have now been ten weeks at home, & I have eight more weeks before me to be spent in Ireland; my brain has gradually been clearing, & I commence to quiet down somewhat & to find reflection possible. This morning after I rose, I noticed that the world & its cares were uppermost in my mind, & I felt the symptoms of disgust & discontent swelling within me: I prayed & felt calmer; I read & the verses that spoke to my heart were "And that ye study to be quiet, and to do your own business," and "Humble yourselves therefore under the mighty hand of God, that He may exalt you in due time". Why shd. I trouble myself about the honors of this world? Why shd. I worry myself if they are long in coming? Why shd. I be disquieted if looking back on the past, I have not taken those steps most calculated to gain those marks of honorable recognition for me? To the boy beaten, the medal seemed to be the only thing worth living for; to the first in the class, the value of the medal ceased the moment it was obtained. To the outsiders, an A.B. seems something grand; the Bachelor of Arts hardly ever thinks of it after he once has it. Thus then to me who have not the C.B., or the K.C.B., those letters seem to have a charm about them, which I am sure would be dispelled by possession. Granted that the medal, the B.A., the C.B., are all marks of summits attained: they record the past, & are starting points for future efforts, but just as it is often the outside horse that wins the race, and just as many men, besides the snobs who have cut their initials on them, may have visited remarkable places, so, too, in life — in its work, in usefulness, & best of all in the self-conciousness of noble aim, brave endeavour, & true success — the men whose names have neither A.B. nor C.B. to take them, are generally men who live more really, & whose deeds are less likely to prove hollow as drums, or barren & without good fruit.^{71}

This train of thought — fermenting, unheard, for some time back, — has been bubbling up this morning as the result of a feeling that I have not been spending my leave as advantageously, as pleasantly, or as wisely, as time & opportunities wd. have allowed. In this way: instead of seeking the acceptance of the men in authority in Europe — not only in England, but on the continent — men, to whom my position wd. have proved reason for knowing me, & to whose doors my connexion with the Chinese Mission wd. have brought me so easily, and whose friendship might have been useful to me in the present & in the future, I have been staying quietly at home: I have not gone to theatres — concerts — balls — dinners — receptions — "drawing rooms" &c. &c. &c; I have not hunted for recognition, & I have not attempted to set agoing those things which wd. have arrived <u>directly</u> at securing "crosses and ribbons". Instead of being everywhere & living gaily, I have been spending my time quietly in the country with my sisters, & have avoided, instead of sought for, even those little marks of attention which country people cd. have shown, without breaking in much on my quiet or my time.

Now: the question is, have I been acting wisely? Ninety-nine, out of a hundred, wd. say I have been foolish not to avail myself to the utmost of the opportunities I have had of going about, of knowing, & of becoming known. The simple fact of the matter is that I take no pleasure in "going about", that I don't care for the trouble of "becoming known", & that I could not be bored by giving so much of my short time to the hunting down even [?] to be known. I might have been acquainted with men high in rank & office: the possibility is, they wd. have "dropped" me after I had once been to their houses: I might have got acquainted with some influential people, through whom I might have procured C.B. at least, but wd. a C.B., got in such a way, have ever seemed valuable to me, however much the possession of its might have made me higher in the estimation of others? I confess: to have C.B. or K.C.B. wd. please me: but ought the want of it — the not having of it — to make me unhappy? Decidedly not. We cannot get everything: we must give up part or whole of some good things in order to procure part or whole of others: and had I remained in London, or gone about everywhere with the Chinese, I could not have had the satisfaction of being so much with my friends. At the same time: I can now see that my better plan wd. have been to have remained in London to the end of June, & to have spent the whole of July & August quietly at home. But I need not be discontented: "into each life some rain must fall": it is not given to men to see beforehand, & wisdom — which is to the individual rather the sigh over the wished past that produces contentment than the lesson which guides future action — cannot be got except in exchange for mistakes: we have to pay out a good many coppers, before we get a sovereign in exchange.

Besides my morning lesson is "Learn to be quiet"; & to wait for the "due time". "Let the dead past bury its dead": play out the game in accordance with the present state of the boards [?]; if you try to tack on to a past that has <u>not</u> even [?] a future[,] that only wd. accord with that past, the result must be failure. Having therefore gone in for quiet, & not notoriety, let quiet & not notoriety be sought for during the remainder of your leave. You have

certain work to do, before going to China: do that work, & don't bother yourself about C.B.s, or "presentations" or every of the hundred and one things,
which might (or might not) have been, but to seek for which now, wd. simply be to play a game that the cards don't warrant — or to fight a fight with
an unknown enemy, but off from one's resources, without a base, & trusting
to chance for supplies. From such folly, may I be delivered: may I be free
from such "vanity & vexation of spirit." Nothing is more difficult than to
look at realities firmly as they are; we always look at what we see through the
distorted medium of an insufficient experience, or through the discolored
glass of our own hopes & wishes; and there is no more uncommon sense
than common sense. I have life & health & strength: in a few years — I know
not how soon, — all three will be gone: am I to work for the bread that perisheth, or for the name on earth that is so soon forgotten? No: let the bread
be regarded as bread that perisheth, & the name as the name that is to be
forgotten: don't leave the straight track in pursuit of any such butterflies.
March boldly on: keep your eye fixed on the end: the little gate that leads
from this to another world, & so work that your works may follow you there.
Just fancy saying in Heaven, "O I was introduced to Lord A. whose
influence with Lord B. got me presented at Court & prepared for me the
C.B!" Rather pleasanter, I fancy, to be able to look down upon the work
accomplished that was given to be done. For it is a fact that the honors, I.E.
stars &c., go more by favour than by merit; but (while I allow my little hand
has some little work to do) great work is done only by those who can do it.
Now: am I to go in for "butterflies", or for "work"?

[Four stars across the page, with Hart's usual squiggles between the second and third]

With me Pin has always been pleasant in the extreme, & has shewn himself a man of great good sense. Bowra & De Champs, on the contrary, continually tell me that he is selfish, arrogant, overbearing, &c. &c. &c. Now I
know how prone one is to misrepresent — how [word illegible, underlined]
one is to it, unintentionally — and I must not allow myself to be drawn aside
from my own plans by the opinions of men who, for such opinions, may have
interested motives, or who, without interested motives, may form them
through an unconscious & self-deceiving self-imposing on, misrepresenta-
tion, or who form them under the influence of irritation, &c. My aim has
been 1°. to get the Chinese govt. to send officials to Europe; in that I have
succeeded; 2°. to get the European govts. to receive & kindly treat such
officials; in that I have succeeded better than I expected; 3°. to cause Europeans to be pleased with & take more interest in the Chinese; in that too I
have succeeded; 4°. to cause the Chinese officials to carry away with them
pleasant (their time is too short to admit of their being instructed) memories
of foreign lands; in that, too, I have so far succeeded. Now these four points
gained, am I to spoil everything by such action, as would make it impossible
to secure the attainment of the other ends yet hoped for? Those other ends
ought to be noted down, and then we shall be able to consider the steps to
be taken (in the face of present appearances) to make certain of their being

gained. I aimed (and aim) at 5°. having Pin made a t'ang kwan or Minister for Foreign Affairs, on return to China; 6°. getting the govt., by his aid, to look kindly on some of the arts and sciences of the West; 7°. inducing China to appoint Embassies abroad; and 8°. establishing a sensible & rational kind of friendship between China & other countries. Such are the ends I have had in view, in working for years back to bring about this mission: am I to be such an ass as to spoil everything by intemperate, hasty, or injudicious action now? Pin may have his faults; no doubt, he has; who hasn't? But if I go in against him, and successfully, the Mission will have been a total failure; if I go against him, unsuccessfully, he will never be my friend, & I shall not gain the other objects in as satisfactory a way as cd. be wished for. Now, I don't think I could go against him successfully: Häng Ke & the others wd. pull Pin through; and I can't see that I am called upon to go against him atall, for I have not the fullest reliance on either the good temper, judgment or tact of either Mr. B. or De C., and such being the case, how foolish it wd. be to go in against Pin unsuccessfully! So my plan is to take no notice of their petty squabblings & squallings. The machinery in the mill makes a noise, but if, to get rid of the noise, we stop it, where are we to get our linen? I have my own work to do: my aims are not selfish ones—I aim at the general good—I aim at ends which all wish for, which none are working for, & which all will applaud: aims apart, or viewed as determining action, my plan is to keep Pin in a good temper, to make him as powerful as possible, & to keep him as a friend in power. Will he "kick" when he has the upper hand? Will he "bolt"? I think not; I must chance it, however: to go to a distant country, you must run risks; you cannot examine every plank of the vessel,—you cannot determine beforehand the winds that will blow,—you may be drowned or you may arrive safely,—but if you have to go, you must start, & by ship. Now, I have this international voyage to make, I must go on with it, my ship is Pin—I have already embarked, got half over, and I shall go on. I must keep an eye on B. & De C. for the future, however: I don't think they'll do for places where either the plainest common sense or tact are required; they can't look around corners, & they won't make allowances.

[Asterisks along the bottom of the page]

MONDAY, 16 JULY 1866: Went to L'burn today with 'Doty' Hughes, & dined at Mary's. Mr. Guard & Cha were also there. After dinner went to some fruiterer's garden, and ate Strawberries, Raspberries, &c.: noticed that I had so long wished for proved to be less agreeable than the reminiscences of the past had caused me to expect. After tea Mary's youngest child (born St. Patrick's Day, 17 March last) was christened: called Robert Hart, after me.[72]

TUESDAY, 17 JULY 1866: Doty left today.

WEDNESDAY, 18 JULY 1866: Went to D'lin by the 2 train, & spent the evening from 7 to 11 1/2 with Hessie. Introduced to Sandy, who resembles Maggie much.

THURSDAY, 19 JULY 1866: Ordered a lot of things, shirts, & under clothing at Carringan's. Sandy dined with me; spent the evening with Hessie.

FRIDAY, 20 JULY 1866: Gave instructions to Messrs. Taylor, Mackesy, and Mortimer, Solicitors, 7 Dawson Street, to draw up settlements.
Spent the day with Hessie (whom I saw at the Riding School) from 12 1/2 @ 11.

SATURDAY, 21 JULY 1866: Spent the morning with Hessie; called at the Solicitors. Came home, accompanied by Sarah (& by Mrs. Bredon & Miss Saurin as far as P'down) by the 5 train. Took tea at Mary's.
Found a lot of letters awaiting me. The Chinese were in St. Petersburg on the 16th. They had seen the King of Sweden, & been well (too well) treated. Pin threatened to report to the Supt. of Russia the gov. of Abo, for opening a box (Customs' search)!
Letter, very affectionately worded, from de Meritens who is now recovering. He says the Govt. wd. like him to go out on the 19 Augt. & assist the Chargé d'affaires at P'King to put through the idea of sending Chinese Commissioners to the Exhibition in Paris.

SUNDAY, 22 JULY 1866: A beautiful morning: up & dressed for fatigue-duty (tattoo work) at 7.20. Today I must arrange all my proceedings for the next month, & must answer & write all necessary letters.

MONDAY, 23 JULY 1866: After breakfast had a long talk with my father relative to the points in which he & James Maze differ respecting their partnership. In the evening walked into Lisburn and had a talk with James. I hope I'm not "meddling to muddle".

TUESDAY, 24 JULY 1866: Left Ravarnette in the evening en route for Aberdeen.

WEDNESDAY, 25 JULY 1866: At Guinwik at daylight: at Glasgow at six; at Bridge of Allan, with Dick about one. Drove out in the afternoon to Doon Castle, saw the bed in which Queen Mary slept, & the window through which Hume escaped. B. of Allan is a lovely locality.[73]

THURSDAY, 26 JULY 1866: Left Dick at 10; at Perth about 1; telegraphed to Brazier, who, with his wife, met me on the platform about 4. Walked out with Brazier, who in appearance is not much changed. He has a nice family, three sons and one daughter.[74] Aberdeen a granite city—cold.

FRIDAY, 27 JULY 1866: Drove out with the Braziers to Mrs. White's where we lunched. Walked a good deal, and tired in consequence. Dined with the minister, M. Bourverie. In the evening saw some curious things in Brazier's laboratory.[75]

SATURDAY, 28 JULY 1866: Called on Winchester's father, on the Harry family, & on Wilke.[76]
Arranged with Brazier to let him have £400 before June next. Left Aberdeen at 4.

SUNDAY, 29 JULY 1866: At Rugby at 7 1/2; went to Mrs. Clarkes' but found Meadow's children had gone to London.[77] Left Rugby at two, & put up at St. James's Hotel, Piccadilly, about 7.

MONDAY, 30 JULY 1866: Campbell & Hippisley (fair chaps) breakfasted with me. Campbell is to go out with me as Secretary & Auditor: salary £1200 a year from 1st October. To O.B.C. [Oriental Bank Corporation]; Emanuel's; Mayall's, &c. Mrs. Turien & her son called: don't take to him. Knew her once.[78]

TUESDAY, 31 JULY 1866: Hughes dined with me at the Club. To Trinity House about Chefoo lights. Cartwright's brother called.[79]

WEDNESDAY, 1 AUGUST 1866: Adkins breakfasted with me:[80] also Hannen. Dined with Adkins & then went to carnival.

THURSDAY, 2 AUGUST 1866: Gordon to breakfast: Gave him £100 to buy presents for Chinese friends.

FRIDAY, 3 AUGUST 1866: Campbell dined with me at Club, & we then went to the "Adelphi" & saw "Helen"—a Mr. Johannes Von Gumpach called (introduced by Campbell) to apply for chair of Mathematics & Astronomy: he is an erudite German, speaking English & French equally well— age 47 —: I think he'll do.

Sent £100 to Hessie, & £50 to Sarah; drew £100 present for Cha, & £50 for self.

SATURDAY, 4 AUGUST 1866: Went to Pinline [?], but found the little Meadows were still at Penge: went to Penge & saw them: they are not much changed in appearance; have forgotten their Chinese, but speak English well: sent their "love & kisses to Pappa, Mamma, & little sister". Anna thought she remembered me: they recollected the names of the dogs — "Don", "Guess", "Fan".[81]
Went again to Emanuels' & Maynall's — Ordered lots of things at Swift's.
Left London at 8 1/2 for Paris with Campbell.

SUNDAY, 5 AUGUST 1866: At Paris at 7 1/2: put up at Hotel de Douvres [?] with the Chinese.
Called on Champion: he recommends M. Billequin for Chemistry &c. has no one for French, & has a Butlar [?] "in her eye" but no work.[82] Very tired.

MONDAY, 6 AUGUST 1866: Appointed M. Anatole Billequin, [indistinct word] de Chemie, to the "Chair of Chemistry at Peking", salary £600 a year from 16 Augt.
Appointed M. Mouillesaux who (with his mother & brother accompanied by de Meritens), introduced by M. Billonet, called: to be third Interpreter. He seems a nice young fellow.[83]
Meritens & Campbell dined with me, & we then went to the "Chatelaine" & saw "Andrillon", a gorgeously got-up piece: drove through the Champs Elysées & Bois de Boulogne: magnificent place, this Paris!
Champion sent me a lot of Peking photographs.
Met Schmidt (of Fletcher & Co.) at the theatre.[84]

TUESDAY, 7 AUGUST 1866: Warmer today. Wish it was [sic] Saturday. Longing to be home again. Longing to see Hessie.
Letter from FitzRoy tells me he has had to dismiss Cliquet & Gibbs: & that Baker must go too.[85]

[Last entry in this volume of the journal; the next is dated 1 January 1867.]

CHAPTER ELEVEN

Perspectives and Hypotheses

Robert hart's journals from 1863 to 1866—the substance of this volume—will speak with many voices as historians come to use them. What do they say to us now? Let us lay out a few broad perspectives.

HART AS AN INTERMEDIARY

In chapter 1, we see a Sino-foreign, and more specifically an Anglo-Ch'ing, partnership taking shape in the early 1860s. Victorian Britain begins to play a role in the power structure of the newly semi-colonial late Ch'ing empire. An Anglo-Ch'ing sea-and-land condominium is created by British sea power on the China coast. The British navy enables the opening of the first 5 treaty ports in the 1840s and then suppresses Chinese piracy to protect maritime trade. In the late 1850s British seapower makes possible the seizure and government of Canton by the Anglo-French Allied Commission from early 1858 to mid-1861. It facilitates the 1858 treaty settlement at Tientsin and its enforcement by the Anglo-French capture of Peking in 1860. It helps open the Yangtze to foreign trade in 1861. And finally it contributes to the defense of Shanghai against the Taipings and the recapture of Soochow and environs in 1862–1864. The French partnership-cum-rivalry with Britain in the conquest of Peking and in the recovery of Ningpo and Hangchow from the Taipings has throughout been secondary to the British leadership.

Basic to the Anglo-Ch'ing cooperation is the Ch'ing decision to turn from warfare to appeasement. If you can't lick them, join them. In the Anglo-Ch'ing condominium thus created along the coast and up the Yangtze, Robert Hart emerges as a Ch'ing employee who is building a new revenue collectorate for the new foreign office, the Tsungli Yamen. Hart becomes a mediator in Anglo-Chinese relations at Shanghai and the principal channel of communication at Peking. Through the 11 customs houses that Hart has added in 1861–1864 to his predecessor's original 3, a growing foreign-trade revenue accrues to the account of the Peking government. By 1866 it has paid off the Anglo-French indemnity of 1860 and has financed Sino-foreign military contingents as well as training programs, dockyards, arsenals, foreign-language schools, and even exploratory missions abroad. While these innovations are taking shape, Hart becomes the chief point at which British and Chinese interests can be reconciled in policy.

In the early 1860s Peking's acceptance of British semi-partnership concerning law and order on the coast was a creative forward step for China. Britain, though rivaled by France, Russia, and even the Americans, for the moment dominated both trade and diplomacy in East Asia. Peking, though still beset by rebellions, was able to reassert the legitimacy of the Manchu ruling house and the Confucian-minded social order that it led. Anglo-Ch'ing cooperation was institutionalized largely through the Customs Service arm of the Tsungli Yamen.

Our chapters 3 and 5 show Hart's dexterity in becoming simultaneously a trusted servant of the Tsungli Yamen and a dictator over the Customs Service. These seemingly two-faced relationships were actually in the Chinese style. They attest to the social scientists' observation that Confucian teachings as well as legalist practices led to a Chinese acceptance of arbitrary authority and a dependence upon it by those subordinate in status.

In day-to-day practice Hart was the personal intermediary between the British and other legations in Peking and the leading ministers of the Grand Council who headed the Tsungli Yamen. In this role Hart could foster a greater degree of mutual Sino-foreign understanding than more formal and direct confrontations could possibly have achieved. In the early 1860s patient, informed, and extensive conversation was the only way to bridge the linguistic and conceptual gap between China and the Western powers. Ideas of the autonomy of national sovereignty, of the equality of nation states, of the sanctity of treaties, and of the mutual benefits of commerce were part of the working vocabulary of Western diplomacy. In the other direction, Hart could explain Chinese concepts of the sanctity of ancestral example, the moral responsibilities of the ruler as enjoined by Confucianism, the need for reciprocity in human relations, and the necessity of hierarchy in the social order as well as its proper expression in ritual — all of which provided the foundation for imperial China's concept of "state dignity" (*t'i-chih*), as Hart translated the term.

Hart also had the good fortune to establish a working relationship with the rising Chinese official in Sino-foreign relations in the lower Yangtze provinces, Li Hung-chang. As Governor of Kiangsu from

1862 to 1865, Li was well on his way to becoming China's chief protagonist for using Western arms, ships, technology, and learning in the "self-strengthening" movement of the 1870s and 1880s.

What Hart learned from his contact with influential metropolitan and provincial officials gives him an outlook that becomes important in chapter 7, when he puts forward ideas for reform. He now understands much more about Ch'ing administration; for example the special importance of "outsiders" in the Chinese power structure — whether the Manchu rulers at the top (whose paranoid political style and patronage of traditional culture reflected their precarious position as alien conquerors outnumbered 100 to 1), the multi-ethnic Bannermen (a vast and expensive hereditary elite living more or less separately from the Chinese and closely tied to Manchu interests), Western civil and military employees like himself (always subject to surveillance, suspicion, and resentment), or Chinese officials operating in unfamiliar territory by virtue of the "rule of avoidance" (and therefore at the mercy of local clerks and runners). All this is part of a broader perception of traditional China.

CHINA'S DOMESTIC TRANSFORMATION

By the mid-1860s Hart had come to understand that the rebellions of the mid-nineteenth century had changed irrevocably the relationship between Peking and the provinces. As a basis for this new view, Hart learned something of the land-based counterpart to the waterborne Anglo-Ch'ing condominium on the China coast. It consisted of a new arrangement between Peking and the provinces, or more specifically between the Manchu dynasty and Chinese provincial elites. The chief significance of this domestic movement was that it marked a broadening of the base of participation in the Ch'ing government. We have just mentioned the inclusion in that government of foreign-derived military power and trade administration. The domestic counterpart to this foreign participation in the late-Ch'ing power structure was the rise of Chinese gentry commanders in the Yangtze provinces, who supported their new armies by the new likin taxes on the local market economy. To be sure, this local provincial militarization was accompanied by a vehement reassertion of the T'ung-chih Restoration's principles of imperial Confucianism; but these expressions of principle were all the more vehement for being so largely ineffective. As usual, changes in the old order of thought, ideals, and values lagged far behind the rapid changes in the economy, material technology, and social structure.

In the 1850s the imperial Confucian state still rested in theory on the economic foundation of agriculture. Its proper revenue, therefore, came from the land tax. This tax was light, usually under 10 percent, and its collection was naturally inefficient because of the difficulty of avoiding squeeze (illegal gain) on the part of the collectorate. The cost of gathering the land tax has been estimated as using a fifth to a quarter of the amount collected, but one wonders whether this estimate takes full account of the squeeze put on the peasant taxpayer at tax-collection time by the yamen runners and other ruffians who regularly shortchanged and overcharged him.

In the Confucian scheme of things, commercial taxes were a less than admirable means of procuring revenue, since the pursuit of profit through trade was itself ignoble. But when the Taipings captured Nanking in 1853, they disrupted land-tax collections over a wide area, forcing the embattled Ch'ing government to seek new sources of revenue. It was no accident that trade taxes were activated by the inauguration of likin in Anhwei province in 1853 and of the foreign Inspectorate of Customs at Shanghai in 1854. The threat of rebellion brought foreigners and Chinese provincial elites together as allies of the Manchus, making possible not only the suppression of the Taipings but also China's first halting steps toward modernization. Just as the Ch'ing dynasty's acceptance of foreign support fostered Hart's rise as I.G., Peking's final acceptance of Chinese gentry leadership in the provinces fostered the rise of Li Hung-chang.

In the simplest of terms, the state found itself trying to catch up with the growth of the Chinese economy. The result was not only a shift in the balance of political power, but also a profound change in the class structure of late Ch'ing China. Foreign supervision of Maritime Customs after 1854 produced no such change — primarily because the Inspectorate provided no new opportunities for either individual financial gain or enhanced social leverage. But likin administration was another matter. Charged as an excise tax on goods held by shopkeepers in inventory and as a transit tax on goods transported by merchants on trade routes, likin immediately became an essential source of government income at the local level. Collecting stations rapidly proliferated into province-wide hierarchies of bureaux at the prefectural, county, and market-center levels. This meant new jobs and new opportunities for gain on the part of the likin collectors, the provincial treasuries, and the Board of Revenue at Peking, each of whom grabbed a piece of the action.

During the early 1850s, provincial elites ("gentry") who had previously been excluded from military affairs and from land-tax collection began to organize, lead, and supply armies, and to take an active role in raising the new commercial taxes that helped to finance militia and mercenary forces. They thus not only acquired enormous local power, but also began to assume responsibilities traditionally undertaken by merchants. At the same time, the increase in the sale of degrees as a revenue source brought rich merchants more fully into the social orbit of the Chinese elite. By the twentieth century the process of fusion was so complete that members of the local elite were now often called gentry-merchants or merchant-gentry. Meanwhile likin had become a deeply entrenched vested interest.

The likin tax illustrated, at least to Hart and a number of other reform-minded Westerners, the great deficiency of Ch'ing administration: its lack of sufficient central-government control over fiscal and military affairs. In Hart's eyes this "temporary" tax for local military purposes should never have been necessary in the first place. It is true, of course, that the I.G.'s advocacy of greater centralization was in part a matter of administrative self-interest. He knew from painful first-hand experience that the dynasty's tendency to "localize responsibility" could easily threaten his own authority (as in the Hammond case; see 26 July 1864); and he had seen that modernizing experiments such as the Lay-Osborn Flotilla and the Ever-Victorious Army could fall victim to the caprice of local officials in the absence of adequate central-government control. These experiences and others prompted Hart at various times to seek direct authority over Ch'ing financial and military affairs, and to view his own Foreign Inspectorate as the logical modernizing model for the empire as a whole.[1]

Hart genuinely believed that administrative centralization was in China's best interest. He put the matter this way in his journal entry of 25 January 1865: "To exist the [Ch'ing] govt. must do this: it must acquire strength, and it must centralise. . . . To get strength, it must have money, & to procure money it must remodel its taxation." Hart had in mind nothing less than the complete restructuring of the land tax and the elimination of corruption in all realms of tax collection, including likin. Indeed, he would have welcomed the abolition of all transit levies. Unfortunately for the I.G., the easy money provided to local officials by the likin tax discouraged any effort at empire-wide fiscal reorganization, just as certain successful ad hoc adjustments in the Ch'ing military during the 1850s and 1860s made more fundamental institutional changes seem unnecessary. Intended as a temporary expedient, likin became a solid fixture of the local Chinese scene well into the twentieth century.[2]

Although the likin tax got started in parallel with maritime customs collections on foreign trade, there was one great difference between these two critical sources of revenue: The Customs with its substantial salaries for the foreign and Chinese collectors had a comparatively high cost of collection—compared, that is, with Western tax collectorates—but peculation was kept to a bare minimum. Not so with likin. The provincial networks of likin stations and collectorates expanded in every province, and peculation could not be controlled. Heavy surcharges, "customary fees," and repeated collections were added on, barriers proliferated, and soon a merchant transporting his goods to a city market might find his way obstructed and his hoped-for profit preempted by half a dozen or a dozen likin stations whose demands could not be avoided. Land-tax collectors had devised numerous ways to peculate, but likin collectors fairly outdid them. Domestic commerce became host to a ubiquitous parasite.[3]

These evils flourished, as Hart repeatedly pointed out, because no statutory provision had been made to pay for the upkeep of the government establishment. Officials' salaries, raised early in the eighteenth century, had become purely nominal. Bureaucrats were expected to be tax farmers—that is, to pay in a set quota and keep the rest. Since the host of several hundred clerks and runners at a county yamen had to be fed, the county magistrate (once he had paid his own gatekeeper and personal advisers on law and finance) let them live off what unofficial but customary fees they could get. It was a competitive life, ripe for abuse. To combat corruption in this government of men, there was no legal system to guarantee them a living—simply a system of doctrine-of-the-mean morality and ethical principles to ameliorate their conduct through exhortation. Only extreme cases of corruption could be censured.

Incorruptibilty was thus the principal feature that set the foreign-run Customs apart from the rest of the Ch'ing tax system. Corruption had always been a main target of Chinese reform movements; but now to the Confucian rhetoric was added the foreign example. Inevitably Hart, the advocate of Western ways, was drawn into the reform program of the T'ung-chih Restoration.

THE PROVENANCE OF REFORM PROPOSALS

We have seen in chapter 7 that, when Hart gave Tung Hsun a preview of the reform ideas later embodied in his "Bystander's" memorandum, Tung remarked that they resembled ideas already advanced by the Soochow scholar Feng Kuei-fen. Feng was the scion of a landed Soochow family who had a distinctive career as a scholar, adviser of high officials, and leading member of the Soochow gentry with wide connections among persons of influence. When Lin Tse-hsu was at Soochow as Governor of Kiangsu (1832–1837), before he was put on the stage of world history by being sent to extirpate opium at Canton in 1839, Feng had been one of Lin's secretaries. After taking his metropolitan degree in 1840, he served in the Hanlin Academy and as an imperial examiner and then as director of an academy. Came the Taiping seizure of Soochow in 1853, Feng Kuei-fen exemplified the trend toward gentry participation in local government and military defense. He became head of the Soochow Militia Commission in 1853, authorized (although not an official) to recruit and supply militia forces. Feng's leadership in the Soochow Supply Bureau led him both to seek reforms against tax corruption and to become part of the Chinese establishment in Shanghai. Feng was a prime mover among the Soochow gentry in advocating the appointment of Li Hung-chang to govern Kiangsu province. Feng may well have contributed to hiring of the 7 steamships that brought Li's Anhwei Army to Shanghai early in 1862. At any rate, he had been active in likin administration for Li at Shanghai and had written and distributed his reform essays well before Hart had his long session with Governor Li in May of 1865. Hart's "Bystander's View" ventured on several points that Feng had already dealt with.

When we find Hart, like Feng, inveighing against the rule of avoidance and rapid turnover in office, which weakened the power of the magistrate to control the yamen clerks and runners, we should remember the much-admired Ku Yen-wu. In the early Ch'ing he had put his finger on the key problem of official responsibility and local leadership by advocating that county magistracies be made hereditary (like the positions of clerks and runners). Thus the magistrate could more readily control his underlings. Feng's solution to the problem of yamen corruption, as we have noted, was to replace clerks by regularly appointed civil-service degree-holders and to elect salaried headmen as administrators at the village level. Since many of these ideas had been circulating in one form or another for years, we must accept the probability that Hart, like Wade, was unconsciously advocating measures that came from a widespread climate of Chinese reform opinion.

It was not, after all, in a vacuum that Hart and Wade did their thinking, but as peripheral participants in Chinese official life. They read the *Peking Gazette* regularly, they were daily in touch with their Chinese scholar-assistants, with translators or "writers," as well as with mandarins in substantial posts at all levels. Hart's writer Sun, who reported his correspondence to the Shanghai Taotai, to say nothing of the garrulous Pin-ch'un in Peking, were two-way communicants always ready to convey the political gossip to their foreign employers. Wade and Hart were more capable of echoing Chinese ideas than of originating them. In other words, they picked up and reflected such Chinese sentiments as appealed to them. They did not represent foreign research centers or a consensus of Sinologists.

We should remember, too, that the Wade and Hart memoranda were written for Chinese readers, not Westerners. Indeed, we have thus far been unable to find an English version of Hart's "Bystander's View."[4] This circumstance lends credence to an idea that may apply to Hart's relationship with the Tsungli Yamen as a whole; namely, that the nature of China's traditional bureaucratic defense system instinctively encouraged Hart to put forward ideas that would endanger any other Ch'ing official who expressed them. Certainly the political hazards were real enough. We know, for example, that even such powerful officials as Tseng Kuo-fan and Li Hung-chang refused to advocate the more radical ideas of Feng Kuei-fen, and that the ministers of the Tsungli Yamen were constantly worried about "losing face"—either by interfering in foreign affairs at the local level or by urging foreign-inspired reform. Wen-hsiang responded to one of Hart's many pleas for help in modernizing China by stating simply: "What's the use of my taking in hand your projects? Who is there outside to cooperate with us? Pu-hing [*pu-hsing*, "it cannot be done"]."

The result was that Hart—whether consciously or not—became a mouthpiece for the more progressive of his Ch'ing employers at the capital, as well as for his colleagues in the provinces. He could suggest domestic reforms and changes in China's system of foreign relations without taking the same political risks. Meanwhile, his many conversations both at the Yamen and with officials in treaty-port areas contributed to the growth of his ideas. They were not monologues but genuine exchanges of fact and opinion, as Hart's journals plainly indicate. He knew better than constantly to harp on Westernization to save China. Instead he absorbed the Yamen ministers' sense of problem and practical concern in China's domestic and foreign affairs. His receptivity led them to take him into their world of discourse, raising for us the interesting question of how far his ideas represented theirs.

Hart's importance as a T'ung-chih reformer, in any case, was not a matter of his having a particularly innovative outlook. His only truly radical notion—a high degree of administrative centralization at the metropolitan level—found no Chinese supporters at all, not even Feng Kuei-fen. Rather his significance lies in his ability to articulate reformist sentiments officially, or at least publicly, with an authority derived from his dual status as a foreigner and a Ch'ing official. Put simply, Hart made it easier for the Tsungli Yamen to pursue its unpopular task. We may assume, for instance, that, without the Hart-Wade memoranda of 1865–1866 to forge a path, it would have been far more difficult for the Tsungli Yamen to broach with provincial officials the issues of treaty revision that had to be raised in anticipation of negotiations with the British Minister, Rutherford Alcock. As it developed, the Tsungli Yamen's circular letter of late 1867, and the "secret correspondence" from the provinces in response to it, produced no major surprises, no political waves.[5]

The intellectual background of Hart's thinking on China's political economy will thus have many aspects. In addition to taking into account the influence of various strains of Chinese reformist thought, we might consider the fact that Benthamite utilitarianism had come to fruition in Britain in the early decades of the century, and that Jeremy Bentham's private secretary and acolyte, John Bowring, who had edited Bentham's *Life and Works* in 11 volumes and served ten years in Parliament, had become British Consul at Canton in 1849. Later, as Minister at Hong Kong, Sir John had pushed for the extension of the Shanghai Foreign Inspectorate to all the treaty ports. Hart's journal was at a confluence of several strains of thought — Chinese and Western — that should repay further research.

HART'S INFLUENCE—THE ALCOCK CONVENTION OF 1869

While we do not present in this volume the text of Hart's journals of 1867 to 1869 (which would require another book) we may draw upon them to show briefly how the Sino-British negotiations of 1867–1869 over the revision of the Treaty of Tientsin (1858) reveal the ironies and ambiguities of Hart's unique position as a metropolitan middleman and reformer. On the one hand, he was genuinely sympathetic with Great Britain's desire for expanded trade and for Western-style "progress." On the other, he was sensitive to China's political realities and committed to helping the Ch'ing government resist unreasonable foreign demands. It was a delicate and difficult balancing act. Hart's journal entries for the period testify to his integral involvement in the complex negotiations. His role went well beyond what the official record — Chinese or Western — indicates. To be sure, he was by all accounts the dominant member of the 5-man Mixed Commission established in early 1868 to conduct preliminary talks on treaty revision. But he also worked continuously behind the scenes, corresponding, as well as meeting privately, with Ch'ing and British representatives at all levels. Alcock trusted him, as did the Tsungli Yamen.

Wen-hsiang, we discover, relied almost entirely on Hart. The two Chinese members of the Mixed Commission, named Hsia and Ts'ai, were low-ranking members of the Yamen with no diplomatic leverage, and, although they consulted often with Hart on questions related to treaty revision, they had no diplomatic prestige at all. Hart's journal entry of 27 June 1868, indicates that Wen-hsiang told "the great I.G." that he expected him to do 80 percent of the negotiating with Alcock—an estimate he soon revised upward (on 14 July) to "nine parts . . . instead of eight."

It is difficult to know the exact degree to which Alcock's views were influenced by Hart. Alexander Michie, in his biography of Sir Rutherford, asserts that, despite Hart's obvious pro-Chinese sympathies, the British Minister, "so far from regarding the inspector-general as an opponent, commended him to the Foreign Office as a valuable auxiliary." Wade, he says, "clung to the same belief for a good many years longer." From Michie's standpoint, Hart's influence in the making of England's China policy was enough to "tie the hands of the British Government for a whole generation."[6] We can assume, then, that Hart indeed helped soften the official British position in the face of constant demands by British merchants to apply ever greater pressure on China. In so doing, however, he was forced to take sides against those whose modernizing views he basically shared.[7]

Particularly ironic was Hart's defense of the dynasty against a charge he had been making all along—that the Ch'ing central government lacked sufficient power and authority to operate effectively. The chief complaint on the British side was that Peking seemed unwilling or unable to enforce the provisions of the treaties at the local level. The most pressing practical matter involved finding a way to protect the goods of foreign trade from internal transit taxes and other levies in excess of the 2 1/2 per cent provided for by the Treaty of Tientsin (see chapter 1 on transit dues). As the British put the matter to the Tsungli Yamen: "of what use . . . is a Treaty giving the right to trade on payment of certain fixed duties, if the Emperor's officials in the provinces can at their pleasure increase these without limit, in the passage through the interior of the staple articles constituting the trade? . . . Under the head of leking [likin] taxes, and transit dues chiefly, but under an indefinite variety of names and pretexts, exactions over and above what by Treaty they are entitled to levy, amounting to from

7 to 100 per cent. of the original cost, are raised before foreign goods can reach the hands of the consumers in the interior."[8]

Hart, in representing the Chinese position, "took the high ground of maintaining, with subtle dialectic, that the protection foreigners claimed was not in fact given by the treaties." He admitted that likin and other internal levies were an impediment to trade, but argued that the purpose of the transit pass was "to protect goods only while actually in transit between two given points, namely treaty port and specified inland place, or vice versa." Transit passes, he went on to say, were never intended to "protect goods from such levies as production and consumption taxes or local municipal charges." To the Western merchants and many consuls this was pure heresy, but it made sense to the Chinese, and in fact to Lord Clarendon.[9]

Eventually, the British and Chinese representatives reached a compromise whereby foreign goods were to pay the basic import duty and 2 1/2 percent transit duties simultaneously at the port of entry without option and regardless of destination, after which the goods might circulate freely in the 9 provinces that had treaty ports. Native produce destined for export was subject to all domestic taxes, but vouchers were to be given upon payment; if the produce were then exported, the Maritime Customs at the port of exit would refund any sum in excess of the 2 1/2 percent. The sale of transit passes would thereby be stopped, and merchants engaged in legitimate export trade could claim their refund from a reliable agency.[10]

Other features of the final version of the Alcock Convention were: modifications in the most-favored-nation clause; the concession of China's right to establish a consulate in any British port, including Hong Kong; and agreements to establish bonded warehouses in China, sanction foreign assistance in the working of Chinese coal mines, raise the import duty on opium and the export duty on raw silk, accept the rules for courts of joint investigation in Customs cases, permit temporary foreign residence in the Chinese interior for trading purposes, authorize inland navigation by foreign sailing vessels (but not steamship, except on Poyang Lake), establish certain landing stages on the Yangtze River, open the ports of Wenchow and Wuhu (against the cancellation of Kiungchow on Hainan Island), and adopt a written code of Chinese commercial law. Although Alcock told Hart privately on 17 September that he didn't like the revised treaty because it was "too pro-Chinese," he defended the convention publicly, stating that "no country or Western government has ever before made such liberal concessions to foreign trade [as China]."[11]

The concessions did not come easily, and Alcock's position was not always so accommodating. As may be imagined, there were many twists and turns of diplomacy during the protracted negotiations. The ministers of the Tsungli Yamen reported, for example, that Alcock was alternately courteous and overbearing with them. At one point, during the fall of 1868, anti-foreign outbreaks in several parts of China caused the British Minister to abandon his moderate stance temporarily and sanction gunboat diplomacy. Meanwhile, Burlingame's flights of rhetorical fancy on his trip to Europe and the United States seem to have produced a false sense of confidence on the part of the Tsungli Yamen. Even Hart, an ardent supporter of the Burlingame Mission from the very outset, deplored the apparent effect his statements had on hardening the attitude of the Tsungli Yamen.[12] As late as the first week of October 1869, a formal agreement still had not been reached, but on 9 October, Hart gleefully announced in his journal: "Last Saturday, a deadlock: today all settled." Prince Kung and his associates, representing China, and Alcock, representing Great Britain, signed the so-called Alcock Convention on 23 October 1869.

Sadly for China and Hart, the Alcock Convention was never ratified. Fierce opposition from British merchants, both at home and in China, torpedoed the agreement, forcing the British government to refuse ratification. The merchant consensus was that Britain had yielded far too much to China, that the 1858 treaty would be more congenial to British interests than the revised version. From a Chinese perspective, the Tsungli Yamen lost considerable face, not to mention faith in Western-style diplomacy. Wade later described Wen-hsiang as "thirsting for revenge because of the discredit and inconvenience our rejection of the Convention has occasioned."[13]

Predictably, Hart emerged from the negotiations both a goat and a hero; the British merchants and treaty-port press vilified him for his pro-Chinese sympathies, while the Chinese tended to glorify him. On 20 November 1868, Hart received a promotion to the rank of Provincial Financial Commissioner (*pu-cheng shih-ssu;* 2b) for his services to the dynasty. The Tsungli Yamen's memorial requesting the honor emphasized his contributions to the treaty-revision process as well as his devoted service as Inspector General.[14] The honor was, perhaps, small satisfaction in view of the ultimate fate of the Alcock Convention, but it did represent the Ch'ing government's public acknowledgment of his value to the dynasty as an administrator, spokesman, and diplomat. To Hart, we know, such recognition mattered greatly.

In the 1870s, the I.G.'s star continued to rise, and, by 19 July 1874, his inveterate desire to be "objective" (and nobody's fool) led him to advance 21 reasons for his "general success in life." Among these are: "a good constitution"; the capacity to work long hours at his desk; wide reading; a "quick intelligence"; the ability to be "a good listener"; intellectual and personal honesty; a good memory; thoroughness; a logical, careful, and methodical approach to matters; a "fairly equable temper"; the knack of yielding a position without abandoning it; reliability; patience; dedication; courage; self-confidence; and loyalty to his employers, the Chinese. He admits to having a "gloomy" manner, to finding "little pleasure in life." Business, he says, "is my first consideration. I let nothing take me from it: I give up everything for it." He concludes: "In fact, I'm a safe sort of hardworking, modestly-gifted, many-sided, equal-tempered, and inwardly, God-fearing & heaven-seeking, man: I don't suppose I'll 'set the Yangtsze on fire',—neither do I fear much a struggle against its current." (He also tells us that his 7 pages of self-appraisal took an hour and a quarter to write.)

Not all of Hart's contemporaries saw Hart the way he saw himself. Although most foreigners and Chinese appreciated his intelligence, energy, dedication, and honesty, nevertheless his autocratic style did not always go down well with his subordinates. A few of his employees, notably Paul King, criticized him publicly, while one of the instructors Hart had hired for the T'ung-wen kuan, Johannes von Gumpach, sued him for high-handed and deceitful practices, calling him "a thorough egotist—unscrupulous and ambitious selfishness personified."[15] A number of Chinese were likewise hostile to Hart at one time or another; and even the I.G.'s friend and "ally," Li Hung-chang, once described him as "quite contentious" (*shen-hen*), and willing to exert himself on China's behalf only because he coveted a high salary.[16]

Whatever their personal opinions of Hart, his employment served as a constant and humiliating reminder to Ch'ing officials of the regime's administrative inadequacies, including the inability of either the I.G. or the central government to train sufficient numbers of Chinese to assume Hart's multifarious responsibilities. The aim of self-strengthening was clearly to learn the methods of the Westerners "without having always to use their men."[17] Yet here was Hart, wearing all kinds of Chinese hats, seemingly indispensable. The predictable outcome was that Ch'ing officials were torn between relying on Hart and trying to do without him. Throughout the T'ung-chih era— and indeed throughout his career—Hart's influence therefore waxed and waned according to the Ch'ing government's sense of crisis. At times he felt utterly indispensable. On 3 December 1872, for instance, he tells us that in their negotiations with the foreign ministers, the members of the Tsungli Yamen feel his support is essential, and that without it "they are certain they'll not get the minister's [*sic*] consent to any proposal. Such is my position with them now." On the other hand, Hart wrote periodically of being virtually ignored by the Yamen, as if meeting him were some sort of "favor" granted by its members.[18]

Paradoxically, Hart's principal limitation as a T'ung-chih reformer was also his greatest asset — his unique position as a Westerner in the Ch'ing metropolitan bureaucracy. For although he did good service to the dynasty, and was by his own admission and the testimony of others "a Chinese agent," as "completely Chinese in his sympathies as a Chinese himself," Hart remained a foreigner. As such, his loyalties were impossible to assure. His employers in the Tsungli Yamen lamented that he had not been "born a Chinese," so that he could talk more authoritatively about moral principles (*tao-li*). Contrary to their hopes, he never became fully Sinicized by marrying a Chinese, changing to Chinese clothes, and becoming a Ch'ing subject.[19] In one particularly telling exchange with his Chinese writer during 1867, the writer asked Hart whether he would wear Chinese regalia or Western clothes if the Ch'ing Emperor were to grant him an audience. Hart replied: "if I wore Chinese dress, I shd. [should] have to perform the Chinese ceremony, but, being a foreigner, I cannot k'ot'ow, & therefore I shd. wear foreign dress."[20] Undoubtedly such views found their way to Hart's employers, who must have questioned his commitment to the dynasty, or at least to Chinese cultural values.

There were even reasons for the Chinese to fear Hart as a security risk; he knew so much about the inner workings of the Ch'ing bureaucracy and the Chinese military.[21] Although on balance his actions and writings — both public and private — over half a century of service to China attest to his fidelity to the Ch'ing government, at least a few journal entries suggest precisely the sort of sentiments that Ch'ing officials feared. On 25 July 1867, for example, he wrote that the Chinese "have been treated kindly, & fed on 'lollipops' too long; a change of treatment . . . would do them good." He went on to say in obvious frustration that the Tsungli Yamen has "got into such a way of doing nothing that it would be almost a pleasure to see it 'in a fix'. I don't expect it to do anything that it is not made to do. . . . We must feel our way; but if I can get the Yamen into a dilemma — in favor of progress — I will."

THE CUSTOMS AND IMPERIALISM

The expression of such sentiments brings us to the modern perspective on the Customs under Hart as a handmaiden of imperialism. In Hart's day, the self-congratulatory Western idea was that late imperial China received from the West the boon of "progress," though with some backsliding. Western observers saw China in the second half of the nineteenth century entering into the community of nations and viewed the unequal treaties as a slightly skewed extension of international law. The Chinese, however, were slow to see the value of international law. The Japanese, by contrast, would aggressively assert their sovereign rights after 1868. Having at once begun a rights-recovery movement involving judicial reform and other steps to do away with the unequal treaties, by 1896 they had succeeded.

China's sovereignty remained impaired until 1943. This was due less to circumstances such as the rejection of the Alcock Convention, and the greater British imperialist pressure imposed on China than on Japan, than to China's lack of the idea of itself as a nation-state. Absence of nationalism was a psychological as well as an intellectual phenomenon. From the manifold provisions of the treaties, which were legal statements of foreign rights and privileges, it was plain that all the foreign establishment of merchants, consuls, missionaries, ports, gunboats, and foreign trade were controlled by a body of rules and regulations. Anyone who mastered this body of law could use it in self-defense as well as for growth or aggression. Yet Chinese lawyers did not appear even in Hong Kong until the 1880s.

The problem, again, was primarily one of incentives. The traditional Ch'ing civil-service examinations, which survived without significant change until 1904, made no effort to test candidates in either international or domestic law; Chinese society continued to disesteem law in principle as well as practice. Finally, after China's defeat in the Sino-Japanese War of 1894–1895, Chinese nationalism became a potent enough force to overcome traditional prejudices on a significant scale. But the damage had already been done. China fell decades behind Japan in the modernizing race, losing a province (Taiwan) as part of the bargain. During the twentieth century, the framework of Chinese assumptions has undergone radical changes, from liberalism to Marxism to market socialism in economic matters, and from dynastic authoritarianism to Communist Party dictatorship to bureaucratic socialism or the like in political matters. Because the change in world outlook on the part of Chinese scholars has been so great in the last 120 years, the Chinese view of Robert Hart and the Customs has shifted enormously.[22]

Two things characterize the role of the Maritime Customs Service under Hart in the nineteenth century. First is the wide variety of projects and institutional arrangements that contributed to China's modernization and entry into the outside world. Second is the fact that, by the end of Hart's long service, the Customs had become the agent of imperialist subjection of China—a convenient device to collect taxes that could pay foreign loans and indemnities to the profit of foreign bond-holders. In general terms, one may see the modern improvements getting started in the first half of Hart's regime up to the 1880s and the imperialist exploitation taking hold increasingly thereafter. It can hardly be denied that the Customs Service taking shape in the early 1860s contained the seeds of the imperialist domination that would bear fruit in the first part of the twentieth century.

Students of the Customs are therefore saddled with phenomena that were both benevolent and malevolent toward the Chinese people. Although possibly this is no greater than the ambiguity that attaches to much of modern history, yet in the 1990s it presents a considerable problem of interpretation. The record provides a basis both for an apologetics and a denunciation. We cannot attempt to settle this ongoing question here. Yet the fact remains that, in working for the Tsung-li Yamen, Hart was essentially working for the Ch'ing dynasty. A Chinese official of the Yamen like Tung Hsun was just enough representative of Chinese scholarship to maintain the official myth of dyarchy. Wen-hsiang, Pao-yun, and others were either Manchus or Chinese Bannermen. Thus, when Hart strove for the accretion of central power to Peking, he was in his own mind furthering the creation of a Chinese nation-state with a more effective government. But, in the view of later Chinese nationalists, Hart was fostering the continued rule of a non-Chinese dynasty of conquest. Like the British and other diplomats, he found little occasion to champion the latent force of Chinese nationalism that would later emerge. In effect, he was propping up the old order in a time of incipient revolution and change. The weaknesses and evil habits that he saw in China, the official corruption and the continued opposition of interests between Peking and the provinces, he could not attack in the name of Chinese nationalism.[23] Seen in the broadest scope of history, Hart and the Customs were trying to strengthen and preserve a political order that was already doomed. Fortunately for Hart, by the end of the dynasty in 1911 he, like it, had become part of history.

Foreigners' Positions in Imperial Maritime Customs

FROM *SERVICE LIST* FOR 1875

REVENUE DEPARTMENT
In-Door Staff

Inspector General and Commissioners (23)*

Deputy Commissioners (12)

First Assistants: A (10)   B (10)

Second Assistants: A (10)   B (10)

Third Assistants: A (10)   B (10)

Fourth Assistants: A (10   B (10)

Unclassed (5)
Clerk, Harbour Master's Office, Shanghai
Gas Engineer
Printing Office Manager, Shanghai
Assistant Printer
Mining Engineer

Out-Door Staff

Tide Surveyors

Chief Tide Surveyor (1)
Tide Surveyors (16)   [14]**
Assistant Tide Surveyors (9)
Boat Officers (3)

Examiners

Chief Examiner (5)
Examiners (20)
Assistant Examiners (40)

Tidewaiters

First Class (20)
Second Class (30)
Third Class (35)
Probationary (24)

*Numbers in parentheses signify actual number in each category in 1875.
**Numbers in brackets signify the number in that category before 1868.

413

Note:

In-Door Revenue Staff was much the same when Hart became I.G.—same positions, same people in the Customs Service.

Out-Door Revenue Staff was much more limited in 1863. Of the *Tide Surveyors* 14 had joined the Customs before 1867, but only 8 had been Tidesurveyors.

Of *Assistant Tide Surveyors*, 4 had held that rank earlier, but all 9 had joined the Customs by 1863.

There were no *Boat Officers*, though all 3 had joined the Customs.

There were no *Examiners* of any grade before Sept. 1867.

There were no *Tidewaiters* before 1873.

Of the *Coast Staff*, one (Nils Peter Andersen) had joined by 1863, but there were no Commanders, Officers, or Engineers before 1870.

The *Marine Dept.* did not exist before 1871.

Size of staff:

By the 1875 Service List the numbers of Chinese were:

First Class Clerks	282
Skilled Employees	478
Official Servants	324
Coast	145
	1,229

The largest Office was Shanghai with 26 (foreign In-Door Staff); next, Peking, with 11; and Canton, 10.

Between 1863 and 1867 the following from the In-Door Staff left the Service:

Inspector General   Resigned: 1
Commissioners   Resigned: 3   Deceased 3
Deputy Commissioners   Resigned: 2
Clerks   Resigned 17;   Discharged 11;   Deceased 3

In the Out-Door Staff the changes were far more numerous: men came and went, were discharged or died, so the figures fluctuate considerably.

The following seven letters from Robert Hart to E. C. Bowra of the Pin-ch'un mission are from the Morse collection of Hart letters in the Houghton Library of Harvard University.

Inspector General's Office.

PRIVATE

Dear Mr. Bowra,

I have only got time for one line, and that is to say, that we hope to get to Shanghai in time to leave by the French mail of the 17th or 20th March. Be at Hongkong on the 24th at the latest. We shall probably return to China by the French mail in September: but that point is not yet settled.

The official is not a <u>Kin-chae</u>, but he is nominated by the Yamen and goes 'foreign' by Imperial Decree.

Yours truly,

ROBERT HART

8th Feb. 1866.

Ravarnette House,
Lisburn
2nd. June   (1866).

Dear Mr. Bowra,

I am in receipt of your notes of the 26th and 31st and am glad to learn that things go on so well. Yours of the 31st only arrived last night: too late for a telegraphic message. Should the Prince wish Pin to attend a <u>levee</u>, let him go (accompanied by yourself of course): <u>but don't let him take his flute</u>!

I received the "Owl" and a number of the "Telegraph"; many thanks for them. The "Owl" did not strike me as being very bright, and the other paper seemed a little unfair. Another paper, I think from you, shows that Colonel Sykes* wants to know something of the mission. I enclose a Memo. to which I wish you to adhere as far as you can: it is, however, necessarily of an Indian-rubber-like material, and will bear either stretching or compression. If Pin wants more money on Hungku's account let him telegraph at once; and do

*Colonel Sykes, M.P., was a vocal critic of British policy in China.

415

you yourself by telegraph acknowledge receipt of this letter with its enclosures one of which is a cheque for £1,500 (No. 3 45479 in your favor on O.B.C. [Oriental Bank Corporation]) Send the telegram to me at

Imperial Hotel,
Portadown,
Co. Armagh,

where I shall be for the next five days (after which my address will be Ravarnette House).

I have a lovely rolling country before me, rich with young crops, trees and hedge-rows, and I am enjoying myself far more than I did in London. With kind regards, Yours truly, ROBERT HART

Dear Mr. Bowra,

Thanks for your letters: the last received is dated the 10th inst.

I can readily understand the difficulties you have to contend with, and you may rest assured that if, by keeping the end in view, you make the best of them, your services will not be unappreciated. Three things I regard as of major importance: (1) that people generally should be pleased with the Chinese; (2) that the Chinese, while having their eyes opened, should not be bored too much; and (3) that the Government although it did authorize me to expend whatever sum I pleased, should not be alarmed by the expenditure. It was civil of the F.O. to offer to appoint someone to go with the Mission: I did not suggest it; it was also considerate for the F.O. to nominate the Major, for he had had experience with the Japanese, but his name was brought forward before I could ask for anyone else: and, in short, we have every reason to be thankful to the F.O., however much we may be put out by the peculiarities of the agent. Him, however, I gave distinctly to understand that his assistance would be necessary only when asked for. You must just take things at their best, and not at their worst.

If requisite, the programme sent you can be varied, but I marked out simply what I wish the Mission, if possible, to do. I hope to see you off for America by the first opportunity in September; it would not do for the Mission to return without having at least visited Washington.

I cannot possibly go to London today to see Pin Tajin; nor would it be of any use for him to come in this direction to find me. I am continually on the move, and cannot say on what days I shall be at home, or on what days I shall be in parts of the country where railways are unknown. I may pick you up in Hamburg or Copenhagen; but I cannot be sure. I am most likely to meet you next in Brussels.

I send you a couple of letters just received from China; one of them looks like a note from myself, as far as the address is concerned. I have not received any telegram from you relative to your movements. Keep me informed, please, of your times for starting and destinations.

Tell Pin, with my compts., that he may set his mind at rest as to being in China in proper time.

I have nothing fresh to say to you. If I write to the continent I shall send my letter to the care of the Secretary of Legation (British) at Copenhagen, Stockholm, St. Petersburg, or Berlin. You had better ask for them at each place.

With kind regards to De Champs and our Chinese friends,

Yours very truly,

ROBERT HART

In which "Times" is your letter? I have not seen it.

Ravarnette,

13th June 1866.

My dear Mr. Bowra,

I got your telegram late last night, and I may as well write in reply as send you a short and enigmatical response.

I cannot conveniently go to London till Monday; I shall, however, then go. You may therefore remain there until my arrival, and we can then, in full conclave, settle the route etc.

Yours truly,

ROBERT HART

14 June, 1866

Lisburn

10th July, 1866.

Dear Mr. Bowra,

I received your telegram from Stockholm yesterday and, fearing you might know nothing about the Swedish Treaty, I gave you the hints contained in the reply telegraphed to you last night.

I presume that you will be in St. Petersburg on Monday the 16th, stay there five days, and go on to Berlin making a stay there of five days also, and after leaving Berlin visit Krupp's Gun-factory at Essen; proceed to Brussels. You will be in Brussels, I assume by the 30th July; remain there four days, and then go on to Paris. You ought to be in Paris by the 5th August, and you will remain there until the 15th, when the party must start for Marseilles to return to China by the mail of the 19th August ([left blank]). When I last saw him, Pin was so anxious to return to China that he was with difficulty persuaded to remain willingly until the 18th August; I do not suppose he has as yet changed his mind. Carry out the above arrangements: five days in St. Petersburg, five days in Berlin, and four days in Brussels. I shall join the party in Paris on the 13th or 14th August. As soon as you have got the party safely in Brussels, you can hand over charge to De Champs and return to England; from England you will please to return to Paris by the night mail of the 14th August, so that I may see you when you rejoin the party prior to starting for China.

Write to me from Berlin, and let me know (1) what the expenses have been from leaving England until arrival there, and (2) what sums you may have in hand.

Tell Pin that Wän Seang has been made [Hart used the wrong character for *shang* in rendering *Li-pu shang-shu,* President of the Board of Civil Appointments].

Man's "Customer" won the "Derby", and his "Sambo" the steeplechase; my "Ting Chae" won the Teentsin cup. Murray got the Lady's purse, and Bismark the Customs' cup.

Weather here cold and wet.

Yours very truly,

ROBERT HART.

Sound Pin and his son as to the willingness of either or both to allow the latter to remain in Europe for a year: and let me know what they say.

Dear Mr. Bowra,

I have just got your note dated the 5th July written at Copenhagen. I am sorry to hear your work still continues to be difficult and unpleasant. The only way to alleviate the discomfort is to shorten it. Passages will be taken for the party by the mail of the 19th August. I wish you (i.e. the party) to be in Paris on the 5th or 6th August and to remain there until the 15th. Hasten your other arrangements so as to ensure the carrying into effect of this wish.

Yours truly,

ROBERT HART.

Lisburn,

11th July, 1866.

Dear Mr. Bowra,

Your note from Stockholm is just to hand. I wrote the other day to St. Petersburg, and I now add these few lines to repeat what I stated in that letter. Be in Paris by the 5th August, and make such stay at St. Petersburg, Berlin, and Brussels as you think proper: I imagine five days each at the two former, and three days at the last will suffice.

I am going to Paris next week, and I shall take passages for the party by the mail of the 19th August; you may tell Pin that I do not envy him his trip home, as he will have the warmest weather for the Red Sea, and the end of the typhoon season for the China Sea.

Should any remark be made relative to the short visits paid to Russia and Prussia, you will please to explain that Pin's instructions were to be back again in China in six months' time, and that he is afraid to be absent longer.

Yours truly,

ROBERT HART.

13th July, 1866.

The following eight letters from Robert Hart to his fiancee, Hester Bredon, written between 17 June and 18 August 1866 while Hart was "home," are a welcome addition to the file on Hart. They are part of a miscellaneous collection from the Hart family archives that turned up in 1990 at the University of Hong Kong. The material deals mainly with Hart's later years in China—boxes of letters, memorabilia concerning his children, invitations, guest lists, photographs, programs. Their indiscriminate array has been brought into some kind of investigative order by Ms. Elizabeth Sinn of the History Department, from whom we received our copies. We much appreciate her help.

You are the dearest girl in all the world, Hessie! Dearer to me every day; far dearer now than a week ago. I cannot explain to you how much I enjoyed the halfhour in the train the other morning, or how happy—quietly and yet triumphantly happy—I felt, as I sat with your hands in mine. Do you remember that you took off your gloves, and that afterwards you "fidgetted" a little with your hands? Do you know what I thought? Simply this: that you felt as happy as I did myself, and that the <u>unrest</u> of your hands denoted a desire to hug or a wish to be hugged? Was I right? My darling! it is so pleasant to have you near me; it is such a "bore" to be away from you! And yet, until you are altogether mine, we shall be but little with each other. Just fancy: it is already forty-eight hours since I saw you, and twice that number of hours have yet to go by before we can again meet! I permit myself to believe that you are just as anxious for the time of separation to finish as I am, and I think that with you that time passes more slowly than with me; I have to travel and to work and, with a mind occupied in spite of itself with other matters, I almost find the days too short, whereas with yourself, you are more than ever cut off from engaging in those things which would make time fly. Allow me to condole with you, my little girl, and to express a hope, that, when you do get hold of me again—I hope on Thursday evening next—you will "make much of me": I do not think it a disgrace to one's manhood, to confess to a liking to petting and being petted.

Yesterday we (that is my father and myself) went to Omuthe [?] Park. The day was a horribly cold one: the train by which we travelled was a very slow one: it was continually stopping—"backing and filling"; and we did not arrive until after two o'clock. I sat for half an hour in the drawing room, and then took a walk around the grounds with W. Woodhouse. Mrs. Woodhouse then appropriated me, having found us in the conservatory where we had taken shelter from the rain, and took me back to the house, where I had an hour's gossip with the girls and Miss Saurin. After that came a five o'clock dinner and, while the two <u>paterfamiliases</u> sipped punch, I resumed my position in the Wren [?] room, & found myself "in for it." Led on by young W. Woodh. the ladies commenced to "quiz"; I attempted to enact the part of innocence personified, — I don't know with what success, but, altho allusions were made by them to the Church, the Armagh road, my visits to Portadown, &c. &c. &c. your name did not come out atall: and while I was standing a heavy fire, M. Woodhouse came in, and said that he cannot be so inhospitable as to tell me I must either go or stay; I at once said good-bye, jumped into the cart, and drove back to the Railway Station. My father remained at Portadown: by the way, he said he won't call on you on Monday. I came on home and, almost dead with cold (just fancy; the fields between Morin [?] & Lisburn were white with snow!) paid as much attention to tea as did even Dr. Johnston. Query: is there a 't' in that ever-to-be-revered name, or not? I think not.

When passing your house, I looked at all the windows in the rear, and, though I saw nothing actually, I fancied somebody there, and <u>felt</u> <u>my</u> <u>heart</u> <u>going</u> <u>out</u> <u>towards</u> <u>her</u> with a warmth of feeling — of contented and confident love, that it never knew before. Watch for me on Thursday evening next at $5.^{35}$ p.m.; that is the time the 2 o'c train, by which I shall come from London, ought to pass your home; if you see <u>anything</u> <u>white</u> outside the window of my carriage, you may guess whose hand holds it.

I go to London tomorrow, via Holyhead: I shall be in Dublin on Thursday morning, as it is my intention to return by the same route, leaving London on Wednesday evening; I may possibly see your mother in Dublin, as I shall be there from 9 a.m. to 2 p.m.

Now my darling — my own little girl, I must say good-bye: with best wishes, and best love, till Thursday evening, dearest Hessie, goodbye.

Ever yours,
Robert Hart
Sunday evening, 17th June, 1866.

[Written down the middle of the folded sheet:]
I had almost forgotten to say that my sisters think as highly of my darling girl (if that were possible) as I do myself.

[23 July]

Dearest Hessie,

I am still at Ravarnette, & shall not be able to leave it until tomorrow night; certain family affairs of a vexatious kind call for my friendly interference, and to my own 'Celestial' cares I now find others added of a not less annoying kind. I hope, however, to arrange matters before this time tomorrow, and, should what I am about to propose be approved of, I think I shall have done a good work.

I now enclose, in duplicate, the document which Mrs. Wright is to sign in the presence of a witness; let her keep one copy, and do you yourself retain the other. I also enclose £15 No. H37908, 8 May, 1866 for £10 on Bank of England, and a Bank Post Bill 18398, 13 July 1866 endorsed to H. Leigh, on Bank of England for £5, to be handed to her.

Whose sewing machine does she use? Had I not better tell Smith Elder Co. to send one out to China at once with the saddles & other things I am about to order? 'Twould save trouble.

I found a lot of letters awaiting me on my return, and I have now to go at what remains to be done by me before returning to China, in a serious and energetic way. The work I have now to do will, however, cause me to be absent for a longer time than I anticipated. I shall not leave Paris to return to Ireland until the 9th August, and I shall only be back in time to be at Cha's wedding which has to be put off (owing to my absence) until the 16th. I fear our own will not be able to take place on the 22nd but, at all events, do you go on with arrangements so as to be ready for that day. I don't wish it to be deferred, and if I can get things in order to admit of its taking place then, so much the better.

My head is too full of business today to allow me to write you a gossiping, love-making letter, I must ask you to write to me while away; I shall write every second or third day, and shall tell you where to write to. Until you again hear from me address your letters to me at the

Royal Thames Yacht Club
7. Albemarle Street,
Piccadilly,
London

I suppose I shall next see you in Portadown about the 13th of August: what a long time for us to be separated — quite three weeks! I shall be much occupied, but nevertheless my thoughts, even when most busily engaged, will not be altogether without you: even consciously, or less consciously, you will be in all my plans. Now darling, I must say good-bye: a thousand kisses to you my own pet, my darling Hessie.!

With best love,
Ever yours,
Robert Hart

Ravarnette
23 July 1866

[Folded and addressed to:]

Miss H. J. Bredon
4 Upper Buckingham St.
Dublin

[24 July]

Dearest Hessie,

It has occurred to me that my yesterday's note may have caused you unnecessary anxiety. When I spoke of additional troubles, I did <u>not</u> mean troubles affecting you and me: I now fear that I wrote so vaguely as to lead you to think difficulties respecting <u>settlements</u> might have arisen, but it was not to such matters that I alluded. My father and Mr. Maze have some difficulties and differences concerning the arrangement of <u>their</u> partnership affairs, & it was the attempt to settle those differences that kept me at home till now. No, my darling, as afar as I am concerned, there is nothing occurring to interfere with what you & I are looking for—our union. My sweet pet: it is such a horrible thing to be away from you—such a horrible thing to have to go through another three weeks without seeing you! Why dearest, I shd like to have you always within the same four walls—to have you at my side—to talk to you about every occurrence—and to feel, whether you spoke it our not, your sympathy in all my affairs! I do hope I shall be able to carry you off and have you all to myself on the 22nd of August: I don't want a day longer to pass by before I can have the <u>right</u> to take you with me wherever I may have to go. Be ready yourself, darling, for <u>that</u> day & I shall do all I can to have my affairs in readiness too.

With best love,

My own darling little girl,

Ever yours,
Robert Hart
Lisburn, 24 July 1866.

I really start this evening.

17. Bon Accord [?] Square
Aberdeen
Friday, 27th July 1866

My dearest Hessie,

You cannot expect a very long letter from a traveller, but I love you too dearly to think of permitting too many days to go by without thinking of you in that way which (so perceptible to myself, as it must be when it is embodied in writing) is most likely to prove welcome to your own sweet self.

I had a beautiful night for crossing to Glasgow; I was not atall seasick, but I had a most vicious attack of tooth-ache, the recollection of which I don't know whether I ought to laugh or to shudder. At Glasgow I merely remained a couple of hours to wash and breakfast, after which I came on to the Bridge of Allan where I remained with Mr. and Mrs. Dick, from noon on Wednesday until about the same time on Thursday; while with them I went to the Doon [? a blot here] Castle near Dunthane, a place at which Queen Mary slept (I saw her bed &c) and from which Hume escaped. I send you a 'blue-bell' picked up on the grounds of the Castle. B. of Allan is a lovely place, &, so far as I have yet seen it, Scotland is infinitely superior to Ireland. Yesterday I telegraphed from Perth to the Braziers, & on my arrival at Aberdeen Mr. and Mrs. B. were on the Railway platform to meet me. I was delighted to see my old friend, but our lives have run in such different tracks since we last met that we are a little strange to each other. They have four children, three boys & a girl: a very nice little family, and, so far, admirably brought op. I shall leave them tomorrow, & hope to be in London on Sunday afternoon: I shall spend a few hours at Rugby on my way south. Aberdeen is a very clean-looking city; the houses are large and commodious . . .

[Two copies of the first page came, and none of the third.]

Rugby, 29th July, 1866

My darling Hessie,
    I have had my journey to Rugby (from which I now write), I might say, for nothing; M. Meadow's little daughters (don't be jealous, dear; they are aged nine and eleven respectively) left this for London on Thursday last, and, except that I have got their London address and their photographs, my 'pilgrimage' has done nothing more than show that I am not inattentive to the claims of friendship. M. Meadows was the first Consul whom I served in China; he is now a merchant resident in Teentsin, and, he & myself having been intimate friends for a dozen years, I readily volunteered, when saying aurevoir in March, to carry a parcel to his children, & visit them in person. The little girls are now near the Chrystal [sic] Palace, &, if I can spare three or four hours, I must go see them on Tuesday or Wednesday. Meantime I am here, at an old fashioned English Inn, waiting for the train; it is now a quarter past twelve, & I must remain here until two o'clock. The query is how to pass the time? The answer to that query is: think of, & write to my own darling little girl! Is that satisfactory? Is it pleasing to you, that after a week's separation, my first thought when I sit down with nothing to do, should be 'you'? My darling! Is it to be always thus? Are you and I to continue cooing in this way to the end of the chapter, or, shall I at some future date, be handed over to the jeers of the public, & the tender mercies of a British jury, for having "stamped on the wife of my buzzum?" Now that I propose that query, & reflect on the way you & I sat together for a while the last day we met, I think that such a physical feat or feet would be an impossibility, for it strikes me forcibly that you, who have the advantage of me in — may I say? — weight, could take me by the back of the neck between your finger and thumb, &, setting me up on the fire-place, render it utterly impossible for such 'lord of his creation' to commit an act, so much to be reprobated — and, having got thus far, I wonder where the end of the sentence is to come from!

423

I left Aberdeen yesterday at 4^{15} P.M., and arrived here this morning at half past seven. The night was cold, & as you may suppose, I do not feel very fresh this forenoon: by the way, it is afternoon now. I enjoyed my stay with the Braziers very much: they & their friends at Aberdeen did all they could to make the visit pleasant, & the only thing they failed to do, was to enduce me to stay for a longer time with them. I shall be in London before 5 o'clock, & I intend to rest quietly this evening, so as to be ready for the work that must be done tomorrow. I wonder shall I find my letters from you at the Yacht Club? I expect one, & I hope for two. I think it possible that you may have got my note from Aberdeen yesterday forenoon, & that you may have sent me a few lines to cheer me by last night's steamer: should there be no letter from you at the Club, I shall be horribly disappointed, & I shall at once find it necessary to have recourse to my cigar-case in order to smother the hunger-of-love, and to calm the 'nervous irritability' with which I am certain to be afflicted. However: I look upon it as certain that I shall find a letter from your own sweet self awaiting me there. In all probability there will be other letters, too, whose <u>absence</u> might be preferable to their presence: but we must take the bad with the good,— only, mark you, shd. I chance to receive disagreeable letters from others, & not a line from you, I shall have to stagger along under a load of unmitigated evil. It's all very well to say 'no news is good news'; but I prefer <u>you</u> to your <u>photograph</u>, & a <u>line</u> from you to an empty <u>inference</u>. Should cares and troubles too much pester, I'll bear them all while loved by Hester: snap scornful fingers at all pain, so long as there is truth in Jane. don't think there is my poetry—those rhymes, but there is a pleasant vein of <u>'sentimentality'</u>.

Now darling: the end of the sheet; so I'll write no more, but shall merely indulge in pleasant reveries, in which you will be the chief object. Goodbye, my pet, for a couple of days, & be sure you write as often as you can! With best love, Ever yours,

Robert Hart

Thursday [August 2, 1866, St. James Hotel]

My darling Hessie,

I feel very much inclined to write and re-write the three words with which I have commenced until the sheet is filled. I am constantly thinking of my darling: I call her my love, my pet, my treasure, my own little girl, and my dearest! But if I were to continue to write so lovingly, I fear you would think I had taken leave of my senses, and that you would not fail to consider me a very 'spoon'[?]. The fact is, my darling, I am miserably and abominably fond of you: so fond of you, that I am almost angry with you for having laid hands on me! Why did you seize me, you witch? Your loving letter of the 31st was not opened by me until about midnight last night. When I had finished reading it, the first words that came to my lips were "God bless my darling girl!" Can you analyze that, do you think? <u>I</u> can: for I felt you were a pure, generous, sensible, high-minded, loving girl, and I felt that you had given me your heart, with <u>very</u> <u>little</u> reservations indeed. And, my darling, my idea in saying, 'God bless my darling girl,' was simply this: "What a good girl she is & how she loves me! I hope I'll never do anything to make her love me less, or to render her unhappy. Heaven forbid! God bless my darling girl!" You can comprehend that, dearest, can you not?

I wish, Hessie, you were here with me. I do not like to be alone; it is not good. I don't know how a woman feels, for I'm not a woman; but, as far as I am concerned, now that I have said to you what I have said, I should just like to have you constantly by my side, and <u>to never see another woman in the world</u>! You are all that I want; but while you are absent—while I am without you—while I have not got you—I feel as if I had nothing, and as if I wanted everything! I shall not write a day after the 22nd; twenty days more, my darling! What a horrid bore it is to be away from you, and that too just at a time when we should both of us so much like to be together! I have regretted one thing very much, & it is this. I am very fond of the country—of strolling about through the fields, & of enjoying the trees & hedge-rows; & and I should find the country doubly pleasant were you in it with me, & I should find your company doubly enjoyable had I it in the country. So far we have only had city or town life together & our <u>tenderness</u> has been within four walls: I wish we could have (before marriage) a walk or two together in the country, with fine weather: not unless you come to Ravernette on Saturday the 11th to stay until Tuesday the 14th: do you think you could manage [arrange?] that? I'll give you—I'll give you 'ever so many kisses' if you do!

Of course, dear, about Ravernette, you must just do whatever your Mamma wishes you to do. I shall not be angry with you, whether you go or whether you stay away. <u>I</u> am a considerable favorite with the Hart-folk here, & those of them that know you like you too. My mother, I am sure, feels sorry every day that goes by without having seen <u>the one</u> that is to be her son's wife, and she would be delighted, beyond expression, to have you down there for as long a time as you could stay.

I am still in London, & don't think I shall go to Paris until Saturday night. I shall return from Paris on Wednesday night & shall be here again on Thursday and Friday. I shall go to Dublin on Friday night & on Saturday, I shall go north: but I commence to have my doubts about whether I shall or <u>shall</u> <u>not</u> make any stay at Portadown on Saturday. if I go on to Ravernette on Saturday (11th) I shall return for a few hours to Portadown on Monday: that is, supposing I don't find you at Ravernette. By the way, would <u>you</u> think it "absolutely wrong" to spend a few days there? And if so, why so?

My <u>cartes</u> [?] are not finished yet; they will not be ready for me until my return from Paris. I shall then let you have as many as you like. Remember, I want some more of yours: the sitting, full face set

10 1/2 a.m.

*　　*　　*　　*

4 p.m.

Those stars represent an interval of almost six hours. Col. Gordon breakfasted with me at eleven; Consul Adkins was here from 12 1/2 to one; Secretary Campbell then came in, followed by M. or rather Herr Johannes von
Gumpach, an eminent German scholar who applies for the Chair of Mathematics & Astronomy in our College at Peking; at 3 Capt. Forks [?], R.N.
came in, and at 3 1/2 Webster of the consular service appeared. It is now
four o'clock, & having got rid of my visitors with whom I did a good deal of
business, I go on with my letter writing. I must finish this letter to you first
of all, after which I have letters to write for China.

My China letters arrived two nights ago: satisfactory on the whole, for
affairs are going along quietly, but unsatisfactory in some respects, for certain individuals have been misbehaving. The sooner I am back there again,
the better for general interests viewed from our standing point.

I hear that the P&O steamers (English) will be very much crowded during the next few months. I have not yet taken [?] our passages, but, as we
go by the French Mail (which service is not much [word unclear] by English
[word unclear]), I do not think there will be any difficulty, the more especially as the French generally smooth the way for officials.

Your letter of the 31st, in what it says about 5-franc pieces, will be
attended to; but I fear the gold coins of that value are all the same size. I
shall see, however; and, if the same size, I shall get you 5-franc & 10-franc
pieces.

You say you have got "almost" everything you want; I take advantage of
the word "almost" to send you the enclosed. Don't be offended, like a good
girl! You and I are sufficiently intimate to allow of such a familiarity on my
part & we are so soon to be so closely allied that you have almost the right
to ask for it supposing you wanted it.

Now my pet, I cannot give you any more of my time. Goodbye: with best
wishes, & best love, my darling, my dearest Hessie,

Ever Yours,

Robert Hart

St. James Hotel

3rd August [on the same sheet of paper, written perpendicular to the rest of
the letter]

A thousand thanks, Hessie darling, for your note of yesterday and for the
news it contains. They will be delighted to see you at Ravernette, and most
of all, my mother: she is a plain old country body, who has never been away
from home, but she is a dear, goodhearted, woman, and whose [?] loving
must often be allowed to make up for intellectual qualities, a good life and
kind intentions must be permitted to atone for the absence of 'West End
Graces': which means, that my people are country-folk, but that I love them

just as much as if they could sport the "strawberry leaf." Now like a good girl, do one thing for me: go to Ravernette on Saturday the 11th for as much [word unclear] as you like, and stay until Tuesday or Wednesday the 14th or 15th. Will you do so, like a good girl? You can't imagine how much it will delight me to have you with me in the country for a few days! Country life is so pleasant; at least I enjoy it amazingly for I require quiet: and with you near me, it will be doubly enjoyable. If you don't do this, we'll only have a few hours together before the 22nd, for when I go home on the 11th I shall stay with my sisters until the 20th, & nothing will "budge" me.

I could not post this yesterday. I have been very busy, & have been greatly worried; however, all the worry will be over in another week, & then for home! and then for Hessie.

My darling, I think you're a very good girl, and I think that in you I have found my good angel: it isn't that I want to be constantly kissing you or anything of that sort, but the fact is that when you are in the room with me I seem to breathe a different atmosphere, and then I feel a sensation of quiet & repose which is something I have never known before. Your proximity gives me content, banishing all restlessness. You are like my favorite color (green): my eye is always pleased when it has you within range of vision, whether looking at you directly, or merely catching a side-sight of your outline. Well dear, another week will see me on my way to Ireland, and maybe I shall be [word unclear] be glad to have you by my side once more!

If you don't want the enclosed, don't send it back by post; you can use it when you see Mrs. H. Meantimes don't be angry with me for sending it. It is only love that prompts the act. My darling pet; I kissed the drop of black sealing wax! Imagine a kiss [picture of a heart?] in return. Ever yours,

[unclear—looks like T'er's]

Friday

Ravarnette House
15 Augt. 1866

My dearest Hessie,

The note in the one I received from you this morning was from W. Taylor, telling me that he had received the cover dispatched from your house on Monday, & that he would take care to apprise the proper office of your extraordinary desire to be married to "the other Party." I have written today to W. Fitzgerald, and my note was as short as it could be under the circumstances; since dispatching it, a query has suggested itself to me, viz. whether or not I have to communicate with the incumbent of St. Thomas's Church atall? Do you know, my dear? Have I to tell him, or will W. Fitzgerald do all that business? Being "unaccustomed" to this sort of thing, I don't know what to do or what to leave undone, and the fact of our being about to be married away from home, where neither of us are known, makes matters all the more difficult.

You noticed that I looked very serious the other day, when you were joking me about my having repeated several times "unaccustomed as I am to this sort of work", & you remarked that I almost seemed to be speaking as if I were conscious of a necessity to exculpate myself. You were blushing very deeply at the time. What made me look serious was this: I was wondering whether you did, or did not, doubt my truthfulness. From the way you blushed, I inferred that you had heard of my doings in <u>1856</u> — ten years ago — and from your remarks that I talked like one conscious of requiring an excuse, I further inferred that you were inviting my confidence. I don't know how far I was right in either inference. You may remember, I said, however, that I was not going to tell you what a fool I had been in the past, & I said, "Remember, Hessie, you are marrying me <u>for the future</u>." I am of a somewhat peculiar disposition — indeed I believe, now I think of it, that I am "self-willed": my disposition is of this sort, that if my own consciousness of good intentions were trifled with, I would neither attempt to deny the truth of a charge of which I was innocent, nor would I admit to the truth of one in reference to which I might chance to be guilty. To be doubted or distrusted by you, Hessie, would for me be the greatest of all earthly calamities: I have materials in me for great good, or for great evil: and were any distrust on your part to turn me in the wrong direction, I fear I shd be a curse to myself & to others. Now, my dear, when I said the other day, "unaccustomed &c. &c. &c. . . . " I meant that I had never spoken to a clergyman in the way of asking him to marry me. But the fact is that, in 1856, I was as near getting married as any man ever was that didn't get married: a very serious affair it was, I assure you, but the young lady's papa did not think me rich enough, — the affair was knocked on the head, — and in <u>three</u> months from the day on which the catastrophe occurred, she was married to another man who had more money — who was fonder of her than I was — who suited her much better, & she has been his wife for the last ten years, and is now a fat little dowdy, with ever so many children. I have not seen her for about ten years. I did not intend to tell you anything about this matter, but it occurred to me the other day from the way you spoke, and coupled with the way you blushed, that you had heard something about it, and that <u>you</u> were thinking of it when I, not thinking of it atall, spoke in a way which led you to think I was trying to conceal it. My dear! I conceal nothing, but I make no unnecessary revelations! If you would like me to do it, I could tell you how I have spent every year since I went to China, but for you to ask for such an account would be for <u>you to stoop</u> to take off the boot which conceals the <u>earthern foot</u>! I had a fondness for the other girl, and had her father said, "yes", we shd have been married! Thank Heaven he said <u>no</u>! She got over it very quickly, for, as I have said above, she was married to another man <u>three</u> months afterwards: she sent me her wedding cards, & I called to congratulate her on her marriage! I got over it quickly too — in one way: but I immediately took an immoderate dose of Byron, thought I had been harshly dealt with, turned down my collar, and began a life of dissipation the thoughts of which make me now disgusted with myself to an extent that renders life miserable when the past is thought of. From that slough I, however, gradually emerged, and,—though the temptings of old Adam make themselves felt now & then,—I have for the last two years at least led a blameless life, and have gone through the temptations of London & Paris life in a way that satisfies me that the wild oats of youth have been sown—but this is not the way to talk of so serious a subject, nor is it the way to write to so pure a girl as yourself. I should not have asked you to become my wife had I not preferred you to others. I should not have thought of marriage did I not prefer a quiet and virtuous wife: and I feel sure enough of myself for the future to think, and to be certain, that in it—in the future—nothing will be done by me to pain my wife, or call forth form her a blush for me.

You must not let what I have written pain you, my darling! I write <u>this</u> and <u>thus</u>, because I love you, and because I want you to trust me. Had it not been for your own blush, and for your own words, I should not have written thus, but, being what I am, I cannot deny anything that I have ever done, nor attempt to appear <u>to you</u> any other than what I really am. You love me for what I am; you will not distrust me for what I have been. I don't know whether other men would write in this way: <u>I</u> can only be <u>myself</u>: I <u>could</u> put on a face to others, but to you, Hessie, I cannot. I wish I had not to write in this way, but men generally don't attain my age without having gone through both fire and water; I have gone through both, but I flatter myself the result has been of a kind which burns out sores, and washes out stains. I know I am a purer and better man than I was five years ago, and I don't think a girl likely to be made unhappy who trusts her future life to me. Darling Hessie, <u>this</u> <u>day</u> <u>week</u>! Your note this morning was only too short, but of course you had nothing to say, & what you did say—you sent me your <u>love</u> and a <u>kiss</u>—suffices.

I have been very busy all day, & have got through nearly all the work I must do before marriage. I have half a mind to run up to Dublin before the end of the week, but I fear I cannot manage it. I begin to think more & more that <u>my</u> place is <u>inside</u> you—my darling girl! When you are with me—when you are mine—you may rely upon it with the most simple confidence that I shall be wholly and entirely yours. With best love: what better proof of entire love than such a letter as I have now written?—my darling Hessie,

Ever yours,
Robert Hart

Since I wrote my name I got a letter from W. Taylor saying that he inscribed the papers with the [?] & that all will be ready for me when I call on Tuesday morning.

Ravarnette House

Lisburn

18th August 1866

Thanks, a thousand thanks, my dearest little girl, for your letter — your kind, good, <u>sensible</u>, loving letter! Believe, my pet, that the future will be all you can wish it to be! I need not <u>promise</u> you anything: I know myself well enough <u>now</u>, to feel certain that nothing will henceforth be done by me to pain your heart, or make you regret that you confide in me. As I once before said, my honor, my affection, and my self-interest, all combine to make me do all that would tend to secure your happiness, and to refrain from doing anything that would cause you the slightest uneasiness. You are my own darling sweetheart now, and, as my wife — which, thank God! you will be in four days more — you will only be loved the more, and the more carefully provided for. God bless you, my darling, and make your life as happy a one as I now wish it to be!

*   *   *

I wrote to W. Fitzgerald some days ago, but I have not since heard from him. Last night, I wrote to Robert to ask him to supplement my previous letter. In that letter, I merely said that you and your mamma wished Mr. F. to be the officiating clergyman, & that I very willingly added my request to yours: & I further said that he would find a room ready for him at Morrison's on Tuesday, if his arrangements admit of his coming to Dublin. If he fails us, we shall have to get one of the curates to tie the knot.

This morning I have written to Dr. Stanford as you suggested; not knowing any other address, I have addressed the letter to St. Thomas' Church, Marlborough St. I dare say there is a sexton and as the letter goes by the 2 p.m. train today, it will be in the sexton's hands as soon as <u>this</u> can be in yours.

By the way, have you had your cards (Mrs. Hart) ordered yet. If not, pray order some at once — not to send out anywhere but because you may want them when away with me.

I had a frightful bout of tooth-ache & neuralgia yesterday. The cold and damp brought it on, and I was almost mad with it; after the fit was over (it lasted about three hours) I felt as fatigued as if I had walked twenty miles, and felt sick as if thoroughly done up. I hope it will not come on Wednesday next: were it to do so, I fear you would be wishing for another travelling companion! Dress <u>quietly</u> for the travelling part of the work, as I don't wish your dress to be a speaking intimation to all the word: "Come look at me, I'm just married!"

I shall go up by the 2 train on Monday, and shall spend an hour with you in the evening: but mind, you must not ask me to stay late.

With best love, my own darling Hessie, Ever from

Robert Hart

Notes

PREFACE

1. *Entering China's Service*, p. 325.

CHAPTER ONE – ROBERT HART IN CHINA'S HISTORY

1. See, for example, Philip C. C. Huang, *The Peasant Economy and Social Change in North China*; and for a synthesis of recent scholarship, consult Lloyd E. Eastman, *Family, Field and Ancestors*: chapters 4–7; also Susan Naquin and Evelyn Rawski, *Chinese Society in the Eighteenth Century*, chapters 1, 2, 4, 5, and 6, passim.
2. See Richard J. Smith, "China's Employment of Foreign Military Talent." On the immediate Jesuit precedent, consult Jonathan Spence, *To Change China*, chapter 1.
3. "Not meeting" (the proper time, *shih pu yü*) is the name given to a type of poem or rhyme-prose (*fu*) that was used especially in the Early Han dynasty to express the frustration of a scholar qualified for office in the newly developing Han bureaucracy yet not chosen by the emperor: Some of these *fu* were implicitly critical of the ruler, but more prudent writers like Tung Chung-shu stressed the idea of timeliness, the times being unpropitious." See Hellmut Wilhelm, "The Scholar's Frustrations."
4. On Ch'ing decrepitude and the Western invasion of the mid-nineteenth century, see the various chapters in *The Cambridge History of China*, Vols. 10 and 11. Hu Sheng, *Ti-Kuo chu-i yü Chung-kuo cheng-chih*, vigorously denounces the Western invasion of China and the Ch'ing dynasty's feeble response.
5. The opium settlement of 1858 is summarized in Hosea Ballou Morse, *The International Relations of the Chinese Empire*, 1, 554–555.
6. On the opium problem, see Jonathan Spence, "Opium Smoking in Ch'ing China."
7. On these tariff arrangements, see Stanley F. Wright, *China's Struggle for Tariff Autonomy*; on opium taxation at the ports as of 1868, table, p. 231. The only early circular on opium is *Inspector General's Circulars* no. 2 of 1864 requesting data on native opium competing with foreign. On transit duties, see *ibid.*, no. 9 of 1861 and no. 3 of 1864. On

exemption and drawback certificates, see Stanley R. Wright, *Hart and the Chinese Customs*, 85 et passim and John K. Fairbank, *Trade and Diplomacy on the China Coast: The Opening of the Treaty Ports 1842–1854*, 313–322; *Inspector General's Circulars* nos. 2, 3 and 8 of 1861; no. 5, 12 and 20 of 1863. On coast trade duty, *ibid.*, nos. 4 and 19 of 1863.

8. On the late Ch'ing fiscal system, see Yeh-chien Wang, *Land Taxation in Imperial China 1750–1911*, chapter 1. A more recent and detailed study of an earlier era is Madeline Zelin, *The Magistrate's Tael*. On the general fiscal situation, see Marianne Bastid, "The Structure of the Financial Institutions of the State in Late Qing."

9. These letters are in the Morse Collection of the Houghton Library, Harvard University.

10. See Mary C. Wright, *The Last Stand of Chinese Conservatism*, 18 ff. See also note 12 below and our chapters 3 and 7.

11. *North China Herald*, 3 November 1860 and 21 December 1861.

12. See Wright, *The Last Stand*, chapters 4 and 5. Cf. Kwang-Ching Liu, "The Ch'ing Restoration," esp. 415–423, 477–490. Hart was convinced that the real leader of the Restoration reform effort was Wen-hsiang. (Journals, 12 July 1867)

13. Richard J. Smith, *China's Cultural Heritage*, 46–50, 110–117. See also Hart's journal entry for 26 July 1864.

14. Liu, "The Ch'ing Restoration," 411.

15. Journals, 26 July 1864. The following discussion of Ch'ing administration is drawn primarily from Smith, *China's Cultural Heritage*, chapters 3 and 4; see also Fu Tsung-mao, *Ch'ing-chih lun wen-chi*; Yang Shu-fan, *Ch'ing-tai chung-yang cheng-chih chih-tu*; and Li Kuo-ch'i, "Ming-Ch'ing liang-tai ti-fang hsing-cheng chih-tu chung tao ti kung-neng chi ch'i yen-pien."

16. Journals, 22 November 1864; *Inspector General's Circulars* no. 4 of 1865; etc. On the problem of gift-giving, see also Thomas Metzger, *The Internal Organization of Ch'ing Bureaucracy*, 322–325; Zelin, *The Magistrate's Tael*, 55 ff.; Chang Te-ch'ang, *Ch'ing-chi i-ko ching-kuan ti sheng-huo*, 56, 63, note 37. Chang, 70 ff. provides numerous examples of the types and amounts of gifts given (*k'uei-tseng*).

17. See Kwang-Ching Liu, "The Limits of Regional Power in the Late Ch'ing Period: A Reappraisal."

18. Consult Jason Parker, "The Rise and Decline of I-hsin, Prince Kung, 1858–1865," 204–236; also Wu Hsiang-hsiang, *Wan-Ch'ing kung-t'ing shih-chi*, 102–111.

19. W. F. Mayers, N. B. Dennys, and Charles King, *The Treaty Ports of China and Japan*, 385. Cf. also *North China Herald*, 28 January 1865 "[As] soon as the pacification of . . . [Kiangsu] province rendered residence at Soochow safe, the thousands of natives who thronged the streets of the foreign settlements of Shanghai shook off the enforced

yoke of cleanliness and municipal ordinances, and hastened back to dirt, freedom, and Soochow." For a discussion of Shanghai during the 1860s, see Leung, Yuen-sang, "The Shanghai Taotai"; Betty Beh-T'i Wei, *Shanghai: Crucible of Modern China*, esp. 64 ff; C. B. Maybon and J. Fredet, *Histoire de la Concession Française de Changhai*, 186–228; also *TPTK*, III, 443–533.

20. For perspective on Amoy's commercial role, see Chin-keong Ng, *Trade and Society: The Amoy Network on the China Coast, 1683–1735.*

21. Susan Mann Jones, "Ningpo Pang and Financial Power at Shanghai," 73 ff. See also Andrea Lee McElderry, *Shanghai Old-Style Banks (Ch'ien-chuang) 1800–1935*; and Susan Mann Jones, "Finance in Ningpo: the 'Ch'ien chuang,' 1750–1880."

22. *North China Herald*, 21 July 1860. On the role of compradors, see Yen-p'ing Hao, *The Comprador in Nineteenth Century China.*

23. Richard J. Smith, *Mercenaries and Mandarins*, 13–14; see also *Wu Hsu tang-an-chung ti T'ai-p'ing t'ien-kuo shih-liao hsuan-chi* (hereafter *WHTA*), 39–50, 63–120 ff.

24. James Polachek, "Gentry Hegemony," esp. 240–245. See also Stanley Spector, *Li Hung-chang and the Huai Army*, 45 ff.

25. Cited in Smith, *Mercenaries and Mandarins*, 193.

26. Ibid., 156. See also Stanley Wright, *Hart and the Chinese Customs*, 243–244.

27. Our discussion of the "Soochow Massacre" is taken primarily from Smith, *Mercenaries and Mandarins*, 144–149, 152–153, 160–162. See also the illuminating documents in *WHTA*, 282 ff. For a harsh critique of Li Hung-chang's actions by a scholar sympathetic to the Taipings, consult Jen Yu-wen, *The Taiping Revolutionary Movement*, 503–505.

28. BPP 63 (3408) 1864, 23–24, Gordon to Bruce, 6 February 1864. See also Li's letter to Gordon of 4 January 1864 in *TPTK shih-liao*, 357–358.

29. BPP 63 (3408) 1864, 25–29, Hart to Bruce, 6 February 1864.

30. Ibid., 16–17, "Proclamation by Li, Footae of Kiang-soo, &c.," 14 February 1864, differs somewhat from the *North China Herald*'s translation. For further discussion of the proclamation and its proper translation, see the *North China Herald*, 7 January 1865.

31. Smith, *Mercenaries and Mandarins*, 148–149. On d'Aiguebelle's Franco-Chinese contingent, see ibid., 163–164; also Steven A. Leibo, *A Journal of the Chinese Civil War*, and chapter 5. The correspondence between Li and Gordon in 1864 indicates growing closeness and cooperation after the breach. See *TPTK shih-liao*, 358–375.

32. *LWCK*, Memorials, 6:52b.

33. Juliet Bredon, *Sir Robert Hart*, 91.

34. Smith, *Mercenaries and Mandarins*, 164. For details, including Prince Kung's communication to Bruce acknowledging Hart's role, consult *TPTK shih-liao*, 370, 418–421, 431–432.

35. Gordon Papers, Ad. Mss. 52,386, Hart to Gordon, 17 May 1864.

CHAPTER TWO—JOURNALS

1. During the siege of Soochow by Ch'ing forces and the Ever-Victorious Army, the Taiping defenders were torn by dissension. On 4 December 1863, the Mu-wang, T'an Shao-kuang, a leader strong for continued resistance, was assassinated by his brother "kings" (*wang*), who preferred to negotiate for surrender. See Kuo T'ing-i, *TPTK jih-chih*, 1035–1038; Charles Curwen, *Taiping Rebel*, 143–144; and Jen Yu-wen, *The Taiping Revolutionary Movement*, 503–505. These sources, among others, provide maps and chronological discussions that make the last stages of the Ch'ing-Taiping War comprehensible. Andrew Wilson, *The "Ever Victorious Army,"* xxxi–xxxii, provides a chronology of the EVA's operations for the period 1862–1864 that is rendered in romanizations similar to those of Hart.

2. J. McLeavy Brown, from Northern Ireland like Hart, was Assistant Chinese Secretary at the British Legation in Peking. Hart had dined with his former Ningpo boss, John Armstrong Taylor Meadows, on 26 August in Tientsin on his way to Shanghai (see *Entering China's Service*, 309). Young C. M. Bowra, then in his first Chinese post at Tientsin, included in his journal for March 1863 a thumbnail sketch of Meadows among the callers at the office: "Next came Meadows, who had started in the Consular Service, but taken a Chinese wife and resigned, done tolerably well in commerce, and is now, I dare say, worth £50,000; a good Chinese scholar, a capital man of business and a first rate Amphitryon, his dinners being much the best here." Meadows was also the Tientsin correspondent for the *North China Herald*. Edward Charles Macintosh Bowra, "Manuscript diary 20 March–24 Dec. 1863," in the Library of the School for Oriental and African Studies, University of London; and Charles Drage, *Servants of the Dragon Throne*, 70.

3. Le Footae: Li *fu-t'ai*; Governor Li Hung-chang.

   Sun was Hart's Chinese writer (personal secretary), who rendered his spoken Chinese into documentary style. For an example of Sun's work, see *WHTA*, 205.

4. General W. G. Brown was the successor to General Charles Stavely as Commander-in-Chief of the British forces in China. He had arrived in Shanghai to take charge on 31 March 1863.

5. Lay, who had been instructed by the Tsungli Yamen to settle the accounts for the disbanded Lay-Osborn Flotilla with Hart, supplied a general statement for most of the funds assigned to the project, and departed from Peking on 21 November for Shanghai. The month of December he spent there, reconciling the details of the accounts with Hart; he would begin his trip home on 9 January 1864. The accounts were not finally settled for another two years.

6. Seang-jang taou-le: *hsiang-jang tao-li*.

7. Prince von Sayn Wittgenstein had been left in charge of Prussian and other German interests after the departure of the Graf von Eulenberg in 1861; the next official Minister would be M. von Rehfues, arriving in May 1864. The Prussian treaty had deferred for 5 years the right to establish a permanent legation in Peking; Wittgenstein wished to press for one sooner, but was advised by other foreign envoys not to raise the question for the time being. He was therefore residing in Shanghai.

8. Though W. S. F. Mayers is listed in the official *Foreign Office List* of personnel for both 1863 and 1864 as Interpreter at Canton, he seems obviously to have been in Shanghai. He had come to China in June 1859, and by December of that same year was already serving as Interpreter to a British military commission on the recommendation of Sir Frederick Bruce (then Mr. Bruce). On the question of the Neutrality Act and Bruce's policies in 1863-1864, see Smith, *Mercenaries and Mandarins*, 24-25, 36, 47-49, 152-156.

9. Tseng Kuo-fan, now an Imperial Commissioner in charge of suppressing the rebellion, had been organizing militia and fighting the Taipings since 1855. Li Hung-chang had originally served under him.

10. Quinsan, also referred to as Kwan-shan (see Hart's journal entry 21 January 1864): K'un-shan. This hill city on the deltaic plain, once the seat of a Taiping force and arsenal, had been taken by Gordon at the end of May 1863 and became his headquarters.
   "tsan": *ts'an.*

11. Pa: Pa Hsia-li, Sir Harry Parkes. Parkes had gone to England on home leave in October 1861. He returned to China in 1864 to serve for a short time as Consul at Shanghai, but in 1865 was named Minister to Japan, a post he held for the next 18 years.
   Woosieh: Wu-hsi.

12. By "Tartars," Hart means Manchu Bannermen.

13. Baron Eugène de Meritens, formerly an Interpreter for Baron Gros, was an early commissioner, who had been appointed by Lay and installed by Hart initially at Tientsin in 1862.
   Though Lay had made a start at setting up the Customs Service, he had scarcely put the first few ports into action before he left for Europe and other preoccupations. Before Hart's time each Customs House had acted in a decentralized system, each Commissioner acting conjointly with his Chinese colleague, the Superintendent of Customs at that port, and both disinclined to conform to policy laid down by a centralizing office, the Inspectorate. It required firmness, tact, and a steady hand to hold the many reins now put into the new Inspector General's hands. See H. B. Morse, *The Trade and Administration of the Chinese Empire*, 360, for a summary.

14. Tsung Ming: Ch'ung-ming; an alluvial island about 40 miles long at the mouth of the Yangtze River, opposite Woosung.

A shroff was a native money-handler engaged to test coins, separate the base from the genuine, and manage exchange generally.

15. M. Chevrey Rameau was French Vice-Consul at Shanghai. Bovet Bros. & Co., a firm based at Church Street, Shanghai, was headed by G. Bovet and F. Tobler.

The Customs was still obliged to assert its statutory prerogatives at Shanghai, 10 years after the inauguration of the foreign inspectorate.

16. Captured Taiping soldiers in this period were often recruited into anti-Taiping forces as an alternative to decapitation. Both Li Hung-chang and Gordon employed them. Col. Phayre may be Col. Favre of the French army. The French had a counterpart of the EVA at Ningpo, as well as a small foreign-officered contingent in the Shanghai area. See Kuo T'ing-i, *TPTK jih-chih*, Appendixes, 159–172.

17. Mei: Mei Li-teng, de Meritens' Chinese name.

18. Thomas Dick, who had become the first Customs Commissioner in Hankow in 1862, would take over from Hart as Commissioner at Shanghai in January.

19. Hale, Mongan, and Hewlett were all British diplomatic officials. See *Entering China's Service*, 185, 228, 341–342.

20. William Hyde Lay (brother of H. N. Lay), who had been steadily advancing in the Consular Service since joining it in 1853, was now Acting Vice-Consul at Shanghai (June 1863–October 1864).

21. This was James Duncan Campbell, who had gone back to England in November on the *China* after the Lay-Osborn fleet was disbanded. After 1868 he would become Hart's "Non-Resident Secretary," i.e. London agent for the Customs Service. See *The I.G. in Peking*.

22. The Taotai (circuit intendant) in question could be either Wu Hsu, who also served as Superintendant (*tu-tai*) of the Ever-Victorious Army, or his replacement as Taotai in 1863, Huang Fang, former Acting Magistrate of Shanghai. Wu Hsu continued to be involved in the EVA's affairs even after he had been cashiered. Huang resigned because of illness in March 1864, and was replaced as Acting Taotai by Ying Pao-shih until June 1864, when Ting Jih-ch'ang assumed the regular post. See Kwang-Ching Liu, "The Confucian as Patriot and Pragmatist," 22–23 and notes; also *WHTA*, 144–146, 169–172; *TPTK shih-liao*, 411–416.

23. Kirby & Co., manager E. C. Kirby, were owners of a foreign hong in Ningpo.

James Brown was in charge of the Ningpo Customs as 3rd-class clerk from 8 April 1863 to 1 November 1864.

24. Cf. Hart's self-evaluation of 19 July 1874 discussed in chapter 11.

25. Rev. William Muirhead was a minister of the London Missionary Society, based in Shanghai.

26. Hillsboro was the village near Portadown in Northern Ireland to which Hart's parents had moved during his boyhood.

27. Richard Whately (1781-1863), Archbishop of Dublin, was a prolific

writer on religious and philosophical topics. "On search after infallibility, considered in reference to the danger of religious errors aris-
ing within the Church in the primitive as well as in all later ages"
was his discourse at an ordination ceremony on 22 August 1847.

28. Andrew Patton Happer was a medical missionary of the American
Presbyterian Mission who had been working in China since 1844.
His son, of the same name, was to join the customs in 1879.

29. Major Morton had been in command of a unit of the Ever-Victorious Army under Ward in Chekiang at the time Ningpo was re-
captured from the Taipings in 1862. See Smith, *Mercenaries and
Mandarins*, 68.

The Beloochee Mess was that of the 29th Belooch Regiment.

30. Robert C. Antrobus of Lindsay & Co., former Chairman of the
Shanghai Chamber of Commerce, had had a somewhat belligerent
correspondence with H. N. Lay in the *Times* of London while Lay
was in England, concerning rights of foreign merchants on the
Yangtze.

The Shanghai Volunteers were civilians enrolled as militia, subject to call.

31. On this issue, see Smith, *Mercenaries and Mandarins*, 146–147.

Choo fun: *ch'u-fen*.

lew jin: *liu-jen*.

32. For an account of the capture of the steamer *Firefly* by rebels, see
Entering China's Service, 315.

33. After the fall of Soochow, a large number of captured guns and
munitions were given over to General Ching (Ch'eng Hsueh-ch'i) of
the imperial forces, who had participated in the siege with Gordon.
This provided him with "a very good artillery under one of Major
Gordon's old officers, Captain Bailey." Thus equipped, Ch'eng and
Bailey were detailed to capture P'ing-wang, a fortified post held by
the rebels on the Grand Canal and considered a threat to the security of Soochow. See A. E. Hake, *Events in the Taeping Rebellion*, 398.

34. The average price of rice per picul (*shih*, c. 133 pounds) fluctuated
between 1 and 2 taels for most of the Ch'ing period, including the
19th century. The Taiping Rebellion, however, inflated prices
throughout the empire. See Hsiao Kung-chuan, *Rural China*, 381.
According to a Chinese diarist (Yao Chi) writing in the early 1860s,
the price of rice in the Shanghai area was nearly 9,000 cash per
picul (about 7 taels at the prevailing exchange rate). *Hsiao ts'ang-sang
chi*, 26 June 1862, reprinted in *TPTK*, VI, 503. Yet the price Hart
quotes at Nanking is about 4 times this amount, presumably an
effect of the Ch'ing blockade of the Taiping capital.

35. The *Elfin*, a Customs steamer, had been seized by James L. Hammond, clerk at large for the Customs at Kiukiang, in June 1863. See
Entering China's Service, 274.

36. F. Kleinwachter was a German who had joined the Customs in February 1863.

  F. E. Wright, who had joined in October 1859, would soon become Acting Deputy-Commissioner at Shanghai.

  Staff Assistant-Surgeon A. Moffitt, who had organized the medical department of the Ever-Victorious Army into a highly efficient branch, was one of Gordon's most valued officers. Smith, *Mercenaries and Mandarins*, 130.

37. *Tsung-pan* were the all-important chief secretaries who handled Yamen business. See chapter 3.

  Kung-han were "official letters" or communications between offices of equal status, presumably used in both directions between Hart and the Yamen secretaries. (To the Yamen Ministers he wrote *shen-ch'eng*, reports.) Here he evidently refers to his own filing system in which letters he received are under *shui* (perhaps representing his Chinese title as I.G., *tsung shui-wu ssu*) and letters he sent are filed under *kung*, official.

38. Frederick R. St. John had been 2nd Secretary at the British Legation in Peking since October 1862.

  J. Mackey, now a 1st-class clerk at Tientsin, took charge officially at Newchwang as deputy Commissioner on 12 April 1864, with W. L. Sibbald as Assistant.

39. William Baker, a 1st-class clerk, took over from Mackey in Tientsin, where he remained until December 1865.

40. Kea-Hing: Chia-hsing.

  Hsieh Wae-lung: Hsieh Wae-lung must be Ts'ai Yuan-lung; see Kuo, *TPTK jih-chih*, 1045–1046.

  Keang-yen: Chiang-yin

41. Stuart Man (listed in the Customs records as J. A. Man) had been H. N. Lay's secretary in the Customs and transferred to serve under Hart.

42. Neither Robert Swinhoe nor William Lay transferred from the Consular Service to the Customs. Their willingness to do so, however, is indicative of the fact that both services were looked upon by ambitious young men as proper avenues to advancement.

  R. Wadman, a merchant at Ningpo during Hart's term there, had probably not seen him for 5 years.

43. Hart's itinerary is hard to trace without the uniform spelling of later romanization. Furthermore, even Chinese sources of the day often differ on the characters used to render place names. A useful guide is Yin Wei-ho's *Chiang-su liu-shih-i hsien chih*. It seems likely that the boats started on 19 January along the Wu-sung River. At 9 the next morning they were at Wong Doo (Huang-tu), about equidistant from Tsing poo (Ch'ing-p'u) on the south and Kea-ting (Chia-ting) on the north. On the 21st at noon they arrived at Kwan-shan (K'un-shan; Quinsan), but found Gordon away. Heading almost due west,

they arrived the next day at Soochow and saw Li Hung-chang, who advised them to go to Muh-tuh (Mu-tu), 20 miles southwest. There they found they had missed Gordon yet again, and spent 5 miserable days of rain and wind traveling through marshes, heading for Tung-t'ing shan, between Wu-chiang and Hu-chou. But on the way, learning that Gordon was not there either, they headed back to Soochow, where they arrived on 29 January. Two days later, at Quinsan (where they had been on the 21st) they finally caught up with Gordon.

Bridge of "a thousand autumns": Ch'ien-ch'iu ch'iao.

44. Chung Wang foo: Palace of the "Loyal King" (*Chung-wang*, Li Hsiu-ch'eng).

Major William Brennan had been with the Ever-Victorious Army since the days of Ward. In February 1863 he was with Captain John Yates Holland at the disastrous defeat at T'ai-ts'ang, but in April redeemed himself when, under Gordon, his regiment was the first over the wall in the capture of that city.

Failure to secure prompt and regular payment was a persistent problem with the Ever-Victorious Army under Gordon. See Smith, *Mercenaries and Mandarins*, 131–138, passim.

Rhodey: Major Rhode was commander of the Ever-Victorious Army's Second Battalion, and in mid-1863 joined Li Hung-chang's Anhwei Army as a drill instructor. Later, after the EVA had been disbanded, he joined the Taipings in Fukien. Smith, *Mercenaries and Mandarins*, 162; Kuo, *TPTK jih-chih*, Appendixes, 168, 177.

45. Mondi: Perhaps Wondi; i.e. Huang-ti.

Jiu-tsin-keaou: Chiu-ch'in ch'iao ("nine-peak bridge"). Probably an alternative rendering for Chiu-feng ch'iao, which can also be translated "nine-peak bridge."

46. WooChow foo: Hu-chou.

Too-Chuh: Perhaps Tu-ts'un.

47. Dza-boo-dziaou:? Dziaou is undoubtedly Hart's transliteration here of *ch'iao*, bridge. A glance at Yin Wei-ho's work (see note 43) confirms Hart's point about placenames and bridges in the canal-laced delta.

48. WanKin: Perhaps Wang-chia ts'un.

49. Ta Eding: Ta Wei-t'ing.

50. Gordon's interpreter, according to Hart, was incompetent. See Smith, *Mercenaries and Mandarins*, 138; also note 56 below.

The adopted son of the Na-wang (Kao Yung-k'uan), was named Kao Sheng-piao. See Kuo, *TPTK jih-chih*, 1037. See also the summary of Gordon's reports on the "Affairs at Soochow" in BPP, 63 (3408) 1864, 7–11.

Ganwhuy: Anhwei province.

51. Wae-quau-dong: Wai-kua t'ang. The *Hyson*, Gordon's "flagship," was a small iron paddle steamer about 90 feet long and 24 feet wide, with a 32-pounder cannon at her bow and a 12-pounder howitzer at her stern. Wilson, *The "Ever-Victorious Army"*, 134.

52. Commander Davidson was the brave and talented captain of the *Hyson*.

    Major Tapp, commander of the Ever-Victorious Army's heavy artillery, had been wounded in the siege of Soochow.

    Major Kirkham, who had served for some time with the Ever-Victorious Army's first battalion, was Gordon's adjutant-general at the capture of Soochow. Indeed he was wounded on 27 November during that action, but apparently not seriously. See chapter 6, note 101.

    Show-fei: *shou-pei*.

53. Pwan Tajin: P'an *ta-jen*; P'an Ting-hsin, one of Li Hung-chang's best and most trusted Anhwei Army officers. *Ta-jen* indicates official status here.

    Mandel: Perhaps Captain Maunder of the first battalion, Provost Marshal of the EVA.

    Li was not interested in seeing arms dealers because he was already well supplied with shot and shell by Halliday Macartney from an arsenal the latter had organized at Sung-chiang, former headquarters of the EVA. At Feng-ching, one of the preliminary battles preceding the capture of Soochow, this ammunition had been successfully tested against the Taipings. In addition, Macartney was engaged on Li's behalf in contracting for the machinery and equipment previously designed for the supply of ammunition to the Lay-Osborn Flotilla. Agreement was reached in January, and after various delays the workshop was put into action in April 1864.

54. Hart's long letter to Sir Frederick Bruce, actually dated 6 February 1864, is quoted at length in chapter 1 above.

55. The two taotais were Huang Fang and Wu Hsu. See note 22 above. Hart's reference to Ting may be to Ying Pao-shih, one of the founders of the Defence Committee or United Defence Bureau (Hui-fang chü). See Kuo, *TPTK jih-chih*, 844. But Ting Jih-ch'ang, who would soon replace Huang as Taotai at Shanghai, was also actively involved in local defense at this time.

    One of the two Chins is almost certainly Ch'en Fu-hsun. See Spector, *Li Hung-chang and the Huai Army*, 288, Table 17; also Hart's journal entries of 5 March and 20 April 1864.

56. Hart was preparing to detach Herbert E. Hobson from his post in the Customs in order to give Gordon a competent interpreter. See note 50 above. Hobson, who had joined the Customs in 1862, left Shanghai on 4 April to join Gordon; see Hart's entry of 11 April.

57. John Markham was Acting British Consul at Shanghai.

58. In his cover letter forwarding Li Hung-chang's proclamation to the British Minister, Markham reported that Hart had helped Li Hung-chang to draw it up. See BPP, 63 (3408), 16, Markham to Bruce, 23 February 1864.

59. Ibid., 6–7, Bruce to Gordon, 25 January 1864. See Morse's discus-

sion of this letter in the context of British repeal of an Order in Council sanctioning enlistments of army officers in the Chinese service. H. B. Morse, *The International Relations of the Chinese Empire*, II, 105.

60. Colonel L. S. Hough was Commandant of the 29th Belooch Regiment.

61. C. W. de St. Croix, British in spite of his name, had entered the Customs Service in 1863.

Lieutenant Jebb of the 67th Regiment was later to succeed Gordon at Feng-huang shan, the training camp for Chinese soldiers. See Hart's journal entry of 14 November 1864; also chapter 5.

F. W. R. Clements was a lieutenant in the Royal Engineers.

62. Ting-heang hein: T'ung-hsiang hsien.
Han-yin chow: Hai-yen chou.
Keahing foo: Chia-hsing fu.
Kwan-ping: *kuan-ping*.
WooChow: Hu-chou.

63. W. F. Mayers and Hart were to have a lifetime antagonism over the rights and responsibilities of the Consular vs. the Customs services. Mayers modeled himself on the militant Harry Parkes, who was also anti-Customs and who, one remembers from Hart's Canton journals, went around that city tearing down Chinese proclamations. (But time wrought a kind of poetic justice, for Mayer's son, F. J. Mayers, was to have a long and distinguished career as Commissioner of Customs. See Wright, *Hart and the Chinese Customs*, 441.)

64. See note 22 above.

65. William Macpherson had succeeded Thomas Dick as Acting Commissioner at Hankow on 7 October 1863. William Breck, a clerk with Russell & Co. in Hankow, also served as U.S. Consul there. Anson Burlingame, U.S. Minister to China, served from 1861 to 1867. According to Tidewaiter W. Gray, Peterson referred to "this G-d-m Customs House," and said "I hate every son of a b- belonging to it." In Macpherson's rather idiosyncratic view, the use of foul language ("God damn" and "son of a bitch") was "equivalent to a prohibition of the presence of Customs officers on board." Several crewmen of the *Hu Kwang* disputed Gray's claim under oath, and merchants at Hankow criticized Macpherson for his rude treatment of the agent of the steamer, claiming "It is by such acts of discourtesy that much unpleasantness, if not hostility, is created between the Customs officials and members of the mercantile community." Correspondence and affadavits relating to the *Hu Kwang* (or *Hu-quang*) controversy are printed in the *North China Herald*, 5 March 1864 and 16 April 1864.

66. George F. Seward was U.S. Consul General in Shanghai.

Chinkiang and Kiukiang were treaty ports on the Yangtze River; the city of I-cheng (Eching) lay a few miles up river from Chinkiang. C. Kleczkowski served as Commissioner at Chinkiang from November 1863 to March 1864. William Breck, now at Hankow, had previously been at Kiukiang.

In 1863, David Williams, an American, was arraigned before the American Consul at Shanghai and convicted of piracy and murder, and a warrant for his execution was issued by Burlingame in Peking; on 29 February 1864 he was removed from the British jail to that of the Consulate, where the next day he committed suicide.

67. Thomas Adkins was British Vice-Consul at Chinkiang.

Li's proclamation, dated the 15th day of the 12th month of the 2nd year of the T'ung-chih reign (23 January 1864) is translated in the *North China Herald*, 20 February 1864. Li argues that "Soochow is plainly an interior place where foreigners have no right even to rent land for the purpose of building houses. Much less can they purchase land and houses in utter disregard of Treaty stipulations."

Ying paou she: Ying Pao-shih.

68. Dr. F. C. Sibbald, M.D., was surgeon at the Shanghai Hospital and Dispensary. Since the letter had been in transit for over 2 weeks, he was obviously not at the moment in Shanghai; possibly he was serving as a medical officer with the troops.

69. Dr. Wong was almost certainly Huang K'uan (Wong Fung; also Wong Foon, Wong Fun, etc.). Huang had taken a medical degree at the University of Edinburgh and became the Customs Medical Officer in Canton in 1863 — a position he held until his death in 1878. See Paul Cohen, *Between Tradition and Modernity*, 318–319, note 3; also Wilson, *The "Ever-Victorious Army,"* 268; Arthur Hummel, ed., *Eminent Chinese of the Ch'ing Period (1644–1912)*, 403.

C. A. Lord, who had joined the Customs in 1859, was Interpreter at the Canton office under George B. Glover as Commissioner. He was to become Acting Commissioner at Chinkiang from 1864 to 1866.

70. Vaucher Frères of Shantung Road, London Mission Compound, was a Shanghai trading firm headed by Fritz Vaucher.

Remi, Schmidt & Cie, Bund French Concession, was headed by Remi de Montigny and Edouard Schmidt. (*China Directory*, 1864)

71. Mr. Cowie headed the firm of Cowie & Co., Woosung Road in Shanghai.

D. Gilmour was a clerk at Dent & Co., Shanghai.

P. O. B. Twigg headed the Shanghae Carting Co., Woosung Road in Shanghai.

Wright may possibly have been W. A. Wright, Assistant Harbor-Master, Shanghai.

Carts of the foreign firm evidently competed with native transport.

72. George Tyson, a merchant of Queen's Road.

Drawbacks, as we have indicated, were refund certificates for duty paid on goods imported into China but unsold and to be re-exported, such certificates to be used only toward payment of other duties. See chapter 1.

73. Leang Tae Hoo: *Liang-t'ai* Hu.

Hwang Sun Sang: Huang *hsien-sheng*, Mr. Huang.

Transit certificates or passes were issued for foreign imports sent inland after having already paid import duty at the port of entry. (See chapter 1.) Both native merchants and foreign importers complained about infringements under the system, which was one of the first matters of discussion by Hart during his early visit to Peking in 1861. His I.G. Circular No. 8 of 1861 (4 November 1861) had outlined the system as then practiced, but it remained for years a bone of contention between the Chinese, who felt defrauded of income at river ports, and foreign merchants, who objected to paying any provincial levies.

Tso Chetai: Tso *chih-t'ai*; Governor General Tso Tsung-t'ang.

Keen-wuh, possibly a garble for *chien-tu*, superintendents of customs.

74. For a discussion of Hart's translation of Li Hung-chang's proclamation, see our chapter 1; also Hart's journal entry of 20 March 1864 and notes.

75. G. W. Talbot was a merchant connected with the firm of Olyphant & Co.

76. Thorne Brothers & Co. of Shanghai was headed by Joseph Thorne, Cornelius Thorne, and John Andrew Maitland. F. G. Reed of Queen's Road was an auctioneer.

The British consul at Shanghai was on the level of the Shanghai taotai, not of the Kiangsu governor (*fu-t'ai*); hence Parkes should have sent Li Hung-chang a *shen-ch'eng* (report) rather than a *chao-hui* (communication between equals).

Cheheins: *chih-hsien*. Sometimes rendered by Hart "Cheheen."

77. James Henderson, M.D., was a missionary of the London Missionary Society.

Ma Loo Mun; Ma-lu men. "House," may refer to a brothel in Nanking Road.

The *North China Herald* of 16 April 1864 reports the capture of Dore's alleged murderer, A-king.

78. William Lent had joined the Customs as a clerk in its early days, January 1855, apparently at the invitation of Lay, and in 1857 was Secretary in the Shanghai office. He resigned in May 1863 with the rank of Deputy Commissioner.

H. Tudor Davies had served with Hart as Acting Inspector General during the last few months of Lay's absence in England. He was Commissioner at Shanghai at the time of his death in June 1863.

79. R. A. Jamieson was the Editor of the *North China Herald*.

Louis Cliquet, a Frenchman, had been in the Customs since April 1863, but was to resign after only 3 years, in August 1866.

80. The *Tsatlee*, one of Gordon's steamers, was not seen again until 10 March at Kashingfu where, not knowing that General Ching (Ch'eng Hsueh-ch'i) was besieging the town, her crew tried to run her into the city. At the barrier across the creek she was stopped and taken. The "foreigners" who had seized her at Shanghai were to have received £20,000 for her from the rebels. The ringleaders were tried and one of them, Morris, who had also been engaged in the capture of the *Firefly*, was sentenced to 10 years' penal servitude. The *Confucius* and *Pluto* had previously been used by the Ever-Victorious Army. See Hake, *Taiping Rebellion*, 398; Smith, *Mercenaries and Mandarins*, 98.

    Pitman was one of Sherard Osborn's men who had helped take the Flotilla to China. Hart had apparently offered him the post of captain of the *Elfin*; see Hart's journal entry for 31 March 1864.
81. David Reid was a Shanghai merchant.

    Yuyaou (Yü-yao) was the city 15 miles west of Ningpo which Captain Roderick Dew had taken on 11 August 1862, with the support of a joint force from the Ever-Victorious and other Ch'ing armies. It was in this campaign, a month later, that Frederick Ward had been killed. We cannot tell whether Hart wrote Drew or Dew. See Morse, Vol. 2, on Captain Roderick Dew.
82. Marcus Robert Mercer, in the Customs since July 1863, was a clerk at the Shanghai Customs office.

    Kung Kwan: *kung-kuan*, i.e., the Customs Office.
83. William Pustan & Co., headed by William and Thomas Probst, were merchants on Barrier Road, Shanghai.

    Keahing: Chia-hsing.
84. Hoo chaw: *hu-chao*; passport or other similar identifying document.
85. *Doctor Thorne*, one of Anthony Trollope's series of Barsetshire novels, was published in London by Chapman and Hall in 1858.
86. Minhong: Min-hang, a stretch of the Whangpu above Shanghai.
87. Chapoo: Cha-p'u; Keashon: Chia-shan; Hae yen: Hai-yen; Ping-hoo: P'ing-hu; Tung heang: T'ung-hsiang; Hae-ning: Hai-ning; Shih mun: Shih-men. For dates of submission, see Kuo, *TPTK jih-chih*, map number 9 (no pagination). Although all the above-named places were in Chekiang, they submitted to Li Hung-chang's forces.
88. W. Watson was assistant tide surveyor for the Customs at Shanghai.
89. T. Bertolini had been agent for the Services Maritimes des Messageries Imperiales, Shanghai.
90. Tso-che-tae: Tso *chih-t'ai*. *Chih-t'ai* is the epistolary designation for governor general (*tsung-tu*).

    Ehing: I-hsing.
91. wei-yuen: *wei-yuan*.

    Yih-peih Keun-ho: *yü-pei chün-hsu* [?], preparations for military supplies. [?]

    Thomas Dick was the Shanghai Customs Commissioner, succeeding Hart.

Ninqua: the name sounds like that of a Chinese hong merchant.
92. Woo: probably Wu Hsu
93. CheHeen: see note 76 above.
    Twan San: Tuan or T'uan San
94. Twan laou yay: Tuan (or T'uan) *lao-yeh*, the "venerable" Mr. Tuan or
    T'uan; *lao-yeh* is an honorific term.
    Chang sun sung: Chang *hsien-sheng*, Mr. Chang.
95. Le Yang: Li-yang.
    Paou Chou: Pao Ch'ao, from Szechwan, one of Tseng Kuo-fan's
    best Hunan Army field commanders.
    Ningkuo: Ning-kuo.
96. Emile de Champs, a Frenchman like Meritens, went into the Cus-
    toms in June 1864 as a 4th-class clerk. He died less than 10 years
    later, as a commissioner. For his role in the Pin-ch'un Mission, see
    our chapter 9.
        J. H. Chichester, an American, came into the service, as Hart
    says, in April 1864 as a 4th-class clerk, but remained only 2 years
    before resigning in 1866.
        C. P. Butler was a clerk in the Shanghai office.
97. For Hart's office clerk and Chinese writer, Sun, to be reporting pri-
    vately to the Taotai would be standard operating procedure.
98. Le-yang: Li-yang.
    E-hing: I-hsing.
    Ta-poo-keaow: Ta-p'u ch'iao.
    Shih-wang: Shih-wang, the "Attendant King," Li Shih-hsien.
    Kin-tan: Chin-t'an.
    Ayah: *Ai-ya*, a general expression of lament or surprise.
99. M. E. Towell, British, had joined the Customs in June 1861; J. Jacques
    and Henry Aeneas Sidford, also British, had joined in September 1863.
100. Mayers includes the Chinese text in the *North China Herald*, 19 March
    1864 (*ch'i-hsien Li-i t'ou-hsiang sha Mu-ni hsien Lou-men ting-ch'i-lai-ying mien-
    chien ts'eng-ts'eng wei Ko tsong-ping so chih yeh*) and appends to it "a literal
    translation" of the characters: "At first, the negociations entered into, to
    surrender, to slay the rebel Mo, to deliver up the Low Mun, to appoint
    a time for coming to the camp for an interview, step by step, were what
    Major Gordon knew." For the entire controversy, see the *North China
    Herald*, 27 February, 5 March; 19 March 1864; 7 January 1865.
101. Ying yuen: Ying Yuan.
102. The joint tribunal, or court of joint investigation, consisting of the
    superintendent of customs, the foreign consul concerned, and the
    commissioner of customs, was established in June 1864 to deal with
    disputes over confiscations and fines. See chapter 3; also Morse, *Inter-
    national Relations*, II, 151–152.
103. During his 3 years at the Queen's College in Belfast, Hart had
    boarded with Dr. John Aicken, a well-known Wesleyan physician
    and surgeon, and an old friend of the family.

104. Fuh Shan: Fu-shan; Chang-shoo: Ch'ang-shu. Gordon had forced the submission of I-hsing and Li-yang during early March, but suffered severe repulses at Chin-t'an and Hua-shu later in the month. During April, however, he would redeem himself by capturing Hua-shu and defeating the Taipings in the area of Chiang-yin and Ch'ang-shu. See Smith, *Mercenaries and Mandarins*, 148.

105. This was Hart's letter of 6 February 1864, reporting on his trip of 9 January–4 February to Gordon's headquarters. Lord Russell was Foreign Secretary, soon to succeed Palmerston as Prime Minister.

106. Thomas Sutherland (later Sir Thomas), a year older than Hart, after graduating from the University of Aberdeen had entered the service of the Peninsular & Oriental Co. and was in China for some years representing that organization. He was to be the Chairman of its first Board.

   The Customs Commissioner at Amoy was George Hughes; at Swatow, Henry Dwight Williams.

107. Wilkie Collins's *No Name*, a novel in 2 volumes, had been published in London by Sampson, Low in 1862. Hart in Shanghai was reading more recently published novels than he had been able to get hold of in Ningpo.

108. Tsung-ching: Presumably a garble for *tsung-ping* (brigade-general), Gordon's official Chinese title.

109. Brown, Peking: J. McLeavy Brown.

   R. J. Forrest was Acting Consul at the British Consulate in Ningpo.

110. On his return, Henry A. Burgevine had gone to Peking, where he made a favorable impression on both Burlingame and Bruce, who joined in urging Prince Kung to reinstate him. In Shanghai, however, he found a different story, for Li Hung-chang had no intention of reinstating him. Hence in August he took the step that would alienate all sympathy: With a band of his followers he seized the steamer *Kajow* (*Keorjeor, Kao-ch'iao*, etc.) and entered the service of the Taipings. For the bizarre events surrounding Burgevine's checkered career in China, see Smith, *Mercenaries and Mandarins*, 108–114, 120–122.

111. Ma-urh, Ma Erh, "Ma number two," a servant — now named Ma Te-lin.

   Urh-kih, *erh-ko*, second elder brother, still Ma-urh.

112. Woo Sieh, Wu-hsi (Wusih).

   Chung Wang: the "Loyal King," i.e., Li Hsiu-ch'eng.

   Gordon had marched north and on 21 March had attempted to take the city of Chin-t'an, across a canal that led close under its wall. The defenders maintained ominous silence until the men for the assault were embarked in boats, whereupon every sort of missile rained down on them. Gordon was struck just below the knee by a ball from the wall and had to return to his boat. Major Brown, brother of the general, took Gordon's flag up the breach, but he too was wounded, as were 9 other officers including Col. Kirkham. In the morning the troops fell back on Li-yang. See Hake, *Taiping Rebellion*, 425–427; also Hart's journal entry for 28 March below.

113. George Glass Lowder, stepson of Rutherford Alcock, had joined the Customs in August 1863 and was a 2nd Assistant in the Shanghai office.

R. A. Brown was commander of the *Ringdove*, a despatch vessel of 5 guns, soon to return to England. See Hart's journal entry for 20 April 1864.

114. Ningpo, taken by Li Shih-hsien, the "Attendant King" (*Shih-wang*), on 9 December 1861, was recovered by Capt. Roderick Dew, R.N., and Lt. Kenny of the French navy, on 10 May 1862. *TPTK jih-chih*, 833, 892–93. At this time, however, Li Shih-hsien was in Chekiang. The "Wang" Hart refers to is therefore probably the "Loyal King," Li Hsiu-ch'eng, then at Fu-shan. See Wilson, *The "Ever-Victorious Army,"* 223.

115. Ch'eng Hsueh-ch'i was mortally wounded in the recapture of Chia-hsing. See Kuo, *TPTK jih-chih*, 1056; also note 150 below.

Foo: *fu*.

Heën: *hsien*.

116. WaeSoo: Hua-shu.

Kan urh tze: *kan erh-tzu*.

Tsze Wang: The so-called Tsze Wang is most likely Li Jung-fa, also known as Li Shih-kuei — see Kuo, *TPTK, jih-chih*, 1058 and his Appendix p. 21.

For an account of this episode, see Hake, *Taiping Rebellion*, 434–436. He lists the officers killed as: Capt. Gibbon, Lt. Lethbridge Pratt, Capt. Hughes, Lt. Dowling, Lt. Polken, Capt. Chinkoff. Still other spellings of their names, listed by regiment, are given in the memorial erected in 1866 at the entrance to the public garden in Shanghai. See Morse, *International Relations*, II, 112; also Wilson, *"Ever-Victorious Army,"* 385.

Le-Yang-Keaou: Li-yang ch'iao.

117. TanYang: Tan-yang.

Keiu-yung: Chü-jung.

118. Leang: Liang Su, Hart's servant.

119. On Bruce's letter to Gordon of 12 March 1864, see BPP 63 (3408) 1864, pp. 22–23.

120. Prosper Giquel, a former French naval officer, had been a leading figure in the Sino-French forces operating out of Ningpo against the Taipings. After he joined the Customs Service in October 1861, he remained at Ningpo as Commissioner from November 1861 to April 1863, when he went on leave and was temporarily replaced by James Brown. He was now writing from France to signal his return; he would resume charge at Ningpo in November 1864. See also chapter 5.

121. The Neviuses, John L. and Helen Coan, were a missionary couple Hart had known well at Ningpo in 1854–1855. See *Entering China's Service*, 50, 53–54.

122. Chaloner Alabaster, who had been in the Consular Service since the age of 16, was Interpreter at the British Consulate in Shanghai.

123. Pu Kow: P'u-k'ou. According to Kuo, *TPTK jih-chih*, 1061, Gordon occupied Hua-shu on 11 April. Chü-jung was taken by Pao Ch'ao's forces on 12 April.

124. The *Alabama* was one of 3 cruisers built by subterfuge for the U.S. Confederacy in British shipyards in 1862 in an effort to end the Union blockade of the South. As a neutral, Britain had no right to allow warships for either side to leave its shores or use its port; hence the United States sent England a bill for the 257 merchantmen destroyed by the ships during the time they were active. The bill, known as the *Alabama* claims, was not settled until 1872. Now, it seemed to Hart, China was knowingly taking on a similar liability.

125. Hung Hsiu-ch'üan, the founder of the Taiping movement, had adopted the title T'ien-wang (Heavenly King). He was to be a suicide two months hence, in June, as Nanking was assailed and captured. Dissention and fratricidal conflict had plagued the Taipings since the first disastrous power struggle in 1856.

126. France considered herself the protector of the Roman Catholic missionary establishment in China, many of the priests and nuns being French in origin. Only a few years hence, in June 1870, France and China would approach the brink of war over the Tientsin Massacre.

127. W. F. Jackson of Jackson & Co. is listed in the *China Directory* of 1864 as a merchant of Ningpo.

Keou-Kwan: possibly *chiao-kuan*, lit., educational official.

Wänchow: Wen-chou, Chekiang.

Twan Taoutae, Tuan Taotai, was known as a barbarian handler at Ningpo. See John K. Fairbank, *Trade and Diplomacy on the China Coast*, 345–346; also *Entering China's Service*, 66, 85, and 352–353, note 34.

128. A. E. Lebrethon de Caligny, of the French navy, had with Prosper Giquel, then Commissioner of Customs at Ningpo (see note 120 above), organized a Franco-Chinese contingent to emulate the Ever-Victorious Army in the neighborhood of Ningpo in late 1862. On 18 January 1863, however, it was repulsed before Shao-hsing, and Le Brethon was killed in action. He was replaced by Paul d'Aiguebelle.

Major Cooke had served under General Holland, Ward's successor, in the siege of T'ai-ts'ang in February 1863. His force, drilled by instructors supplied from British troops in Shanghai, numbered about 1,500 men. On the British and French contingents at Ningpo, consult Kuo, *TPTK jih-chih*, 164–167; also Leibo, *A Journal of the Chinese Civil War*, passim.

129. Hermann Henkel, a German, had joined the Customs in July 1863

as a 3rd-class clerk. Two years later, however, he was to be discharged while still at the same rank.

130. The Taotai (also Superintendent of Customs) at Ningpo was Shih Chih-o.

131. H. F. W. Holt is listed in the British *Foreign Service List* as Acting Interpreter at the Ningpo Consulate in 1864. The *China Directory* of 1864 calls him an Assistant at the British Consulate and packet agent, Ningpo. Hwang is evidently a deputy of Hu Taotai.

132. she-yay:? *Shih-yeh* is a standard term for a business or an occupation, but it does not describe a position or a relationship. Hart's use of the term here is not clear.

133. The Prefect at Ningpo was Peen Paow-cheng (Pien Pao-cheng?).

Yang-tseang-tuiy: *yang-ch'iang tui*, foreign arms corps; presumably in this case LeBrethon's contingent.

134. Hart's interview with the merchants highlights some of the areas of tension to be found along the 3-sided power structure — commerce, diplomacy, customs. The merchants wanted wider trade, easier access to the interior, less red tape. The foreign consuls — and above them the foreign ministers — wanted strict observance of the treaties. The Customs, representing the Chinese government, wanted accommodation of the two within legal bounds, to facilitate the maximum collection of duties. And to the third side of the conformation Hart was to add constantly throughout his career the long-range objective of improving conditions in China for the benefit of all commerce, both Chinese and foreign, but especially British.

The merchants named here are listed under the foreign hongs (businesses) at Ningpo in the *China Directory*: W. F. Jackson, whom Hart had met on the ship from Shanghai; R. Rayner of Rayner & Co.; W. Smith, Marshal of the U.S. Consulate; A. N. Brown, agent for Dent & Co.; C. E. Cerruto of Johnson & Co.

135. Chao-paou-shan: Chao-pao-shan, at the entrance of the Yung River. Hwang and Hoo Taoutae: See note 131.

Governor General Tso Tsung-t'ang's forces, including LeBrethon's Franco-Chinese contingent, now under Paul d'Aiguebelle, captured the Chekiang provincial capital of Hangchow on 31 March 1864, two weeks before Hart was in Ningpo.

Chow-le question: Perhaps this refers to levying of likin (*ch'ou-li*).

136. On Paul d'Aiguebelle, see chapter 5. Like Cooke, d'Aiguebelle once held a city ransom to force the Chinese authorities to pay his contingent.

137. L. Verney was in 1864 the French Vice-Consul at Ningpo.

138. Although James Brown was never appointed commissioner by Hart, he was temporarily in charge twice after leaving Ningpo in November 1864: from 21 April 1866, to 23 January 1867 as Acting Commissioner at Foochow; and from 19 September to 30 October 1867 as Deputy Commissioner-in-Charge at Shanghai.

139. Emil Westergaard, a Dane, came into the Customs in June 1862 as a tidewaiter, a post in the so-called "Out-Door Service"; sometime thereafter he was transferred to the "In-Door Service"—a somewhat rare occurrence—and was a 3rd-class clerk at his death in February 1867.

J. F. Fisher is listed in the *China Directory* for 1864 as an Assistant at the Ningpo Customs Office, along with Westergaard. Another Fisher, Henry James Fisher, had a subsequent career in the Customs, but this one seems not to have been listed again.

140. R. J. Forrest, the Acting British Consul at Ningpo; H. Hubbard, a clerk for Dent & Co., Shanghai.

141. Mo Be: Mo Pi?

142. Wo-po shih-lim-pow: Presumably an expression of his fear (po: *p'a*) over the sound of the explosions (pow: *pao*).

143. Waesoo: Hua-shu (see note 123).

144. Lew Fantai: Liu *fan-t'ai*, i.e., Liu K'un-i, (Kiangsi) Provincial Treasurer.

Tseang Fantai: Chiang *fan-t'ai*, Chiang I-li, (Chekiang) Provincial Treasurer. In fact, Ma Hsin-i became Governor of Chekiang from 1864 to 1867.

145. It was not surprising that Hart should not have known Wo-jen, who was anti-foreign and opposed to the policy of Westernization begun by Prince Kung and Wen-hsiang. A Grand Secretary since 1862, Wo-jen was also head of the Board of Revenue.

Paou tsun:? (Pao-yun?)

Kuan-wen had been since 1853 a prominent figure in the fight against both the Taipings and the Niens. In 1864, after the fall of Nanking, he was given the hereditary rank of 1st-class earl, in recognition of his cooperation with Tseng Kuo-fan, Hu Lin-i, and other Hunan generals.

Tsäng Kwo fan: Tseng Kuo-fan.

Lo Ping-chang, as Governor of Hunan from 1850 to 1860, was another who had a long career of opposition to the Taipings. In view of his success in Hunan he was ordered in 1860 to Szechwan, where he secured the submission and death of a Taiping leader who had been harassing the province for more than a year. After the fall of Nanking he too was rewarded with high honors.

Tso Chetae: Governor General Tso Tsung-t'ang.

Kin-ts'a: *ching-ch'a* ("capital inspection"), a triennial evaluation of metropolitan officials; the provincial counterpart was known as the *ta-chi* ("grand reckoning")

P'ing lun: *p'ing-lun*, a critique. Perhaps *p'ing-lun* refers generally to a discussion or critique, and *ching-ch'a* is a technical term indicating the evaluation of metropolitan officials (and all governors and governors general) every 3 years. See Metzger, *The Internal Organization of Ch'ing Bureaucracy*, 126.

146. Ganhwuy: Anhwei province.
     <u>Tsih-Ke-heen</u>:?
     Shang Yu: *shang-yü.*
     Le Hung chang yih neng te-leang tsze-e, <u>fow</u>? Perhaps something
     like *Li Hung-chang i neng te-liang tse-i fou*; i.e., Li Hung-chang will also
     be able to consider his responsibility, will he not?
147. <u>Chin King</u>, perhaps Ch'en Ch'ing.
148. "The other Chin": probably Ch'en Fu-hsun. See note 55 above.
     tung neën: t'ung nien; gained a civil-service-examination degree
     in the same year.
     Shin Footae: Shen *fu-ta'i*, Shen Pao-chen, Governor of Kiangsi.
149. The *Vulcan* was a steam troopship commanded by A. C. Strode. On
     the *Ringdove*, see note 113 above.
     Ch'eng Hsueh-ch'i, Hart's General Ching, was mortally wounded
     at Chia-hsing in March and died on 15 April at the age of 35. On
     hearing the news Gordon was reported to have burst into tears, and
     later called Ch'eng "the most likely man to have reformed the Chi-
     nese army." Smith, *Mercenaries and Mandarins*, 166. A native of T'ung-
     ch'eng, Anhwei, when that city fell into the hands of the Taipings,
     Ch'eng allied himself with the rebels, but in May 1861 went over to
     the side of the government at Anking.
150. R. K. Douglas was in the British Consulate at Tientsin.
     Henderson:?
     Robert Montgomery Martin (1803–1868) wrote prolifically on
     political and economic matters relating to the British empire, includ-
     ing *British Relations with the Chinese Empire* (1832); *China: Political, Com-
     mercial, and Social* (1847); etc.
151. E. Godeaux had been French Consul at Hong Kong.
152. WänChow: Wen-chou, Chekiang. There were already 3 ports with
     Customs offices on the Yangtze: Chinkiang, Kiukiang, and Hankow
     (see note 66 above). Since Hart himself had made the arrangements
     for these ports, his reference here to "a third port" is unclear.
153. Dr. W. Lockhart was surgeon at the British Legation in Peking, as
     well as medical missionary at the Chinese Hospital there.
154. On the theme of Anglo-French rivalry in China, see chapters 5 and 7.
155. Story's "Reminiscences" appear as an appendix to Hake, *Taeping
     Rebellion*.
156. C. D. Williams was agent for A. Heard & Co. in Hankow. J. A. Web-
     ster served as Acting British Consul at the treaty port. The principal
     antagonists were J. Mackellar, Robert Wadmore, and J. H. Evans.
     See the *North China Herald*, 16 April 1864, and note 65 above.
157. These excised lines probably refer to Hart's Chinese "wife," Ayaou.
     See *Entering China's Service*, 151–154, 230–232, etc. See also our chap-
     ter 6, note 65, and chapter 10, note 68.
158. W. S. Schenck was an American who had entered the Customs Ser-
     vice in June 1861.

Ke-ling: Ch'i-ling was Governor General of Fukien and Che-kiang in 1862 and became Tartar General at Foochow in 1863.

159. Baron de Meritens was the older man, but junior in service (having joined the Customs in December 1861). George B. Glover joined in August 1859.

HART'S LOOSE-LEAF TRAVEL NOTES (28 APRIL–15 MAY 1864)

[In pencil in the margin:] Visit to Gordon at Chang Chowfoo <u>May</u> <u>1864</u>.

<u>Thursday,</u> <u>28th</u> <u>April</u>: left S'Hae at 10. northbound above Markham's farm at 3.

<u>Friday</u> <u>29th</u> <u>April</u>: five o'c: got near Quinsan.

Saturday 30th—: have got to Heou Ading [Hsiao-wei-t'ing].

<u>Sunday</u> <u>1st</u> <u>May</u>: arrived at Soochow at 9. Lou mun [Lou Gate]. at 10 h left the gate on the [west?] side: at 7 oc hr; from [indistinct] got to Woo-sih [Wu-hsi].

<u>Monday</u> <u>2nd</u> <u>May</u>: left at 5: many corpses [?]: many boats going up: at ChangChow at 5. Met [?] Le Footae.

Tues 3rd May. called on Le Footae: 2 letters from T.L. Yamen: went to [indistinct].

Wd. 4 May. Rode round city wall: proposal on part of Kiangsi men to <u>surrender</u> [undecipherable]. Saw San ta jin [Li Ho-chang]. Le Ai dong [Li Ai-t'ang; also known as Li Heng-sung, a Green Standard commander—ostensibly Gordon's co-commander. See Smith, *Mercenaries and Mandarins*, 129–130, 138, 141, 159] called.

Monday [should be Thursday] 5 May: Paid Boatmen (?) $30 & $50: Cook $2 & $15. Two Rebels Keang Pei [*chiang-pei*, north of the Yangtze]. Luy Chow men carried out.

Friday 6 May: Last night 30 men came over from the branch; & this morning a small boy slipped down. 3 wangs: Tso Wang (Hwang his tz [Tso-wang, Huang Ho chin]) Hoo Wang (Chin Aochi szi [Hu-wang, Ch'en K'un-shu]) and Leih Wang [Lieh-wang, surnamed Fei]: about <u>20000</u> people in the city. With some <u>4000</u> fighting men. Rain. [See Kuo, *TPTK jih-chih*, p. 1068.]

Saty. 7 May: Morning fine: rebels out; flags on wall: snake or fish [?]: Called on Footae: can <u>80000</u>: approves of <u>Hwang</u> <u>Shu</u>; wants the Foochow money.

On return to S'hae:

    1. to write to M [?] 6th & 8th mons Tls <u>80 000</u>

    2. to write to Le Footae Tax on Opium too high.

    3. . . . . .Tin 1/2 duty.

    4. . . . . .money handed to Ting [Ying?; Ting Jih-ch'ang or Ying Pao-shih]

    5. . . . . .about the breaking up of the force.

Sunday 8th. Fine day. Footae called. Called on Le ai Dong [Li Heng-sung, as above].

Monday 9th. Rain.

Tuesday 10th. Fine: Bombarding: to attack tomorrow.

Monday [sic; must be Wednesday] 11th. Bombardment: attacks. cf. 2:3 [?]
    City taken: entry 4th, 6th day [indistinct]

Thursday 12th. Left ChangChow; [indistinct; seems to refer to the palaces
    (*fu*) of the wangs, including the Tso-wang and Lieh-wang; see entry
    for 6 May above]

Friday 13th — At Woosih at 9 am: rain.

Saturday 14th — Sailor died; put in stockade: wet morning.

    at Soochow at 11: left Low Mun at 2: at Kwanshan [K'un-shan] at
    11 P.M.

Sunday 15th Beautiful day: started at daylight.

[On back of this sheet is a list of 19 things to do at Shanghai, most of which
have been crossed out. Items 5 and 17, although not crossed out, remain
illegible]

    1. Letters to Li & Gordon on break-up of the force

    5. [?]

   10. Remittance to Lay

   14. To arrange for $16097 from Hong Kong

   15. [?] to Gordon

   17. [?]

(Not yet done: arrange passage to Hankow for 2 of Gordon's men.)

   18. Preparations for going to Peking:

72. 6 doz	Champagne	Cheese	Shirts
90. 9 ''	Sherry	Butter	
18. 6 ''	Beer	Tea	
18. 6 ''	Porter	Crackers	
24. 2 ''	Brandy	Pepper	
	Sodawater	Mustard	
	Burgundy	Oil	
		Vinegar	
		Sauces	
		Pickles	
		Salt	
		Candles	

CHAPTER THREE — PEKING 1864: ESTABLISHING THE I.G.'S STATUS

1. See John K. Fairbank and Ssu-yü Teng, *Ch'ing Administration: Three
   Studies.*

2. Our account is much indebted to S. M. Meng, *The Tsungli Yamen.*
   See also Liu Hsiung-hsiang, *Ch'ing-chi ssu-shih nien chih wai-chiao yü hai-
   fang,* and Ch'en Wen-chin, "Ch'ing-tai chih Tsung-li Ya-men chi ch'i
   ching-fei, 1861–1884." Fu Tsung-mao, *Ch'ing-chih lun wen-chi,* I, 1–63,
   offers an excellent analysis of the relationship between the Tsungli
   Yamen and the Grand Council.

3. W. F. Mayers, *Treaties between the Empire of China and Foreign Powers*, 85–86. Cf. Fairbank and Teng, *Ch'ing Administration*.
4. Meng, *Tsungli Yamen*, 22. The Ministry of Foreign Affairs in the 20th century would be translated straightforwardly as Wai-wu pu or Wai-chiao pu. But the term "Office for Management" or Tsungli Yamen seems to have originated in the Chinese text of the Russian Treaty of Tientsin in 1858 as a circumlocution that avoided raising any constitutional issue.
5. Ibid., 25, quoting Judge Hornby and Mrs. Conger. See also Liu Hsiung-hsiang, *Ch'ing-chi*, 4–5; Tung Hsun, *Huan-tu wo-shu shih lao-jen tzu-ting nien-p'u* (hereafter Tung, *nien-p'u*), 1:35b–36a, 40b–41a. Later the Yamen apparently moved. L. C. Arlington and William Lewisohn wrote in 1935 that "the Tsungli Yamen was situated in the street north of the Wai Chiao Pu Chieh [Foreign Ministry Street]," which opened off of Hatamen Street on the east side. At the back of the Yamen was the T'ung-wen kuan. L. C. Arlington and William Lewisohn, *In Search of Old Peking*, 148–149. For a vivid but rather cynical description of the way normal business was conducted at the Yamen, see E. H. Parker, *China's Past and Present*, 207 ff. Cf. United States, Department of State, *Papers Relating to Foreign Affairs*, 1865–1866, part 2, 445–449.
6. Fu Tsung-mou, *Ch'ing chih* I, 29–30, 37, 74–76.
7. Yang Chia-lo, ed., *Hsin-hsiu Ch'ing-chi shih san-shih-chiu piao*, section 2, chart 6, contains a list of Tsungli Yamen Ministers from year to year, indicating names, ethnic background, and concurrent positions.
8. On his career, see Ralph Covell, *W. A. P. Martin: Pioneer of Progress in China*. Among Martin's works in Chinese was *Ko-wu ju-men* (An introduction to science), 1868.
9. W. A. P. Martin, *A Cycle of Cathay*, 346.
10. See the views of Wang K'ai-yun and Tseng Kuo-fan, cited in Jason Parker, "Prince Kung," 230.
11. Cited in Mary Wright, *The Last Stand*, 71.
12. Martin, *A Cycle of Cathay*, 361–362. Cf. Wang Chia-chien, "Wen-hsiang tui-yü shih-chü ti jen-shih chi ch'i tzu-ch'iang ssu-hsiang."
13. Martin, *A Cycle of Cathay*, 360.
14. Ibid., 355, 358. See also F.O. 17/431, no. 245, Wade to Russell, 27 October 1865. For Tung's interest in the T'ung-wen kuan, see, for example, Tung, *nien-p'u*, I, 37a, 42b, 45a, 46a, etc.
15. See C. S. Ch'ien, "An Early Chinese Version of Longfellow's 'Psalm of Life'." Ch'ien traces how the Chinese poem, written on a fan, was sent to Longfellow, who on 30 November 1865 gave a dinner for Anson Burlingame, then American Minister to China, in honor of the fan. Later, the Chinese poem was preserved in a collection entitled *Chiao-hsien sui-lu* (The commonplace book of the Palm Pavilion),

published in 1872 by Fang Ch'un-shih. Fang had been a Secretary in the Tsungli Yamen since 1861, and Tung had asked him to help revise W. A. P. Martin's translation of Wheaton's *International Law* (see chapter 7). Tung also wrote a poem for Burlingame on the eve of his departure for Europe and the United States. See Richard J. Smith, "China's Early Reach Westward," 89; also U.S. Department of State, *Papers Relating to Foreign Affairs*, 1865–1866, part 2, 448–449.

16. The letters of A. B. Freeman-Mitford in *The Attaché at Peking* shed additional light on the personalities of Heng-ch'i and several other members of the Tsungli Yamen, including Prince Kung.

17. Spector, *Li Hung-chang and the Huai Army*, 32–37. For background, see Fairbank, *Trade and Diplomacy on the China Coast*, 430, and Smith, *Mercenaries and Mandarins*, 15–16, 42–57, 75–77, 83.

18. See, for example, Hart's journal entries for 27 June 1864, 29 August 1864, and 16 October 1864.

19. See Meng, *Tsungli Yamen*, 24 ff.

20. *Kung-han* indicates a "communication between administrative organs that are not subordinate one to another." Fairbank and Teng, *Ch'ing Administration*, 90.

21. Tung, *nien-p'u*, II, 49.

22. Chester Holcombe, *The Real Chinaman*, 93–94.

23. See, for example, 17 June 1864; 26 June 1864; 4 July 1864; 8 August 1864; also chapter 4, note 30; Tung, *nien-p'u*, I, 45b–46a.

24. Meng, *Tsungli Yamen*, 31.

25. Martin, *A Cycle of Cathay*, 341.

26. Meng, *Tsungli Yamen*, 41–43.

27. Ibid., 36 ff. Martin, *A Cycle of Cathay*, 339, provides an illuminating account of the way provincial authorities ignored the authority of the Tsungli Yamen.

28. Cited in Smith, *China's Cultural Heritage*, 249.

29. Immanuel C. Y. Hsü, *China's Entrance into the Family of Nations*, 202.

30. For the first 15 years, the circulars were numbered consecutively within each year, totaling 9 in 1861, 2 in 1862, 25 in 1863, 17 in 1864, 13 in 1865, 15 in 1866, and so forth up to 61 in 1875. Thereafter the circulars of the second series were numbered cumulatively, and by the end of Hart's tenure were being designated in 4 figures.

31. Morse Collection. See chapter 5, note 13.

32. See *Entering China's Service*, chapter 5.

33. U.S. Department of State, *Papers Relating to Foreign Affairs*, 1865, part 3, 437. Cf. Hart's circular to the Foreign Ministers of 16 March 1867 in *Papers Relating to Foreign Affairs*, 1868, part 1, 470. For Burlingame's response to Hart's initial request, see *Papers Relating to Foreign Affairs*, 1865, part 3, 436–437; also chapter 4, note 47.

34. See Stanley Wright, *Hart and the Chinese Customs*, 840–844; also 270–271, 832–833.

35. Cited in Leibo, *A Journal of the Chinese Civil War*, 39.

36. Gordon Papers, Ad. Mss. 52,386, Macartney to Gordon, n.d. Among the many Customs personnel involved in the years covered by this volume were Giquel, Eugene de Meritens, H. E. Hobson, E. C. Bowra, E. de Champs, and O. H. Brown. See *Yang-wu yun-tung* (The foreign affairs movement), III, 471 ff.; *LWCK*, Memorials, 10: 4a–5a; etc.

37. See Hart's journal entries for 22 August 1864 and esp. 3 February 1865: "Today I wrote note to Sir F. Bruce, sending him my 'Memo on the Working of the Inspectorate.'"

38. By 1935 the paper work necessary merely to get a foreign ship into a treaty port would include delivering to the Customs: a consular report (stating nationality, name type of vessel, registered tonnage, master, nature of cargo, where from, and consignee); an arrival report; a ship's national register; a manifest of cargo in identifiable detail; a tonnage dues certificate if any; a list of sea and ship's stores; a list of arms and ammunition for self-defense; a fumigation certificate; a clearance record if from a Chinese port; a list of passengers. See Stanley Wright, *Code of Customs Regulations and Procedure*, 15.

39. See *China no. 1 (1865): Foreign Customs establishment in China*. Presented to both Houses of Parliament by command of Her Majesty, 1865.

40. See journals, esp. 17 and 20 June 1864; also Morse, *International Relations*, II, 150–152. Hart submitted the regulations in a *shen-ch'eng* or "statement" such as he normally used to address them. By the Treaty of Nanking, subordinate British officers were to address Chinese high officers by this kind of document. In 1844 the American and French treaties followed suit. See Fairbank and Teng, *Ch'ing Administration*, 94.

41. Stanley Wright, *Hart*, 357–358.

42. Morse, *International Relations*, II, 152.

43. Ibid.

44. See the *North China Herald*, 23 December 1865 and 7 July 1866 for excellent contemporary accounts of the rules and procedures of the Mixed Court. See Ching-lin Hsia, *The Status of Shanghai*, 44. As was the case with Hart's Joint Investigation Rules, however, modifications were made in the structure and procedures of the Mixed Court in the latter part of the 1860s to reflect more closely the realities of Sino-foreign relations. See Morse, *International Relations*, II, 133.

45. The fact that Hart's journal at all times refers to the Misses Li in the plural, never to one alone, probably means that in heterosexual encounters in Peking during the 1860s, as in political encounters in the 1960s, one always took along a friendly witness who could corroborate one's own story of what transpired.

CHAPTER FOUR—JOURNALS

1. Hart had maintained his headquarters at Shanghai rather than at Peking, in response to the wishes of both the Tsungli Yamen and the British Minister. It was felt to be advisable to keep his function commercial rather than political; his presence in Peking might have seemed to nudge it toward the latter. The service was so new to China, however, and the regulation of foreign trade so beset by unfamiliar complications, that the Yamen found it increasingly comfortable to consult with so knowledgeable and compatible a Westerner as Hart. After another year of these periodic sessions in Peking, Hart, on 28 October 1865, was asked by the Yamen to make his residence in Peking.

   Hosewoo: Ho-hsi-wu. Ho-hsi-wu was the second important taxing station for goods in northbound Grand Canal traffic. The first portion of tax was paid at Lin-ch'ing, and the last at the Ha-ta Gate (Ch'ung-wen men) in Peking. See Susan Mann, *Local Merchants and the Chinese Bureaucracy*, 227; also chapter 8, note 2.

   Chang Kea Wan: Chang-chia wan.

   Kowlan Hootung: Kou-lan hu-t'ung. The lane of Hart's residence in Peking. The term *kou-lan* was used to designate prostitutes' quarters, a fact Hart fails to remark upon in his journal.

   Leang: Liang Su, Hart's servant.

   Albert L. Brett, British, had joined the Customs in 1862, but would have only a few years in China before his death in 1874.

   Ching lin: Ch'eng-lin, one of the Yamen secretaries general (*tsung-pan*).

2. For fuller discussions of the individuals mentioned in this paragraph, see chapters 3 and 5.

   Ching: Ch'eng-lin. Hart often uses only the sound of the first character of two-character Manchu names in his transliterations.

   Tsae: Presumably Ts'ai Shih-chün, like Ch'eng-lin also a *tsung-pan*. Wha-t'ing: *hua-t'ing*.

   Baron von Rehfues (called de Rehfues in early accounts, and always by Hart) was Prussian and then German Minister to China from 1864 to 1873. His predecessor, Prince von Wittgenstein, had left Peking without succeeding in establishing a legation there (see Hart's journal entry for 16 December 1863). Von Rehfues also failed in his first attempt; he would leave Peking later in June without having had his official visit returned by Prince Kung.

   Pechele: Pei Chih-li. The Gulf of Chihli is the body of water off the Yellow Sea which includes the ports of Chefoo on its west, and Port Arthur on its northeast. It was indeed nearly landlocked (a *mare clausum*), its navigable opening to the China Sea between Chefoo and Port Arthur only 60 miles across.

   Shin King: Sheng-ching refers administratively to the city Shen-

yang (Mukden), capital of the Manchu homeland in southern Manchuria (Liao-tung).

3. Sir Frederick Bruce was merely going on leave; he would not be
replaced as Minister (by Sir Rutherford Alcock) until 1865.

"Elfin": The *Elfin* (Ai-li-fen) was one of several steamers chartered
by Yang Fang and Wu Hsu, ostensibly for use by the Ever-Victorious
Army under Burgevine and Holland. See their correspondence in
WHTA, 179–194. The steamer had been confiscated in 1863 (see
Hart's journal entries of 9 and 17 June 1864), perhaps because of the
questionable activities of Yang and Wu. For their malpractices regarding steamers, see Smith, *Mercenaries and Mandarins*, 97.

4. When Gordon left China in the fall, it was with the rank of *t'i-tu*, or
Provincial Commander-in-Chief (translated for him as Field Marshal), as well as a peacock feather (*hua-ling*), the prestigious yellow
riding jacket (*huang ma-kua*), a gold medal (*pao-hsing*), and 4 different
sets of military regalia (*chang-fu ssu-hsi*), each appropriate to his new
rank. He persistently refused the 10,000 taels he had been offered
for the recapture of Soochow, much to the embarrassment of the
Ch'ing authorities. From the British government Gordon received a
brevet lieutenant-colonelcy, and somewhat later the Companion-
ship of the Bath. He was pleased with his Chinese outfits, in one of
which he had his photograph taken. See Demetrius C. Boulger, *The
Life of Gordon*, I, 122–123; also Smith, *Mercenaries and Mandarins*,
161–162; and *IWSM, T'ung-chih*, 22: 18a–19a and 25: 27b–28a;
TPTK shih-liao, 357–358 and 370.

Assistant-Surgeon Moffitt was responsible for a vast improvement in the medical services of the Ever-Victorious Army under
Gordon. He later married one of Gordon's sisters.

5. TsungHow: Ch'ung-hou, Superintendent of Trade for the Northern
Ports.

Alisch: Alexander Alisch & Co. were merchants of Tientsin.

6. Hsieh: Hsueh Huan, a Chinese minister of the Tsungli Yamen.

hoo hwan: *hu-huan*.

The Portuguese had been in Macao (Ao-men) for 300 years, under
the jurisdiction of the Chinese government. In 1849, however, taking
advantage of China's temporary weakness, the Portuguese Governor
declared the port to be under the sole jurisdiction of Portugal. In 1862,
again at a moment of strain for the Chinese, Portugal sent an envoy,
Isodoro Francisco Guimaraes, to negotiate a treaty, which was indeed
signed at Canton on 13 August 1862, by Heng-ch'i of the Tsungli
Yamen and Ch'ung-hou, Superintendent of Trade for the Northern
Ports. Two years were allowed for ratification. The sticking point was
a provision to recognize the status quo in Macao. Before the 2 years
were out, China had recovered sufficiently to refuse ratification. See
Morse, *International Relations*, II, 116–117; also Hart's journal entry for
17 June 1864 and chapter 8, note 10.

7. Siamen: Hsia-men, Amoy.
8. J. McLeavy Brown was Assistant Chinese Secretary, and T. Watters a student interpreter at the British Legation.
   Breck: William Breck, a clerk with Russell & Co. in Hankow who also served as U.S. Consul there.
9. Sze-kwan: *ssu-kuan*.
   Tang Kwan: *t'ang-kuan*.
   Hart's house in the Kou-lan *hu-t'ung*, where the Customs language students stayed, was located just south of the street leading to the southerly east gate known as Ch'ao-yang men or Ch'i-hua men.
10. Hart refers here to several young Bannermen who were then studying foreign languages at the Tung-wen kuan or Interpreters' College in Peking. This small school, mandated in 1861 at the same time as the Tsungli Yamen, was an outgrowth of the treaties of 1858 and the need for a sound diplomatic understanding of the foreign treaty texts on the part of the Ch'ing government. As initially organized, the T'ung-wen kuan consisted of 3 classes — English, French, and Russian — the languages of the first major treaties signed with China. The English class, taught by the Rev. S. J. Burdon, was opened in June 1862. After Hart became I.G., he took a vigorous interest in promoting and expanding the college that gradually developed from this small beginning. See chapter 7; also Morse, *International Relations*, III, 471–478; and Knight Biggerstaff, *The Earliest Modern Government Schools in China*, passim.
11. Thus the guests were: Sir Frederick Bruce, British Minister; Frederick R. St. John, 2nd Secretary; J. McLeavy Brown, Assistant Chinese Secretary; John G. Murray, Assistant and Accountant; A. Vlangali, Russian Minister; N. Glinka, 1st Secretary; D. Pestshouroff, Interpreter; M. Jules Berthemy, French Minister; M. Fontanier, Interpreter; Anson Burlingame, U.S. Minister; S. Wells Williams, Secretary and Interpreter; Ch'ung-lun from the Tsungli Yamen.
12. The "holiday" to which Hart refers was the Festival of the Upright Sun (*Tuan-yang chieh*), popularly known as the Dragon-Boat Festival.
13. Gaou-mun: Ao-men, Macao.
14. Shang-leang pan-le: *shang-liang pan-li*.
    The Portuguese Minister in 1864 was José Rodrigues Coelho d'Amaral, who was also Governor of Macao.
15. Shin: Shen Pao-chen, Governor of Kiangsu.
16. In 1860–1861 there was an insurrection in Syria together with conflict between Moslem Druses and Christian Maronites, many of whom were massacred. The powers gave France a mandate to intervene, and an expeditionary force restored order.
    Lao Tsung kwang: Lao Ch'ung-kuang, Governor General of Yunnan and Kweichow.
    Yun-kwei tsung-tuh: *Yun-Kuei tsung-tu*.
    T'seen Tetuh: T'ien *t'i-tu*, Provincial Commander-in-Chief T'ien.

In 1861, Green Standard forces under T'ien Hsing-shu had murdered a French priest while attacking a Christian community, an incident that outraged the French government. See chapter 7, note 33; also note 25 below.

keuen: *ch'üan.*

17. Dudley Edward Saurin was a 2nd Secretary at the Legation; E. Solbe, C. F. R. Allen, and T. Watters were student interpreters.

18. Transit Office: presumably a transit duty office. Although Newchwang had been designated one of the 14 treaty ports in 1858 at the Treaty of Tientsin, it was not opened until May 1864.

19. William Tarrant was the fifth editor of the *Friend of China,* a weekly publication begun in Hong Kong in 1842 and subsequently published in Canton under Tarrant. The *Friend of China* was extremely hostile to British and French support for the Ch'ing government against the Taipings.

20. Henry Burgevine, the American mercenary commander of the Ever-Victorious Army, had been dismissed from the imperial forces in January 1863 for insubordination, assault, and robbery. He later defected to the rebels in August, and was arrested in November by the American Consul at Shanghai. Partly to get him out of the way and to close a regrettable incident, the Americans deported him to Japan. In June 1864, however, he returned to China and joined the Taiping cause a second time. The Chinese, who had previously posted a reward for his capture dead or alive, were understandably incensed at the American government's failure to discipline its renegades. A year later, in May 1865, he was taken prisoner and turned over to the Chinese authorities. Sent by them to Soochow, he was drowned on the way, supposedly accidentally. See chapter 2, note 110; also chapter 5, note 20.

21. Chueen Keaou: *ch'uan-chiao.*

22. Ping k'ow: *p'ing-k'ou.*

23. J. Mcleavy Brown, a contemporary of Hart's, had been born in Northern Ireland and, like Hart, educated at the Queen's College.

24. Baron Eugene de Meritens, Commissioner of Customs at Foochow, was at the time involved in the training of Chinese troops and would soon lead them against Taiping remnants at Chang-chou. See chapter 5.

George Hughes was Commissioner of Customs at Amoy.

25. Pih Tang: Pei-t'ang, the "North Church," or cathedral, originally built within the Forbidden City on land granted to French missionaries in 1703. See Hummel, *Eminent Chinese,* 330.

Te'en Tetuh: T'ien *t'i-tu;* see note 16 above. Although T'ien had been Acting Governor of Kweichow, he is referred to in Chinese documents of the mid-1860s as "a cashiered provincial commander-in-chief."

26. Hwang Ma-kwa: *huang ma-kua.*

Sse-tao E-fuh: *ssu-tao i-fu*. Hart seems to be using *tao* as a numerative, but the proper term here is *hsi*. *TPTK shih-liao*, 418–421 provides a detailed breakdown of the different uniforms given to Gordon, and acknowledges Hart's role in the matter.

27. Nanking, the last major stronghold of the Taipings, was under siege by Tseng Kuo-ch'üan, but would not fall until mid-July. Success came about through the combined pressures of the forces of Li Hung-chang in southeastern Kiangsu, Tseng Kuo-ch'üan at Nanking, and Tso Tsung-t'ang in Chekiang. Immediately after the disbandment of the Ever-Victorious Army, Gordon traveled to Tseng Kuo-ch'üan's headquarters with Capt. Smith of the *Elfin*, intending, according to Smith, "to examine the strength of the place, to see all the Chinese officials and men in high places, and to try and induce them to allow him to bring his siege-train . . . to assist them to take the place." See Smith, *Mercenaries and Mandarins*, 167, 184.

28. The question of bonding was a prickly one that would still be under discussion, but not settled, in the 1880s. The necessity for having at the ports special warehouses or receiving hulks for the storage of opium, before payment of likin, focused attention on bonding in general — a privilege sought by merchants from the earliest treaty days but resisted by Chinese authorities. In 1853 Alcock had set up in Shanghai an improvised bonding system which soon failed. He would remember this, however, in his Convention of 1868, in which Hart, as a member of the commission for treaty revision, would have a hand. See Stanley Wright, *Hart and the Chinese Customs*, 590–593.

29. *Ad captandum* (vulgus): in order to please (the mob), emotional.

30. The problem of Chinese-Manchu tension existed throughout the Ch'ing period, and was accentuated in the 1850s and 1860s by the anti-Manchu thrust of the Taiping Rebellion. Mary Wright goes too far in asserting that by the 1860s the Manchus "were, for all practical purposes, Chinese." Wright, *The Last Stand of Chinese Conservatism*, 56. For some relevant journal entries, consult 26, 28 June and 4 July 1864; 8 August and 23 October 1865; 2 January 1866; etc.

31. A mule and a "bloke": presumably a mule and a muleteer.
    Wenchow would not be opened with a Customs office until 1877.

32. Kih Keaou, tsue heur: *ko-chiao ch'uan-hsueh*. See also Hart's journal entry for 31 August, 1864.

33. seang-fu: *hsiang-fu*. A form of mental and physical exercise.
    K'e: *ch'i*.
    Hwang-leu-tang: *huang-liu t'ang*, presumably a disorienting potion.

34. The clause allowing the French the right to own land in the interior was inserted only in the Chinese version of the Sino-French convention of 1860, not the authoritative French version.

35. How-poo-taou: *hou-pu tao*. "Expectant" generally refers to degree-holders awaiting substantive appointment. The man turns out to be Pin-ch'un; see chapter 9.

36. A. H. Layard had been Lord Russell's Under-Secretary in the Foreign Office when H. N. Lay in 1861 was arranging for the Lay-Osborn Flotilla.

Henry Thomas Liddell, baronet (later first Earl of Ravensworth and Baron Islington), had in 1855 succeeded to the peerage and sat for Liverpool.

37. At this time, Burgevine had not yet joined the rebels. See note 20.

38. Hart's memorandum to Bruce would be printed as China No. 1 of 1865 in the *Parliamentary Papers* (BPP).

39. Burlingame's circular, dated 15 June 1864, was called "Public Relations of Foreigners with the Chinese: The U.S. Minister at Peking to the U.S. Consul General, Shanghai." See Morse, *International Relations*, II, 137 and Appendix A, 419–424.

40. Ping Laou Yay: Pin *lao-yeh*, "His excellency," Pin-ch'un. *Lao-yeh* here suggests that he was formerly an official.

41. We have discussed this circular (No. 8, dated 21 June 1864) at some length in chapter 3.

42. Dybböl (German, Düppel) was a town in S. Jutland on the coast of Denmark, the scene of struggles between Danes and Germans in the 1840s. It was held by Denmark from 1860 until its recapture by Prussians in 1864. Thereafter it was held by the Germans until 1920.

43. William Maxwell, British, had joined the Customs Service in September 1862 as a 3rd-class clerk, and was now Commissioner at Tamsui. He died in September 1865.

44. The Rev. Joseph Edkins was the London Missionary Society's representative in Peking whose text, *Chinese Conversations*, Hart had used in Ningpo. See *Entering China's Service*, 97 and 354 note 48.

45. Hart's departing Prussian Minister was Prince von Wittgenstein.

Wän Chow: Wen-chou, Chekiang.

Kin Chae: *ch'in-ch'ai*.

46. N. Glinka, the Russian Secretary-of-Legation at Peking.

47. See also entry for 14 July.

48. Tonnage dues, levied by the Chinese government, were based on a fixed fee per ton of the registered capacity of foreign vessels trading in the treaty ports. Vessels from abroad were obliged to pay such dues not later than 48 hours after arrival, but were permitted to make that one payment cover trading at several or all of the treaty ports on the same voyage. Under the Treaty of Tientsin it was stipulated that the certificate issued on payment of these dues should confer exemption from further levy for a period of 4 months. Hong Kong presented a special problem, being recognized as a foreign place, but it was included in the list of eligible ports; now it was being proposed that Saigon (for the French) and Manila (for the Spanish) be also added. See Wright, *Hart*, 291–293.

49. p'o: *p'o*, push or compel [?].

tsih-fei: possibly *chih-fu*, to bring to subjection [?].

50. Murray: J. G. Murray, Assistant at the British Legation.

Bowra: Presumably W. A. Bowra, of Bowra & Co., a ship chandler of Queen's Road, Hong Kong.

51. Shin-ke ying: Though called in English the Peking Field Force, the Shen-chi ying (Divine Mechanisms Camp) had been one of the 3 Ming army training camps at Peking under the Yung-lo Emperor in the early 1400s "with the primary task of training the troops in the use of firearms." See Edward Dreyer, *Early Ming China: A Political History 1355–1435*, 192. During the late Ch'ing period (1862), it was established for the training of a corps of Bannermen in the use of modern firearms. It was under the charge of Prince Kung, with Wen-hsiang as one of its directors. See Kwang-Ching Liu and Smith, "The Military Challenge," 204.

Shin ke miaou swin: *shen-chi miao-suan* [?], "ingenious plan of the divine instrument." Possibly the source of the Shen-chi ying's name.

Foo Tsiang Keun: Fu *chiang-chün*, Tartar General Fu; possibly Fu hsing. See Kuo, *TPTK jih-chih*, Appendix, 151. Fu-hsing began his career in Kwangtung, became a Tartar General at Hsi-an (Sian) in 1856 and, although cashiered after the breaking of the siege of Nanking in that year, was allowed to retain his position. See Chang Ch'i-yun et al., eds., *Ch'ing-shih*, 6: 4791–4792 (*lieh-chüan* 204).

52. KewChow: Ch'u-chou [?]

yin te'en: *yin-t'ien*.

Han-shoo peaow: *han-shu piao*.

Tseih Yay: Ch'i-yeh; see note 64 below.

Nan Yuan: Nan-yuan, a drill ground in the southern part of Peking.

53. Ting chai: *ting-ch'ai* can mean orderly, office boy, or official messenger. Here, Hart indicates that the use of a red cart would require that he be attended by an office boy on horseback.

54. Tung Tajin: *ta-jen* (lit. "great man") here indicates that Tung Hsun is a high official.

According to Hart's letter to Burlingame, the Commissioners in charge of the treaty ports in 1864 consisted of 5 British, 3 Americans, 3 French, and 1 Prussian—but "not one American . . . who can be said to have any knowledge of Chinese." In response to Hart's request for 3 young college-educated gentlemen from the United Sates, Secretary of State William Seward entrusted the selection to the presidents of three colleges (including his own). They nominated E. C. Taintor (Union), E. B. Drew (Harvard), and F. E. Woodruff (Yale), all of the class of 1865. The 3 Americans already in the Customs were G. B. Glover, J. L. Hammond (both of whom had joined in 1859), and W. S. Schenck (in 1861). There had been one other American in the Service—William Wallace Ward (brother of the American Minister, appointed by Lay), who had joined in January 1860 as a Commissioner and resigned in

May 1863. See Morse, *International Relations*, II, 140 and notes.

55. Koo lang soo: Ku-lang-su, an island in Amoy harbor used for foreign residence.

56. Kwei tsze: *kuei-tzu*.

    Le-Yang-Tang: Li-yang t'ang; presumably a church or churches.

    Kwo: *kuo*; can mean either country or dynasty in this context.

57. Tsun-wan puh Ko ta na-Ko siaou swan pan: *ch'ien wan pu-k'o ta na-ke hsiao suan-pan*; i.e. we certainly must not be small-minded (niggardly) in this matter.

    tsze-seih-teih: *tzu-se ti*, of a reddish-purple color.

58. Shin ching: *shen-ch'eng*.

59. tsun and seih: *tsun* [?]; *se*, sex [?].

60. The question of duties on opium had been troublesome from the start. The Tientsin treaty had legalized its import and specified its tax. In addition, it had stipulated that the drug should be sold by the importer only at the treaty port of entry, that it could be conveyed into the interior only by the Chinese, and that further taxation in transit should be solely at the discretion of the Chinese authorities. This left the Chinese provincial authorities free to tax it further when outside the treaty ports. See our discussion in chapter 3 above.

61. H. C. J. Kopsch, British, had joined the Customs in January 1862, and was now a student interpreter under Macpherson at Hankow.

62. After having his offers of assistance politely declined by Tseng Kuo-ch'üan, Gordon met with other Chinese military officials, including Tseng Kuo-fan at Anking, and was again refused. Irked, he complained privately that the Chinese were averse to change and that he doubted they could manage to take Nanking "for some time." But exactly a month later, on 19 July, the Hunan Army captured the rebel stronghold after mining it in the traditional fashion. Smith, *Mercenaries and Mandarins*, 167.

63. Hart had known the Martins, an American Presbyterian missionary couple, in Ningpo in 1854. See *Entering China's Service*, 37–38, 40, 42.

    Tsing Poo Hoo tung: Tsung-pu *hu-t'ung*, a major street in Peking.

64. Tih-shing mun: Te-sheng men, the North Gate. Of Peking's 2 northern gates, this is the one on the west.

    Tseih Yay: *Ch'i-yeh*. The Seventh Prince was I-huan, Prince Ch'un. In 1861 he was made a lieutenant-general of a Banner, an adjutant-general, and a Chamberlain of the Imperial Bodyguard. In 1862 he became assistant to his half-brother, Prince Kung, who commanded the Peking Field Force. See Hummel, *Eminent Chinese*, 384.

    John Ramsey McCulloch (1780–1864) began in 1841–1842 publication of his *Dictionary, practical, theoretical and historical, of commerce and commercial navigation*, which ran through many editions with up-to-date supplements.

65. Sir Rutherford Alcock was then Minister to Japan; Capt. Forbes may have been Charles Stewart Forbes, who was to become Marine Commissioner in the Customs in 1868; R. C. R. Owen was a barrister of Queen's Road, Hong Kong; and R. A. Jamieson was Editor of the *North China Herald*. See also chapter 10, note 49.
 Charles Hannen was then Commissioner at Chefoo.

66. Taou-le: *tao-li*.

67. Yang-tsiang tuy: *yang-ch'iang tui*.
 The Duke of Cambridge (George Frederick Charles, 1819–1904) had already by 1864 had a distinguished military career culminating after the Crimean War with an appointment in 1862 as field marshal. His command was marked throughout by reorganization and innovation in military procedures.

68. The Four Books (*ssu-shu*) consisted of the *Analects of Confucius*, the *Book of Mencius*, the *Great Learning*, and the *Doctrine of the Mean*. They were considered fundamental to Confucian education in the Ch'ing period, and quotations from these works not only served as topics for the examination system, but were also used in argumentation. See Smith, *China's Cultural Heritage*, 47–49, 84, 111–118.

69. Frederick R. St. John and Dudley Edward Saurin were both 2nd Secretaries at the British Legation.

70. Hoo Poo: Hu-pu.
 Hart's plan for a fleet had two aims: to combat piracy and smuggling, and to strengthen China's hand in general. It did not come to fruition until 1879 and the 1880s, when Campbell in London was instructed to oversee the building of several ships. See the index of *The I.G. in Peking*, under "Cruisers."

71. The business of the Spanish Minister's residence in Peking dragged on into the autumn, hinging on the completion of a treaty satisfactory to both parties. Sinibaldo de Mas, the Minister, relied for translation of documents upon a French interpreter, Fontainier, a circumstance that Hart felt only created misunderstandings and further delays. In September it seemed to be settled that de Mas could live in Peking after a wait of 3 years; yet Hart's journal of October 1865 records his presence at a dinner in the capital.

72. Chun-Kuen Wang: Ch'un-chün wang. I-huan, the First Prince Ch'un, had been made a Prince of the 2nd Degree (Chun-wang) in 1850 on the ascension of his brother to the throne.
 Ts'eih yay: Ch'i-yeh, the Seventh Prince; i.e. Prince Ch'un above.

73. chih sin-Koo: *ch'ih hsin-k'u*, lit., "eat bitterness."

74. In fact there were a number of distinctions between Manchus and Chinese, including laws stipulating that the two ethnic groups were not to intermarry. See note 30 above.

75. The 48 Manchus were sent to learn the manufacture of foreign-style weapons at Soochow. See *LWCK*, Memorials, 7: 17a–19a. According

to Li Hung-chang's memorial, the men and their 12 servants did not arrive in Shanghai until 23 July 1864.

76. William C. Chambers (1800–1883) was the compiler of many reference works: *Chambers' Information for the People* (1832); *Chambers' Biographical Dictionary* (1849), etc. With R. Chambers he edited many more such works. Others besides Hart realized the need for making available Western ideas on science. John Fryer, for many years from 1860 on involved in this endeavor as teacher, editor, and translator, would in 1885 translate "Homely words to aid government" from W. and R. *Chambers' Educational Course*. See Adrian A. Bennett, *John Fryer: The Introduction of Western Science and Technology into Nineteenth-Century China*, 100.

77. sze-leu chang; perhaps *shih-liu chang*, suggesting a cart 16 (Chinese) feet (*ch'ih*) long. [Note: This cannot mean 16 *chang*, as each *chang* is almost 12 feet in length.]

78. This phrase, taken from the *Classic of Poetry*, refers originally to refinement and cultivation of character.

79. Walter Thurlow Lay (8 years younger than Horatio Nelson Lay) had come to China in 1859, and with his brother's sponsorship had been accepted by Bruce as supernumerary interpreter on condition that he should not defect to the Customs. In 1862, however, while H. N. Lay was in England, Walter took a Customs post with Bruce's acquiescence. He was now Interpreter for the Customs at Kiukiang.

J. L. Hammond had been clerk-in-charge at Kiukiang since the departure of Commissioner W. W. Ward in May 1863. The new Commissioner who would replace him in September 1864 was F. W. White.

"My strong circular": No. 8 of 21 June 1864.

80. Franz Wilzer, who had joined the Customs in January 1857, was then Commissioner at Tientsin. He remained in correspondence with Hart after returning to Germany, and in the 1880s sent a German governess for the Hart family. His son, A. H. Wilzer, joined the Customs in 1887 and had a long career in the service.

Tso Chetae: Tso *chih-t'ai*, Governor-General Tso.

In late August 1864, before the Ever-Triumphant Army had been disbanded, Paul d'Aiguebelle, Prosper Giquel, and other French officers assisted the forces of Li Hung-chang and Tso Tsung-t'ang in the recovery of Hu-chou in Chekiang. See Leibo, *A Journal of the Chinese Civil War*, based on Giquel's diary.

81. Forbes may have been the Capt. Forbes mentioned by Hart on 1 July; J. Sparrow Knight was a clerk in the Customs office at Shanghai. It is not clear why, after seeing Burlingame, they were going to Newchwang (see next day's journal entry). J. Mackay was Acting Commissioner there from April 1864 to May 1865. Knight had joined the Customs in the preceding January and would resign in 1866.

82. Chin: perhaps Yamen secretary Ch'en Ch'in. See *IWSM, T'ung-chih,* 27: 16a.
83. Tchang-hsing: Ch'ang-hsing. See Kuo, *TPTK jih-chih,* 1080.
84. Rev. Wilhelm Lobschied of the Rhenish Mission had his headquarters in Wyndham St., Hong Kong.
85. Ya-too: possibly *ya-t'ung,* toothache.
86. M. Duchesne is listed in the *China Directory* for 1864 as Consul Honoraire Chancelier at the French Legation, and also as Interpreter; M. Fontanier was of course the official Interpreter; M. Pichon was Attaché.
87. The ships named were part of the Lay-Osborn Flotilla.
88. San fuh: *san-fu.*
89. Lo To Sung-mao: *lo-t'o sung-mao*; camels' hair, loose.
    Lo To Jiang: presumably *lo-t'o jung*; camels' wool.
90. hipped: vexed. Earlier hypped, der. hyp, short for hypochondria.
91. ming-gan: *ming-an*
92. Dr. John Dudgeon came to Peking in 1864 to take charge of the London Missionary Society's hospital there, succeeding Dr. Lockhart. He was to join the Customs Service in 1865 and also become Professor of Anatomy at the T'ung-wen kuan.
    sequa: *hsi-kua.*
93. The Chinese government's right of confiscation for fraud and smuggling was long disputed. The Britisher W. H. Medhurst, "the warrior Consul," as he was called, was particularly vehement in maintaining that under the extraterritoriality rights of the Tientsin Treaty only a Consular Court could decide such cases. Bruce disagreed, and meanwhile Lay, when on leave in London, had consulted leading legal authorities on the powers and status of the Chinese Customs. The consensus was that the Chinese government "retained the undoubted right to make and enforce its own revenue laws within its own territory, the ordinary mode of enforcing such laws being the seizure and confiscation of goods in respect of which the infringement of the law had been committed; that if the Chinese government exercised this right of confiscation unjustly redress could be sought only by diplomatic proceedings; that confiscable goods on board a British steamer in Chinese waters could be seized by the Chinese authorities without a warrant from the British consul." These opinions, though they strengthened the hand of the British Minister and the Chinese authorities, did little to dissipate the feelings of rancor and distrust on the part of British merchants. See Wright, *Hart,* 355; also chapter 3 on the "four regulations."
94. Henry William Dent, a merchant Consul, was the representative of Dent & Co. on Yangtze Road in Shanghai. The headquarters of the firm was on Queen's Road, Hong Kong.
95. Ta Kung paou: presumably the Hall of High Heaven (Ta Kao T'ien

467

or Ta Kao-Hsun-T'ien) in Peking, where the Emperor traditionally prayed for rain.

96. Rev. William H. Collins was a representative of the Church Missionary Society in Peking.

97. paou t'oo-tsze: *pao tu-tzu*, lit. "a violent stomach."

98. Thomas B. Macaulay's "Minute on Indian Education" (1835) was a blueprint for vernacular education for the mass of people in India, based somewhat upon the system currently in existence in New York and New England, as well as in Prussia, and advocated for France and England. Macaulay was then a member, and later President, of the General Committee of Public Instruction. The problem in India, as in China, involved a decision as to whether to promote such education in English or in the native tongue. See Clive, *Macaulay*, 364–376.

99. 800 le a day: 800 *li*; i.e., about 222 miles a day by horse post—the top speed. For an account of the capture of Nanking, consult Yu-wen Jen, *The Taiping Revolutionary Movement*, 529–532.

100. WänChow (also Wäan Chow): Wen-chou, Chekiang.

Newchwang, opened by the treaty of 1858, began to function as a treaty port in 1864. Nanking, on the other hand, was not added to the list until 1899.

Hoopih: Hupeh.

101. Keentuh: *chien-tu*.

jin pun shën: *jen pen shan*, elipsis from the first line of the *Three-Character Classic*, i.e., *Jen chih ch'u hsing pen shan* ("At man's beginning, his nature is fundamentally good.")

tao chih i-te ch'i-chih i-li yu-chih ch'ieh ko: from the Confucian *Analects*, book 2, chapter 3.

102. shwuy-wuh-sze: *shui-wu ssu*.

103. leën ping: *lien ping*.

chih-tih-choo: [?]

104. Cha-tsze: *cha-tzu*.

Tsae Taoutae: Ts'ai Taotai, superintendent of customs at Kiu-kiang.

fan-jen: fan-jen. Perhaps in the original despatch *fan* was the character for "barbarian," rather than the character for "all," which is also pronounced *fan*.

Taou-le: *tao-li*. Hart refers here to the orthodox Confucian principle that man's nature is fundamentally good.

105. J. Aplin Webster was 1st Assistant at the British Consulate in Hankow.

106. Prata Island and Reef (modern Tung-sha tao) are in the South China Sea, southwest of Taiwan.

107. In 1867 Chinese merchants were allowed to own foreign-style ships legally. See Kwang-Ching Liu, "The Confucian as Patriot and Pragmatist," 40. It was not until 1873 that the dragon ensign was used to identify Customs ships and property; this was a yellow triangular

flag with a red sun and a blue imperial dragon. The rectangular flag drawn by Hart in the margin here was adopted in 1889. See *The I.G. in Peking*, letter 753 and note 2.

108. Hart refers here to the expansion of the T'ung-wen kuan's curriculum. He seems to imply that Caine and Thomas were British since he states that other "officers" might be from *"foreign* countries."

It seems probable that the Caine Hart had in mind was the British Consul at Swatow, although, as it turned out, he never had any connection with the T'ung-wen kuan.

The Rev. J. R. Thomas of the London Missionary Society was (according to Freeman-Mitford, writing in 1866), famous in China for being "the converse of St. Mathew, having left the church to go to the Customs." He was by then a great linguist, fluent in Russian, Chinese, Japanese, and Mongol. Having quarreled with his brother missionaries, as we see here, he entered the Customs Service and was stationed at Chefoo, where Freeman-Mitford met him. Soon, however, he returned to the church and lived with other missionaries in Peking. An inveterate traveler, he embarked on an American ship for a trip to Korea (having been shipwrecked in a previous attempt), but not one of the party was ever seen again. A report reached Peking that the Koreans had burned the ship with all hands in the Han River near Seoul. Freeman-Mitford, *The Attaché in Peking*, 205 and 208 note 2. Presumably this ill-fated ship was the famous *General Sherman* (Tyler Dennett, *Americans in Eastern Asia*, 419).

109. One of the earliest treaties entered into by China with a European power was the Kiakhta Boundary Treaty of 1727–1728, which dealt with trade and boundaries and, more important, provided for the establishment of a Russian ecclesiastical mission in Peking.

Keuen Ping: *ch'üan-ping.*

Count Kleczkowski, French, had joined the Customs in March 1860, had been Commissioner at Tientsin in 1862, and was now Commissioner at Chinkiang.

110. Keung Chow Foo: Ch'iung-chou fu, on Hainan Island.

111. Taou-le: *tao-li.*

sing-tsing: *hsing-ch'ing*, lit. "nature and feelings."

Keaou: *chiao.*

Ching: *cheng.*

112. lih tsew: *li-ch'iu*, beginning of autumn. It fell on 7 August 1864. Hart was not yet in the 7th month; 30 July was the 27th day of the 6th month.

113. Generally speaking, the names given to foreigners consisted of characters whose pronunciation approximated the sound of the foreigner's last name. They often (but not invariably) had felicitous meanings. For example, Te-shan means "moral and good."

114. In July Gordon, now Li Hung-chang's close personal friend, began training about 1,000 Chinese in foreign methods at the Feng-huang-

shan camp near Ch'ing-p'u. By mid-August Gordon wrote of the troops' "great progress" but complained of the tedium of instruction, which he could no longer endure. See chapter 5.

115. Nanking fell on 19 July 1864. By this time, Hung Hsiu-ch'üan, "the Heavenly King," had indeed died, although accounts differ as to the cause of his death. Tseng Kuo-fan's report that Hung's son had "filled his palace with firewood and burned himself to death" was incorrect, as was the assertion that no rebels escaped. In fact, the "Young Sovereign" had been personally escorted out of the city by Li Hsiu-ch'eng, the "Loyal King," who soon thereafter was captured. According to Li's "confession," he provided his own war-horse for Hung's son's escape from Nanking and took an inferior horse himself. The "Young Sovereign" was finally captured later in the year and executed on 18 November 1864, much to the relief of the Ch'ing government. See Jen, 528–536; also Curwen, *Taiping Rebel*, 25–27, 154–155.

    Keun-Ke-choo: Chün-chi ch'u.

    Gan-King: Anking.

116. HooChow: Hu-chou fell on 27 August and was occupied by imperial troops the next day.

117. <u>Keuen</u>: *ch'üan*.

118. Hart's journal entry for this date reflects his abiding concern with matters of status and protocol. All Ch'ing civil and military officials were divided into 9 degrees of rank (*p'in*), each of which was subdivided into 2 classes, *cheng* (conventionally designated "a") and *tsung* ("b"). The lower the number, the higher the rank, although military rank was considered inferior to civil rank. For information on various kinds of imperial audiences, consult Silas Wu, *Communication and Imperial Control in China*.

    Yin-Keen: *yin-chien*.

    Che-heen: *chih-hsien*, civil rank 5b.

    Show-fei: *shou-pei*, military rank 7b.

    Chaou-keen: *ch'ao-chien*.

    tang: *t'ang*.

119. Hart has the 2 forms of salutations reversed. There were about a dozen different formal salutations in Ch'ing China, ranging from the full kowtow (3 kneelings and 9 prostrations—each prostration accompanied by a ritualized hitting of the head on the ground) to a variety of different bows. See Smith, *China's Cultural Heritage*, 231–233; P. Simon Kiong, *Quelques mots sur las politesse Chinoise*, chapter 2.

    Kih-t'ow: *k'o-t'ou*.

    P'ing-t'ow: *p'ing-t'ou*.

120. Ting Chae: *t'ing-ch'ai*.

    Ma-urh: Ma-erh.

121. <u>ling che</u>: *ling-ch'ih*.

122. Shang-yuen: *shang-yuan*.

chung-yuen: *chung-yuan*.

hia-yuen: *hsia-yuan*.

Kea-tsze: *chia-tzu*. *Chia-tzu* denotes the beginning of a cycle. *Chia* and *tzu* are the first set of paired characters in the traditional Chinese sexegenary cycle.

123. Kea King, Taou Kwang, Heen Fung: Chia-ch'ing (1796–1820), Tao-kuang (1820–1850), Hsien-feng (1850–1861). Reign-names for the 3 emperors preceding the T'ung-chih Emperor (1862–1874).

Pih-leen Keaou: Pai-lien chiao; a religious sect that helped inspire widespread rebellion in the late 18th and early 19th centuries.

Tseih wih Kwafoo: ?

124. Keen-lung: Ch'ien-lung (1735–1796).

Kang-he: K'ang-hsi (1661–1722).

Yung-ching: Yung-cheng (1722–1735).

Yung-luh: Yung-lo (1403–1424).

Ping-ting Kwei-keen (Yuen chaou): *P'ing-ting kuei-chien* (Yuan ch'ao), a Yuan dynasty book showing that the *ping-wu* and *ting-wei* years of every cycle were unlucky. See Hart's entry for 19 August 1864 and note 148 below.

125. Tsäng Kwo fan, Kwan Wen, Tsang Kwo Tseuen & Le Hung Chang: Tseng Kuo-fan, Kuan-wen, Tseng Kuo-ch'üan and Li Hung-chang.

Hou-tsëo: *hou-chueh*.

Pih-tsëo: *po-chueh*.

Chang Wang: probably the Chung-wang, Li Hsiu-ch'eng.

Kan Wang: Hung Jen-kan. In fact, it was the Fu-wang, Hung Jen-ta, who was captured at this time, not Hung Jen-kan. See Kuo, *TPTK jih-chih*, 1086, 1104. See also chapter 6, note 22.

According to Tseng Kuo-fan's personal secretary, Chao Lieh-wen, who was on the scene at Nanking, "After the city was breached I estimate that apart from the vigorous rebels who were killed in the fighting, very few others were killed. Most of them carried stuff out of the city for the soldiers, or helped them find buried treasure, after which they were let go. . . . Nine out of ten of the bodies of those killed in the streets were of old people, but children of under two or three were also cut down for fun. Amongst those crawling on all fours in the streets there was not a single woman of under forty. . . . The Governor [Tseng Kuo-ch'üan] made a proclamation throughout the city that innocent people were not to be killed or women carried off. But the various commanders . . . were only interested in pillage themselves and completely disregarded the order." See Curwen, 26–27.

126. Ching Taoutai: Ch'eng Taotai.

127. Pin-ch'un's son mentioned here was probably Kuang-ying. See chapter 9.

She-she: *shih-shih*.

Ke-lin: Ch'i-lin?

Keu jin: *chü-jen.*

128. Tae tsze tae-paou: *t'ai-tzu t'ai pao.*

Paou: Pao-yun.

Keun-Ke: *Chün-chi.*

Kung-laou: *kung-lao.*

Teaou-ting: *t'iao-t'ing.*

Chao Meng was Chief Minister of the state of Chin in the region of modern Shansi province during the Chou dynasty 737–420 B.C. See Legge, *Tso-chuan* V, 569 ff. esp. 574, 581.

Aut Caesar, aut nulles: either Caesar or nobody.

129. tsëe: *ch'ieh.*

130. Kan-new-urh: *kan-nü-erh.*

Hoonan hag: old woman from Hunan province.

131. FuhKeen Seun foo: Fukien hsun-fu.

Kwo-Kea: *kuo-chia.*

Te-che: *t'i-chih,* state structure and prestige. For Hart's understanding of this term, see also *Entering China's Service,* 254, 281, 287 and 336.

Teen Tetuh: T'ien *t'i-tu,* Provincial Commander-in-Chief T'ien Hsing-shu.

Hart has miswritten a character here — probably *ai,* "to hinder, obstruct, or interfere."

132. Hwang-te: *huang-ti.*

Shun-chi: Shun-chih (1643–1661), reign-name of the first Manchu Emperor of China.

133. T'ou-urh-pin ting taë: *t'ou-erh-p'in ting-tai.*

hwaling: *hua-ling.*

paou-sing: *pao-hsing.* Background on this award is given in *IWSM, T'ung-chih,* 15: 14a–15.

fung luh: *feng-lu.*

134. Ch'in at Teentsin: Ch'en [?] at Tientsin.

135. The Ward Claims were made by the family of F. T. Ward, first commander of the Ever-Victorious Army, against Yang Fang and Wu Hsu (see chapter 1). The arbitration, litigation, and diplomatic negotiations surrounding these and related claims spanned nearly four decades after 1862, raising but not completely answering the question of whether Yang and Wu were acting as private individuals or as representatives of the Ch'ing central government in managing the affairs of the Ever-Victorious Army. See Richard J. Smith, "The 'God from the West': A Chinese Perspective," 144–145.

136. she: *shih,* "yes," right [?].

puh-she: *pu-shih,* "no," wrong [?].

137. Charles A. Lord, who had joined the Customs in 1859 and had recently been Interpreter at Canton, was from 1864–1866 Acting Commissioner at Chinkiang.

The report that there was no fighting at Nanking was clearly false. See notes 115 and 125 above.

138. F. W. White had been in the Service since August 1859 and from 1864 to 1866 would serve as Acting Commissioner at Kiukiang. J. L. Hammond, who had been clerk-in-charge there, resigned; see Hart's journal entry for 4 August.
139. Pandy: a stroke on the palm with a cane or strap as a punishment.
140. On these individuals, see notes 2 and 16 above. Lao Ch'ung-kuang was a relatively progressive individual, with some experience in foreign-training programs. See *YWYT*, 3: 459–461.
141. In the early 1860s Capt. Tardif de Moidrey had formed in Shanghai a small contingent of foreign-trained Chinese artillerymen which fought against the Taipings. When LeBrethon was killed in the battle for Shao-hsing near Ningpo, Tardif took command, but was himself killed on 19 February 1864. See Kuo, *TPTK jih-chih*, Appendix, 165–167.
142. mons: Latin, mountain
    <u>mus</u>: Latin, mouse.
    Tae Shan yew zün, säng hia she ko k'o seaou tih haou-tsz: *T'ai Shan yu tsun shang-hsia shih-ko k'o-hsiao ti hao-tzu*): "In all of exalted Mt. T'ai there are [only] ten ludicrous mice." See note 125 above.
143. Kin-chae: *ch'in-ch'ai*
    Chae-she: *ch'ai-shih*.
144. urh-moo-tsin: *erh-mu-ch'in*; lit., "second mother."
    The Widow Bedott was the pseudonym of Frances Miriam (Berry) Whitcher (1811–1852), an American whose *Widow Bedott Papers* ran through many editions. It was part of the Library of Wit and Humour, originally published in *Neal's Saturday Gazette*.
    Ta-jin: *ta-jen*. Perhaps Hart told them of his impending rank. See note 133 above.
145. Hëen Fung, the Wän tsung heen Hwang te: The Hsien-feng Emperor, I-chu, died on 22 August 1861. He was canonized as Hsien-huang-ti, with the temple name Wen-tsung.
146. Gan-ting Mun: An-ting men; the gate on the east side of the northernmost city wall of Peking.
    Yuë ching: *yueh-ch'eng*; the courtyard between the outer and inner gateways of the gate complex, i.e., the area within the barbican walls.
147. <u>Shun-che</u> mun: Shun-chih men; the gate on the south wall of the Manchu (Inner) City, west of the Front Gate (Ch'ien-men).
    <u>Kwo-haou</u>: *kuo-hao*.
    <u>Hung-wo</u> Mun: Hung-wu men.
148. Yuen chaou: *Yuan-ch'ao*.
    Ming mô: *Ming-mo*.
    Ping Kwei-Keen: *Ping-kuei-chien*. See note 124 above.
    Ping wu: *ping-wu*; 33rd combination in the cycle of sexegenary characters.
    Ting wei: *ting-wei*; 34th combination in the cycle of sexegenary characters.

149. Osborn had settled his accounts for the repatriation of the force by the summer of 1864. The inability of the British government to resolve problems connected with the disposal of the vessels for 2 years, however, delayed reimbursement to the Ch'ing government until mid-1867. For detailed figures involved and methods of calculation, see Jack T. Gerson, *Horatio Nelson Lay and Sino-British Relations, 1854–1864*, 196–197.

150. Laou Kwan (*lao-kuan*): the old ("native") customs.

151. yün-ke: *yun-ch'i*.

    Fung shwuy: *feng-shui*; lit. "wind and water," meaning the geomantic influences of a natural setting upon a human situation.

    swan-ming: *suan-ming*.

    On the prevalence of fortunetelling techniques at all levels of Ch'ing society, see R. J. Smith, "'Knowing Fate': Divination in Late Imperial China." According to Martin, *A Cycle of Cathay*, 355, 358, Tung Hsun in fact did believe in *feng-shui*, despite his remarks to Hart.

    Walker or Valki? (Text unclear.)

152. The term "astronomy" here probably means "astrology;" Tseng's belief in various fortunetelling techniques is well known. See Smith, "Knowing Fate," esp. p. 171, note 56.

153. Yuen-tsze: *yuan-tzu*.

154. As illustration, we are told that Mao Tse-tung's father encouraged him to acquire a classical education after losing a lawsuit because of an apt Confucian quotation used by his opponent. Edgar Snow, *Red Star over China*, p. 126.

155. Hart probably refers to Joseph Butler (1692–1752), an English prelate and theologian.

156. Pierre Piry had joined the Customs Service in November 1857 and was now a 2nd-class clerk at Kiukiang. He resigned from the Service in 1898. His son, A. T. Piry, would have a long career in the Customs from 1874 to 1909, and from 1901 would be head of the Customs-run Imperial Post Office; his grandson, Alphonse Piry, would join in 1905.

157. Martin, *A Cycle of Cathay*, 235 ff., documents his educational efforts.

158. Le tseay tseay: Li *chieh-chieh*.

159. Shing-ke Ying: Shen-chi ying, the Peking Field Force.

160. On W. A. P. Martin's translation of Wheaton, see chapter 7.

161. Lung fuh-tze: Lung-fu ssu, Temple of Prosperity and Happiness, was a dilapidated Ming temple near the Eastern Four Arches (Tung ssu-p'ai-lou), where a 2-day fair was held 3 times each month, inaugurated in the Yung-cheng era (1723–1736). The courtyards were filled with merchants' stalls or displays on the ground offering everything imaginable in a modern department store or supermarket — a fascinating sight and very lively. See Arlington and Lewisohn, *Old Peking*, 183, 352; and Juliet Bredon, *Peking: A Historical and Intimate Description of its Chief Places of Interest*, 458–461.

fung kew, fung shih: ?

Kwang-meaou: *kuang-miao*; go sightseeing at the temple. [?]

Pa-le-keaow: Pa-li ch'iao. When fighting their way to Peking in 1860, the French captured the "Eight-li Bridge" (Pa-li ch'iao), a landmark on the Tientsin-Peking Road. The French commander later became "Le Comte de Palikao."

162. Kih-Keaou chuen heueh: *ko-chiao ch'uan-hsueh*.

163. Tow-shoo che-chë: *t'ou-shu chi-ch'i*. Lit., to "throw at the rat and avoid [hitting] the crockery." The general implication is that one should consider the consequences of one's actions, although the phrase was used with particular reference to overcautiousness, half-hearted measures, or "the failure to impeach a corrupt official for fear of involving the prince."

164. Pootung Point, opposite the lower end of the Bund at Shanghai.

165. Tsün Mun: Presumably Ch'ien men, the Front Gate.

Shun chi mun: Shun-chih men.

Se Sze Pae Low: Hsi ssu-p'ai-lou; the Western Four Arches.

Hoo Kwo she: Hu-kuo ssu, Temple of Protecting the State, near the Western Four Arches (Hsi ssu-p'ai-lou), where fairs were held several times a month. See Arlington and Lewisohn, *Old Peking*, 205, 352.

166. Leang: Liang Su, Hart's servant.

Teentsin Hoo-kwan: Tientsin *hu-kuan*.

167. Chaou-yang mun: Ch'ao-yang men; gate on the east wall of the Manchu (Inner) City; also known as the Ch'i-hua men.

Puh tso leen: *pu tso lien*.

168. Afang was Hart's long-time servant.

Chang Kea Wan (Chang-chia-wan) and other stopping points on the road from Peking to Tientsin are discussed in chapter 5.

169. Leang Kea Yuen: Liang-chia yuan; lit., "Liang family courtyard."

William Baker, clerk at the Tientsin Customs.

170. John Hanna was the Tientsin agent for Dent & Co.

171. Rev. J. R. Thomas of the London Missionary Society. See note 108 above.

Payne may have been the R. H. Payne who had been 3rd Assistant in the Amoy Customs in 1863.

172. Shing King: Sheng-ching, "flourishing capital," i.e. the early base of the dynasty in southern Manchuria, Liao-tung.

173. Yingtsze: Ying-tzu or Ying-k'ou, port (and foreign settlement) for Newchwang, 30 miles away.

Meadows: Thomas Taylor Meadows, who was then British Consul at Newchwang.

174. Mu-kow-ying: Mo-kou-ying, old name for Ying-k'ou.

175. Two Pedders are listed in the *China Directory* of 1864 as residents of Tientsin: Frederick Pedder, a merchant with the P. & O. at Tien-

tsin, as was J. Pedder. The applicant was perhaps related to W. H. Pedder, long at Hong Kong, now the British Consul at Amoy.

176. Sha-Kwo-mên: Sha-wo men, gate on the east wall of the Chinese (Outer) City, also called the Kuang-chu men.

177. J. M. Hockly had joined the Customs in May 1862; he would be Acting Marine Commissioner in 1868, when he died.

Thomas Dick, Commissioner of Customs at Shanghai; M. R. Mercer, clerk.

Baron de Meritens had been on leave from his post as Commissioner at Foochow from 13 July to 4 August 1864. According to the record in *The Customs Service: Officers in Charge, 1859–1921*, he was in charge during all of June, and only temporarily turned over responsibility to F. N. May, a clerk, on 13 July.

178. She-tsän: Shih-tseng. The Hoppo represented the Imperial Household Department as Superintendant of Customs at Canton.

179. Kaou-ch'ieh Meaow: Kao-ch'ieh miao, a temple.

Rev. W. C. Burns was a missionary of Amoy.

180. Two ports on Formosa were manned by Customs officers at this time. Tamsui, in the north, had W. Maxwell as Assistant-in-Charge from September 1863 to January 1864, after which he transferred to Takow near the South Cape, where he remained until October 1865. He was succeeded at Tamsui by J. W. Howell. See Hart's journal entry of 7 May 1865 for an account of his own visit to Taiwan.

181. Chin Chaou Ting: Ch'en Chao-t'ing [?]. See chapter 6, note 32.

Yu: probably Yü-ch'ing, Shih-tseng's predecessor as Hoppo.

Häng: probably Heng-ch'i.

182. Foo Tseang-keun: Fu *chiang-chün*.

T.T.M.: Thomas Taylor Meadows. M. C. Morrison was British Consul at Chefoo. P. J. Hughes, who succeeded him, had been Vice-Consul at Hankow.

183. C. W. Murray and W. T. Mercer were both from Hong Kong; the former was a merchant, head of Birley & Co., Queen's Road, and the latter, Colonial Secretary. The *Manilla* was a store vessel of 4 guns, commanded by J. Burnett.

Col. Yonge: An officer named C. W. Yonge is listed in the *China Directory* as from the 29th or 2nd Belooch Regiment.

184. She-she joo-e: *shih-shih ju-i*, "everything as you wish."

F. T. Ward and Halliday Macartney, both foreign adventurers, had received Chinese military rank for their efforts against the Taipings. Hart, a civil official, felt degraded by the comparison.

185. On 3 December 1864, Li Hung-chang requested that Hart be given brevet rank as a provincial judicial commissioner (*an-ch'a shih hsien*), citing as justification Hart's exemplary service as Inspector General, the importance of foreign customs revenues in financing the Ch'ing-Taiping war, and Hart's valuable role as a negotiator and mediator. *LWCK*, Memorials, 7: 56a–b. The imperial rescript in

response (10 December 1864) referred the matter to the Tsungli Yamen. Prince Kung and his colleagues quickly memorialized the Throne, echoing Li's sentiments and asking that his request be granted as a means of encouraging Hart. Significantly, their memorial made reference not only to Hart's useful services but also to Gordon's receipt of brevet rank (1b) as a provincial commander-in-chief (*t'i-tu hsien*). A rescript dated 17 December 1864 bestowed the civil rank of provincial judicial commissioner (3a) without further remark. See *IWSM, T'ung-chih*, 30: 1a–b, 12b–13b.

Wän-che: *wen-chih.*

Nee-tai heën: *Nieh-t'ai hsien. Nieh-t'ai* is the epistolary designation for a provincial judicial commissioner (*an-ch'a shih*).

fung-keuen: *feng-ch'üan*

tuy-tsze: *tui tz'u.*

fuh-suh: *fu-se.* The matter of foreign employees changing to Chinese dress and becoming Chinese subjects was of considerable concern. See Smith, "China's Employment of Foreign Military Talent"; also Smith, *Mercenaries and Mandarins*, 162–164.

186. On tonnage dues, see note 48 above. Hart's purpose was to centralize the revenues so collected into a fund to be used for improvements where most needed. Between 1 January 1865, when the provision took effect, until 31 March 1868, when in accordance with a second application the Yamen authorized the appropriation of 7/10s tonnage dues for the purpose, the fund amounted to some Tls. 100,000 — known as the I.G.'s account "C." From it was drawn the cost of a lighthouse for Chefoo, 2 lighthouses for Ningpo, and marks and buoys for Amoy and Tientsin. Wright, *Hart*, 295.

187. Shin Ching's Choo Tieh: Probably a large compilation sponsored by the K'ang-hsi Emperor. K'ang-hsi's temple name was, however, Sheng-tsu, not Sheng-cheng.

Shang-yü: Presumably the K'ang-hsi Emperor's "Sacred Edict," *Sheng-yu hsiang-chieh.*

188. Tsing-Shih Kwan: Perhaps Ching-shih kuan; the "capital" (*ching-shih*) school.

189. Ying min: *Ying-min.*

190. fung-shway: *feng-shui*; see note 151 above. According to widespread belief, any construction undertaken without reference to *feng-shui* principles would bring bad luck to the area in question.

191. Ta-jin: *ta-jen.*

Hia Liaou Yay: Hsia *lao-yeh*; "His Excellency," Mr. Hsia, probably a Yamen secretary.

192. Pay yay: *Pa-yeh*, Eighth Prince.

che-chuh lai tuh: *Che-chu* [?] *lai-te*; someone from Che-chu.

Tsen foo-jin: *ts'an fu-jen*: participating wife. [?]

193. Kung Kwan: *kung-kuan.*

CHAPTER FIVE – HART AT WORK: FACETS OF ADMINISTRATION

1. Stanley Wright, *China's Struggle for Tariff Autonomy*, 166.
2. Ibid., 26, 231. See also Kwang-Ching Liu, "The Ch'ing Restoration," 513 ff and Li Kuo-ch'i. "Ming-Ch'ing liang-tai ti-fang hsing-cheng chih-tu chung tao ti kung-neng chi ch'i yen-pien," 159 ff.
3. Stanley Wright, *Hart*, 213, 282. Wright lists the "Customs office allowance" at successive dates as follows:

   1859 Tls. 675,333, including Tls. 100,000 for a preventive force in the Canton Delta

   1863 Tls. 700,200, then raised to 742,200

   1876 Tls. 1,098,200, etc. until in

   1898 Tls. 3,168,000 for a staff of 5,118 at 30 ports.

   See also ibid., 223, note 43, for a summary table 1876–1929.
4. Wright, *China's Struggle*, 231.
5. On confiscations, etc. see *Inspector General's Circulars* nos. 1, 8, and 9 of 1863; nos. 4, 5, 9, and 10 of 1864; and no. 3 of 1865.
6. Enclosure in *Inspector General's Circulars* no. 4 of 1864.
7. See H. B. Morse, *The Chronicles of the East India Company Trading to China, 1635–1834*, passim.
8. On tonnage dues, see *Inspector General's Circulars* nos. 7 and 21 of 1863; nos. 1 and 12 of 1865; no. 3 of 1866; no. 2 of 1868; no. 25 of 1870.
9. On the I.G.'s accounts, see *Inspector General's Circulars* nos. 24 and 25 of 1863; and nos. 1, 3 and 6 of 1865.
10. See *Inspector General's Circulars* no. 13 of 1865; no. 14 of 1866; and nos. 6 and 9 of 1867.
11. See Gerson, *Horatio Nelson Lay*, 58, citing the *North China Herald*, 26 May 1855, and Robertson's letter to Bowring of 3 December 1855.
12. See *Inspector General's Circulars* nos. 2 and 3 of 1867.
13. For a brief history of the Customs Service by a later Commissioner of Customs, bringing it up to 1950, see B. Foster Hall, *The Chinese Maritime Customs: An International Service, 1854–1950*.
14. H. B. Morse procured copies of Hart's personal letters to a dozen early Commissioners, quoted some of them in volumes 2 and 3 of *The International Relations of the Chinese Empire*, and deposited the remainder in the Houghton Library (cited as Morse Collection). The pressed copy books of S/O letters from Morse to Hart and H. F. Merrill to Hart are also in Houghton.
15. Mayers, et al., *Treaty Ports of China and Japan*, 375.
16. See Kwang-Ching Liu, *Anglo-American Steamship Rivalry in China, 1862–1874*, tables, 39, 54–55, 71.
17. See Hart's journal entry for 25 January 1865; also *IWSM*, *T'ung-chih*, 30: 12b–13a.
18. See Fairbank, *Trade and Diplomacy on the China Coast*, passim. S. W. Williams, *The Chinese Commercial Guide*, 59–60, indicates some of the hazards that steamers usually could avoid.

19. Robert Irick, *Ch'ing Policy toward the Coolie Trade 1847-1878.*
20. Most of our information on the ports has been drawn from Mayers, et al., *Treaty Ports of China and Japan.* See also Fairbank, *Trade and Diplomacy* and Liu, *Anglo-American Steamship Rivalry.*
21. On the Burgevine affair, consult Martin Ring, "The Burgevine Case and Extrality in China, 1863-1866." According to Li Hung-chang's memorial of 14 June 1865, William Winstanley, formerly an officer in the Ever-Victorious Army and a close acquaintance of Burgevine's, turned the American adventurer in to the Customs authorities. See *IWSM, T'ung-chih,* 37: 39a. This was not the first time foreign Customs personnel had become involved in the capture of Western mercenaries who had joined the Taipings. See, for example, ibid. 34: 7b-8a. Predictably, Wade used the Burgevine case as a text "to lecture China on the need for literal observation of the treaty articles," and even got Prince Kung to order Robert Hart to have his Kiukiang Commissioner of Customs go in person to get an imprisoned British subject (Mansfield) out of jail, lest he suffer the same fate as Burgevine. (Ring, 146-147) For fascinating details of the situation at Amoy, see "Retrospect of Events in China and Japan during the Year 1865," *Journal of the North China Branch of the Royal Asiatic Society* (1866), esp. 142-148.
22. On the Foochow foreign-training program, see Smith, *Mercenaries and Mandarins,* 185; also *Yang-wu yun-tung* (The foreign affairs movement), III; 471-473, 477-478, 482, 597-605.
23. See Ellsworth C. Carlson, *The Foochow Missionaries, 1847-1880.*
24. Journals, 8 November 1864. On Ting as a reformer, see Jonathan Ocko, *Bureaucratic Reform in Provincial China.*
25. F.O. 228/367, Parkes to Wade, 29 July 1864; Gordon Papers, Ad. Mss., 52,387, Hart to Gordon, 17 May 1864. On the question of foreign rivalries, see Smith, *Mercenaries and Mandarins,* 162-164 and Leibo, *Journal of the Chinese Civil War,* 39, 48-49; also *Yang-wu yun-tung,* 3: 451, 464, 466, etc.
26. Cited in Leibo, *Journal of the Chinese Civil War,* 39.
27. *IWSM, T'ung-chih,* 25: 27a-b; also 32: 35b-37a. The following discussion of the training camp at Feng-huang-shan is taken from Richard J. Smith, "Foreign-Training and China's Self-Strengthening: The Case of Feng-huang-shan, 1864-1873."
28. Most of the information on the treaty ports in this section is drawn from Mayers, et al., *Treaty Ports of China and Japan,* unless otherwise indicated.
29. See William T. Rowe, *Hankow: Commerce and Society in A Chinese City 1796-1889.*
30. Mayers, et al., *Treaty Ports of China and Japan,* 451.
31. Ibid., 485.
32. Ibid., 487. Both the water and land routes from Tientsin to Peking are clearly indicated in the map of Shun-t'ien prefecture in *Ch'in-ting ku-chin t'u-shu chi-ch'eng,* Vol VIII, *Chih-fang tien* (Administrative divisions), 98.

CHAPTER SIX—JOURNALS

1. Tsung How: Ch'ung-hou, Superintendant of Trade for the three northern ports of Tientsin, Chefoo, and Newchwang.

2. Alexander Alisch & Co. were merchants of Tientsin; J. Livingston was a merchant of Tientsin; Stuart Man was Hart's secretary, formerly employed by Lay. William Lent resigned the Customs service in May 1863 after having been a Deputy Commissioner at Shanghai. Schmidt may have been either J. M. Schmidt, a shipbuilder with Knoop & Co., or E. Schmidt of S. Remi & Co., merchant, both of Shanghai.

   The 67th Regiment had stayed at Tientsin, at the Taku Forts, to insure payment of the indemnity.

3. Pwan Tajin: P'an ta-jen; his excellency P'an. Presumably the Taotai at Chefoo.

   M. C. Morrison was British Consul at Chefoo.

   J. Pignatel is listed in the *China Directory* for 1864 as storekeeper, Chefoo.

   Charles Hannen had been Commissioner at Chefoo since March 1863.

4. Ting Taoutae: Taotai Ting Jih-ch'ang (later to be Governor of Kiangsu) was associated with Li Hung-chang in the administration of the training camp at Feng-huang shan. For Ting's administrative outlook and practices, see Ocko, *Bureaucratic Reform in Provincial China*.

   Chaou Chow: Ch'ao-chou, a prefectural city (*fu*) in Kwangtung; see note 85 below.

   tsan: *ts'an*.

   Tsan-seang: *ts'an-chiang*.

   Footae: *fu-t'ai*; governor, i.e., Li Hung-chang.

   shang-leang: *shang-liang*.

   Achik: Tong Achik, a corrupt linguist; see journal entries for 19–29 November 1864.

5. Chang Chow: Chang-chou, Fukien (not to be confused with Ch'ang-chou, Kiangsu—also sometimes spelled Chang Chow—which was recovered by the Ever-Victorious Army and Li Hung-chang's forces in May 1864). Chang-chou was occupied by the Shih-wang, Li Shih-hsien, on 14 October 1864 and not recovered until mid-May 1865. See note 98 below.

   Hoo Chow: Hu-chou, Chekiang.

   Meritens: Baron Eugene de Meritens, Commissioner of Customs at Foochow, had established a foreign-training program there. See chapter 4, note 24; also *IWSM, T'ung-chih*, 30: 12a–13b.

6. Herbert E. Hobson had been detached by Hart for duty as an Interpreter in the Ever-Victorious Army under Gordon. He was now involved in Gordon's foreign-training program at Feng-huang-shan. See Smith, "Foreign-Training and China's Self-Strengthening"; also Smith, *Mercenaries and Mandarins*, 168-171.

Le Yang rebels: Taiping soldiers taken into the Ever-Victorious Army after the recovery of Li-yang in March 1864.

Harry Parkes was the British Consul at Shanghai. On his interference in the affairs at Feng-huang-shan, see journal entries for 22 and 24 May.

7. shih: *shih*; ming: *ming*.

Fung Wan Shan: Feng-huang-shan.

keang-kew: *chiang-chiu*; i.e., to obviate or dispose of, deal with, put up with.

Pwan Fantae: P'an *fan-t'ai*; Provincial Financial Commissioner P'an (see note 3 above).

Chuen-chang: *ch'uan-ch'ang*. This shipyard became the famous Kiangnan Arsenal, begun by Ting in 1865. See Thomas Kennedy, *The Arms of Kiangnan*.

8. James Cock is listed in the *China Directory* of 1864 as a merchant of Shanghai, in the firm of Watson & Co.

9. Albert F. Heard was a member of the firm of Augustine Heard & Co. in Shanghai.

Wan Chou and Chinchew: Wen-chou in Chekiang and Ch'üan-chou in Fukien.

Foochow, near the mouth of the Min River, had been opened as a port in 1842, with a Maritime Customs Office established in 1861.

10. Seward: George F. Seward, American Consul at Shanghai.

Miss Delano was American, daughter of the Russell & Co. partner possibly memorialized in Franklin Delano Roosevelt's name.

11. Jebb: Lieutenant Jebb was of the 67th Regiment. On the politics of his succession to Gordon as head drill instructor at Feng-huang-shan, see Smith, "Foreign-Training and China's Self-Strengthening"; also Smith, *Mercenaries and Mandarins*, 168–171.

Pwan: P'an. P'an Ting-hsin, one of Li Hung-chang's most capable Anhwei Army officers.

12. Hoo Kwang-ting: Probably Hu Kuang-yung of Chekiang, a buying agent for Tso Tsung-t'ang. See C. John Stanley, *Late Ch'ing Finance: Hu Kuang-yung as an Innovator*.

Hwang Seën Sang: Huang *hsien-sheng*; Mr. Huang.

Tso Kung-paou: Tso *kung-pao*; honorific term for Tso Tsung-t'ang, who had just been designated a hereditary earl (*po-chueh*) for his military accomplishments. See Kuo, *TPTK jih-chih*, 1109.

Gae-min, yung ping: Perhaps *kai-min yung-ping*; lit. "reforms the people and uses troops [well]." If the first word in the phrase is Gan (i.e. *an*) instead of Gae, it would mean "gives security (*an*) to the people and uses troops [well]."

13. F. E. Kleinwachter was a German who joined the Customs in 1863; Emile de Champs, a Frenchman, went into the Customs in June 1864. Hart had left Kleinwachter in charge of his Peking office.

14. Doughty: ? See chapter 8, note 23.

15. This Mayers seems to have been a brother of W. S. F. Mayers, Interpreter at the British Consulate at Shanghai. For the dispute between Hart and W. S. F. Mayers over the Soochow Incident, see chapter 1. Chaloner Alabaster had come to China from the British Foreign Office in 1855 and served as Interpreter not only for the Legation in Peking, but also for the anti-Taiping Allied Forces in the Shanghai area during the period 1862–1864.

16. Andrew Wilson, on the staff of the *China Mail* since 1857 and its editor from 1858–1860, did not write a life of Gordon, but in 1868 published *The "Ever-Victorious Army,"* based on Gordon's "Private Journal and Correspondence," among other published and unpublished sources.

17. Le Footae, Li *fu-t'ai*. Li Hung-chang, was appointed Acting Governor General (epistolary designation, *chih-t'ai*) of Liang-chiang at Nanking.

    Woo Tang: Wu T'ang, whom Hart later described as a "Fung-shuyist fogey" (journal entry for 19 January 1868), became involved in the establishment of the Foochow Shipyard, and soon thereafter received an appointment as Governor General of Min-Che at Foochow. Meanwhile, Kuo Po-yin, involved in treaty negotiations with Denmark at Shanghai, became Acting Governor of Kiangsu. See *IWSM, T'ung-chih*, 42: 17b–18a; 45: 59b; 46: 31b; 48: 21b.

    Tseng Kuo-fan, having played a leading role in suppressing the Taipings, would soon have to face the Nien rebels. In mid-November, he and Li Hung-chang met to discuss strategy against the Niens. See Kuo, *TPTK jih-chih*, 1110; also note 39 below.

    Hoo Pih: Hupeh province.

18. C. A. Lord, Acting Commissioner of Customs at Chinkiang. Circular No. 9, of 4 July 1864, specified yearly returns of trade.

19. Prosper Giquel, Commissioner of Customs at Ningpo from November 1861 to April 1863, had been on leave in France for about a year, and was now back at Ningpo.

20. Wuhu: Wu-hu; Tatung: Ta-t'ung; Ganking: Anking. All unopened ports upriver from Nanking.

21. Tong Achik. The linguist's surname was undoubtedly T'ang; his given name, Achik, sounds distinctly Cantonese.

22. The progressively minded Kan-wang, Hung Jen-kan, together with several other Taiping leaders, including the "Young Monarch" (successor to the T'ien-wang, Hung Hsiu-ch'uan) escaped into Kiangsi province during the latter half of 1864. Hung Jen-kan was captured by Ch'ing forces on 9 October 1864 and the "Young Sovereign" on 25 October of the same year. Both were executed in November after writing their "confessions." See *TPTK jih-chih*, 1104, 1106, 1110 and 1111. The Chung-wang's companion "of the same sing" (*hsing*, surname) was Hung Jen-ta. See ibid., 1086.

23. Tong Akue: brother of Tong Achik.

Le Kipbu: His surname is Li; his given name, like those of the T'ang brothers, sounds Cantonese.

transportation: exile.

Ja san Keh'rh: Presumably put in a portable wooden stock (cangue; *chia*), perhaps one accommodating 3 people (*san-ke jen*).

24. Hart's description of Gordon is right on target; for a discussion of the British commander's personality and his role at Feng-huang-shan, consult Smith, *Mercenaries and Mandarins*, 124–126, 147–148, 153, 159, 169–170, 227 note 7.

25. Henry Kingsmill of Queen's Road, Hong Kong, was a barrister; S. W. Maud was a lieutenant in the Royal Engineers based in Hong Kong.

26. Munshang: *men-shang*; lit. gatekeeper, refers generally to deputies, attendants, and other underlings. Hart is probably mistaken about the number of blows with the bamboo; there was no such punishment in the Ch'ing legal code. One hundred blows would have been severe.

Pootung: *pu-t'ing*; the colloquial designation of a *tien-shih* (district police chief and jail warden.).

Hing Poo: Hsing-pu.

27. Wen-chou was not taken, but the problem of foreign mercenaries joining the Taiping remnants at Chang-chou remained a matter of considerable concern to the Ch'ing authorities. See note 5 above and notes 95, 98, and 100 below.

28. Captain Davidson was a brave and talented officer of the Ever-Victorious Army. Brown was presumably J. McLeavy Brown, Assistant Secretary at the British Legation. Like Hart he had been born in Northern Ireland and educated at Queen's College.

29. Wong Ashing: Probably Huang Sheng, a colleague and friend of Dr. Wong Fung (Huang K'uan; see chapter 2 note 69). He, like both Huang K'uan and the famous Yale graduate Yung Wing (Jung Hung), had been educated abroad. During the 1850s and 1860s, Huang Sheng served as superintendent of the London Missionary Press in Hong Kong. See Paul Cohen, *Between Tradition and Modernity*, 318, note 3.

30. The Rev. J. R. Thomas of the London Missionary Society, as Hart indicates, was a great linguist. See also chapter 4, note 108.

The Rev. William Muirhead was associated with the Shanghai branch of the London Missionary Society.

31. The *Hankow*, a vessel of Russell & Co. with Capt. P. Bennett in charge, left Hong Kong at 8 a.m. every Monday, Wednesday, and Friday.

G. B. Glover, an American who had been in the Customs since 1859, had returned to his post as Commissioner at Canton in May from a year's leave.

32. Chang (also "old Chang"—possibly Chang Hsiao-t'ang?), Luh (Lu), Chin (Ch'en?) and Sha (Hsia?) were apparently functionaries in the

Hoppo's yamen. Chin is perhaps Chin Chaou Ting, referred to in Hart's journal entry of 15 October 1864. He seems to have been Hart's temporary writer.

33. Minqua had been a hong merchant whose portrait was painted by Chinnary. This man was perhaps the son of the original Minqua.

Kwo Footae: Kuo *fu-t'ai*; Governor Kuo Sung-t'ao had been appointed Grain Intendant at Soochow in 1862 and served as Acting Governor of Kwangtung from 1863–1866. He would later (1876) become China's first minister abroad. Tseng Kuo-fan's 4th daughter, Tseng Chi-ch'un, married Kuo's eldest son, Kuo Kang-chi.

shen-yu-chow-le: *shen yu ch'ou-li*; [?]

34. Tseën Kea: Ch'ien-*chia*.

Kwang Chow foo: Kuang-chou fu; short for *chih-fu* (prefect).

Taetae: *t'ai-t'ai*.

Urhfoojin: *erh fu-jen*.

D. B. Robertson was British Consul at Canton.

Foo and Nanhae: presumably through the Canton Prefect and Nan-hai Magistrate.

Hsieh: Hsueh Huan, now a Minister of the Tsungli Yamen.

35. Fung (Ting-yew): Feng T'ing (Ting ?)-yu; or perhaps Mr. Feng (who is presently at home in mourning for one of his parents; *ting-yu*)

Suin Poo: *hsun-p'u*.

Na-jin shih tsae sha pang-tsoo wo-min-teih: *Na jen shih-tsai shih [?] pang-chu wo-men-ti*.

36. M. Chevrey Rameau was French Vice-Consul.

37. Possibly Oliver H. Perry, American Consul at Canton. On drawbacks, see chapters 1 and 3.

38. C. F. M. de Grijs is listed in the *China Directory* for 1864 as Dutch Consul at Amoy.

39. laou-ta-jin: *lao ta-jen*. In fact, both Tseng and Li would soon be deeply involved in the campaign against the Niens, whose forces in Hupeh had been amplified by Taiping remnants under Lai Wen-kuang. Tseng was appointed Imperial Commissioner for the suppression of the Nien Rebellion in late May, 5 days after the death of Prince Seng-ko-lin-ch'in (Senggerinchin) on 20 May. Li took over as Imperial Commissioner after Tseng's resignation in early December 1866.

40. George Henry Fitzroy, who had served with Hart as "exercising conjointly the functions of Inspector General" during Lay's absence, had been Commissioner at Shanghai from 1861 to July 1863, when he went on leave. The news that he had resigned was premature, since he served again as Commissioner at Shanghai from December 1865 to April 1868, when he did resign.

Franz Wilzer had been Deputy Commissioner at Swatow from October 1860 to March 1862, when he returned to his native Hamburg on leave. After his resignation in 1864, he carried out occasional personal commissions for Hart in Germany.

41. "Miss Breadon" may well have been Hester Jane Bredon (the surname was spelled both ways), whom Hart was to marry two years later. Several of his relatives seem to have had this match in mind.

42. Samuel Mossman finally published *General Gordon's Private Diary of His Exploits in China* in 1885, after the book had been serialized in the *North China Herald*, of which he had been the editor from 1861 to 1865.

43. William Cartwright, a midshipman in the British Navy, had been recruited by Lay for the Customs after the disbanding of the Lay-Osborn Flotilla. Assigned to the In-Door Staff (rather than the Out-Door, for which his seaman's skills might seem to have fitted him), he quickly rose to prominence because of his unusual proficiency in Chinese. By November 1866, he would be Chinese Secretary at the Inspectorate in Peking.

    William Baker, a Britisher who had joined the Customs in 1861, was a clerk in the office at Tientsin. The Meadows commenting on his behavior was therefore probably Hart's old associate from Ningpo days, J. A. T. Meadows — now a Tientsin merchant.

    D.T.: presumably delirium tremens.

    C. Amy had been a tidewaiter connected with the Customs at Shanghai under Thomas Dick.

44. I. des Amorie Van der Hooeven is listed in the *China Directory* for 1864 as a merchant of Macao.

    Thomas Adkins was the British Vice-Consul at Kiukiang; John Moore the Spanish Consul at Shanghai.

45. Mao Chetae: Mao *chih-t'ai*; Governor General Mao Hung-pin. Mao served as Liang-Kwang Governor General from 1863 to 1865.

    Kwo Footae: Kuo *fu-t'ai*; Governor Kuo Sung-t'ao. See note 33 above.

    Tse Nan: Chi-nan (Tsinan).

    Yu-she: *yü-shih*.

    Tsung-tuh: *tsung-tu*. *Chih-t'ai* (see above) is the epistolary designation of the same office.

    Hoonan Kwan-hwa: Hunan *kuan-hua*, i.e. Hunan-accented Mandarin Chinese.

46. Mao Tajin: Mao *ta-jen*; His excellency, Mao Hung-pin. The foreign drill program had begun in 1862 under the supervision of Lao Ch'ung-kuang, then Liang-Kwang Governor General, and the British Consul at Canton, D. B. Robertson, although French instructors also became involved. See *YWYT*, 3: 459–466, 468–470, 481, etc.

    The Hoppo (Chinese Superintendent of Customs for the province of Kwangtung) was Yü-ch'ing.

    she-pan: *shih-pan*.

47. Chang Seaou-tang: Chang Hsiao-tang. [?]

    K'ow-teen Wu: Wu K'ao-t'ien. [?]

    Sew-tsae: *hsiu-ts'ai*.

paou-keu: *pao-chü.*
Keaou-kwan: *chiao-kuan.*

48. Hart's offer was never accepted by Thomas Adkins, and was not accepted until 1873 by J. McLeavy Brown, who in 1864 was Assistant Chinese Secretary at the British Legation in Peking. The salaries offered reflect the range for posts in larger and smaller ports. Thomas Dick in Shanghai was getting 6,000 taels a year, as was de Meritens in Foochow, whereas Giquel in Ningpo was paid 3,600.

C. M. Bowra did not become a Commissioner until 1868, having in the meantime served as Interpreter with the Pin-ch'un Mission that went to Europe with Hart in 1866, as did also Emile des Champs. These offers reflect Hart's early struggles to maintain a high level of competence in the so recently formed Customs Service. The young men serving in junior posts had obviously not had time to equal the caliber of those already established in the Consular Service.

49. Nee-tae: *nieh-t'ai;* rank 3a. On Li's memorial, see chapter 4, note 185.

50. Tang: Mr. T'ang assisted M. C. Morrison and Harry Parkes, both of whom had been diplomats and interpreters at Canton and Amoy in the 1850s. See Fairbank, *Trade and Diplomacy on the China Coast,* 475–477.

51. old Chang: see note 32 above.

tsan: *ts'an.* This impeachment, together with what Hart describes as Kuo Sung-t'ao's "hasty" approach and lack of foresight, may help explain why he was "unaccountably discharged" from his post as Governor of Kwangtung in 1866. Cf. J. D. Frodsham, *The First Chinese Embassy to the West,* xxxii.

Keujin: *chü-jen.*
fung: *feng.*
Lin Kea: Lin-*chia.*

52. Woo keu-jin: *wu chü-jen.*
Kwang chow foo: Kuang-chou *fu;* Canton prefecture.
Hia-sze-foo: [?]
Taoukwang: Tao-kuang Emperor, reigned 1821–1850.

53. Te-muh: *t'i-mu.*
Books: The Four Books.
wän chang: *wen-chang.*
Shimtih Heen: Shun-te hsien (county).
Choo-kaou: *chu-k'ao.*
Chang: probably Chang Hsiao-t'ang; see note 32 above.

54. Hio-tai: *hsueh-t'ai.*

Han lin: The Hanlin Academy was a prestigious training ground for officials, where top-level degree-holders performed various ritual, editorial, and pedagogical functions for the Emperor until they received other bureaucratic appointments.

Wu-tsung-yaou: Wu Ch'ung-yueh was the fifth son of the famous hong merchant Wu Ping-chien. Like his father (and grandfather,

Wu Kuo-ying), he was known to foreigners as Howqua. He died in 1863.

Woo: Wu

Tae tae: *t'ai-t'ai*.

55. Lo Tun-yen was a high ranking supporter of the anti-foreign gentry in the Canton area during 1858. He, together with Lung Tuan-hsi and Su T'ing-k'uei (hence Hart's reference to "Lo-Lung-Soo notoriety), had received the Hsien-feng Emperor's secret approval to oust the foreign enemy from Canton. See *Entering China's Service*, 363 note 30. In the 1860s he was a factional enemy of Prince Kung and Wen-hsiang. See chapter 8, note 14.

Hoo Poo Shang Shoo: Hu-pu *shang-shu*.

56. Deprivation of rank was a first step toward severe punishment, since degree-holders and "button-holders" enjoyed a number of special privileges and legal immunities. Ocko's *Bureaucratic Reform in Provincial China*, chapter 4, provides an illuminating glimpse into the Ch'ing legal process at the local level as well as Ting Jih-ch'ang's particular approach to law. See also chapter 5.

57. George Hughes was Commissioner of Customs at Amoy. The two provincial commanders-in-chief (*t'i-tu*) mentioned in Hughes's letter were Kao Lien-sheng and Huang Shao-ch'un. See Kuo, *TPTK jih-chih*, 1115.

58. K'ow-Kung: *k'ou-kung*. In fact, as Charles Curwen and others have noted, Tseng Kuo-fan did not publish the entire version. Rather, he edited the Chung-wang's "deposition" in order to "win approbation and avoid the censure of a suspicious court." See Curwen, 17–46.

sha-hae: *sha-hai*.

tow-heang: *t'ou-hsiang*.

59. A picul (*shih*) was equal to approximately 133 pounds. Acheen was evidently a Cantonese tea merchant. There were several Deacons in Macao, any one of whom might have been Hart's informant: A. Deacon, acting consular agent for Great Britain, Macao; J. B. Deacon, merchant, Macao; Ernest Deacon, tea taster, Macao, the last two being members of the firm of Deacon & Co.

60. Tseang Taeyay: Chiang *ta-yeh*. His excellency Chiang; perhaps the reference is to Chiang I-li, who would become the Governor of Kwangtung following the dismissal of Kuo Sung-t'ao. *IWSM, T'ung-chih*, 31: 1b, 42: 58b.

Tsze How Kung: Tz'u-hou kung. [?]

61. Lo Ping-chang had been Governor (*hsun-fu*) of Hunan from 1850 to 1860, during which period he worked closely with Tseng Kuo-fan in campaigns against the Taipings. Yeh Ming-ch'en had been Governor of Kwangtung from 1847 to 1852, and Governor General of Liang-Kuang from 1852–1857.

Nanhae heen: Nan-hai hsien. Nan-hai is the county in which Canton is located.

t'ow-tsze: t'ou tzu. [?]

Lo Ping-chang and his Taiping adversary, Hung Hsiu-ch'üan (the Heavenly King), were both born in Hua-hsien, Kwangtung.

62. The Rev. Andrew Patton Happer, M.D., was a medical missionary at Canton; Andrew, his son, would enter the Customs Service in 1879.

63. She-tsang: Shih-tseng, the new Hoppo at Canton, replacing Yü-ch'ing.

Chin: See note 32 above and 73 below.

64. Douglas Lapraik & Co. had steamships on the Hong Kong-Shanghai run.

65. William Lobschied was a member of the Rhenish Mission. (Possibly this private business concerned sending Hart's three children by Ayaou to England.)

66. A trio of prominent Hong Kong businessmen: Thomas Sutherland, superintendent of the P. & O. Co. on Queen's Road; Warren Delano, Jr., of Russell & Co., Queen's Road; and A. B. Neilson of Olyphant & Co., Queen's Road East.

Lady Robinson was the wife of Sir Hercules Robinson, Governor of Hong Kong.

Robert Swinhoe, now Vice-Consul at Tamsui, Formosa (Taiwan), was an old friend of Hart's early days in China, and already on his way to becoming a famous botanist.

67. William Maxwell was Assistant-in-Charge at the port of Tamsui from September 1863 to January 1864.

68. Sir Rutherford Alcock was on his way home from Japan, where he was British Minister.

69. Augustine Heard, Jr., was one of the heads of the firm of Augustine Heard & Co; John E. Ward had been U.S. Commissioner to China from 1859 to 1860, when he resigned and was succeeded in 1861 by Anson Burlingame as U.S. Minister.

70. Keang-pih: *chiang-pei*; lit., north of the (Yangtze) River. On the "geographical and psychological cleavage" between the areas north and south of the Yangtze in Kiangsu, see Ocko, *Bureaucratic Reform*, 21–26. Hupeh was, of course, well to the west of Kiangsu, but it too was divided by the Yangtze.

Kaou & Hwang Tetuh: See note 57 above.

Kwo Sunglin: Kuo Sung-lin, formerly one of Tseng Kuo-fan's Hunan Army commanders, fought together with Liu Ming-ch'uan in campaigns against the Taipings at Hu-chou in Chekiang and later against the Nien rebels in North China.

Dr. Lockhead served as a surgeon in the British army. See Kuo, *TPTK jih-chih*, Appendix, 174. On the question of such decorations, see Smith, *Mercenaries and Mandarins*, 162–164.

71. sin-pun-shen: *hsing pen shan*. The phrase comes from the *Three-Character Classic*.

72. Chan, Luh and Chang: see note 32 above; also entry for 29 January, 1865.
    George B. Glover was Commissioner of Customs at Canton.
73. Lieut. R. E. Crane was Commander of the Royal Artillery, Hong Kong. He had left Hong Kong however, before Hart's offer reached him. See Hart's journal entry for 26 January 1865.
74. Fa-te: Fa-ti, near Canton.
    Te'en tsze Matow: *T'ien-tzu ma-t'ou.*
    Kungkwan: *kung-kuan.*
    Kwei-shing-gen: *kuei sheng-an. Kuei* means to kneel, and *sheng-an* refers to inquiring after the sacred emperor's well-being.
75. According to widespread Chinese belief, the 8 characters (*pa-tzu*) of a person's "nativity" (i.e. time of birth: 2 each for the year, month, day, and hour) could be used to determine that person's destiny. For each person, certain activities on particular days were considered either auspicious or inauspicious. For society at large, the official state calendar (*shih-hsien shu*) and popular almanacs (*t'ung-shu*), both issued annually, designated a wide range of both ritual and mundane activities "appropriate" (*i*) or inappropriate (*pu-i*) for virtually every day of the year. See Smith, "'Knowing Fate'" and "A Note on Qing Dynasty Calendars."
76. Mrs. Chalmers, wife of the Rev. John Chalmers of the London Missionary Society; Mrs. Condit, wife of the Rev. I. M. Condit of the American Presbyterian Board; Mrs. T. Sampson, wife of the agent of British West Indian Emigration; Mrs. Happer, wife of A. P. Happer, M.D., of the American Board of Commissioners for Foreign Missions.
77. Thomas B. Macaulay, best known for his *History of England*, served from 1834 to 1838 as a member of the Supreme Council of India. His *Essays* include a number on Indian affairs. Robert Clive had served as a soldier and administrator in India in the 1750s and 1760s.
78. Nee-tae: *nieh-t'ai.* The decree was issued on the 19th day of the 11th month (i.e. 17 December 1864). Hart seems disappointed that the decree did not include reference to the praise of both Li Hung-chang and the Tsungli Yamen.
79. In this case, the decree was both issued and received on the same day.
80. She ta-jin: Shih *ta-jen;* "his excellency." Shih-tseng.
    teen Ke: *tien-ch'i?*
81. Congou was a kind of black tea from China. A catty (*chin*) was about 1 1/3 pounds; a picul (*shih*), about 133 pounds.
82. Che-tae: *chih-t'ai.*
    Kwei shing gan: *kuei sheng-an* (see note 74 above). The issue was not, of course, the Emperor's status, but rather the status of the Hoppo in relation to the Governor General (*chih-t'ai*).
    Kwang-chow-sze: Kuang-chou *ssu* [?] Canton administration [?]; or perhaps Kuang-chou *shih,* i.e. city.

Hiotae: *hsueh-t'ai*.

pae-pae: *pai-pai*. The ceremonies attending receipt of the official seals of office, like many other ritual events, had to await an auspicious day. See note 75.

Wan Show Kung: Wan-shou kung; lit., Longevity Temple; presumably the "Birthday Temple" mentioned above in the journal entry.

Chao-e: *ch'ao-i*.

tsow-tsan: *tsou-ts'an*.

83. Sze ta-jin: Shih [?] *ta-jen*. Possibly Shih-tseng, the Hoppo (see note 80 above), although Hart usually renders the *shih* sound either "she" or "shih." If not Shih-tseng, presumably a local official with whom Mao Hung-pin did not get along. See journal entry for 2 February 1865.

84. Yu ta-jin: Yü *ta-jen*; "his excellency," Yü; Yü-ch'ing, former Hoppo.

85. Yu-Tsing: Yü-ch'ing.

Chaou Chow: Ch'ao-chou; a major Kwangtung city 35 miles inland from Swatow. The treaties of 1858 had "opened" Ch'ao-chou for consular representation, but Swatow (which had been added in parentheses after Ch'ao-chou), had become the treaty port. As Hart's journal entry suggests, popular resistance at Ch'ao-chou had prevented the foreign powers from establishing a consulate there.

86. Stuart was manager of the Oriental Banking Corporation, the first foreign bank to operate in China; it had established branches in Hong Kong (1845) and in Shanghai (1848).

87. Major J. B. Edwards of the Royal Engineers, based at Hong Kong.

88. Edwards was thinking about assuming command of the British training program at Canton, a role analogous to Gordon's at Feng-huang-shan. On the problem of foreign rivalries there and elsewhere, see chapter 5; also Smith, "Foreign-Training and China's Self-Strengthening"; *YWYT*, 3: 461–472, 477–482, etc.

T. G. Luson had been in charge of the Customs Office at Canton during Glover's leave.

89. Price and Lister were evidently new recruits for the Customs, recently arrived at Hong Kong. Since their names do not appear in later *Service Lists*, they must not have stayed long.

90. old Chang: probably Chang Hsiao-t'ang; see notes 32 and 51 above.

For a summary of the procedures and pitfalls of Chinese emigration, see Morse, *International Relations*, 2, 163–184; also Irick, *Ch'ing Policy toward the Coolie Trade, 1847–1878*. Emigration to the gold fields of the United States and Australia was relatively free; that to Cuba, the West Indies, and Central and South America took the form of "contract labor," in which abuses were many.

91. mun shang: *men-shang*.

Yu-Kwan: Hoppo 1843.

Leang: Liang *men-shang* of the new Hoppo.

Chang: *men-shang* of the new Hoppo.

Nuy-woo-foo: Nei-wu-fu. The Imperial Household Department was the principal financial agency of the Ch'ing rulers. See Preston Torbert, *The Imperial Household Department*. The "scheme" refers to Hart's proposal of 2 February.

92. Laou: Lao. Lao Ch'ung-kuang had been Governor General of Kwangtung and Kwangsi from 1859 to 1862.

93. Tseung-Keun: *chiang-chün*.

Juy-lin: Jui-lin.

Fantae: *fan-t'ai*.

Le Han chang: Li Han-chang; Li Hung-chang's elder brother.

Yen-tae: *yen-t'ai*.

two Hoppos: Yü-ch'ing and Shih-tseng.

chung-t'ang: *chung-t'ang*.

94. Swatow, at the mouth of the Han river 170 miles northwest of Hong Kong, had been opened as a Customs port by Lay in January 1860. The people of the district had always had a reputation for piracy and turbulence, with many kidnappings and much hostility to foreigners. This hostility was not lessened by foreign merchants promoting the coolie trade; hence Hart's worry about the safety of a Customs House. See also note 85 above.

fung-shwuy: *feng-shui* (geomancy).

Dircks & Co. were commission merchants at Swatow.

A. S. Preston was an Assistant in the Swatow Customs, and G. W. Caine the British Consul there.

Shoopan: *shu-pan*. On accountants in the Customs Service, see Wright, *Hart*, 272.

Mrs. Richardson was the wife of T. W. Richardson of Bradley & Co., a merchant of Swatow.

The United States Consul at Swatow was C. W. Bradley, Jr.

95. White Dogs: Well-known island landmarks a few miles south of the seaward entrance to the Min River.

Sha' Peak: Presumably Sharp Island Peak, a prominent landmark guiding vessels through the Min River estuary.

Baron Eugene de Meritens was Commissioner of Customs at Foochow. Rhode and Co. refers to the foreign mercenaries who had joined the Taiping remnants at Chang-chou. On 11 April 1865, de Meritens, together with Kuo Sung-lin, Kao Lien-sheng, and Huang Shao-ch'un inflicted a severe defeat on the troops of the Shih-wang, Li Shih-hsien, that left 3 or 4 thousand Taiping troops dead. See *TPTK jih-chih*, 1122.

Ying Tseang-keun: Ying *chiang-chün*; Tartar General Ying-kuei. See note 98 below.

Seu Footae: Hsu *fu-t'ai*: Governor Hsu Tsung-kan. See 99 below.

May: F. N. May, an Assistant who had joined the Customs in 1859.

Meade: H. Meade was a tide surveyor in the Customs at Amoy. The Haekwan Chang Hooling: *Hai-kuan* (Superintendant of Customs) Chang Hu-ling.

Gov. Genl. Tso: Tso Tsung-t'ang.

Yen-Ping-Foo: Yen-p'ing prefectural city.

A. R. Hewlett was Interpreter at the British Consulate, Foochow.

Nan-tae: Nan-t'ai. The foreign settlement on the south side of the Min River.

George Hughes, the object of de Meritens' envy, was the Customs Commissioner at Amoy.

The one of the Lay brothers who was then at Foochow was Walter Thurlow Lay, not William, as Hart seems absent-mindedly to have written. William was in the British Consular Service. Walter had been in the Customs at Kiukiang.

96. Kwang: probably Kuang-hsing; see note 99 below.

97. William Maxwell had been Assistant-in-Charge at the port of Tamsui (the other port on the island of Formosa), from September 1863 to January 1864, when he was succeeded by J. W. Howell; in Takow he was in charge from March 1864 as Assistant-in-Charge, but in 1865 became Commissioner. He died on 3 October 1865. "Taewan" in this entry refers to T'ai-wan fu, the prefectural capital until Taiwan was made a province in 1885. This city is now known as T'ai-nan.

Mrs. Swinhoe was the wife of Robert Swinhoe, British Vice-Consul at Tamsui, who published a number of botanical studies during his career in China.

98. W. H. Pedder was the British Consul at Amoy. He traveled to Chang-chou on 14 February 1865. Kuo, *TPTK jih-chih*, 1118.

Gerard: On Gerard's attempt to run with the hares and hunt with the hounds, see Kuo, *TPTK jih-chih*, Appendix, 177.

She-wang: Shih-wang, Li Shih-hsien. Li had occupied Chang-chou since 14 October 1864, but lost the city on 15 May 1865 to the combined forces of Kuo Sung-lin, Kao Lien-sheng, and Huang Shao-ch'un.

Chin Kin-lung: Ch'en Chin-lung. Joint memorials by the Min-Che Governor General, Tso Tsung-t'ang, and Fukien Governor Hsu Tsung-han (15 February 1865) and Foochow Tartar General Ying-kuei and Governor Hsu Tsung-han (12 March 1865) describe the interception of the letter from Li Shih-hsien to Pedder, the deposition and execution of Ch'en Chin-lung, and the role played by Hart and especially Amoy Commissioner of Customs George Hughes (Hsiu-shih). See *IWSM, T'ung-chih*, 31: 3a–b; 8a–b; 14a–15b.

Commander A. J. Kingston was in charge of the *Perseus*, a British steam sloop with 17 guns.

99. HaeKwan at Amoy: Hart has miswritten the character for Kuang. The person in question is probably Kuang-hsing. See *IWSM, T'ung-chih*, 30: 12a–b.

Kung-poo: Kung-pu.

Wen-hsiang's *tzu* was Po-ch'uan.

100. Colonel Rhode, who had been associated with Gordon, joined the rebels after the disbanding of the Ever-Victorious Army. Indeed, Gordon's recommendation of a Chinese medal for him was countermanded when Hart pointed out that Rhode had joined the rebels in Fukien after leaving the imperial service. Butler too had been originally in Gordon's forces. See Kuo, *TPTK jih-chih*, Appendix, p. 177; Smith, *Mercenaries and Mandarins*, 162, 185.

101. Yang and Kuo Tetuh: Yang Ting-hsun and Kuo Sung-lin. See Kuo, *TPTK jih-chih*, 1126.

Martin and Kirkham: Captain Martin and Colonel Kirkham were both former Ever-Victorious Army officers who remained in the Ch'ing military service after disbandment of the EVA. Kuo, *TPTK jih-chih*, Appendix, 162–153.

Kaou: Kao Lien-sheng. See Kuo, *TPTK jih-chih*, 1126.

102. James Porter had been First Assistant in the Customs at Amoy since 1864; James Jones had also been there the same length of time.

103. James Tait of Tait & Co., agents for the P. & O. Steam Navigation Company, was a merchant at Amoy. He had been active in the coolie trade.

104. Kwang: Probably Kuang-hsing (see notes 97 and 100 above).

105. Mrs. Delano was the wife of W. Delano, Jr., of Russell & Co., on whom Hart had called in Hong Kong on 15 January. Mrs. Vaucher's husband was A. E. Vaucher of Vaucher & Co.

Mrs. Pauncefoote: Perhaps Mrs. J. P. Paunceforte, wife of the barrister of D'Aguilar St., Hong Kong.

William Lamond was the manager of the Oriental Bank in Hong Kong.

106. These appointments represent the 13 ports that were open when Hart became I.G., plus Newchwang, which had been added in 1864.

James Veith Leonard, formerly an Assistant with Dent & Co., had been at Swatow since 1862, first as Assistant-in-Charge, then as Acting Commissioner, and now would become Commissioner. Henry Dwight Williams had been at Swatow since 1862, first as Assistant-in-Charge, then as Acting Commissioner, and now would become Commissioner.

107. Hart's social calls included visits to the wives of diplomats, merchants, doctors, and lawyers, among them: T. Markham, British Vice-Consul at Shanghai; P. Hazeon, merchant with Wilkinson & Co.; Henry S. Grew, a Shanghai merchant with John Silverlock & Co.; J. A. S. Coghill, M.D., surgeon; F. B. Eames, counsellor at law; E. C. Essex, a merchant with George Barnet & Co.; W. G. Cuthbertson, Shanghai agent of the Central Bank of Western India.

108. When the civil war was nearly over, and foreign pressure eased, the powers of Prince Kung were apparently too great for the comfort of

the ambitious Empress Dowager, Tz'u-hsi. Thus, on 2 April, he was deprived of all his offices, on several vague charges, such as carelessness in his conduct at court. After urgent pleas by his supporters he was reinstated as head of the Tsungli Yamen on 7 April, and of the Grand Council on 8 May, but he no longer held the rank of Prince Counsellor. On this episode, consult Jason Parker, "The Rise and Decline of Prince Kung," 193–236, esp. 204–229.

109. Kan Pan: *kan-pan*; "manager of general affairs," known as the "Number One boy" in general foreign-treaty-port parlance. Hart has provided characters for all of the names in this journal entry (see Glossary-Index), although sometimes they are written incorrectly. No figures are given to go with the dollar signs for wages except in the case of the gatekeeper.

110. Andrew Happer was a medical missionary. Jamie was Hart's younger brother, who would have a career in the Customs.

The *Hyson* had been a gunboat in the Ever-Victorious Army.

111. Mrs. Coutts was the wife of G. W. Coutts, of Watson & Co., Shanghai.

112. For the Feng-huang-shan training camp, see notes 6 and 11 above. William Winstanley, a former Ever-Victorious Army officer, would be Jebb's successor as head drillmaster. Cardew, Lempriese, Hall and Hobson had all been involved in the foreign training of Chinese troops in the Shanghai area. Hobson, originally on loan from the Customs Service to interpret for Gordon (see chapter 2 note 56), was involved in translating the details of Western drill into a Chinese drill book at Feng-huang-shan. See Smith, "Foreign-Training," 96.

Soochow, K'un-shan, Ch'ing-p'u, and Sung-chiang were all strategic cities to the west of Shanghai; Hangchow Bay was south.

113. Yu Footsaeng: Yü *fu-chiang*, Colonel Yü. This was Yü Tsai-pang, who together with Yuan Chiu-kao and P'an Ting-hsin were all officers in Li Hung-chang's Anhwei Army. Yü and Yuan served as battalion commanders for the Feng-huang-shan camp. P'an, headquartered at Sung-chiang, was the Chinese commandant (*t'ung-ling*) of the camp. P'an and Yü would later lead troops from the Feng-huang-shan camp against the Niens, just as Kuo Sung-lin led Chinese forces from the camp against Taiping remnants at Changchou. See Smith, "Foreign-Training," 88–90, 93, 97.

114. Lung Chow-foo in GanHwuy: Lung-chou, Anhwei.

Keang Pih: *chiang-pei*; see note 70.

115. For Li Hung-chang's problems with Parkes, see Smith, "Foreign-Training," 86–88, 91; also *LWCK*, Letters, 8: 67a–68a.

116. Kin Chae: *ch'in-ch'ai*.

Tsae Seang: *tsai-hsiang*.

Clearly Hart did not accept, or perhaps even appreciate, Li's point that extraterritoriality should be a two-way street.

117. Sha Cheun: *sha-ch'uan*; this type of junk was known to foreigners as a "Kiangsu province trader."

Hangkia: *hang-chia.*

<u>fa</u> <u>tsze</u>: *fa-tzu.*

118. Le san ta-jin: Li san-ta-jen; "his excellency, the third Li." Li Ho-chang, one of Li Hung-chang's younger brothers, commanded the Kiangsu Governor's "personal guard unit" (*ch'in-ping*) against the Taipings during 1862–1864. See Spector, *Li Hung-chang and the Huai Army,* 100.

119. <u>paou-pei</u>: *pao-pei.*

120. <u>tsung</u>: accounting [?]

121. Tsang chung-t'ang: Tseng *chung-t'ang*; Tseng Kuo-fan.

<u>Tsemmo-hao-ne</u>: *tsen-ma hao-ni.*

122. For Burgevine's fate, see note 126 below.

123. Prosper Giquel eventually received the rank of brigade-general (*tsung-ping*; 2a) for his efforts in the recovery of Hu-chou on 24 August 1864. See *IWSM, T'ung-chih,* 37: 30a. Although his rank was indeed of the 2nd class (as compared to Hart's 3rd-class civil rank), military rank was considered inferior to civil rank. See chapter 4, note 118. Hart's remarks on Giquel's rank reflect a longstanding personal rivalry with his ambitious French subordinate.

124. In May 1865 Tseng Kuo-fan was ordered to take command in Shantung against the Nien bandits, and Li Hung-chang was made Acting Governor General at Nanking in his place. Later, in 1866, when Tseng had failed to win swift victory, Li would be made Imperial Commissioner to direct the campaign.

Tsäng Wang: Seng-wang. Prince Seng-ko-lin-ch'in (Sengerrinchin), a Mongol prince, was ambushed and killed in action against the combined forces of Taiping remnants and Nien rebels, led by Lai Wen-kuang. See note 39 above.

Yün-ching-Hsian: apparently a corruption of Wu-chia tien. See *TPTK jih-chih,* p. 1127.

Lew Fantae: Liu *fan-t'ai*; Provincial Financial Commissioner Liu Hsun.

125. Ta-tsing: Ta-Ch'ing.

Tsang Wang yay: Seng *wang-yeh*; the honorable Prince Seng; as above, note 129.

Shanghai Hsien: Shanghai *hsien.*

126. On 25 June 1865, about a month after his arrest in mid-May, Burgevine drowned in a boating accident while in the custody of the Ch'ing authorities. *TPTK jih-chih,* p. 1134. Butler's death is discussed in Hart's journal entry of 7 May 1865.

127. For the slow development and ultimate fate of this railway idea, see David Pong, "Confucian Patriotism and the Destruction of the Woosung Railway, 1877."

128. The term *wei-jan* here suggests "not yet."

129. The Taotai at Hankow was Ch'en Lan.

The Viceroy (Governor General) of Hupeh and Hunan was Kuan-wen.

130. Robert Wetmore was with Jardine Matheson in Hankow, as well as on the Municipal Council there. K. R. Mackenzie was a merchant of Hankow; G. Grant Gordon a clerk with Mackeller & Co.

There are two Hankow men named Evans listed in the *China Directory* for 1864: E. H. Evans was with Dent & Co. and M. P. Evans with Hogg Brothers.

Halkett: This may have been Richard Webb Halket, who had joined the Customs in 1862.

Mr. Wadman may well have been the merchant whom Hart had known in Ningpo in 1854. If so, he was now connected with the firm of another of Hart's Ningpo acquaintances—J. A. T. Meadows, of Meadows & Co., in Tientsin.

131. Charles Thomas Mande was with the British Legation.

For Albert Brett's financial troubles, see Hart's journal entry of 25 November 1864.

132. F. W. White, who had joined the Customs in 1859, was Acting Commissioner at Kiukiang from 1864 to 1866. P. J. Hughes was Britain's Acting Consul at Kiukiang.

Ta-laou-yay shwo Shwuy Keaou: *T'a-lao-yeh shuo shui-chiao.*

CHAPTER SEVEN—ANGLO-CH'ING REFORM MEASURES

1. Journals, 14 August 1864.
2. Cited in Mary Wright, *The Last Stand of Chinese Conservatism*, 21-22.
3. Ibid., passim. Polacheck, "Gentry Hegemony," offers a cynical assessment of the Restoration. The most balanced view is in Kwang-Ching Liu, "The Ch'ing Restoration."
4. See Liu, "The Ch'ing Restoration," 485-486.
5. Ibid., 447 ff.
6. Cited in Wright, *The Last Stand*, 180-181.
7. See Kuo T'ing-i and Kwang-Ching Liu, "Self-Strengthening: The Pursuit of Western Technology"; also David Pong, "Keeping the Foochow Navy Yard Afloat: Government Finance and China's Early Defence Industry, 1866-75"; and Kennedy, *Arms of Kiangnan.*
8. Liu, Kwang-ching and Richard J. Smith, "The Military Challenge: The Northwest and the Coast."
9. Cf. the writings cited in Liu, "The Ch'ing Restoration" and Wright, *The Last Stand.* See also the analysis in Jason Parker, "Prince Kung," 248 ff.
10. See Kwang-Ching Liu, "Politics, Intellectual Outlook, and Reform: The T'ung-wen Kuan Controversy of 1867."
11. On standard Restoration themes, see I-hsin (Prince Kung), *Lo-tao t'ang wen-ch'ao,* esp. preface, 1a; 1: 5b-6b, 14b-15b, 17b-19a, 22b-25a, 27a-29b; 2: 25a-26a. For Prince Kung's concrete administrative ideas, see esp. ibid., 3: 4a-6a, 10a-11a; 4: 15a-16b, 38a-39b.
12. *IWSM, T'ung-chih,* 48: 4a.

13. Ibid., 25: 3a; F.O. 17/408, Bruce to Russell, 12 June 1864. Cf. Hart journals, 17 June 1864. For Wen-hsiang's modernizing views, consult Wang Chia-chien, "Wen-hsiang tui-yü shih-chü ti jen-shih chi ch'i tzu-ch'iang ssu-hsiang."

14. Wen-hsiang, *Wen Wen-chung-kung tzu-ting nien-p'u* (hereafter Wen-hsiang *nien-p'u*), 3: 44a–56a.

15. On Wen-hsiang's views on ritual and morality, see, for example, ibid., 3: 53a, 55a–58a, etc. On the system of cycles, see ibid., 3: 42b. On the State Calendar, consult R. Smith, "Ch'ing Dynasty Calendars."

16. Tung Hsun, *Huan-tu wo-shu shih lao-jen tzu-ting nien-p'u*. Tung's essay on Western military assistance, *Yang-ping chi-lueh*, is reprinted in Hsiang Ta, et al. eds., *T'ai-p'ing t'ien-kuo*, 2: 529–564.

17. See Tung, *Huan-tu wo-shu shih lao-jen tzu-ting nien-p'u*, 1: 35b–52b.
    Lo-pin (for Robert) was Hart's *tzu* or style name, chosen in maturity.

18. U.S. Department of State, *Papers Relating to Foreign Affairs* (also known as *Foreign Relations of the United States*), 1866, part 1, p. 488, Williams to Seward, 26 December 1865. On Hsu's *Ying-huan chih-lueh*, see Drake, *China Charts the World*. Hart described T'an T'ing-hsiang, who became a Minister of the Tsungli Yamen in 1865, as "retrograde decidedly." Journals, 3 January 1866.

19. On Li and his advisers, see Kwang-Ching Liu "The Confucian as Patriot and Pragmatist," and "The Ch'ing Restoration." The quotation from Kuo comes from Frodsham, *The First Chinese Embassy to the West*, xxx.

20. On Feng's ideas, see Lü Shih-ch'iang "Feng Kuei-feng ti cheng-chih ssu-hsiang." Also Ocko, *Bureaucratic Reform*, 175–176; Wright, *The Last Stand*, 65–68, 91–94, 165–167.

21. Kuo and Liu, "Self-Strengthening," 503. A recent appraisal of Feng's proposals is in Min Tu-ki, *National Polity and Local Power: The Transformation of Late Imperial China*, 105–107 *et passim*.

22. Kwang-Ching Liu, "The Ch'ing Restoration," 488.

23. Kwang-Ching Liu, "The Confucian," 34–35.

24. For examples of Hart's acute awareness of China's administrative problems, see his journal entries for 23 December 1863; 2 July 1864; 5 July 1864; 27 July 1864; 22 November 1864; 30 December 1864; 25 January 1865; 24 May 1865; 24 July 1865; 24 October 1865; 2 January 1866; etc.

25. Gordon Papers, Ad. Mss. 52,386, Hart to Gordon, 7 October 1863. See also Hart's journal entries for 2 August 1864 and 20 January 1865.

26. On the Chinese missions of exploration, see chapter 9; on coastal improvements, see, for example, U.S. Department of State, *Papers Relating to Foreign Affairs*, 1868, part 1, 467–470.

27. Martin, *A Cycle of Cathay*, 222, 233–234. For additional background, consult Hart's journal, 25 July and 27 July 1865; also Hsü, *China's*

Entrance into the Family of Nations, 127 and 237 note 16; Wright, *The Last Stand*, 237–238.

28. In a carefully worded memorial received by the Throne on 30 August 1864, Prince Kung and his associates in the Tsungli Yamen made their appeal for support of Martin's translation project on the grounds that it would provide China with a means of resisting Western pressure and refuting Western claims. The Yamen Ministers pointed out that many foreigners had become accomplished students of the Chinese language, that Westerners had investigated Chinese law for their own purposes, and that they had already translated the Ch'ing Penal Code (*Ta-Ch'ing lü-li*). The Yamen went on to emphasize that Martin (Ting Wei-liang) was anxious to follow the precedent of Matteo Ricci and others who had "established good reputations in China." *IWSM T'ung-chih*, 27: 25a–26b.

29. On Hart's early support of Martin's translating and educational activities, see his journal entries for 20, 22 and 25 August 1864.

30. *IWSM, T'ung-chih* 40: 10b.

31. Ibid., 40: 12a–13b. F.O. 17/431, no. 257, Secret and Confidential, Wade to Russell, 2 November 1865.

32. F.O. 17/431, no 245, Secret and Confidential, Wade to Russell, 27 October 1865. Hart's memorandum, for which we have found no English version, appears in *IWSM, T'ung-chih*, 40: 13b–22a. For a contemporary evaluation of the memorandum by Chiang Tun-fu, an associate of the famous translator Wang T'ao at Shanghai, see Chiang Tun-fu, *Hsiao-ku-t'ang wen-chi*, 3: 15a–22b, reprinted in Ko Shih-chün, *Huang-ch'ao ching-shih wen-hsu-pien*, 104: 1a–4b. For recent Chinese assessments, consult Ch'en Shih-ch'i, *Chung-kuo chin-tai hai-kuan shih wen-t'i ch'u-shen*, 29–30, 93–96 and Lu Han-chao, *Ho-te chuan*, 89–97, esp. 96. Looking ahead to see Hart's "Bystander's View" in perspective as the beginning of a process of advising China in formal terms, we should take note of a much longer, more detailed, and more masterful summary entitled "Inspector General's Proposals for the Better Regulation of International Relations," dated by Hart at Peking 23 January 1876. Morse, *The International Relations of the Chinese Empire*, II, 440–474, Appendix D. See also chapter 11, note 9.

33. T'ien Hsing-shu, Acting Governor of Kweichow, was in charge of suppressing the Miao rebels. In 1861 his Green Standard forces murdered a French priest while attacking a Christian community. The case dragged on for years, and, although he was eventually sentenced to be banished to Sinkiang, the sentence was never actually carried out. For a summary of the affair, see Wang Wen-chieh, *Chung-kuo chin-shih shih shang ti chiao-an*, 44–51; also *IWSM, T'ung-chih*, 35: 10b–12b; 39: 34a–35a, etc. On Ch'ao-chou, see chapter 6, note 85.

34. *IWSM, T'ung-chih*, 40: 10a–12a.

35. The text of Wade's memorandum is in ibid., 40: 24a–36a. See also F.O. 17/431 no 245, Secret and Confidential, Wade To Russell, 27

October 1865 and no. 257, Secret and Confidential, Wade to Russell, 2 November 1865.

36. Cf. *IWSM, T'ung-chih*, 40: 22a and 40: 36a.
37. Ibid., 40: 10b–11b; also 41: 36b–40b; see also note 32 above for contemporary Chinese evaluations.
38. Ibid., 40: 12a–13b.
39. Ibid., 41: 43a.
40. See the summary in Wright, *The Last Stand*, 263–268; 273–276; also Hsü, *China's Entrance into the Family of Nations*, 158–160.
41. See, for example, *IWSM, T'ung-chih*, 41: 30a, 41a–b.
42. Ibid., 41: 45a–b, 64b–65a; 42: 59b–60a, 63a.
43. See, for example, ibid., 41: 27a, 43a–b, 44a, 48b, 49b, etc. Consult Smith, *China's Cultural Heritage*, 248–249.
44. On the problem of anti-missionary sentiment, see, for example, Cohen, "Christian Missions and Their Impact to 1900."
45. Smith, "Foreign-Training and China's Self-Strengthening," 85. On other foreign-training programs and their problems, see also *Yang-wu yun-tung*, 3: 441 ff., esp. 3: 471–72, 477–479, 483–484, 491–498, and 510.
46. See Kwang-ching Liu, "Politics, Intellectual Outlook and Reform," 92–93; also Biggerstaff, *The Earliest Modern Government Schools in China*, 101–102, 104, 105.
47. *IWSM, T'ung chih*, 42: 64b–65a. Nonetheless, Hart's memo received considerable attention subsequently from both Chinese and foreign observers. See Martin, *A Cycle of Cathay*, 413; Hart's journals, 4 and 24 June 1869; *North China Herald*, 18 September 1891.
48. Cited in S. Y. Teng and John Fairbank, comps., *China's Response to the West*, 119.
49. Smith, *Mercenaries and Mandarins*, 186–190, esp. 188.
50. The contrast with Japan is striking. See Richard J. Smith, "Reflections on the Comparative Study of Modernization in China and Japan" and "The Reform of Military Education in Late Ch'ing China, 1842–1895."
51. Bredon, *Sir Robert Hart*, 111.

CHAPTER EIGHT—JOURNALS

1. Lan Keang Sha: Lan-chiang-sha, commonly known by foreigners as the Taku Bar.

Chow Ta-jen: Chou *ta-jen*; "his excellency," Chou.

Tsze-chuh-lin office: Tzu-chu-lin; name of the foreign settlement in Tientsin.

The troops from Sung-chiang under P'an Ting-hsin were connected with the Feng-huang-shan training program established in 1864 by Charles Gordon with remnants of the Ever-Victorious Army.

Hart's remarks on regular payment were occasioned by his experience with the EVA.

Too-fei: *t'u-fei*. The "bandits" from Honan and Shantung were in fact the Nien rebels.

2. Liang Su was Hart's servant; Stuart Man, his personal secretary.

Yangtsun: Yang-ts'un; Ho-see-woo: Ho-hsi-wu; Matow: Ma-t'ou; Chang-Kia Wan: Chang-chia-wan; Yu Kea Wei: Yu-chia wei; Sha-hoo-men: Sha-wo men (a major gate on the east side of the Outer [Chinese] city of Peking); Kow-lin Hoo-tung: Kou-lan *hu-t'ung* (the lane where Hart lived and where the Peking Inspectorate General of Customs office was located). Ha-ta-men, officially known as Ch'ung-wen men, was a major easterly gate on the south wall of the Inner (Manchu) City. It was the location of the notorious Peking Octroi, and also served as the primary checkpoint for official visitors to the Tsungli Yamen. See *IWSM, T'ung-chih,* 24: 22a.

3. Sze-kwan: *ssu-kuan*. Note that the higher-ranking officials (*t'ang-kuan*)—Wen-hsiang, Heng-ch'i, Ch'ung-lun and Tung Hsun—sent their cards back.

4. Tsae: Ts'ai Shih-chün, a *tsung-pan* (Secretary General) of the Tsungli Yamen.

Hsüeh: Hsueh Huan; a former Minister of the Tsungli Yamen.
Han lin Peen-Shoo: *Han-lin pien-hsiu.*
Tsae Show-Ke: Ts'ai Shou-ch'i?

5. For the development of the arsenal at Soochow under Ting Jih-ch'ang, see Kennedy, *The Arms of Kiangnan: Modernization of the Chinese Ordnance Industry 1860–1895.*

6. Wade published a number of works on the Chinese language throughout his career. Among them was *Yu-yen Tsu-erh Chi [Yü-yen tzu-erh chi]: a Progressive Course in Colloquial Chinese* (1867; 2 vols) on which he must have been working at the time of his conversations with Hart. See also note 103 below.

7. Ma-urh: Ma Erh, Hart's servant.

Hoppo: Hart refers here to the former Hoppo, Yü-ch'ing, who had recently returned to the Imperial Household Department. See chapter 6, note 46.

Hwang-tsun: Huang-ts'un.

8. Tung Ta-jen: Tung *ta-jen*; "his excellency," Tung Hsun.

Foo Tseang Keun: Fu *chiang-chun*; Tartar General Fu; Fu-hsing. See Chang Ch'i-yun, et al., eds. *Ch'ing-shih,* VI, 4791–4792 (*lieh-chuan,* 204); also chapter 4, note 51.

9. The Russian Minister was A. Vlangali, and the Secretary, N. Glinka. M. de Bellonnet was French Secretary of Legation (Hart spells his name variously). Emile de Champs, a Frenchman, had joined the Customs Service in June of 1864.

10. For background on the "Portuguese question," see chapter 4, note 6. Relations with Portugal over Macao had been strained since 1849,

when the Portuguese Governor, availing himself of the troubles between England and China, ejected the Chinese Customs and declared the port of Macao to be under the sole jurisdiction of Portugal. The Chinese thereupon removed the Customs Houses from Macao and reestablished them at Whampoa, to which the Chinese merchants and their families likewise relocated. In 1862 Portugal had again seized the opportunity when the power of the Chinese government was at a low ebb, and dispatched an envoy to negotiate a treaty. This treaty was signed in August 1862, with two years allowed for the exchange of ratifications. The "objectionable" article in the treaty had to do with the continuation of the status quo in Macao; the French proposition was evidently that there should be a Chinese Customs House again at Macao, with the Commissioner at Canton. In the end, the Chinese refused to ratify.

Sir R.A.: Sir Rutherford Alcock, newly appointed British Minister. On Frederick Bruce, his predecessor, M. Jules Berthemy (France), Anson Burlingame (the United States), and A. Vlangali (Russia), see chapter 4, note 11.

"Presentation" refers to the presentation of the Foreign Ministers to the Chinese Emperor in audience. Immemorial custom required the performance of the full kotow (*k'o-t'ou*; 3 kneelings and 9 knockings of the head) in the Emperor's presence, but the Western Ministers, although intent on securing an audience in recognition of their diplomatic status, refused to contemplate a gesture of self-abasement so far in excess of that required before their own sovereigns. The minority of the T'ung-chih Emperor gave the Ch'ing authorities a pretext for delaying the audience issue, but it remained a stumbling block to Sino-foreign relations. (As it turned out, the first audience was held, without kotow, on 29 June 1873.)

The ChaoChow issue involved the failure of the Ch'ing authorities to open the treaty port of Ch'ao-chou to foreign consular representation. For the background, consult chapter 6, note 85; see also Hart's journal entry of 17 December 1865.

11. William Baker was clerk at the Tientsin Customs Office. There is a Thomas Menzies listed in the *China Directory* as a clerk at the Central Bank of Western India, Shanghai—possibly the one to whom Hart refers. Tsung How (Ch'ung-hou) was Superintendent of Trade for the three northern ports of Tientsin, Chefoo, and Newchwang, with his residence in Tientsin.

12. For background on Hart's propositions, see his journal entries for 23 December 1864; 2 February 1865; 14 February 1865; etc. Note also his entries for 2 and 3 August 1865.

Paou ta-jin was, of course, "his excellency," Pao-yun, a Grand Councillor and one of the original members of the Tsungli Yamen.

13. J. McLeavy Brown was Assistant Secretary at the British Legation; John G. Murray, assistant and accountant.

14. Hoo-poo: Hu-pu. Lo Tun-yen had been a high-ranking supporter of the anti-foreign militia movement at Canton during 1858; he was now an influential metropolitan official and part of a court faction opposing Prince Kung and Wen-hsiang. Kwang-Ching Liu and Smith, "The Military Challenge: The North-West and the Coast," 206.

15. Tung-ling: Tung-ling. The Eastern Tombs of the Ch'ing rulers were located northeast of Peking. Although the Hsien-feng Emperor (r. 1850–1861) had died in August 1861, he was not actually buried until the 9th month of the 4th year of the T'ung-chih reign (20 October–17 November 1865).

    Wen-hsiang was from Mukden, Manchuria, and during his career he was given several assignments involving the suppression of bandits in his home area (see note 108 below); hence his interest in Newchwang, where William MacPherson was now Commissioner of Customs.

16. William Cartwright became Hart's secretary in August 1865 and served until 4 November 1866.

17. "fash": Scottish, meaning worry or trouble (from Old French, *fascher*).

18. M. de Bellonnet was Secretary, and M. Fontanier, Interpreter, at the Establissement Diplomatique in Peking. E. Blancheton had been Interpreter in the French Consulate at Canton in 1864. In Hart's estimation, Fontanier was a very poor translator. See, for example, his journal entries of 11 June 1864 and 17 and 21 August 1865.

19. "The fleet" was, of course, the Lay-Osborn Flotilla.

    George Glass Lowder was the stepson of Sir Rutherford Alcock, on his way to China to succeed Frederick Bruce as British Minister. See note 156 below.

20. Hart indicates the intercalary month by using the character *yu* (again) before "5th month" rather than the more conventional term *jun*.

21. Gordon: presumably Charles G. Gordon, former Commander of the Ever-Victorious Army. See chapter 1. Forbes is probably Captain Charles Stewart Forbes; see note 74 below.

22. Oliver H. Perry was U.S. Consul in Canton.

    Canton-Fatshan railway: This plan, to link Canton by rail with the commercial and manufacturing center of Fo-shan, about 30 miles away, was not implemented.

    Sir Macd Stephenson: Sir Macdonald Stephenson.

23. By August 1864, William Cartwright, Edward C. Bowra, F. E. Kleinwachter, and Emile de Champs had all been given new appointments in the Customs Service (see Hart's journal entry of 24 August 1865). Bowra and de Champs would later accompany the Pin-ch'un Mission (see chapter 9). Hamilton and Doughty, as their scores suggest, made no mark on the Customs. See, for example, Hart's later annotation to his journal entry of 14 November 1864.

24. *hinc ille lachrimae*: hence these tears.

25. Che: presumably a Secretary (*chang-ching*) at the Yamen.

Ching: Probably Ch'eng-lin, who began his career in foreign affairs during the early 1860s. He started out as a Secretary in the Tsungli Yamen after assisting with the establishment of the T'ung-wen kuan, was promoted to General Secretary (*tsung-pan*) in 1864, and by 1869 had become a full Minister of the Yamen. During 1865 he was temporarily detached to serve as Superintendant of Customs as Newchwang. See *IWSM, T'ung-chih*, 4: 38b; 15: 14a; 26: 8a; 44: 4b–6a and 45: 64a; also Hart's journal entries for 1 August 1865 and 25 December 1865. Macpherson was being called to Peking to discuss the question of transit dues. See entries for 3, 4 and 8 August 1865; also 29 and 30 October 1865.

James Mongan, who had entered the Consular Service only a few months ahead of Hart, had been a friend of his on his first arrival in Hong Kong and later on visits to Ningpo. They had corresponded frequently over the years. He was now Acting Consul at Tientsin and Li Hung-chang's liaison with the British military authorities remaining at the Taku forts.

26. Williams was probably S. Wells Williams, Secretary and Chinese Interpreter at the U.S. Legation. The Rev. Joseph Edkins represented the London Missionary Society in Peking. A. R. Hewlett was a consular interpreter, whom Thomas Taylor Meadows, then British Consul at Newchwang, considered "the best man in the consular service now." See Hart's journal entry for 20 July 1865.

A. B. Freeman-Mitford, who had been in the Foreign Office since 1863, arrived in China in April 1865. His letters written during the next two years were published as *The Attaché at Peking* (1900). He became Lord Redesdale.

Robert Alexander Jamieson, who would later join the Customs as consulting surgeon, was from 1863 to 1866 Editor of the *North China Herald*.

27. Like Hart, J. McLeavy Brown had been born in Northern Ireland and educated at the Queen's College, Belfast.

28. It will be recalled that the clause allowing the French missionaries the right to own land in the interior was inserted only in the Chinese version of the Sino-French convention of 1860, not the original and authoritative published French version. See Hart's journal entry of 19 June 1864. For a translation of the Chinese text, consult Mayers, *Treaties between the Empire of China and the Foreign Powers*, 73, footnote to article 6.

29. Seng-ko-lin-ch'in (Senggerinchin) died on 20 May 1865. See chapter 6, notes 39 and 124. The entry of Seng-ko-lin-ch'in's body and rituals surrounding his burial are noted by the metropolitan official Weng T'ung-ho in his diary, *Weng T'ung-ho jih-chi p'ai-yin-pen* (hereafter, Weng, *jih-chi*), I, 289.

Ping tsih mën: P'ing-tse men; the southerly of the two major gates on the west wall of the Inner (Manchu) City.

Wan-min-san: *wan-min san.* Such umbrellas, made of red silk or satin and inscribed in gold with the names of donors, were presented to popular officials.

30. Chin Chaou-ting: Ch'en Ch'ao-t'ing; a member of the former Hoppo Yü-ch'ing's staff. See Hart's journal entry of 15 October 1864.

31. Luh ming-sung: Lu Ming-sung? Like Ch'en Ch'ao-t'ing (above), Lu was a member of Yü-ch'ing's staff. See chapter 4 note 181 and chapter 6, note 32; also Hart's journal entry of 4 January 1866 and note 184 below.

32. wei fen: *wei-feng?*; i.e., awe-inspiring reputation. Or perhaps Hart simply means "position" (*fen-wei*) and has transposed the characters.

yung: *yung.*

Puh-tsuh-mow: *pu-chih mou.*

33. See note 15 above. Wen-hsiang's autobiography indicates the security problems that could arise during the extended period between an emperor's death and his actual interment. See Wen-hsiang, *nien-p'u,* 3: 45a–b.

34. The so-called *Peking Gazette* (*Ching-pao*) of 16 July (the 24th day of the intercalary 5th month of the 4th year of the T'ung-chih reign) reported the confiscation of the *fu* of Hua-feng, the Prince of Su (Su *ch'in-wang*), including the charge that he was "ignorant of basic principles" (*pu-chih ta-t'i*)." For additional detail on this fascinating case, see Weng T'ung-ho's diary entries for 18 July 1864 and 1 August 1865. Weng, *jih-chi,* I, 289, 291.

Wang-yay: *wang-yeh.*

King-fei: *ching-fei.*

35. tsze-teen: *tz'u-tien.* See Weng, *jih-chi,* I, 289.

Hoo-tung: *hu-t'ung*; i.e. the Customs establishment, located on Kou-lan Lane in the Inner (Manchu) City.

36. Brown: probably J. McLeavy Brown.

37. Yutsing: Yü-ch'ing; the former Hoppo, a member of the Imperial Household Department.

Nan Hae: Nan-hai; one of the "three lakes" to the west of the Forbidden City, in the Imperial City. The Emperor was also praying for rain at this time. See Weng, *jih-chi,* 1: 289–290.

38. Ching-lin: Ch'eng-lin; Thomas Taylor Meadows was the British Consul at Newchwang.

39. Tseih-yay: Ch'i-yeh. The Seventh Prince was I-huan, Prince Ch'un (Ch'un *ch'in-wang*).

40. T.T.M.: Thomas Taylor Meadows.

41. San-Fuh: *san-fu.*

42. "Face" (*mien-tzu*) was a central concern of traditional Chinese culture. It had to do with an acute sense of status and a fear over public "loss of dignity," which might afflict institutions as well as individ-

uals. On "face," consult Hsien Chin Hu, "The Chinese Concepts of 'Face,'" esp. 47–48, 57, 59, 62–64. In this case, Wen-hsiang laments the double bind of inviting scorn from both provincial officials and the Western powers. For a personal example, involving Hart's servant, Ma Erh, and de Champs of the Customs Service, see note 79 below.

43. The term *ch'eng-k'ou* or "city port" could be construed both broadly and narrowly; naturally enough, the more encompassing the term, the more room for the extension of foreign privilege.

44. "Ting's powder" presumably refers to powder manufactured at Ting Jih-ch'ang's Soochow arsenal.

45. When Shanghai merchants in 1865 formed a company to make a railway from Shanghai to Wu-sung, a distance of some 10 miles, they encountered a host of difficulties, ranging from Chinese fears over the disruption of local *feng-shui* to various forms of resentment over foreign influence. After more than a decade of negotiations and false starts, about 5 miles of the line were built. They were soon dismantled by the Ch'ing authorities, however. For background, see chapter 6, note 132.

46. The treaty negotiated by Sinibaldo de Mas with the assistance of the French interpreter Fontanier, was signed at Tientsin on 10 October 1864, ratified by the Queen of Spain on 14 May 1866, but not ratified by the Chinese until 10 May 1868. See Mayers, *Treaties*, 165.

47. Hing-poo: Hsing-pu. Parkes's term for the prison—"dread portals"— was undoubtedly inspired by his personal experience as a captive of the Ch'ing government during the Sino-Western negotiations of September 1860.

Hart has the relationship slightly wrong; H. P. McClatchie, who had been in the Consular Service since 1865, was the nephew of Sir Harry Parkes, not his brother-in-law.

Rev. William H. Collins was a representative of the Church Missionary Society in Peking.

48. K.: Probably Count Kleczkowski, French Commissioner of Customs at both Tientsin (1862) and Chinkiang (1864).

49. The new Belgian Minister was A. t'Kint de Roodenbeke, also known as Auguste T'Kint. Tung Hsun and Ch'ung-hou negotiated from the Chinese side. See Tung, *nien-p'u*, 1: 47b. Hart's journal entry of 6 August 1865 suggests that the new Belgian Minister was keenly interested in the possibility of changes in China's treaty with Denmark, signed at Tientsin on 18 July 1863. The Belgian treaty was signed on 2 November 1865 and ratified at Shanghai on 27 October 1866. See Mayers, *Treaties*, 138, 144.

The ships of the Lay-Osborn Flotilla were in process of being sold during 1865–1866. The British government proposed to make up the difference between what China had paid and what it would receive from the proceeds. The only cause for "alarm or concern" might have been, in the case of the ships, delays of settlement; and in that of the Belgian Ambassador, the fact that China was reluctant to receive further Western envoys in Peking.

50. P'ei-poo questions: ? Perhaps the reference here is to difficulties in the northern part (*pei-pu*) of the Chinese empire, e.g., Newchwang, where T. T. Meadows was British Consul. Wen-hsiang's antipathy toward Meadows may have been particularly strong because of the latter's well-known pro-Taiping sympathies during the early 1860s.

Hoo Poo: Hu-pu.

51. Wen-hsiang's concerns about the "proposed Town-Dues" at Shanghai are not clear. There were several local taxation proposals afloat at the treaty port during 1865–1866. See for example, the *North China Herald*, 7 April 1866.

52. Kin chae: *ch'in-ch'ai*. Although the term usually refers to an imperial commissioner, the sense here is clearly "a foreign minister."

53. Baron Eugene de Meritens was Commissioner of Customs at Foochow; Thomas Dick, the same at Tientsin; Prosper Giquel, at Hankow; and William MacPherson, at Newchwang. Dick had previously been posted at Shanghai, Giquel at Ningpo, and MacPherson at Hankow. Although all the above Commissioners were among those recommended by Li Hung-chang for imperial commendation in 1866, de Meritens and Giquel received special notice for their contributions against the Taipings, which included the establishment of foreign-trained Chinese contingents at their respective treaty ports. See *IWSM, T'ung-chih*, 39: 21a–22b.

54. Fung-yih (Feng-yih) and Teh-ming (Tih-ming), both students at the T'ung-wen kuan, would soon accompany Hart on the so-called Pinch'un Mission to Europe; see chapter 9; also note 210 below. Tung Hsun records a "great examination of all the students of the T'ung-wen kuan" on 17, 18, and 19 November 1865, while Hart was away from Peking. Tung, *nien-p'u*, 1: 48b.

55. MacPherson's trip was remarkable because he had to cross the Gulf of Liaotung, the northwest arm of the Yellow Sea. Lin (or Liu) was no doubt Ch'eng-lin's secretary (she-yang is probably garble for *she-jen*). For Ch'eng-lin's background, see note 25 above.

56. Soo-la: *Su-la*; a Manchu term, indicates a Bannerman unattached to a particular Banner.

Wang-yay: *wang-yeh*; here, Prince Kung.

Le She-heën: Li Shih-hsien; the Taiping Shih-wang (Attendant King) was still active in Fukien province. He was killed on 23 August 1865, by his rebel colleague, Wang Hai-yang. See Kuo, *TPTK jih-chih*, 1138.

57. Hang-teen: *hang-tien*.

58. Hoo-Poo Tang-Kwan: Hu-pu *t'ang-kuan*; Presumably Lo Tun-yen. See note 14 above.

59. Puh-hing: *pu-hsing*.

60. P. J. Hughes was Britain's Acting Consul at Kiukiang.

    D. & Co.: Dent & Co.

    WuSueh: Wu-hsueh, a designated Yangtze River docking area. See *IWSM, T'ung-chih*, 63: 30b.

61. Wo Chung-t'ang: Grand Secretary Wo-jen, like Lo Tun-yen a factional enemy of Prince Kung and Wen-hsiang.

62. On the problem of transit dues, see our chapters 1 and 11; also note 25 above and notes 73 and 75 below.

63. yih Kae twan: The sense of the passage seems to be "once you begin (*i-k'ai*) there is no end (*tuan*)."

    sha chuen: *sha-ch'uan.*

64. The central versus provincial governments' competition to tax the opium trade was noted in chapter 1.

    San Woo Poo-Keun: *san-wu pu-chüan.* That is, 3.5 cash (*wen*) for every 1,000 cash or tael (*liang*).

    Yang-yoh Keuen: *yang-yao chüan.*

    Ya-teë-heang: *ya-t'ieh hsiang.* See also note 77.

65. Chuen Keuen: *ch'uan-chüan.* See Hart's journal entries of 2 and 4 August 1864.

66. Maou Chetae: Mao Hung-pin was Governor General of Kwangtung and Kwangsi from 1863 to 1865.

    Kwan-hwa: *kuan-hua.*

    Keen-tuh: *chien-tu.*

67. L. Bols was head of a special mission from Belgium, 1862–1865, resident in Shanghai. He was succeeded by Auguste t'Kint de Roodenbeke as Minister in 1865.

68. Pe-fang-tih-jin: *pi-fang ti jen.*

    Puh pei-fuh: Perhaps *pu p'ei-fu;* "(We) do not respect (that viewpoint)." Wade was himself aware of his legendary lack of tact.

69. Admiral James Hope in 1861–1862 had been in general command, with Admiral Protet, General Staveley, and General Ward, of the foreign troops fighting in the region around Shanghai. In 1861 he had led an expedition up the Yangtze to Hankow, where Kuan-wen, Governor General at Wuhan, refused to accept the terms of the 1860 settlement. Kuan-wen had won many honors for his battles against the Taipings, especially in cooperation with Tseng Kuo-fan, and in the capture of Nanking.

70. For Hart's contact with the individuals mentioned in this paragraph, see *Entering China's Service.* "Cha" is Hart's younger sister, Charlotte.

71. show-kow juh-ping: presumably a garble for *shou-k'ou ju-p'ing.*

72. M. Lemaire was Interpreter at the French Consulate in Shanghai.

    tsun puh tsun: *chun pu-chun;* allow it or not [?].

    shih-kwan: perhaps *shih-kuan,* to manage things experimentally.

73. Tonnage dues were basic to Customs revenue, and constantly subject to complaints and re-interpretations. See, for example, Hart's

journal entry of 23 September 1865 and note 116 below. For background, consult Wright, *Hart*, 291-294; also chapter 4, notes 48 and 186.

For problems related to opium and transit dues at Newchwang, see Hart's journal entries for 3, 4, and 8 August 1865; also 29 and 30 October 1865; *IWSM, T'ung-chih,* 34: 36b-37b; 44: 4b-6a.

74. Captain Charles Stewart Forbes was surely writing about the possibility that the Chinese government might purchase some of the ships from the Lay-Osborn Flotilla, now for sale in England. Indeed, in 1866, rather sooner than Hart had hoped, the *Amoy* and the *Keangsoo* were sold to Forbes acting as agent for the Chinese.

75. Charges for "unloading goods" (*lo-ti*; discussed in Wright, *Hart,* 379), as well as the "half-duty" (*pan-shui*) on opium, were considered transit taxes, like likin. See *IWSM, T'ung-chih,* 34: 36b-37b; 44: 4b-6a. Hart's journal entry for 21 August indicates that Wade did not accept the arrangements.

76. P'ang Show: *pang-shou.*

77. Wade had been one of the original Board of Inspectors when the foreign Inspectorate of Customs was set up in Shanghai in 1854. He had served, in spite of his wish to return to his consular duties, until replaced by Lay in May 1855. See *Entering China's Service,* 161-168.

78. D: perhaps Despatch; or Dent & Co. [?]
    Shin-chin: *shen-ch'eng.*
    Tung Kwan: *Tung-kuan.*

79. This incident illustrates the Chinese concept of "face" discussed above (note 42). As a Chinese Customs official, de Champs possessed a sense of dignity that required no less than a kowtow of apology from Hart's servant Ma Erh. Ma Erh's refusal left no option for him but to leave the I.G.'s service. He returned on 15 August, however, having no doubt kowtowed to de Champs. The process must have required some form of mediation, perhaps facilitated by Hart himself.

80. Ravarnet was the family home of Hart's father, Henry, after 1854. See Wright, *Hart,* 163.

81. Mrs. Twinem: wife of James Twinem, a new British employee in the Customs Service.

82. The "Customs Gazette" was issued periodically and printed in the *North China Herald* to apprise the public of recent appointments in the Customs Service. Number 3 of the "Gazette" appeared in the *Herald* of 2 September 1865; number 4, in the 24 March 1866 edition; number 5 in the 21 April 1866 edition.

William Cartwright was Hart's secretary until 4 November 1866.

3d C.C.: 3rd-class clerk, later 3rd-class assistant, was only one notch above the lowest, or beginning, grade of 4th class in the Customs Service.

83. E. C. Taintor (Union College) and F. E. Woodruff (Yale) had been

recommended to Hart for the Customs Service by the American Minister, Anson Burlingame. For background, see chapter 4, note 54.

84. Prince Kung's "difficulty" refers to the time in April and May 1865 when he was deprived of all of his offices and then gradually reinstated to all but the position of Prince Counsellor. See chapter 6, note 108.

85. The Spanish treaty, negotiated by Sinibaldo de Mas with Fontanier's "assistance," was signed by the principal Chinese negotiators, Hsueh Huan (Hart's "Hsieh") and Ch'ung-hou.

    F: Fontanier.

86. By "over 23 years of age" Hart meant the youth was too old. He preferred to have his new recruits right from the time they finished their education.

87. Minnie Edgar was a relative from Hart's mother's side of the family.

88. Hart had boarded in the house of Dr. John Aicken in Belfast during part of his time at the Queen's University.

89. E-wang: I-wang. Prince Kung's personal name was I-hsin.

90. On the opium half-duty question, see note 75 above.

    The Japan tonnage dues concession was presumably application of the "4 months' clause," first included in the British Treaty of Tientsin, which stipulated that after payment of tonnage dues coasting vessels would be exempt from any further levy of such dues for a period of 4 months. See Wright, *Hart*, 293; also Hart's journal entry of 1 September 1865.

91. James Henry Hart, now 19 (Robert Hart's age when first he went to China), seems to have had other ideas. But he joined the Customs later, in August 1867, as a 4th-class clerk and had a long career there, lasting until a year before his death at 56 in 1902.

92. neë-tae: *nieh-tai;* Fan-tae: *fan-t'ai.* Hart, it seems, was hinting at promotion (from rank 3a to 2b). For background, see his illuminating journal entries of 17 and 18 October 1864. Also chapter 4, note 185 and chapter 6, note 78.

    fuh-seih: *fu-se.* Used here, the term *fu-se* means official clothing or regalia.

93. "Braves" refers to temporary imperial armies (*yung*) raised to combat rebellion. After disbandment such soldiers were often disruptive, and sometimes became involved in anti-foreign incidents. The Ch'ao-chou question persisted into 1866, but a breakthrough occurred when Caine, the British Consul at Swatow, was received as an official guest of the Ch'ao-chou Taotai. See Hart's journal entry for 17 December 1865.

94. On Hart's relatives see *Entering China's Service.*

    William Maxwell, who was Commissioner at Tamsui, died on 3 October 1865. James Jones became Acting Commissioner at the same port in 1869. J. Scharfenort had been an Assistant in the Customs at Canton.

95. Hart may be quoting Sir D. B. Robertson, who had come to China in 1844 as one of the earliest appointments to the Consular Service there, and who had had a long and distinguished career.

96. tseuen-keuen ta-chin: *ch'üan-ch'üan ta-ch'en*; formal translation, Minister Plenipotentiary. Tung Hsun, *nien-p'u*, 1: 47b, dutifully records this appointment.

97. The Moorheads were close friends of the Hart family. See *Entering China's Service*, 357, note 75. James Henderson, M.D., had been a representative of the London Missionary Society in Shanghai.

98. Li refers to the first character of the Prussian Minister's Chinese name, Li Fu-ssu; *ta-jen* indicates "his excellency."

99. On the sequence of events leading up to the Pin-ch'un Mission, see chapter 9; also Hart's journal entries for 5 and 6 April 1866.

100. H. Octavius Brown had joined the Customs in 1864 and was a 3rd-class clerk at Tientsin.

101. The telegraph was presumably on display, as negotiations were underway for a telegraph line from Russia to China. See, however, note 119 below.

102. Tung Chih mên: T'ung-chih men; the northerly gate in the east wall of the Manchu City.

103. Wade did not have a chance to devote himself wholly to philology until his retirement in 1881 at the age of 65, when he became the first Professor of Chinese at Cambridge University. By this time he had already produced several works on the Chinese language. See note 6 above.

104. "The free exchange of people is no less useful than that of merchants."

105. Luh Tae Yay: Lu *ta-yeh*; "his excellency" Lu. This man is probably not Lu Ming-sung (see notes 32 and 37 above), who normally would not deserve such an exalted title. Hart's journal entry of 29 January 1865 suggests, however, that Luh and Chin peculated to the tune of 200,000 tls. (each?) while at Canton in the service of the Hoppo, Yü-ch'ing; this would have been more than enough to buy 1,500 *mou* (about 250 acres) of land at 5 taels per *mou*. Such savings and such an estate would have made Lu a very wealthy man by 19th-century Chinese standards.

106. Yu-tsing: Yü-ch'ing.

Tetuh Kwän Show: *t'i-tu* Kuan-shou; Provincial Commander-in-Chief, Kuan Shou [?]

Tseang-Keun: *chiang-chün*.

107. Foo Keen Tuh: *fu-chien-tu*; Tsung Kan Men: Ch'ung-wen men or Ha-ta men. The position of Assistant Supervisor of the Peking Octroi, located at the Ch'ung-wen Gate, was lucrative but not prestigious. See chapter 4, note 1.

Yu Tsing: Perhaps the former Hoppo Yü-ch'ing temporarily assumed some of Ch'ung-hou's trade related duties because the latter was so busy negotiating treaties during 1865–1866.

108. Kung Poo Shang-shoo: Kung-pu *shang-shu*. Wen-hsiang's visit to the Eastern Tombs (Tung-ling) to inspect the Hsien-feng Emperor's final resting place (see notes 15 and 34 above) was indeed a pretext. He had repeatedly "asked for leave" to bring his mother back to Peking from Mukden, but as banditry threatened southern Manchuria he was sent northward with the Peking Field Force (Shen-chi ying) to suppress it. He started out with only about 2,500 soldiers, but, on being informed that the mounted bandits numbered 30,000, he asked for 1,500 additional troops from Ch'ung-hou's foreign-training program at Tientsin. See Hummel, ed., *Eminent Chinese of the Ch'ing Period*, 854.

109. "sung po-po": *sung po-po*.

110. The 22nd article of the French Treaty of Tientsin concerned the payment of tonnage dues and various exemptions. See Mayers, *Treaties*, 65. Although the French treaty specified tonnage dues of 1/2 tael (5 mace) per ton for vessels over 150 tons, the British treaty provided for payment of only 4/10 tael (4 mace) for vessels of the same size. Ibid., 16. The French naturally invoked the "most-favored-nation" clause in order to lower their tonnage dues.

111. sze-kwan: *ssu-kuan*.

   From this and other journal entries, we can see that those who complained that Hart was "as completely Chinese in his sympathies as the Chinese themselves" were close to the mark. See *Entering China's Service*, 328, 332.

112. Foo Tseang Keun: Fu *chiang-chün*; i.e. Fu-hsing. General Fu's participation did not, however, relieve Wen-hsiang of overall responsibility for suppressing the "mounted bandits" (*ch'i-ma tsei*) in Manchuria.

   Technically, S. Wells Williams was not U.S. Minister but Secretary of Legation and Interpreter; General Vlangaly and M. von Rehfues were indeed Ministers, of Russia and Germany respectively. Hart habitually referred to von Rehfues as de Rehfues.

   As to telegraphs, the Chinese continued reluctant. Telegraphic communication was not established between Shanghai and San Francisco (via London) until 1871; nor was it on the Chinese mainland until 1881. As with railroads, Chinese resistance to telegraphs was based on a number of factors, not least fears over the disruption of *feng-shui* and concern over foreign economic penetration and domination of the interior.

113. Amoor presumably means the former Chinese Maritime Province, acknowledged as Russian in 1860. Vladivostok was its main port.

   Foo Too-tung: Fu *tu-t'ung*. Hart may still be referring to Fu *chiang-chün* (see note 112 above). In the early 1860s he was posted in Peking as an Acting Lieutenant General (*tu-t'ung*) of the Bordered Red Banners. See Chang Ch'i-yun, et al., eds. *Ch'ing-shih*, VI, 4791–4792 (*lieh-chuan*, 204); also chapter 4, note 51.

   Tsung Wän mên: Ch'ung-wen men.

114. Chaouchow: Ch'ao-chou.

Teen tetuh: T'ien *t'i-tu*. In 1861 Ch'ing troops under T'ien Hsing-shu murdered a French priest. Although cashiered as a Green Standard provincial commander-in-chief (*t'i-tu*), he remained unpunished. For background, see chapter 4 note 16.

Leang Kwang Tsung-tuh: Liang-Kuang *tsung-tu*.

Sze cheun Chetae: Szechwan *chih-t'ai*.

che King-chung: *chih ch'ing-chung*; lit. "knows the weight of . . ."

115. A-tajin: A *ta-jen*; "his excellency," Alcock. The British Minister's full Chinese name was A Li-kuo.

Lay, it may be remembered, had as Inspector General been ordered to make his headquarters in Shanghai, since the Tsungli Yamen did not relish the thought of so prickly an official always in close proximity. The Foreign Ministers, for their part, were wary of too close an association of diplomatic and commercial policies. Hart, however, was a different matter. The Tsungli Yamen found him congenial and reliable as a consultant along the strange pathways of foreign relations with the West; and with the foreign diplomatic corps he also maintained easy contact. By October 1865 he would be invited, with "the Prince's devoted approbation," to make his headquarters in Peking. See *Entering China's Service*, 319-320.

116. Hart evidently had in mind detachments of the foreign-trained forces from Feng-huang-shan and Sung-chiang that had recently seen duty against the Taipings in Fukien and were now engaged against the Nien rebels in north China.

117. Colonel Kirkham served as a captain and then major in the Ever-Victorious Army's First Battalion. He also accompanied the Ch'ing forces from Feng-huang-shan that went to Fukien in the spring of 1865.

118. Tsae Laou-Yay: Ts'ai *lao-yeh*; presumably "his excellency" Ts'ai Shih-chün, a Secretary General of the Tsungli Yamen (see note 4 above).

Crane and Burgevine: The events surrounding the deaths of Crane, an Englishman, and Burgevine, the former American Commander of the Ever-Victorious Army, in late June 1865, are described in Thomas Kingsmill, "Retrospect of Events in China and Japan during the Year 1865," 145-148.

119. Wei yuen Chang: *wei-yuan* Chang.

Ke-ma-tseih: *ch'i-ma tsei*.

120. How common a practice it was for merchants to serve as "vice-consuls" or "acting consuls" in less prestigious ports can be seen by consulting the *China Directory*. In 1864, for instance, Swatow had T. W. Richardson serving for the Netherlands, C. W. Bradley, Jr., for the United States, and H. A. Diercks for both Denmark, and Hamburg, Lubeck, and Bremen. In Amoy, A. R. Johnston acted for France, Portugal, and the Netherlands, and Walter Mourilyan for Denmark. At Hankow, C. D. Williams was Officiating Consul

for Russia. Britain alone seemed to maintain a regular official from the Consular Service in every port.

121. shin-chin: *shen-ch'eng*. The request was finally granted in 1867.

122. M. R. Guierry was a Roman Catholic missionary in Ningpo, and Rev. J. H. Gray the British consular chaplain at Canton.

123. James Leighton Brown was named Deputy Commissioner of Customs at Shanghai. See Hart's journal entry for 22 October.

124. Hart usually referred to his Chinese memorandum on reform (*Chü-wai p'ang-kuan lun* or *P'ang-kuan chih lun*) as a "Bystander's View". He was now nearly at the point of sending it to Prince Kung, which he did on 6 November 1865.

     Kang He: K'ang-hsi, reigned 1661-1722.

     Le teen: Li T'ien: ?

125. Boyd & Co. of Amoy were agents for Lloyds.

126. The "Soo Chow man named Fung" was Feng Kuei-fen, one of Li Hung-chang's most talented and foresighted advisers. His essays were collected in a book entitled *Chiao-pin-lu k'ang-i*. See chapter 7.

     de Billagnet: This seems to be M. de Bellonnet, the French Secretary of Legation.

     C. Bismark was an Interpreter at the German Legation.

127. Lough Neagh is a lake 17 miles long in county Antrim, Northern Ireland, the largest lake in the British Isles.

128. In Szechwan there was to be for years a state of friction between the Roman Catholic missionaries and the gentry. In August 1865, only 3 months after the mission was established, the Abbé Mabileau was killed. In the years following there were various episodes of converts killed, houses burned, etc., culminating in January 1869 when Abbé Rigaud was killed and the mission buildings pillaged and burned.

129. Juy Ling: Jui-lin, Governor General of Liang-Kwang. Hart had met Jui-lin when the latter was Tartar General at Canton in February 1865.

130. Kwei-tsze: *kuei-tzu*.

     new-urh: *nü-erh*. Apparently the Spanish Minister garbled the expression for "tabby cat" (*nü mao-erh*).

131. Gustav Detring, a German who had joined the Customs in April 1865, was to have a long career in China, ending in 1908.

132. Hart miswrites the character *shen* in Shen-chi ying.

     'Saou ta tsze': *sao* Ta-tzu.

     Han Man tsze': Han Man-tzu.

     Yang Kwei-tze: *yang kuei-tzu*.

133. William Cartwright was Hart's newly appointed personal secretary.

     Juy Chung-tang: Jui *chung-t'ang*: Grand Secretary Jui; i.e. Jui-lin, Governor General of Liang-Kwang. Jui-lin had previously served as a Grand Secretary, hence Hart's use of the honorific term *chung-t'ang*.

     F. W. White was Acting Commissioner at Kiukiang 1864-1866.

     Kang-chou-foo: Kan-chou *fu*, in Kiangsi.

134. Wang Chaou-Ke: Wang Ch'ao-ch'i. Hart refers here to an impeach-

ment case involving the censor, discussed briefly in Weng, *jih-chi*, 300–302.

135. Kaou-Kea: *kao-chia*.

136. Kung Poo: Kung-pu.

137. J. Porter was Assistant-in-Charge at Amoy.

G. Kleczkowski, French, had joined the Customs in 1860 and was Commissioner at Amoy from 1865 to his death in 1867. It must have been over the accounts in Chinkiang that he and Lord were squabbling, for Kleczkowski had been Commissioner there in 1863–1864, and C. A. Lord, who had joined the Customs in 1859, succeeded him.

138. This was the Rev. W. A. P. Martin, whose school Hart previously called the Tsing-Shih Kwan (Ching-shih kuan? See chapter 4, note 191). Martin had been translating Wheaton's *Elements of International Law* into Chinese, and would soon begin teaching English at the Tung-wen kuan. From its modest origins as a school for training interpreters, the T'ung-wen kuan gradually expanded under Hart's watchful eye, and in late 1865 the I.G. received authority from the Tsungli Yamen to recruit several additional Western instructors. Dr. Martin became the first president of the school in 1869. See Martin's historical overview of the College in H. B. Morse, *The International Relations of the Chinese Empire*, 3: 471–478, Appendix F.

139. Brown: Probably J. McLeavy Brown, since the others were diplomats. N. Glinka had been Secretary at the Russian Legation in Peking.

140. chih-jung: *chih-jung*.

lang-p'i: *lang-p'i* means wolfskin; the additional "and" is just one of Hart's occasional slips of the pen.

141. lun: *lun*. Hart's "Bystander's View." Wade actually wrote two "Secret and Confidential" letters to Lord Russell on Hart's memorandum, one dated 27 October 1865 and the other 2 November 1865 (F.O. 17/431, nos. 245 and 257 respectively).

142. Tuh Foo: *tu-fu*; a contraction of *tsung-tu* and *hsun-fu*.

143. As it developed, Alcock soon became Hart's admirer and even confidant. Sir Rutherford's biographer, Alexander Michie, goes so far as to assert in *The Englishman in China during the Victorian Era*, II, 164, that the I.G.'s influence over Wade and Alcock constrained British policy in China for an entire generation.

144. The term *tzu-k'ou* refers here to transit taxes (*tzu-k'ou shui*), collected at local stations. For background on the problem of transit dues at Newchwang and the opium half-duty, see notes 25 and 77 above.

145. Wusueh: Wu-hsueh.

146. Morrison: perhaps M. C. Morrison, British Consul at Chefoo.. de Billagnet: M. de Bellonnet. Williams: presumably S. W. Williams.

147. chaou-huang: a miswrite for *chao-hui*, a communication between equals, used between the Yamen and the foreign Ministers.

For the contributions of Brown, Lovatt, and others in the foreign-style military training programs at Tientsin and at the capital, see *YWYT,* 3: 475–476, 478–479, 483–484, 488–491. Brown and Lovatt were awarded the Chinese military rank in 1867 for their efforts.

148. Edward B. Drew (Harvard 1865), was one of the 3 Americans recruited for the Customs by the U.S. Minister Anson Burlingame. The other 2 who joined at Burlingame's invitation were E. C. Taintor and F. E. Woodruff.

Pwan Ta-jin: P'an *ta-jen*; the Taotai at Chefoo.

149. William H. Lay was Vice-Consul at the British Consulate in Shanghai. He and Walter Thurlow Lay were brothers of Horatio Nelson Lay.

Tih-shing: Te-hsing?

150. Simpson: Clare Lenox Simpson had joined the Customs in 1861. Presumably B. Lenox Simpson, who wrote as Putnam Weale in the early 20th century, was his son.

151. Propser Giquel and Paul d'Aiguebelle had already established their reputations as advisers and assistants to Tso Tsung-t'ang, and would soon (13 December 1865) be rewarded with high Chinese military rank for their efforts against the Taipings. Kuo, *TPTK jih-chih*, 1145. They were to Tso what Hart and "Chinese" Gordon were to Li Hung-chang. For background, see chapter 4, note 81, and chapter 6, note 128. Giquel, who had recently been transferred from Ningpo to Hankow, would resign as Commissioner of Customs in 1866 to become Director of Tso's Foochow Shipyard.

152. According to Giquel, Hart had wanted the Foochow Shipyard to be under the direction of the Customs Administration; but when Giquel broached the matter to Tso, Tso refused. Giquel claimed he was quite willing to let either Hart or the French government take control of the shipyard, and that he only "reluctantly" concluded it would be best to resign from the Customs Service. For the controversy surrounding Giquel's resignation — including the dubious French charge that Hart privately encouraged Baron Eugene de Meritens to undermine the Foochow project — see Steven Leibo, *Transferring Technology to China: Prosper Giquel and the Self-Strengthening Movement*, 84–87.

153. Sir Edmund Hornby had been asked by Hammond to go to China as Chief Judge to organize the judicial service, as he had already done in Turkey. Hornby arrived in Peking during the summer of 1865, and, although he was apparently civil enough to Hart at their first meeting, he became increasingly scornful of Hart's position as a loyal employee of the Ch'ing government and chafed over the I.G.'s failure to call on him subsequently. (*Autobiography*, 238–240)

C. A. Winchester had been British Consul at Ningpo during Hart's extended stay there, and later Officiating Consul at Canton at the time Hart resigned from the Consulate to enter the Customs.

154. Geoffrey Milburne Hart was the younger of Robert's two brothers.

These gifts are typical of Hart's open-handedness and unsolicited generosity toward his family throughout his career. Mary, his older sister, married to a somewhat ineffectual linen merchant, obviously needed the largest sum, disguised as a loan but surely never repaid.

Presumably his payment to a private account at Smith, Elder & Co. in London was for the bookkeeper to whose care he was about to entrust his 3 small children by his Chinese "wife," Ayaou. See chapter 2, note 157; chapter 6, note 65; also *Entering China's Service*, 151, 153–154, 230–232, etc. In June 1875, when Hart wrote to his London agent, James D. Campbell, about the education of these children, he recalled that he had sent them to England in 1866, when they were aged 6, 4, and 1. *The I.G. in Peking*, letter 124 and note 1.

155. F. Neville May, who had joined the Customs in 1859 and who was to have a long career in China, was now clerk at Shanghai.

156. Meadows: J. A. T. Meadows, Hart's early associate at Ningpo, now a merchant.

Mongan: James Mongan, British Consul at Tientsin.

George: George Glass Lowder, Sir Rutherford Alcock's stepson, had a somewhat lackluster career in the Customs, being in 1865 an Assistant at Shanghai. He died during home leave in 1880. Alcock, as the inventor of the Foreign Inspectorate, naturally felt justified in giving advice on Customs policy.

157. Miss L.: Amy Henrietta Lowder, Mrs. Alcock's daughter, sister of George Glass Lowder.

158. J. Mackey, who had been in the Customs since 1861, was 1st-class clerk at Tientsin, but would soon become Acting Commissioner at Newchwang. Hart himself exercised general supervision over the T'ung-wen kuan until W. A. P. Martin assumed the presidency in 1869.

159. Seu Ke-yu: Hsu Chi-yü, who in 1847 had been appointed Governor of Fukien and supervisor of commercial dealings with foreign nations, incurred the enmity of many Chinese in his efforts to establish relations of mutual confidence. Thus in 1851 he was denounced and dismissed from office. In the mid-1860s, however, as the Taiping forces moved northward, he took charge of organizing volunteers in Shansi; and in 1865 he was summoned to an audience and appointed to the Tsungli Yamen. In 1869 he retired on the grounds of old age and ill health, and died in 1873. On his book and career, see Drake, *China Charts the World*.

160. Brown: J. McLeavy Brown.

161. Teih-mao-wang: T'ieh-mao wang. This term refers to princes by right of perpetual inheritance—descendants of the "eight great houses" (*pa ta-chia*) that assisted in the Ch'ing conquest of China. One of these princes, of the 2nd degree, was designated Shun-ch'eng chun-wang. See also note 35 above.

162. Presumably, the "Inspectorate of Literary Establishments" could

have been set up by the Tsungli Yamen, as was the Tung-wen kuan, to be placed under Hart's general supervision.

163. For Hart's early study of the Chinese language, see *Entering China's Service*, 16, 42–44, 65, 67, 68, 76, 92, 110, 138.

164. Keentuh: *chien-tu*. Sha-hoo-kwan: Sha-hu kuan; the Customs Office at Sha-hu-k'ou. See *IWSM, T'ung-chih*, 44: 5b.

165. Brown: James Leighton Brown had been originally assigned to Shanghai.

166. Hart was to recruit these instructors during his home leave. See chapter 9.

167. Actually, G. H. Fitzroy, then Commissioner at Shanghai, was appointed Acting Inspector General from April through October 1866 during Hart's absence.

168. Hart had persuaded Pao-yun that the Chinese government should contract a foreign loan to support suppression of Muslim rebellions in northwest and southwest China.

   Yang: Yang Yueh-pin, Governor General of Shensi and Kansu, a veteran of the Ch'ing-Taiping War.

   Yun-Kwei: Yunnan and Kweichow.

   pa-wuh: *pa-wu*; i.e., a way of handling things.

   She-lang: *shih-lang*.

169. Tsung-ping heen: *tsung-ping hsien*. At the same time Tso Tsung-t'ang requested that Paul d'Aiguebelle receive brevet rank as a *ti-tu* (provincial commander-in-chief) and the honor of wearing the yellow riding jacket (*huang ma-kua*)—the same honors Gordon had been awarded in 1864.

170. Ke-ma-tseih: *ch'i-ma tsei*.

171. Nikolaevsk, a seaport town near the mouth of the Amur River, was a regional center for salmon fishing.

172. Amy Lowder would marry Charles Hannen in 1874.

173. Seu Ke-yu: Hsu Chi-yü.

   T'an T'ing-hsiang, who served in the Tsungli Yamen from 1865 to his death in 1870, had wide-ranging administrative experience, both as a provincial and as a metropolitan official, but little direct contact with foreigners prior to serving in the Yamen. Chang Ch'i-yun, et al., *Ch'ing-shih*, 6: 4849 (*lieh-chuan* 213).

174. The convention was not signed until 1877.

175. Ken: ? Presumably the sound of the first character of the priest's Chinese name. Heng-ch'i, however, pronounced it Heng (Hang). Such confusion of foreign names in Chinese transliteration was common at the time.

   Ching-too: Ch'eng-tu, provincial capital of Szechwan.

176. Shan-Hai-Kwan: Shan-hai kuan, the pass at the eastern end of the Great Wall.

177. John G. Murray was Assistant and Accountant at the British Legation.

178. Chang Kia Kow: Chang-chia k'ou was a city of military and com-

mercial importance in Chihli province, just inside the Great Wall — the starting point of camel caravan routes to Urga. Through it had traditionally passed a large amount of the Chinese tea trade with Russia. Kalgan was the Mongol name for Chang-chia k'on, located just beyond the Great Wall in Inner Mongolia.

179. Pwan Taoutae: ? Perhaps P'an *ta-jen* at Chefoo. See chapter 6, note 3; note 148 above.

Yang Yao-ping: Yang Yueh-pin.

180. Ting She chang: Perhaps Hart means Ting Jih-ch'ang, whom he once described in his journal (8 November 1864) as "a thin man with a bad mouth but very intelligent eye which when he is in earnest flashes with meaning."

181. Tso-too Yu-she: *tso-tu yü-shih*.

Le Ho-neen: Li Ho-nien, soon to be transferred from Hupeh to Honan. The other two Li's were Li Hung-chang, governor of Kiangsu, and his brother, Li Han-chang, Governor of Hunan. The "lately appointed Governor of Hoopih [Hupeh]" was Cheng Tun-chin. The years 1865–1866 witnessed an uncommon number of provincial transfers. See Ch'ien Shih-fu, *Ch'ing-chi chung-yao chih-kuan nien-piao*, 190.

Keun Ke: Chün-chi. The deceased Le was Li T'ang-chieh. The Emperor's tutor was Li Hung-tsao. He had been appointed to instruct the Hsien-feng Emperor's only son in 1861, and, when the child ascended the throne a year later, the two Dowager Empresses appointed Li as one of 4 tutors to the young monarch. In 1866, after various promotions, Li was made Vice-President of the Board of Revenue and a Grand Councillor. See also Hart's journal entry for 2 January 1866. Li Hung-tsao, like Wo-jen, Lo Tun-yen, and Weng T'ung-ho, was a factional enemy of Prince Kung and Wen-hsiang. See Kwang-Ching Liu, "The Ch'ing Restoration," 505–506.

182. Hans: Han.

Man: Man.

Yang: *yang*

Hwuy: *hui*.

183. heen che: *hsien-chih*.

184. Luh meng seng: Lu Ming-sung? See note 31 above.

185. Thomas: Perhaps the Rev. J. R. Thomas, an inveterate traveler. See chapter 4, note 108.

Ching lin: Ch'eng-lin. At this time, Ch'eng-lin was still on temporary leave from the Tsungli Yamen, acting as Superintendant of Customs at Newchwang. See note 25 above.

Yang tseang tuy: *yang-ch'iang tui*. Ch'ung-hou established a foreign-training program in the early 1860s that not only produced a "foreign-arms corps" for the defense of Tientsin, but also assisted in instructing other Ch'ing forces in the use of Western weapons, including troops from the Peking Field Force (Shen-chi ying). See *YWYT*, III, 443–458; also note 158 above.

186. Kuan Koo: ? Takoo Wei Yuen: Ta-ku *wei-yuan*; an underling representing the Imperial Commissioner at the Taku Forts.

These forces, led by P'an Ting-hsin, were presumably from the Feng-huang-shan training program, rather than from Ch'ung-hou's Tientsin program.

187. Tsae laou yay: Ts'ai Shih-chün.

Ping: Pin-ch'un, Hart's writer since mid-1864, did in fact go with Hart to England.

188. Nee-tae: *nieh-t'ai*. Ta-jen ("great men") here refers to the *t'ang-kuan* (high officials) of the Tsungli Yamen.

189. G. Kleczkowski, Commissioner of Customs at Amoy, was reporting ongoing talks between Paul d'Aiguebelle and Tso Tsung-t'ang concerning the Foochow Shipyard.

190. The indemnities imposed by the Conventions of Peking (1860) — 8 million taels each to Great Britain and France — had been paid off by 1866. For background on the use of the Customs Service as a debt-paying agency, consult Wright, *Hart*, 148–149.

191. *Analects* (*Lun-yü*) book 4, chapter 18: "The Master [Confucius] said: "In serving parents, a son may gently remonstrate with them, but if he sees that they are determined not to follow [his advice], he will again be reverential and not go against [them]. . . . "

192. Ta-Ka puh näng puh-pan: *ta-kai pu-neng pu-pan*.

193. Kea-ying Chow: Chia-ying chou. The Taiping leader Wang Hai-yang had managed to establish himself in Chia-ying chou, Kwang-tung, in December 1865, and maintained his base there until February 1866. On 1 February he died, and a week later his force was annihilated. In 2 days of fighting from 7–9 February, 10,000 Tai-pings were reportedly killed and over 50,000 surrendered. Kuo, *TPTK jih-chih*, 1148–1150.

194. P'ang-pan: *pang-pan*; Foo-tsung pan: *fu tsung-pan*.

195. He-she: Perhaps "Hart [-related] matters" (Ho-*shih*).

Fantae heën: fan-t'ai *hsien*. In fact, Hart would not receive this coveted honor until 20 November 1868. See *IWSM, T'ung-chih*, 69; 24a–b.

tsung-le shwuy-loo shwuy-wuh sze: *tsung-lishui-lu shui-wu-ssu*. Hart emphasizes "sea and land" (*shui-lu*) here.

Kiakhta, on the northern border of Outer Mongolia just east of the Orkhon River, was on the caravan route 150 miles north of Urga. It did not, however, in Hart's time become a Customs post.

196. You-le: *yu-li*; travel in the sense of a tour. See also letter of 8 February to Bowra in Appendix B.

197. Foo-tsung-pan: *fu tsung-pan*; San pin heen: *san-p'in hsien*. Pin-ch'un's son Kuang-ying, a Secretary in the Imperial Household Department, received brevet 6th rank along with Te-ming, and Feng-i, both of whom previously held 8th rank as minor officials in the T'ung-wen kuan. Yen-hui was a T'ung-wen kuan student. Chan

Afang was Hart's personal servant. Edward Bowra, posted at Canton, and Emile de Champs, at Chefoo, were both accomplished translators.

Hing-chwang Ying: *hsing-chuang ying*; i.e. luggage.

198. Although the loan plans with Stuart never bore fruit, Tso Tsung-t'ang did secure a foreign loan of 1.2 million taels, guaranteed by the Superintendents of Customs at the treaty ports, to help finance the Ch'ing campaign against the rebels in Shensi and Kansu. On the financial arrangements, see Liu and Smith, "The Military Challenge," 227–228.

199. MacPherson, who was Commissioner at Newchwang, remained there until January 1868, so obviously the sealed orders were not used.

Chang-chia k'ou propositions: See Hart's journal entry of 29 December 1865 and note 191.

200. *tai-chih tai [?]*. The idea is that the Commissioner at Shanghai will act on Hart's behalf. J. F. W. Vernimb, a German, had joined the Customs on the recommendation of Commissioner Wilzer, arriving in Shanghai in May 1865. He resigned in April 1866 while still a 4th-class clerk. Evidently something about him stirred unpleasant memories for Hart, for in January 1869, writing James Campbell in London with instructions about hiring new German recruits for the Customs in Europe, he concluded, "Don't re-engage Vernimb if he applies." *The I.G. in Peking*, I, 42. James Twinem, British, had recently joined the Customs. J. Coolidge had been a clerk in the Customs at Kiukiang.

201. M. Pinchon was Attaché at the French Legation.

202. David F. Rennie, medical officer for the British Legation guards in the early days of residence for foreign diplomats in Peking, was a dinner companion at Minister Bruce's during Hart's first visit to Peking in 1861. With Bruce's blessing he was keeping a diary of day-to-day occurrences during these momentous days, and Hart's reports of conversations with Prince Kung and the Ministers of the Tsungli Yamen were grist to his mill. The account was published as *Peking and the Pekingese* in 2 volumes (1865). Actually, no secrets were betrayed, but Hart was irked at what might seem an indiscretion on his part. *Entering China's Service*, 241.

203. Yue Hae Kwan: Yueh *hai-kuan*; lit., Canton Customs, i.e. the Hoppo's long-lived establishment, now supplemented by the Maritime Customs as regards foreign trade under treaties.

Chow le: *ch'ou-li*; perhaps short for *ch'ou li-chin*; "to levy likin."

204. Wade's memo was entitled "Hsin-i lueh-lun" (A brief discussion of new proposals). It occupied over 26 pages of text, and, although similar to Hart's memorandum in many respects, its tone was more ominous. See chapter 7.

CHAPTER NINE—TRAVELS TO EUROPE 1866

1. *Entering China's Service*, 300.
2. See Mary Wright, *The Last Stand*, 260-261; 273; Frodsham, *The First Chinese Embassy to the West*, xxiv–xxv.
3. Journals, 20 February 1866; *IWSM, T'ung-chih*, 39: 1a–b.
4. Journals, 2 March 1866; cf. *IWSM, T'ung-chih*, 39: 2a–b; *Ch'eng-ch'a pi-chi* (Notes on a mission of investigation), p. 1b.
5. Freeman-Mitford, *The Attaché at Peking*, 226.
6. See Knight Biggerstaff, "The First Chinese Mission of Investigation Sent to Europe" in Biggerstaff, *Some Early Chinese Steps toward Modernization*.
7. For a discussion of the Chinese accounts, see ibid., 43; on Bowra's diary, consult Drage, *Servants of the Dragon Throne*.
8. *Ch'eng-ch'a pi-chi*, 1a–2a; cf. journals, 7, 8 and 10 March 1866 and our chapter 5.
9. Martin, *A Cycle of Cathay*, 373. "Minghuang" in the last line refers to a T'ang-dynasty Emperor known for his fondness for women.
10. Biggerstaff, "First Chinese Mission," 45. On Pin's early experiences with trains, see *Ch'eng-ch'a pi-chi*, 16b, 17b, etc.
11. Drage, *Dragon Throne*, 141. For the comparison between England and France, see *Ch'eng-ch'a pi-chi*, 24a. Pin-ch'un's description of Great Britain is typical of his diary entries for each country he visited. He notes, for example, the general location, names, and dimensions of the British isles, together with a brief overview of English history since Roman times (the Han period, in Pin-ch'un's words). His main emphasis is on Britain's political leadership, but he draws no comparisons between, say, Queen Victoria and the Empress Dowager Tz'u-hsi. *Ch'eng-ch'a pi-chi*, 23b–24a. One gets the impression that Pin-ch'un understood about as much of the history and culture of the countries he visited as do most modern Western visitors of China after a 3-week tour.
12. Drage, *Dragon Throne*, 143-144; cf. *Ch'eng-ch'a pi-chi*, 21a–b. See also Biggerstaff, "First Chinese Mission," 44-45.
13. *Ch'eng-ch'a pi-chi*, 26a. In fact, Gordon did speak with a lisp, and struck a number of observers as rather effeminate.
14. For the seven letters Hart wrote between 2 June and 13 July 1866 in response to appeals for guidance from E. C. Bowra, see Appendix B.
15. For Pin-ch'un's other activities in England, see Drage, *Dragon Throne*, 145 ff.; also Biggerstaff, "First Chinese Mission," 47.
16. Journals, 15 July 1866. See also Morse, *International Relations*, II, 188, esp. note 12.
17. Most of the preceding discussion has been drawn from Drage.
18. *Ch'eng-ch'a pi-chi*, pp. 59a–b. Cf. *IWSM, T'ung-chih*, 46: 17a–b.
19. Morse, *International Relations*, II, 188.
20. Ibid., 187, esp. note 8; journals, 9 January 1867. For contemporary

and later evaluations of the mission, see Freeman-Mitford, *The Atta-ché at Peking*, 226; Alexander Michie, *Englishman in China*, II, 137; Big-gerstaff, *Some Early Chinese Steps toward Modernization*, 51–52.

21. On the Burlingame Mission, consult Smith, "China's Early Reach Westward." Like the Pin-ch'un Mission, the Burlingame expedition was financed by Customs revenues and Hart was an early and ardent supporter of it. See, for example, journals, 24 November 1867.

22. *IWSM, T'ung-chih* 55: 27a; 56: 11a.

23. Frodsham, *First Chinese Embassy*, xl–xli; Morse, 3: 476; *The I.G. in Peking*, I, 397–398. For Hart's influence on the permanent mission, see ibid., I, 197 ff., esp. letters 130, 136, 140, 142, etc.

24. On his Chinese wife and children, see ibid., I, 25; also *Entering China's Service*, 151, 153–54, 191, 192, 210, 218–219, 230–232.

25. Juliet Bredon, *Sir Robert Hart*, 3.

26. *The I.G. in Peking*, 2: 1479.

27. On von Gumpach, see chapter 11, esp. note 15.

28. Hart indicates "end" in his journal entry with the Chinese character *le*, signifying past tense. It may be added that, despite the I.G.'s well-established reputation for liking pretty young women, he remained faithful to Hessie. See Paul King, *In the Customs Service*, 238–239.

CHAPTER TEN–JOURNALS

1. Johannes von Gumpach was appointed Professor of Astronomy at the T'ung-wen kuan, though Hart had been warned that he would be troublesome. He was, and in 1868 Hart discharged him. Von Gumpach, in turn, sued Hart. For the gory details, see Wright, *Hart*, 334–347.

2. Dudley Edward Saurin was a friend of A. B. Freeman-Mitford: they had both arrived in China to serve at the British Legation in the spring of 1865. For Ha-ta-men and other points on Hart's route, see chapter 8, note 2. The trip of 80 miles between Peking and Tientsin would have to be made by cart or on horseback at this time of year, for the river would have been frozen since November.

3. Tsung How: Ch'ung-hou; Commissioner for the Northern Ports.
   Wei-yuen: *wei-yuan*.
   Kung-kwan: *kung-kuan*.

4. Thomas Dick, who had been Commissioner of Customs at Shang-hai, was on home leave, and would return in 1866 to become Com-missioner at Tientsin; Miss Laurie was the daughter of P. G. Laurie of Jardine, Matheson. Charles G. Gordon, former commander of the Ever-Victorious Army, had become a good friend of Hart's, and would visit him in London (see note 40 below).

5. For Hart's earlier contact with Aunt Brady, see *Entering China's Service*, 321. Miss Hester Jane Bredon was, of course, to become Hart's bride.

6. Although there are three Hendersons listed as tidewaiters or tide surveyors in the *China Directory,* none could be David Marr Henderson, who later had a distinguished career with the Customs, for he did not join Hart's service until 1869. H. Octavius Brown and Captain Lowatt were involved in training Chinese troops in the Peking-Tientsin area.

   Kirin (Chinese: Ch'i-lin) was the official Japanese name for Yunki, a city in eastern Manchuria, on the left bank of the Sungari River, long an important trade center for lumber and tobacco. Wenhsiang in fact gained a number of significant victories against the "mounted bandits" (*ch'i-ma tsei*) in this area and returned to Peking in midsummer, bringing his aged mother with him.

7. The party consisted of Pin-ch'un, his son Kuang-ying, Te-ming, Feng-i, and Yen-hui, all Manchus. Yaou must have been one of the 7 servants, although it is rather peculiar that he would be sitting across from Pin-ch'un, who was so much higher in status.

8. Emile de Champs had been posted to Chefoo after a period of language training at Peking under Hart's supervision. Luson was Acting Commissioner at Chefoo from 1865 to 1868. Drew is presumably E. B. Drew, a young American recently recruited into the Customs Service. "Lay" might have been Walter Thurlow Lay, though he was not posted to Chefoo at this time; or George Tradescant Lay of Barnet & Co., Shanghai; or William Hyde Lay, Acting Vice-Consul at Shanghai from 1863–1864. The Taotai at Chefoo was surnamed P'an.

9. It is possible that Hart was disappointed in the tide surveyor because he knew other more capable people of the same name. George Carter Stent, for example, who would join the Customs in 1869, was the author of Chinese-American dictionaries, translations, etc.

10. George Henry Fitzroy was Commissioner of Customs at Shanghai from 1861 to 1863 and 1865 to 1868. He was appointed Acting Inspector General during Hart's absence in 1866. See Hart's journal entry for 23 March 1866. William G. Howell of Barnet & Co. was a merchant of Shanghai. "Boyce" was probably Captain Boys of the *Barossa,* a corvette sent to Shanghai for the use of Sir Edmund Hornby in making his official visits to each of the open ports in China and Japan.

11. The Messageries gave Hart a very good rate for passages to Marseilles. Their notice in the 1864 *China Directory* quotes passages from Hong Kong for a cabin with one bed at $1,154. At the rate of 715 taels per thousand dollars, his 573 taels would have amounted to about $802.

   Hall & Holtz were storekeepers and ship chandlers of Shanghai.

   On Hart's accounts, see Wright, *Hart,* 283. Account "B" was for fines and confiscations; account "Z" was Hart's personal account. See *The I.G. in Peking,* letter 90.

12. William Baker, who was 1st-class clerk at Tientsin from 1864 to 1866, resigned in October 1866. See also Hart's journal entry for 23 March 1866.

13. F. N. May, who had joined the Customs in 1859, was an Assistant at Foochow under Baron Eugene de Meritens, Commissioner.

14. Brown is presumably H. O. Brown.

15. Saigon, capital of Cochin China, had been captured by the French in 1860.

16. William H. Fittock had been British Vice-Consul at Shanghai.

17. Ching: probably Ch'eng. A blue hat button (*lan-pao-shih*) signified 3rd rank.

    Pae: *p'ai*.

    Chung Kwo: *Chung-kuo*.

18. Hart's journal entries indicate that he could already get by in French, albeit haltingly.

19. In fact, the Pin-ch'un expedition was nothing more than a mission of exploration by a few low-ranking Chinese functionaries. It certainly did not imply a recognition of other nation-states as equals, for China continued to hold on to its Sinocentric tributary view of the world. See Smith, "China's Early Reach Westward." Cf. Hart's lengthy journal entry of 15 July 1866.

20. Kwang-ying was Pin-ch'un's third son.

21. Pulo (Pulau): a Malay term meaning island, was often used with the names of islands in the Malay Archipelago.

22. Hwang-tsin-Wang: Huang ch'in-wang; Prince Huang. One of the 10 sons of the Yung-cheng Emperor (r. 1722–1735). Kuei-liang, father-in-law of Prince Kung, was one of the founding members of the Tsungli Yamen just before his death in 1862. See Hummel, ed., *Eminent Chinese of the Ch'ing Period*, 380–384; 428–430; 915–919, passim. The Tao-kuang Emperor reigned from 1820–1850.

    On degrees of mourning in Chinese society, see Smith, *China's Cultural Heritage*, 65–68. A full 27 months of mourning was the rule for the death of a parent (*chan-ts'ui*). It is not clear why the daughter of Prince Huang observed only 9 months of mourning (*ta-kung*) for her father, especially since she had not yet married. Had she been married, she would have mourned about a year (*tzu-ts'ui*) for the death of a parent.

23. Hart's point was that Pin-ch'un should be given as much status as possible.

24. Galle, capital of Southern Province, Ceylon, port of call on the Indian Ocean. Hart had stopped there in 1854 on his way out to China.

25. For an example of Hart's inability to "illustrate my opinions" in conversation with Dick, see his journal entry for 20 December 1863 (chapter 2).

26. The references to the "proposed 'Reform'" pertain to the Second

Reform Bill, which eventually passed in August 1867 after being vigorously discussed during the summer of 1866. Workers were demanding voting reform, which eventually extended the suffrage in both boroughs and counties, increasing the electorate from roughly 1 million to 2 million.

27. George Canning had been a member of a Liberal Cabinet in 1822 and succeeded to the Prime Ministership in 1827, but died soon after.

28. Sir Francis Palgrave (1788–1861), an historian famous for his antiquarian studies, was best known for the 4-volume *History of Normandy and England* (1851–1864). He was also the author of a *Handbook for Travellers to Northern Italy.*

29. The Rev. Andrew Patton Happer was a medical missionary at Canton; his son, also named Andrew, would enter the Customs Service in 1879.

30. Aden, once the capital and port of South Yemen, was held from 1839 to 1937 by Britain and governed as a part of India.

31. "Norris" may be *Lorna* (see Hart's journal entry for 20 April). Hart's handwriting is especially cramped in the journal entries for his period of leave, making unfamiliar names especially difficult to decipher.

32. The Suez Canal was not opened until 1869. Up to that time, travelers went overland from Suez to Cairo, and thence to Alexandria for a ship to Mediterranean ports.

33. W. Schmidt was connected with the firm of Fletcher & Co. of Queen's Road East, Hong Kong.

34. Mt. Horeb or Mt. Sinai was where, according to the Bible, Moses received the Law; located in the Gebel Musa on the Sinai peninsula.

35. The expressions *chin-shih wen-tzu* and *chung-ting-wen* both refer to ancient forms of Chinese writing. The study of inscriptions taken from Shang and Chou dynasty stones and bronze artifacts such as bells (*chung*) and cauldrons (*ting*) was particularly well developed in Ch'ing times. Hart has miswritten the character *ting.*

36. Ferdinand de Lesseps, a French engineer, was in charge of work on the Suez Canal. Abdel Kader was a well-known Arab leader in Algeria, who died in 1883.

37. Messina: a city in northeast Sicily, on the strait of the same name which separates Sicily from Italy. Reggio was the city opposite, on the toe of Italy. Scylla and Charybdis were presumably two landforms in the Straits of Messina representing the mythical figures of the same name.

38. The Strait of Bonifacio runs between the islands of Corsica and Sardinia. Magdalena Island is at the mouth of the Strait. Giuseppe Garibaldi, in whose guerrilla forces Frederick T. Ward once reportedly fought before he formed the Ever-Victorious Army in China, had captured Naples and Sicily in 1859, thereby contributing to the unification of Italy.

39. George Hughes was on leave from his post at Amoy, where he was Commissioner from 1864 to 1875. Charles Hannen had been Commissioner at Chefoo 1863–1864 and would return this year as Commissioner at Kiukiang. Pin-ch'un's diary records visits on 18 May from all three of these commissioners and Hart, each of whom, Pin-ch'un noted, was "on leave" (*kao-chia*). Charles Gordon, who saw Hart on 5 May, also visited with Pin-ch'un on 18 May—the same day Pin-ch'un saw Hughes and Dick. See Pin-ch'un, *Ch'eng-ch'a pi-chi*, 24a, 26a.

40. Robert Hart was the eldest of a family of 10 children. The next in age was Mary, a year younger than he (1836–1916) and married to James Maze, linen merchant of Lisburn. Geoffrey (1856–1884) was the youngest, born two years after Robert left for China, and now only 10; James Henry ("Jamie"; 1846–1902) was now 20 and looking for a career, which Robert would soon provide. Cassie was Hart's younger sister Anne Marie Catherine (1848–1922), who would have been only 18 at the time. Another younger sister, Charlotte ("Cha"; 1842–1868) was then 24.

41. From 1846 to 1850 Hart had attended the Wesleyan Connexional School in Dublin, later called Wesley College.

42. Andrews: Professor Thomas Andrews was Vice-President of the Queen's University and Professor of Chemistry, with whom Hart had studied that science for at least a year.

43. In 1836, a year after Robert Hart's birth, his parents had moved to Milltown, where his father, Henry Hart, in partnership with John Smyth, ran a small distillery. When that burned down, the Harts returned to Portadown, where his father became an employee in the Old Distillery, owned by two brothers, William and David Hutcheson. This firm, however, went into bankruptcy in 1843, and Henry Hart became manager of a distillery built by Hercules Bradshaw, near Hillsborough—a fair-sized enterprise, employing over 40 men. See Wright, *Hart*, 162–163. It was probably to this latter business that Robert in 1866 went to visit old friends.

The Miss Moorheads were Maggie and Mary, the daughters of long-time Hart family friends from Hillsborough. Hart had previously corresponded with both of the daughters, as well as the two Moorhead sons, Robbie and Henry. See *Entering China's Service*, 223, 228, and 357, note 75. Three Moorheads would eventually find careers in the Customs: first, the father, R. B. Moorhead, who went out to China in 1868, and then his two sons in the 1880s—another instance of Hart's tendency to find places for family and friends.

44. H. Dent: Henry and John Dent were merchants in charge of Dent & Co., Shanghai.

Webster may have been J. A. Webster, who had been in the Consular Service in China since 1856, but would be dismissed in 1868. On the other hand, the Webster whom Hart saw four days later he identified as "O.B.C." (Oriental Banking Corporation) Webster.

E. Waller was a merchant of Tientsin.

45. The Paynes may have been the family of Rowland H. Payne, who had been 3rd Assistant in the Customs at Amoy, but who had died in September 1863. There was also a W. N. Payne, who had been 1st Assistant at the British Consulate in Canton.

46. The Kings would seem to have been related by marriage to Hart's secretary, Stuart Man. Paul H. King, Man's nephew, was to join the Customs in 1874.

47. James Webster had been acting agent for the Oriental Banking Corporation (O.B.C.) in Shanghai.

48. Laurence Oliphant, author of *Elgin's Mission to China and Japan* (1859), had been Lord Elgin's secretary.

    Ninian Crawford was in the firm of Lane, Crawford & Co., ship chandlers, of Shanghai.

    Lay: Horatio Nelson Lay.

    Edmund Hammond had been Under-Secretary in the Foreign Office when Hart went to London in 1854 for his interview before leaving for China.

    A later member of the Alston family, Sir B. F. Alston, was British Minister to China in the early 1920s. Since the Alston whom Hart saw was from the Foreign Office, it would seem that this was a family of career diplomats.

49. Captain Charles Stewart Forbes had commanded the *Keangsoo*, flagship of the Lay-Osborn Flotilla. In November 1865 Forbes, who had also traveled to Japan, provided Hart with a memorandum on Chinese affairs in which he gave estimates for the cost of gunboats suitable for use in China. According to Stanley Wright, Hart saw a good deal of Forbes in London during 1866, although Hart mentions him only two or three times in his diary. See Wright, *Hart*, 298.

    Franz Wilzer had resigned as Commissioner of Customs at Tientsin in 1864, but continued to carry out occasional personal tasks for Hart. His son, A. H., joined the Customs Service in 1887.

    Kahn: Possibly Julius Kahn, merchant, of Reiss & Co., Hong Kong.

50. Lord Clarendon was the British Foreign Secretary.

51. Sir John Francis Davis had been appointed in 1833 as 3rd Superintendent of Trade for British subjects in China; on the death of Lord Napier by malaria in 1834, he succeeded to the chief superintendency. He had been for many years in China with the East India Company, and was one of the few foreigners at that time who had studied the Chinese language.

52. "The Baron" was Eugene de Meritens.

53. James Duncan Campbell, whom Hart had already met when he was in China with Lay as Chief Secretary and Auditor, and who would return to China on the same ship with Hart and his bride, had been in England for two years recovering from an accident which broke

his thigh. For Hart's long correspondence with Campbell, who served as the I.G.'s London agent from 1868 to 1907, see *The I.G. in Peking.*

54. Charles Hannen did not quite meet Hart's deadline; he was Commissioner at Kiukiang from 6 December 1866 to 17 September 1867.

55. Ravarnet (which Hart usually spelled Ravarnette) was the family home of Hart's father, Henry, after 1864.

56. From 31 May to 5 June is a fairly rapid courtship, but both were ready for the event. Robert Hart, as we have seen, came home determined on finding a bride; and Hester Jane Bredon was craving a wider world than Portadown. See also Hart's entry of 11 June.

57. See Appendix B for Hart's letter of the same date to E. C. Bowra of the Pin-ch'un Mission.

58. Aunt Edgar: One of Hart's mother's sisters, perhaps the wife of Richard Edgar. See *Entering China's Service*, 3, 84, and 133.

59. Thomas Shillington: ? See ibid., 138.

60. Dr. Bredon died on 16 May, and so now it was up to the eldest brother, Robert E. Bredon, to give the official consent for the family. He would later be in the Customs Service himself, and indeed succeeded Hart briefly as I.G.

61. Willie Aicken was the son of the Dr. John Aicken in whose house Hart had boarded during part of his time at Queen's College.

62. "The past" to which Hart refers concerns his relationship with the Chinese woman Ayaou, by whom he had 3 children. In 1866, before leaving for home, he had sent his "three wards," as he called them, to be in the charge of the wife of the bookkeeper at Smith, Elder & Co., with whom he did business.

63. Sir Macdonald Stephenson, an expert on railroads, was the author of *Railways in Turkey* (1859).

W. A. Rawlinson, who had joined the Customs in 1863, would be "permitted to resign" in August 1871.

64. Wesley Guard was to marry Hart's sister Charlotte, "Cha."

65. Athlone was an urban district on the Shannon, in north central Ireland, a center for salmon fisheries and for the manufacture of woolen and linen goods. It had been stormed in 1691 by William of Orange. Hart mentions the celebrations of the "Orangemen" in his journal entry of 12 July.

66. Professor George Lille Craik, a literary critic and historian, had held the Chair of English Literature and Modern History in Hart's day at the Queen's College.

67. James Maze was Robert Hart's brother-in-law; Mary, Hart's sister. James was also the father of Frederick W. Maze, who later became I.G.

68. K'e-ma tseih: *ch'i-ma tsei*; note 6 above.

tsieh: *tsei*; as above, bandits.

69. For the Orangemen, see note 64 above. The term refers generally to the Protestant Irish, especially of Ulster.
70. Perhaps Hart's transactions had to do with establishing a fund for Hessie.
71. While he was in England, Lay had been awarded (on his own application, it turned out) the honor of C.B. (Companion of the Bath). Hart seems obviously to have been envious.
72. Robert Hart Maze joined the Customs Service from 1884 to 1897, when he resigned.
73. Guinwik is Wigtown, across the North Channel of the Irish Sea from Belfast.
74. Professor Brazier seems to have been a family friend, or possibly he had been connected with the Queen's College while Hart was there. Typically, Hart provided careers for the three sons—James Russell, Henry Woodhouse, and William—who all entered the Customs Service beginning with James in 1878. Hart was also to be godfather to James's second child.
75. Mrs. White was presumably the wife of F. W. White, then Commissioner of Customs at Takow.
76. Winchester's father was probably parent of the British Consul, Charles Winchester, whom Hart had known in Ningpo. See Wright, *Hart*, 137–139.
77. Meadow's children: the children of John Meadows, younger brother of the better-known British Consular official Thomas Taylor Meadows. Hart had known both men in China.
78. Alfred E. Hippisley would join the Customs in October 1867.
79. Trinity House: government building housing the lighthouse administration.
    Cartwright: brother of William Cartwright.
80. Thomas Adkins was a British consular official. He would become Vice-Consul at Shanghai on his return to China.
81. Penge is an urban district in Kent, 6 miles south of London, and part of Greater London.
82. A. A. Billequin would continue as Professor of Chemistry at the T'ung-wen kuan until 1893. He became the author of a chemistry text and a Franco-Chinese dictionary, as well as the translator of the Code Napoleon into Chinese.
83. A. Mouillesaux de Bernieres joined the Customs in April 1867. He appears in the *Service Lists* as A. Mouillesaux until 1880, and after that as A. M. de Bernieres.
84. W. Schmidt was connected with the firm of Fletcher & Co. in Hong Kong.
85. L. Cliquet and J. H. Gibbs had both been clerks in the Customs at Shanghai.

CHAPTER ELEVEN – PERSPECTIVES AND HYPOTHESES

1. See, for example, journal entries for 16 February 1868, 18 April 1869, and 4 January 1875.
2. See Smith, *Mercenaries and Mandarins*, 192–193. For Wade's views on taxation as a problem of Central government authority, consult Michie, *Englishman in China*, II, 164; also his detailed memorandum of December 1868 in *Correspondence Respecting the Revision of the Treaty of Tientsin* (BPP, China, no. 5, 1871), pp. 429–467, esp. p. 444. Cf. Kwang-Ching Liu, "The Limits of Regional Power."
3. For Restoration critiques, consult Mary Wright, *The Last Stand*, 167–168. Western attacks on the system were incessant, as the negotiations over the Alcock Convention indicate. See notes 10–12 below.
4. We have also not come across an English version of Wade's "New Proposals," although we have not searched systematically for one. James Cooley's study of Wade, *T. F. Wade in China: Pioneer in Global Diplomacy 1842–1882*, cites only the Chinese text in his discussion of the Wade memorandum.
5. Knight Biggerstaff, "The Secret Correspondence of 1867–1868" in Biggerstaff, *Some Early Chinese Steps toward Modernization*, 54–68. See also Mary Wright, *The Last Stand*, 271–277. Hart's journal entry of 28 October 1865 makes it clear that the memo was a means of acquainting provincial officials with the difficulties involved in the Yamen's management of China's foreign relations.
6. Michie, *Englishman in China*, II, 164.
7. See, for example, the proposals by the Tientsin foreign community in *Correspondence Respecting the Revision of the Treaty of Tientsin* (BPP, China, no. 5, 1871), 87–90. Hart's emphasis on moderation is reflected in his "Note on Chinese Matters," 30 June 1869, included as an appendix in F. W. Williams, *Anson Burlingame and the First Chinese Mission to Foreign Powers*, 285–298. Cf. J. Ross Browne's response in ibid., 298–314 and the memorandum by Wade cited in note 2 above.
8. *Correspondence Respecting the Revision of the Treaty of Tientsin* (BPP, China, no. 5, 1871), 93, 97, and 190–193.
9. Michie, *Englishman in China*, II, 213; Wright, *Hart*, 377–379, 392, note 59; Hart journals, 16 January 1868.
10. Mary Wright, *The Last Stand*, 287–288. For the negotiations, see BPP, China. No. 5 (1871), 187, 190–213, 218–20, 222–23. Cf. Wright, *Hart*, 379–380; Michie, *Englishman in China*, II, 210–222.
11. Journals, 17 September 1868; Mary Wright, *The Last Stand*, 286–291.
12. On the effect of the Burlingame Mission, see Smith, "China's Early Reach Westward," esp. 102–103. On the negotiating process, aside from Hart's own reflections in his journal, consult Mary Wright, *The Last Stand*, 279–294, 390, note 132; also Michie, 2, 160–166.
13. Mary Wright, *The Last Stand*, 290–293.

14. *IWSM, T'ung-chih,* 69: 24a–b. Morse, *International Relations,* III, 470–471 lists the many honors Hart received from both the Chinese and foreign governments over the years.

15. For King's critical evaluation of the I.G. see *In the Chinese Customs Service,* 237–247. On the von Gumpach case, consult Wright, *Hart,* 335–348.

16. See for example, *LWCK,* Memorials, 6: 53a–b; *IWSM, T'ung-chih,* 55: 8a. Hart's journal of 16 April 1867 suggests that Li was not entirely off mark. The Chinese, he writes, "use us just so long as they see we suit their purposes . . . [and] we must just see that they pay us properly for the works we effect."

17. Smith, *Mercenaries and Mandarins,* 188.

18. Journals, 5 February 1868; 2 January 1872; 3 September 1874; 4 January 1875.

19. *IWSM, T'ung-chih,* 55: 8a. On Hart's pro-Chinese sympathies, see *Entering China's Service,* 331–332. The issue of changing to Chinese clothing and settling in China as a Chinese subject first appears in his journals on 18 October 1864. For historical background, consult Smith, "Employment of Foreign Military Talent."

20. Journals, 16 July 1867.

21. Cf. Smith, *Mercenaries and Mandarins,* 181.

22. For some recent appraisals, see Ch'en Shih-ch'i, *Chung-kuo chin-tai hai-kuan shih wen-t'i;* Lu Han-chao, *Ho-te chuan;* and Wang Ching-yu, *Ho-te yü chin-tai Chung-Hsi kuan-hsi;* Ch'iu K'o, *Chü-nei p'ang-kuan che-Ying-jen Ho-te yü Chang-kuo chintai wai-chiao.* Cf. Hu Sheng, *Ti-kuo chu-i yü Chung-kuo cheng-chih,* passim, and Hai-kuan tsung-shu yen-chiu shih, ed. *Ti-kuo chu-i yü Chung-kuo hai-kuan.* Other opinions on Hart may be found in the Proceedings of the First International Conference on the Chinese Maritime Customs (Hong Kong, 30 November–2 December 1988), forthcoming.

23. Significantly, the problems of bureaucratic factionalism, central government versus provincial power, inefficiency, and fear of over-reliance on foreign experts and foreign technology faced by Hart and his supporters in the 19th century remain very much alive in contemporary China. Richard P. Suttmeier points out, for example, that China's political system continues to be afflicted by bureaucratic rivalries and "has yet to find 'the right formula' for the relationship between centralization and decentralization of its political and administrative institutions." Furthermore, he identifies widespread problems of insecurity and mistrust in China, as well as "a powerful unresolved tension . . . between the perception of the technological superiority of . . . foreign technology and the belief that China should be able to provide all or most of these systems itself." This "technological nationalism," which has both political and psychological overtones, "has not solved the problem of reliance on foreign science and technology; it has probably

made it worse." See Suttmeier, "Science, Technology, and China's Political Future—A Framework for Analysis," in Simon and Goldman, eds., *Science and Technology in Post-Mao China*, esp. 378–379.

Bibliography

Arlington, L. C. and William Lewisohn. *In Search of Old Peking.* Peking, Henry Vetch, 1935.

Banno, Masatake. *China and the West, 1858–1861: The Origins of the Tsungli Yamen.* Cambridge, Harvard University Press, 1964.

Bastid, Marianne. "The Structure of the Financial Institutions of the State in Late Qing." In Stuart Schram, ed., *The Scope of State Power in China.* Hong Kong, Chinese University Press, 1985.

Bennett, Adrian A. *John Fryer: The Introduction of Western Science and Technology into Nineteenth Century China.* Cambridge, East Asian Research Center, Harvard University, 1967.

———. *Young J. Allen, Missionary Journalist.* Chicago, University of Chicago Press, 1983.

Biggerstaff, Knight. *The Earliest Modern Government Schools in China.* Ithaca, Cornell University Press, 1963.

———. *Some Early Chinese Steps toward Modernization.* San Francisco, Chinese Materials Center, Inc., 1975.

BPP. See Great Britain, House of Commons. British Parliamentary Papers (or British Sessional Papers).

Boulger, Demetrius, C. *The Life of Gordon.* London, T. Fisher Unwin, 1896.

———. *The Life of Sir Halliday Macartney.* London, John Lane, 1908.

Bowra, Edward Charles Macintosh. Manuscript diary. In the Library of the School for Oriental and African Studies, University of London.

Bredon, Juliet. *Sir Robert Hart: The Romance of a Great Career.* London, Hutchison & Co., 1909.

———. *Peking: A Historical and Intimate Description of Its Chief Places of Interest.* London, T. Werner Laurie, Ltd., 1924.

Bruner, Katherine F., John K. Fairbank, and Richard J. Smith, eds. *Entering China's Service: Robert Hart's Journals, 1854–1863.* Cambridge, Council on East Asian Studies, Harvard University, 1986.

Cady, John F. *The Roots of French Imperialism in Eastern Asia.* Ithaca, Cornell University Press, 1954.

Carlson, Ellsworth C. *The Foochow Missionaries.* Cambridge, East Asian Research Center, Harvard University, 1974.

Chang Ch'i-yun, et al., eds. *Ch'ing-shih* (History of the Ch'ing dynasty). Taipei: Kuo-fang yen-chiu yuan, 1961.

Chang Te-ch'ang. *Ch'ing-chi i-ko ching-kuan ti sheng-huo* (The life of a late Ch'ing metropolitan official). Hong Kong, Chung-wen ta-hsueh, 1970.

Chang Yu-fa, "Foochow ch'uan-ch'ang chih k'ai-ch'uang chi-ch'i ch'u-ch'i fa-chan" (The founding and early development of the Foochow Shipyard), *Chung-yang yen-chiu-yuan chin-tai-shih yen-chiu-so chi-k'an* 2 (June, 1971).

Ch'en Shih-ch'i, *Chung-kuo chin-tai hai-kuan shih wen-t'i ch'u-shen* (A preliminary investigation into questions regarding the history of China's recent maritime customs). Peking, Chung-kuo chan-wang ch'u-pan she, 1987.

Ch'en Wen-chin, "Ch'ing-tai chih Tsung-li Ya-men chi ch'i ching-fei, 1861–1884" (The Tsungli Yamen and its financial support, 1861–1884), *Chung-kuo chin-tai ching-chi shih yen-chiu chi-k'an* 1.1 (November, 1932).

Ch'ien, C. S. (Chung-shu), "An Early Chinese Version of Longfellow's 'Psalm of Life,'" *Philobiblon* 2.2 (March 1848).

Ch'ien Shih-fu, ed. *Ch'ing-chi chung-yao chih-kuan nien-piao* (A chronological chart of important officials of the Ch'ing period). Peking, Chung-hua shu-chü, 1959.

Ch'in-ting ku-chin t'u-shu chi-ch'eng (Imperially approved complete collection of writings and illustrations, past and present). Peking, 1726; Taipei reprint, Ting-wen shu-chü, 1977.

China Directory.

China Mail.

China, The Maritime Customs: Documents Illustrative of the Origin, Development, and Activities of the Chinese Customs Service. 7 vols. Shanghai, Inspectorate General of Customs, 1941.

China no. 1 (1865): Foreign Customs Establishment in China. London, Harrison and Sons, 1865.

Ching Tun-fu. *Hsiao-ku-t'ang wen-chi* (Collected prose of the Sounds of the Past Hall). Shanghai, 1868.

Ch'iu K'o, *Chü-nei p'ang-kuan che—Ying-jen Ho-te yü Chung-kuo chin-tai wai-chiao* (An outside observer on the inside—The Englishman Robert Hart and China's modern foreign relations). Sian, Shen-hsi jen-min ch'u-pan she, 1990.

Ch'ou-pan i-wu shih-mo (Complete record of the management of barbarian affairs), Hsien-feng and T'ung-chih reigns. Peiping, Palace Museum photolithograph, 1930. Abbrev. *IWSM*

Chung-kuo k'o-hsueh yuan chin-tai-shih yen-chiu-so, comp. *Yang-wu yun-tung* (The foreign affairs movement). Shanghai, Jen-min ch'u-pan she, 1961). Abbrev. *YWYT.*

Clive, John. *Macaulay: The Shaping of the Historian.* New York, Knopf, 1973.

Clyde, Paul Hibbert. *United States Policy Toward China: Diplomatic and Public Documents 1839–1939 Selected and Arranged.* Durham, Duke University Press, 1940.

Coates, P. D. *The China Consuls: British Consular Officers, 1843–1943.* Hong Kong, Oxford University Press, 1985.

Cohen, Paul. *Between Tradition and Modernity: Wang T'ao and Reform in Late Ch'ing China.* Cambridge, Harvard University Press, 1974.

—— and John E. Schrecker, eds., *Reform in Nineteenth-Century China.* Cambridge, Council on East Asian Studies, Harvard University, 1976.

——. "Christian Missions and Their Impact in 1900." In J. K. Fairbank, ed., *The Cambridge History of China,* Vol. 10 (Late Ch'ing, 1800–1911. Part 1). London, New York, and Melbourne, Cambridge University Press, 1978.

Cooley, James. *T. F. Wade in China: Pioneer in Global Diplomacy 1842–1882.* Leiden, E. J. Brill, 1981.

Covell, Ralph, *W. A. P. Martin: Pioneer of Progress in China.* Washington, D.C., Christian University Press, 1978.

Correspondence Respecting the Revision of the Treaty of Tientsin. Originally published as BPP, China, no. 5 (1871); reprinted in one volume by the Chinese Materials Center, Inc., San Francisco, 1975; original pagination.

Curwen, Charles C., *Taiping Rebel: The Deposition of Li Hsiu-ch'eng.* Cambridge, Cambridge University Press, 1977.

Dean, Britten. "Sino-British Diplomacy in the 1860s: The Establishment of the British Concession at Hankow," *Harvard Journal of Asiatic Studies* 32 (1972).

——. *China and Great Britain: The Diplomacy of Commercial Relations, 1860–1864.* Cambridge, East Asian Research Center, Harvard University, 1974.

Dennett, Tyler. *Americans in Eastern Asia.* New York, Barnes and Noble, 1941.

Drage, Charles. *Servants of the Dragon Throne.* London, Peter Dawnay, 1966.

Drake, Fred W. *China Charts the World: Hsu Chi-yü and his Geography of 1848.* Cambridge, East Asian Research Center, Harvard University, 1975.

Dreyer, Edward L. *Early Ming China: A Political History, 1355–1435.* Stanford, Stanford University Press, 1982.

Eastman, Lloyd E. *Family, Field and Ancestors: Constancy and Change in China's Social and Economic History, 1550–1949.* New York, Oxford University Press, 1988.

Elvin, Mark and G. William Skinner, eds. *The Chinese City between Two Worlds.* Stanford, Stanford University Press, 1974.

Fairbank, John King. *Trade and Diplomacy on the China Coast: The Opening of the*

Treaty Ports 1842–1854. Cambridge, Harvard University Press, 1953; Stanford University reprint, 1964.

———, ed. *Chinese Thought and Institutions.* Chicago, The University of Chicago Press, 1957.

———. "The Creation of the Treaty System." In John K. Fairbank, ed. *The Cambridge History of China,* Vol. 10 (Late Ch'ing, 1800–1911. Part 1). London, New York, and Melbourne, Cambridge University Press, 1978.

———, ed. *The Cambridge History of China,* Vol. 10 (Late Ch'ing, 1800–1911. Part 1). London, New York, and Melbourne, Cambridge University Press, 1978.

———, Katherine Frost Bruner, and Elizabeth MacLeod Matheson, eds. *The I.G. in Peking: Letters of Robert Hart, Chinese Maritime Customs, 1868–1907.* 2 vols. Cambridge, Harvard University Press, 1975.

———, and Kwang-Ching Liu, eds. *The Cambridge History of China,* Vol. 11 (Late Ch'ing, 1800–1911, Part 2). London, New York, and Melbourne, Cambridge University Press, 1980.

———, and Ssu-yü Teng, *Ch'ing Administration: Three Studies.* Cambridge, Harvard University Press, 1961.

Feng Kuei-fen. *Chiao-pin-lu k'ang-i* (Protests from the Chiao-pin Study). Taipei, Wen-hai reproduction of 1898 edition, 1971.

F.O. See Great Britain, Public Record Office. Foreign Office General Correspondence, China (F.O. 17); Consular and Embassy Archives (F.O. 228).

Foster Hall, B. *The Chinese Maritime Customs: An International Service, 1854–1950.* National Maritime Museum, Maritime Monographs and Reports, No. 26, 1977.

Fox, Grace. *British Admirals and Chinese Pirates, 1832–1869.* London, Kegan, Paul, Trench, Trubner & Co., 1940.

Freeman-Mitford. A. B. *The Attaché at Peking.* London, Macmillan, 1900.

Frodsham, J. D. *The First Chinese Embassy to the West: The Journals of Kuo Sung-t'ao, Liu Hsi-hung and Chang Te-i.* Oxford, Clarendon Press, 1974.

Fu Tsung-mao. *Ch'ing-chih lun wen-chi* (Collected works on Ch'ing institutions). Taipei, T'ai-wan shang-wu yin-shu kuan, 1977.

Gerson, Jack J. *Horatio Nelson Lay and Sino-British Relations 1854–1864.* Cambridge, East Asian Research Center, Harvard University, 1972.

Gordon Papers. Manuscript Division, British Museum Library.

Great Britain, House of Commons. British Parliamentary Papers (or British Sessional Papers). Abbrev. BPP.

———. Public Record Office. Foreign Office General Correspondence, China (F.O. 17); Consular and Embassy Archives (F.O. 228).

Gregory, J. S. *Great Britain and the Taipings.* New York, Praeger, 1969.

Hai-kuan ts'ung-shu yen-chiu shih, ed. *Ti-kuo chu-i yü Chung-kuo hai-kuan* (Imperialism and the Chinese maritime customs). Peking, K'o-hsueh ch'u-pan she, 1957–1959.

Hake, A. E. *Events in the Taeping Rebellion.* London, W. H. Allen, 1891.

Hao, Yen-p'ing. *The Comprador in Nineteenth Century China: Bridge between East and West.* Cambridge, Harvard University Press, 1970.

——— and Wang Erh-min, "Changing Views of Western Relations, 1840–95." In John King Fairbank and Kwang-Ching Liu, eds. *The Cambridge History of China,* Vol. 11 (Late Ch'ing, 1800–1911, Part 2). London, New York, and Melbourne, Cambridge University Press, 1980.

Holcombe, Chester. *The Real Chinaman.* New York, Dodd, Mead & Co., 1895.

Hornby, Sir Edmund. *Sir Edmund Hornby: An Autobiography.* Boston and New York, Houghton Mifflin, 1928.

Hsia Ching-lin. *The Status of Shanghai: A Historical Review of the International Settlement.* Shanghai, Kelly and Walsh, 1929.

Hsiang Ta, et al., eds. *T'ai-p'ing t'ien-kuo* (The Taiping Heavenly Kingdom). Peking, Shen-chou kuo-kuang she, 1952. Abbrev. *TPTK.*

Hsiao I-shan. *Ch'ing-tai t'ung-shih* (General history of the Ch'ing dynasty). Taipei, Shang-wu yin-shu kuan, 1962.

Hsiao, Kung-chuan. *Rural China: Imperial Control in the Nineteenth Century.* Seattle, University of Washington Press, 1967.

Hsieh, Pao-Chao. *The Government of China (1644–1911).* Baltimore, The Johns Hopkins University Press, 1925.

Hsü, Immanuel C. Y. *China's Entrance into the Family of Nations: The Diplomatic Phase, 1858–1880.* Cambridge, Harvard University Press, 1960.

Hu, Hsien Chin. "The Chinese Concept of 'Face'." *American Anthropologist,* n.s. 46 (1944).

Hu Sheng. *Ti-kuo chu-i yü Chung-kuo cheng-chih* (Imperialism and Chinese politics). Peking, 1952. In English translation as *Imperialism and Chinese Politics.* Peking, Foreign Language Press, 1955.

Huang, Philip C. C. *The Peasant Economy and Social Change in North China.* Stanford, Stanford University Press, 1985.

Hummel, Arthur W., ed. *Eminent Chinese of the Ch'ing Period (1644–1912).* 2 vols. Washington, U.S. Government Printing Office, 1943.

I-hsin (Prince Kung). *Lo-tao t'ang wen-ch'ao* (Essays from the Hall of Delighting in the Way). Peking, n.d. (1867).

Inspector General's Circulars, First Series, 1861–1875. Shanghai, Statistical Department of the Inspectorate General, 1879.

Irick, Robert Lee. "Ch'ing Policy toward the Coolie Trade, 1847–1878." PhD dissertation. Harvard University, 1971.

IWSM. See *Ch'ou-pan i-wu shih-mo.*

Jen (Chien) Yu-wen. *The Taiping Revolutionary Movement.* New Haven and London, Yale University Press, 1973.

Jones, Susan Mann. "Finance in Ningpo: the 'Ch'ien chuang,' 1750–1880." In W. E. Willmott, ed., *Economic Organization in Chinese Society.* Stanford, Stanford University Press, 1972. *See also* Mann, Susan.

———. "The Ningpo Pang and Financial Power at Shanghai." In Mark Elvin and G. William Skinner, eds., *The Chinese City between Two Worlds.* Stanford, Stanford University Press, 1974.

Kennedy, Thomas L., *The Arms of Kiangnan: Modernization of the Chinese Ordnance Industry 1860–1895.* Boulder, Westview Press, 1978.

King, Frank H. H. *Money and Monetary Policy in China 1845–1895.* Cambridge, Harvard University Press, 1965.

King, Paul. *In the Chinese Customs Service: A Personal Record of Forty-seven Years.* London, Heath Cranton, 1924.

Kingsmill, Thomas. "Retrospect of Events in China and Japan during the Year 1865," *Journal of the North China Branch of the Royal Asiatic Society* 2 (1865).

Kiong, P. Simon. *Quelques mots sur la politesse Chinoise.* Shanghai, Catholic Mission Press, 1906.

Ko Shih-chün, comp. *Huang-ch'ao ching-shih wen hsu-pien* (Continuation of Ch'ing dynasty writings on statecraft). Taipei, Wen-hai facsimile of 1901 edition, 1972).

Kuhn, Philip A., "The Taiping Rebellion." In John K. Fairbank, ed. *The Cambridge History of China,* Vol. 10 (Late Ch'ing, 1800–1911, Part 1). London, New York, and Melbourne, Cambridge University Press, 1978.

Kuo T'ing-i. *T'ai-p'ing t'ien-kuo shih-shih jih-chih* (A daily record of historical events of the Taiping Heavenly Kingdom). Chungking, Shang-wu shu-chü, 1946. Taipei reprint, Shang-wu shu-chü, 1963. Abbrev. *TPTK jih-chih.*

——— and Kwang-Ching Liu, "Self-Strengthening: The Pursuit of Western Technology." In John K. Fairbank, ed. *Cambridge History of China,* Vol. 10 (Late Ch'ing, 1800–1911, Part 1). London, New York, and Melbourne, Cambridge University Press, 1978.

Latourette, Kenneth Scott. *A History of Christian Missions in China.* London, Society for Promoting Christian Knowledge, 1929.

Legge, James. *The Chinese Classics.* 5 vols. 1893–1895. Reprint Taipei, 1966.

Leibo, Steven A., ed. *A Journal of the Chinese Civil War.* Honolulu, University of Hawaii Press, 1985.

———. *Transferring Technology to China: Prosper Giquel and the Self-Strengthening Movement.* Berkeley, Center for Chinese Studies, 1985.

Leung, Yuen-sang, "The Shanghai Taotai: The Linkage Man in a Changing

Society." PhD dissertation. University of California at Santa Barbara, 1980.

Li Hung-chang, *Li Wen-chung-kung ch'üan-chi* (Collected works of Li Hung-chang). Taipei, Wen-hai reproduction of 1908 edition, 1962. Abbrev. *LWCK*.

Li Kuo-ch'i. "Ming-Ch'ing liang-tai ti-fang hsing-cheng chih-tu chung tao ti kung-neng chi ch'i yen-pien" (The function and development of the taotai in the local administrative system of the Ming and Ch'ing dynasties), *Chung-yang yen-chiu-yuan chin-tai-shih yen-chiu-so chi-k'an* 3.1 (1972).

—— et al., eds. *Chung-kuo ti-fang-chih yen-chiu: Ch'ing-tai chi-ts'eng ti-fang-kuan jen-shih shan-ti hsien-hsiang chih liang-hua fen-hsi* (Research on Chinese gazetteers: A quantitative analysis of the careers of local officials in the Ch'ing dynasty). Taipei, 1975.

Lindley, A. F. *History of the Ti-Ping Revolution*, London, Day and Co., 1866.

Liu Hsiung-hsiang. *Ch'ing-chi ssu-shih nien chih wai-chaio yü hai-fang* (Forty years of foreign relations and maritime defense in the late Ch'ing period). Chunking, San-yu shu-tien, 1943 [?]).

Liu, Kwang-Ching, *Anglo-American Steamship Rivalry in China, 1862–1874*. Cambridge, Harvard University Press, 1962.

—— . "The Confucian as Patriot and Pragmatist: Li Hung-chang's Formative Years, 1823–1866, *Harvard Journal of Asiatic Studies* 30 (1970).

—— . "The Limits of Regional Power in the Late Ch'ing Period: A Reappraisal," *Ch'ing-hua hsueh-pao*, n.s., 10.2 (July 1974).

—— . "Politics, Intellectual Outlook, and Reform: The T'ung-wen Kuan Controversy of 1867." In Paul A. Cohen and John E. Schrecker, eds. *Reform in Nineteenth-Century China*. Cambridge, East Asian Research Center, Harvard University, 1976.

—— "The Ch'ing Restoration." In John K. Fairbank, ed., *The Cambridge History of China*, Vol. 10 (Late Ch'ing, 1800–1911, Part 1). London, New York, Melbourne, Cambridge University Press, 1978.

—— and Richard J. Smith, "The Military Challenge: The Northwest and the Coast." In John King Fairbank and Kwang-Ching Liu, eds. *The Cambridge History of China*, Vol. 11 (Late Ch'ing, 1800–1911, Part 2). London, New York, and Melbourne, Cambridge University Press, 1980.

Lu Han-chao. *Ho-te chuan* (Biography of Robert Hart). Shanghai, Jen-min ch'u-pan she, 1986.

Lü Shih-ch'iang. "Feng Kuei-feng ti cheng-chih ssu-hsiang" (The political thought of Feng Kuei-fen), *Chung-hua wen-hua fu-hsing yueh-k'an* 4.2 (February, 1971).

LWCK. See Li Hung-chang, *Li Wen-chung-kung ch'üan-chi* (Collected works of Li Hung-chang). Taipei, Wen-hai reproduction of 1908 edition, 1962.

MacGillivray, Donald, ed. *A Century of Protestant Missions in China, 1807–1907.* Shanghai, American Presbyterian Mission Press, 1907.

Mann, Susan. *Local Merchants and the Chinese Bureaucracy, 1750–1950.* Stanford, Stanford University Press, 1987.

Martin, W. A. P. *A Cycle of Cathay or China: South and North with Personal Reminiscences.* New York, Fleming H. Revell Co., 1897.

Maybon, C. B. and J. Fredet, *Histoire de la Concession Française de Changhai.* Paris, Plon, 1927.

Mayers, W. F. *Treaties between the Empire of China and Foreign Powers.* Shanghai, J. Broadhurst Tootal, 1877. Reprinted by Ch'eng-wen Publishing Co., 1966.

——— . *The Chinese Government: A Manual of Chinese Titles, Categorically Arranged and Explained with an Appendix.* Shanghai, Kelly and Walsh, 1897.

——— , N. B. Dennys, and Charles King. *The Treaty Ports of China and Japan: A Complete Guide to the Open Ports of Those Countries, together with Peking, Yedo, Hong Kong and Macao.* London, Trubner and Co.; Hong Kong, A. Shortrede and Co., 1867.

McElderry, Andrea Lee. *Shanghai Old-Style Banks (Ch'ien-chuang) 1800–1935.* Ann Arbor, University of Michigan Center for Chinese Studies, 1976.

Meadows, Thomas Taylor. *The Chinese and Their Rebellions.* London, 1856. Stanford, Academic Reprints, 1958.

——— . *Desultory Notes on the Government and People of China and on the Chinese Language.* London, W. H. Allen & Co., 1847.

Meng, S. M. *The Tsungli Yamen: Its Organization and Functions.* Cambridge, East Asian Research Center, Harvard University, 1962.

Metzger, Thomas. *The Internal Organization of the Ch'ing Bureaucracy.* Cambridge, Harvard University Press, 1973.

Michie, Alexander. *The Englishman in China during the Victorian Era, as Illustrated in the Career of Sir Rutherford Alcock.* 2 vols. Edinburgh, Wm. Blackwood & Sons, 1900.

Min Tu-ki. *National Polity and Local Power: The Transformation of Late Imperial China.* Ed. Philip A. Kuhn and Timothy Brook. Cambridge, Council on East Asian Studies, Harvard University, 1989.

Morse Collection (of Hart's letters to his commissioners). Houghton Library.

Morse, Hosea Ballou. *The Trade and Administration of the Chinese Empire.* Shanghai, Kelly and Walsh, 1908.

——— . *The International Relations of the Chinese Empire:* Vol. I: The Period of Conflict (1834–1860); Vol. II: The Period of Submission (1861–1893); Vol. III: The Period of Subjection (1894–1911). London, Longmans, Green & Co., 1910–1918.

——— . *The Chronicles of the East India Company Trading to China 1635–1834.* 4 vols. Oxford, Clarendon Press, 1926. Vol. 5 for 1742–1774, 1929.

Naquin, Susan, and Evelyn Rawski. *Chinese Society in the Eighteenth Century.* New Haven, Yale University Press, 1987.

Nevius, John L. *China and the Chinese.* New York, Harper & Brothers, 1898.

Ng, Chin-keong, *Trade and Society: The Amoy Network on the China Coast 1683–1735.* Singapore, Singapore University Press, 1983.

North China Herald.

Ocko, Jonathan K. *Bureaucratic Reform in Provincial China: Ting Jih-ch'ang in Restoration Kiangsu, 1867–1870.* Cambridge, Council on East Asian Studies, Harvard University, 1983.

Parker, E. H. *China's Past and Present.* London, Chapman and Hall, 1903.

Parker, Jason H. "The Rise and Decline of I-hsin, Prince Kung, 1858–1865: A Study of the Interaction of Politics and Ideology in Late Imperial China." PhD dissertation. Princeton University, 1979.

Pin-ch'un. *Ch'eng-ch'a pi-chi* (Notes on a mission of investigation). From the Hart collection, Queen's University Library. Belfast. Prefaces dated 1869.

Polacheck, James, "Gentry Hegemony: Soochow in the T'ung-chih Restoration." In Frederic Wakeman Jr. and Carolyn Grant, eds., *Conflict and Control in Late Imperial China.* Berkeley, University Of California Press, 1976.

——— . "Literati Groups and Literati Politics in Early Nineteenth Century China." PhD dissertation, University of California, Berkeley, 1977.

Pong, David, "Confucian Patriotism and the Destruction of the Woo-sung Railway," *Modern Asian Studies* 7.4 (1973).

——— . "The Vocabulary of Change: Reformist Ideas of the 1860's and 1870's." In David Pong and Edmund S. K. Fung, eds., *Ideal and Reality: Social and Political Change in Modern China.* University Press of America, 1985.

——— . "Keeping the Foochow Navy Yard Afloat: Government Finance and China's Early Defence Industry, 1866–75," *Modern Asian Studies* 21.1 (1987).

——— , and Edmund S. K. Fung, eds. *Ideal and Reality: Social and Political Change in Modern China.* University Press of America, 1985.

Porter, Jonathan. "Foreign Affairs (Yang-wu) Expertise in the Late Ch'ing: The Career of Chao Lieh-wen," *Modern Asian Studies* 13.3 (1979).

Rankin, Mary B. *Elite Activism and Political Transformation in China: Zhejiang Province, 1865–1911.* Stanford, Stanford University Press, 1986.

Rennie, David Field. *Peking and the Pekingese.* 2 vols. London, John Murray 1865.

Ring, Martin. "The Burgevine Case and Extrality in China, 1863–1866," *Papers on China* 22A (May 1969).

Rowe, William T. *Hankow: Commerce and Society in a Chinese City, 1796–1889.* 2 vols. Stanford, Stanford University Press, 1984.

———. *Hankow: Conflict and Community in a Chinese City, 1790–1895.* Stanford, Stanford University Press, 1989.

Simon, Denis Fred and Merle Goldman, eds. *Science and Technology in Post-Mao China.* Cambridge, Council on East Asian Studies, 1989.

Smith, Richard J. "China's Employment of Foreign Military Talent: Chinese Tradition and Late Ch'ing Practice," *Journal of the Hong Kong Branch of the Royal Asiatic Society* 15 (1975).

———. "Foreign-Training and China's Self-Strengthening: The Case of Feng-huang-shan, 1864–1873, *Modern Asian Studies* 10.1 (1976).

———. "Reflections on the Comparative Study of Modernization in China and Japan," *Journal of the Hong Kong Branch of the Royal Asiatic Society* 16 (1976).

———. "The Reform of Military Education in Late Ch'ing China, 1842–1895," *Journal of the Hong Kong Branch of the Royal Asiatic Society* 18 (1978).

———. "The 'God from the West': A Chinese Perspective," *Essex Institute Historical Collections* 114.3 (July 1978).

———. *Mercenaries and Mandarins: The Ever-Victorious Army in Nineteenth Century China.* Millwood, N.Y., KTO Press, 1978.

———. "China's Early Reach Westward: The Burlingame Mission, 1867–1870," *Sino-American Relations* 7.3 (Autumn, 1981).

———. *China's Cultural Heritage: The Ch'ing Dynasty, 1644–1912.* Boulder and London, Westview Press, 1983.

———. "'Knowing Fate': Divination in Late Imperial China," *Journal of Chinese Studies* 3.2 (October 1986).

———. "A Note on Qing Dynasty Calendars," *Late Imperial China* 9.1 (June 1988).

Snow, Edgar. *Red Star Over China.* rev. ed. New York, Grove, 1968.

Spector, Stanley, *Li Hung-chang and the Huai Army: A Study in Nineteenth-Century Regionalism.* Seattle, University of Washington Press, 1964.

Spence, Jonathan. *To Change China: Western Advisers in China 1620–1960.* Boston, Little Brown, 1969.

———. "Opium Smoking in Ch'ing China." In Frederick Wakeman, Jr., and Carolyn Grant, eds., *Conflict and Control in Late Imperial China.* Berkeley, University of California Press, 1976.

Stanley, C. John. *Late Ch'ing Finance: Hu Kuang-yung as an Innovator.* Cambridge, East Asian Research Center, Harvard University, 1961.

Suttmeier, Richard P. "Science, Technology, and China's Political Future— A Framework for Analysis." In Denis Fred Simon and Merle Goldman, eds., *Science and Technology in Post-Mao China.* Cambridge, Council on East Asian Studies, Harvard University, 1989.

Teng, Ssu-yü. *The Taiping Rebellion and the Western Powers: A Comprehensive Survey.* Oxford, Oxford University Press, 1971.

—— and John K. Fairbank, comps. *China's Response to the West, A Documentary Survey 1839–1923.* Cambridge, Harvard University Press, 1954. Reprint, New York, Atheneum, 1969.

T'ien Yü-ch'ing, et al., eds. *T'ai-p'ing t'ien-kuo shih-liao* (Historical materials on the Taiping Heavenly Kingdom). Peking, 1950. Abbrev. *TPTK shih-liao.*

Torbert, Preston. *The Imperial Household Department: A Study of Its Organization and Principal Functions, 1662–1796.* Cambridge, East Asian Research Center, Harvard University, 1977.

TPTK. See Hsiang Ta, et al., eds. *T'ai-p'ing t'ien-kuo* (The Taiping Heavenly Kingdom). Peking, Shen-chou kuo-kuang she, 1952.

TPTK jih-chih. See Kuo T'ing-i. *T'ai-p'ing t'ien-kuo shih-shih jih-chih* (A daily record of historical events of the Taiping Heavenly Kingdom). Chungking, Shang-wu shu-chu, 1946. Taipei reprint, Shang-wu shu-chu, 1963.

TPTK shih-liao. See T'ien Yü-ch'ing, et al., eds. *T'ai-p'ing t'ien-kuo shih-liao* (Historical materials on the Taiping Heavenly Kingdom). Peking, 1950.

Tung Hsun. *Huan-tu wo-shu shih lao-jen tzu-ting nien-p'u* (Autobiographical record of the old man of the Study for Returning to Read My Books). 1892. Reprinted in *Nien-p'u ts'ung-shu* (A collection of reprinted chronological biographies). Taipei, Kuang-wen shu-chü, 1971).

——. *Yang-ping chi-lueh* (A short record of foreign troops). Reprinted in Vol. 2 of Hsiang Ta, et al., eds., *T'ai-p'ing t'ien-kuo* (The Taiping Heavenly Kingdom). Peking, Shen-chou kuo-kuang she, 1952.

United States, Department of State. *Papers Relating to Foreign Affairs* (also known as *Foreign Relations of the United States*). Washington, Government Printing Office, 1863–1867.

Wakeman, Frederic, Jr., and Carolyn Grant, eds., *Conflict and Control in Late Imperial China.* Berkeley, University of California Press, 1976.

Wang Chia-chien. "Wen-hsiang tui-yü shih-chü ti jen-shih chi ch'i tzu-ch'iang ssu-hsiang" (Wen-hsiang's understanding of the circumstances of his time and his thoughts regarding self-strengthening), *Kuo-li T'ai-wan shih-fan ta-hsueh li-shih hsueh-pao* 1 (1973).

Wang Ching-yü. *Ho-te yü chin-tai Chung-Hsi kuan-hsi* (Hart and modern Sino-Western relations). Peking, 1987.

Wang Wen-chieh. *Chung-kuo chin-shih shih shang ti chiao-an* (Missionary cases in modern Chinese history). Fukien, Fukien Christian University, 1947.

Wang, Yeh-chien. *Land Taxation in Imperial China 1750–1911.* Cambridge, Harvard University Press, 1973.

Wei, Betty Beh-T'i. *Shanghai: Crucible of Modern China.* Hong Kong, Oxford University Press, 1987.

Wei Hsiu-mei. *Ch'ing-chi chih-kuan piao* (A chart of officials of the late Ch'ing period). Taipei, Chung-yang yen-chiu-yuan chin-tai shih yen-chiu-so, 1977.

Wen-hsiang. *Wen Wen-chung-kung tzu-ting nien-p'u* (Autobiographical record of Wen-hsiang). 1882. In *Nien-p'u ts'ung-shu* (A collection of reprinted chronological biographies). Taipei, Kuang-wen shu-chu, 1971).

Weng T'ung-ho, *Weng T'ung-ho jih-chi p'ai-yin-pen* (Typeset edition of Weng T'ung-ho's diary). Taipei, Ch'eng-wen, 1970.

Wilhelm, Hellmut. "The Scholar's Frustrations: Notes on a Type of Fu." In John K. Fairbank, ed., *Chinese Thought and Institutions.* Chicago, The University of Chicago Press, 1957.

Williams, F. W. *Anson Burlingame and the First Chinese Mission to Foreign Powers.* New York, Scribners, 1912.

Williams, S. Wells. *The Chinese Commercial Guide.* 5th ed. Hong Kong, A. Shortrede and Co., 1863.

Wilson, Andrew. *The "Ever-Victorious Army".* Reprint edition with marginal notes by John Holland: San Francisco, Chinese Materials Center, Inc., 1977. Original edition, London, Blackwood and Sons, 1868.

Woodcock, George. *The British in the Far East.* London, Weidenfeld and Nicolson, 1969.

Wright, Mary Clabaugh. *The Last Stand of Chinese Conservatism: The T'ung-chih Restoration, 1862–1874.* Stanford, Stanford University Press, 1957.

Wright, Stanley F., *Code of Customs Regulations and Procedures.* 2nd ed. Shanghai, Statistical Department of the Inspectorate General of Customs, 1935.

———, *China's Struggle for Tariff Autonomy 1843–1938.* Shanghai, Kelly and Walsh, 1938.

———. *Hart and the Chinese Customs.* Belfast, William Mullen & Son, 1950.

Wu Hsiang-hsiang. *Wan-Ch'ing kung-t'ing shih-chi* (A true account of the late Ch'ing Court). Taipei, Cheng-chung shu-chu, 1961.

Wu Hsu. *Wu Hsu tang-an-chung ti T'ai-p'ing t'ien-kuo shih-liao hsuan-chi* (Selected historical materials on the Taiping Heavenly Kingdom from the archives of Wu Hsu). Peking, San-lien. 1958. Abbrev. *WHTA.*

Wu, Silas. *Communication and Imperial Control in China: The Evolution of the Palace Memorial System, 1693–1795.* Cambridge, Harvard University Press, 1970.

Yang Chia-lo, ed., *Hsin-hsiu Ch'ing-chi shih san-shih-chiu piao* (A newly revised edition of thirty-nine charts [on officials] of the late Ch'ing period). Taipei, Ting-wen shu-chu, 1973.

Yang Shu-fan. *Ch'ing-tai chung-yang cheng-chih chih-tu* (The Ch'ing dynasty's system of central government). Taipei, T'ai-wan shang-wu yin-shu kuan, 1978).

Yin Wei-ho. *Chiang-su liu-shih-i hsien chih* (Gazetteer for Kiangsu's sixty-one counties). Taipei, 1936.

YWYT. See Chung-kuo k'o-hsueh yuan chin-tai-shih yen-chiu-so, comp. *Yang-wu yun-tung* (The foreign affairs movement). Shanghai, Jen-min ch'u-pan she, 1961).

Zelin, Madeline. *The Magistrate's Tael: Rationalizing Fiscal Reform in Eighteenth Century China.* Berkeley, University of California Press, 1984.

GLOSSARY/INDEX

[Chinese words or phrases are indexed as they were spelled by Hart, and by him either underlined or not. Wade-Giles romanizations follow in parentheses. Chinese characters are given only when used by Hart.]

Harvard East Asian Monographs

49. Endymion Wilkinson, *The History of Imperial China: A Research Guide*

50. Britten Dean, *China and Great Britain: The Diplomacy of Commercial Relations, 1860–1864*

51. Ellsworth C. Carlson, *The Foochow Missionaries, 1847–1880*

52. Yeh-chien Wang, *An Estimate of the Land-Tax Collection in China, 1753 and 1908*

53. Richard M. Pfeffer, *Understanding Business Contracts in China, 1949–1963*

54. Han-sheng Chuan and Richard Kraus, *Mid-Ch'ing Rice Markets and Trade, An Essay in Price History*

55. Ranbir Vohra, *Lao She and the Chinese Revolution*

56. Liang-lin Hsiao, *China's Foreign Trade Statistics, 1864–1949*

57. Lee-hsia Hsu Ting, *Government Control of the Press in Modern China, 1900–1949*

58. Edward W. Wagner, *The Literati Purges: Political Conflict in Early Yi Korea*

59. Joungwon A. Kim, *Divided Korea: The Politics of Development, 1945–1972*

60. Noriko Kamachi, John K. Fairbank, and Chūzō Ichiko, *Japanese Studies of Modern China Since 1953: A Bibliographical Guide to Historical and Social-Science Research on the Nineteenth and Twentieth Centuries, Supplementary Volume for 1953–1969*

61. Donald A. Gibbs and Yun-chen Li, *A Bibliography of Studies and Translations of Modern Chinese Literature, 1918–1942*

62. Robert H. Silin, *Leadership and Values: The Organization of Large-Scale Taiwanese Enterprises*

63. David Pong, *A Critical Guide to the Kwangtung Provincial Archives Deposited at the Public Record Office of London*

64. Fred W. Drake, *China Charts the World: Hsu Chi-yü and His Geography of 1848*

65. William A. Brown and Urgunge Onon, translators and annotators, *History of the Mongolian People's Republic*

66. Edward L. Farmer, *Early Ming Government: The Evolution of Dual Capitals*

67. Ralph C. Croizier, *Koxinga and Chinese Nationalism: History, Myth, and the Hero*

68. William J. Tyler, tr., *The Psychological World of Natsume Sōseki*, by Doi Takeo

69. Eric Widmer, *The Russian Ecclesiastical Mission in Peking during the Eighteenth Century*

70. Charlton M. Lewis, *Prologue to the Chinese Revolution: The Transformation of Ideas and Institutions in Hunan Province, 1891–1907*

71. Preston Torbert, *The Ch'ing Imperial Household Department: A Study of its Organization and Principal Functions, 1662–1796*

72. Paul A. Cohen and John E. Schrecker, eds., *Reform in Nineteenth-Century China*

73. Jon Sigurdson, *Rural Industrialism in China*

74. Kang Chao, *The Development of Cotton Textile Production in China*

75. Valentin Rabe, *The Home Base of American China Missions, 1880–1920*

76. Sarasin Viraphol, *Tribute and Profit: Sino-Siamese Trade, 1652–1853*